MARKETING MANAGEMENT

The Big Picture

CHRISTIE L. NORDHIELM
University of Michigan

MARTA DAPENA-BARÓN
University of Michigan

WILEY

VICE PRESIDENT & EXECUTIVE PUBLISHER	George Hoffman
EXECUTIVE EDITOR	Lisé Johnson
SENIOR ACQUISITIONS EDITOR	Franny Kelly
DEVELOPMENTAL EDITORS	Leslie Kraham
	Elisa Adams
PROJECT EDITOR	Jennifer Manias
EDITORIAL ASSISTANT	Jacqueline Hughes
EDITORIAL OPERATIONS MANAGER	Yana Mermel
DIRECTOR OF MARKETING	Amy Scholz
ASSISTANT MARKETING MANAGER	Puja Katariwala
CONTENT MANAGER	Michael Olivo
SENIOR PRODUCTION EDITOR	Anna Melhorn
SENIOR PHOTO EDITOR	Mary Ann Price
PHOTO RESEARCHER	Teri Stratford
DESIGN DIRECTOR	Harry Nolan
SENIOR DESIGNER	Tom Nery
COVER IMAGE	© Johner Images/Johnér Images/Corbis

This book was set in Kepler Std Light 10/12 by Aptara and printed and bound by Donnelley Willard. The cover was printed by Donnelley Willard.

Founded in 1807, John Wiley & Sons, Inc. has been a valued source of knowledge and understanding for more than 200 years, helping people around the world meet their needs and fulfill their aspirations. Our company is built on a foundation of principles that include responsibility to the communities we serve and where we live and work. In 2008, we launched a Corporate Citizenship Initiative, a global effort to address the environmental, social, economic, and ethical challenges we face in our business. Among the issues we are addressing are carbon impact, paper specifications and procurement, ethical conduct within our business and among our vendors, and community and charitable support. For more information, please visit our website: www.wiley.com/go/citizenship.

Evaluation copies are provided to qualified academics and professionals for review purposes only, for use in their courses during the next academic year. These copies are licensed and may not be sold or transferred to a third party. Upon completion of the review period, please return the evaluation copy to Wiley. Return instructions and a free of charge return shipping label are available at www.wiley.com/go/returnlabel. Outside of the United States, please contact your local representative.

978-1-118-01455-4

Printed in the United States of America

10 9 8 7 6 5 4 3 2 1

This book is dedicated to our parents,
Naomi and Berndt Nordhielm
and Andres Dapena-Prado and Mercedes Baron-Palomera.
They embody a spirit of integrity, hard work,
and a commitment to excellence that guide our work.

ABOUT THE AUTHORS

Christie Nordhielm, Ph.D. is a world-renowned marketing educator, coach, consultant, and speaker. She began her career at the top-ranked Marketing Department at the J. L. Kellogg Graduate School of Management at Northwestern University, where, in 2003 she was selected by students in the full-time MBA program as the L.G. Lavengood Outstanding Professor of the Year. She also has served on the Marketing faculty at the Ross School of Business at the University of Michigan, which adopted the Big Picture framework in 2004, and the University of Chicago. In 2005 Professor Nordhielm founded The Big Picture Partners and began implementing the framework with companies internationally. Her clients include GE, American Express, Johnson & Johnson, Sealed Air, Philips, Ecolab, and a number of small- and medium-size companies.

Professor Nordhielm is the author of several articles and the recipient of the Ferber Award for best article based on a dissertation published in the *Journal of Consumer Research*. She also appears regularly on television and radio and is frequently quoted in the press on a variety of marketing topics. Professor Nordhielm received her Ph.D. and MBA from the Graduate School of Business at the University of Chicago.

Marta Dapena-Barón, Ed.D. combines an academic and pragmatic approach to marketing. A founding partner of The Big Picture Partners, she has taught strategic marketing and pricing to executive audiences at a variety of Fortune 100 companies around the world. Dr. Dapena-Barón has served on the Marketing faculty at the Johnson School of Business at Cornell University and at the Ross School of Business at the University of Michigan. At the University of Michigan, she is also a faculty affiliate in the Masters in Entrepreneurship Program, where she teaches Entrepreneurial Marketing Strategy.

Prior to founding The Big Picture Partners, Dr. Dapena-Barón was the Vice President for Marketing for GE Capital; as a strategy consultant for McKinsey & Co., she advised clients in a variety of industries on the American and European continents. She also spent several years at ABN AMRO Bank in a variety of roles, serving as Director of Strategy to the North American Chairman, directing the ecommerce function for the Global Trade business line, and advising and financing infrastructure privatization projects in Latin America.

Dr. Dapena-Barón holds a Doctorate and a Masters in Education from the University of Pennsylvania, an MBA in finance and international business from the University of Chicago, and a BA in Economics summa cum laude from Kenyon College.

HOW THIS PROJECT CAME TO BE

MARKETING HAS RUINED MY LIFE.

It began shortly after my graduation from the Graduate School of Business at the University of Chicago. I took a job in client service with the Leo Burnett Company, then a premier advertising agency in the world, working as Assistant Account Executive on a variety of packaged-goods accounts ranging from candy bars to cat food. Not long after my start date, I began to notice small changes in what had previously been routine behaviors for me. Most notably, what was once a quick trip to the grocery store each Saturday morning swelled into a three-hour marathon during which I studiously reviewed the pricing, packaging, and promotional tactics of the products lining the aisles of my local supermarket.

My friends and roommates quickly learned to refuse my invitations to join me "to pick up a few things at the store." At home things were no better; my TV viewing habits had taken a turn for the worse. The notion of a "commercial break" disappeared. Instead of turning away from the television to chat with friends or family during the ads, I insisted on turning up the volume and scrutinizing each execution with rapt attention (often jumping for the VCR to tape a spot of particular interest). I was soon politely but firmly excluded from any social events involving sports or drama on TV. In just a few months, my experience of two rather mundane activities, grocery shopping and watching television, had been permanently transformed by my choice of profession.

I eventually left the warm company of my cherished companions at Leo Burnett (Morris the Cat and Ernie Keebler) to take what I saw at the time as my dream job: Director of Marketing and Promotion for WXRT Radio in Chicago, a (then) independent, alternative rock-and-roll music station. I entered the wonderful world of free CDs, record-release parties, and backstage passes believing I had truly found happiness. Moreover, I was hopeful that my unfortunate habits in the grocery store and the TV room would eventually fade, and that I would be re-endowed with the status of "normal" by my friends and family.

These hopes were dashed the night of my very first concert in my new position. I was happily ensconced in the VIP section at a Grateful Dead concert, but I found myself not lost in a reverie regarding the inner truths of the lyrics of the great Jerry Garcia, but instead wondering whether we should develop customized after-concert programming promotions to align with the touring schedules of key bands. I was horrified to realize that while everyone around me was partying and having fun, I was *working*.

The inevitable conclusion I reached that night was that marketing had ruined my life. I had developed the unfortunate habit of analyzing examples of marketing whenever I encountered them, which, in today's world where marketing is virtually impossible to avoid, meant every minute of every day. Marketers are responsible for constructing much of the cultural landscape in which we live. It is virtually unimaginable that a person in a developed country could look around without experiencing a logo, a selling line, or a product placement in print, radio, TV, or Internet advertising.

As a consumer and citizen, I may bemoan the state of a world in which billboards are more ubiquitous than trees, but as a marketing professional I have come to recognize this new landscape as a reference library of carefully planned and executed marketing plans. From the perspective of a marketing manager, each advertising exposure is an opportunity to learn from other managers. These communications are literally a window into the marketing strategy of all firms competing in the marketplace.

When I realized this, I became determined to become a marketing educator, so that I, in turn, could ruin the lives of countless students in the same way that mine had been ruined. This book is the culmination of 27 years of this pursuit. As such, it is not intended to be the "frozen knowledge of the field," a definition my colleague John Deighton once offered for most textbooks, but rather a lens through which a student can view everyday experiences, and in doing so, improve his or her skills as a marketer.

—Christie Nordhielm, January 2013

PREFACE

From a marketing perspective, the materials in this book were designed to achieve the first goal of any well-conceived product: to meet a need. Initially, this need was our own. Our students were nearly unanimous in their dissatisfaction with various marketing textbooks made available to them. Common concerns were:

- ■ **"I don't understand how this all fits together."** As complex marketing problems loom larger, our response has been to try to break things down into smaller and smaller parts. This has led us further into the realm of specialization and away from the wisdom that a holistic, integrated approach imparts.[1] Most attempts to solve this problem in the past have been organizational in nature and reflected in a variety of "team" approaches. Unfortunately, by changing an organizational structure without changing the strategic approach, we usually create just another illustration of the reorganizational adage: "different tree, same monkeys." Organizational changes alone cannot create integration if our approach to marketing problems continues to be analytic as opposed to synthetic in nature. Yet the traditional "textbook" approach to marketing, whether implemented by individuals or teams, is inherently analytic—problems are broken down and considered as separate issues instead of as interrelated components in a dynamic system. Without an integrated approach, the marketing manager is simply solving a series of unrelated problems instead of considering how a change in one element of the marketing plan will influence myriad other strategic and executional variables.

- ■ **"It's an encyclopedia, not a textbook."** When we first started teaching marketing, we heartily believed in the "more is more" theory and were quite happy to assign a text that could also be used for weight training. We very quickly learned that one of the primary functions of a teacher (or a text) should be to identify a reasonable amount of high-value information for students. The encyclopedic nature of many marketing textbooks makes them uniquely unsuited for this purpose.

- ■ **"I get brain freeze when I try to do a case."** The second thing we learned from our students was that the more comprehensive the approach being taught, the less able students are to attack a marketing problem. This difficulty has increased each year as the complexity and dynamic nature of marketing environments has

---

[1]This is not to say that marketers should never use analytics when facing marketing problems. Analytical tools can be quite valuable, but only if they are used in the context of an integrated methodology. The tools available should never dictate the approach taken to business strategy—instead, the strategic approach should dictate the tools employed.

increased. We are no longer in a position to offer a laundry list of possible solutions to students. Instead we must work to develop a useful framework that students can internalize and then customize to meet their needs. Effective business people don't achieve success by citing examples; they do it by making decisions. Thus this text is designed to assist students in making marketing decisions. By providing a decision aid, we hope to help students cut through the overload of information that will assault them when making marketing decisions in the future. The structured approach presented here should help students to assess the relevance of information and then use relevant information more effectively.

- **"Marketing is 'soft . . .'."** Unfortunately, the end effect of all this complexity is the "nobody's right/nobody's wrong" syndrome. In the end, it is impossible to "prove" whether a particular strategy is the right one. This situation has sadly made it seem that the best talkers are the best marketers, and as a result marketing seems "soft" to those of us who appreciate logic and fact. The framework presented here cannot claim to make proof possible; however, it does make logical argument the preferred method for approaching marketing problems rather than flowery speech. In particular, the case analysis format leaves no room for written or verbal embellishments that can often hide illogic and wishful thinking.

- **"This textbook is boring!"** A colleague of ours once said, "It's a textbook, it's *supposed* to be boring!" And this certainly has seemed to be the case. Boredom, of course, is the evil force that haunts students and professors alike. It destroys any possibility for true learning. Captain Kangaroo elegantly stated this fact many years ago: "It is better to entertain someone and hope that they learn than to try to teach someone something and hope they are entertained." We have found that, given the proper tools, students are actually quite willing and able to entertain themselves, especially as they begin to see fruits of their labor. The materials presented here have been designed as a response to the above concerns.

The purpose of the Big Picture is therefore as follows: *to provide a set of materials that will enable students to attack marketing problems by utilizing an integrated framework and associated tools designed to help them analyze, prioritize, and then solve these problems.* The framework is presented in Figure P.1, and we refer to it throughout the text. The basic learning process using the framework breaks down as follows:

1. **Identify.** Using the Big Picture framework, students utilize fact, logic, and assumptions to identify key marketing variables, both strategic and executional. This stage in the process requires stepping through the entire framework to develop a basic overview of the corporate strategy.
2. **Prioritize.** Based on the assessment of key variables and evaluation of their interrelationships, the student identifies what he or she believes to be the most important problem in the case. This prioritization hones in on a particular part of the framework that has been identified as the area of greatest opportunity. While there may be numerous problems in the case, the student learns the importance of prioritizing these problems in order to appropriately allocate resources.
3. **Express.** Using a highly structured write-up format, the students present and support their choice of problem and accompanying solution. Because the goal-impediment-solution format is simple and quite sparse, any weakness in analysis

becomes immediately evident to the student. He or she then can step back and reassess the analysis and prioritization. The format also quickly provides a common vocabulary for students to use when discussing cases in a group setting.

We have found that students easily grasp these three steps, which allows them to quickly assess marketing problems in the classroom. The simplicity of the approach enables them to practice outside the classroom as well; they quickly find themselves evaluating marketing problems they encounter in their daily lives through the lens of the Big Picture. That is perhaps the single greatest advantage of this approach compared with that of traditional marketing texts: The core knowledge of the framework is absorbed quickly, and this knowledge thus resides in students' minds instead of in their textbooks.

Over the course of the semester, students' learning is enhanced not because they simply continue to read and memorize more material, but because they are afforded a wide variety of opportunities both inside and outside the classroom to apply their growing knowledge and skills. Because the Big Picture approach is integrated, a student never performs a single marketing activity (e.g., pricing) without considering all the other elements of the Big Picture, and how these elements affect and are affected by the immediate decision (e.g., how pricing fits within the overall entity's strategy). The need to consider every element of the Big Picture whenever a marketing decision is to be made reinforces in the student's mind what all the elements of the Big Picture are and how they interrelate. A student of the Big Picture approach never becomes

The Big Picture Framework

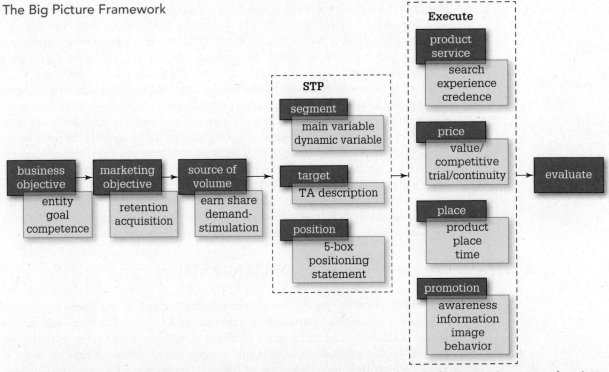

Figure P.1 The Big Picture framework is organized as a series of chapters that present the fundamental concepts of marketing strategy and execution as a series of decisions. Although the framework is presented linearly, and the text moves through the framework from left to right, students are encouraged to use the framework as a system in which all elements must always be in alignment. Thus, we view the framework as a circular decision-making system.

skilled in one marketing element (e.g., segmentation) without practicing all the other marketing elements. This leads to a stronger, more effective marketer in the long run.

OVERVIEW

Over the last few decades, business education and practice have been focused on addressing the firm's problems from a functional perspective, where strategies and the execution of those strategies are considered separately. The departure point for most MBA-level texts and courses that deal with finance, operations, or accounting is an assumption that the strategy of the firm has been set and remains constant while the functional practitioner executes a specific aspect of that strategy. Conversely, strategy courses generally focus on the interactions among market players, the impact of emerging trends on the firm and its industry, and customers and suppliers as homogenous groups. However, the reality that firms face today is characterized by problems that cannot be solved by perfecting single business processes in isolation. Successful decision-making requires a keen understanding of the firm and its environment as self-balancing systems, where a change in one variable has repercussions in a variety of other variables.

As our environment grows increasingly complex, it is only natural that we attempt to break things down into small pieces to unravel them. However, when this phenomenon occurs in organizations, individuals risk losing sight of the overall objective of the firm. It has been widely recognized that companies need to perfect both supply and demand processes if they are to be successful. It is now also widely recognized that companies face a marketplace so competitive that they cannot afford to address strategy and execution separately or measure strategic and executional processes against different objectives. The Big Picture attempts to address this challenge.

The Big Picture is an integrated framework designed to help marketing students analyze and solve the myriad marketing problems they will face during their careers. The framework emphasizes the dynamic nature of marketing by presenting key marketing topics as a set of interrelated chapters, as opposed to separate chapters representing independent topics. Beginning with the high-level strategic topic of business objective, it identifies areas where a marketer must prioritize and make key decisions, then highlights how those decisions affect other elements of the framework. The continuous referencing of the framework and numerous illustrations of key concepts, using the case analysis format, encourages marketers to actively utilize the framework for solving marketing problems and thus internalize the approach.

ORGANIZATION

The primary text for the Big Picture consists of 14 chapters and offers a complete overview of an integrated strategy-through-execution process. The framework allows students to understand strategic marketing as a system in which changes in one aspect of the plan affect other aspects, and where strategic decisions have executional ramifications. This interrelatedness of the chapters forces a discipline and unity of purpose that results in efficient decision-making. From a user perspective, the power of the Big Picture lies in the economies it brings to decision-making: once a strategic decision has been made, executional decisions become simplified.

Chapter One: Ethics and Tools of Responsibility. Because ethics are integral to marketing decisions, it is vital to address this topic earlier rather than later. This chapter emphasizes the importance of considering ethical issues *during* case analysis or strategy development rather than after. It sets the tone for our consideration of specific marketing topics by addressing ethical issues relating to each chapter of the framework.

Chapter Two: Business Objective. The point of departure of the Big Picture framework is the definition of three fundamental decisions that guide the definition of the firm's marketing strategy. Those three decisions are the selection of the *Fundamental Entity, Core Competence,* and *Business Goal.* The fundamental entity is the corporate unit for analysis purposes. The firm's competence is an integrated set of organizational skills that differentiates it in a substantial and sustainable way; core competences (also called core capabilities in the strategy field) are unique in the category, they are supported by and support the company's organizational resource base (also called strategic assets), and they are linked to customer benefits—and thus are subject to constant renewal through a process of market-based feedback. The business goal is a single-minded objective the company will attain in a predefined timeframe and that will guide decision-making in the firm. The answers to these three questions are the strategic pillars of our marketing strategy.

Chapter Three: Marketing Objective. This chapter focuses on the question of what is a customer. Defining a customer in a strategic manner is key to tying our customer-based metrics of *acquisition* and *retention* and customer profitability to the rest of the strategy of the firm. This chapter also deals with the activities and metrics that surround the customer acquisition and retention efforts. Only with an understanding of acquisition and retention resource allocation and revenue contribution can we evaluate the relative efficiency of the firm's commercial efforts. This chapter also addresses the topic of customer loyalty. We define a customer as being loyal when he or she has a preference for our brand and behaves accordingly by purchasing it, and/or engaging with it, and/or recommending it to others. Finally, the chapter introduces emotional or *heart* loyalty, functional or *head* loyalty, and *habitual* or hand loyalty.

Chapter Four: Source of Volume. This chapter presents the concepts of earn share and stimulate demand. In an earn share strategy, we choose to grow at the expense of an identifiable competitor or segment. In a stimulate demand strategy, our growth comes from expanding the competitive playing field for all companies in that category. This chapter combines the decisions of Marketing Objective and Source of Volume to derive the Strategic Quadrants. It then provides a high-level explanation of how the choice of a particular Strategic Quadrant drives the more tactical choices we make in the executional portion of the framework.

Chapter Five: Segmentation. This chapter presents the different types of segmentation variables available to the marketer and offers a pragmatic approach to rationalizing our markets by using just two variables—*the main variable,* that is, the principal benefit customers seek when purchasing a product or service, and the *dynamic variable,* or the benefit that differentiates the product from the category leader. If the firm elects to pursue a *stimulate demand* strategy, it will emphasize the main variable; if it implements an earn share strategy, it will build its execution around the dynamic variable.

Chapter Six: Targeting. Targeting is the process by which we describe the audience we want to reach through our execution and sales efforts. Within the Big Picture framework, the target audience is very specifically defined in terms of its behavioral, attitudinal, and aspirational characteristics. This chapter provides a succinct discussion of how to create a crisp definition of whom we are trying to reach.

Chapter Seven: Positioning. In this chapter, all the strategic elements of the Big Picture developed so far coalesce into a single message to be delivered to the target audience. This chapter highlights the importance of linking target customers' attitudes, needs, and behaviors to the company's customer proposition or key takeaway. This chapter further explains how to develop positioning statements to both marshal internal tactical resources and guide the firm's strategic advertising and communications efforts.

Chapter Eight: Product. This chapter addresses the executional aspects of brands and products. Here we present products as bundles of benefits rather than as static feature sets. Thinking of products as benefit bundles adds a dynamic element to the product life cycle concept, because products can be continually augmented by layering customer benefits and thus maximizing the company's investment in its product portfolio. This chapter also defines product attribute types (search, experience, credence) and shows how to use them differentially depending on the firm's strategy.

Chapter Nine: Product as Service. The expansion of the service sector has created a trend toward the "productization" of services and strategies such as "mass customization." There are many advantages to service standardization, including the application of traditional marketing, operations, and economics principles to service industries where they have not been used before. While recognizing these parallels, this chapter explores three key attributes of services that make them unique. These are intangibility, which makes brand-building for service companies more challenging; the inability of services to be inventoried or inspected, which makes product failures harder to prevent; and simultaneous production and consumption, which adds a performance element to services not present for hard goods.

Chapter Ten: Pricing. This chapter explores pricing strategies and tactics—and explains why making that distinction is crucial. Pricing strategy is defined as the company's long-term and overall approach to pricing given its strategy and positioning. Price implementation is integrally linked to the company's STP (Segmentation, Target, Positioning) decisions as well as to its executional decisions. The pricing chapter explores cost-based, competitive-based, value-based, and strategy-based approaches to setting prices. It also considers how other framework decisions affect pricing decisions.

Chapter Eleven: Channels. This chapter explains the function of distribution channels in the transmission of information and products throughout the value chain. Distribution decisions and tactics are considered in light of the necessary alignment between the channel strategy and the firm's overall strategy. In this chapter we discuss structural channel decisions of length, breadth, and depth in the context of the Strategic Focus of the firm. We then turn our attention to the customer benefits of channels.

Chapter Twelve: Promotion. A commonly held belief that the objective of advertising is to "sell" leads many companies to purchase advertising that is not aligned with their strategy and is therefore ineffective in advancing it. This chapter explores the different types of advertising objectives (awareness, information, image, behavior), how to categorize ads by their objective, and how to design advertising to match the company's strategic positioning.

Chapter Thirteen: Market Research. This chapter introduces basic market research techniques and the process steps required to successfully complete marketing research projects.

Chapter Fourteen: Metrics. Building upon the market research chapter, in this chapter we discuss specific means for assessing the relationship between our marketing strategy and our operational metrics, which track our implementation efforts. We also address evaluation metrics from an input and an output perspective, again tying strategy and execution to the results of that strategy.

KEY FEATURES

Opening Case: Each chapter begins with a brief current case study intended to elucidate a key issue raised in that chapter. These cases reflect Big Picture concepts put into practice.

Digital/Social Media examples: Social media and digital marketing are now a key element in our marketing toolkit. However, if these tools are not used strategically they will represent wasted resources. Social media boxes and additional illustrated real-world digital and social media examples in each chapter are designed to demonstrate the appropriate, effective use of these tools in many types of firms.

New Products/Innovation: Innovation continues to be a crucial aspect of marketing. Highlighted boxed examples of new products and innovations in each chapter represent marketing thinking that will lead to sustainable growth, as opposed to short-term sales.

Customer Focus: While marketers constantly talk about customer focus, we often lose this focus when we move to execution. Boxed Customer Focus examples in each chapter are intended to remind the reader that there are still many opportunities to enhance this focus.

Global Marketing: Global marketing issues are highlighted in boxes in many chapters to highlight real examples from around the world.

Review and Discussion Questions: At the end of each chapter, a set of review and discussion questions is provided to help students internalize the chapter's information.

Marketing Tools: To enable students to make effective use of the framework and quickly translate theory into practice, we present a number of Marketing Tools in chapter appendices.

ADDITIONAL MATERIALS

In addition to the book, the Big Picture concepts are illustrated through a web-based software tool, the Big Picture Simulation, created with generous support from Johnson & Johnson. Users of the Big Picture simulation can build interactive business case studies and access case studies already built and available through the web. The simulation was created to capture the complexity of the strategic issues companies face when trying to implement a strategy in the face of customer and competitive realities. Users can access it through the Big Picture website at www.bigpictureonline.com.

The Big Picture website also contains advertising examples and links to other articles, web sites, and recommended books pertaining to the marketing and strategy topics explored throughout the Big Picture. These materials were chosen to reflect the dynamic and messy nature of marketing problems and problem solving, which calls for a disciplined approach provided by a framework. At the same time, the ability to pursue a topic in greater depth opens up the possibility of discovery so important to problem solving. Properly applied, the framework will allow marketing students to reduce the uncertainty associated with marketing decisions, thereby increasing their ability to generate a wider range of potent solutions to the specific problem. Perhaps more importantly, the framework enables the marketer to assess decisions on an ongoing basis, engaging in a process of continuous learning in the area of marketing.

Student and Instructor Resources

Marketing Management: The Big Picture is supported by a comprehensive learning package that assists the instructor in creating a motivating and enthusiastic environment. And, students will find additional tools for study and practice. Visit the Book Companion Site at www.wiley.com/college/nordhielm.

Instructor's Manual. This comprehensive manual includes learning objectives, chapter outlines, lecture notes, and suggested answers for all questions found in the text.

PowerPoint Presentations. This robust set of PowerPoint slides includes outlined material from each chapter, relevant figures and examples, and lecture notes. An *Image Gallery*, containing jpg files for all the figures in the text, is also provided for instructor convenience.

Test Bank. This comprehensive Test Bank includes true/false, multiple-choice, and short-essay questions that vary in degree of difficulty. All the questions are tagged to learning objectives and difficulty level. The *Computerized Test Bank* allows instructors to modify and add questions to the master bank and to customize their exams.

Practice Quizzes. This online study tool, with quizzes of varying levels of difficulty, helps students evaluate their progress through each chapter. Since the Practice Quizzes have been written by the Test Bank author, students can be prepared to see similar questions on exams.

The Case Method Appendix. This online appendix presents a description of a case analysis format that can be used in conjunction with this text. This appendix includes discussions of the importance of developing strategy prior to attempting to find solutions. The goal-impediment-solution approach is a key tool students will use throughout the course as they analyze marketing issues and learn to re-state the problem, explain their approach, and defend their solutions clearly and concisely.

Student-Developed Life Cases. Big Picture framework students at the MBA level have applied framework to a short and 'live' case. In contrast to a more traditional method, where faculty presents a known case for students to analyze, Big Picture faculty might encourage students to choose and write a case of their authorship on a current topic of interest and using a carefully designed template. The students who have prepared the case will then take a leadership role in managing the discussion of these mini-cases. The rest of the students in the class and the faculty, will receive the written case materials ahead of the class meeting to enable a rich in-class discussion of the case. In this way the class maximizes the relevance of the cases to the students' business lives and also provides an opportunity for them to became intimately acquainted with the case format, so widely used in the business curriculum.

The 'live' case approach has been used in a number of MBA-level classes already and sample cases are available as reference.

The Big Picture Simulation. As previously described, the Big Picture simulation is a web-based software tool based on The Big Picture framework, and created to build interactive business case studies. The tool is used to illustrate key framework concepts and break through the apparent complexity of strategic marketing issues and concepts by elucidating the key relationships between marketing variables, in particular, the target audience, customer decision drivers, customer behaviors and their financial impact, within a dynamic market environment.

The Big Picture simulation offers students the opportunity to apply framework concepts within a virtual market environment. Given key company, customer and competitive assumptions, the simulation generates results showing how specific investments result in customer attitudinal and behavioral changes and how those can affect firm performance and market growth.

Please refer to www.bigpicturepartners.com for an updated list of simulated case studies and other software tools immediately available. Or, ask your Wiley representative for more information on packaging a Simulation with your textbook.

ACKNOWLEDGMENTS

In 2003 I walked in to teach my MBA marketing class at the Kellogg Graduate School of Management without a textbook. I had finally admitted to myself what my students had been telling me for years, that a new approach to marketing thinking was needed. I had my ideas about what this approach should be, but they were untested and somewhat radical. I decided to place my faith in my students and explain to them that I would be sharing these ideas with them throughout the course, inviting them to challenge and strengthen the framework I had begun to develop. They did just that, with passion, intellect, and a sense of humor I have come to expect in Kellogg students. The framework, the first version of this book, was essentially a collaborative effort of literally hundreds of the greatest students in the world. These included Meta Marshall, John Kim, Gang Kong, and especially the original "Dream Team" of Brian Fox, Justin Crotty, Sophie Hawkins, Sarah Rafanelli, and David Weiss, among many, many others. Students at the University of Michigan also provided invaluable input and support.

Two friends and colleagues at Kellogg, Angela Lee and Victoria Husted Medvec, have provided undaunted and invaluable support over these many years. We would also like to specifically thank two colleagues at the University of Michigan for their energetic backing and specific contributions in implementing this framework, Christie Brown and Rajeev Batra.

A number of practitioners have been instrumental in providing input and support for the framework, and putting it into action. It is a diverse group, but they all share a passion for strategic thinking and ethical practice in business. These include Drew Boyd, Shelly Cropper, Martin Potjer, Christophe Beck, Toni Bentfeld, Fred Virgin, Beth Bogan, and many other friends and supporters of the framework from around the world.

We like to think of this framework not as a finished product but as an ongoing process of understanding marketing as a system—dynamic, complex, and infinitely interesting. Toward this end, we hope to continue to rely on and engage with friends and colleagues around the ideas put forward in this framework as we move through the next century of marketing.

In addition, we'd like to thank the numerous reviewers who have provided invaluable feedback along the way:

Reviewers

Aaron Ahuvia, *University of Michigan, Dearborn*

Lerzan Aksoy, *Fordham University*

Verl Anderson, *Dixie State College*

Wasim Azhar, *University Of California, Berkeley*

Sandy Becker, *Rutgers University*

Charles Besio, *Southern Methodist University*

Parimal Bhagat, *Indiana University of Pennsylvania*

Darron Billeter, *Brigham Young University*

Dave Bourff, *Boise State University*

Christie Brown, *University of Michigan*

Frederic Brunel, *Boston University*

Michael Capella, *Villanova University*

Russell Casey, *Pennsylvania State University, Worthington Scranton*

Pradeep Chintagunta, *University of Chicago*

S. Chan Choi, *Rutgers University, Newark*

Kelly Cowan, *Portland State University*

Mark DeFanti, *Providence College*

Gary Gephardt, *University of Florida*

Albert Greco, *Fordham University, Lincoln Center*

Curtis Haugtvedt, *Ohio State University*

William Heath, *Baruch College*

Steven Huff, *Brigham Young*

Eleanor Huser, *Fairleigh Dickinson University*

William C. Johnson, *Nova Southeastern University*

Sertan Kabadayi, *Fordham University*

Harrychand Kalicharan, *Nova Southeastern University*

Mark Kay, *Montclair State University*

Lisa Klein Pearo, *Cornell University*

Nanda Kumar, *University of Texas at Dallas*

Aparna Labroo, *University of Toronto*

Angela Lee, *Northwestern University*

Shibo Li, *Indiana University*

Jeremy MacLaughlin, *Southwest Baptist University*

Joan Meyers-Levy, *University of Minnesota*

Chip Miller, *Drake University*

Avinandan Mukherjee, *Montclair State University*

Jyotsna Mukherji, *Texas A&M International University*

Richard Murphy, *Jacksonville University*

Lynn Murray, *Pittsburg State University*

Hieu Nguyen, *California State University, Long Beach*

Nicholas Nugent, *Florida Southern College*

Tracy Padron, *University of Colorado*

Koen Paulews, *Dartmouth College*

Dennis Pitta, *University of Baltimore*

Carolyn Predmore, *Manhattan College*

George Priovolos, *Iona College*

Jan Saykiewicz, *Duquesne University*

Hope Schau, *University of Arizona*

Larry Schramm, *Oakland University*

Kabir Sen, *Lamar University*

Christina Simmers, *Missouri State University*

Barry Soloff, *Baruch College*

Nancy Stephens, *Arizona State University*

Geoffrey Stewart, *University of Louisiana, Lafayette*

Tracy Suter, *Oklahoma State University*

Michael Voss, *University of Central Arkansas*

Qiyu Zhang, *Loyola University Maryland*

Focus Group Participants

Piotr Chelminski, *Providence College*
Pradeep Chintagunta, *University of Chicago*
Kelly Cowan, *Portland State University*
TC Dale, *Portland State University*
Curtis Haugtvedt, *Ohio State University*
William C. Johnson, *Nova Southeastern University*

Hieu Nguyen, *California State University, Long Beach*
Ravi Shanmugam, *Santa Clara University*
Christina Simmers, *Missouri State University*
Barry Soloff, *Baruch College*
Andres Terech, *University of California, Los Angeles*

Survey Respondents

Alan Ammann, *Pensacola State College*
David Andrus, *Kansas State University*
Wasim Azhar, *University of California, Berkeley*
Vishag Badrinarayanan, *Texas State University*
George Bercovitz, *York College, City University of New York*
Julie Britton, *Duke University*
Erin Cavusgil, *University of Michigan, Flint*
Mark Collins, *University of Tennessee*
Jim Curran, *University of South Florida, Sarasota-Manatee*
Kathryn Davis, *Huston-Tillotson University*
Michael Denning, *Arizona State University*
Timothy Donahue, *Chadron State College*
Laura Downey, *Purdue University, West Lafayette*
Robert Evans, *Texas A&M International University*
Melissa Fisher , *Ohio State University*
Ed Forrest, *University of Alaska, Anchorage*
Robert Girondi, *Temple University*
John Grabner, *University of North Texas, Denton*
BettyJean Hebel, *Madonna University*
Jim Jarrard, *University of Wisconsin, Platteville*
Peter Johnson, *Fordham University*
Vishnu Kirpalani, *Bloomsburg University*
Christine Lai, *State University of New York College at Buffalo*
vivek madupu, *Missouri Western State College*
Denny McCorkle, *University of Northern Colorado*

David Nasser, *Georgia State University*
Leonardo Nicolao, *Texas Christian University*
Louis Nzegwu, *University of Wisconsin, Platteville*
Jenny Olson, *University of Michigan*
Robert Owen, *Texas A&M University, Texarkana*
Robert Pitts, *College of Charleston*
Brenda Ponsford, *Clarion University*
Barbara Quaintance, *University of Central Florida, Cocoa Campus*
Peter Raven, *Seattle University*
William Rhyne, *Notre Dame de Namur University*
William Rice, *California State University, Fresno*
Darrell Scott, *Idaho State University*
Carol Scovotti, *University of Wisconsin, Whitewater*
Tiebing Shi, *Northwest Missouri State University*
Stanley Slater, *Colorado State University, Fort Collins*
William Smith, *University of Southern Mississippi*
Paul Solomon, *University of South Florida*
William Steiger, *University of Central Florida*
James Stock, *University of South Florida*
Jon Stuart, *University of South Florida*
Tracy Suter, *Oklahoma State University*
Frank van Vliet, *University of Baltimore*
Paula Wolper, *University of Findlay*
Wei Zhang, *Iowa State University*

BRIEF CONTENTS

CONTENTS

MARKETING MANAGEMENT
The Big Picture

chapter one

"A good name is more
valuable than great wealth."

–Cervantes, Don Quixote, p. 603

TOOLS AND RESPONSIBILITIES

After studying this chapter you should be able to:

1. *Describe the structure of the Big Picture framework*
2. *Identify the main principles of Ethical Practice in Marketing*
3. *Distinguish between personal and business ethics issues*
4. *Integrate ethical questions into the Big Picture framework*

Ben and Jerry's: Ethical Standards as an Integral Part of the Brand Image

Ben and Jerry's was founded in 1978 in Vermont by Ben Cohen and Jerry Greenfield and quickly gained national acclaim, not only for its ice cream made with natural ingredients but also for its quirky and socially responsible approach to running a business. The Company's mission statement has three interrelated components covering Social Impact, Product, and Economic goals. The social mission statement component is "To operate the Company in a way that actively recognizes the central role that business plays in society by initiating innovative ways to improve the quality of life locally, nationally and internationally."

The Company lives up to this mission with a series of specific initiatives and operating practices. It sources organic ingredients and gives preference to suppliers that follow sustainable and environmentally conscious practices. For example, since 2009 Ben and Jerry's has been using Forest Stewardship Council (FSC) certified paperboard instead of regular paperboard for its ice cream pint containers. FSC certification means the pulp used in the paperboard is from forests managed for the protection of wildlife habitat, maintenance of biodiversity, and forest sustainability. Since December 2011, after receiving approval from the US Environmental Protection Agency

© Kevin Foy/Alamy

(EPA), Ben and Jerry's has been using hydrocarbon (HC) freezers that are significantly more energy-efficient, with lower global warming potential than standard freezers.

Ben and Jerry's was acquired by Unilever in 2000. Since then, observers have raised concerns that the company might struggle to maintain its socially and environmentally responsible values. However, Ben and Jerry's has preserved its ethical stance since the acquisition. At the end of 2012 it became the first subsidiary of a publicly traded company to be named a certified B corporation. According to the B Lab website, "B Corps are certified by the nonprofit B Lab to meet rigorous standards of social and environmental performance, accountability, and transparency." Ben and Jerry's also plans to become "an entirely fair-trade-sourced company by 2013." The company's charter states that its founders or the board will consider the community, employees, and social impact as well as shareholder profit when making a business decision. ■

Sources: Goldmark, Alex. "Ben and Jerry's becomes a B corporation," *Fast Company*, October 22, 2012, http://www.fastcoexist.com/1680771/ben-and-jerry-s-becomes-a-b-corporation.

Roberts, Genevieve. "Ben and Jerry's builds on its social-values approach," *The New York Times*. November 16, 2010. http://www.nytimes.com/2010/11/17/business/global/17iht-rbofice.html?pagewanted=all&_r=0. Accessed April 24, 2013.

Company website, http://www.benjerry.com/activism/mission-statement. Accessed March 12, 2013.

Company website, http://www.bcorporation.net/what-are-b-corps/the-non-profit-behind-b-corps. Accessed August 12, 2013.

Company website, http://www.benjerry.com/activism/mission-statement. Accessed March 12, 2013.

Marketing is, at its heart, not a science or an art, but a *discipline*. It requires problem solving and, most importantly, making decisions under uncertainty in a complex, dynamic environment. The most effective marketing managers are looking not for the right answers, but rather for the right tools to help them make the right decisions. This book is intended to do more than simply present information about marketing; its goal is to help you build a set of tools, and to use them in an efficient and disciplined fashion. In this chapter we introduce the organizing framework for these tools and then discuss the ethical responsibilities we must consider as our skill and experience with these tools grow.

THE BIG PICTURE FRAMEWORK

Many texts and courses assume the strategy of the firm has been set and remains constant while the functional practitioner executes a specific aspect of that strategy. The truth, however, is that today's environment is characterized by problems that cannot be solved by perfecting single business processes in isolation. Successful decision-making requires a keen understanding of the firm and its environment as a self-balancing system, in which a change in one variable ripples out to affect a variety of others.

As our environment grows increasingly complex, it is only natural that we attempt to break things down into small pieces them. However, when this phenomenon occurs in organizations, we risk losing sight of the overall objective of the firm while making the issues more complicated instead of more controllable. To be effective, companies facing a need to find tools and approaches that can *organize* and *synthesize* information and decision-making in a cohesive manner.

The **Big Picture Framework** is an integrated framework designed to help you analyze and address the myriad marketing problems you will face during your career. While we present it in this text in a series of chapters, you should think of it as a set of interrelated aspects of marketing, each of which affects and is affected by the others. This is the essential philosophy of our approach: marketing decisions should not be made in a vacuum, but rather in context. Each choice we make, from strategy through execution, should be *aligned* and *consistent* with our other choices. In theory, this goal of alignment seems quite obvious and simple; in a complex and dynamic environment, however, it represents one of the greatest challenges we will face as marketers.

Figure 1.1 will be our primary touch point as we seek to meet this challenge. Throughout the text, we will constantly refer to this diagram to ensure that, as we dive into a particular topic, we do not lose sight of how this topic relates to the bigger marketing picture. The dark blue boxes represent the chapter topics; the light blue boxes represent the key questions we will consider in each chapter. But this figure is more than a roadmap of the chapters. It is intended to keep us honest in our efforts to align our marketing strategy and execution. In each chapter we will also "zoom in" on a particular facet of the framework and learn the key marketing concepts and definitions related to that area.

The first three chapters present high-level, strategic topic areas: business objective, marketing objective (customer focus), and source of volume (competitive focus). These are represented by the boxes on the left side of the diagram. In the center of the framework we present segmentation, targeting, and positioning (STP), the crucial link between strategy and execution. Finally, we address execution: product/service, pricing, distribution, and communications.

The Big Picture framework. An integrated framework designed to help you analyze and address the myriad marketing problems you will face during your career.

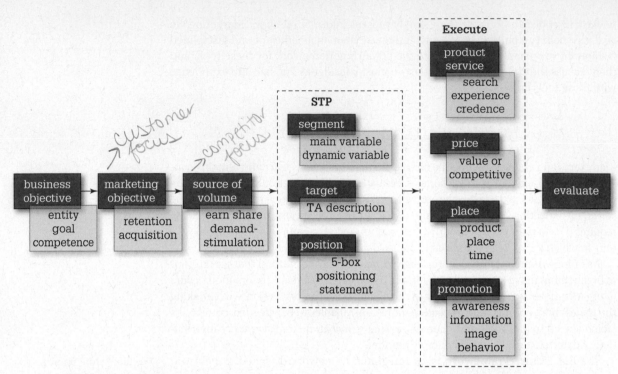

Figure 1.1 The Big Picture framework execution by linking strategic decisions to their executional implications as the firm moves through the marketing process. The dark blue boxes represent the chapter topic; the light blue boxes represent the key questions we will consider in each chapter.

Business Objective (Chapter 2)

Many managers begin their strategic analysis with a competitive analysis. While understanding the competition is indeed important, the first order of business is really to understand the strengths, weaknesses, and goals of our own firm. This understanding will drive and direct our subsequent decisions about competitive analysis and, ultimately, execution. In this chapter we ask three fundamental questions. Taken together, the answers to these questions about our business objective will set the groundwork for the rest of our strategic analysis.

1. **Who are we as a firm?** The answer defines what we call the **fundamental entity.** Our choice of fundamental entity determines the perspective from which we will conduct our strategic analysis, whether brand by brand or from a more global, corporate perspective. Because we will develop our business objective specifically for our Fundamental Entity, this first step of specifying who we are is crucial.

2. **What are we good at?** This answer identifies our **core competence,** those key skills that will drive sustainable growth. These are our source of differentiation, and our deep understanding of these competencies will be crucial as we move through the Big Picture framework.

Fundamental entity. Our choice of fundamental entity determines the perspective from which we will conduct our strategic analysis, whether it be brand by brand or from a more global, corporate point of view.

Core competence. Key organizational skills that drive sustainable growth. The core competence is the source of differentiation for the firm.

3. **Where are we going?** The answer is of course our *goal*. A well-specified *goal* will serve as more than simply a standard for judging performance; it will help us prioritize our actions and our resource allocation in a strategic and ultimately more efficient manner.

The decisions we make to answer the three questions at this early stage of the Big Picture framework process are certainly challenging. Some managers essentially avoid making them by creating complex strategic documents that serve only to muddle the issues. Our job as managers is not to confuse, however, but to clarify, and our first step toward arriving at an elegant, well-defined marketing plan is to make a clear and concise statement of our business objective.

Marketing Objective (Chapter 3)

After identifying our firm's skills and goals, we turn our attention to the customer in Chapter 3. Who is our customer, who might become our customer, how many people are in each category, and what kind of loyalty would we like to develop in them? With this information about our marketing objective we will begin to assess how to allocate our resources between growing our business with our current customers and attracting new ones. This analysis will be the foundation for a strategic perspective on our growth by using *customer value* as the key metric instead of *product* value.

Source of Growth (Chapter 4)

Next, in the Big Picture framework, we evaluate our competitive opportunity. Here, based on our understanding of our firm and our customer focus, we can assess the source from which our growth will come. We will choose between two options: We can focus on gaining share from a competitor or segment, or we can "grow the pie" by stimulating demand in a particular industry or category. In effect, we will be deciding whether to invoke a competitive comparison or, as a market leader, increase interest and usage in the category. Our decisions here and in Marketing Objective will determine our **strategic focus**, the key intersection of customer and competitive attention that represents our best strategic opportunity.

Segmentation, Targeting, and Positioning (Chapters 5, 6, and 7)

Segmentation, targeting, and positioning form the crucial link between strategy and execution. It is here that we will decide how to further focus our efforts, identifying the attitudes and behaviors of our ideal target market and considering how our consumers and potential consumers view our offerings relative to the competition.

Product

Product represents the first executional chapter in the Big Picture framework. As we move into this area, we need to build on our strategic foundations and consider how we can execute in a disciplined fashion the strategic decisions we made. Our products are more than simply what we sell; they are a crucial point of contact between the firm and the customer. We will explore how to do more than sell our products; we'll also investigate how to use them to build customer equity.

Service as Product

We consider services separately from hard goods because there are clear strategic and tactical differences between them. In particular, we will consider the fact that services are *intangible*, that they are *performed* not produced, and that their performance affects customer satisfaction and loyalty.

Pricing Strategy

Pricing is not simply a means of capturing revenue and profits. In reality, pricing decisions are pervasive throughout the Big Picture framework, and they affect everything from source of growth to segmentation and positioning to distribution and product strategy. In the end, a sound pricing strategy is built on a sound strategic approach to all elements of marketing. For this reason we can see pricing as a *symptom* of either healthy or unhealthy marketing practice.

Channel Strategy

Channel planning and management form a complex and dynamic process for directing the flow of product, money, and information. Since a channel structure can be difficult to modify once in place, we must be particularly mindful of the short- and long-run implications of our decisions. First and foremost we must ask ourselves what value each channel member adds to our end product, and how we can increase this end value efficiently and effectively.

Communications Strategy

In the age of digital marketing and social media, communications strategy has become simultaneously more tactical and more strategic. The number of communications tools available to us has proliferated rapidly, making it harder to judge which might be most effective. For this reason we must build our communications strategy on a firm strategic bedding, letting our strategy drive our selection of tools, instead of tools driving our strategy.

Metrics

In the final chapter we address the all-important topic of marketing metrics: how to measure the impact of our actions. With appropriate metrics we can begin to evaluate the effectiveness and efficiency of our marketing actions and take steps to improve them. We visit this topic last because we cannot consider which metrics to use until we understand our strategic and tactical objectives. Given that understanding, we can review our plans and identify where and how we can measure the impact of our actions.

In each of these chapters we present key tools for developing and integrating strategy with execution. As our skills grow as marketers, so does our responsibility to practice in an ethical manner, which we discuss next.

ETHICAL PRACTICE IN MARKETING

Most issues of integrity we face are not big issues but small ones, yet the accumulated weight of our choices has an impact on our sense of self.

—*Nathaniel Branden*

As practitioners, professors, students, and human beings, we must make decisions daily that rely on our personal ethics. The firm can and should play an important part in supporting a culture that encourages employees to make ethical managerial decisions as well. In the end, ethical practice results not from an inspiring corporate mission or values statement, but rather from the everyday actions of the people who work there.

The Challenge of Studying Ethics

Ethics are the "moral judgments, standards, and rules of conduct by which we live."[1] We can consider ethics in terms of (1) what we personally consider to be the *right* or *moral* choice, and (2) what impact our actions will have on ourselves, our firm, our customers, and society as a whole. In theory, then, in order to be perfectly ethical we simply have to (1) always know what is right and (2) be able to accurately predict the impact of our actions on ourselves and everyone else.

In practice, of course, this seems like an almost impossible task. It is precisely because the topic of ethics is complex and subjective that we must devote greater thought and effort to identifying our own system of ethics, improving it, and applying it consistently every day. **Ethical practice** is our ongoing effort to act in accordance with the guiding moral principles we have identified that reflect our assessment of right and wrong. Just as we can develop skills as marketers, we also can develop skills as *ethical* marketers by considering not just the strategic and executional implications of our decisions, but their ethical implications as well. And just as marketing is a discipline, the ethical practice of marketing is a discipline as well.

As we discussed above, the emphasis of this book is on marketing as a system in which changes in one part have an impact on other parts. This interconnectedness holds true for ethical practice as well. If we consistently consider our ethical responsibilities at the corporate level, we will instinctively apply them at the level of implementation. In contrast, if ethics are not integral at the corporate level, we should not be surprised when they are not evident in the everyday practice of our employees.[2]

Ethics. The moral judgments, standards, and rules of conduct by which we live.

Ethical practice. Our ongoing effort to act in accordance with the guiding moral principles we have identified that reflect our assessment of right and wrong and to consider the impact of our actions.

---

[1]Taylor, Paul W. (1975). *Principles of Ethics: An Introduction*, Encino, CA: Dickenson Publishing Company, Inc.

[2]For additional resources on business ethics, see the society for business ethics (societyforbusinessethics. org.).

Do the Right Thing...

Our first task, then, is simply to *do the right thing*. By definition this requires us to make a personal and subjective assessment of what we consider right and wrong. In most societies and cultures what is considered "right" is judged by the moral virtues described by Aristotle in his Nicomachean Ethics.[3] These virtues include courage, temperance, generosity, honesty, fairness, gentleness, and justice. The practice of these virtues is believed to lead to individual happiness, and to also benefit society as a whole.

As managers, we may extend these virtues to consider whether the organization is acting in an ethical manner. For example, Ben and Jerry's might be considered organizationally generous and magnanimous because it limits the difference between its highest- and lowest-paid employees. And just as individual virtuousness can lead to individual happiness, the virtuousness of a firm can lead to "happiness" of a different sort. An ethical firm can enjoy advantages in recruiting employees, greater employee retention, lower liability, greater brand equity, and, ultimately, more sustained growth. Organizations such as Ethisphere publish annual assessments of firms based on their ethical virtues.

It is often argued that because the notion of right and wrong is inherently subjective, we should not consider it in business. And while it may in fact be difficult to assess right and wrong in certain business situations, there are many more in which it is actually quite straightforward. Most people can agree, for example, that causing harm to another individual is not right. As managers, citizens, and human beings, we cannot escape the need to consider ethics by arguing that the issues are too complicated or too subjective. Instead, we must do our best, on a daily basis, to live in accordance with our values.

Ethisphere is an international think-tank dedicated to advancing ethical business practices. Every year it compiles a list of the world's most ethical companies.

Have a Positive Impact...

The second piece of the ethics puzzle is the impact of our behaviors on others. While we can debate and even disagree about what is right and what is wrong, the impact of what we do is usually much easier to see. There are three variables to consider as we address this aspect of behavior.

Whom Are We Affecting?

When we make a decision as managers, we must consider a number of different "stakeholders." These include ourselves, other people in our firm, our customers, our shareholders, our partners, and society as a whole. Our greatest ethical challenges arise when there is a conflict between one or more of these groups. For example, food scientists at Kraft Foods understand that products with fairly high quantities of sugar such as Jello Gelatin, Chips Ahoy Cookies, and Fruity Pebbles Cereal are preferred by children, and that producing and marketing these types of products will likely result in higher sales, more profits, and a higher return on investment for shareholders. Unfortunately, the children consuming these products will experience higher rates of obesity, diabetes, and heart disease and will incur higher health care costs for their families, their future employers, and ultimately society as a whole.

---

[3]Aristotle. *Nicomachean Ethics*. Translated by Martin Ostwald. New York: Macmillan, 1962.

CUSTOMERFOCUS

SALT, SUGAR, FAT: ETHICS AND THE FOOD INDUSTRY

In his book, *Salt, Sugar, Fat*, the Pulitzer-prize winning writer Michael Moss explores how some of the largest packaged-food companies in the world have contributed to the obesity epidemic. Moss conducts his research at companies like Kraft and General Mills and details their science-based approach to developing food that becomes addictive. He also interviews a variety of marketers from the food industry, some of whom have left their jobs full of remorse, and builds a compelling case against an industry that has targeted the world's most vulnerable population, using cartoon characters and other tactics to get children 'hooked' on food that is unhealthy and habit-forming. In doing so, food and bever-

Mark Rightmire KRT/NewsCom

age giants were making calculations not just about current profitability but also about the long-term potential for customer lifetime value. For example, as reported by Moss, Coca Cola's marketing efforts focused on attracting customers who over time would become heavy users of Coke products by drinking more than 1,000 cans of Coke annually. Moss details how boards of directors of major food companies instructed their managers to prioritize shareholder profits over kids' health.

Ethical issues are pervasive in marketing, and the individual marketer must be conscious of how the strategy of the company aligns with his or her personal views and ethical stance. ■

Sources: Mowbray, Scott. "You Really Can't Eat Just One, and Here's the Reason," *The New York Times.* March 17, 2013. http://www.nytimes.com/2013/03/18/books/salt-sugar-fat-by-michael-moss.html?pagewanted=all. Accessed April 30, 2013.

Boeschenstein, Nell. "How the Food Industry Manipulates Taste Buds with 'Salt Sugar Fat,'" *Blog post.* NPR. Org. http://www.npr.org/blogs/thesalt/2013/02/26/172969363/how-the-food-industry-manipulates-taste-buds-with-salt-sugar-fat. Accessed April 30, 2013.

When we perceive conflicts between the "good" of different stakeholders, such as investors and children, we face an ethical decision. Kraft Foods decided to continue producing some sugary cereals but to stop promoting them to children under twelve. The initial impact was generally believed to be a loss of revenue. However, the company arguably saw a positive impact on brand equity, particularly among parents, as it promoted its Smart Choice Program as the first in the industry to voluntarily apply nutrition criteria to products advertised to young children. The challenge for Kraft's marketers, of course, is to quantify the net impact of this decision.

What Is the Quantifiable Impact of Our Decision?

After we have identified the stakeholders affected, we must attempt to estimate and quantify the net impact of our actions. We must therefore determine (1) our unit of measurement and (2) our time frame. As marketers, we most often measure our impact in economic terms like revenue, profits, market share, and share price. However, there are other quantifiable outcomes of our actions. For example, if we make unethical decisions we increase our risk of legal liability. Kraft's parent company, Altria (formerly Philip Morris), was party to a lawsuit between 46 state Attorney Generals and the four largest tobacco companies that was ultimately settled for more than $200 billion. The settlement required, among other things, that defendants fund an anti-smoking advocacy group that ran several compelling anti-smoking advertising campaigns. This settlement was the culmination of a decades-long legal action regarding the connection between cigarettes and lung cancer and other health problems, and it represents a financial estimate of the negative impact of the actions of the tobacco companies on the health and well-being of the citizens of the 46 states in the suit.

Some effects may be difficult to quantify. For example, Whole Foods Markets actively supports local and organic farmers. This support has a number of positive benefits: it gives Whole Foods more credibility with its customers and quite possibly a higher stock price for its shareholders. In addition, the use of local farmers reduces gas consumption, which reduces shipping costs as well. Reduced shipping distances in turn reduce traffic congestion, pollution, and health problems in the community that are associated with bad air quality. Such benefits are hard to measure but no less important. As we improve our ability to quantify these secondary benefits, we are better able to provide logical support for decisions we personally believe to be ethical.

What Is the Probability That Our Ethical Decisions Will Have a Positive Impact?

The task of quantifying the impact of our decisions is challenging. As managers, we must go further and assess the *probability* that these outcomes will occur. For example, top management at the four largest tobacco companies was quite aware that, if they lost in court, the outcome would be massive settlement costs. Unfortunately, they did not accurately assess the *probability* that such a judgment would come to pass. Thus, in addition to estimating the potential *magnitude* of a negative or positive outcome, we must also try to figure out how *likely* it is.

In industries ranging from healthcare to automotive, this is an important and complex issue. Consider the case of Toyota, which in 2010 had to recall approximately 8.5 million cars and trucks worldwide. Not all these vehicles were faulty; however, once a certain number of failures had been observed in a particular model, all vehicles of that model had to be recalled because of the potential for injury or death of Toyota drivers.

A decision like the one Toyota faced requires (1) estimating the cost of the different actions, and (2) estimating the probability that each outcome might occur. This type of **expected value** analysis helps us to assess complex ethical situations and consider the potential impact of our actions in a more systematic manner. Expected value is a statistical term defined as the mean of a random variable. For example, suppose we flip a coin 10 times and obtain $5 every time we get heads and lose $3 every time we get tails. We can calculate the expected value of this game as follows:

$$E = 10 \, (p_{heads} \times \$5 - p_{tails} \times \$3) = \$10$$

where

$$E = \text{expected value}$$
$$p_{heads} = \text{probability of getting heads (0.5)}$$
$$p_{tails} = \text{probability of getting tails (0.5)}$$

Similarly, for larger uncertain events we can estimate the probabilities of certain outcomes and estimate the dollar impact of each, obtaining an expected value by adding the product of the probabilities and values of each outcome. Because we are dealing with estimates of events that are uncertain, this exercise will not give us an objective answer; it will, however, help to clarify the issues. The basis of ethical practice is consistency, and systematic approach to the considering the potential impact of our actions is one way to enhance our consistency.

...and Achieve Sustainable Growth

The second reason to engage in ethical practice is that it leads to long-term profitability. In the short run, it is certainly possible that a firm might make substantial profits by ignoring its ethical responsibilities; we can always choose to mislead consumers about our product in order to acquire income we would not otherwise have earned. If we are interested only in generating one-time sales, this approach may work; however, the source of profitability for most ongoing ventures is *revenue streams from retained customers*. We achieve these revenue streams only by consistently delivering on our value proposition, and that consistency is a cornerstone of ethical practice.

In extreme cases, customers can address a company's ethical deficiencies by recourse to the legal system. In most other situations, they simply seek other suppliers when they recognize that a company is not engaging in ethical practices. Arguably, then, ethical practice not only preserves but also significantly enhances the value of the firm. The most frequently cited example is Johnson & Johnson's response to a series of customer deaths after someone injected cyanide into Tylenol capsules on shelves in several stores in 1982. Following its now-famous ethical credo, which begins: "We believe our first responsibility is to the doctors, nurses and patients, to mothers and fathers and all others who use our products and services," Johnson & Johnson immediately informed customers and pulled all of its Tylenol product from shelves, incurring a significant cost. It did not put the brand back into distribution until it had developed new tamper-proof packaging. Although it could have argued that it was not to blame, Johnson & Johnson instead reacted quickly and took more than its share of responsibility for the incident. This action saved the brand and created long-lasting goodwill for the company. It was also the right thing to do.

PERSONAL ETHICS AND BUSINESS ETHICS

When we address ethical issues as managers we must, at the core, consider our personal ethics, our beliefs about right and wrong. A discussion of our personal beliefs is not within the scope of a marketing text; however, we cannot pursue ethical practice in marketing (or any field) without them. During the job search process, for instance, we will implicitly or explicitly evaluate whether the ethics of the firm align with our own. From the firm's perspective, it is important to provide a clearly established and ethical code. This code cannot be simply a set of vague positive statements; it must be a guide for day-to-day decision-making. Perhaps the simplest and most straightforward example is Google's informal code of conduct: "Don't be evil."

Of course, this simple statement quickly inspires the question: "What is evil?" Like individuals, firms need to define for themselves the terms "good" and "evil," "right" and "wrong" and effectively communicate their meanings to everyone in the firm. The ethical code these words define can become more than a set of empty statements; it can be a guide for day-to-day decision-making. As Nathaniel Branden states in *The Six Pillars of Self-Esteem*:[4] "Most issues of integrity we face are not big issues but small ones, yet the accumulated weight of our choices has an impact on our sense of self." This same philosophy can apply to the decisions we make as managers.

---

[4]Branden, Nathaniel, *The Six Pillars of Self-Esteem*. New York, NY, England: Bantam Books, Inc. (1994).

Thus, our goal as managers is to ensure that our firm's ethics are aligned with our own. If they are not, we must consider taking the steps necessary to *do the right thing*. When the firm's ethics are aligned with our own, then by building on this foundation, we can begin to understand and explore how we can make a positive difference to our peers, consumers, our society, and ourselves.

Toward this end, one of the first questions we should ask ourselves as marketers is, "Do I believe that, using the tools of marketing, I can get people to do what they would not otherwise have done?" If the answer is *yes*, then our ethical responsibility is clear: if we *can* change people's attitudes and behaviors with the tools we are learning to use, we must consider whether and how these changes *should* occur. If we spend more time and resources marketing cigarettes and alcohol than health clubs and language learning software, we can reasonably expect that use of "vice" products might increase, while use of "virtuous" products might decrease. As our skill with marketing tools grows, our consciousness of our responsibility must grow as well. This awareness will lead to better, more ethical practices that will eventually become habitual. It is this *habit* of ethical practice that we must develop to be truly effective marketers.

ETHICS AND THE BIG PICTURE FRAMEWORK

With the Big Picture framework we seek to achieve integration between execution and strategy; nowhere is this more important than with regard to ethics. A strong, clear statement of corporate values is the first step in the process; the strategy and execution that supports that statement reveals the true integrity of the firm and its employees.

By engaging in ethical practices, we establish a pattern of behavior that will stimulate ethical thinking at every stage of the Big Picture framework. The discussion below, structured around the elements of the framework in Figure 1.2, outlines just a few possible issues that may arise as we move from strategy to execution. This will serve as a foundation for continued dialog as we move into the content of the book.

Business Objective: Very often, business ethicists will speak of the conflict between a firm's responsibility to its shareholders and its responsibility to customers and the community. If a company takes a long-term perspective, however, these objectives will actually be aligned: corporate equity (and therefore profitability) will be enhanced when customers and the community see the corporation as trustworthy, and the firm will thrive in a society that is healthy and prosperous. At a more basic level, if the community of consumers served by the firm is prosperous, they will have more money to buy the firm's products.

Henry Ford demonstrated this idea in action in 1914 when he introduced a minimum wage of $5 and profit sharing at his factories. This move improved worker satisfaction, decreased turnover, and in the end actually *lowered* labor costs for Ford. And his higher-paid workers were now able to afford the cars they were building, further increasing satisfaction as well as Ford sales. The right thing to do was also the best thing to do in order to accomplish Ford's business objective. Therefore, the time frame on which the

Consumption of vice products and virtuous products can be linked to the level of marketing dollars spent promoting them. For example, Philip Morris's promotional efforts in the 1950s motivated millions of people around the world to smoke. The number of people who smoke today has declined drastically as the industry's promotional spending on cigarettes has decreased. Similarly, the growing sales of health and organic foods can be traced to increased promotional spending by food companies and grocery stores.

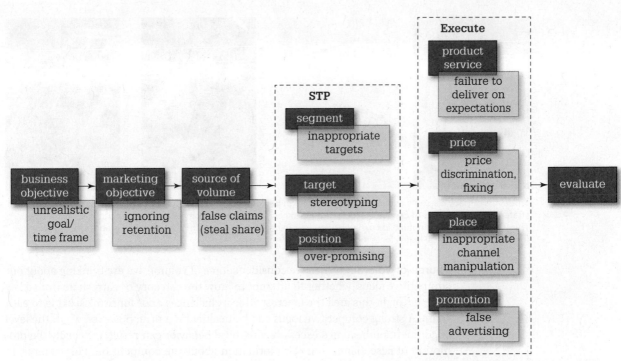

Figure 1.2 Ethics and the Big Picture framework. Ethical issues (in the orange boxes) are pervasive along the strategy-execution continuum of the Big Picture framework.

corporation chooses to focus will have perhaps the greatest influence on its ethical practice. If it is short term, there is much greater danger that performance pressures will lead to unethical practices.

Ensuring that the business objective is ethical is critical. Business objectives that aren't grounded in strategic reality will often lead to unethical behavior as managers attempt to meet impossible goals. While a stretch goal can motivate, an out-of-reach goal can lead to disaster.

Marketing Objective: A firm primarily engaged in *acquiring* customers is at greater risk of acting in an unethical fashion than one seeking growth from existing customers. The reason is that the tendency to over-promise is strong. Certain industries, such as residential construction and new car dealers, have a very high percentage of first-time or one-time customers. Not surprisingly, firms in these industries are at greater risk for ethical (and legal) violations.

In contrast, a focus on *retaining* customers can naturally move the firm toward more ethical activities, because growth through retention comes from delivering on our promises consistently, over time. This type of behavior generates brand loyalty that in turn generates sustainable growth. Over-promising doesn't work if you are seeking to retain customers, because once they experience disappointment, they will often find someone else with whom to do business. This is why most successful firms commit substantial resources to quality control and customer satisfaction.

In 1914, Henry Ford introduced a minimum wage standard across all his factories of $5 per day. At that time the average wage for factory workers was $2.34 for a 9-hour workday. This action is often cited as an example of business ethics that had a long-term effect on the manufacturing industry overall and helped create the middle class in America. This move by Henry Ford was not only ethical but it was also an effective cost-saving measure because increasing the average wage for workers in his factories resulted in a sharp reduction in his workforce turnover rate and a large increase in productivity, and of course, profits for Ford.

GILKIS-Emielke van Wyk/GettyImages   moodboard/Cultura/Getty Images   Dan Brandenburg/Getty Images   © Sogno Lucido/Shutterstock

Producers of baby car seats and mortgages draw a high percentage of first-time users and tend to focus on acquisition strategies, while makers of cereal and ketchup tend to have long-term customers and focus on retention strategies. This is logical given the natural life cycle of customers in both types of industries. However, the absence of a retention focus can create ethical issues for companies and their employees.

Source of Volume: When we consider source of volume, we are thinking about our competitive focus, whether to attempt to grow the category or earn share from a key competitor. In this area the greatest ethical challenges arise for firms seeking to earn share. A strong competitive focus can be healthy for a firm; however, when the level of competition becomes excessive, unethical behavior can result, especially the promotion of false claims and misinformation about the competition. For example, in the early 2000's Hyundai and Kia sought to earn share from market leader Toyota. Unfortunately, pressures to achieve this objective led the firms to overstate both horsepower and fuel economy for several of their models in their ads. This resulted in class-action lawsuits for false advertising.

Segmentation, Targeting, and Positioning: When we engage in segmentation, targeting, and positioning, we decide whom we want to speak to and what we want to say. In some cases our choice to target a particular segment can lead us into dangerous areas. The most obvious (and highly regulated) example is marketing to children, because it is quite easy to manipulate children with appealing characters and arguments. In 1997 the Federal Trade Commission charged R. J. Reynolds with "causing substantial injury to the health and safety of children" by its use of the "Joe Camel" cartoon character in advertising. One study published in the *Journal of the American Medical Association* found that 6-year-old children were as familiar with Joe Camel as they were with Mickey Mouse.[5]

Thus, particularly when we are dealing with key demographic segments such as children or the elderly, or segments that for any reason might be subject to undue influence, we must exercise particular care. While we may find it quite easy to leverage marketing tools to change beliefs and behaviors of certain segments, we should not always take advantage of these tools.

© Steve Skjold/Alamy Limited

© Featureflash/Shutterstock

A 1991 study published in the *Journal of the American Medical Association* found that six-year-old children were as familiar with Joe Camel as they were with Mickey Mouse.

Product: Ethics issues can arise when products fail. As discussed above, many companies face difficult trade-offs when they experience these failures and must consider recalling their products. The trade-off is generally between potential lost profit and damaged reputation from a recall, and potential risk to human life if no action is

[5]Fischer, Paul M., MD, et al. "Brand logo recognition by children aged 3 to 6 years," *JAMA 1991* 266: 3145–3148.

taken. How and when to deal with product failures are two of the most challenging ethical issues for marketers.

Product failures arise from insufficient quality control in the design and manufacturing stages of product development. Unfortunately, quality control efforts take time and money, and as the environment becomes increasingly complex and dynamic, firms face pressures to develop and launch products more and more rapidly. The stress of meeting product-launch deadlines can sometimes result in shortcuts that bring problems later. If and when failures do occur, the ethical health of the company is quickly brought into public view.

Price: In most countries, pricing practices are highly regulated, and laws dictate many pricing decisions that have an ethical component. In general, these laws prevent firms from taking actions that have a negative impact on price competition. In addition, firms face constraints regarding where and how they can communicate price information, and these constraints vary widely from industry to industry. Because pricing regulations are often complex, the greatest ethical pitfall we face as managers is the risk that we will fail to either understand or abide by these regulations.

MCT/Getty Images

Because pricing is tied directly to profitability, managers often face severe ethical challenges in this area, particularly when they are pressed to meet unrealistic profit targets. While regulations provide strong incentives to price in an ethical fashion, the immediacy of profit pressure is nonetheless quite profound. From this perspective, issues of pricing ethics are often tied to goals that are set in the strategic chapters of the Big Picture framework—business objective, marketing objective, and source of volume. As discussed above, these goals must be realistic, so that we are not tempted to violate ethical or legal rules in order to achieve them.

Making unit price information readily available on grocery store products adds transparency for consumers and is an example of an ethical pricing practice.

Place (Channels): Channels are the conduits through which we make and keep promises to customers. The greater the distance between the firm and the customer, the greater the chance that promises might be made and broken without the firm's knowledge. This possibility poses a danger to the firm from a marketing, ethical, and even legal standpoint. Thus, our greatest ethical challenge here is channel alignment and coordination. We must (1) ensure that each and every channel member clearly understands what needs to be delivered, and (2) enforce standards throughout the channel that enable this delivery. In general this is best accomplished when a **channel leader** such as Walmart or Intel emerges. A channel leader is a company that holds the greatest power in the distribution channel; as a result, it is able to set standards for how the channel will be managed and bring channel members together around key activities and behaviors. Then other channel members align much more quickly and efficiently.

Channel leader. A company that holds the greatest power in the distribution channel; as a result, it is able to set standards for how the channel will be managed and bring channel members together around key activities and behaviors.

Promotion: Advertising and promotion are areas known to be susceptible to ethical violations that range from false or misleading advertising to failure to fulfill rebates. On a broader scale, we as marketers must consider whether and how advertising increases materialism, sometimes to the detriment of the society. Products that are marketed more heavily will likely be used more; if these products are detrimental to users, then whether and how to promote them become ethical issues (See Box on page 18).

social**media**

Challenging Fake Popularity Ratings on the Web

Attempts to build "buzz" and positive ratings can tempt firms into questionable ethical territory. Recently a number of companies have developed software that can create fake followers in social media outlets such as Twitter and Facebook to provide positive ratings and/or a sense that a product is more popular than it really is. In 2012 Marco Calzori, a professor of corporate communications at IULM University in Milan, made the news when he asserted that 54% of the followers of a rising star in Italy, the comedian-turned-political figure Beppe

Marco Calzori, a professor of corporate communications at IULM University in Milan, made the news when he asserted that 54% of the followers of a rising star in Italy, the comedian-turned-political figure Beppe Grillo, were fake.

Alessia Pierdomenico/Bloomberg/Getty Images

Grillo, were fake. Calzori developed an algorithm that can distinguish real followers from fake automated ones, which he calls 'bots.' He has already proved that many of the followers of both international and Italian brands like @Cocacola and @IKEAITALIA are fake, and he demonstrated how easy it is to commit this type of fraud by purchasing 50,000 of his fake Twitter followers for $20. However, the revelation that Grillo's followers were fake generated outrage among his real followers, who responded with hate emails directed to Calzori.

Sources: Vogt, Andrea. "Hot or bot? Italian professor casts doubt on politician's Twitter popularity," *The Guardian UK*, July 22, 2012. http://www.guardian.co.uk/world/2012/jul/22/bot-italian-politician-twitter-grillo. Accessed April 28, 2013.

Kitchen, Michael. "Some brands may buy fake Twitter followers: Report" April 26, 2013. *The Wall Street Journal. Market Watch*, http://articles.marketwatch.com/2013-04-26/industries/38821082_1_fake-twitter-followers-twitter-accounts-new-study-highlights. Accessed April 28, 2013.

Unfortunately, these strategic issues are the least of our ethical challenges. As advertising tools become increasingly sophisticated, marketers face increasing tests at the executional level. For example, in the area of social media, marketers are constantly seeking to obtain positive reviews or ratings in order to boost product sales. In order to accomplish this, they may hire "brand ambassadors," members of the target audience who are paid to promote a specific product among their peers. Red Bull promoted its energy drink on college campuses using this tactic. The intended audience may or may not know that the positive opinions being expressed about the product are not entirely objective. Further, since the firm does not fully control the message the ambassadors are relating, there can be unintended negative consequences. Some Red Bull ambassadors, for example, chose to showcase the product by mixing it with vodka. The combination of caffeine and alcohol can be particularly dangerous when consumed in excess.

Peter Bolter/Mirrorpix/NewsCom

A popular drink on college campuses, Red Bull increased consumption through college-age brand ambassadors who promoted the product to their peers, sometimes by mixing it with alcohol.

Market Research: Psychology and other social sciences have defined very clear methodologies for collecting information from people and conducting experiments in a manner that is not emotionally or physically harmful. As marketers, we do need a clear understanding of the customer, but we cannot obtain it at the customer's expense. For this reason the ethical manager should always consider the research methodology, keeping in mind the effect it will have on the research subjects.

Perhaps the greatest concern in marketing research and ethics today is the issue of privacy. Firms such as Google and Facebook have unprecedented access to consumer information. In some cases consumers are quite aware of this fact; for example, most Google users understand that the ads they see on their search screen are customized based on what sites they have visited. Fewer users may be aware that Google and other firms also scan users email accounts to identify potential marketing opportunities. As mobile devices that transmit location data proliferate, these firms can now begin analyzing this information to customize messaging at a whole new level.

Consumers choose to trade their privacy for the expected benefit of a more customized and possibly convenient Internet or mobile experience. Firms ask their users to consider this trade-off when they agree to specific terms of use when setting up an

GLOBALMARKETING

(DIGITAL/GLOBAL): COMPARING PRIVACY REGULATIONS IN THE UNITED STATES AND EUROPE

Companies like Facebook, Google, and Amazon, among many others, store and use private data collected from customers around the world. The proper use and protection of that data have become a major ethical issue an increasing number of companies must face.

Governments worldwide have different regulations about how personal data can be collected and used, resulting in very different approaches to privacy protections. The European Union (EU) uses a single set of rules, created in 1995 and due for a major revision in 2014, for any company seeking to do business in Europe or handling data belonging to any EU citizen, even if that person is based in another country. The new privacy rules provide one clear set of regulations protecting more than 500 million people in the EU and will be enforced by local authorities. All companies with more than 250 employees will have to name data protection officers, in charge of ensuring privacy compliance within organizations and of promoting transparency about what data is being collected and for what purpose. Organizations will also have to obtain each individual's consent before collecting any data.

In case of a data privacy breach, companies will have just 24 hours to notify those affected. The new rules also grant consumers the right to be forgotten, meaning they must be able to delete their data once the organization using it no longer has any legitimate reason to keep it. Fines will be charged for privacy violations; current proposals suggest they could reach 2% of a company's sales.

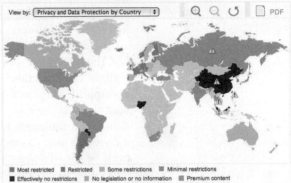

World Privacy Regulations Heat Map. Forrester Research maintains a World Map showing privacy regulations by country. The map is color coded to indicate the relative level of privacy restrictions in different parts of the world. Source: http://heatmap.forrestertools.com/

Privacy laws in the United States exist at the federal and state levels, creating a relatively complex patchwork of rules that both companies and individuals might struggle to understand. Overall, U.S. privacy laws allow companies to collect more data about individuals and to use it more freely than in Europe. A more stringent EU approach to privacy will mean that U.S. companies working with EU citizens will have to significantly tighten their privacy practices. ■

Sources: Singer, Natasha. "An American quilt of privacy laws, incomplete," *The New York Times*. March 30, 2013. http://www.nytimes.com/2013/03/31/technology/in-privacy-laws-an-incomplete-american-quilt.html?pagewanted=all. Accessed April 27, 2013.

"Myth-busting: What the Commission proposals on data protection do and don't mean." European Commission website, http://ec.europa.eu/justice/newsroom/data-protection/news/121207_en.htm. Accessed April 27, 2013.

account. Because these agreements are so dense and voluminous, users rarely review them in detail before "checking the box." Thus, satisfying legal concerns does not mean that the marketer has demonstrated proper ethics. Often when ethical violations are committed these firms are publicly chastised in the social media world, and their reputations can be damaged as a result. Further, around the world countries are attempting to protect the privacy rights of their citizens through legislation as discussed in the previous Social Media box. Today more than ever it is not enough to simply ensure that we have covered ourselves legally. We must make a clear and honest assessment of the ethical implications of our use of individual consumer data.

We've touched briefly on ethical issues at various stages of the Big Picture framework, as a starting point for a deeper consideration of ethical practice that will continue throughout the text. This is, of course, only the beginning; for managers, ethics is not simply a matter of theory but one of practice, and our ethical "muscle" will develop as we face and make proper decisions throughout our careers. As we embark on this process, we should consider a foundational aspect of ethical marketing practice that relates to the firm's overall skill level. Often, ethical challenges in business arise when there is a mismatch between expectations and abilities. At any stage in the marketing process, we may agree to produce results that cannot realistically be achieved given the firm's skills and resources, or our own. Instead of admitting to this fact and adjusting objectives accordingly, we may be tempted to resort to unethical behavior on behalf of the firm. How do we avoid this outcome?

The best way to mitigate the problem of challenging objectives, for both the firm and the individual, is to continue to enhance our skills and close the gap between abilities and expectations. The tools presented in this book are intended to help you accomplish this objective at the individual level, and, ultimately, as a key influencer in your firm. As the competitive environment becomes increasingly complex and dynamic, the challenges to practitioners seeking to operate in an ethical manner will increase as well. To successfully address these challenges, ethical marketing practice must be considered not as a topic, but as a philosophy for conducting business every day. We can begin by referring not to ethics but to ethical *practice*, to remind ourselves that this area is not just theory but action.

□ SUMMARY

1. Describe the structure of the Big Picture framework

The emphasis of this book is on marketing as a system, in which changes in one part have an impact on other parts. The Big Picture is an integrated framework designed to help you analyze and address the myriad marketing problems you will face during your career. While it is presented in this text in a series of chapters, you should think of it as a set of interrelated aspects of marketing, each of which affects and is affected by the others. This relationship holds true for ethical practice as well. If we consistently consider our ethical responsibilities at the corporate level, this approach becomes almost instinctual at the level of implementation. In contrast, if ethics are not integral at the corporate level, we should not be surprised that they are not evident in the everyday practice of our employees. The Big Picture framework helps to align and integrate marketing strategy and execution by linking strategic decisions to execution as the firm moves through the marketing process.

2. Identify the main principles of Ethical Practice in Marketing

Ethics are the moral judgments, standards, and rules of conduct by which we live. We can consider ethics in terms of (1) what we personally consider to be the right or moral choice, and (2) what impact our actions will have on ourselves, our firm, our customers, and society as a whole. Ethical practice is our ongoing effort to act in accordance with the guiding moral principles we have identified that reflect our assessment of right and wrong and to consider the impact of our actions. Just as we can develop skills as marketers, we also can develop skills as ethical marketers, by considering not just the strategic and executional implications of our decisions, but their ethical implications as well. Ethical practice in marketing requires that we do the right thing, we try to have a positive impact, while striving to achieve profitability for our company. Doing the right thing requires us to make a personal and subjective assessment of what we consider right and wrong. In most societies and cultures what is considered "right" is judged by Aristotelian moral virtues. These virtues include courage, temperance, generosity, honesty, fairness, gentleness, and justice. The practice of these virtues is believed to lead to individual happiness, and to also benefit society as a whole. To have a positive impact, we must act thoughtfully and consider whom we are affecting by our actions, what the result of our actions is, and the probability that these effects will take place. Finally, ethical practice and profitability should complement, rather than conflict with, each other.

3. Distinguish between personal and business ethics issues

Ethics is the moral code that guides our decision-making; our personal moral code should guide our professional code. As marketing managers we have a responsibility to ensure that our firm's ethics are aligned with our own. If they are not, we must consider taking the steps necessary to *do the right thing*. When they are, then by building on the foundation of personal and firm ethics, we can begin to understand and explore how we can make a positive difference to our peers, consumers, our society, and ourselves. We will master ethical decision-making when thinking about ethics becomes habitual and is integrated into our marketing decision-making routines.

4. Integrate ethical questions into the Big Picture framework

While business ethics is often taught as a separate subject, our strong belief is that it is more effective to integrate ethical thinking into our decision processes from strategy development through execution. Ethical issues arise at each step of the marketing framework. Having overly aggressive and short-term goals in our business objective can encourage unethical behavior. In Marketing Objective we look at acquiring and retaining customers. Overly aggressive acquisition objectives can help create an organizational environment where customers are 'forgotten' once they have purchased our product. This is not only bad for our customers; it is also bad for our brands and our business in the long term. When thinking of our overall competitive approach in the Source of Volume chapter, we need to be particularly careful to ensure that our efforts on behalf of our brands do not lead to unethical practices, especially the promotion of false claims and misinformation about the competition. The ethical treatment of other companies comes into focus again when we think about our distribution partners; our ethical behavior must extend to ourselves, our employee partners, competitors, and channel members. Finally, in collecting market research information it is critical that we maintain transparency and follow an ethical approach to information gathering and privacy.

☐ KEY TERMS

Channel leader. (p. 17) A company that holds the greatest power in the distribution channel; as a result, it is able to set standards for how the channel will be managed and bring channel members together around key activities and behaviors.

Core competence. (p. 6) Key organizational skills that drive sustainable growth. The core competence is the source of differentiation for the firm.

Ethical practice. (p. 9) Our ongoing effort to act in accordance with the guiding moral principles we have identified that reflect our assessment of right and wrong and to consider the impact of our actions.

Ethics. (p. 9) The moral judgments, standards, and rules of conduct by which we live.

Expected value analysis. (p. 12) A technique that can help us estimate the potential impact of our actions in a systematic manner by considering the probability of an event and the value of the outcome.

Fundamental entity. (p. 6) Our choice of fundamental entity determines the perspective from which we will conduct our strategic analysis, whether it be brand by brand or from a more global, corporate point of view.

Goal. (p. 7) Company goals function as success criteria and also help prioritize our actions and our allocation of resources.

Strategic focus. (p. 7) The key intersection of customer and competitive attention that represents our best strategic opportunity.

The Big Picture framework. (p. 5) An integrated framework designed to help you analyze and address the myriad marketing problems you will face during your career.

☐ QUESTIONS FOR DISCUSSION

1. Imagine you are the marketing manager for Acme Pharma, a company that sells drug A, which treats a rare disease that sometimes afflicts elderly cancer patients. Acme is in the final stages of getting FDA approval for a new cancer-fighting drug called drug B. Drug A has been on the market for over five years and is prescribed to thousands of patients globally; it is the major driver of profitability for your company. Your firm has just received a copy of a new clinical research study, funded by an insurance company, that finds drug A to be less effective than your firm claimed in the clinical data presented for FDA approval. The study says drug A helps some patients, but not as much as your company claims; even worse, it produces many and more serious side effects than previously thought. If the study is released to the public right now, it will tarnish your company's reputation and might affect not just drug A but also drug B's approval process. The new drug is due to be approved within the next week.

   (a) What are the ethical dilemmas confronting your firm and you personally?

   (b) Should your company try to prevent or delay the public release of the insurance company study?

   (c) Are there ethical actions your firm can take that will help minimize the reputational and financial damage the new data will likely cause?

2. Identify and discuss the specific ethical issues facing marketers in the following industries:

   (a) Restaurants

   (b) Casinos

   (c) Wineries

   (d) Breakfast cereal

   (e) Cigarettes

3. Identify at least one ethical issue that could arise in each of the following topics within the Big Picture framework.

   (a) Business objective goal

   (b) Marketing objective

   (c) Product

   (d) Price

   (e) Promotion

□ RESOURCES

Branden, Nathaniel, *The Six Pillars of Self-Esteem*. New York, NY, England: Bantam Books, Inc., 1994.

Branden, Nathaniel. *Honoring the Self: The Psychology of Confidence and Respect*. New York, NY, England Bantam, Books, 1985.

Chonko, Lawrence B., and Shelby D. Hunt. "Ethics and marketing management: An empirical examination," *Journal of Business Research* 13.4 (2012): 339–359.

Hunt, Shelby D., and Scott Vitell. "A general theory of marketing ethics," *Journal of Macromarketing* 6.1 (1986): 5–16.

Hunt, Shelby D., and Arturo Z. Vasquez-Parraga. "Organizational consequences, marketing ethics, and sales force supervision," *Journal of Marketing Research 30* (1993): 78–78.

Velasquez, Manuel G., and Manuel Velazquez. *Business Ethics: Concepts and Cases*. 5th ed. Upper Saddle River, NJ: Prentice Hall, 2002.

chapter two

"Oh, the many talents that
remain undiscovered
out there, and the many
neglected intellects and
unappreciated skills."

Don Quixote, p. 769

THE BUSINESS OBJECTIVE

After studying this chapter you should be able to:

1. *List the business objective decisions*

2. *Describe the concept of Fundamental Entity: Who are we?*

3. *Identify the advantages and disadvantages of different branding strategies*

4. *Define the core competence: What do we do best?*

5. *Define the core business: What business are we in?*

6. *Define business goals: Where are we going?*

7. *Integrate the Business Objective decisions with other Big Picture decisions*

Walmart's International Expansion

The giant U.S. discount retailer Walmart launched an international expansion plan in the 1990s, first going to Mexico and then opening its first Chinese store in Shenzhen in 1996 and in Germany in 1998. The discount retail chain was hoping to replicate its low-margin large-volume business model, so successful in the United States, in both Germany and China. However, the company quickly ran into major problems.

In the United States, Walmart is famously antilabor union. However, in both Germany and China, governments mandate labor union representation for workers. The company acquiesced in both countries. In Germany, Walmart also had to accommodate to paying workers much higher salaries than in the United States and allowing them to work shorter hours.

In addition to running into labor problems, Walmart, known to possess a logistics and supply chain core competence in the United States, ran into major problems with sourcing and merchandising in both Germany and China. Germany's CEO David Wild admitted large-scale failures in sourcing: "Many of our (product) buyers in Germany were Americans. Some real goof-ups occurred as a result. Like, did you know that American pillowcases are a different size than German ones are?" he asked. Walmart Germany ended up with a huge pile of pillowcases it couldn't sell to German customers. Sourcing was also an Achilles heel for the company in China. Initially, fish and meat were offered as they were in the United States, dead and packaged in Styrofoam. However, Chinese consumers perceived prepackaged fish and meat as old merchandise and would not buy it. Walmart China now offers live fish, frogs and turtles

Chinese Walmart: Walmart has adapted its merchandising to accommodate Chinese consumer demands and its stores now sell live fish and bull frogs, among other things.

for consumers to pick out and also displays meat uncovered. In addition to offering U.S. cosmetic products, Walmart China also offers Chinese beauty products, such as ones made with sheep's placenta, believed to reduce wrinkles.

Sourcing and labor problems prevented Walmart from implementing its expansion model fully in Germany. And because the Company's low price low profit margin model makes it dependent on large volumes for profitability, Walmart was never able to reach sufficient scale to sustain its German operation. By 1999, Walmart closed its operations in Germany at an estimated cost of $1BLN. The company has been more successful in China where it acquired Trust-Mart. As of August 5, 2010, Walmart had 189 units in 101 cities throughout the country. ■

Sources: Naughton, Keith. "The great Walmart of China; to move into China, America's biggest and most successful retailer had to learn its business all over again." *Newsweek,* October 30, 2006. Print.

"Walmart in China Factsheet." Walmart Corporate website. http://www.Walmartchina.com/english/walmart/index.htm#china. Accessed April 12, 2012.

To be successful a company requires skills or competencies in a number of areas, from sourcing and raising capital to product development and commercialization. Company competencies are contextual; that is, they are relative to the market environment within which the company operates. Sourcing and merchandising practices in one country might not work in another country. As companies plan for international expansion, they need to plan for competencies that translate to new markets and for those competencies that will need to be developed anew. The question of how to plan and develop competencies that enable companies to create value for customers that is distinct from other companies in their industry is perhaps the most important question we must pose in establishing our marketing strategy.

THE BUSINESS OBJECTIVE DECISIONS AND WHY THEY MATTER

The Big Picture framework presents a series of topics that progress from broadest and most strategic to narrowest and more executional. Decisions in the Business Objective chapter of the framework initiate the strategic portion of the Big Picture. The framework topics correspond to a series of decisions managers must make to guide the marketing strategy of a company; we will advance from left to right in the model in order to proceed from strategy to execution/tactics and not the other way around. Too often marketers get caught up in the daily routine of executional decisions—pricing, the next advertising campaign, or the latest competitive crisis—and they neglect their carefully developed long-term strategy. The Big Picture framework is helpful here, because it not only defines a process for developing a strategy, but also ensures that we adhere to the appropriate tactics necessary for its execution. Thus, as we move through the framework, decisions become more tactical in nature, but our strategic goal always drives these decisions. We should be constantly checking for **strategic alignment** is a consistent relationship between our strategy and the actions we take based on that strategy.

Because they drive and limit all our later decisions, the choices we make in the early chapters of the framework are the most important, and often the most challenging, decisions we will make. In fact, their difficulty often tempts us to skip over them and get down to the business of execution. In an extremely simple environment it is possible to survive by making executional decisions — looking for breakthrough products, technologies, or even communications campaigns that will drive growth in the short run. However, as the competitive landscape becomes more complex and resources become more constrained, it grows is increasingly less effective to execute without a strategy, and ultimately it is not sustainable. Instead, we must face the day-to-day challenges that emerge and persist by making and adhering to higher-level strategic decisions.

The first step in developing a reasoned marketing strategy is identifying our primary *business objective*. In doing so, we ask four essential questions:

1. Who are we? (fundamental entity)
2. What are we good at? (core competence)
3. Where are we going? (goal)
4. What is our main business? (core business)

The answers to these questions should be specific and actionable. The business objective is neither a mission statement, a value statement, nor a statement of corporate philosophy. While mission and vision statements may inspire, they usually do not instruct. In contrast, a properly framed business objective will serve as a key point of reference and a decision aid as we move through the framework: every executional decision we make should align with this primary objective. It is the first means by which we can ensure that strategy and execution are tightly integrated.

THE CONCEPT OF FUNDAMENTAL ENTITY: WHO ARE WE?

The American Marketing Association offers this definition of brand: A name, term, sign, symbol, or design, or a combination of them which is intended to identify the goods or services of one seller or a group of sellers and to differentiate them from those of competitors (AMA, 1960). A more practical definition might be: A brand is a collection of beliefs consumers hold about a company, product, or service. Brands can be represented by names, signs or symbols, color combinations, or logos and are **strategic assets** of the firm. A strategic asset is a resource of the company that is supported by a core competence and critical to differentiating the brand. Within the Big Picture framework we distinguish the term *brand* from a related term, which we call the **Fundamental Entity.**

The Fundamental Entity question is the first one we ask ourselves in developing our marketing strategy. It asks, Who are we? In other words: From what perspective should the company develop its marketing strategy, given how customers think of the firm? We define the Fundamental Entity as the brand level from which we conduct the strategic analysis and which reflects the customer perspective regarding who we are. It might be the corporate brand, a brand line, or a product brand, depending on the company's brand structure. For example, if we are working for Nabisco, the corporate brand is Nabisco, the brand line might be Nabisco Crackers, and the product brand might be Ritz. Whatever the case, the Fundamental Entity mirrors the consumer perspective of the brand.

The question of who we are is thus essential and highly strategic, and when we develop new products we should not relegate branding decisions to the end of the development process along with package and logo design but should address them at the very initial stages. This practice of thinking of brand tactically at the end of the product development process is particularly prevalent in business-to-business (B2B) contexts, where, at the extreme, a product might be conceptualized, developed, tested, and priced before it is named. In many B2B organizations branding is considered a tactical question to be made at lower levels, a matter of selecting catchy names, logo designs, or slogans on a business card. In contrast, in many business-to-consumer (B2C) firms, branding decisions are made at higher levels but without paying enough attention to the implications for those "on the ground" who must execute on them. In reality our choice of branding strategy has implica-

Strategic asset. A strategic asset is a resource of the company that is supported by a core competence and is critical to differentiating the brand.

Fundamental entity. The brand level from which we conduct the strategic analysis. The Fundamental Entity might be the corporate brand, a brand line, or a product brand, depending on the company's brand structure.

tions for our customers, our company, and our competitive decision-making. Here is why:

1. Customers: How do our customers think of us? Do they think about separate products, identifying each with distinct benefits (iPhone or iPad?)? Or do they associate the overall brand benefit with our corporate brand and then select a product with a specific functional benefit (do they associate design for simplicity with Apple and then choose an iPhone to communicate, an iPad for portable entertainment, and an iPod for music listening)? What comes to our customers' minds first, the product brand or the corporate brand?

2. Company: How do we organize our brands? Are products organized by brand or is there strong cooperation across product groups under one brand? When we launch a new product do we start from square one, determining the benefits of the product and positioning (as do Microsoft Xbox and Windows), or do we launch new products with the objective of delivering a predefined benefit (BMW performance)?

3. Competition: When we do competitive analysis, who do we include in our competitive set? An umbrella brand by definition will have more competitors in more categories and must plan accordingly. In contrast, distinct branding approaches lead to a narrower competitive picture. When doing the analysis on behalf of P&G we will need to consider competitors in all major categories where that company operates. If instead we look at just Head and Shoulders, we will be interested only in shampoo competitors.

Hence, our choice of Fundamental Entity will affect our entire marketing and organizational strategy. A single, broad Fundamental Entity calls for one overarching Big Picture analysis in which we evaluate our products based on their contribution to the overall value of the Fundamental Entity. For example, the BMW brand allocates more promotional resources to its M-series sedans than are proportionate to its sales. One reason for this relatively large resource allocation is that the M-series is the product line most representative of the overall brand benefit 'ultimate driving performance.' In contrast, an organization with multiple Fundamental Entities will also have multiple distinct goals and activities for each of the FE's, and distinct or unrelated customer benefits. For example, Procter and Gamble sells shampoo to make hair shiny, Pantene, as well as shaving razors, Gillette. For each of these Fundamental Entities, we will develop a separate Big Picture analysis.

© Chen Fei/Xinhua Press/Corbis

Our Fundamental Entity determines the lens through which we analyze and make all subsequent marketing decisions. A company may undertake a strategic analysis of its operations and decide to develop a strategy for an internal unit, such as HR, Finance, or the Eastern division. However, customers do not care about how our company is organized or what channels we sell though. They are not buying a division or a strategic business unit but a product, a brand, and ultimately a benefit. Our choice of Fundamental Entity should reflect this fact and be made with the consumer in mind. The marketing manager should think about how we want the customer to experience and categorize the product or service being offered, and define the Fundamental Entity based on that customer perspective.

Ultimately, the choice of Fundamental Entity has a significant impact on how the customer views the firm and how the firm markets to the customer. The firm delivers products or services; however, the identity of the firm, is represented by the brand. Given the crucial importance of brand, it therefore makes sense to conduct our analysis from this perspective.

DIFFERENT BRANDING STRATEGIES AND THEIR ADVANTAGES AND DISADVANTAGES

The AMA and marketing academics offer theoretical definitions of brand; marketers have debated for years about what "brand" really means in practice. Many believe a brand is a promise a company makes to its customers about the benefit they will derive from using its product or service. This is true but incomplete. A **brand** is actually a *collection* of beliefs—a core belief the customer holds about the product or service, and then a compilation of memories, experiences, observations, information, and stories from others that support and reinforce the core belief. The quantity, importance, vividness, and believability of these thoughts influence the strength of the customer's opinion about the product or service. This opinion—what the product or service *means* to the customer—is the essence of that product or service's brand. For example, Nike means 'self-empowerment through sports,' and McDonalds means 'convenience.'

In this book we distinguish three broad types of brand strategies: distinct branding, hybrid branding, and umbrella branding. Figure 2.1 shows some examples of companies that organize their brands in each of these types. We discuss each brand type in some detail next.

> **Brand.** A name, term, sign, symbol, or design, or a combination of them which is intended to identify the goods or services of one seller or a group of sellers, and to differentiate them from those of competitors. In practice, the brand is synonymous with the overall benefit the company promises to deliver to its customers.

> **Umbrella branding**
> A branding approach whereby the company uses just one brand for all of its products and services.

Umbrella Branding

An **umbrella brand** represents a family of products that delivers the same value proposition. Each product may deliver a unique functional benefit (a specific toothpaste may deliver a "whitening" benefit), but all products within the umbrella also deliver

Distinct branding	Hybrid branding	Umbrella branding
FEs = distinct brands	FE = brand line	FE = umbrella element
▪ P&G	▪ Marriott-branded hotels	▪ BMW
▪ Altria	▪ Porsche Cayenne	▪ Four Seasons hotels
▪ Starwood hotels		

Figure 2.1 Distinct branded companies go to market under separate brand names, whereas umbrella-branded companies go to market under the corporate brand. Hybrid-branded companies go to market combining a corporate and a product brand name.

a common higher-order benefit (everything beneath the Crest umbrella delivers the benefit of healthy teeth).

McKinsey & Co., a business consulting firm and Target each deliver a distinct value proposition to the customer. Target's is "Expect More. Pay Less." McKinsey promises "To help leaders make distinctive, lasting, and substantial improvements in performance, and constantly build a great firm that attracts, develops, excites, and retains exceptional people." When the entire company delivers a common value proposition, we define the entire company as the Fundamental Entity. The specific products and services the company offers are essentially *features* of the brand, just as the performance, reliability, weight, and torque of a Makita® power drill are features of that brand. For an umbrella brand, the equity delivered through products and services accrues to a single brand name. Not having additional names or logos focuses the attention, memory, and emotion of the customer onto this single umbrella brand.

Distinct Branding

At the other end of the spectrum is a **distinct** branding strategy, in which a firm may offer several products or groups of products with distinct meanings, brand names, and logos. For example, Procter & Gamble offers Gillette shaving products, Tide detergent, and Lacoste fragrances. Each delivers a different benefit, often to a different target audience. From the perspective of the Big Picture framework, each brand in a distinct-branded company is a separate Fundamental Entity, with a separate strategic analysis. Resources will generally be allocated to these Fundamental Entities based on financial considerations like return on investment or diversification, rather than on positioning decisions. Note that for a distinct-branded company, like Procter & Gamble, each brand underneath the corporate brand might function as its own umbrella. Crest toothpaste, for example, sits under the P&G family of brands but products ranging from Crest Pro-health toothpaste with a 'healthy teeth' benefit, to Crest Whitening Strips for 'white healthy teeth,' to Crest Toothbrushes to promote 'clean healthy teeth.'

Distinct branding. A branding approach whereby the company creates different brands for its different products and services.

Hybrid Branding

Many firms find themselves somewhere between umbrella- and distinct-branding strategies. These firms may develop a **hybrid** strategy, using a corporate brand to capture the benefits of the umbrella while supporting a sub-brand to further distinguish the product in the marketplace. For example, 3M uses its corporate name as an umbrella for many of its consumer products but also maintains the Post-it brand umbrella, as well as distinct product brands like Scotch Guard. It also markets a broad array of industrial products derived from its core competence in chemical engineering; some of the company's operating units follow an umbrella-branding strategy, and others a distinct-branding strategy. Ideally, a hybrid strategy offers the best of both worlds, allowing the firm to realize umbrella efficiencies while maintaining flexibility.

Unfortunately, many hybrid strategies spring not so much from sound strategy as from tactical decisions that, over time, result in an incoherent product portfolio. All too often a firm is loathe to let go of its umbrella brand, even when the positioning of that umbrella doesn't fit the intended positioning of a new product being

Hybrid branding. A branding approach that combines two brands—the corporate brand plus separate brands— to designate differences in product or service lines.

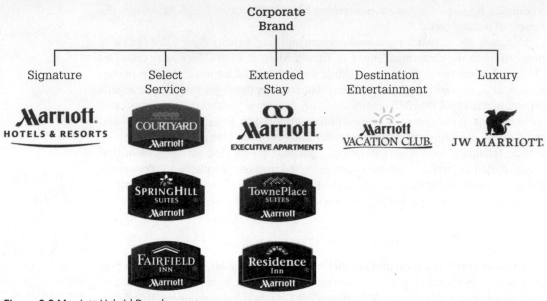

Figure 2.2 Marriott Hybrid Brands.
© Marriott International Inc. Used with permission.

launched. For example, in 2004 United launched Ted Airlines to compete in the low-cost air travel market. Although the company developed a separate brand for the venture, marketing it as "warm, friendly, and casual" with no first-class cabin but with its own Ted-branded in-flight entertainment channels, Ted flights often used United planes. While United hoped to earn share from Southwest, the low-cost airline leader, the Ted brand ceased operations in January 2009. United had failed to distinguish it from the negative associations consumers had with the parent firm; there was simply not enough separation between the two brands for Ted to really take flight.

Some companies develop hybrid brands to efficiently serve different market segments with diverse needs. For example, Marriott developed different hotel brands to fit different usage occasions (business trips, families with kids, longer-term stays) and different price points (see Fig. 2.2). All were marketed as sub-brands of the Marriott Corporation. However, this proliferation of choices might have the unintended effect of confusing the consumer. This is especially the case when consumers are new to the brand and might feel overwhelmed by the choice and apparent lack of differentiation between sub-brands.

Another example of the perils of hybrid branding is the Cadillac Catera, launched by General Motors in 1997. Advertising and positioning for the Catera were intended to appeal to a younger target audience than the Cadillac brand attracts, and the car was meant to take advantage of Cadillac's existing equity while energizing and updating the corporate brand. Unfortunately, the exact opposite occurred. The Cadillac name caused consumers to question the veracity of Catera's claim to hipness, and Catera's positioning likely offended die-hard Cadillac owners. In this case the hybrid brand represented the worst of both worlds.

Comparing Branding Approaches: Umbrella vs. Distinct Branding

Because choosing brand structure is a strategic decision, we must consider the costs and benefits of each option in light of our overall company strategy. The most obvious benefit of an umbrella strategy is the marketing efficiency we can realize with it. Once consumers are aware of the brand positioning, the costs associated with new product launches are substantially reduced, especially when the identity of the umbrella brand and the positioning of the new product are obviously connected. For example, Porsche is well positioned to launch new high-performance cars; it would be less efficient for Porsche to launch an economy car. In the 1980s, Harley Davidson was able to extend its brand beyond motorcycles and into fashion because the brand identity extended easily into this new category. In contrast, despite the amazing market power of the Michael Jordan name in the 1990s, a fragrance bearing his name was not successful. The success of an umbrella strategy depends on how many profitable products and services can be launched that both capitalize on and contribute to the positioning of the umbrella brand.

In addition to delivering marketing efficiencies, umbrella branding creates additional efficiencies within the organization. Decision-making is streamlined across products; many executional decisions concerning positioning, product, distribution, and pricing do not need to be revisited with each new product introduction. For example, Coach makes the same promise of quality and luxury to all its customers. Because these decisions affect a large number of current and future products, we tend to make them with a longer-term view, an approach that generally benefits the brand over time.

The potential costs of an umbrella strategy mirror the benefits. The good news is that umbrella branding allows all of the firm's products to take advantage of the corporate brand; the bad news is that a failure of any one of these products can have a harmful effect on the entire product line. Consider Toyota Motor Corporation, an umbrella brand heralded as the model for reliable manufacturing within the auto industry. Toyota recalled 7.1 million vehicles in 2010 due to a number of alleged technical problems, most notably unintended acceleration. Toyota was named in dozens of U.S. state and federal lawsuits for not initiating recalls quickly enough. The company settled these lawsuits in December 2012 for $1.1 billion[1]. While not all Toyota models were included in the recall, all models suffered. Toyota's sales also suffered, and its U.S. market share fell from 17% in 2009 to 15.2% in 2010. While the immediate financial impact of the recall was tremendous, the long-term impact to the brand value is much harder to estimate. This is especially true because reliability was at the core of the Toyota brand image, so the recall posed questions about the very essence of the company's brand meaning.

---

[1]Toyota Makes Legal Troubles Go Away for $1 Billion - Business - The Atlantic Wire, December 12, 2012. http://www.theatlanticwire.com/business/2012/12/toyota-makes-legal-troubles-go-away-1-billion/60350/#.UQqcGVeguRM.gmail. Accessed January 31, 2013.

© The Proctor & Gamble
Company

P&G's Pampers and Luvs Diaper
Brands are sold by the same
company but offer different
customer benefits and appeal to
different customer segments.

In addition to being more expensive when there is a product failure, umbrella branding also limits positioning options and competitive behavior. The positioning of the umbrella brand will naturally constrain the types of markets and products we might pursue, as well as the marketing decisions that we will make later in the Big Picture analysis. The Disney Company, for example, cannot lend its brand name to entertainment products that run counter to the family positioning it has so carefully developed over decades.

These constraints also can extend to other strategic decisions such as source of volume, a topic we'll discuss in Chapter 4. Consider Google, a brand that enjoys #1 status as an online search engine and whose brand name has become a commonly used verb. Given that Google is perceived as a market leader, competitors and consumers look to the company to set the pace in any category in which it participates, even where it is a new entrant. This widespread expectation is now part of the Google brand image, and if Google were to act like a #2 brand in entering a new category, it would affect consumer perception of the entire brand and across all categories. Thus, the corporate umbrella dictates the benefit and the competitive behavior of all the product lines that carry its name.

In contrast to the umbrella-branded firm, a firm that offers a large number of products, each delivering a unique benefit to the customer, and that follows a distinct branding approach, faces more decisions and expense. It must position and fund each of its brands to stand on its own. For example, The Procter & Gamble Company markets dozens of brands in a variety of product categories from toilet paper to pharmaceuticals. These brands have distinct names and are positioned differently, and while the P&G name can be found on the package, it is not a major element driving consumers' purchase decision.

In fact, because it funds distinct brands, P&G can participate in the same product category with brands that are seemingly competitive, thus serving a broader spectrum of consumers than a single-brand company. For example, in the diaper category, P&G owns two brands, Luvs and Pampers. These brands actively compete against each other in a way that does not seem inconsistent to consumers: Luvs is positioned as a lower-priced brand and sells at 30–50% less than Pampers. In contrast, the Disney Corporation promotes products ranging from online video games to water parks. Each product prominently features the Disney name and adheres to the overall Disney image. These products are intended to complement, as opposed to compete, with each other. Disney pursues an umbrella-branding strategy, while P&G pursues a distinct-branding strategy.

The greatest cost associated with a distinct-branding strategy is lost marketing efficiency. Each distinct brand must be supported by a separate marketing budget and committed organizational resources or it will quickly falter in the face of competition. In addition, it takes longer to build share for a newly launched distinct brand than for a new umbrella-branded product, because it takes time to create awareness of the new brand. It is thus crucial to be realistic about the potential time and money costs of a distinct-branding strategy.

Sometimes an umbrella organization will choose to implement a distinct brand strategy for certain brands. BMW maintains umbrella branding for the majority of its products worldwide, yet it purposefully chose a distinct-branding strategy for the MINI (as it did when it acquired Rolls Royce in 1999). Unlike the BMW brand, the MINI positions itself as an affordable way to express your personality, an entry-level car with spunk. As the graphics on the MINI homepage load, for example, a welcome screen entices visitors to explore any of the 10,000 unique design combinations across the brand. Prices range from about $19,000 to $25,000 for basic models.

While BMW shares its brand equity and confers allure on MINI through dealerships that carry both brands, MINI maintains a separate marketing budget and a distinct branding strategy.

Despite the costs, the appeal of a distinct-branding strategy is strong, particularly given the dynamic nature of most industries, because it is flexible. Under this strategy the firm is free to pursue new markets, new customer segments, and new positioning strategies. Furthermore, a failure of one product, while not ideal, will not have the repercussions that it might under an umbrella strategy. For example, when P&G had to retire Olestra, a fat-free food additive, due to safety concerns, the P&G brand suffered little beyond the direct financial loss from that brand.

The diversified portfolio yielded by a distinct-branding strategy enables the firm to explore new opportunities while minimizing the risk to existing franchises. If a distinct-branding strategy is chosen, a separate Big Picture analysis should be developed for each distinct brand. This is different from umbrella and retail branding, in which a single Big Picture analysis—a single-brand strategy—will drive all decision-making. While the flexibility associated with distinct branding is certainly a benefit, it can also engender undisciplined, short-term thinking. Regardless of whether it pursues an umbrella or distinct-brand strategy, the firm must consider the long-term implications of its product development decisions (see Fig. 2.3).

Key factors to consider in selecting a branding strategy (and eventually a Fundamental Entity) are:

- **Time frame:** Firms that need short product-development timetables may consider an umbrella strategy in order to speed time-to-market and boost efficiency since the different product brands do not need to build awareness independently. Firms requiring the flexibility to change positioning as consumer trends change might prefer a distinct-brand strategy.

- **Robustness of brand positioning:** Some brand positionings are extendable across a wider variety of product/market/consumer segments. In particular, benefit-oriented, as opposed to feature-based, positionings tend to be more robust and more appropriate for umbrella branding.

MINI Cooper advertising emphasizes its fun positioning, whereas BMW advertising emphasizes its driving performance positioning.

© Nicola Margaret/iStockphoto

• Umbrella Branding	• Distinct Branding
1. marketing efficiency	1. more expensive
2. stremlined decision-making	2. increased decision-making
3. engenders long-term thinking	3. engenders shorter-term thinking
4. constrained positioning options	4. flexible positioning options
5. constrained new market entry	5. flexible new market entry
6. constrained source of volume	6. flexible source of volume
7. impact to overall umbrella of product failure	7. offer 'some' protection against liability in case of product failure

Figure 2.3 Umbrella vs Distinct Branding.

GLOBALMARKETING

GLOBAL ISSUES: LOCAL VERSUS GLOBAL BRANDS

In 1983 Theodore Levitt of Harvard Business School published a paper titled "The Globalization of Markets." Levitt essentially argued that consumer tastes and needs around the globe were converging, primarily due to advances in technology. As a result of this convergence, companies should focus on offering the same products around the world and in creating global brands. Levitt essentially argued that globalization was leading to the extinction of traditional differences in national tastes. In part, Levitt's paper seemed to have been a response to the rapid proliferation of brands in the 1980s. At that time, Chrysler offered car buyers over 1 million automobile configurations; Black & Decker sold 19 types of irons; and Colgate and Crest each offered more than 35 types and packages of toothpaste. Levitt would have argued that these companies should be rationalizing their brands.

In 1999, Unilever CEO Antony Burgmans announced that the company would cull 1,200 of its 1,600 brands to focus on the 400 that accounted for approximately 90% of the company's profits. "It will be a massive operation," he said. While shareholders received the news with enthusiasm and the company's share price has greatly outperformed the market index since then, Unilever's drastic brand rationalization does not completely validate Levitt's thesis. In fact, ample evidence suggests that consumers can become attached to local brands and reject global ones. For example, as part of a broader brand globalization effort in 2000, P&G renamed its popular "Fairy" laundry detergent in Germany "Dawn" to position the latter as a global brand. There was

Some of Unilevers' brands.
Reproduced with kind permission of Unilever PLC and/or Unilever NV and /or their group companies

no change in the product's formulation. But by the end of 2001, P&G's market share of Dawn in Germany had fallen drastically. While Fairy was a familiar and trusted brand to German consumers, Dawn did not have that bond with them. Even though the company changed the brand back to Fairy, its market position in Germany did not recover.

Brands help to establish a company's identity in the local market; they are the point of contact between the company and the consumers it is hoping will become loyal followers. However, maintaining strong brands requires significant and continued investment. Having fewer strategic brands can help companies obtain significant economies of scale in their production and commercial processes. Today, most global consumer product giants like Unilever, P&G, and Nestlé spend billions of dollars to acquire and maintain a careful mix of local and global brands. ∎

Sources: Interbrand Brand Channel blog post. http://www.brandchannel.com/features_effect.asp?pf_id=253. Accessed March 12, 2012.
Frost, Randall. "Should global brands trash local favorites," *The BBC news website.* http://news.bbc.co.uk/2/hi/business/440012.stm. Accessed March 12, 2012. Levitt, Theodore. "The globalization of markets," *Harvard Business Review*, May/June 1983, Copyright © 1983 by the President and Fellows of Harvard College.

- **Product risk:** If the risk of product failure is high, or the negative impact of such a risk is high, a distinct-brand strategy is recommended to mitigate this risk.

- **Firm competencies:** Certain competencies align better with distinct or umbrella strategies. For example, a firm implementing an umbrella strategy must possess the marketing abilities to implement and maintain a consistent positioning across all its product lines. In contrast, a firm implementing a distinct-branding strategy with multiple brands will likely need strengths in product development and commercialization (such as speed to market).

We must consider that companies grow over time, and their brands do as well. For example, Procter & Gamble launched the Crest Toothpaste brand nationally in the

1950s as the first toothpaste with therapeutic properties. Competing against Colgate, Crest grew rapidly after the American Dental Association (ADA) endorsed the brand as an effective treatment against tooth decay in 1960, the first time it had issued such an endorsement. Crest became a leading brand in the toothpaste market, and P&G later extended it into toothbrushes, whitening dental strips, dental floss, mouthwash, and other products in the teeth-cleaning category—wherever the brand benefit of tooth health would resonate. Over time the Crest brand has become its own umbrella within the Procter & Gamble family of brands.

Procter & Gamble also owns Oral-B, a brand of toothbrushes and dental floss. The Oral-B Brand lives side by side with Crest under the Procter & Gamble family of brands, and it competes with Crest since both brands sell toothbrushes. This reflects Procter & Gamble's decision that the company overall is better off by having two well-recognized brands in the tooth care category than just one. Oral-B was the original manufacturer of Glide dental floss, but when Procter & Gamble acquired Oral-B, it rebranded Glide as Crest Glide. Since 2010, however, Glide has been reintroduced under the Oral-B brand as Glide Pro-Health Floss. These brands afford great flexibility as Procter & Gamble decides how to best address changes in the category, and the fit between product innovations and the already-established brand meaning of Oral-B and Crest. A firm's choice of branding strategy is ultimately a reflection of the company's overall objectives and the market environment. A strategy that reflects this perspective is likely to be consistently more successful in the long run.

Relationship of Fundamental Entity to Branding Strategy

The Fundamental Entity represents the perspective from which we will conduct our Big Picture analysis. For a firm that markets a single brand and does not plan to develop additional brands in the future, the Fundamental Entity is quite simple: all

social**media**

The Pantene Umbrella Brand Establishes a Global Positioning

In 2006 P&G adopted a new global positioning for its shampoo brand, Pantene, accompanied by the global tag line 'Shine. I believe I can.' The positioning is based on a research study done in collaboration with the Oxford Hair Foundation. Using eye-tracking technology, researchers identified that people's eyes are drawn to visibly shiny hair. The idea behind the new positioning is creating a belief that having shiny hair will make women more self-confident by helping them shine inwardly and outwardly.

Daniel Acker/Bloomberg/ Getty Images

Sources: "Pantene repositions itself as the brand that helps women 'shine,'" Agency FAQS!. September 12, 2006. http://www.afaqs.com/news/story/16013_Pantene-repositions-itself-as-the-brand-that-helps-women-%E2%80%98shine%E2%80%99. Accessed March 15, 2013.

Neff, Jack. "P&G, Lever battle for sexes in dandruff wars," *Advertising Age*. May 21, 2012. http://adage.com/article/news/p-g-lever-battle-sexes-dandruff-wars/234861/. Accessed February 11, 2013.

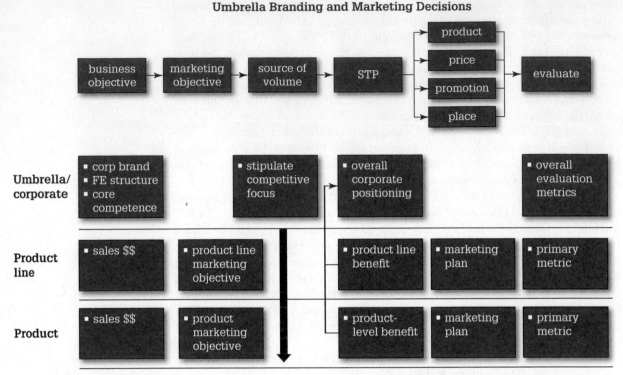

Figure 2.4 The umbrella-branded company chooses one overall benefit, and each of its product lines and products within them must deliver on that overall brand benefit or deliver a benefit that is highly aligned with to the overall umbrella benefit.

analysis will be done from the perspective of that brand. This approach also will hold for a retail or corporate brand such as Target or McKinsey & Co., as mentioned above. Although both firms offer a variety of products, these are marketed under a single umbrella brand that represents the Fundamental Entity. For a firm pursuing a clear umbrella strategy, the Fundamental Entity will be that umbrella brand, and a single Big Picture analysis will be completed. In this case, one overall strategy will be identified for the brand as a whole, and distinct products only will be considered at the segmentation and execution decision level. In essence, the individual products offered under the brand umbrella are *features* of that brand. The decision whether and how to introduce new products will be made always with the umbrella positioning in mind (see Fig. 2.4).

In the case of multiple distinct brands within the same firm, we must undertake analyses for multiple Fundamental Entities. At the corporate level, the firm may address the interrelationships between these various brands. For example, P&G will monitor its overall presence in the diaper category by looking at the Luvs and the Pampers brands jointly. However, for the purpose of marketing analysis, each distinct brand should be treated as a single Fundamental Entity with its own Big Picture analysis. Therefore, there will be as many Big Picture analyses as there are distinct brands (see Fig. 2.5).

Distinct Branding and Marketing Decisions

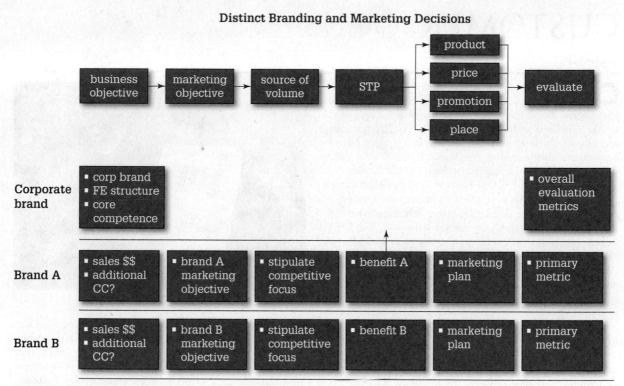

Figure 2.5 The distinct-branded company has more strategic flexibility throughout the entire marketing framework. Specifically, it can deliver diverse and even conflicting benefits (reliability and innovation, or premium quality and low price) through each of its brands.

For firms pursuing a hybrid strategy, the choice of Fundamental Entity is less clear. Whether they develop one analysis for the umbrella or several for the sub-brands depends on the relative importance they place on the positioning of the umbrella and the sub-brands, and on the degree of independence they desire for the sub-brands. If corporate equity is considered most important and the sub-brands do not require strategic independence from the overall umbrella, the Fundamental Entity should be the umbrella brand; if not, an analysis of multiple Fundamental Entities, one for each sub-brand, might be in order.

Porsche, for example, could elect to market its brand under its corporate umbrella by emphasizing the corporate positioning of "Sports high Performance." Although there are efficiencies to this approach, there would also be some potential constraints. It would emphasize similarities between the Cayenne and the Porsche product line; and from a customer focus perspective, the Cayenne would naturally be targeted at retained Porsche customers. If it were instead considered a separate Fundamental Entity, the Cayenne might be positioned on "functional performance," rather somewhat different from the overall Porsche product line. Cayenne's marketing managers might also decide that its relationship with existing customers (who are attracted to Porsche for its high performance reputation) is not as critical to the new model's success and might more naturally lean toward a customer acquisition strategy. The key with a hybrid strategy is to maintain consistency

CUSTOMERFOCUS

COACH

Coach, the famous manufacturer of women's leather bags, owed its initial success to designing serious and simple bags for women who were achieving leadership positions in business in the 1970s. The company was known for designing understated but elegant bags in dark colors and featuring simple buckles and little decoration. When it was acquired by Sara Lee Corporation in 1985, women's place in the workforce had started to shift again, and by the mid-1990s many more women were in positions of power in business and felt secure enough to show more femininity in the workplace. In the 1990s, women's business attire became more relaxed and more varied, and that trend extended to their accessories.

Coach might have missed this shift in the market had it not been by a single-minded focus on its customers and the collection of customer data that allowed the company to track purchases at a customer level, customer longevity and other metrics. This customer-based discipline was enforced by the CEO, Lew Frankfort, who invested heavily in a customer tracking system. This system detected that in places like Japan, women were defecting from the brand in favor of more design-forward manufacturers.

Coach evolved its designs just in time, and by the year 2000 it was selling bags in non-leather materials, in a variety

© Allen Eyestone/ZUMA Press /Corbis

of colors, and also expanding its product range by also selling wallets, glasses, and of other fashion items. Today Coach spends more than $5 million per year on product testing, conducts more than 40,000 one-on-one interviews with customers each year, and has expanded its customer database to almost 10 million entries. Its product portfolio moves with, rather than follows, its customers. ■

Sources: Slywotzky, Adrian. "How Coach learned to know, not guess, what customers want," *Olyver Wyman Journal*, http://www.oliverwyman.com/media/OWJ-UpsideofStratRisk.pdf. Accessed August 12, 2013.

Binkly, Christina. "Coach comes around to reclaim its iconic look." *The Wall Street Journal*. July 13, 2012.

'E-commerce strategy, client-analysis focus help Coach Bag Sales.' http://searchcio.techtarget.com/video/E-commerce-strategy-client-analysis-focus-help-Coach-bag-sales Accessed January 30, 2012.

throughout the analysis by honoring the Fundamental Entity decision throughout all subsequent decisions.

WHAT WE DO BEST: CORE COMPETENCE

Core competence. A skill of the firm that is pervasive throughout the organization and can lead to a sustainable, competitive advantage.

A **core competence** is a skill the corporation possesses that results (or might result, in the case of a startup) in a sustainable competitive advantage. This skill enables the firm to generate one or more strategic assets, which in turn generate products or services. Further, the core competence is pervasive throughout the organization and cannot be easily imitated by competitors. For example, Apple has a core competence in the design of easy to use consumer electronics, seamlessly integrating software and hardware across a variety of products. This skill has generated a number of strategic assets, among them strong customer loyalty, fruitful strategic partnerships with programmers, and the Apple Store, the most successful consumer electronics retail chain

GLOBALMARKETING

COCA-COLA AND GLOBAL DISTRIBUTION

The Coca-Cola Company possesses a core competence in distribution, which allows it to deliver its product to every country in the world. As of 2012 Coca Cola was sold in every country, with the exception of Cuba and North Korea (due to trade embargo restrictions in those countries). ■

Soe Than WIN/AFP/Getty Images

in the United States by sales per square foot.[2] These assets in turn enable Apple to develop and improve its products, which integrate all forms of media into one convenient platform, thus delivering the benefit of accessibility and connectivity.

Perhaps the best way to understand a core competence is to understand what it is not. It is not a patent, a copyright, a particular product, large customer base, or brand equity; these are strategic assets, and they are static. A core competence helps the firm *produces* these types of assets. A core competence in customer relationship management, for instance, might create a large customer base; a core competence in marketing might create strong brand equity; and a core competence in product innovation might produce a large portfolio of patents and products. The key here is to focus on the input, the set of skills that produce the asset, as opposed to the output, the asset itself.

Figure 2-6 illustrates the relationship between core competence, strategic assets, and products. The concept of core competence matters only if you are hoping to stay in business for the long term. In the short run, a strategic asset or two usually will generate earnings. In order to generate a stream of earnings over a longer period of time, however, it is generally necessary to utilize a core competence to create a stream of strategic assets, and profitable products, over time.

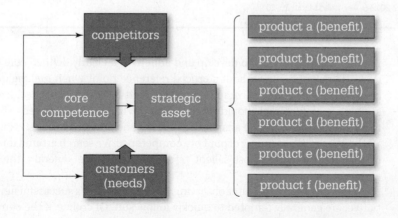

Figure 2.6 This figure illustrates two important characteristics of core competencies. First, the core competence leads to strategic assets and, in turn, those lead to customer benefits delivered through products and services. Secondly, the core competence is defined within the market context, which means that the core competence is defined relative to the competitors in the category and must enable the delivery of meaningful benefits to customers.

[2] Elmer-DeWitt, Phillip "Apple stores top Tiffany's in sales per square foot, again," *Money. Cnn* November 13, 2012, www.techfortune.cnn.com/2012/11/13.

NEW PRODUCTS/INNOVATION

The four television broadcast networks in the United States—ABC, CBS, NBC, and Fox (owned by News Corp)—have seen very stiff competition in the last 20 years. First, the growth of cable channels, particularly the popular HBO and Showtime channels, decreased the overall audience for network television. Then, the adoption of TiVo and DVRs allowed viewers to pre-record shows and skip commercials, endangering networks' revenue source. TV watching is still the country's number one pastime, with viewers devoting at an average of four hours and 39 minutes per day. However, people between 12 and 34 are now watching less TV and more digital content. As a result, networks are losing ratings they covet, leading to a precipitous decline in advertising income, and each has had to redefine its core business. Are they in the television broadcast business, the media business, or the entertainment business?

Most have decided they are in the media and entertainment business. ABC, NBC, and Fox, for example, have accepted an online video streaming model in the form of their joint venture, Hulu.com. CBS developed its own site, TV.com. By committing themselves to the entertainment programming business, these firms can protect themselves from inevitable future technology shifts. While they have not fully developed a sustainable business model (online video advertising is still in its infancy), by redefining their core business they can be more flexible in conquering this challenge. ■

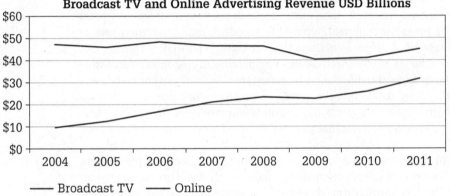

Broadcast TV and Online Advertising Revenue USD Billions

—— Broadcast TV   —— Online

Source: "IAC Advertising Revenue Report, 2011," Interactive Advertising Bureau; Television Bureau of Advertising. http://www.iab.net/media/file/IAB_Internet_Advertising_Revenue_Report_FY_2011.pdf. Accessed June 30, 2012.

Sources: Stelter, Brian. "Youths are watching, but less often on TV," *The New York Times.* February 9, 2012.

Minato, Charlie. "ComScore: Here's how much online ad spending will increase this year." businessinsider.com. http://www.businessinsider.com/online-ad-spending-will-increase-18-in-2012-2012-6. Accessed March 20, 2012.

A company that fails to develop and adhere to a clearly defined core competence runs the risk of being without a crucial reference point when making decisions and being swayed by competitive actions, in effect letting competitors decide its corporate strategy. Which market should we enter next? Which customer needs should we seek to satisfy? How should we adapt our products and services to satisfy our customers? Without an understanding of our core competence, we search around for other points of reference, and the most salient reference points are generally the activities of competitors.

Marketing managers, after observing a key competitor's successful new market initiative, are generally tempted to quickly follow suit. Of course, if the competitor's initiative is strategically sound and based on its own core competence, it will almost certainly dominate all imitators in the marketplace. Or the competitor's initiative could be tactical in nature and not based on any sound strategy, making any decision

GLOBALMARKETING

GENERAL MOTORS DEVELOPING A GLOBAL MANUFACTURING CORE COMPETENCE

After General Motors declared bankruptcy in 2010, the company announced a move away from decentralized manufacturing platforms to global car platforms. This move was aimed at improving its manufacturing competencies, creating efficiencies and greater product reliability. The first car model to move to a common global manufacturing process was the Ford Focus. And by 2012, GM announced a goal of manufacturing 80% of all its vehicles on global platforms. ■

Jeff Kowalsky/Bloomberg/ Getty Images

Sources: Rutenberg, Jim and Jeremy Peters. "2 American automakers rebut claims by Romney," October, 30, 2012. NYTimes.com. December 17, 2012. "Barra, Mary. GM's next CEO?" *CNN Money*. http://management.fortune.cnn.com/2012/12/17/gm-mary-barra/.

---

to follow suit even less wise. Either way, a reactive strategy will eventually lead the company astray.

It is unambiguously better to set a course based on a clear understanding of the corporation's core competence. Since effective strategy is core competence-driven, it is critical to select a single core competence to focus on when setting marketing strategy. A select group of firms (like NBC, ABC, and CBS featured in the Innovation box on page 42) may have developed multiple core competencies. One of these, however, is most likely dominant—the most important factor in the company's sustained success.

In order to identify this dominant core competence, managers should evaluate how different competence might drive key marketing decisions. They can then choose to focus on the core competence that seems to generate the most logical or advantageous set of decisions: Given our core competence, what products are we likely to develop? By answering this question, we can test our definition of our core competence, and refine our understanding of the business we are in. Are we in the computer business or the information business? The two possible answers to this question lead to two very different product portfolios. We may be better able to execute our strategy with one portfolio than the other.

Given our core competence and likely product portfolio, who is our competition? Although this question seems obvious, answering it after we have defined our core competence provides a more informed answer. We often consider our competition to be the one or two companies that currently present threats to our business. In doing this we automatically align our business objective with that of the competition. The irony of this situation becomes clear when we consider that our competitors are likely looking at *us* to identify *their* core competencies. With nobody looking beyond the immediate industry, the vision necessary for healthy category growth is replaced with shortsighted, reactionary thinking.

The corollary to this observation is that the competitor most affected by category growth—the market leader—has the greatest incentive (and the biggest responsibility) to look beyond the narrowly defined category for competitors. It is critical for

NBC, for example, to understand its dominant core competence as being a "skill at creating branded entertainment." A focus on this core competence rather than on other important, but less critical, competencies (like TV broadcasting or affiliate management) allows NBC to see its competition not simply as the other three major broadcast networks, but also as other cable networks, video games, movie theatres, and other online activities (e.g., social networking sites). If it understands its core competence as the ability to deliver an engaging entertainment experience with a unique flair, NBC will make different marketing decisions than if it thinks its core competence is TV production. These decisions will affect everything from advertising, to production and programming choices, to talent acquisition, to the portfolio mix of genres of entertainment. These strategic choices highlight the importance of fully understanding the firm's core competencies, as well as the importance of investing to defend and expand upon our core competence.

Core Competence vs. Competence

Its core competence is certainly not the only skill the firm possesses. For example, Intel has a core competence in nanotechnology; Target has a core competence in mechandising. Of course, Intel's management is still concerned with cost containment, and Target is not a slacker when it comes to innovation. Some level of competence in all the tasks of the corporation is prerequisite to success in the marketplace. The *core* competence, however, is the skill set that uniquely distinguishes one company from another.

Why is it so important to articulate our core competence? Because understanding our core competence will help us to develop a sustainable, as opposed to temporary,

GLOBALMARKETING

GANGNAM STYLE AND CORE COMPETENCE

The South Korean pop sensation "Gangnam Style" reached 1 billion YouTube views in 2012, becoming the most widely viewed video ever at that time. In successfully launching and promoting the song, the artist Psy used winning tactics for social media promotion. He allowed others to imitate his work: the song was published without copyright so people would create their own online parodies, helping create a self-sustaining promotional push for "Gangnam Style." Psy also cleverly used crowd sourcing, inviting the entire South Korean dance community to contribute moves for the horse dance featured in the song. This created an early captive audience for the song.

Mark Sisson/Rex Features/AP Images

"Gangnam Style" may be the most famous pop music export from South Korea, but it is not an isolated phenomenon. It can even be said that South Korea possesses a core competence in pop music. The country has created an entire genre known as K-pop, and its music industry is adept at identifying global music tastes and using those customer insights to launch mega artists like Psy. ∎

Sources: Ryun Chang, Dae. "Marketing, Gangnam Style," September 20, 2012. *HBR Blog Network.* Accessed February 11, 2013.

competitive advantage. Consider Amazon. If Amazon had conceived of its core competence as distribution of books, it would have considered its competition to be solely other booksellers such as Barnes & Noble and Borders. Such a narrow focus would have prevented it from developing sophisticated supply-chain logistics to efficiently ship everything from books to groceries worldwide. Amazon's core competence is in developing algorithms that enable it to accurately predict consumer purchase interest across a variety of product categories. By continuously developing this competence and the strategic assets of its logistics systems, Amazon is able to compete not just with Barnes & Noble, but also with Walmart.

Integrating Core Competence with Marketing Strategy

A well-conceived core competence is never forgotten, because it drives every decision the firm makes, from product development to pricing to positioning to long-term acquisition strategy. For example, Johnson & Johnson's core competence, its skill at ethical decision-making, is embodied in its credo and is ever-present in the minds of its workers. The credo is prominently displayed in its offices and is reported to be a significant driver in decision-making (see Fig. 2.7). This core competence might mean Johnson & Johnson's products are not always perceived as highly innovative, but J&J customers expect a very high level of reliable performance. To many parents and medical practitioners, Johnson & Johnson is synonymous with trust.

By definition, a company must limit the number of competencies on which it focuses. While there is no magic number, it is difficult to find organizations that have more than two or three true core competencies, and these are often related and synergistic. For example, the Four Seasons Hotel's core competence at training its staff is combined with core competencies in hiring and service operations to deliver a differentiating benefit of excellent customer service to its guests. Any firm considering supporting several competencies should also consider whether and how those competencies might integrate with one another.

Core Competence and the Fundamental Entity

The firm should also consider the relationship of the Fundamental Entity to its core competence. Firms may elect to invest in core competencies at the corporate level and allow multiple Fundamental Entities to profit from them. For example,

Our Credo

We believe our first responsibility is to the doctors, nurses and patients, to mothers and fathers and all others who use our products and services. In meeting their needs everything we do must be of high quality. We must constantly strive to reduce our costs in order to maintain reasonable prices. Customers' orders must be serviced promptly and accurately. Our suppliers and distributors must have an opportunity to make a fair profit.

We are responsible to our employees, the men and women who work with us throughout the world. Everyone must be considered as an individual. We must respect their dignity and recognize their merit. They must have a sense of security in their jobs. Compensation must be fair and adequate, and working conditions clean, orderly and safe. We must be mindful of ways to help our employees fulfill their family responsibilities. Employees must feel free to make suggestions and complaints. There must be equal opportunity for employment, development and advancement for those qualified. We must provide competent management, and their actions must be just and ethical.

We are responsible to the communities in which we live and work and to the world community as well. We must be good citizens — support good works and charities and bear our fair share of taxes. We must encourage civic improvements and better health and education. We must maintain in good order the property we are privileged to use, protecting the environment and natural resources.

Our final responsibility is to our stockholders. Business must make a sound profit. We must experiment with new ideas. Research must be carried on, innovative programs developed and mistakes paid for. New equipment must be purchased, new facilities provided and new products launched. Reserves must be created to provide for adverse times. When we operate according to these principles, the stockholders should realize a fair return.

Johnson & Johnson

Figure 2.7 The Johnson and & Johnson credo is posted in all corporate offices and serves as the ethical guide for employee's decision-making. This ethical approach to decision-making could be a core competence of the company.

Credo used by permission of Johnson & Johnson.

as illustrated in Table 2-1, all marketers at Procter & Gamble take advantage of corporate core competencies around product development and marketing. Regardless of whether someone works in the shampoo, diaper, or detergent business, there are centrally-administered functions from which all employees in the firm can draw. In addition to drawing from a corporate core competence, each of the brands operating in separate businesses might need to develop additional core competencies to compete in each of their distinct business categories, and as they enter new markets, they might need to develop even more core competencies by geography. In these situations the Fundamental Entities of the corporation benefit from the substantial corporate resources available to develop and sustain the core competence.

In contrast, McDonald's seeks to deliver the primary benefit of convenience under a single brand name all over the world. Because it delivers a single customer benefit, all its locations will draw from the same corporate core competence related to food operations. However, given its global reach and because convenience is understood differently throughout the world, McDonald's might need to develop some additional local core competencies in order to deliver convenience everywhere. For example, in the United States the firm leverages a core competence of operational efficiency and training to deliver food consistently and quickly at its drive-throughs and in the store. In Turkey, in contrast, McDonald's provides home delivery, because this fits the definition of convenience in this region. The company must develop and leverage a local core competence in single-unit transportation logistics that is not necessary in the United States.

Finally, J&J Medical delivers medical devices to patients and doctors across a variety of procedures (orthopedics, metabolic surgery, colorectal surgery, etc.). The company will require a core competency different from the J&J Consumer core competency for all its medical device products. And if necessary, each local company in the different regions of the world may require additional core competencies if local competitive conditions require it.

Although identifying and defining the core competence is critical, individual marketing managers may sometimes feel constrained by the fact that they are unable to define or change the core competence of their firms. Aligning the organization around the core competence definition, and prioritizing investment initiatives accordingly—that is, by emphasizing projects that reinforce or enhance it and de-prioritizing other projects—is critical to developing focused strategies and executional plans. Even when management has not officially identified and prioritized a core competence, individuals and teams have much to gain from agreeing on one as a way to focus their efforts.

Table 2.1 The Relationship of Fundamental Entity Structure to Core Competence

Example	Fundamental Entity/ Brand Strategy	Number of Benefits	Level/Number of Competencies
Procter & Gamble	Distinct	many and different	corporate/distinct/regional
McDonald's	Umbrella	one	corporate/regional
J&J Medical	Hybrid	many and related	corporate division/regional

WHAT BUSINESSES ARE WE IN?:
CORE BUSINESS

The notion of core competence is linked to the concept of **core business.** Essentially, we need to answer the question: "What business are we in?" The core business of the firm is the central focus of a company's activity. Strategic core business definitions are based on a customer benefit rather than a technology, product, or process.

Theodore Levitt best articulated the importance of this question in his now-classic *Harvard Business Review* article, "Marketing Myopia."[3] Levitt highlighted the difference between being in the *transportation* business and being in the *railroad* business, or between the *information* business and the *newspaper* business. This comparison illustrates the crucial difference between companies that define their business by focusing on customer benefit and those that focus on product function. By considering this distinction, the corporation does more than simply pay lip service to the popular notion of customer-driven marketing. A clear understanding of the true business of a corporation, satisfying a customer need, provides a blueprint for future product development and enables more efficient decision-making at all levels of the organization. For example, as described in Table 2-2, J&J may consider different core business and customer benefit definitions depending on their choice of fundamental entity.

Thinking about the relationship you would like to create with customers when defining a Fundamental Entity can deliver a significant advantage to the company. At the MacWorld Conference in January 2007, Apple Computer changed its name, and hence, its Fundamental Entity, to Apple Inc. This signaled a shift in focus from solely developing personal computers (Macs) to delivering much broader experiences for consumers throughout their daily activities.[4] The same day it changed its name, Apple also released the new iPhone and Apple TV, illustrating clearly its strategic evolution from a computer company to a consumer electronics company. Technology bloggers and traditional media sources alike commented that the new name solidified the strategic changes Apple had introduced in 2001 with the release of iTunes and the iPod.[5] When he introduced the convergence of several media devices in one iPhone in 2007, Steve Jobs, CEO of Apple, cited computer scientist Alan Kay, saying "People who are really serious about software should make their own hardware."[6] By combining the development and production of software and hardware under one Fundamental Entity—Apple Inc.—Jobs erased internal conflict

© Veronika Lukasova/ ZUMAPress/Corbis   © James Leynse/ Corbis   © Hou Yuxuan/ iStockphoto

Apple computer logo through the ages: Apple Computer rainbow logo used from 1976 to 1988; the black and white Apple Computer logo used from 1988–2007, and the new Apple Logo (without the word 'Computer') still in use today.

Table 2.2 Fundamental Entity, Core Business, and Benefit

Fundamental Entity	Core Business	Customer Benefit
J&J Consumer Products	Consumer packaged goods	Trust
Johnson's Baby	Baby care	Trust/Purity
Johnson's Baby Shampoo	Baby hygiene	Gentleness

[3]Levitt, Theodore. "Marketing myopia," *The Harvard Business Review,* 1960.

[4]Honan, Mathew. "Apple drops 'Computer' from name," *Macworld,* January 9, 2007.

[5]Kahney, Leander. "Apple Inc. drops the 'Computer,'" *Wired.com,* January 9, 2007.

[6]Greelish, David. "An interview with computing pioneer Alan Kay," *Time Tech,* April 2, 2013.

social**media**

Dell Uses the Social Media Channel As Launch Pad for New Services Model

The increased pressure on margins in the computer hardware business has driven iconic brands like Dell or IBM to increase software and services as a way to improve profitability. This transition at Dell illustrates how a company can transition its core business, in whole or in part, by using a mix of acquisitions and organic growth.

Dell entered the services business by acquiring Perot Systems in 2009, with over 40,000 employees, dedicated to providing systems integration services and consulting. Dell's own prowess in the social media space gave the company the idea of creating a service solution by reselling its services. Most large companies track chatter and other activity on the Internet related to their brands. Over the last years, as the volume of social media activity has increased, it has become costly and more difficult to keep track of what is being said and whether and how to react. In 2011, Dell was tracking over 25,000 daily mentions of its brand and its product on the Internet from a central command cen-

ter in Texas. In 2012, the company decided to offer that same infrastructure to ten clients on a pilot basis. These clients included the American Red Cross, Aetna, and Kraft Foods.

Justin Sullivan/Getty Images

In commenting on Dell's entry into the social media services business, some industry analysts questioned the computer company's ability to succeed in a market space where media agencies have already established reputations and acquired a client base. A key question that would be helpful in predicting Dell's potential for success is, what core competence is most helpful in providing social media listening services: is it one related to technical expertise or to knowledge and expertise in traditional media?

Sources: *Cotton, Delo.* "Dell launches new unit to provide social-media strategy to brands group: will compete with agencies, as well as start-ups and enterprise computing firms;" December 4, 2012. http://adage.com/article/digital/dell-launches-unit-providing-social-media-strategy-brands/238594/.) Accessed August 12, 2013.

Dell Corporate website (www.content.dell.com/). Accessed January 31, 2013.

about who the company was. Moreover, by reframing Apple's core business, Jobs afforded his company the flexibility to continue to innovate technologies to enhance consumers' lives.

WHERE ARE WE GOING?: THE GOAL

After articulating the core competence of the corporation, managers must identify the specific goal. While firms often use goals as criteria, such as for providing performance incentives, in fact the primary purpose of a goal is to serve as a *decision aid*. The most effective marketing manager can make difficult decisions consistently and efficiently. If the goal statement is good, it will serve as a reference point for accomplishing this objective. For example, a clear primary business objective "to increase *revenues* by 20 percent" enables the manager to evaluate potential projects in terms of their fit with this goal. An acquisition campaign designed to bring in new customers aligns with this goal. A price increase may not if the customer base is price-sensitive. On the other hand, a price decrease that increases share but doesn't increase revenues would clearly conflict with this goal. For example, during its first few years of business Amazon.com priced its products at a level similar to other online retailers while investing very heavily in predictive data analytics and logistics to acquire customers.

In contrast, if the primary business objective is to increase *profits* by 10 percent, an effective action toward this goal might be to reduce marketing spending or other operational costs and to focus on maintaining the existing customer base. The manager may be willing to trade share for profits in this case. After expanding its business by reaching out to new customers from the 1970s through the 1990s, Gillette shifted its emphasis to marketing to its retained users and developing new, more valuable, and more expensive products. In contrast, a business that sets increasing market share as its goal will often be willing to sacrifice some profit to achieve volume growth. For example, in 2006 Nortel's CEO, Mike Zafirovski, said the company would achieve at least a 20% share of any market in which it participated or would pull out and reallocate research and development resources elsewhere.[7] While he was not telling managers to lower prices, he was giving them a clear direction when faced with a tradeoff between share and profits.

By constantly referring to the goal, we can efficiently evaluate alternatives, ensuring consistency and integration of strategy and execution. Using a goal statement as a decision aid can help us uncover inconsistencies between tactics and the overall strategic goal. For example, a corporate goal of enhancing profit is inconsistent with adopting deep discounts on slow-selling items; conversely, an overall strategic goal of increasing market share is inconsistent with adopting a premium pricing strategy. The simple act of using the goal to align execution with strategy will enhance efficiency and effectiveness.

If the manager finds he or she is making decisions that run contrary to the primary objective, one of two things needs to happen. The manager needs to either stop making these contrary decisions, or rethink and modify the primary objective so the objective and actions align. If neither happens, the goal statement quickly will become meaningless, and strategic control of the corporation will be undermined.

The second function of a goal is to define *performance criteria*. If we carefully quantify our goal statement and time frame, we will be able to refer back to it and determine objectively whether we have accomplished what we set out to do. If we have not, we can begin to assess why not. Perhaps the goal was unrealistic, or perhaps the strategies we implemented to achieve it were not effective. Whatever the case, if we have truly used the goal as a decision aid, our evaluation at this stage will, at a minimum, yield important lessons for future decision-making.

Goal Criteria

Whenever a decision is made in the Big Picture, a goal is set. For example, when we decide to "earn share" in the Source of Volume chapter of the Big Picture, we set a goal to convert a specific percentage of sales from a specific competitor in a specific time period. Each lower-level goal should be developed in the service of achieving a higher-level goal. For example, if the business objective is to increase revenues by 20% in one year, the goal we set when considering the appropriate marketing objective (say, to acquire 200,000 new customers in one year) must facilitate achievement of the business objective's goal.

Likewise, the decision to earn five share points from the market leader (Source of Volume) must result in the 200,000 new customers required by our customer objective

---

[7] Gubbins, Ed. "Nortel CEO sets market share goals," *Connected Planet*, February 23, 2006. http://connectedplanetonline.com/finance/news/nortel_zafirovski_goals_022306/. Accessed January 30, 2013.

decision (Marketing Objective), which in turn will result in 20% revenue increase stipulated by the business objective. This process of determining lower-order goals based on how to best fulfill higher-order goals runs throughout the entire Big Picture. Each goal links naturally to lower- and higher-level goals, and in the end each always promotes the goal set as the company's business objective. By articulating goals at each stage of the Big Picture, we can clearly identify successful strategies and diagnose failures. In order to accomplish this, every goal statement must be measurable, time-dependent, single-minded, realistic, and integrated. Let's look at each of these characteristics.

1. **Measurable:** Because one purpose of a goal is to serve as a standard for measuring performance, it must be measurable. The simplest way to ensure this characteristic is to quantify the goal. "Provide superior-quality products" sounds good but is a worthless goal statement; we have no way of knowing whether or when we have achieved this nebulous aim. We can quantify it, however, by adding hard statistics such as number of customer complaints, product return rates, or changes in third-party evaluations. Goals that we can measure objectively in dollars, volume, units, percentage points, customers, and so on generally work best because they are communicated most easily to others and are most easily recognized when attained. For example, Jeff Bezos, CEO of Amazon famously called the culture in his company a 'culture of metrics.' The giant online retailer tracks its performance against more than 500 measurable goals, and while that number may seem overwhelming, it is less so because nearly 80% of those measurements relate to customers. Bezos is known for running meetings with an empty chair in the room and asking his employees to imagine a customer is sitting there, as a way to focus the conversation on bringing value-added to customers.[8]

2. **Time-Dependent:** For a goal to be measurable, we must know *when* we are going to measure it. The time frame aspect of the goal statement provides almost as much information as the goal itself. If a business objective is expressed with an extremely short time frame, it is likely the corporation is facing some sort of crisis. On the other hand, a long time frame such as three to five years suggests that short-term concerns are well in hand and the corporation is ready to expand its horizons. The time frame over which we hope to reach a goal (say, to increase sales by $200,000) will greatly influence the way we go about achieving it. Accomplishing it over the next quarter may require a completely different marketing strategy than doing it over three years.

3. **Single-Minded:** The most challenging, and most important, criterion to adhere to is single-mindedness. If a goal is not single-minded, it cannot serve as a decision aid. A goal statement such as "increase share by 5% and profits by 2%" does not help us choose between investing in a competitive advertising campaign and investing in a cost-saving machine. These goals must be prioritized. It is quite likely that they are related: an increase in market share actually may lead to an increase in profits. In this case the corporate goal (the promise to share-

---

[8] Anders, George. "Inside Amazon's idea machine: How Bezos decodes the customer," *Fortune Magazine*, April, 4, 2012. http://www.forbes.com/sites/georgeanders/2012/04/04/inside-amazon/. Accessed January 30, 2013.

GLOBALMARKETING

MANAGING SHAREHOLDER EXPECTATIONS THROUGH GOAL SETTING: "IT'S ALL ABOUT THE LONG TERM"

We believe that a fundamental measure of our success will be the shareholder value we create over the long term. This value will be a direct result of our ability to extend and solidify our current market leadership position. The stronger our market leadership, the more powerful our economic model. Market leadership can translate directly to higher revenue, higher profitability, greater capital velocity, and correspondingly stronger returns on invested capital.

In this excerpt from the 1997 letter to shareholders, Jeff Bezos, the CEO of Amazon.com, warned that his com-

Emmanuel Dunand/AFP/GettyImages

pany takes a very long-term approach to the business. With this short and carefully worded paragraph, Bezos was implying that, realistically, Amazon would not be profitable for several years. In subsequent letters in 1998 and 1999, he referred back to this paragraph to justify his company's lack of profitability. Bezos was very successful in adjusting expectations and explicating the company strategy. Despite negative or very low profitability at first, Amazon became a favorite stock of investors, trading at a huge price/earnings ratio. ■

Sources: 1997, 1998, and 1999. Letter to Shareholders. Amazon Annual Reports. Accessed on January 12, 2013.

---

holders) is likely a profit increase, with a strategy of increasing market share. This market-share strategy will be categorized as the business objective goal in the Big Picture.

The fact that a goal is single-minded does not mean we should ignore reasonable constraints. For example, if our stated goal is to increase unit sales by 10 percent, our implicit assumption is that this increase will be achieved within current spending constraints. Hence, while our goal does not explicitly address profitability, it still does not provide us free rein to disregard cost issues.

4. **Realistic:** A goal is not a vision statement; it is not intended to inspire, but rather to direct. An unrealistic goal will be worthless as both a decision aid and a standard for judging; people will either ignore it or be demoralized by it. In the worst case, they may resort to unethical or illegal business practices to achieve it, damaging the firm in the long run.

5. **Integrated:** All business objectives should link naturally to higher- and lower-level objectives. A business objective of increasing unit volume should lead to marketing and operations objectives that also support this goal. Further, the core competence of the firm must be reflected throughout the Big Picture analysis.

Many students and managers find it difficult to identify one primary goal; they argue that a corporation has a number of objectives, all of which are important. For example, Clorox stated the following in its 2008 annual report:

We've grown our business despite the challenging economic environment

Today, Clorox people continue to strive for excellence, even in the face of tough economic times. Since fiscal year 2008, we have delivered solid results despite the economic recession and the ongoing challenges of the economy. We have grown sales an average of nearly 3 percent during this period. Importantly, we have also delivered strong total stockholder returns of 59 percent, compared to an average of 47 percent by our peers and 16 percent by the S&P 500. In the last eight years, we have repurchased nearly 40 percent of our outstanding shares. Between share repurchases and increases in total annual dividends paid to stockholders, we have returned more than $5 billion in cash to our stockholders since fiscal year 2005.

And, in keeping with tradition, strong governance and values underpin our financial performance. Corporate responsibility (CR) is embedded in all aspects of our business, and we continue to step up our CR efforts because we believe doing the right thing is simply good business.[9]

Like many companies, Clorox wants everything, not just for its consumers, but also for its employees. Unfortunately, this promise to shareholders is worthless as a decision aid. If Clorox's marketers tried to accomplish all its goals in parallel, with equal vigor, they would undoubtedly fail. Without a primary goal that supersedes all these, both efficiency and consistency in decision-making will suffer, and ultimately the performance of the firm will suffer as a result.

If, on the other hand, goals are *prioritized* from the outset, we make one very difficult decision right now (choosing the primary goal), but we save ourselves the pain and suffering of making hundreds of difficult and potentially sub-optimal decisions over the coming year. What is more important to our firm right now, profits or revenue? The sooner we grapple with this issue, the sooner it will be resolved. If we choose revenue as our primary objective, does this mean we will spend wildly and with no regard for cost control? Of course not. Cost control is likely a secondary objective and will be an ongoing concern, as will a number of other objectives. But, as this example shows, when we are forced to choose between profits and revenues, we know which way to go, and *we will go the same way every time.*

INTEGRATION:
BUSINESS OBJECTIVE AND THE BIG PICTURE

While the focus of this chapter has been on the business objective, each chapter in the framework will have an associated goal statement. For example, in the Marketing Objective chapter we will identify and quantify a primary goal of either acquisition or retention; in the Source of Volume chapter we will select and quantify either an earn share or stimulate primary demand goal, and so on. Each of these goals should meet each of the criteria we identified. In this way we develop a model that reflects how we believe our marketing strategy will work. Our primary assumption with this model is that by accomplishing the goals we have set for executional chapters such as Product and Pricing, we will in turn achieve the higher-level strategic goals we have set for Segmentation, Targeting, Positioning, Source of Volume, and Marketing Objective, and will finally achieve our business objective. If we fail to reach our overall business

---

[9] 2012 Clorox Company Annual Report. CEO Letter. http://annualreport.thecloroxcompany.com/ceo-letter/. Accessed January 30, 2013.

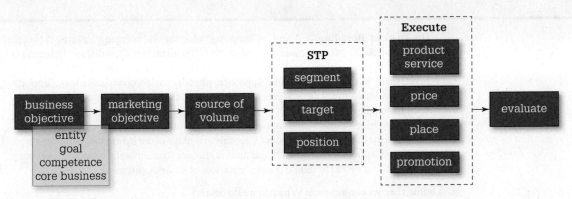

Figure 2.8 In the Business Objective chapter we consider the fundamental questions of our company's strategy, including Fundamental Entity, Goal, Core Competence, and Core Business.

objective goal, we should be able to look at our lower-level goals to identify what in the framework needs fixing.

In summary, these key elements are necessary to complete the business objective segment of the Big Picture: Fundamental Entity: Who are we? Core Competence: What do we do better than anyone else? Goal: Where should we go? Core Business: What business are we in?

☐ SUMMARY

1. Because they drive and limit all our later decisions, the choices we make in the early chapters of the framework are the most important, and often the most challenging, decisions we will make.

   The chapter identifies essential business objective decisions:
   1. Who are we? (fundamental entity)
   2. What are we good at? (core competence)
   3. Where are we going? (goal)
   4. What is our main business? (core business)

2. **Describe the concept of Fundamental Entity: Who are we?**
   The Fundamental Entity is the brand level from which we conduct the strategic analysis. The Fundamental Entity might be the Corporate Brand, a Brand Line, or a Product Brand, depending on the company's brand structure.

3. **Identify the advantages and disadvantages of different branding strategies.**
   We distinguish three broad types of brand strategies.
   (a) **Umbrella Branding:** a branding approach whereby the company uses just one brand for all its products and services.

(b) **Distinct Branding:** a branding approach whereby the company creates different brands for its different products and services. The main benefit of distinct branding is flexibility in positioning. The main drawback of distinct branding is cost.

(c) **Hybrid Branding:** a branding approach whereby the company uses the corporate brand across multiple products and services but also creates separate brands to designate differences in product or service lines. We can identify a hybrid brand because two different brand names appear next to each other, one for the company and the other for the product or product line. The advantage of the hybrid branding approach is that launching individual brand lines is cheaper than umbrella branding. However, the risk of hybrid branding is a potential loss of strategic discipline.

4. Define the core competence: What do we do best?

The core competence is a skill that leads to a sustainable competitive advantage. Core competencies create and support strategic assets, which are the key resources the company employs to create customer benefits. The strategic asset, like any asset, can increase or decrease in value depending on how it is managed. With continued careful investment in the core competence, the strategic asset will continue to grow. If we choose instead to use the asset without investing in it, we can deplete it until it is no longer of value. For example, FedEx has a core competence at logistics. This skill was used to create a logistics system for global package delivery. The strength of this skill and the quality of the resulting strategic asset allowed FedEx to deliver the customer benefit of reliability.

5. Define the core business: What business are we in?

The core business of the firm is the central focus of a company's activity. Strategic core business definitions are based on a customer benefit rather than a technology, product, or process. Any potential key benefit must tie back to the strategic asset and core competence. If the key benefit cannot be linked to a strategic asset and competence, it can be duplicated by competitors and will not be a source of sustainable competitive advantage for the firm.

6. Define business goals: Where are we going?

For the purpose of Big Picture Analysis, this goal must be single-minded, realistic, measurable, and linked to higher and lower-level goals. For a goal statement to be valuable, it must serve as a decision aid; that is, it must provide direction to the manager faced with an executional decision. If a goal statement has multiple parts, such as to simultaneously "increase profits, share, and revenue," then it provides no direction for managerial decision-making. Goal metrics should be aligned: improvement in one would naturally cause another to improve. Based on our time frame, we must identify the most important goal for the firm.

7. Integrate the Business Objective decisions with other Big Picture decisions.

The Big Picture framework organizes the key strategy and executional decisions of the firm and integrates them. Each chapter of the framework represents a topic with associated analyses and goals. By integrating all these topics and identifying their interrelationships, we gain the ability to learn from our mistakes. If we fail to reach our overall business objective goal, we should be able to look at our lower-level goals to identify what in the framework needs fixing.

☐ KEY TERMS

Brand. (p.30) A name, term, sign, symbol, or design, or a combination of them which is intended to identify the goods or services of one seller or a group of sellers, and to differentiate them from those of competitors. In practice, the brand is synonymous with the overall benefit the company promises to deliver to its customers.

Core business. (p. 47) The core business of the firm is the central focus of a company's activity.

Core competence. (p. 40) A skill of the firm that is pervasive throughout the organization and can lead to a sustainable, competitive advantage.

Distinct branding. (p. 31) A branding approach whereby the company creates different brands for its different products and services.

Fundamental entity. (p. 28) The brand level from which we conduct the strategic analysis. The Fundamental Entity might be the Corporate Brand, a Brand Line, or a Product Brand, depending on the company's brand structure.

Hybrid branding. (p. 31) A branding approach that combines two brands—the corporate brand plus separate brands— to designate differences in product or service lines.

Strategic asset. (p. 28) A strategic asset is a resource of the company that is supported by a core competence and is critical to differentiating the brand.

Umbrella branding. (p. 30) A branding approach whereby the company uses just one brand for all of its products and services.

☐ REVIEW AND DISCUSSION QUESTIONS

1. Three highly successful car companies, Toyota, Mercedes Benz, and BMW, are positioned on different benefits. Toyota is known for selling highly reliable cars; Mercedes Benz prides itself on offering ultimate comfort through its high-status luxury sedans, best represented by its E-class models; and BMW is known for selling cars that deliver 'the ultimate driving performance,' epitomized by its M-class cars. Comment on how each company might define core competencies to deliver the benefits of 'reliability, 'comfort,' and 'driving performance.' Discuss in terms of 'skills,' 'strategic assets,' and 'connected benefits.'

2. Comment on the pros and cons of each branding structure— umbrella, distinct, and hybrid— for a company operating in each of the environments described below.

   (a) A company with highly innovative products that capture consumer trends.

   (b) A technology company that sells products in different but related product categories (such as home electronics, appliances, and high-end sound systems).

   (c) A construction company that builds custom-designed homes in all regions of the country.

3. Imagine that you are the marketing manager for a small division within a large multinational company. The division has one successful brand and was independent until the large multinational company purchased it last year. How would the choice of a Fundamental Entity—either the multinational brand or the division's single brand—affect the choice of a business objective goal for your division?

4. Explain the difference between a core competence and competencies. Now, re-read the beginning chapter vignette, which discusses Walmart's market entry challenges in Germany and China. List the competences and core competencies you think a company like Walmart would need to be successful in the Chinese markets. How might the market environment and customer expectations in that country affect Walmart's ability to differentiate its business on low price?

☐ APPENDIX: MARKETING ANALYSIS AND PLANNING

Marketing Tool #1: Core Competence Audit

As the core competence is critically important to a company's strategy, most marketing strategy analyses should begin by evaluating the company's core competence. This marketing tool offers a structured approach to auditing a company's core competence. We organize core competence research and validation into two separate tasks: Identify and Measure. During the Identify phase we do research to define the core competence. During the measure phase we look for metrics that will allow us to track the specific core competence skills over time.

Identify the Core Competence

We can identify a short list of potential core competencies by answering some basic questions about the company:

1. **What are the strategic assets of the firm?** These are the tangible and intangible assets that bring tremendous value to the company and that are relatively unique and valuable to the company. For example: Does the company have unique products, patents, specialized staff, or manufacturing facilities? A really strong brand?

Do some Internet research to try to figure these out. Also, go to social media sites and blogs to figure out what the 'crown jewels' of the company might be. If the company is public, look for annual reports and listen to investor calls or podcasts, if they exist, to discover the major assets of the company.

2. **Why do customers purchase from the company?** We can interview customers and ask this open-ended question to learn about the main benefits the company offers. We can also use secondary data such as blogs, and product and service review boards. What do people like about products and services of this company? Research and interviews can help us triangulate what is most appealing to customers about this company.

3. **What are the core skills of the firm that lead to those strategic assets, which, in turn, generate customer benefits** (Fig. 2A.1)? We might use research from secondary sources to find out what industry experts think is really unique about the firm. We are looking for skills that span several departments or functions in the firm, rather than sitting in just one area of the company. We 'back into' these, so make a list based on the information you have gathered so far. This list is really just hypothetical, but it is useful because it will help you narrow your research going forward. Note that the arrows in Figure 2A.1 indicate that skills, assets and benefit items should be related.

Once you have done some research, complete a CSB tool by filling in specifics for the descriptions in Figure 2A.2 and look for linkages between skills (competences), assets, and benefits. Look for places where there are clear connections and also identify where the connections are not as clear.

Select two (three at most) core competencies. Be sure they describe skills that are:

(a) Pervasive in the organization; that is, they are shared across several functional areas (sales, marketing, customer service, operations, finance, HR, and so on).

(b) Hard to imitate by competitors.

(c) In need of specific investment and specific hiring and training policies in the company.

(d) Linked to customer benefits.

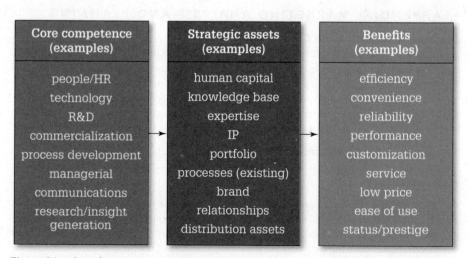

Core competence (examples)	Strategic assets (examples)	Benefits (examples)
people/HR	human capital	efficiency
technology	knowledge base	convenience
R&D	expertise	reliability
commercialization	IP	performance
process development	portfolio	customization
managerial	processes (existing)	service
communications	brand	low price
research/insight generation	relationships	ease of use
	distribution assets	status/prestige

Figure 2A.1 Sample core competencies, strategic assets, and benefits (CSB) tool.

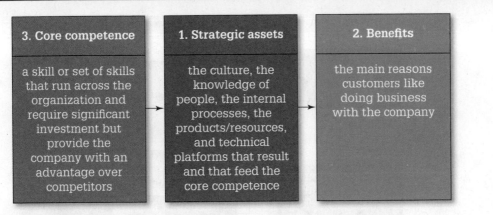

3. Core competence	1. Strategic assets	2. Benefits
a skill or set of skills that run across the organization and require significant investment but provide the company with an advantage over competitors	the culture, the knowledge of people, the internal processes, the products/resources, and technical platforms that result and that feed the core competence	the main reasons customers like doing business with the company

Figure 2A.2 The basic CSB tool.

Measure the Core Competence: Cross-Industry Benchmarking

Try to come up with two or three ways to measure each core competence. A helpful way to do this is by identifying a core competence benchmark, that is, a company in a different industry with a similar core competence, and one for which we can identify process-level metrics that will allow us to track our Company's core competence. If we were working on a customer-service related core competence, we would probably want to track the amount and type of employee training that happens in the company, the types of processes used to recruit employees, the processes used for capturing and categorizing complaints, the types and number of tools the company uses to establish and maintain relationships with customers, and so on.

For example, if we identified "Human Resource Processes for Customer Service" as our core competence, then we are looking for another company in a different industry which excels and this same type of skill set. The Ritz Carlton Hotels are known for having this very type of core competence, and they would be a great benchmarking company, especially if we operate in a different industry.

So the key to measuring the core competence is identifying a benchmark—a company in a different industry with the same or very similar core competence—that can help us set up metrics and targets for our company. We measure the core competence by:

- Generating two or three examples of companies in other industries with similar core competencies.
- Describing the skills of the benchmark companies by thinking about a customer's experience with the company and how the company is able to satisfy a customer in a specific way. (Is it good at training people, at sourcing raw materials, at innovating, at manufacturing and bringing things to market, and operating reliably every time, and so forth?)

Marketing Tool #2: Calculating Strategic Goals: The Revenue Tree

In choosing a revenue goal for the company, we should start by understanding how many customers we have and how much those customers purchased in the last year. As shown in Figure 2A.3, we can estimate the revenue goal for the next year (or period) by estimating:

(a) **Revenue from current customers.** This is our estimate of the number of customers we already have and we think will stay with us into the next period multiplied by the average purchase per customer.

(b) **Growth from retention.** This is based on the number of existing customers we think will increase the volume and/or the value of their purchases from us.

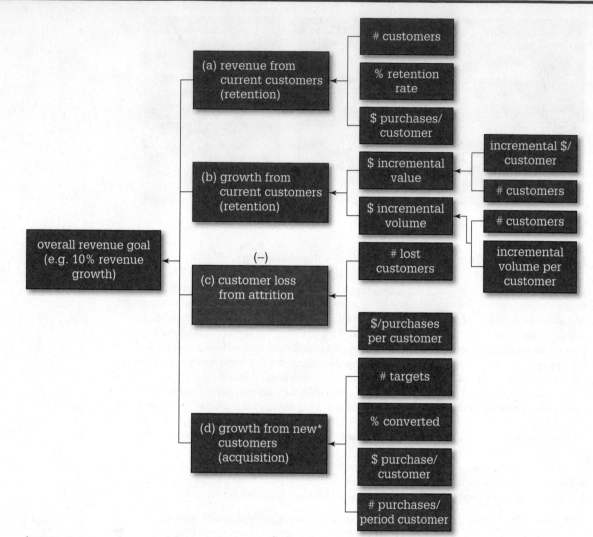

* new customers can be acquired from outside the category or from a competitor

Figure 2A.3 Revenue goal tree.

    (c) Customer attrition. This will be a negative number, which is based on the number of customers we think will leave the firm, and the dollar amount of purchases they represent.

    (d) Growth from acquisition. This is our best guess as to how many customers we will acquire, based on the number of customers we are targeting, expected conversion rates, revenue per customer purchase, and expected purchases per customer.

Setting goals requires a detailed estimate of how many customers we will acquire and how many we will retain, and how many purchases are likely to come from each of these customer groupings. (We go through these calculations in more detail in Chapters 3 and 4.)

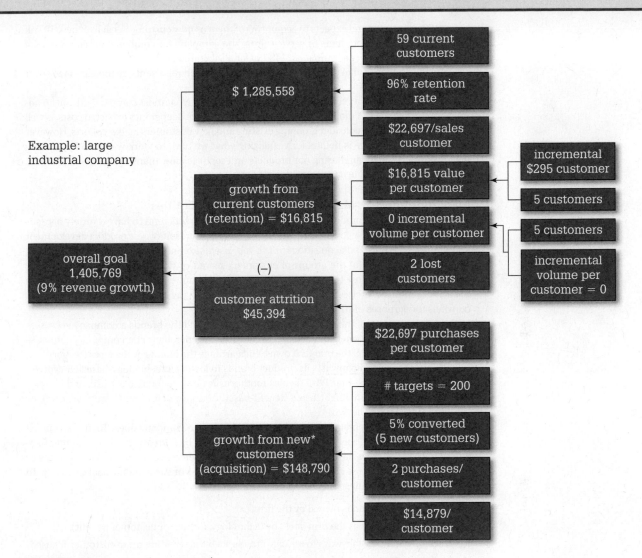

Example: large industrial company

Figure 2A.4 Revenue goal tree example.

In Figure 2A.4 we present an example of a revenue goal tree for a large industrial company that currently has 59 customers and an annual attrition rate of 4% (or 96% retention rate). This company estimates that its customers will purchase on average $22,697 of products and services from the company in the next period. The company has historically retained 96% of its customers, so it expects to lose 2 of the current 59, or the equivalent of $45,394 of revenue. For the 57 customers it retains, the company expects to be able to grow revenues by a combination of selling additional products and services (this is generally called *upselling*) and price increases, and therefore increase revenues per customer by $295, or $16,815 for all 57 retained customers. Now we turn our attention to the acquisition side of the tree. The company will target 100 companies and expects to acquire 5% of them as new customers; each of these 10 will initially purchase two products or services from the company for combined initial revenue of $14,879 per customer or an estimated $148,790 for all acquired customers. Adding the expected revenues, we get an annual revenue goal of $1,405,769, which represents an increase of 9% over last year's revenues.

This revenue tree is a very simplified exercise relative to what most companies do on an annual or monthly basis. A more complete analysis would delve deeper into expected costs as well as revenues and would consider grouping existing and new customers in like-cohorts. However simple, the revenue tree is helpful for visualizing what we have to work with and for drawing insights about who is purchasing our products and services, how many are entirely new to us, and how many have done business with us before.

Marketing Tool #3: Mapping the Fundamental Entities

Large companies with products and services in diverse markets tend to have a variety of product brands that have been created organically over time as a result of new product development and brand extensions and acquisitions. It is a very useful exercise to map a company's brands, clearly distinguishing: (a) the groups of customers served or their business category, (b) the benefits provided to those customers and (c) how the customer groups and the benefits relate to each other. This exercise also helps us understand how many fundamental entities the company has for purposes of strategic analysis.

In developing one of these maps we are looking to list all the brands a company possesses and to group them by benefit-based categories. You can generally visit a company's corporate website to find a list of all the brands it owns. Then arrange the brands by business category. You might find that the company lists its product brands following a technology-based categorization (below you can see that P&G divides toothbrushes into manual, electrical, and battery-operated). The company might use a benefit-based category definition (beauty vs. care), or some combination of the two.

Try this exercise by first mapping the brands just as the company does. Then ask yourself whether other possible ways of categorizing brands might be better aligned to customer benefits. Finally, look across the brands and ask yourself whether the company could rationalize or extend brands and pursue additional business opportunities or garner additional efficiency. To recap, the steps in building and using a brand map are:

(1) Develop a list of brands owned by the firm.

(2) Arrange the brands as the firm does (by technology, feature, or customer benefit).

(3) Develop other possible ways to arrange brands such that they are more customer-focused.

(4) Look for opportunities to rationalize brands.

(5) Look for opportunities to extend Fundamental Entity (primary) brands.

Figure 2A.5 shows a partial brand map for Procter & Gamble's (P&G) Dental Care Division. Crest's primary benefit is 'preventing tooth decay', or encouraging 'Healthy Teeth'. The brand has been extended from toothpaste into toothbrushes, floss, dental rinse, and whitening strips, prompting the introduction of a series of sub-brands.

P&G also introduced other brands that complement and in some instances compete with Crest. For example, within the Rinse category, the Scope brand was launched in the 1960s by P&G to deliver the benefit of 'fresh breath'. Oral-B, originally a toothbrush brand purchased in 2006, is primarily known for electric toothbrushes that carry the Professional, Triumph, or Pulsonic sub-brands. However, P&G realized that the brand benefit Oral-B offered, 'technical oral care', could be used in other places in the mouth, so the company decided to extend that brand to the Floss product line.

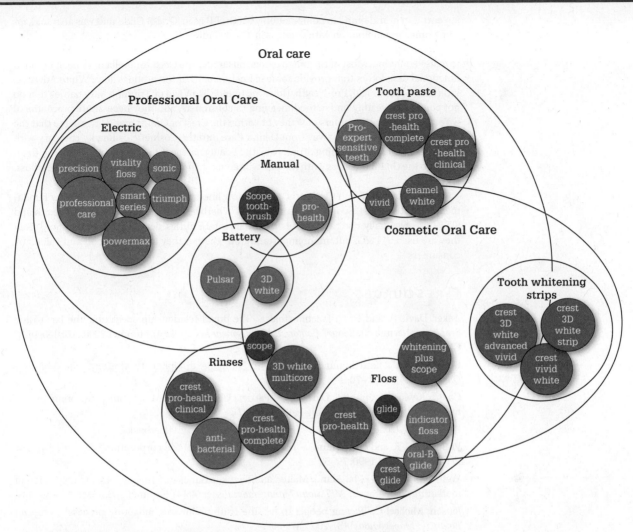

Figure 2A.5 A partial brand map for Procter & Gamble's (P&G) Dental Care Division.
Source: See P&G corporate website. "Leadership Brands." (http://www.pg.com/en_US/brands/index.shtml). Accessed April 12, 2012.
Please see this source for updated information about P&G's brands.

Within the toothpaste and rinse lines, P&G has tried to preserve the essence of Crest and its focus on the healthy teeth benefit by creating the Pro Health sub-brand. Managing a portfolio of brands that have traditionally functioned as distinct from each other with different positionings is made complex by corporate pressures to maximize profits, using existing brands to launch new products, and extending and commingling brands. The risk in extending and commingling brands is that the brand meaning might become obscure and the consumer might become confused. Although Crest and Oral-B have different meanings to customers, P&G makes some attempts to present them as complementary; for example, they have shared websites and they also now share some sub-brands. For example, the Pro-Health, the Vivid, and the Scope brands show up on Crest and on Oral-B products. Also, Glide Floss appears as an independent brand; it appears as a hybrid brand in combination with Oral-B as in 'Oral-B Glide' and was also sold, for some time, in combination with Crest, as in 'Crest Glide.'

The proliferation of products and brands around the original brands also has the potential to cause confusion. Most of the brand extensions under the Crest umbrella have been branded functional descriptors that provide some indication of what the product does: White Advance, Indicator floss, Clinical, Pro-Health. However, brands like Vivid or Triumph have names that do not convey any readily understood meaning to consumers, and they necessitate promotional work to explain to consumers how they fit within the Crest or Oral-B brand lines. Note that the Crest brand was extended away from Dental Care into the Cosmetic or Beauty category with the introduction of Whitening Strips. Now the Beauty category forms a large part of the Crest and also the Oral-B business, with not just whitening strips, but also toothbrushes, rinses, floss, and so on.

Within the P&G Tooth Care and Dental Beauty lines, there seem to be the following Fundamental Entities: Crest, Scope, Glide, and Oral-B. Whether other brands such as Pro-Health and 3D White eventually rise to the level of 'Fundamental Entities' depends not just on how often they are used by P&G, but, more importantly, on whether they are understood and valued by consumers.

☐ RESOURCES

Aaker, David A. and Erich Joachimsthaler. "The brand relationship spectrum: The key to the brand architecture challenge," *California Management Review* 42(4), Summer 2000, ABI/INFORM Global: 8–23.

Coyne, Kevin P. and Somu Subramaniam. "Bringing discipline to strategy," *The McKinsey Quarterly* 4, 1996: 61–70.

Coyne, Kevin P., Stephen, J. D. Hall, and Patricia Gorman Clifford. "Is your core competence a mirage?," *The McKinsey Quarterly* 1: 40–54 (1997).

Drucker, P. F. (2006). *The practice of management*, NY Harper Paperbacks.

Prahalad, C. K. and Gary Hamel. "The core competence of the corporation," *Harvard Business Review*, May–June 1990: 79–90.

Webster, Frederick E. Jr., Alan J. Malter, and Shankar Ganesan, "The decline and dispersion of marketing competence," *MIT Sloan Management Review* 46(4), Summer 2005, SMR 176: 34–43.

Jensen, Michael C. "Paying people to lie: The truth about the budgeting process," *European Financial Management* 9(3), 2003: 379–406.

Levitt, Theodore. *Marketing imagination:* New York. Simon and Schuster, 1986.

☐ END NOTES

Claburn, Thomas. "Apple drops 'Computer' from corporate moniker." *InformationWeek.* January 9, 2007. http://www.informationweek.com/news/global-cio/showArticle.jhtml?articleID=196802415. Accessed May 22, 2009.

Coach Inc. "Coach Annual Report 2007." *Coach Annual Report 2007.* June 30, 2007. http://ww3.ics. adp.com/streetlink_data/dirCOH/annual/HTML1/coach_ar2007_0041.htm. Accessed May 26, 2009.

Collins, Glenn. "Company news; Ten years later, Coca-Cola laughs at 'New Coke'." *The New York Times.* April 11, 1995. http://www.nytimes.com/1995/04/11/business/company-news-ten-years-later-coca-cola-laughs-at-new-coke.html?scp=1&sq=new%20coke%20marketing%20blunder&st=cse. Accessed May 26, 2009.

Hafner, Katie. "Inside Apple stores, a certain aura enchants the faithful." *New York Times*. December 27, 2007. http://www.nytimes.com/2007/12/27/business/27apple.html?_r=1&scp=1&sq=sales%20per%20square%20foot%20at%20apple&st=cse. Accessed May 28, 2009.

The Coca-Cola Company. "Mission, vision & values." May 26, 2009. http://www.thecoca-colacompany.com/ourcompany/mission_vision_values.html. Accessed May 26, 2009.

Wharton, Knowledge @. "What's in a name change? Look at Apple." *Forbes.com*. January 25, 2007. http://www.forbes.com/2007/01/25/apple-microsoft-motorola-ent-sales-cx_kw_0125wharton.html. Accessed May 22, 2009.

chapter three

"One Thing owned is better
than two things promised. . ."
—Cervants, *Don Quixote, page 614*

MARKETING OBJECTIVE

Customer Focus

After studying this chapter you should be able to:

1. *Explain the value of a customer orientation*
2. *Contrast different definitions of a customer*
3. *Identify three types of customer loyalty*
4. *Explain the strategic implications of customer acquisition and retention*
5. *Integrate the marketing objectives within the Big Picture*

Using a New Product to Bring Customers to the Franchise: Apple iPhone

Spencer Platt/Getty Images

In January 2007, Apple Inc. introduced the iPhone, its entry in the smartphone market. The iPhone was immediately hailed as revolutionary, not because it offered many new features—other devices at the time offered similar voice and email communications as well as entertainment and productivity options—but rather because of its differentiated design and ease of use. As it had done before with the Mac and iPod, Apple had again capitalized on its core competence in interface design, instead of simply reacting to competition by launching a feature-driven incremental innovation.

The success of the iPhone prompted millions of consumers to switch wireless carriers, since initially ATT was the only wireless company in the United States to support the device. It also drove software developers to release small software programs called applications or 'apps' specifically designed for the iPhone, despite the fact that Apple used a proprietary software platform.

And the iPhone's popularity of course benefited Apple directly, not only from a sales and profitability standpoint but also by increasing brand equity for the entire franchise. The iPhone generated a "halo effect" whereby consumers, especially if they were new to the Apple brand, transferred the positive associations of the new device to other Apple products. There is strong positive correlation between iPhone sales and Mac sales. The iPhone in effect has functioned as a customer acquisition tool for Apple, prompting millions of PC users around the world to switch to Macs and eroding Microsoft's dominance in both the smartphone and the computer markets. While overall PC sales grew by only 2.3% following the iPhone's release, Mac sales grew at an astonishing 16.4% during the same period. As Needham and Company analyst Charlie Wolf said, "We believe that the halo effect emanating from the iPhone is even stronger than that surrounding the iPod. After all, the iPod is a relatively simple device while the iPhone is arguably a mini-computer wrapped in a phone's form factor."

By depending on its core competence in product design, Apple was able to grow Mac sales by attracting new customers to the brand umbrella without lowering its computer profit margins. Although the iPhone was also attractive to existing Apple customers, it propelled the Apple brand primarily because it appealed to customers who had never before relied on Apple for their personal data storage and communication needs. In developing the iPhone, Apple made a strategic choice to focus on acquiring new customers to the Apple franchise. ∎

Sources: Oliver, Sam. "Apple's iPhone 'halo effect' lifts Mac to 16.4% sales growth." *Apple Insider* December 1, 2009. Accessed December 12, 2012. http://appleinsider.com/articles/09/12/01/.

Troianovski, Anton. "Free iPhone to escalate low-end fight." *The Wall Street Journal.* October 5, 2011. Accessed December 12, 2012. http://online.wsj.com/article/SB10001424052970204524604576611353925098240.html.

THE VALUE OF DEVELOPING A CUSTOMER ORIENTATION IN THE FIRM

Apple's strategic choice highlights a challenge that every marketing manager faces: optimally allocating resources between customer acquisition and customer retention activities. Now that we have identified the fundamental entity, core competence, and goal, we turn our attention to the company's source of growth: customers.

The focus on individual customers distinguishes marketing from other strategic disciplines, which generally focus on companies as the strategic actors. It is the response of our customers, not of markets or companies, that will determine whether our marketing plan results in success or failure. Marketers allocate very significant resources to understanding and improving customer loyalty to their brands because there is evidence that *satisfied* customers tend to be more loyal, and **customer loyalty** is a driver of company profits. Customer loyalty is generally defined as the combination of repeat purchases and commitment to a brand on the part of a customer; both attitudinal and behavioral components are necessary for loyalty to exist. Companies who have lots of loyal customers benefit directly and indirectly from this loyalty. Loyal customers have higher repurchase rates and longer relationships with their preferred brands; they are also more likely to recommend the brands they prefer to friends, family, and colleagues at work.

In this chapter we explore the concept of **Customer Lifetime Value**—or the value of a customer to the company throughout the life of his or her relationship with the firm. Research has shown that we can in fact estimate the value of a firm by adding together the values of its individual customer relationships. This method of calculating the value of a company has been shown to be a better predictor of long-term share price performance than financial analysis alone (Gupta and Lehmann, 2005).

As marketers, we are charged with *creating and capturing value*: the repository of this value creation and capture is not the product, but the customer. Product, price,

Customer loyalty. Customer loyalty is generally defined as the combination of repeat purchases and commitment to a brand on the part of a customer; both attitudinal and behavioral components are necessary for loyalty to exist.

Customer Lifetime Value (CLV). The total net present value of current and future profits that a particular customer will generate over the lifetime of his or her relationship with a firm. $CLV = \$m(r/1 + r - d)$, where m is the \$ margin per customer, r is the retention rate, and d is the weighted-average cost of capital of the company or discount rate.

social**media**

Customer Acquisition: Futbol

Hugely popular elsewhere in the world, futbol has only recently become popular—as soccer— in the United States, thanks in great part to efforts by the U.S. Soccer Federation. In 1998, the Soccer Federation created "Project 2010" aimed at making soccer as popular in the United States as football, and a big push went into introducing kids to soccer by funding school soccer leagues. Acquiring customers early through these leagues has paid off. The U.S. TV audience for the 2010 World Cup final between Spain and the Netherlands was more than 24 million strong.

Ali Al-Saadi/AFP/Getty Images

Sources: Pinto, Pedro. "Shouldn't the United States be better at soccer?" CNN Blog. July 11, 2011. http://worldsport.blogs.cnn.com/2011/06/16/shouldnt-the-united-states-be-better-at-soccer/. Accessed August 12, 2013.

Kaplan, Thomas. "Soccer's growth in the U.S. seems steady." *The New York Times*, 22 July, 2010.

Customer acquisition.
A series of activities designed to bring new customers to our brand or franchise, including awareness creation, information delivery, and activities designed to encourage trial.

Customer retention.
Activities designed to help keep customers longer.

distribution, and communication strategies are simply means of building equity among our customers and then capturing that equity. In particular, we are concerned with **customer acquisition:** attracting new customers to the brand franchise, and **customer retention:** maintaining and strengthening the relationship between these customers and the franchise. These two seemingly simple concepts, when used in a disciplined fashion, are key levers of our marketing strategy.

Customer Acquisition

The first goal of any firm is to acquire customers. This is obvious for new and growing firms, as well as an ongoing concern for those engaged in new market development. In addition, all firms will experience a natural level of customer attrition and will need to replace these customers in order to achieve sustainable growth. Because these customers are usually newly acquired, they are experiencing our products and services for the first time. In others, customers have left our franchise and we are charged with the task of bringing them back. In the first case we are starting from the beginning; we must generate awareness, disseminate information about our brand, and convince potential customers to try our products or services. If we seek to reacquire customers, we may be faced with the further task of convincing former customers who may have left the franchise due to product or service failures that we have new and/or different offerings that will satisfy them. In either case the task of customer acquisition requires substantial time and money resources, a fact we must consider during the marketing planning process.

social**media**

Zingerman's Uses Early Customer Acquisition

Chris Borrelli/Chicago Tribune/MCT/Getty Images

Zingermans started in 1982 in the college town of Ann Arbor, Michigan. The company has grown from its original deli business by acquiring customers as students and cultivating the relationship as those customers go on to the next phase of their lives. It now consists of eight separate operations, including two restaurants, a bake house, a coffee company, and a catering company that all sell premium food products, plus an executive training company. Through its successful mail order and online catalogues, and thanks to a highly committed and socially active clientele, the company retains its customers after they graduate and even if they leave Michigan.

Each business has its own organizational structure but maintains the same standards and commitment to the company's values, so customers have a consistent experience throughout all eight businesses. Zingerman's stands for a particularly liberal and empowering management ideal that captures the atmosphere of the town where it is headquartered.

Sources: Company website www.zingermans.com. Accessed January 1, 2013.
Burlinghan, Bo. "The coolest small company in America." January 1, 2003. *Inc. Magazine.* http://www.inc.com/magazine/20030101/25036.html. Accessed February 11, 2013.

While **customer acquisition** is necessary, all *newly acquired customers are not created equal*. If, for example, we seek to acquire customers with a price promotion, we will likely attract more price-sensitive customers who may not properly value our products in the long run. This is why we should always engage in *acquisition with retention in mind*, taking a strategic approach to our customer acquisition that will ensure the long-term success of our venture.

Customer Retention

If we cannot efficiently and effectively retain our customers, we will not experience sustainable growth. A high customer retention rate is generally an indicator of the overall health of the firm, product/service performance, and customer loyalty. A strong

social**media**

Acquisition and Retention Dynamics and Online Music Sharing (a.k.a. Piracy)

The Internet has rocked the music industry by fundamentally changing the power structure in the distribution channel, taking power from the music labels and traditional radio stations and shifting it to individual listeners via technology and innovative pricing. Starting in 1999, when Napster was created, many listeners decided to share their music libraries through peer-to-peer networks rather than buy songs. Although Napster was banned in 2001 after being successfully sued for copyright violations by the Recording Industry Association of America, music piracy continued. In the first half of 2012, U.S. listeners illegally downloaded 759 million songs using BitTorrent downloading software.

Many artists have spoken out against piracy, notably Eminem, Metallica, and Madonna. However, others became quite vocal defenders of music sharing. For example, an independent band called *Dispatch* credited Napster with its ability to headline *New York City's Madison Square Garden* with no formal promotion or radio play, selling the venue out for three consecutive nights. Still, why would any artist encourage piracy?

The music industry is subject to two phenomena studied by economists. The first is the *free-rider problem*, which describes the inefficiencies created in a market when people consume products without paying for them. In the music market, people who download music they have not

paid for are "free-riding"—that is, not paying for the value of what they consume.

The second problem is *network externalities*, which occur when the value of a product or service increases the more people use it. As people download and share tracks, other listeners hear music they would not have otherwise been exposed to. Researchers have found that peer-to-peer sharing lowers the cost of customer acquisition for lesser-known artists. In marketing we think of music as a product rich in 'experience attributes', something you have to sample to know whether you like it or not. This makes it really difficult for unknown artists to break into the market unless they can be heard.

The free-rider problem, network externalities, and the fact that music is an experiential product help explain why Madonna dislikes the idea that inspired Napster and Dispatch likes it. Sales for mega-stars are negatively affected by free downloads; sales for lesser-known artists are actually increased by them. Lesser-known artists are working on *customer acquisition* as their marketing objective; and acquisition costs are lowered by free downloads due to the network externalities effect. Mega artists are working on *retaining* their fans with each new song and album; for them, the negative effect of free riders on sales is higher than the positive effect of network externalities because their music is already well known.

Sources: Ellyatt, Holly. "Florida city named pirate capital of music world." March 8, 2012. CNBC. *http://finance.yahoo.com/news/music-industry-fights-conquer-piracys-104812479.html*. Accessed April 9, 2013.

Borland, John. "Unreleased Madonna single slips onto Net." CNET News. *http://news.cnet.com/2100-1023-241341.html*. Accessed March 12, 2012; Gopal, Bhattacherjee, and GL Sanders. 'Do artists benefit from online music sharing?' *The Journal of Business* 79: 3 (May 2006), 1503–1533.

retention rate can also simply be the result of non-marketing or external competitive factors; for example, many air travel routes are owned almost exclusively by one airline, and customers are therefore forced to "select" this carrier. Very often firms will attempt to lock customers in with a long-term contract. In addition, some firms benefit from a force referred to as "network externalities;" this situation arises when high market share of a brand or product type in one category drives consumption in another. For example, the dominance of VHS video players in the 1980's meant that sales of VHS tapes were higher than those for the competing standard, Beta. While these external factors can result in strong customer retention, the source of this retention is not necessarily higher satisfaction with the product. In the long run, the best way to achieve sustainable growth is to generate retention by developing and selling products that customers value.

Just as we should have a goal of acquisition with retention in mind, we should also seek to achieve *retention with acquisition in mind*. This occurs when the source of our retention rate is customer loyalty as opposed to external factors. When customers are loyal to our product for the right reasons, they are far more likely to recommend our brand to potential customers. This *word-of-mouth* effect can have a substantial impact on our acquisition rate.

In a strategic marketing context, therefore, acquisition and retention, while distinct concepts, are interrelated. However, the specific activities we engage in to achieve acquisition are quite different from those for retention. Therefore, we must carefully specify the nature of acquisition and retention as it relates to the customer, the category, and the firm.

DEVELOPING A CUSTOMER DEFINITION

Who is our customer? Is it someone who has recently purchased the product, or someone who purchases it infrequently but never purchases the competition? Is it someone who buys the product when it is available but buys the competition when it is not? Before we can articulate our acquisition and retention goals, we must have a clear definition of the prospective, acquired, and retained customer. These three types of customers obviously represent a continuum, with potential customers farthest away from our ideal retained customers in their behavior and attitude toward our product, and acquired customers somewhere in between the two. Obviously the distinction between these three types of customers is subjective; however, we must have clear criteria for membership in each of these groups in order to count customers, and ultimately to measure our marketing effectiveness and efficiency.

Behavioral Customer Definitions

The obvious approach to defining a customer is to observe and measure behaviors. Three common behavioral metrics are frequency of purchase, recency of purchase, and volume of purchase. We can consider these behaviors relative to competition (how frequently did my customer buy my product compared to the competition?) or on an absolute basis (how many total units did she buy from me last month?).

Recency, Frequency, and Monetary value (RFM) analysis is an example of a database behavioral marketing metric and consists of ranking customers by examining how recently they have purchased (recency), how often they purchase (frequency), and how much they spend with the company (monetary). RFM analysis is based on the marketing axiom that "80% of your business comes from 20% of your customers." Marketers for non-profit organizations often use RFM to target their mailings to people most likely to make donations based on their past donations. The reasoning behind RFM-based targeting is simply that the best predictor of future behavior is past behavior. In RFM analysis, customers are grouped into percentiles and assigned a ranking number of 1,2,3,4, or 5 (with 5 being highest) for each RFM parameter. The three scores together are referred to as an RFM "cell." The database is sorted to identify the "best" customers in the past, with a cell ranking of "555" being ideal.

RFM analysis does have some shortcomings. A company must be careful not to over-focus on customers with the highest rankings, because that risks annoying the best customers. Also, RFM analysis looks only at the revenue side of the profitability equation and should be complemented with profitability analysis (such as Customer Lifetime Value) to identify customers who negotiate discounts or consume a lot of customer service resources; these accounts can be unprofitable despite generating a lot of revenue. Finally, we must be careful not to ignore customers who could be cultivated to purchase more if we paid more attention to them.

While behavioral metrics like RFM can help us identify acquired and retained customers, there may be strategic reasons for choosing one over the other. For example, if we have excess capacity we may focus purely on increasing unit sales and define a customer as one who purchases large quantities of our product. On the other hand, in an intensely competitive market with lots of customer switching, recency or relative frequency of purchase may be more important. In order to make sure our execution and strategy are well integrated, we need to choose the behavioral metric that best reflects our strategic goals and environment.

Having selected the behavioral metric, we next will specify the points at which we judge our customer to have transitioned from potential to acquired, or from acquired to retained. For firms with an existing customer base, it is often easiest to first identify our "ideal" retained customer. In our dreams, what would all our customers look like in terms of behaviors? For example, the ideal Starbucks customer will drive or walk for up to 30 minutes, passing other coffee shops, to purchase a cup of Starbucks. The ideal Allstate customer has not just auto insurance, but also homeowners and a life insurance policy. The ideal De Beers customer receives a diamond ring in celebration of her engagement, then asks for diamond jewelry on her birthday, and decides to purchase a second diamond ring later in life to celebrate her professional accomplishments.

"Ideal" customers such as these represent value for the firm not just today, but on an ongoing basis. They are the foundation of a firm that enjoys sustainable growth. We can use behavioral information to begin to identify these ideal customers using a metric know as customer lifetime value (CLV).

© fstop123/iStockphoto

De Beers launched a campaign in 2003 to create heavier usage of diamonds, by appealing to women to purchase diamonds for themselves beyond their engagement.

Customer Lifetime Value

Customer lifetime value (CLV) is the total net present value of current and future profits that a particular customer will generate over the lifetime of his or her relationship with our firm. The concept of customer lifetime value (CLV) has become increasingly popular as customer data has become more accessible. A simplified formula allows us to calculate CLV by considering (1) how much profit we earn from a particular customer over a particular time period and (2) how long he or she will stay with us. The final aspect of the CLV formula is the time value of money; the formula places less weight on profits made in later years. When customer retention rates are constant over time, the formula looks like this:

$$CLV = \$m(r/1 + r - d)$$

where

      r is the customer retention rate
      $\$m$ is the dollar profit margin per customer
      d is the company's discount rate

CLV is a powerful tool for marketers because it provides a guide for how much we should invest to acquire customers. For most companies, the average CLV is between 1 and 4.5 times the per-customer profit margin ($m).[1] Also, the CLV formula is more sensitive to changes in the retention rate than to changes in the margin per customer; in other words, CLV is elastic to the retention rate (see the accompanying box on this concept). This finding reinforces the importance of customer retention rates, even though many firms focus more on profit margin per customer. We explore the customer lifetime value calculation in more detail in the Marketing Analysis and Planning Tools section of the chapter.

CLV analysis can help us specify our ideal retained customer. Furthermore, by looking at different behaviors relative to CLV, we can begin to identify a continuum over which our customer may travel on the way to becoming an ideal customer. Figure 3.1 provides an illustration for three different firms. For Allstate, it makes sense to target as potential customers brand-new drivers or current drivers with a competitor's policy. The newly acquired customer is one who has just purchased an auto policy. However, the source of Allstate's long-term profitability is its retained customers, defined here as those who have purchased homeowner's and life insurance policies in addition to their auto policy. This assessment is quite different for Starbucks: the potential customer may be a coffee drinker who brews coffee at home, the acquired customer is one who stops at Starbucks when convenient, and the retained customer actively seeks out Starbucks, walking or driving past other coffee shops to get there.

Where do we draw the line between potential, acquired, and retained? That is a decision each manager must make based on the particular characteristics of the industry, the firm, and the brand. Very often the CLV metric provides important insight here; for example, many insurance firms observe a marked jump in CLV for customers who purchase two or more products. In the end, the decision is a subjective one. How-

---

[1]Gupta, Sunil, Donald Lehmann, and Jennifer Ames Stuart. "Valuing customers," *Journal of Marketing Research* (2004): 7–18.

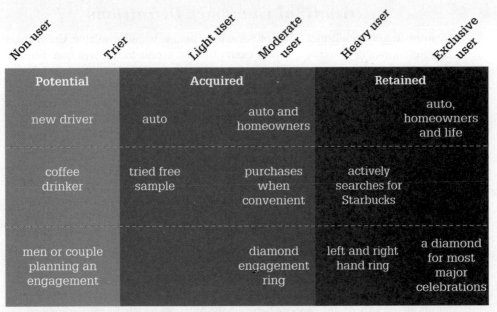

	Non user	Trier	Light user	Moderate user	Heavy user	Exclusive user
	Potential		**Acquired**		**Retained**	
	new driver	auto	auto and homeowners			auto, homeowners and life
	coffee drinker	tried free sample	purchases when convenient		actively searches for Starbucks	
	men or couple planning an engagement		diamond engagement ring		left and right hand ring	a diamond for most major celebrations

Figure 3.1 The acquisition/retention continuum.

ever, it is crucial that once we set these subjective definitions of acquired and retained customer, we apply them consistently. Without consistent definitions, the firm cannot conclusively assess the effectiveness and efficiency of marketing efforts. When CLV is utilized strategically and consistently, it can be an extremely useful tool for analyzing and capitalizing on behavioral information.

social**media**

Hotmail: Acquisition through Retained Customers

Hotmail.com was launched by Microsoft and grew very rapidly by relying on retained customers for new-customer acquisition. When customers of the free web-based service sent an email, a promotional message at the bottom invited the recipient to obtain a free Hotmail account. This clever tactic was quite novel at the time and

© scanrail/iStockphoto

was very effective for Hotmail. Competition from advertising-free email, particularly Gmail, prompted Microsoft to phase out Hotmail at the end of 2012 and offer users free Outlook. com email addresses.

Sources: Jones, Steven and Ovide Shira. "Microsoft reboots Hotmail as Outlook.com," *The Wall Street Journal.* July 31, 2012.

Halliday, Josh. "Microsoft hopes for sunny outlook as Hotmail retired," *The Guardian UK.* August 1, 2012.

Attitudinal Customer Definitions

In some industries a broad range of behavioral data is widely available. Companies like Netflix.com or Amazon.com, for example, have access to massive quantities of detailed behavioral data for every one of their customers. Using complex algorithms, these firms mine their data to make product recommendations to current customers based on past purchases. Amazon's information is already so rich and complete that it is doubtful whether information about customer attitudes would significantly improve its recommendations.

While online companies have a natural repository of behavioral data, some brick-and-mortar firms have also developed a core competence at predictive data mining, and they rely on this skill as a source of competitive advantage. For example, Capital One, a U.S. credit card company, applies information about a consumer's spending behavior, risk profile, demographics, and responsiveness to previous campaigns to efforts that target specific offers to customers. In grocery stores, the United Kingdom's Tesco uses innovative database marketing in its Club card program, which collects detailed purchase information about all its repeat shoppers. By identifying what its most valuable shoppers prefer, Tesco modifies its product mix to better serve this customer group and significantly increase its loyalty. Understanding customer buying habits also lets Tesco differentiate between the items for which customers are and are not price-sensitive. This knowledge gives it the power to adjust product pricing to consumers' changes in price-sensitivity.

For many other firms, however, behavioral data is not readily available in sufficient quantities to assist in strategic decision-making. This is often the case for business-to-business companies with a few large customers and manufacturers of consumer and industrial durable products such as cars, appliances, and computers. These companies might have limited customer data because they have few customers or because the frequency of purchase is low. It is also hard to rely on behavioral data for certain products that are purchased irregularly based on specific and changing needs, such as baby products and vacation packages.

When behavioral data is sparse or inconsistent, the firm will need to add *attitudinal* information in order to assess customer acquisition and retention. To do so we must examine our customers' beliefs about our product and its benefits. Would they recommend the product to others? If and when they were ready to replace the product or re-enter the category, would they consider our brand again? We can combine this attitudinal data with behavioral data to draw richer and more meaningful definitions of potential, acquired, and retained customers.

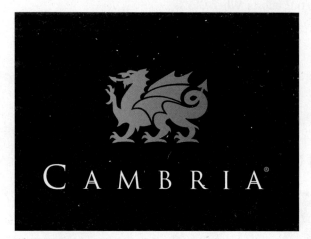

When measuring customer loyalty for infrequently purchased products like countertops, companies cannot just use behavior as a proxy for preference but must also take attitudes into account to know whether someone is loyal to the brand.

Source: http://countertopsz.com/wp-content/uploads/2012/07/cambria-countertops.jpg.www.cambriausa.com

Consider Cambria, a producer of manufactured stone countertops. Consumers purchase these countertops when they are remodeling a kitchen or a bathroom. The average interval between such purchases is about 10 years, during which time that customer has little or no contact with the company. However, customers' attitudes toward the brand indicate how well the product has performed, and whether they will be recommending it to others. These attitudes help predict Cambria's future sales.

Therefore, marketers must collect and assess not just behavioral data but attitudinal data as well. This information helps us assess how loyal our customers are. The nature of this loyalty may vary from industry to industry, from firm to firm, and from customer to customer.

THREE TYPES OF CUSTOMER LOYALTY

Discussions of brand loyalty often revolve around "fanatical" customers, those users who are actively engaged with the brand at all levels. One commonly cited example of this type of user is the Apple loyalist, often defined (and self-defined) as a "zealot" for the brand. While this type of loyalty is potentially profitable, many other less extreme examples of customer loyalty are equally sustainable for the firm. The discussion below outlines three types of loyalty that have quite different strategic implications.

Heart Loyalty

Like the Apple fanatic, the heart-loyal customer is highly involved with the brand, and this involvement is emotional in nature. Very often a heart loyal will use the brand as a self-description: "I'm an Apple person." Thus, a competitor that criticizes the brand is, in effect, criticizing the brand user. The brand is a part of the customer's identity.

We define **heart loyalty** as an emotional attachment to a brand. There are strong relationship aspects to heart loyalty; the product is invested with human qualities and the customer has a bond with this brand. Like a friend, the brand makes the customer happy. The customer defends and promotes the brand when speaking to others. And, as in some interpersonal relationships, the brand can even "betray" the friendship by failing to deliver on the product promise. The consumer will be anxious to "forgive" the brand for performance failures, at least to a point.

Heart loyalty. Customer loyalty based on personal identification with the brand.

There is good news and bad news associated with this deep, emotional relationship. The good news is that heart loyalty is quite immune to competitive attacks, because the consumer will actively defend the brand like any other aspect of his or her identity. The bad news is that the consumer may have exceptionally high expectations based on the nature of the relationship, and it may sometimes be difficult for the firm to sustainably fulfill these expectations. In the case of major or sustained product failure, the strength of the emotional bond between consumer and brand can quickly become a liability if the customer, once an active advocate for the product, now becomes a potent detractor. For some firms, the potential negatives of heart loyalty outweigh the benefits. Luckily, this is not the only type of loyalty a firm can seek to establish.

Head Loyalty

Like heart loyals, **head loyals** are highly engaged. Their involvement is rational, however, rather than emotional in nature. Head loyals are customers whose brand preference is based on an objective assessment of the brand, evaluating performance data, ingredients, ratings, and other characteristics. While a heart loyal might "love" the product, a head loyal will talk about its specific strengths. Thus, the self-identity of the head loyal comes not from the brand itself, but from his or her ability to evaluate the brand's performance.

CUSTOMERFOCUS
ANTHONY BOURDAIN'S LOYALTY TO GLOBAL KNIVES

Heart loyals identify with the brand and can be very effective brand promoters. Chef Anthony Bourdain in his best-selling book, *Kitchen Confidential*, exalts the merits of Global Knives (www.global-knife.com) and tells his readers to 'replace all their kitchen knives with a single Global chef's knife." He further affirms his passion for this Japanese knife brand in a 2006 interview:

What is the crucial gadget in the kitchen?
A properly-maintained knife. I use the Japanese Global knives, as do a lot of my cook and chef friends. They're light, one-piece, so there's no wood handle to fall off or rivets that are likely to come undone. They hold an edge well; they're thin but strong.

Do they get thrown in the dishwasher with everything else?
My knife never goes into the dishwasher, ever, ever, ever. That would be a sin. I'm constantly washing my knife.

Anthony Bourdain endorses the Global Knife brand

Like a Samurai's sword — after he slices someone in half, the hero always gives it a good wipe before putting it back in the scabbard. ■

Adam Taylor/ABC/Getty Images

Sources: http://www.katezimmerman.ca/writing/chefs/bourdain.html. Kate Zimmerman's interview with Anthony Bourdain, professional chef, for the *Weekend Post*, downloaded November 23, 2011. "What Knives to Buy?" *Blogpost*. Accessed April 16, 2013.
http://www.flyertalk.com/forum/diningbuzz/1194385-what-knives-buy.html

Head loyalty. Customer loyalty based on specific benefits of a brand, such as product performance.

Hand loyalty. Customer loyalty characterized by habitual repurchase and low interest in product information, that is, low commitment to the brand.

© Roel Smart/iStockphoto

Morton Salt

The nature of the brand/consumer relationship therefore is quite different for head loyals. It is transactional, as opposed to transformational. We define **head loyalty** as rational involvement with a brand, based on the benefits the brand delivers. As long as the brand delivers based on the identified criteria, the head loyal remains loyal. However, if another brand can clearly demonstrate an advantage on the criteria of interest, the head loyal consumer will change brands. In essence, the head loyal customer is always asking the brand, "What have you done for me lately?"

Hand Loyalty

Not all loyalty is high-involvement loyalty. In some cases, the consumer will consistently purchase one brand but, when asked why, will respond with a shrug. **Hand loyal** customers are habitually loyal; these are customers who use products or services simply because they have used them for a long time and they work. We call **hand loyalty** *low involvement* loyalty in contrast to the other two types because hand loyals are generally not interested in product features and benefits. There are neither identity nor relationship forces at work here.

Brands in categories such as salt, which is relatively low cost and has few features, tend to inspire hand loyalty. We might be surprised to find, however, that even in these categories at least a few customers are emotionally attached (heart loyal) to brands. Brands like Morton Salt have many hand loyals, but also some head

NEW PRODUCTS/INNOVATION

STEALTH INNOVATION: KEEPING A HAND LOYAL

Marketers often see product innovation as the Holy Grail; they assume that more new features mean more consumer excitement and more sales. For hand loyals, however, excitement can be a bad thing, because it jolts them out of their normal purchase habits. Consider the case of Tropicana orange juice, loved by millions of consumers and recognized for its familiar "straw in an orange" on the package. In an effort to update the brand, the company modified the packaging and took the age-old identifier off the package. Hand-loyal consumers, accustomed

Tropicana's traditional packaging (right) and the failed packaging that was eventually recalled.

© David Brabyn/Corbis

to simply grabbing the familiar carton, were caught short when they couldn't find it in the grocer's refrigerator case. Many consumers complained; many more simply reached for a different brand. The packaging "improvement" had disrupted the purchasing habits of core Tropicana customers.

In response to consumer complaints and plummeting shares, the company restored the old packaging. It is likely that future innovations for the brand will be subtle, as opposed to splashy. ■

Source: Elliott, Stuart. "Tropicana discovers some customers are passionate about packaging." *The New York Times*, February 22, 2009. (http://www.nytimes.com/2009/02/23/business/media/23adcol.html?pagewanted=all&_r=0). Accessed January 12, 2012. Tischler, Linda. "Never mind! Pepsi pulls much-loathed Tropicana packaging." *Fast Company*. February 23, 2009. http://www.fastcompany.com/1179702/never-mind-pepsi-pulls-much-loathed-tropicana-packaging. Accessed January 12, 2013.

loyals who perhaps choose it because it offers iodine-added salt, and heart loyals who are emotionally attached perhaps because this brand evokes pleasant childhood memories.

At first blush, this type of loyalty may seem unappealing from a brand perspective. Who wants a consumer who knows little or nothing about the brand? However, hand loyals can be highly profitable for the firm. Their lack of interest in product information means they are unlikely to even consider competitive offers. They are also rarely price-aware and therefore tend to be quite price-insensitive. As long as a firm can maintain consistent quality control and distribution, it can anticipate continued fidelity from its hand loyals.

Ideally, over time, we will capitalize on both behavioral and attitudinal data to enhance our understanding not just of our customers, but also of the relationship between our marketing activities and our customer mix. As we deepen our insight into this relationship, we better grasp the nature of customer loyalty for our brand.

Loyalty and Core Competence

Assessing brand loyalty is not simply an academic exercise; there are major strategic implications in the type of loyalty a firm's customers tend to exhibit. The core competencies of the firm should enable it to deliver benefits valued by that customer type.

For example, a firm that has or desires predominantly hand loyals should be skilled at quality control to deliver a consistent product, and skilled at supply chain management to keep the product in stock. In contrast, firms with head loyals may need competence in R&D, engineering, feature innovation, commercialization, and/or data management in order to deliver the features and observable benefits desired by this customer. Finally, the firm seeking to satisfy heart loyals must be more skilled at developing customer insights, customer relationship management, industrial design, and/or image-based communications.

Given the nature of core competence, it's clear that, in a competitive environment with limited resources, the firm cannot successfully satisfy the needs of all three loyalty types. Apple satisfies the deep emotional and aesthetic needs of its core customers but is regularly criticized by more pragmatic head loyals; Dell consistently delivers the right price/performance tradeoff for its rational customers but leaves heart loyalists rather cold; for many customers a Lenovo Thinkpad laptop is a purchase decision made out of habit—the brand worked reliably in the past and it is simply too complicated (and possibly risky) to consider switching brands in the future.

While each firm may have an ideal customer loyalty type, it is quite unlikely that its customer mix will be made up entirely of this type. The preponderance of Morton salt users may be hand loyal, but there are certainly some heart loyals mixed in who have a deep nostalgic connection to the brand. Further, brand loyalty is not static; a head loyal can transition to heart or hand loyalty, or vice-versa. In many cases this transition represents the move from acquisition to retention: customers are often acquired with information and features that appeal to rationality, but as their relationship with the brand develops, they move to either a more habitual or a more emotional connection with the brand.

Finally, the mix of head/heart/hand loyalty may vary from industry to industry. Arguably, in the early cell phone market most buyers were head loyal, making purchase decisions based on phone features and wireless plans offered. As the industry matured, however, the importance of design began to loom larger, and the percentage of heart loyals in the category increased. The introduction of the iPhone, mentioned at the beginning of the chapter, was a major factor in the creation of heart loyalty in this product category. Yet, as the cell phone category is mature, we can also observe some number of hand loyals who simply continue to purchase the same brand they have always used, not because it is necessarily the best on some measure, but because it is consistently good enough.

As we are assessing loyalty, therefore, we must consider the dynamics of the industry, consumer characteristics, and the core competence of the firm. If we understand these factors, we can leverage marketing tools more efficiently and effectively.

STRATEGIC CHOICES: ACQUISITION VS. RETENTION

We can think of customers as the growth engine of the firm. The firm communicates its value to prospective customers in the hopes of motivating them to try its products or services. Once customers have tried the firms products and services, the company will deploy a series of actions to motivate them to repurchase. It is through this cycle of acquisition and retention that the company creates and captures value and therefore grows.

Balancing Acquisition and Retention Resources

Companies will always be engaged in both acquisition and retention activities and these activities are distinct, requiring different tactics and producing different return on investment. Some market analysts estimate the cost of acquiring a customer to be as much as five times the cost of retaining an existing customer.[1] There are obvious reasons for this difference; customer acquisition requires moving someone through the early stages on the path to retention: from category awareness, brand awareness, and product search to initial purchase.

There are also more subtle costs associated with acquisition retention goals. A newly acquired customer often requires more attention as he or she learns how to effectively use the product or service. Finally, given the fact that our ultimate goal is retention, the newly acquired customer is in many cases our least certain bet, particularly if we have acquired this customer through a tactical price promotion. Despite these costs, however, we must always devote some percentage of our resources to acquisition. The question is how much. What is the optimal balance of acquisition and retention spending?

The U.S. wireless industry provides an interesting case study in customer acquisition and retention tradeoffs. In the 2000–2002 period, new wireless subscription rates were as high as 25–30% per year as customers made the switch from wired to wireless communications. While the industry as a whole was growing rapidly, wireless providers focused on customer acquisition. Providers offered discounts on new handsets, introductory fixed-rate plans, and other incentives to get new customers. The logic of this focus on acquisition relied on the fact that subscribers, once acquired, have a disincentive to switch carriers, because of inertia and high switching costs. **Switching costs** are the costs customers incur if they switch companies; they obviously include financial costs like contract breakage fees, but they can also include more subtle costs, such as the cost of time to apply for a new service or learn to use a new device, and the psychological costs associated with the uncertainty that the new company might not be better than the old one. In industries where switching costs are high, like in wireless services, retention rates tend to also be high, and there is a general tendency for companies to focus on acquisition.

By 2010, when the growth rate of wireless subscriptions had dropped below 5% and per-customer acquisition costs had risen to $400, the industry as a whole had to reconsider. Carriers began looking for ways to improve the efficiency of their customer acquisition activities on the one hand, and also to shift resources from acquisition to retention on the other. Tracking acquisition rates and costs provides insight about how to improve marketing efficiency. But the benefits of understanding the acquisition-retention tradeoff go well beyond short-term efficiency.[2]

> **Switching costs.** The costs customers will incur if they switch companies, including financial costs but also the cost of time to apply for a new service or learn to use a new device.

---

[2]McCall, Margo. "Balance swings to customer retention," *Wireless Week,* February 28, 2007. http://www.wirelessweek.com/Archives/2006/01/Balance-Swings-to-Customer-Retention/. Accessed March 10, 2012.

NEW PRODUCTS/INNOVATION

RETENTION ELASTICITY

Using sensitivity analysis, it is also possible to assess the relative impact of retention rate on customer lifetime value (CLV). This is known as **retention elasticity**. The more elastic retention is, the greater the impact of retention on CLV. The chart below shows the relationship between the retention rate and CLV, using 2% as the discount rate. For example, for retention rates of 80%, a 1% improvement in retention increases CLV by 50%, and for retention rates of 85% a 1% improvement in retention would improve CLV by 15 times, that is, by 4.15%. (See Fig. 3.2.) ■

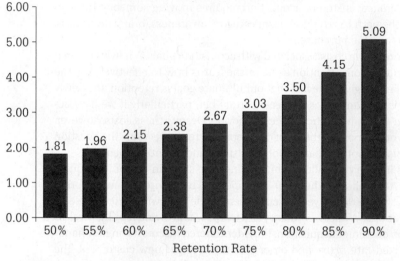

Impact of Retention Rate on CLV

Figure 3.2 Impact of the retention rate on CLV.
This chart illustrates the relationship between retention rate and CLV. The impact of retention rate on CLV increases as the retention rate increases.

Source: Gupta, Sunil; Lehmann, Donald, Managing Customers As Investments: The Strategic Value of Customers in the Long Run, 1st edition, © 2005. Reprinted by permission of Pearson Education, Inc., Upper Saddle River, NJ. School Publishing.

Retention elasticity is the change in customer lifetime value with a 1% improvement in the retention rate.

The topic of acquisition/retention optimization is often addressed by considering CLV, based on our assessment of how much a prospective customer might purchase from us, at what price, and for how long. By estimating potential purchase quantities, margins, and retention time frame, we can begin to get a picture right now of customer value. Customer lifetime value (CLV) is an extremely powerful concept for a number of reasons. First, it changes our frame of reference from product-based metrics such as market share and total sales to a more realistic and strategically powerful customer-based metric. Second, because a key aspect of CLV is the retention time frame, this concept encourages more long-term thinking. Third, by looking at our assumptions regarding margin, predicted sales, and retention time frame, we can get a feel for how these individual factors influence our overall profitability.

GLOBALMARKETING

SUPERMERCADO REY: EVALUATING RESOURCE ALLOCATION AND CLV

The simple exercise of evaluating our current activities to assess whether they have an acquisition or retention objective can yield interesting insights even in markets where panel data detailing customer habits is not readily available. Rey Supermarkets, a leading Central American grocery chain, had made investments in a new loyalty program to enhance its retention rate. The company was also moving rapidly to open new stores in order to acquire new customers before its competitors. Managers assembled a cross-functional team to analyze the allocation of acquisition and retention expenses and revenues.

This analysis showed that Rey was allocating almost 80% of its commercial budget to acquiring customers, but its acquired customers accounted for just 14% of revenues. The team estimated that the retention rate for this customer base was approximately 80%. Based on cost and customer information, the firm determined that it was spending $650 to acquire one customer who in turn would spend $750 each year at its stores. As margins in the supermarket business tend to hover around the single digits (2–4%), a customer who spends $750 yields less than $40 in profits annually to the company (and therefore a CLV of less than $200).[3]

A quick customer lifetime value assessment confirmed what by now seemed obvious, that the company was grossly over-spending to acquire customers. Management redirected its spending toward increasing purchases per customer, moving resources from new store openings to merchandising expenditures in-stores, employee training, and customer service. Within two years the company saw a tremendous increase in sales per customer, company profitability, and customer loyalty as measured by the retention rate. ∎

Source: Authors' Analysis, June 6, 2010.

An accurate assessment of the lifetime value of a retained customer should give us an indication of how much we are willing to pay to acquire that customer. Hypothetically we could use an optimization program, plug in accurate information about costs and impact of spending, and just solve to optimize profits. In fact, many Internet-based firms do just this on an ongoing basis, constantly calculating the lifetime value of a customer and adjusting acquisition spend accordingly. In general, this approach can be quite effective; however, there are two important caveats to consider.

First, any drastic short-term events that affect acquisition or retention will obviously have a short-term impact on our optimization. For example, if an online travel-booking engine such as Hotwire suddenly loses a key airline partner, there will be a short-term shock where retention costs increase and customer retention rates decline, causing CLV to decline sharply. If we respond solely to the numbers, we would theoretically lower acquisition spending to match the new lower CLV. However, the appropriate strategic response would be to *increase* acquisition spending in order to replace our lost customers, despite the fact that the CLV optimization program would not suggest this.

Second and perhaps most important, there is an inherent assumption underlying this optimization problem that resource allocation is a *zero-sum game*, in which case a shift of resources from retention to acquisition will cause an *increase* in acquisition rates and simultaneous *decrease* in retention rates. This could quite possibly lead to a negative feedback loop, as illustrated in Figure 3.3. In this example, the firm shifts

---

[3]The numbers in this analysis are illustrative and do not correspond to actual figures. This has been done to protect the confidentiality of the company.

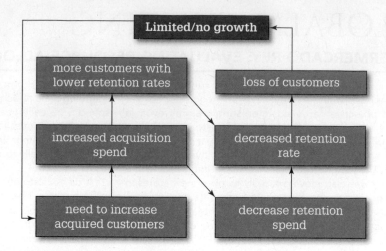

Figure 3.3: Resource allocation as a zero-sum game.

funds from retention to acquisition in order to grow, but the negative impact of this resource shift is to limit growth because it lowers the overall resource available to spend on retention activities. The type of decision-calculus described above seems predicated on the assumption that any increase in retention activity will reduce acquisition, and vice-versa. However, the resource allocation problem does not have to be a zero-sum game; a strategic investment in acquisition can actually lead to an *increase* in retention rates.

This occurs when we think carefully about exactly how we acquire our customers. There are many ways to acquire new customers; we can offer price incentives, or emphasize particular aspects of our products and services. However, if, for example, we acquire a new customer through a price incentive, this customer will likely expect aggressive pricing going forward. Thus, we want to acquire customers with activities that are consistent with our core competence and positioning. We refer to this phenomenon as *acquisition with retention in mind*. As illustrated in Figure 3.4, we can conceive of a scenario where the need to acquire new customers drives the firm to spend strategically, identifying and targeting those potential customers more likely to stay with it over the long run. If we acquire customers who match the attitudinal and behavioral profile of our retained customers, we can anticipate that our newly acquired customers will also be happier in the long run. Thus our spend in acquisition results in an increase in retention rates.

We can observe the same outcome for retention spend: we refer to this as *retention with acquisition in mind*. Many companies seek to retain customers by "locking them in," for example, with a long-term contract. However, this retention-by-force approach will often have a negative impact on customer attitudes toward our brand, and this may translate into negative word-of-mouth. Thus, while our retention rate may increase, our acquisition rate will go down. If, on the other hand, we retain customers by improving their experience and increasing their perceived value, our retention rate *and* our word-of-mouth will improve. This is retention with acquisition in mind. This approach leads to sustainable growth and increases marketing efficiency.

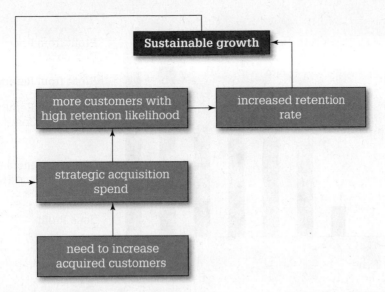

Figure 3.4: Strategic resource allocation.

Acquisition Activities

The specific type of acquisition activities a company uses depends on whether the goal is to bring new users to the category or to attract users from a competitive brand. A common mistake marketers make is to simply engage in random trial-generating activities in order to acquire new customers. While the goal of product trial is obvious, it is not enough to simply get customers to try our product: they have to try it *and like it*.

Trial-based promotions such as high-value coupons, trial-size packaging, and incentive pricing for first-time customers should be considered only if we have determined that, after the consumer tries the product, the experience will be so positive that he or she will continue to purchase it beyond the promotional period. If we are not fairly confident that this will occur, we must take steps in addition to trial-based promotions to increase our chances of keeping these customers. These may include informational advertising to educate consumers about the benefits of our product, product and packaging improvements to make these benefits more salient, and in the case of business-to-business products, substantial sales training designed to communicate effectively these benefits. The bottom line is that trial promotions that are not evaluated based on their potential for creating long-term users are a waste of marketing resources.

The goal for any acquisition expenditure is to obtain a long-term customer. With this goal in mind we likely will need to commit sufficient resources per each new customer to convert not just their usage, but also their attitudes about our brand. Furthermore, acquisition activities should fit within a broader and fully cohesive strategy—these efforts must be part of an integrated strategy.

While the costs of acquiring a new customer are quite high, the benefits may be high as well. Figure 3.5 illustrates the various ways in which a customer can become increasingly more profitable over time. Customer acquisition costs are made upfront

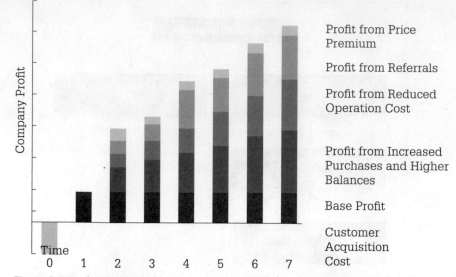

Figure 3.5 Frederick Reichheld reports that retained customers become more profitable over time due to a decrease in the cost of serving them and an increase in their purchases and their willingness to pay.

and then amortized over time. As customers increase their purchases, recommend the brand to other customers, and learn how to navigate the company's customer service and operational processes, they become cheaper to serve. As we project customer profitability, a key consideration is the it will take to recoup the initial investment we have made in acquiring the customer.

As we discussed above, the key metric for determining the value of customer acquisition is the CLV calculation. In some categories, such as diapers or dentures, the lifetime value of a customer is naturally constrained by demographic variables that cannot be altered by marketing activities. For example, a baby will only need diapers for a certain number of years regardless of our marketing efforts. In other categories, however, this lifetime value is affected by activities on behalf of the brand and the category. In addition to this calculation, it is sometimes valuable to calculate an *associated lifetime value,* estimated potential profits that might accrue from friends and associates referred to us by our loyal customer. In any case, it is often quite informative to calculate CLV, no matter how rough the estimate may be at the outset.

In summary, customer acquisition is difficult, risky, and therefore expensive. However, it is a necessary component of any marketing campaign. The key to the development of effective acquisition strategies is to think realistically about the process by which a non-user or competitive user might be converted to a customer.

Retention Activities

Of course, how long our customer continues to use our product depends on our retention spending: monies allocated to persuading our current customers to continue to purchase and perhaps to purchase it in greater quantities or with greater frequency. As we saw above, a dollar spent on retention will go much farther than one spent on acquisition, simply because we do not face the task of building category or brand awareness, but instead need only remind our customer base of the benefits of our product. Retention spending is crucial not just as a means of keeping customers, but also as a signal to discourage competitive entry.

Examples of retention activities include customer loyalty programs (frequent fly/buy rewards), reminder advertising, and continuity coupons (incentives for multiple purchases, in-pack coupons). Product development, particularly line extensions and product improvements, also may be considered retention activities.

Most airlines offer loyalty program benefits to their frequent users to increase retention them to accumulate points for each mile traveled, which can then be cashed in for future travel services. Although this type of loyalty program seems to encourage 'behavioral' loyalty, it does not necessarily improve the customers' perception of the brand and might not be truly effective in generating loyalty. James T. Kane, a corporate consultant on customer loyalty, had this to say about his airline. "I hate you, and I tell everybody I hate you. You could not pay me to get on your airline if I didn't have to. The reason you think I'm a happy customer is I flew 178,000 miles on you last year—but that's because I didn't have a choice." "I'm not loyal," he adds. "I'm just a hostage.[4]" Frequent fliers might continue to fly an airline that provides them elite status in their loyalty mileage program, including perks like free upgrades, priority boarding, and free tickets; even though they don't feel 'attitudinal loyalty.' Airlines like to say that their customers 'have a choice in air travel,' and yet, most of the time there are only one or two choices that meet a traveler's criteria for route and time; thus, from the traveler's perspective there might not be a choice. When customers do not have a free choice of suppliers, companies should be careful not to mistake behaviors for attitudes, or purchases for loyalty. "We don't look on those perks as privileges," Mr. Kane said. "We merely see them as entitlements. To get mine, I had to fly 178,000 miles last year."

In recent years, there has been a strong push for companies to increase their retention activities, given the potential efficiencies associated with this strategy. The increasingly popular practice of CRM (**customer relationship management**) focuses on identifying profitable customers and developing tools to manage their connection with the company and keep them loyal. Very often this includes the use of an IT system that captures information about customer demographics and behaviors and tracks the interactions between firm representatives and the customer. Firms use this information to assess and direct their marketing and sales activities.

Customer Relationship Management (CRM). A set of processes to manage the connection between the company and the customer.

This approach has generated efficiency increases for a number of companies, particularly in sectors such as air travel and financial services. As with any popular tactic, however, it is crucial to maintain a balanced approach to retention activities. An overly aggressive focus on the heavy user can harm relationships with other

---

[4] Sharkey, Joe. January 13, 2008. Travel bug; A million miles vs. a few more smiles. http://query.nytimes.com/gst/fullpage.html?res=9C05E7DA1339F930A25752C0A96E9C8B63.

NEW PRODUCTS/INNOVATION

GROWING THROUGH RETENTION: GILLETTE

Gillette, owned by Procter & Gamble, is the market leader in the men's grooming category, a highly consolidated category that is very active in product development, as competitors constantly innovate to offer their customers an ever-closer shave.

For years, Gillette has focused its marketing efforts on implementing a customer retention strategy. Since the 2005 launch of its Fusion brand, the firm has introduced seven new versions of the popular men's razor. Customers have willingly traded up from the Fusion (2005) to the Fusion Power (2005), the Fusion Power Phantom (2006), the Fusion Power Phenom (2007), the Fusion Power Gamer (2009), the Fusion Power MVP (2009), and the Fusion Pro-Glide (2010).

Gillette's introduction of seven new products in a six-year span nicely illustrates how to capitalize on new-product introduction for retention. Communications for new products make explicit comparisons not to competitors, but to the old generation Gillette product. The firm has not been concerned about cannibalizing its own sales, since the next-generation product is always more profitable to the company, and its high market share makes it unlikely that customers will switch to other brands when new products are launched. Since the 2005 launch of the Fusion, Gillette has maintained a 72% market share in the men's shaving category and increased its pricing by 15% above that of its earlier Mach3 line. The company's marketing communications showcased athletic stars like Derek

Diane Bondareff/AP Images for Gillette

Post on Gillette's UK Facebook Page in December 2010:

Gillette is giving you the chance to take the Fusion ProGlide Challenge! Across the UK, Gillette are challenging men to try their latest razor—the Fusion ProGlide—to show how they are turning shaving into gliding for incredible comfort every day. With 7 innovations including thinner, finer blades* for less tug and pull** this is your chance to try Gillette's most comfortable shave. Free samples, product demonstrations, interactive games and a Free Prize Draw will all be on offer so come along to see how Gillette are turning shaving into gliding.

Jeter and John Cena to appeal to a specific male target audience that cares about performance, and for which Gillette has become synonymous with "breakthrough shaving technology." ∎

Sources: P&G / Gillette Corporate website. http://news.gillette.com/about/history. Accessed April 9, 2012.

Brands, Robert. "Gillette, shaving and the challenge of innovation." *The Huffington Post.* June 10, 2010. http://www.huffingtonpost.com/robert-f-brands/gillette-shaving-and-the_b_607092.html. Accessed April 9, 2012.

http://www.thecentremk.com/Events/Events-Listing/Gillette-Fusion-ProGlide-Challenge. Accessed January 12, 2012.

potentially important customers. Nonetheless, effective retention spending is a vital aspect of any successful long-term marketing plan.

Like acquisition budgets, retention money should be spent with the specific customer in mind. One of the most common examples of retention expenditure is a continuity promotion—a discount on multiple purchases of a product. However, if this promotion does not enhance customer loyalty or prevent switching, we are simply giving money away to customers who were planning on buying our product anyway. Very often, spending on non-price-related retention activities such as advertising and the sales force can be more effective for maintaining long-term loyalty. Regardless of our specific choice of tactics, retention activities target current customers and are concerned with maintaining and increasing perceived value.

INTEGRATION: MARKETING OBJECTIVE AND THE BIG PICTURE

Figure 3.6 places the Marketing Objective Module within the Big Picture framework. Decisions made within the Business Objective chapter have an impact on marketing objective decisions as follows.

Core Competence: Our competencies will have a significant impact on our ability to implement either retention or acquisition strategies. If we intend to rely heavily on acquisition revenue, we likely will want to ensure that we have a core competence in marketing and new product development. Conversely, if we will focus primarily on retention, our key competencies should lie in the areas of customer service and customer research, since these skills will best allow us to understand and fill the needs of our existing customers.

Goal: Our choice of primary metric here will have implications for marketing objective choices as well. For example, if we have selected profitability as our business objective, it is more likely that we will focus on the less-expensive retention objective, whereas if our business objective is revenue or share, we are more likely to increase our focus on acquisition.

FE: Customer definition affects how we count acquired and retained customers. Our definition of the fundamental entity (FE) affects this count as well. Consider the impact of different FE definitions on how we count our customers. Nike is a very powerful umbrella brand, known to consumers around the world. However, as the firm has grown, it has added a number of product lines that may appeal to quite different audiences. A few of these appear in Figure 3.7.

The way we define the Fundamental Entity will have implications for whether we count customers as being targets for acquisition or for retention activities. A company like Nike, which maintains an umbrella brand structure, would count as customers anyone who purchases any of its products. However, if we instead define the FE's as the

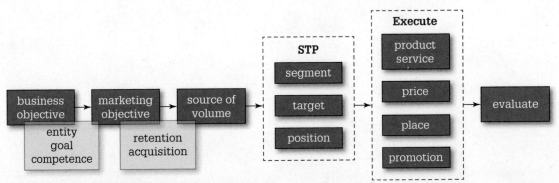

Figure 3.6 The Marketing Objective Module within the Big Picture framework.

Figure 3.7 Relationship of FE to current customer definition

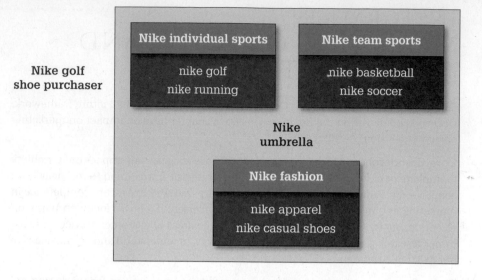

three product groups (nike individual sports, and fashion) each product group would only count customers purchasing products from that group. This matters because whether or not we are counting a particular purchases as a customer will determine whether we plan on using acquisition or retention tactics. Hence, our choice of FE has direct impact on our marketing objective.

We therefore must identify our FE, and then define and count our customers *based on that FE*. If we waver on this point and assess acquisition and retention goals from the perspective of the umbrella one day and from the perspective of distinct brand lines the next, we will not achieve organizational and strategic alignment. Without this alignment, we will never be effective and efficient marketers.

Time Frame. Because acquisition of new customers is generally a more time-consuming process, our time frame in our business objective should reflect this fact. While it may be easy to quickly acquire customers with a price promotion, achieving our strategic goal of acquiring with retention in mind will take substantially longer.

☐ SUMMARY

1. Explain the value of a customer orientation
Customers are the growth engine of the firm. Therefore, developing a customer orientation in the company is critical to achieving sustainable growth. It entails making customers, rather than products, the unit of analysis for firm activities and establishing customer-based metrics to track firm performance.

2. Contrast different definitions of a customer
In creating a working customer definition, we seek to describe a loyal and profitable customer. Customer definitions should generally have behavioral and attitudinal components, because the definition of a loyal customer should be of is someone who repurchases the brand and who also prefers it to similar alternatives. When behaviors are good proxies for attitudinal loyalty, behaviors alone make fine customer definitions. However, there are situations in which behaviors are not good proxies—essentially any time purchase behavior is not necessarily indicative of brand preference—and in those instances we must use attitudes (e.g., 'Would you recommend?,' or 'How satisfied are you?') to define and count customers.

3. Identify three types of customer loyalty
Head loyal customers like a product because of the way it performs; their attachment is more rational than emotional. A company seeking to attract this type of loyalty will need to develop competencies in product innovation and performance communication.

Heart loyal customers hold an emotional relationship with a brand. They feel passionate about their choice and believe it says something about who they are. Companies wishing to attract this type of loyalty should develop a core competence in customer intimacy.

Hand loyalty is based on habit or routine with lower involvement than head or heart loyalty. Hand loyal customers like brands because they are available, convenient, and easy to use. Companies wishing to attract this type of loyalty should develop a core competence in operational excellence or distribution.

4. Explain the strategic implications of customer acquisition and customer retention
Although the efficient marketer is constantly thinking about how to optimize retention and acquisition activities and investment, we need to keep in mind that, when well executed, these activities are complementary. Companies should acquire customers who are likely to remain with the firm and capitalize on retention through word of mouth and social media; in other words, they should acquire with retention in mind and retain with acquisition in mind.

5. Integrate the Marketing Objectives within the Big Picture
Other things being equal, umbrella brands tend toward retention strategies whereas distinct brands are more likely to emphasize acquisition. When we need to improve profitability in a short time frame, we will probably look to retention as our primary marketing objective, because acquisition activities are more expensive and their results more uncertain.

☐ KEY TERMS

Customer acquisition. (p. 68) A series of activities designed to bring new customers to our brand or franchise, including awareness creation, information delivery, and activities designed to encourage trial.

Customer Lifetime Value (CLV). (p. 67) The total net present value of current and future profits that a particular customer will generate over the lifetime of his or her relationship with a firm. $CLV = m \times r/(1 + d - r)$, where m is the $ margin per customer, r is the retention rate, and d is the weighted-average cost of capital of the company or discount rate.

Customer loyalty. (p. 67) Customer loyalty is generally defined as the combination of repeat purchases and commitment to a brand on the part of a customer; both attitudinal and behavioral components are necessary for loyalty to exist.

Customer Relationship Management (CRM). (p. 85) A set of processes to manage the connection between the company and the customer.

Customer retention. (p. 68) Activities designed to help keep customers longer.

Hand loyalty. (p. 76) Customer loyalty characterized by habitual repurchase and low interest in product information, that is, low commitment to the brand.

Head loyalty. (p. 76) Customer loyalty based on specific benefits of a brand, such as product performance.

Heart loyalty. (p. 75) Customer loyalty based on personal identification with the brand.

Recency, Frequency, and Monetary value (RFM). (p. 71) Analysis which ranks customers by examining how *recently* they have purchased (recency), how *often* they purchase (frequency), and *how much* they spend (monetary) with the company.

Switching costs. (p. 79) The costs customers will incur if they switch companies, including financial costs but also the cost of time to apply for a new service or learn to use a new product, and the emotional cost of the uncertainty of working with a different company.

☐ QUESTIONS FOR DISCUSSION

1. Develop customer definitions for specific companies (or types of companies), given the situations described below. For each company, explain the behavioral and attitudinal component of an ideal customer. Also, in each case discuss at least one way to make unprofitable customers more profitable.

   (a) A grocery store implementing a retention strategy, seeking to increase customer loyalty in a very competitive market.

   (b) A manufacturer selling dishwashing machines to restaurant owners. These machines are replaced only every five to ten years, but that requires frequent maintenance. Restaurant owners can purchase maintenance contracts from the manufacturer and from third parties.

   (c) BMW in India

   (d) A company that sells diapers for children between the ages of 0 to 3 years old

   (e) A company that manufactures breakfast cereal

2. A manufacturer of industrial products that has traditionally sold through a direct mail catalogue is now evaluating whether to start using banner ads. The cost of sending one catalogue is $.50; this includes production, printing, and mailing. The company reports that 1 in 1,000 catalogues generally results in a sale .The average customer buys $1,000 worth of merchandise per year. The company's profit margin is 60%. The retention rate of customers acquired through the catalogue is only 50%, since many customers buying from the catalogue order products sold at promotional rates and then move onto another manufacturer. Banner ads will be sent to customers based on sophisticated analyses of their web click-through and purchase patterns, so the customers acquired through banner ads are expected to have retention rates of 80%.The Cost per Thousand (CPM) of reaching customers through a banner ad is $5. The click-through rate for the banner ad is estimated at 1 in 200, and of those who click on a banner ad, 1 in 100 convert to a purchase.

   (f) What is the cost of acquiring customers through the catalogue and through the banner ad?

   (g) Should the company stop mailing catalogues?

   (h) In addition to customer profitability, what other issues should the company consider in making this sales channel decision?

3. Your company is a small power tool manufacturer that operates in a very competitive, global industry. Its products are sold through small hardware stores and through national chains like Home Depot and Lowe's. There are only a handful of competitors selling to the very powerful retailers; the retailers have a good sense for manufacturer margins and negotiate low prices for large purchases. Your company makes a popular line of power drills and other products, like hammers, and mechanical tools that are not very differentiated but have steady sales. Your company currently sells into Lowes but not Home Depot, Lowes is trying to acquire share from Home Depot and it wants your marketing advice.

   • How would you help Lowes design tactics that it could use to acquire heart loyal, head loyal, and hand loyal customers from Home Depot?

   • Which type of customer is easier and which is harder to acquire?

   • What activities might Lowes implement, with your help, to retain each type of customer (heart, head, hand)?

   • Imagine you just received a loyalty categorization market research report indicating that, unlike what you had previously thought, more than 60% of power drill customers heart loyal. What are the implications for your company of having heart loyal customers? And for Lowes?

   • If you wanted to shift hand loyal customers to being head loyal, how might you go about doing that? What are the risks?

Marketing Tool 3.1: The Net Promoter Score

The Net Promoter Score (NPS) is a customer loyalty metric developed by Frederick Reichheld and Bain & Company. (Reichheld, 2003). It uses an 11-point (0–10) scale to measure loyalty by asking customers their willingness to recommend a brand or product to a friend or colleague (Fig. 3A.1). Once we have asked the survey question, we calculate the NPS by taking the percentage of respondents who rate their likelihood to recommend a brand at 9 or 10 and subtracting the percentage who rate it at 6 or less.

A brief example illustrates how to perform the NPS calculation. Imagine, after a service encounter, we ask 100 customers whether, based on their experience, they would recommend the future company to a friend or colleague. This is the question Reichheld believes best correlates with company revenues. The table below presents our hypothetical survey results by rating. Note that in this case the NPS score would be 40−30, or 10.

Rating	0–6	7–8	9–10
Number of Responses	30	30	40

The NPS metric quickly gained acceptance as large companies such as GE, Procter & Gamble, American Express, and others adopted it. Its advantages lie in its simplicity, its conceptual appeal, and the ease with which it can be collected. Reichheld's claim that the 'Would you recommend' question was the only one a company needed as a leading indicator of revenue growth has come under criticism; some research suggests the NPS is not a good predictor of company growth (Reichheld, 2003; Keiningham, Aksoy et al., 2008) and does not outperform other loyalty metrics such as overall satisfaction and repurchase intent (Hayes, 2008).

Ultimately, in order to measure customer loyalty, we do need to measure satisfaction or likelihood to recommend but also tie those questions to the specific service and product benefits of the brand. We should then further correlate those attitudinal measures to actual customer purchases, to better understand which benefits drive behavioral loyalty. The NPS score can be a useful metric, but probably not the magic bullet that Reichheld claimed.

How likely are you to recommend to a colleague or friend?

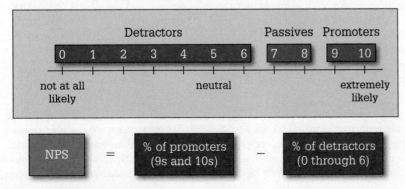

Figure 3A.1 Net promoter score.

Marketing Tool 3.2: Marketing Objective Worksheet: Customer Acquisition and Customer Retention Cost Audit

Before calculating customer lifetime value, marketers should calculate the costs of acquiring and retaining customers. As we discussed in this chapter, average costs of acquisition tend to be higher than average costs of retention. Frederick Reichheld reported that across a number of companies he had analyzed, acquiring a new customer cost six to seven times more than retaining an existing customer. [5] A simple back-of-the-envelope calculation can help us shed some light on the acquisition and retention costs for customers in our company by allocating costs between different types of customers.

(1) Take the company's operating budget for the last calendar year or a recent budget cycle for which you have full information. Start by examining commercial expenses first (cost of goods sold (COGS), selling and administration (SG & A), marketing and promotion) and leave out non-commercial costs, such as legal and depreciation expenses or other fixed costs that cannot be easily allocated to customers.

(2) List all operating budget expenses at a level that will allow you to allocate them to different marketing activities.

(3) For each budget item, ask what percentage was directed toward serving or selling to existing customers (retention) and what percentage to obtaining new customers (acquisition).

- Acquisition costs generally include a large percentage of advertising, promotional, and selling expenses.

- Retention costs generally permeate the entire organization but include a large percentage of customer service and loyalty program expenses if the company has a loyalty program.

The first time we complete this exercise, we will need to make a lot of assumptions to come up with estimates of acquisition and retention costs by customer. Over time we can refine and increase the accuracy of our estimates. We also must agree on the set of behaviors that defines a customer at each stage of the relationship. Without a shared understanding of what constitutes a retained, acquired, and prospective customer, we will not come up with a very reliable estimate.

Here's how a fictitious insurance company, Safety First Inc., completes this exercise. Safety First defines retained customers as customers in good standing (up to date in paying their premium bills) who have had an insurance policy with the firm for at least 1 year. Acquired customers have been with Safety First for less than 1 year. Prospective customers meet a minimum income and wealth threshold and have a need for Safety First's positioning variable.

Safety First will use budget numbers for the last 12 months and allocate its operating expenses by type of customer (acquired or retained). With the help of people in different functions within the company, such as marketing and sales, finance, and operations, Safety First will estimate how much of each line item was spent on acquiring customers and how much on retaining them, as shown in Table 3A.1.

Accurate allocation requires specific knowledge of most of the expenses shown in Table 3A.1 and the answers to questions like:

- Approximately what percentage of sales promotional costs were related to service and product solutions for new and for existing customers?

- What percentage of the brochures produced were for new and for existing customers?

Only a team intimately familiar with the specifics of each expense item will be able to make reasonable fact-based decisions about each initiative. Over time, the marketing organization will adopt a customer orientation and will make acquisition and retention resource allocations before conducting projects and initiatives, so there will no longer be a need to conduct this type

---

[5] Reichheld, Frederick F. "Loyalty-based management," *Harvard Business Review* 71 (1993): 64–64.

Table 3A.1 Safety First Insurance Sample Acquisition and Retention Calculation

Marketing Objective Worksheet					
		retention/acquisition spending allocation			
description	expenditure	acquisition %	acquisition $	retention %	retention $
advertising	$ 100,000	95%	95,000	5%	5,000
sales promotion & items	10,000	95%	9,500	5%	500
brochures	60,000	100%	60,000	0%	0
public relations	250,000	25%	62,500	75%	187,500
product development	90,000	25%	22,500	75%	67,500
customer relations	15,000	5%	750	95%	14,250
Customer Referral programs	-	0%	-	-	-
market research	40,000	80%	32,000	20%	8,000
sales training	20,000	25%	5,000	75%	15,000
broker incentives	150,000	50%	75,000	50%	75,000
call center	40,000	2%	800	98%	39,200
broker commissions	8,400,000	33%	2,772,000	67%	5,628,000
	-	0%	-	-	-
	-	0%	-	-	-
			-	-	-
			-	-	-
*excludes capital expenditures			-	-	-
total:	$ 9,175,000	34%	$ 3,135,050	66%	$ 6,039,950

of forensic analysis. In the meantime, the insights obtained by conducting this type of exercise should help marketers generate support for the customer data storage and analysis resources they need to solidify a customer orientation in the company.

Imagine that a team at Safety First conducted this exercise and estimated that, of $9.17M spent on commercial activities in the last year, 34%, or $3.1M, was spent to acquire customers and 66% or $6.0M to retain customers. To assess the effectiveness and efficiency of the marketing spending, the team also needs additional information about the company's success rate in acquiring and retaining customers and the revenues associated with these activities. Table 3A.2 adds this important detail.

Now we see that Safety First targets a group of 250,000 prospects and in the last year acquired 3% of them for a total of 7,500 customers. Each of those customers generated $400 of revenue during the first year with the company; the team also pointed out that a majority of the customers acquired in the last year were acquired through an auto insurance discount program. Thus, the $400 corresponds to the average annual premium for auto customers. Over time, the customers who stay with Safety First purchase more products from the company than just auto insurance. The most common retained customer profile is of someone who has an auto policy plus a homeowner's policy, and the average revenue for a homeowner's insurance policy is $800. So if a customer stays with Safety First for a second year, he or she will tend to generate $1,200 ($800+$400) of revenue.

After taking a look at the data on retention and acquisition, the team has also discovered that the retention rate for customers during the first year is only 75%, whereas afterwards it goes up to 85%. This is not unusual, since customers tend to defect at the beginning of their

Table 3A.2 Retention/Acquisition Revenue Breakdown

Acquisition	Revenue	Retention	Revenue
Acquisition target population	250,000	Retention target population	35,000
Total acquisition spending	$3,135,050	Total retention spending	$6,039,950
Acquisition conversion probability	3.0%	Retention conversion probability (ongoing)	85%
Total new customers acquired	7,500	Total customers retained	29,750
Revenue per customer, period 1	$400.00	Revenue per customer (ongoing)	$1,200
Total acquisition revenue	$3,750,000	Total retention revenue	$35,700,000
Expenditure per prospect	$418.01	Expenditure per customer	$203.02
Contribution to total revenue	10%	Contribution to total revenue	90%

relationship with a company, and if they stay, they tend to persist. Also, the team suspects that part of the reason the auto customers tend not to stay might be the way they were acquired: through discounted price promotions.

The data in the two tables tells us that Safety First is spending $418 each ($3.1M/7,500) to acquire customers who generate $400 of revenue in the first year. The company is spending just $203 to retain customers who generate $1,200 of revenue. At first blush, it might seem that the company is overspending on acquisition. However, acquisition is required for the company to grow, and many new customers do become retained customers, so we really don't have enough information yet to judge whether Safety First is in fact overspending on acquisition relative to retention. We should take a look at the types of customers the company is acquiring and the types who are successfully retained, as well as the relative profitability of the auto and home-owner product lines. A customer lifetime value (CLV) calculation would be helpful to take this analysis further (see Marketing Tool 3.3).

Marketing Tool 3.3: Customer Lifetime Value Calculation

We now have enough information to calculate year-by-year profitability for the average customer at Safety First (see Marketing Tool 3.2). We assume the customer is acquired in year 0; thus, for that year we include just the $418 of acquisition cost. In year 1 the customer generates a loss of $93 because the revenue from the auto policy does not cover insurance claims, commissions paid to insurance brokers, and other Selling and General Administrative Expenses (SGA), shown as ($93) operating margin in Table 3A.3. There is a 75% probability that the new customer who was acquired an auto policy will stay with Safety First and get a homeowners policy. That policy is more profitable than the auto policy, generating $356 of operating profit.

However, during that second year there is also a 15% probability that the customer will leave; this probability is called the *attrition* or *churn rate* and is 1 minus the 85% retention rate. The probability of collecting the $263 ($359-$93) of net margin in year 2 is just 64% (75%*85%)

Table 3A.3 Abbreviated P&L for Auto and Homeowners Insurance

P&L for 1 Policy	Auto	Homeowners
Gross revenue	$400	$800
Losses	$ 90	$ 40
Broker commission	$200	$201
Net revenue	$110	$559
SGA	$203	$203
Operating profit (Loss)	$ (93)	$356

Table 3A.4 Calculating CLV

The first row in Table 3A.4 shows the operating margin for a customer at Safety First each year, accounting for the discount rate and the retention rate.

	Year 0	Year 1	Year 2	Year 3	Year 4	Year 5	Year 6	Year 7	Year 8	Year 9	Year 10	Year 41	Year 42
Operating Margin		(93.00)	263 00	263.00	263.00	263.00	263.00	26300	263 00	263.00	263.00	263.00	263.00
Acquisition Costs	(418.01)												
Profits per customer	(418.01)	(93.00)	263.00	263.00	263.00	263.00	263.00	263.00	263.00	263.00	263.00	263 00	263.00
Survival Rate		75%	64%	54%	46%	39%	33%	28%	24%	20%	17%	0%	0%
Discount Factor	100%	89%	80%	71%	64%	57%	51%	45%	40%	36%	32%	1%	1%
Customer Profits (annual)	(418.01)	(62.28)	133.66	101.44	76.98	58.43	44.34	33.65	25.54	19.38	14.71	0.00	0.00
Cumulative Customer Value	(418.01)	(480.28)	(346.62)	(245.19)	(168.20)	(109.78)	(65.44)	(31.78)	(6.24)	13.14	27.85	74.15	74.15

(see Table 3A.4 for year 2). The product of the retention rates for each year is called the *survival rate,* and it is the chance that we will collect margin over time given the risk that the customer might leave. In this example, we assume the customer has a constant retention rate of 85% after year 2 and that the operating margin after year 2 is also constant. Each year we also apply a *discount rate* to account for the cost of capital at Safety First. In the example we assumed the discount rate is 12%, so in year 1 the operating margin is also multiplied by $\dfrac{1}{(1 + d)^t}$ where t is the number of years that have gone by. For example, the discount rate for year 1 is $1/(1 + 12\%)^1 = 89\%$, for year 2 it is 80%, and so on.

As shown in Table 3A.4, the customer starts being profitable in year 9, after we have accumulated enough margin to make up the cost of acquiring him or her. Over time, the accumulated value of the customer is $492.16, which net of the $418 of acquisition costs yields $74.15 profitability. A key question the marketing team will need to answer is whether the current acquisition costs and activities are justified, given the average customer's profitability. In this case, it seems they are justified, although not by much. Thus the exercise provides insights into the opportunity both to reallocate resources between retention and acquisition, and to make existing activities within each of those functions more efficient.

We can apply the CLV formula provided in the chapter, CLV = m (r/1 + d − 3), when the margin per customer is constant and we assume the retention rate is also constant. In this example, the customer had different retention and margin rates in the first year and other years. Knowing how to calculate CLV using a discounted cash flow method, as we have done in Table 3A.4, is important for situations in which we cannot apply the constant retention and margin rate assumptions used in the perpetuity formula of CLV. The method shown here also allows us to see how long it takes for the company to achieve *breakeven*—that is, the point in time at which the customer has generated enough revenue to recoup the cost of acquiring the customer.

Marketing Tool 3.4: The Customer Definition

Developing an operational definition of a customer is critically important for the company trying to become more customer focused. The customer definition is also critical for developing good estimates for acquisition and retention costs per customer and customer lifetime value. The marketer will want to define what constitutes a good prospect for the company, and when a customer can be considered acquired and when retained. In developing a customer definition

Figure 3A.2 Company vs. customer value.

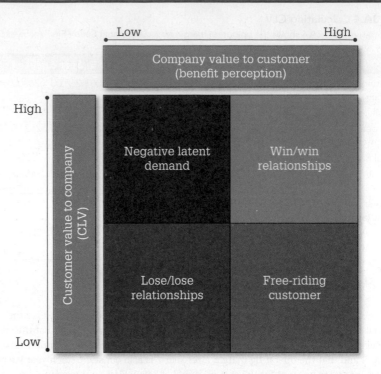

we will want to describe a win-win relationship, that is, a relationship in which the company and the customer both are better off doing business together than not. Figure 3A.2 illustrates the relationship between customer value and company value in this context.

We saw in the chapter that customer loyalty has both attitudinal and behavioral components, and that a good customer definition therefore requires a description of both *attitudes* and *behaviors*. Table 3A.5 summarizes the data we need in order to assemble a useful set of customer and prospect definitions. We need demographic, attitudinal, and behavioral components in our customer definition.

1. We use *demographic* information (age, income level, family characteristics, occupation, and so on) to establish threshold criteria for our target population. This type of information is critically important to define a prospect but not as relevant once we have acquired a customer.

Table 3A.5 Attitudes and Behaviors for Prospects and Customers

Aspects of Customer Definition	Prospect	Acquired	Retained
Demographics	Demographic characteristics of target customers		
Attitudes	A need our company can fulfill	A customer attitude that results from trial of our product or service	A customer attitude that results from repeated use of our product or service
Behaviors	Behaviors indicative of a customer need our company can fulfill	Behavior that reveals the customer has been acquired	Behavior characteristic of a retained customer

CHAPTER THREE MARKETING OBJECTIVE

Table 3A.6 Customer Definition Example for Safety First Insurance Co.

Aspects of Customer Definition	Prospect	Acquired	Retained
Demographics	Families with at least one car and who own a home Annual income >$65k		
Attitudes	Interested in ways to simplify their lives by buying easy-to-use products and services	Feels Safety First experience is simplified	Highly satisfied with Safety First simplified service experience
Behaviors	Repays other financial obligations (e.g., credit cards) on time	Auto insurance or homeowners insurance	Purchases at least two products from Safety First

2. In describing *attitudes*, we are particularly interested in the customer needs we can address through our marketing effort.

3. For *behaviors*, we are interested in recency, purchase frequency, or value that categorizes customers as either acquired or retained.

We also need an estimate of the number of bodies to complete our Marketing Objective calculations; our customer definition is more complete with numerical estimates of the prospects and acquired customers the company is targeting, and the number of retained customers the company has. Finally, estimating CLV for prospects and acquired and retained customers will ensure that we are targeting the right customers from a profitability perspective. We always want to make sure our customer definition corresponds to win-win relationships that result in company profitability and also make customers better off.

Table 3A.6 shows how the customer definition progresses at our fictional insurance company, Safety First (see Marketing Tool 3.2), as the customer moves from being a prospect to being acquired and later retained. Note that the attitudinal row describes the customer in terms of a benefit the company provides. For this reason, we will want to revisit the customer definition once we get to the segmentation, targeting, and positioning section of the Big Picture framework to ensure the benefit in the customer definition is aligned with our segmentation strategy.

☐ RESOURCES

Eggert, Andreas and Ulaga Wolfgang. "Customer perceived value: A substitute for satisfaction in business markets?," *Journal of Business & Industrial Marketing* 17.2/3 (2002): 107–118.

Gupta, S. and D. Lehmann (2005). *Managing customers as investments. The strategic value of customers in the long run*, Wharton School Publishing.

Hayes, B. E. (2008). Measuring Customer Satisfaction and Loyalty: Survey Design, Use, and Statistical Analysis Methods, Asq Pr.

Keiningham, T. L., L. Aksoy, et al. (2008). "Linking customer loyalty to growth," *MIT Sloan Management Review* 49(4): 51–57.

Reichheld, F. F. (2003). "The one number you need to grow," *Harvard Business Review* 81(12): 46–55.

chapter four

"With that fine tempered steel
 whose edge o'erthrows,
 hacks, hews, confounds, and
 routs opposing foes."

"Unheard-of prowess! and
 unheard-of verse!"

"But art new strains invents,
 new glories to rehearse."

—Cervantes, Don Quixote,
page 397

SOURCE OF VOLUME

Competitive Focus

After studying this chapter you should be able to:

1. *Identify the source of volume in performing competitive analysis*
2. *Develop a benefit-based definition of the business category*
3. *Define a stimulate demand strategy*
4. *Define an earn share strategy*
5. *Discuss the difference between earning share and stimulating demand*
6. *Explain how to choose a strategic focus*
7. *Use the 4 Bs as the basis of strategic forecasting*
8. *Integrate the source of volume decision within the Big Picture framework*

Competitive Dynamics in the Coronary Stent Market

In April 2003 the U.S. Food & Drug Administration (FDA) approved a revolutionary implantable cardiac device developed by Johnson & Johnson's Cordis division. A cardiac stent is a cylinder of flexible wire-mesh implanted by cardiologists to treat the coronary artery narrowing that can cause fatal cardiac events. Cypher, Cordis's new stent, was revolutionary because it was coated with sirolimus, a drug shown to dramatically improve post-operative blood clogging. Cypher delivered very superior patient outcomes over bare-metal stents. It had an initial average selling price of approximately $3,500, while bare-metal stents at the time sold for approximately $1,000.

With the introduction of Cypher, Cordis created a new category, the drug-eluting stent (DES) category, which by the end of 2003 had total revenues of $2.8 billion globally (see Figure 4.1). Boston Scientific entered the DES market soon after with a competing stent, Taxus, which had lower pricing and similar patient outcomes, soon making it the market leader. Meanwhile the market continued to grow rapidly by acquiring cardiologist customers who had been non-users of DES stents in the past, including some who had used bare-metal stents and others who might have chosen a different surgical solution or none at all.

In 2006 the DES market was jolted by data indicating that rates of death due to blood clots forming around the stent were significantly higher among DES-treated patients than among bare-metal-stent-treated patients over 2.5 years of follow-up. The FDA held a hearing, and subsequent studies showed that, although blood clots continue to be a concern for some patients, there is no proof of increased mortality with DES stents.

The market has seen dramatic change in the last few years, not only because of the market shock of 2006 but also because competitors drastically changed their behavior. In 2008 a number of new devices entered the market, including Abbott's Xience and Medtronic's Endeavor. Boston Scientific and Cypher both lowered price to compete with the new market entrants, and in 2008 average stent prices fell to about $2,000.

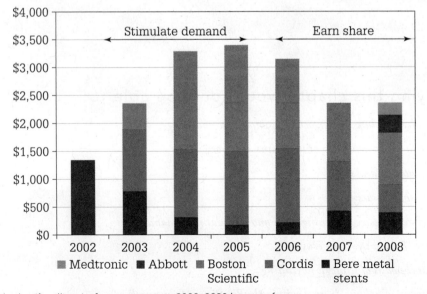

Figure 4.1 Global sales ($ millions) of coronary stents 2002–2008 by manufacturer.
Source: Data from "Boston Scientific." *WikiInvest.*http://www.wikinvest.com/stock/Boston_Scientific_%28BSX%29. Accessed January 30, 2012. Big Picture Partners Analysis.

The other influential dynamic was the decreased importance of patient outcomes. New entrants earned share from the original DES stents by raising the importance of a new benefit, deliverability (the ease with which the stent can be placed in the coronary artery), creating the perception that patient outcome differences among different devices are minimal. Cypher, the market pioneer, went from over 50% market share to 13% share and was perceived as inferior on deliverability, the new category variable (see Figure 4.2). Cordis exited the DES market in May 2011.

We'll see in this chapter how the competitive focus of the firm requires making important choices between stimulating demand (promoting category growth), and between earning share (taking customers away from a competitor.) ∎

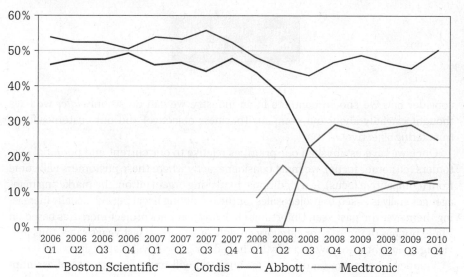

Figure 4.2 U.S. DES unit market share by manufacturer (quarterly 2006–2009). Source: Data from "Boston Scientific." *WikiInvest.* http://www.wikinvest.com/stock/Boston_Scientific_%28BSX%29. Accessed January, 30, 2012. Big Picture Partners Analysis.

— Boston Scientific — Cordis — Abbott — Medtronic

Sources: "Coronary stents do not improve long-term survival," *Science Daily*. University Medical Center. November 8, 2004. (http://www.sciencedaily.com /releases/2004/11/041108013032.htm). Accessed January 18, 2012.
Rankin, Scott "A mini-case of product strategy: The Cypher stent from Cordis," *The Marketing Review* 4 (2004):211–224.
Industry Expert Interviews (2007–2010)

IDENTIFYING THE SOURCE OF VOUME: THE FIRST STEP IN PERFORMING COMPETITIVE ANALYSES

Traditionally, marketers have begun their strategic analysis by looking at markets and competition. A classic approach is to apply **Porter's 5 Forces** (see Figure 4.3) as a means of evaluating competitive threats and buyer and supplier power. The five forces—supplier power, buyer power, threat of competitive entry, threat of substitute products, and threat from existing competitors—provide a systematic means of quickly assessing the competitive space. While this analysis can be helpful, over-reliance on this tool and others that look at competitive forces can lead us to over-emphasize competition, which in turn can lead us to an overly reactive marketing strategy. In extreme cases, the result is a market made up of competitors who are paying more attention to each other than they are to their customers or their own company. Price competition, me-too products, and, ultimately, lack of differentiation can result. Thus, while we must

Porter's 5 Forces.

A framework advanced by Michael Porter that provides a systematic means of quickly assessing the competitive space by highlighting the primary external factors that drive company performance. The five forces are: supplier power, buyer power, threat of competitive entry, threat of substitute products, and threat from existing competitors.

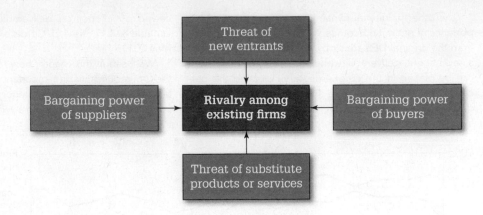

consider how we should compete in an industry, we can do so only *after* we have thought carefully about our company (business objective) and our customer focus (marketing objective).

Once we have established our priorities relative to our current and potential customers (customer focus), we must consider exactly where these customers will come from (competitive focus). In a traditional marketing organization, the marketing manager generally is asked to project sales for the upcoming fiscal period, usually increasing them over the past year. Unfortunately, many planners project increases based on vague notions of industry or category growth, or simply on last year's sales, thus providing no insight into how and why the hoped-for growth will materialize.

Financial managers (and securities analysts) will make these types of assumptions about growth rates because they have limited information, or because they have no influence over the firm's strategy. A marketing manager, however, presumably has a deep understanding of the particular business and has influence over how it will be run in the upcoming period. As marketing managers, we therefore must develop a strategic marketing forecast that leverages our knowledge and skills. To do so we take into account external factors, those outside our control such as population growth and economic trends, just as financial forecasters do. We then augment this information by considering internal factors, those within our control as marketers such as new product launches, increased marketing spending, or changes in segmentation.

We thus control our future not simply by relying on analyst's predictions, but rather by leveraging this knowledge in concert with our strategic decision-making to differentiate our products and our services. We can actively manage marketing activities because these are within our control. These activities will, in turn, influence our sales. A good forecast is thus a realistic assessment of our ability to influence sales, combined with a realistic prediction of events outside our control that might also influence sales.

In Chapter 3 we discussed whether we would focus primarily on acquiring or retaining customers—essentially whether we planned to grow with customers new to our franchise or with customers with whom we already have a relationship. In this chapter we are interested in our current and potential customers' relationship to the competition and the category. Are these consumers currently using our products, competitor's products, or are they not buying in the category at all? These possibilities represent our *sources of volume*: we can generate increases in sales either by expanding the category—thus stimulating demand—or by convincing current category users to switch from a competitor to our brand—thereby earning share. To decide which of these paths to follow, we must have a clear understanding of what consumers are currently doing, how they think about our product and the product category, and how these factors relate to our business and marketing objectives. This information will help us to further refine our strategy and execution.

DEVELOPING A BENEFIT-BASED DEFINITION OF THE BUSINESS CATEGORY

In Chapter 3, our customer focus chapter, we considered customer definition. In this chapter we consider *category* definition: what business are we in? Theodore Levitt posed this question in a compelling fashion in his influential 1960 article *Marketing Myopia*.[1] Levitt described the crucial difference between a product-based and a **benefit-based category definition**. For example, if we are The New York Times, are we in the newspaper business (selling a product) or the information business (selling a benefit)? If we see ourselves as being in a product business, we look at ourselves and perhaps our close competitors. This approach limits our activities, and ultimately our vision; we are much more likely to see ourselves in a declining category, fighting over pieces of a shrinking pie. Today more than ever, technology, operations, and information gains tend to lead to shorter product life cycles. To the extent, therefore, that our category definition is product-based, our category will also be limited in size and time.

Products may come and go; what remains are our customers and the benefits they seek. While the railroad industry may grow or shrink, for example, the market for transportation is quite robust. If we wish to identify a sustainable source of growth for our businesses, therefore, we must look to our customers and define our category based on customer benefits. Products and services are merely a means for delivering these and simply represent the form the benefits take at a certain point in time. Transportation has taken the form of horses, elephants, trains, cars, planes, bicycles, and personal transportation vehicles such as the Segway,[i] to name a few. Currently, hydration is delivered in liquid form by means of bottled water or sports drinks; this benefit could take the form of a pill or gum in the decade to come.

On the other hand, two products that seem the same may deliver entirely different benefits. Most industry analysts consider the iPhone and the Blackberry to be in the same product category; however, most iPhone consumers would agree that their device delivers the primary benefit of entertainment, whereas the Blackberry is more likely considered a device primarily for communication, having fewer apps and less entertainment functionality. Obviously both are smart phones, but each product's growth will stem from the relative importance to the market of the perceived benefits of entertainment vs. communication and the devices' ability to deliver.

Failure to consider the customer perspective will critically constrain our strategic thinking with regard to the customer, the competition, and future product development. For example, if we believe we are in the newspaper business, our competitors are

Benefit-based category definition. The business category (or market) is the field within which companies deploy their products and services and customers satisfy needs through the purchase of products and services. Traditionally, companies defined business categories by adding up their sales of particular types of products; today we do it by adding up the revenues of products that fill a particular customer need.

---

[i] A Segway is an electric-powered self-balancing personal transportation vehicle. For more information about this product, you may see the company website: http://www.segway.com/about-segway/who-we-are.php.

GLOBALMARKETING
DEFINING AND GROWING A GLOBAL CATEGORY: GILLETTE

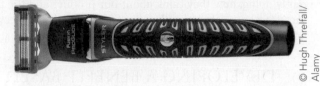

The Gillette brand name has been synonymous with innovation in shaving since 1903, when King Gillette introduced a disposable double-edged razor blade that could be thrown away and replaced when it was dull. What makes Gillette unique is not just its dominance of the shaving category, but the fact that this dominance extends globally. Its research and development, marketing, and commercialization processes offer lessons in how to build a global brand with a homogenous value proposition that is as relevant in Kansas as it is in Delhi, India.

In 1971 the Gillette Company introduced the Trac II, the first razor to carry two separate blades in a disposable cartridge. This shaving system redefined the shaving category by replacing the functional benefit of "hair removal" with the higher-level benefit of "closeness and comfort." The Trac II's first blade not only cut the hair but also pulled it out of the follicle so the second blade could provide a closer shave.

In 1974 competitor Bic introduced a fully disposable razor that became tremendously successful as customers' purchase motivations shifted toward price and convenience. Gillette initially countered with a "Good News" disposable razor, which helped grow the disposable category to 50% of the global market by the 1980s. But the growth in disposables drove down prices. Gillette was able to stem this trend by redefining shaving again with the Sensor shaving system, introduced in 1990. Now the company's strategy was to stimulate demand in the new "shaving system" category, while at the same time eroding the market share of the disposables category. It did not compare itself to disposables because they sold on price and convenience rather than on comfort and closeness.

Since the introduction of the shaving system, Gillette has become the epitome of the global brand—consistently maintaining more than 60% market share in the United States and Europe. The company introduces several products every year and a new razor system every two to five years. Ensuring global success requires a global value proposition, based on research conducted in multiple markets simultaneously. For example, the company spent two years developing the Mach 3 value proposition, testing the product with thousands of men globally.

Once it launches a product, Gillette delivers on the value proposition by ensuring there is enough capacity to satisfy global demand, using global brand names for its products, keeping packaging and look and feel consistent everywhere, establishing consistent pricing around the world, and adopting a military-style approach to product launches by carefully orchestrating and executing every promotional detail. ■

Sources: Rifkin, Glenn (1999). MACH 3: Anatomy of Gillette's Latest Global Launch. Strategy + Business,' April 1, 1999; Gillette Company Website. (www.Gillette.com). Accessed January 1, 2012; Adams, Russell B. Jr., *King C. Gillette: The man and his wonderful shaving device*, Boston: Little, Brown, 1978; Teather, David, "It's Mach 3 versus Quattro as Gillette crosses swords with Schick," *Guardian*, August 15, 2003, p. 16.

Stimulate demand strategy. The market leader's strategy based on growing the category. This is done either by attracting non-users to the category (acquisition) or by motivating current customers of the brand to purchase more or to pay more (retention).

simply the other newspapers being delivered in our market. If, on the other hand, we are in the information business, our competitors will include all forms of information delivery, including television, blogs, websites, Internet news feeds, online social media like Facebook and Twitter, magazines, and radio. If our category definition is driven by consumer benefit, it will be inherently dynamic in nature, changing as consumer needs and perceptions change. As marketers, we can influence these needs and perceptions, thus actively participating in the process of defining and redefining a category over time.

Depending on our strategic objectives and our core competencies, we may elect to broaden or narrow our category definition over time. Consider soft drinks. Coca-Cola, the category leader, has arguably redefined the category from a product-based definition, "bottled beverages," to a benefit-based definition, "refreshment." As Coca-Cola has expanded the category, other competitors have entered and succeeded by creating more narrowly focused categories, such as sports drinks (Gatorade) and energy drinks (Red Bull). These category and segment definitions are dynamic, reflecting consumer needs and interests and the relative success of marketers in identifying and responding to them.

Thus, the question "What business are we in?" is more than simply academic. It reflects a fundamental, strategic decision not just about the competitive environment but also about our customers and our firm's competencies. The answer will drive our long-term investments, our marketing plan, and our day-to-day execution. It provides the foundation on which we identify our competitive focus as either stimulating demand or earning share. It drives our vision and helps us prioritize our actions. Ultimately, the answer will help us to be more effective and more efficient marketers.

Red Bull, a mainstay in the "Energy Drink" market
Source: Red Bull Company website.

STIMULATING DEMAND: GROWING THE CATEGORY

Demand stimulation as discussed in economics texts usually refers to actions and events that spur consumption of commodity categories such as milk or oil. Many of these events are outside the control of marketers. For example, milk consumption increases with the birth rate, but it is unlikely that a marketing manager would encourage couples to have children in order to increase milk sales. On the other hand, it is quite clear that Starbucks marketing actions stimulated demand for coffee consumed outside the home. Our focus will be on examples, such as Second Life in the box on page 107, in which marketing efforts can increase or create interest and activity in a particular segment or category through a **stimulate demand strategy**. With this strategy, the firm focuses not on besting the competition, but rather on growing the entire category.

Some companies, like Starbucks, stimulate demand in an existing category that had been stagnant. Other firms have succeeded in growing "new-to-the-world" categories such as tablet PCs or MP3 players when they were first launched. Finally, a firm may elect to focus on stimulating demand of a sub-segment in an attempt to break away from an existing category. For example, while Red Bull is arguably a soft drink, it was never directly marketed against the market leaders, Coke and Pepsi. Instead, the brand used a stimulate-demand strategy to carve out an entirely new segment from the outset: energy drinks.

This is not to say that Red Bull did not grow at Coca-Cola's expense. Certainly the growth of this new segment has affected Coke and Pepsi sales. Red Bull accomplished its growth, however, not by making a direct comparison to Coke, Pepsi, or the cola segment. Instead the brand chose to *emphasize the category benefit* of increased energy, likely drawing users from Coke, Pepsi, and a variety of other sources and avoiding specific comparisons in the process. This is the essence of a stimulate-demand strategy: no direct comparisons, and an emphasis on the category benefit.

Common marketing wisdom dictates that only the category leader should pursue a stimulate demand approach. There are several sound strategic reasons why. First,

An early Coca-Cola print advertisement highlighting its "Refreshing" benefit and reflecting Coca-Cola's efforts to redefine the soft-drink category.
Source: *Directory Journal Marketing Blog.*

because the leader stands to gain the most from healthy category growth, it makes sense that it should take responsibility for trying to stimulate this growth. When a category grows, competitors will generally capture share of that new demand in proportions roughly equal to their current share. Thus, for example, if McDonald's has a 50% share of a $200 billion market and is successful at stimulating demand to increase by 10%, it can assume, all things being equal, that it will have a 50% share of the newly grown $220 billion market.

One interesting aspect of the stimulate demand strategy is that, for the category leader, creating brand awareness is usually relatively unimportant. The category leader likely already enjoys strong brand awareness, and in mature categories it is often the default brand, the one consumers think of first when they think of that category. For example, when you mention "facial tissues," many consumers think of Kleenex first. It is the default brand. The category leader can take advantage of this status by shifting resources away from brand awareness building and toward other, more profitable activities. This is the essence of an efficient marketing strategy: prioritizing marketing activities based on our specific position in the marketplace and our goals. For a stimulate demand strategy, the first priority is to emphasize the main benefit of the category, the key reason that consumers are or could be interested in that category.

The market leader should almost always pursue a stimulate demand strategy. In some instances it is even appropriate for a product *without* a dominant market position to choose this strategy. For example, in a new-to-the-world category where there are many small players with similar technologies, it might be best for each firm to try to stimulate demand for a segment of the category. By working together to expand the whole pie, small companies can expand the category faster than if they each worked to earn customers from each other. When Wi-Fi broadband Internet connections were first introduced, this was the strategy most players took. Few companies tried to distinguish themselves as preferred providers; instead, they worked to fuel general interest and usage among mobile Internet users.

Category growth comes from three possible sources. We can either (1) attract new users into the category, (2) convince current users to consume our product more often or in greater quantity in order to increase volume, or (3) create new value by convincing existing users to pay more by innovating our product, or by selling additional products and services. We discuss each option next.

Attracting New Users

Path to purchase. The stages that a customer goes through in identifying a need and eventually purchasing, using, and evaluating a product purchase.

In the new user strategy, we are essentially inviting consumers into a category or segment in which they do not currently participate. This strategy is probably the most challenging way to stimulate demand (and also the most expensive), because we are asking our potential customers to move the greatest distance along the **path to purchase** (Figure 4.4). The path to purchase details the decision and action steps the consumer moves through on their way to making a purchase decision. No consumer simply decides, out of the blue, to purchase a product. Consumers must first be aware of a need, develop an understanding of the different options available to them, and then make a choice. After they have made a product choice, their experience with the product will influence their future evaluation and choices.

social**media**

Using Real Money in an Unreal World: Growth in a Virtual Market Stimulates Adjacent Category

The advent of virtual social networks like the one accessed through the popular website Second Life has created an almost surreal market for advertising and media companies. Second Life is a sort of parallel universe; as a customer, you get to choose your appearance and recreate your life in a virtual world. Companies have rushed to these worlds, purchasing billboards, setting up stores, and advertising their virtual and offline products. Even the U.S. Congress has reviewed several bills to tax real incomes generated as a result of these virtual worlds.

© STR/Reuters/Corbis

Sources: Siklos, Richard. "A virtual world but real money." *The New York Times.* October 19, 2006. (http://www.nytimes.com/2006/10/19/technology/19virtual.html?pagewanted=all). Accessed March 1, 2012.

"Virtual Items, Virtual Currency and Public Policy." A White Paper by the Virtual Policy Network. 2012. http://www.virtualpolicy.net/_Downloads/Documents/tVPN_WhitePaper-Virtual_Items_&_Public_Policy.pdf. Accessed April 12, 2013.

When we detail the path to purchase, we can begin to develop specific marketing goals that align with these steps. For example, if our potential customers are not currently using any product in the category, we must build awareness of the category benefits. If, on the other hand, they are already quite familiar with the category and are using a competitor's product, we can presume they already understand the general category benefit, and we may adopt the goal of influencing the way they compare competitive products within the category. Each of these different goals will lead us to consider different marketing tools. If we seek to build general awareness, we may elect to leverage broad-scale communications or a **viral marketing** campaign. If, on the other hand, we wish to influence the way consumers compare our products, we may develop an in-store demonstration of our product benefits vs. the competition's.

Tracking the path to purchase will thus give us insight into the way we allocate marketing resources. For example, first-time expectant parents will likely be entering

Viral marketing. A communications tactic intended to increase awareness using social media as opposed to traditional paid advertising. This awareness spreads like a virus as users come in contact with one another and "infect" their friends and associates with information about a product.

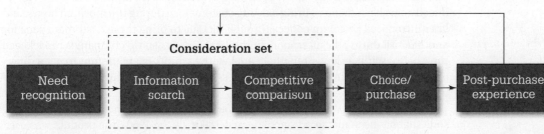

Figure 4.4 The path to purchase.

the disposable diaper category without much encouragement from marketers. We will thus likely spend very little resources on the need-recognition stage of this process, focusing instead on the information search and comparison stages. On the other hand, Toyota has spent substantial resources to generate awareness of, and interest in, the hybrid car category. Arguably this investment has paid off, because consumers who are interested in hybrid cars naturally include Toyota in their **consideration set**, their list of potential brands to choose from, even as the number of hybrid car options grew.

Stimulating New Volume

A second stimulate primary demand strategy is to convince existing users to consume more. This is a more efficient strategy than attracting new users, because we don't need to spend money convincing potential customers to enter the category or even to use our brand. We just need to motivate them to do more of something they already think is a good idea.

Familiar examples of the stimulate new volume strategy include packaging or pricing-based promotions: "Would you like to try the super-jumbo-giant size of popcorn for just a quarter more?" Unfortunately, we sometimes blindly apply this approach without considering the long-term implications of our actions. The ideal strategy convinces consumers to change their attitudes toward consumption behavior on a permanent basis. For example, we may seek to convince consumers to drink orange juice not just in the morning but also with sparkling water for a refreshing afternoon drink. If, on the other hand, we simply lower price or increase package size to encourage higher-volume purchase, we will likely see not a sustainable increase in purchase volume, but rather a short-term bump in sales when consumers simply stock up on the product at the lower price. When consumers engage in such **forward-buying** (also known as pantry-loading), they store the extra product for future use, and overall purchase quantity does not change. This strategy can prove negative for marketers because it creates extreme peaks and valleys in product sales that affect production and distribution efficiencies. Meanwhile, over the medium to long term, brand sales do not increase and might actually go down.

Because of disappointing outcomes like this, many marketers believe new-volume price promotions usually work best with products that cannot be inventoried (like movie popcorn). Unfortunately, this tactical approach can quickly become irritating to consumers who are sick of "suggestive selling" tactics. The ideal approach to generating new volume is not tactical price promotions but rather longer-term, sustainable strategies for increasing demand for our brand. These often mean finding new and/or different ways for the consumer to use the product. For example, McDonald's introduced a breakfast menu to bring existing customers in during the morning hours, and later introduced premium coffees through McCafé to bring these customers back for another visit during the afternoon. In the 1990s, many aspirin companies repackaged their baby aspirin as low-strength, heart-healthy aspirin, in an attempt to get a different group of consumers (older males) to consume a pill a day to reduce the risk of heart attack.

Perhaps the best example of this approach is Arm & Hammer, a brand of baking soda that has been marketed since the mid-1800s. By the 1960s, the product was used

Consideration set. A list of companies or brands that are simultaneously considered by consumers seeking to make a purchase based on a need they have identified or a benefit they are seeking to obtain. As consumers engage in research of a category, they may discover options that were not in their initial consideration set.

Forward buying. The practice of purchasing retail inventory in quantities exceeding current demand, usually motivated by suppliers' offers of temporary discounts.

primarily as a leavening agent in baking. While the brand had achieved extremely high **household penetration**—the percentage of households purchasing the product at least once—the volume of use was extremely low. Through a series of marketing campaigns, the firm promoted awareness of a variety of alternative uses for the product and brand, first as a refrigerator/freezer/garbage disposal freshener, then as a key ingredient in toothpaste, detergents, and other cleaners and deodorizers. These campaigns increased volume for the product by increasing the number of ways to obtain a key product benefit of freshness or deodorization. In each of these products, the brand delivers an added value to consumers familiar with the original product and brand.

Creating New Value

Finally, we can stimulate primary demand by convincing existing customers to trade up, or spend more money on our product. The DeBeers diamond campaign is a classic example of this strategy. The tagline "Is two months' salary too much to spend on something that lasts forever?" has been a tremendously successful effort to increase the amount of money consumers spend on diamonds. American Express cardholders, in response to marketing, aspire to become Black Card holders so they may have the privilege of paying a $5,000 initiation fee and then $2,500 per year to receive "additional benefits." And as the chapter opener shows, Gillette routinely (and successfully) encourages users to trade up to the next multi-blade razor.

DeBeers Print Advertising.

Jamie Rector/Bloomberg/Getty Images

    The key to forming a successful new value strategy is to (1) identify a clear benefit or potential benefit of the existing product, and then (2) identify ways to increase the perceived value of that benefit in order to realize a higher price. Gillette presumably delivers a closer shave with each new model razor; American Express delivers more status with the Black Card. If we cannot successfully increase perceived value through a combination of product features and successful marketing, we will not have a sustainable new value strategy.

EARNING SHARE FROM A COMPETITOR OR A MARKET SEGMENT

So far we've discussed the competitive option of stimulating demand or growing the category. However, if we are not the category leader, and we are not planning to invest in building a new segment, a demand stimulation strategy is not appropriate. Instead of growing the pie, we want to capture a larger slice of the existing pie with an **earn share strategy**. We will thus be far more focused on and reactive to a key competitor or segment: our *earn share target*. We will let our target competitor or group of competitors grow the market, while we focus on earning share from this target by invoking a comparison that places our brand in a favorable light. We may elect to attract new users to our brand, or we may simply try to convince multi-brand users, who are using both our brand and a competitive brand, to switch more of their consumption to us.

Attracting New Users

The most common strategy for earning share is to encourage *brand-switching*, in which consumers decide to switch their allegiance from their current brand to a competitor's brand. This type of behavior is common in durable goods categories such as cars, refrigerators, and clothing. For example, a consumer may previously have been loyal to Diesel jeans but has been convinced that Seven jeans are more fashionable and therefore they stop purchasing Diesels. From a marketing perspective this type of behavioral change is quite challenging to accomplish because it requires convincing a consumer to switch allegiance from a previously preferred and familiar brand. The good news is that each newly converted consumer represents a substantial potential revenue stream for the firm.

Increasing Usage among Multi-brand Users

Alternatively, we may seek not to convert consumers entirely to our brand, but rather to convince them that they should shift the weight of their brand usage behavior in our favor. This is a common goal when our target audience is multi-brand users, who consume more than one brand in a particular category. Frequently purchased product categories such as beer and cereal tend to have a high percentage of multi-brand users; a person who has cereal every morning for breakfast may have two or three favorites from which she selects each day. In these cases we are interested in convincing consumers that they should consume more of our brand instead of the competition's brand. For example, in 2009 General Mills began promoting Cheerios as heart-healthy, suggesting that if consumers consumed the cereal for four weeks instead of their regular brand, they would experience lowered cholesterol levels.

Earn Share: Two Questions

Mac has had a long-standing strategy to earn share from PCs.

We have two key questions to answer in implementing an earn-share strategy. The first question is *from whom?* We must identify the *specific* brand or segment from which we intend to earn share. It is not sufficient to simply say, "from everybody." We can earn share from another brand, as Pepsi has attempted to earn share from Coke, or we can earn share from a clearly defined segment, as Apple has sought to earn share from PC makers. The key here is that we want to leverage our marketing efforts to *invoke a specific comparison.*

When we compare our brand to a well-established brand, like Kleenex or Coke, we are leveraging existing awareness to establish a clear benchmark in consumers' minds; all that remains for us to do is convey how we are differentiated from the benchmark. This is far less challenging than teaching a customer all the benefits of a new category (as in stimulate demand strategies). We can expect our key competitor or group of competitors to handle the task of attracting category users. But a comparison to a vague competitive set such as "other brands" does not leverage existing awareness or the resulting efficiencies. This

GLOBALMARKETING

THE EUROPEAN UNION (EU)—DIRECTIVE ON COMPARATIVE ADVERTISING

The EU adopted Directive 97/55/EC of October 6, 1997, amending Directive 84/450/EEC of September 10, 1984 to regulate comparative and misleading advertising. Since 1997 there has been a lot of controversy about **comparative advertising** in Europe. It is now legal to engage in comparative advertising within the EU. The EU Commission defines comparative advertising as "any advertising that explicitly or by implication identifies a competitor or goods or services offered by a competitor." In the EU, comparative advertising is allowed as long as: it is not misleading; does not create confusion in the marketplace; it relates to products serving the same consumer function or purpose; it does not discredit the competitor's trademark, its name, or its products; it does not use a competitor's protected trademark; and it does not present products as perfect replicas of the competitors. As an aside, in the United States, comparative advertising is regulated by the Federal Trade Commission (FTC) and is allowed and even encouraged as long as comparisons are "clearly identified, truthful, and not deceptive." ∎

Source: "Misleading and Comparative Advertising." European Commission, Consumer Affairs website. (http://ec.europa.eu/consumers/cons_int/safe_shop/mis_adv/index_en.html). Accessed January 12, 2012.

"Statement of Policy Regarding Comparative Advertising." Federal Trade Commission. Washington, DC, 20580. August 13, 1979. http://www.ftc.gov/bcp/policystmt/ad-compare.htm. Accessed April 12, 2012.

---

is why it is critical for us to make a *specific* comparison that has meaning to customers.

That said, it is not necessary to always name names when we implement an earn share strategy. In many global markets it is against the law to specifically mention competitors' brand names; the Global Issues box outlines the approach the European Union elected to follow in 1997. Still, it is always possible to invoke a comparison in consumers' minds. When we mention "the leading brand" in most categories, consumers know to whom we are referring. For example, when Subway launched its "Jared" campaign to promote the healthfulness of its "six grams of fat or less" menu (Figure 4.6), McDonald's was clearly the **source of volume**. McDonald's share of market and mind (as well as the widely known fact that much of its food is high in fat) was so strong that there was no need for Subway to specifically identify it in the advertising. To earn share without naming names, we simply need to provide appropriate clues in our message to consumers.

The second question we must answer after we have identified the key competitor in our segment is: "What is the key advantage of our brand vs. theirs?" Why is a Mac better than a PC? Why is Target better than Walmart? Why is a Lexus better than a Mercedes? This answer will be our *dynamic benefit*, the differentiator we will emphasize as our point-of-difference, and it will be the foundation of our earn share strategy. The dynamic benefit of the Visa Check Card is convenience compared to writing checks; the dynamic benefit of Subway® over McDonald's is low fat.

To successfully implement an earn share strategy, our brand must have a core competence related to this dynamic benefit. The link between core competence and dynamic benefit is the foundation on which the firm develops a sustainable strategy instead of a temporary advantage. If the firm fails to make this link, it is simply promoting a benefit that any competitor in the category could deliver. In essence, the

Mary Ann Price John Wiley & Sons

Comparative advertising. Refers to the practice of advertising products or services relative to other products sold by competitors rather than in absolute terms.

Source of volume. A process by which we attribute customer purchases to groups of consumers in each of the strategic quadrants: retention/stimulate demand, retention/earn share, acquisition/stimulate demand, acquisition/earn share.

---

firm is providing market research for the competition by using its promotional dollars to demonstrate demand for a particular benefit.

This situation can lead to **features wars**. A feature war is a competitive dynamic whereby companies in a business category copy innovations introduced by other competitors rather than innovating based on their core competence. The result is products that are commoditized instead of differentiated. For example, to achieve differentiation, Subway® must have a core skill of processing fresh foods to deliver the benefit of low fat. If it does not, McDonald's will simply match Subway on this benefit, and consumers will make a choice between the two firms based on some other differentiating benefit that McDonald's might deliver better.

A dynamic benefit is different from a main benefit. The **main benefit**, also known as the **category benefit**, is the *primary benefit that attracts consumers to the category*. It is what all members of the category must be able to deliver in order to compete. For the category leader, however, it is a differentiating benefit. McDonald's leads the market in delivering convenience, the main benefit of fast food. Walmart leads in delivering low price, the main benefit of discount retail. In the 1980s Budweiser delivered the main benefit in the beer category of flavor. Flavor was a **cost of entry** for the category; any competitor hoping to garner share had to deliver some acceptable level of flavor, and any beer that did not taste good had little chance of surviving the competition of flavorful beers.

Presuming that Budweiser dominated on flavor, any competitor seeking to enter and survive in the category needed to differentiate itself from Bud by promoting a unique dynamic benefit that at least some consumers are interested in. Imported beers such as Heineken and Corona promoted the differentiating benefit of uniqueness; Miller Lite emphasized the benefit of being "less filling;" other brands such as Asahi Dry and Miller Genuine Draft promoted specific brewing techniques. In a healthy, differentiated category, it is quite easy for consumers to discern specific differences between brands and then make product choices according to their preferences. Firms seeking to survive will attempt to understand consumer preferences, and also to influence them, as they select their dynamic benefit for an earn share strategy.

Features war. When both parties engaged in competition retaliate in succession, their competition is called a *features war* if they primarily compete by trying to improve on each other's product features, or a *price war* if they primarily compete on price.

Main benefit. The primary customer benefit emphasized by the market leader of a category. The main benefit becomes a "cost of entry" into the category because companies wishing to enter that market have to deliver the main benefit to an acceptable level in order to be considered part of the category.

Cost of entry. The cost of entry into a category is the minimum acceptable product or service standard that a company must be able to deliver in order to be considered by consumers in that category as being part of their consideration set in that category.

social**media**

Promoting a Key Benefit Stimulates Demand of the Massively Multiplayer Role Playing Game Category

The explosion of the Internet as a social media channel helped create a wholly new business category of games that naturally includes a socialization component. One of the most famous and successful games was World of Warcraft, inspired by the game *Dungeons and Dragons*. By the end of 2012, World of Warcraft had grown to 10 million subscribers.

Bloomberg/Getty Images

Source: Holsmtrom, Mathias. "What you need to know about 'World of Warcraft' that analysts are ignoring," *Seeking Alpha Blog*, September 21, 2012.

IMPORTANT DISTINCTIONS BETWEEN EARNING SHARE AND STIMULATING DEMAND

Our strategic assumption going in to the market is that the category leader will seek to stimulate demand, and all lower-ranked competitors will seek to earn share from this competitor. The reason is that the category leader benefits most when the category grows. However, we also have the strategic option of *redefining the category*. For example, while it is common for a number-one brand in a category to attempt to stimulate primary demand, a strong market leader may instead choose to broaden the category definition and then pursue an earn-share strategy against a larger segment. Instead of attempting to stimulate primary demand in the fast-food category, McDonald's may instead seek to redefine the category as "dinner" and then attempt to earn share from in-home dining. It is this type of flexible thinking that allows a category leader to continue to lead by constantly considering new and more expansive category definitions.

Conversely, under certain conditions, a smaller player or a new market entrant may elect to implement a stimulate-demand strategy instead of attempting to earn share, even in mature markets. To accomplish this, the brand must conceive of a new, smaller segment, one that it dominates. For example, Gatorade did not enter the soft drink category with an earn-share strategy but rather elected to create a new segment of sports drinks (see Gatorade advertising image). The brand emphasized the category benefit of replenishment, rather than directly comparing itself to other soft drinks where the benefit was refreshment. In doing so, Gatorade became the number-one brand in a new and vital segment and avoided some of the pitfalls it might have faced had it tried to earn share from beverages such as soft drinks or bottled juices.

Because the earn share/stimulate demand decision is a strategic choice, we consider the pros and cons of each option in the following sections.

The 'Be Mike' Campaign Featuring Michael Jordan and other top athletes called on non-users to enter the sports drink category in an example of demand stimulation for a new segment.

Walter Iooss Jr./ NBAE/Getty Images

Stimulate Demand

A key benefit of a stimulate primary demand strategy is that the focus of the brand is on capturing the high ground or thought leadership in the category. It is not enough to simply launch a new feature, or even a new product. The category leader must consistently and successfully identify consumer insights and latent needs that it can respond to by capitalizing on its core competence. A stimulate demand strategy is thus the foundation of sustainable category leadership, and also the key to the continued health of the category. Paying continual attention to the future of the category requires the firm to employ leadership strategies across all aspects of the business including product development distribution, customer service etc.

Furthermore, the category leader would be ill-advised to pursue an earn share campaign. The reason is that an earn share strategy invokes comparisons to a lower-share (and presumably lower-awareness) brand. This activity would likely not only increase awareness of the competitive brand but also call into question the market leader's credibility. In essence, the goal of the market leader is to maintain and protect its leading status by taking a pre-emptive, as opposed to a reactive, approach.

Of course, the downside of the stimulate demand strategy is that it requires significantly more risk-taking than an earn share strategy: The path breaker must always expend more resources. This is why it is so crucial that the innovations created are founded in the firm's core competence. If they are not, the leader will simply be identifying and establishing market demand for low-price imitators.

Earn Share

The good news about the earn share strategy is that, as we've seen, we can use customers' existing awareness and understanding of a competitor's brand in order to communicate something about ours. By invoking a comparison, we capitalize on past investments made by the category leader to create awareness for the category and its primary benefits. This makes the earn share strategy very efficient, at least in the short run.

social**media**

Google Tries to Earn Share from Facebook with Google+

When Google, the undisputed leader in the search engine market, entered the social media market, it threatened the market leader in that category, Facebook, which retaliated. Google had experimented with social media before, but by the Summer of 2010, word leaked out that the company was in the final stages of development of a "Facebook killer" site. On hearing the news, Mark Zuckerberg, CEO of Facebook, called on engineers to work nights and weekends for 60 days to revamp key social features like photos, groups, and events.

By September, Facebook had released a slew of new features, like better grouping tools to mirror Google+ circles. Commenting on the organizational climate at facebook during this time, a member of the product and engineering team said: "[Google] can throw all the money in the world, including hundreds of people, at this. So people were, like, 'This is serious, and we should take it seriously.'" Facebook took drastic measures against Google, including contracting with a public relations firm to plant anti-Google stories in papers and blogs. Facebook also competed with Google by hiring away top talent, including Paul Adams, Google+'s lead social researcher. For its part, Google designed many of the features of Google+ (like photo uploading) to be improved versions of Facebook features.

© franckreporter/iStockphoto

Google's motivation for penetrating the social networking category may well be based on the shift in usage from search-based sites to social-media-based sites. As users move, so will advertisers. Although Google's market share of the $31B search advertising market was over 40% in 2011, Facebook's display-ad revenue was expected to grow 81% in 2011, while Google's display-ad dollars were expected to rise an estimated 34%. It is this fear of losing ad revenue that analysts attribute to Google's aggressive and comparative entry into the social media market. Stifel Nicolaus analyst Jordan Rohan explains, "It's highly unlikely that either Google or Facebook could grow by the billions that investors expect in the display market without engaging directly and stealing market share from the other."

Source: Helft, Miguel and Jessi Hempel, "Facebook vs. Google: The battle for the future of the web," *Fortune*, November 29, 2011. (http://money.cnn.com/2011/11/03/technology/facebook_google_fight.fortune/index.htm) access January 12, 2013; Ulanoff, Lanceed, "Google Plus: The gloves are off." *Mashable.com*, September 20, 2011. Accessed http://mashable.com/2011/09/20/google-vs-facebook-the-gloves-are-off-opinion/.

However, we must still execute the strategy with caution. There are three primary considerations for firms implementing an earn share strategy:

1. *The comparative benefit must be true and discernable, based on our core competence.* If we make a comparative claim and consumers respond positively, our main competitor may simply match us if it has a similar competence.

2. *We must be prepared for competitive retaliation.* Sometimes it is a good thing if our competitors respond, particularly if we have a core-competence-based benefit. Then if the competitor engages, it is likely that overall interest in the benefit will increase. However, we must be sure to clearly establish the link between our brand and the benefit in order to avoid consumer confusion.

3. *We must be sensitive to possible negative reactions from our potential consumers.* Nobody likes to be told they are wrong. If, in the course of our comparative marketing efforts, we demean or insult consumers of the competitive product, we will not succeed in attracting them to our brand. Our arguments in favor of our brand must be presented credibly, be well supported, and be based on a clear understanding of our potential customers' attitudes and opinions.

We must also consider a long-run strategic concern, which is that any money spent in support of an earn share campaign could help to build a long-term perception in consumers' minds that our brand is second-best. In its original incarnation, the Avis Car Rental campaign tag line was: "We're number 2; we try harder." The company gained share based on the success of its marketing campaign; however, as the company gained market leadership in some regions, it then had to choose between weakening the campaign by changing its well-known tagline or starting over with a new and costly campaign. Now it simply claims to "try harder."

In general, we obtain our highest return on marketing investment by staying with a campaign and position for as long as possible. If our long-term plans include a run at category leadership, an earn share approach is likely to be suitable only for a limited time. The move to #1 status will likely require an increase in marketing investment.

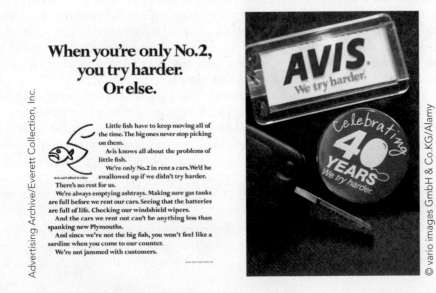

Avis's original campaign in the1960s said "We're No 2; we try harder." Its 1990s campaign said simply: "We try harder," modified to reflect the fact that the company was now achieving No. 1 share positions in some markets.

CHOOSING A STRATEGIC FOCUS

Determining our source of volume is in many cases a lesson in subtle but important distinctions. It is theoretically possible to define many marketing campaigns as either earn share or stimulate primary demand, if we consider only the numbers and not the positioning. For example, much of Gatorade's early volume came from Coca-Cola, the leader in the soft drink category at the time. From a strictly numerical perspective, this is arguably an example of implementing an earn share strategy in the soft drink category; Gatorade definitely took share from Coca-Cola. It did not, however, execute an earn share strategy as we've defined it here, *because it did not invoke a specific comparison to Coke*. Instead of comparing the beverage to Coca-Cola—or even to carbonated soft drinks in general—Gatorade emphasized replenishment, an entirely new benefit for soft drinks. The success of this campaign meant that some consumers reduced consumption in the soft drink category and shifted that demand to the energy drink category, where Gatorade was the category leader.

Similarly, when TV programming became widely available over the Internet thanks to services such as Netflix and Hulu (see image on next page), many consumers elected to cancel their TV cable or satellite subscriptions with companies like Comcast or Direct TV.[ii] However, Netflix and Hulu never invoked a specific comparison to these providers. Instead, they simply emphasized the benefit of a new Internet-based entertainment delivery method. By avoiding a direct comparison, they mitigated the risks of an earn share strategy mentioned above. This approach, avoiding an earn

---

[ii]Comcast is a U.S.-based cable company that distributes TV programming. http://Comcast.com, and its competitor, Direct TV, is a U.S. company which leverages satellite-based technology to distribute TV programming http://www.directv.com/.

share strategy, gives the brand a long-term place to live in consumers' minds, not as a Coke or Comcast "wanna-be" but as a totally new product.

Our decision as to whether to earn share or stimulate demand is thus a strategic choice that is based on a careful consideration of our firm competences, customers, and competitions. Once we have made this choice we can retake it to our choice of customer focus (acquisition or retention) we then have a clear strategic direction for the decisions that follow in the framework. Each of these decisions will be mapped onto a 2x2 matrix illustrated in Figure 4.5. Our choice of marketing objective (customer focus) and source of volume (competitive focus) yields four possible strategic options:

Hulu's commercials first appeared during the 2009 Super Bowl and have since featured several U.S. actors.

1. *Acquisition/Stimulate Demand.* For this option we are trying to attract new users to the category, and we are not interested in making a direct comparison to a particular competitor. If we are successful, we will *grow the category.* Examples of successful acquisition/stimulate demand campaigns abound; any time a new category comes into existence or a dormant category suddenly springs to life, we are likely seeing the results of a successful acquisition/stimulate demand strategy. Examples include the Nike "just do it" campaign, Apple's launch of the iPhone, and Toyota's launch of the Prius Hybrid. In each of these cases the firm succeeded in attracting new users to the category but did not engage in direct comparisons to any other competitor or segment.

	Marketing objective	
	Acquisition	Retention
Stimulate demand	attract potential category users	increase consumption among current users (volume or value)
Earn share	attract competitive brand/segment users	increase consumption among multi-brand users

Source of volume

Figure 4.5 Relationship of source of volume and marketing objective: The strategic focus.

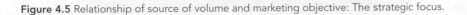

Example of Gillette's continuing retention/stimulate-demand campaign inviting existing consumers to trade up to the latest razor.

2. *Retention/Stimulate Demand.* In this strategic quadrant we are speaking to our existing customers, trying to convince them to either use more of our product or pay more for our product. In the first case we must either identify new usage occasions (use Pledge furniture polish on your countertops) or convince consumers to consume more (replace your Oral-B toothbrush more often). In the many cases we are interested in increasing perceived value for our product by either adding features or communicating added value. Often this is an "upgrade" strategy—we are asking consumers to trade up from their two-blade Gillette razor to a three-blade razor at a higher price. As in all stimulate demand strategies, the competitor is not mentioned here. In general this strategy targets relatively loyal users who already have at least some understanding of our value proposition.

3. *Retention/Earn Share.* Here we are talking about existing users, but we are taking a competitive focus because they are using our product *and* that of a key competitor. They are *multi-brand users* or are consuming from a *brand set.* Our first step is thus to understand why they use more than one brand. In some cases they enjoy variety (eating Raisin Bran three times a week and Cheerios twice, for instance), so we might add more variation to our own product line in order to satisfy their needs. Or they may find either brand acceptable and simply choose the one that is more convenient, in which case our resources might be better focused on controlling distribution in order to ensure the product is easily accessible. In all cases we are looking to increase our total share of consumption, ideally shifting consumers from multi-brand to exclusive users. Because we are taking an earn share competitive focus, we will bend our marketing efforts toward making a specific comparison (e.g., "using Shell gasoline exclusively instead of BP will result in a cleaner engine over time").

4. *Acquisition/Earn Share.* In this quadrant we are again trying to attract new users. However, we are concerned not with attracting them to the category, but rather with wooing them away from the presumed category leader. In this case we will use a specific comparison, emphasizing a clear point of differentiation that is sufficiently powerful to convince consumers to switch from their current brand. Usually what we want is a complete switch, from 100% usage of the competing brand to 100% usage of our brand. We are in essence asking consumers to change their loyalty, as opposed to simply changing their usage patterns. Apple asks consumers to switch from Microsoft; Pepsi asks consumers to switch from Coke; Audi asks consumers to switch from Mercedes. In all these cases the category leader (Microsoft, Coke, Mercedes Benz) built the category, but that is not our concern in this quadrant. Our goal here is to capture consumers *after* they have decided to enter the category by convincing them of the relative merits of our brand vs. the presumed "gold standard."

STRATEGIC FORECASTING: THE 4 Bs

Any firm assessing its current and potential sales will likely find it has both presence and opportunity in all four quadrants. But the actions we take to increase our sales in any one quadrant differ substantially. Our ideal messaging, distribution strategy,

GLOBAL MARKETING

MARKET LEADERSHIP IN THE NORTH AMERICAN BEER CATEGORY

Beer is the most popular alcoholic beverage in Canada and accounts for almost 50% of the volume of alcoholic drinks sold in that country. Labatt is the traditional market leader, and Molson is a close number two. Labatt has also been an innovation leader; for example, it patented a proprietary method to brew ice beer in the early 1990s. However, it was actually Molson that first brought ice beer to the United States, creating the impression there that Molson was the leading brand in Canada, and illustrating how category leadership can shift outside the home market for a brand. ∎

©Lauri Patterson/iStockphoto

Sources: "Ice beer wars," Canadian Broadcast Corporation. April 14, 1993. http://rc-archives.cbc.ca/programs/502-8736/page/3/. Accessed April 22, 2013.

Kenney, Caitlin. "Beer map: Two giant brewers, 210 brands." *Blogentry*. February 19, 2013. Planet Money. NPR. http://www.npr.org/blogs/money/2013/02/19/172323211/beer-map-two-giant-brewers-210-brands. Accessed April 22, 2013.

pricing, and product strategy and execution for acquisition/stimulate demand will look very different from those we use for retention/earn share. If, like most marketers, we face increasing competition and restricted resources, we must *prioritize* our spending. If we simply spread our marketing budget across four different approaches instead, we will be inefficient at best and at worst fail utterly. Hence we must use the **strategic quadrants** to estimate our market potential, assess alternative strategies, and prioritize our spending to maximize our return on marketing investment. Let us explore how to set these priorities.

Our first step toward setting our spending priorities is to assess market potential for each quadrant. This assessment is a forecast, and like any forecast it represents an educated guess based on facts, assumptions, and logic. Available facts include current sales trends in the category, demographic information (population, age, gender, and the like), behavioral trends, and attitudinal trends. We make assumptions about customer definitions, whether trends will continue, what factors might influence them, and so on. Finally, we rely on logic to help us decide what information to collect, how to analyze it, how trends might affect us, and how we might influence trends.

In many industries companies have developed elaborate forecasting models that analyze and synthesize huge amounts of data. Regardless of how sophisticated these models are, they are inherently uncertain: no model enables us to perfectly predict the future. Obviously, we would like our model to be as accurate as possible; an accurate forecast makes operations, service, and financial planning much easier. But a sound forecasting model can do much more: it can aid us in our strategic decision-making if the facts, logic, and assumptions we rely on represent the working reality of the situation we are trying to predict, including those aspects we can influence with our marketing efforts.

To have strategic value, a forecasting model must be intuitively sound and actionable. Our choice of strategic quadrant provides us the foundation for such a model. This tool can serve as a basis for much more complex models that reflect the specifics

Strategic quadrants. The strategic quadrants are a 2 x 2 that results from a combination of the marketing objective decisions (customer focus) and the source of volume choice (competitive focus). There are four strategic quadrants: acquisition/stimulate demand, retention/stimulate demand, acquisition/earn share, retention/earn share.

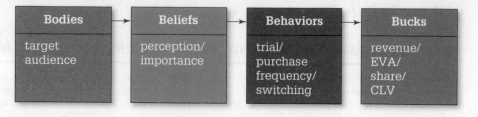

Figure 4.6 The 4 Bs tools illustrate the linkages that must be established between bodies, beliefs, behaviors, and bucks.

of a particular industry and competitive environment. However, no matter how complex we make it, we should not let the model lose its strategic value. We will therefore begin to build it based on our strategic quadrants and the basic elements in any market: consumers (bodies), their attitudes (beliefs), their actions (behaviors), and the resulting sales revenues (bucks). These **4 Bs** and the relationships (see Figure 4.6) between them will form the foundation of our initial forecasting model.

Bodies

Any accurate forecasting model must first assess the number of potential customers. Instead of simply looking at the entire market, we will make this assessment based on our strategic options as discussed below and illustrated earlier in Figure 4.5. By taking this approach we can align our strategic decision-making with our assessment of market potential.

1. For *acquisition/stimulate demand* we are counting customers outside the category, that is, non-users. Obviously, we will not count *all* non-users, but only those who meet the requirements for entering the category. For example, if we are trying to grow the electric car segment, we start by considering target non-users of electric cars *of driving age*.

2. For *acquisition/earn share* we are interested in counting the number of competitive users of the specific brand or group of brands we are targeting. A firm such as Mizuno (maker of sports equipment, clothing, and shoes) might choose to target Nike users; local independent booksellers such as Barbara's Books in Chicago seek to convert consumers from "big box" bookstores such as Barnes and Noble.

3. The measurement task becomes even easier for *retention/stimulate demand*. Here we simply count our current customers. They might be convinced to use our product more frequently or to trade up to other premium products in our franchise.

4. Finally, for *retention/earn share,* we are counting the number of people who use our product as well as the products of a key competitor or segment. These are multi-brand users who we believe might be convinced to switch more of their purchases from our competitor to our brand.

The above discussion illustrates the fact that, as our strategic focus changes, our potential target audience changes. The differences in our target audience described here make it clear that the actions necessary to persuade potential consumers will be different. The reason is that the beliefs they hold, based on their actions and experiences, are different.

Beliefs

In considering the beliefs of our target audience, we are of course concerned with existing beliefs, but perhaps the most important task is to assess *potential* beliefs. This is the core task of marketing: identifying attitudes that we can change in order to influence behaviors. Even more importantly, we are interested in prioritizing these beliefs and identifying the key driver our marketing strategy will focus on. We do not have sufficient resources to influence all beliefs, so we must instead pick those that (1) drive behavior, (2) link to our core competence, and (3) can be effectively influenced through marketing.

The task of assessing beliefs will carry through into our discussions of segmentation, targeting, and positioning in later chapters. For now, we are interested in further refining our market potential assessment by evaluating beliefs in each strategic quadrant. Like bodies, beliefs are quite different in each quadrant, and they require different marketing strategies and execution. These differences are discussed below and illustrated in Figure 4.7.

1. The beliefs of potential customers in the *acquisition/stimulate demand* quadrant are, in general, the most vague and least stable. The reason is that customers in this quadrant may not have even considered entering the category, have likely not collected any information, and simply haven't thought about it. The key question for them, therefore, is unique: Why are you staying out of this category? In some cases the answer is lack of interest or information; in others there is a specific objection ("Smartphones seem too expensive to me").

2. For *acquisition/earn share*, customers may know quite a bit about the category, likely have fairly well formed beliefs about the competitive product they are using, and may have negative attitudes toward our brand. Our primary objective here is not simply understanding why they are using the competitive product, but more importantly finding out what would make them switch. All too often

Figure 4.7 Key attitudinal question by strategic quadrant.

the knee-jerk reaction in this quadrant is to simply try to attract competitive users with a lower price; however, this strategy is rarely effective, because it usually focuses on behaviors instead of beliefs. It is far more sustainable to uncover beliefs about the comparative merits of our products that we might influence. When we change behaviors through a change in customer beliefs, we can expect the behavioral change to be "stickier" than when we simply cut price or change contract terms to motivate customers.

3. In contrast, our customers in the *retention/stimulate demand* quadrant likely have quite strong opinions about our products. They may also think they know more than they do about them, or they may take us for granted. If they have had a bad service or product encounter, they may harbor some ill-will. The key in this quadrant is to clearly understand what our customers already value about our product *and also what they might come to value* as we look for ways to provide more value to them or to motivate them to increase product or service use.

4. Finally, *retention/earn share* customers have experience with our products and those of our competitors. The question here is: Why are they using two brands? In some cases they may be variety-seeking; in others they may simply buy the brand that is more convenient or available at a lower price. An understanding of these beliefs will drive our strategy in this quadrant.

As we explore beliefs, we are interested in estimating (1) how many people are likely to share the particular belief and (2) how likely it is that we could change this belief. Again, we will call upon fact, logic, and assumption to generate our estimate. Of course, a key foundation is some kind of attitudinal research, either sponsored by our firm or available for purchase from a secondary source. In order to collect and use this data effectively and efficiently, we need to let our strategic focus drive our data collection and analysis. If we intend to focus on a retention/stimulate demand strategy, we will spend much of our resources collecting and assessing data about our current customers. In contrast, an acquisition/earn share strategy dictates that we will seek information about competitive users. Our strategy thus drives not only the questions we ask, but to whom we direct them. The alternative is to ask everybody everything and hope we can make some sense of the resulting dataset. While this approach is unfortunately quite common among marketers, it is very rarely effective.

Behaviors

The third element of our model is behaviors. Here, as with attitudes, we are interested in what our target customers are doing now and what we want them to do: their *current* and *desired* behaviors. These behaviors need to be very carefully articulated because we do not want someone to simply buy our product; we want them to try it, or switch brands, or increase frequency of use, or simply obtain more information about our product. What we *want* them to do is determined by *what they are doing now*. The more specific we can be in addressing behaviors, the more efficient our marketing planning and execution will be.

1. Customers in the *acquisition/stimulate demand* quadrant are *not* doing something: they are not buying products in the category. Our goal here is quite difficult,

therefore, because we have to move them from a state of inaction to a state of action. We should be conservative as we define the desired behaviors here. We wish customers would start buying our product regularly, but the first step is to simply get them to try it. The most common mistake marketers make in this quadrant is to be overly optimistic about how far we can move behaviors.

2. For *acquisition/earn share*, the good news is that customers are already buying in the category; the bad news is they are buying the product of another firm. It can sometimes be easier to attract new users to the category than to convince competitive users to switch, which is generally the behavioral objective in this quadrant. Users of competitive brands have expressed their preferences by their actions, and they may have developed strong loyalty to these brands. In the case of durable goods such as the Toyota Prius, described in the Customer Focus box, we may seek to convince consumers to consider (and choose) our brand instead of automatically seeking out the perceived category leader.

3. In the retention/stimulate-demand segment, we are interested in increasing purchase frequency or purchase volume, or in convincing customers to trade up to a higher-priced product. The current and desired behaviors in this quadrant are quite straightforward; we simply identify current and desired frequency, volume, or price paid.

4. Finally, for *retention/earn share* we are looking for *switching* or *substituting* behavior. For example, if consumers are currently choosing Budweiser beer 80% of the time and Miller only when they are looking for a change, we may set our desired behavior as choosing Miller in 35% of beer choice occasions.

CUSTOMERFOCUS

THE TOYOTA PRIUS: EARNING SHARE PRIOR TO PURCHASE

The Toyota Prius first went on sale in Japan in 1997 and was the world's first mass-produced hybrid vehicle. By May 2008, global cumulative sales had reached the milestone 1-million-vehicle mark. Today the Prius is sold in more than 70 countries and regions, with its largest markets in Japan and North America.

The Prius is the clear category leader in the U.S. hybrid car market; in 2007 Toyota sold 250,000, even though more than 10 different hybrid models were available at that time. If we were marketing the Ford Escape, for instance, and we wished to earn share from Prius, we might define the current behavior we wish to change as "driving a Prius." We would then face the nearly impossible task of getting customers to trade in their newly purchased Prius for our Escape. However, consumers engage in a number of behaviors *prior* to purchasing durable goods, and we may be able to earn share by focusing here.

A consumer who has been convinced (presumably by Toyota) to enter the hybrid car category will likely visit a Toyota

© Sjo/iStockphoto

dealer. If we can convince the consumer to also visit a Ford dealer and compare the two cars, we may succeed in earning share at the "research of comparison" stage of the purchase process. Hence, particularly for durable goods, the current and desired behaviors we seek to influence are not purchase behaviors, but rather *information-seeking behaviors*.

Sources: Toyota corporate site. http://www.toyota.co.jp/en/news/08/0515.html. Accessed April 12, 2013; http://www.autoblog.com/2010/10/08/worldwide-toyota-prius-sales-crack-2-million-mark-10-year-annive/. Accessed November 20, 2011.

As we consider these current and desired behaviors, we begin to identify the links between them and the current and desired beliefs we have already identified above. The ability to make this link between beliefs and behaviors is a key skill of the successful marketer. We can uncover the link by assessing key behaviors and then asking ourselves *why*. For example, in the acquisition/earn share quadrant we want to know *why* our target customer uses the competitor's product. Is the reason that it is cheaper than our offering? If this is the case, we may need to educate consumers regarding the specific value our product delivers.

On the other hand, if this customer uses our competitor because he or she believes it is more reliable, we may need to convince her that our product is as reliable and also delivers more features. In both these cases we want to generate the same behavior—switching from a competitive brand; however, our marketing plan will look entirely different depending on which link between belief and behavior we think is most important.

Bucks

The first three steps of the 4 Bs model are the hard part: assessing market size, identifying key beliefs and behaviors, and understanding the relationship between these beliefs and behaviors. Once we have accomplished this, the task of assessing potential revenue is simply a matter of doing the math: if x number of customers increase their purchase frequency by y at a price of z, we will see an $x \times y \times z$ incremental increase in revenues.

The key challenge in this part of the model is really the challenge of maintaining the integration between strategy and execution. Usually the task of measuring "bucks" is assigned to financial managers and not marketing managers. This measurement is a metric that stakeholders and managers use to assess the success of the firm. External and higher-level internal stakeholders may be interested in a variety of financial metrics that may or may not be linked to our marketing strategy. However, the best financial metrics are those with strategic foundations. This is why our primary "bucks" metric should vary from quadrant to quadrant, as illustrated previously in Figure 4.7. We will obviously not ignore metrics that are important to stakeholders; however, from a strategic marketing perspective, our focus should change depending on our strategic quadrant. Strategy should drive our choice of metrics, instead of metrics driving our strategy.

Unfortunately, the most common metric for measuring marketing success is almost always market share. *If we always measure and reward based on market share, we will likely always see marketing plans that emphasize acquisition/earn share tactics.* To avoid this outcome, we must instead identify a key financial metric that is tied to our marketing model and watch this metric carefully. This will enable us to track not only our financial success, but also the success of our specific strategy.

1. As stated above and illustrated in Figure 4.8, for *acquisition/stimulate demand* we are interested in whether we succeeded in incrementally growing the category, and whether we obtained our fair share of this category growth. We want to know whether the category grew *as a result of our marketing efforts*. For example, before Starbucks began actively marketing coffee in the late 1980s, the out-of-home coffee category was stagnant. Starbucks's aggressive

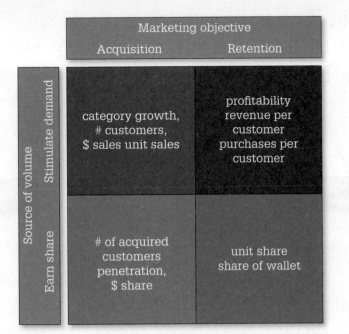

Figure 4.8 Key metrics by strategic quadrant.

marketing plan—including increasing the number of stores, training employees to provide a consistent level of service, offering high-quality coffee, and conducting an active in-store marketing campaign—led to an increase in total category sales for out-of-home coffee. Of course, Starbucks enjoyed the fruits of this labor, but other coffee chains such as Peets and Caribou Coffee also grew during this period. This category growth was clearly the result of marketing efforts.

2. For *acquisition/earn share* we are obviously interested in market share. Ideally, however, we will measure category penetration as well—what percent of total category customers are "ours?" This measure will give us a better feel for total users than total sales will.

3. In the *retention/stimulate* demand quadrant we look at financial metrics that reflect usage and/or willingness to pay. Average price paid and total purchases per customer are common metrics here.

4. If we are implementing a *retention/earn share* strategy, we are interested in our "share of wallet:" of customers' total spending in the category, what percent ended up with us?

In the end, financial metrics have an enormous impact on marketing strategy. Instead of letting the metrics determine the marketing strategy, we should develop what we consider to be the best marketing strategy, and then choose appropriate financial metrics based on that strategy. This approach will ensure that strategy and execution are integrated, which in turn will enable us to use our forecasting model not just to predict the future, but also to develop and tune our marketing strategy and execution.

INTEGRATION:
SOURCE OF VOLUME AND THE BIG PICTURE

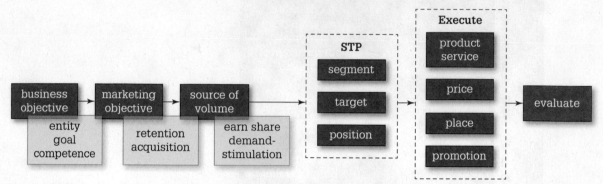

Figure 4.9 The Source of Volume and the Big Picture. The placement of the source of volume module within the Big Picture framework.

One of the great benefits of disciplined strategic thinking is that it affords us greater opportunities for learning. In the case of source of volume, we want to evaluate our results relative to our strategic goals, not just to our sales goals. This means we want to understand the source of our volume gains. If we have implemented an earn share strategy, we should see the bulk of our volume coming from our key competitor, and we should obtain feedback from consumers indicating they selected our brand because it dominated our competitor on the identified, dynamic benefit. If they selected our brand because our competitor was out of stock, we cannot attribute that sale to our strategy. Failure to mistake our good luck for good strategy will hurt us in the long run.

This is where the iterative structure of the Big Picture becomes so valuable. If we find that our current strategy is not the driving force behind our new customers' buying decisions, we can further investigate the true value those customers see in our product. Then we can use this information to refine and improve our Big Picture analysis, perhaps choosing a different go-to-market approach. By carefully analyzing our options and selecting the appropriate strategy, and using research where necessary to confirm our hypotheses, we can develop a clear, single-minded strategy.

☐ SUMMARY

1. Identify the source of volume in performing competitive analysis

Understanding our sources of volume requires an understanding of current and *potential* customers' relationship to the competition and the category. Are these consumers currently using our competitor's products, or are they not buying in the category at all? These two possibilities represent our *sources of volume*: we can generate increases in sales either by expanding the category, a strategy called *stimulating demand,* or by convincing current category users to switch from another competitor to our brand, called *earning share*. To determine which of these paths to follow, we must have a clear understanding of consumers' current behaviors in the category and in regard to our brand, as well as their attitudes.

2. Develop a benefit-based definition of the business category

We can define business categories in terms of features, products, and benefits. Benefit-based category definitions are superior because they most closely mirror the customer perspective. Adopting a definition of the category that mirrors the customers' will focus the marketer on innovation that the customer values. Benefit-based category definitions will also naturally prevent us from being caught off-guard as customers look for new technology-enabled ways to satisfy needs.

3. Define a stimulate demand strategy: Growing the category

To stimulate demand is to focus on expanding a category; this is the responsibility of the market leader. The reason for this is that the alternative to stimulating demand, earning share, is not attractive for the market leader, because this firm stands more to lose than gain by earning share. By earning share the market leader lends credence to its competition, and encourages retaliation. Additionally, over time the category will stop growing if the market leader focuses inwardly and incites features and price wars.

4. Define an earn share strategy: Growing at the expense of competitors or a market segment

A company that is clearly not the category leader may elect to implement an earn share strategy. Companies have two key questions to answer in implementing an earn share strategy. The first question is *from whom?* The company must identify the *specific* brand or segment from which it intends to earn share. It is not sufficient to simply say, "from everybody." Companies can earn share from another brand, or from a clearly defined segment. The key to earning share is that the firm leverages its marketing efforts to *invoke a specific comparison.*

5. Discuss the difference between earning share and stimulating demand

Determining our source of volume is in many cases a lesson in subtle but important distinctions. It is theoretically possible to define many marketing campaigns as either earn share or stimulate primary demand, if we consider only the numbers and not the positioning. A stimulate demand strategy promotes the benefits of the category overall and promotes customer benefits in absolute terms. An earn-share strategy *invokes a specific comparison to another brand or segment.* The success of an earn share strategy cannot be measured by looking at our market share alone, it must be measured by estimating how much of our market share growth has come from a competitive target.

6. Explain how to choose a strategic focus

A company seeking to stimulate demand will avoid competitive comparisons, and will instead focus its marketing investment on emphasizing the category benefit. To earn share from a competitor, a company will invoke a comparison, that is, it will benchmark its products and services, partner with similar distribution channels, and compare all other executional elements to appear incrementally better than its competitor. A foundational discipline of any successful marketer is a focus on the customer and analysis of the market from a customer perspective.

The marketer should understand where the company's volume comes from by analyzing the marketing opportunity in terms of the four strategic quadrants:

- **Acquisition/stimulate demand:** volume comes from customers who are new to the category and the brand.
- **Retention/stimulate demand:** volume comes from current customers loyal to the brand.
- **Acquisition/earn share demand:** volume comes from competitors' customers switching to our brand.
- **Retention/earn share demand:** volume comes from multi-brand users.

7. Use the 4 Bs as the Basis of Strategic Forecasting

The first step toward setting a brand's spending priorities is to assess the market potential for each strategic quadrant. This assessment is a forecast, and like any forecast, it represents an educated guess based on facts, assumption, and logic. Available facts include current sales trends in the category, demographic information (population, age, gender, and the like), behavioral trends, and attitudinal trends. We make assumptions about customer definitions, whether trends will continue, what factors might influence them, and so on. Finally, we use logic to help us decide what information to collect, how to analyze that information, and which assumptions we can safely make. We estimate future sales by making assumptions about all 4 Bs: bodies, beliefs, behaviors, and bucks.

8. Integrate the source of volume decision within the Big Picture framework

Carefully analyzing current sources of volume by strategic quadrant and potential sources of volume allows us to understand strategic options and select an appropriate strategy. As we do this, we will want to bring in market research where necessary to confirm our hypotheses and develop a fact-based, clear, single-minded strategy.

☐ KEY TERMS

4 Bs: Bodies, beliefs, behaviors, bucks. (p. 120) The foundation of any sound strategic marketing investment is thoughtful analysis of the target audience we are trying to reach (bodies), the beliefs we are trying to change (beliefs), the behavioral change we hope will result from the belief change (behaviors), and the financial impact of that behavioral change (bucks).

Benefit-based category definition. (p. 103) The business category (or market) is the field within which companies deploy their products and services and customers satisfy needs through the purchase of products and services. Traditionally, companies defined business categories by adding up their sales of particular types of products; today we do it by adding up the revenues of products that fill a particular customer need.

Comparative advertising. (p. 111) Refers to the practice of advertising products or services relative to other products sold by competitors rather than in absolute terms.

Consideration set. (p. 108) A list of companies or brands that are simultaneously considered by consumers seeking to make a purchase based on a need they have identified or a benefit

they are seeking to obtain. As consumers engage in research of a category, they may discover options that were not in their initial consideration set.

Cost of entry. (p. 112) The cost of entry into a category is the minimum acceptable product or service standard that a company must be able to deliver in order to be considered by consumers in that category as being part of their consideration set in that category.

Earn share strategy. (p. 109) A competitive strategy characterized by comparisons to a company or group of companies (market segment).

Features war. (p. 112) When both parties engaged in competition retaliate in succession, their competition is called a *features war* if they primarily compete by trying to improve on each other's product features, or a *price war* if they primarily compete on price.

Forward buying. (p. 108) The practice of purchasing retail inventory in quantities exceeding current demand, usually motivated by suppliers' offers of temporary discounts.

Household penetration. (p. 109) The percentage of a particular group who use a particular product, product type, or service. For example, the household penetration of smartphones in the United States in June 2013 was 56%.

Main benefit. (p. 112) The primary customer benefit emphasized by the market leader of a category. The main benefit becomes a "cost of entry" into the category because companies wishing to enter that market have to deliver the main benefit to an acceptable level in order to be considered part of the category.

Path to purchase. (p. 106) The stages that a customer goes through in identifying a need and eventually purchasing, using, and evaluating a product purchase.

Porter's 5 Forces. (p. 101) A framework advanced by Michael Porter that provides a systematic means of quickly assessing the competitive space by highlighting the primary external factors that drive company performance. The five forces are: supplier power, buyer power, threat of competitive entry, threat of substitute products, and threat from existing competitors.

Source of volume. (p. 111) A process by which we attribute customer purchases to groups of consumers in each of the strategic quadrants: retention/stimulate demand, retention/earn share, acquisition/stimulate demand, acquisition/earn share.

Stimulate-demand strategy. (p. 104) The market leader's strategy based on growing the category. This is done either by attracting non-users to the category (acquisition) or by motivating current customers of the brand to purchase more or to pay more (retention).

Strategic quadrants (p. 119). The strategic quadrants are a 2x2 that results from a combination of the marketing objective decisions (customer focus) and the source of volume choice (competitive focus). There are four strategic quadrants: acquisition/stimulate demand, retention/stimulate demand, acquisition/earn share, retention/earn share.

Viral marketing. (p. 107) A communications tactic intended to increase awareness using social media as opposed to traditional paid advertising. This awareness spreads like a virus as users come in contact with one another and "infect" their friends and associates with information about a product.

☐ REVIEW AND DISCUSSION QUESTIONS

1. Explain the difference between exogenous market growth and true demand stimulation. Provide some specific examples of each type by pointing to specific markets.

2. You are marketing Tivo, the digital recording device, manufactured by the Sony Corporation. Provide three alternative category definitions for your product. Which one would you choose and why?

3. Which of the following are examples of an acquisition/stimulate-demand strategy ?

   (a) BMW emphasizing the benefit of "performance" to increase sales.

   (b) Milk emphasizing "four glasses per day" to increase sales.

   (c) Orange juice emphasizing that a "breakfast without orange juice is like a day without sunshine" to increase sales.

   (d) (a) and (c) only.

   (e) (a), (b), and (c).

4. Thinking about the Google+ vs. Facebook "earn-share" example in the chapter, write a paragraph describing how either company might have avoided a feature war by focusing on stimulating demand rather than earning share.

5. Provide three examples of companies with low market share that elected to stimulate demand of a new category rather than compete in an existing category, so as to avoid a feature or price war.

☐ APPENDIX: MARKETING ANALYSIS AND PLANNING

Marketing Tool #1: Assessing the Sources of Volume

In the Source of Volume module we deepen our marketing analysis and planning work, moving beyond company business objective decisions and customer focus to consider the impact of the business category and the competitive landscape. In this module we (1) assess our current sources of volume, and (2) select a strategic focus for our brand, based on our current sources of volume and our overall strategic stance and resourcing.

We take an existing company as our example and first review how to calculate current sources of volume. Then we discuss the implications of the current sources of volume and category definition on the choice of a strategic quadrant for purposes of marketing planning. Initially, because we are just assessing what has happened in the past, our sources of volume estimates might leave out "beliefs" if the company we are analyzing has not emphasized a specific positioning statement as part of its customer strategy.

Table 4A.1 Calculating Current Sources of Volume

3 Bs Example for Simple Bank: Current Sources of Volume

Marketing Objective	Source of Volume	Category	Primary Competitors	Bodies	Behaviors (Last Period)			Bucks	
					% Converted / % Retention Rate	Unit Mkt Share (Only for Acq / Stim)	Behaviors (Purchases/ Year)	Price (Last Year)	
Acquisition	Stimulate Demand	Simple banking		20,000	10.0%	5.0%	1	$ 760	$ 76,000
Retention	Stimulate Demand	Simple banking		5,000	96.0%		2	$1,500	$14,400,000
Acquisition	Earn Share	Traditional banking	Large Bank Co	95,000	0.5%		2	$1,450	$ 1,377,500
Retention	Earn Share	Traditional banking	Large Bank Co	500	90.0%		1	$ 500	$ 225,000
Total									16,078,500

Table 4A.1 shows the calculation of current sources of volume for Simple Bank, a small bank that is trying to position itself on simplicity within the larger banking category. In estimating the sources of volume, we are evaluating how well our strategy is currently driving our customer acquisition and retention, and how that activity is generating top-line revenue for the company.

Simple Bank operates in a small market with just 100,000 customers. Of those, a large financial institution, Large Bank Co., has 95,000. Simple Bank has approximately 5,000 customers who on average purchase two products each with average revenue per product of $1,500. Simple is quite successful at keeping those customers, with a retention rate of 96%. Its customers represent 5% of the total market, and 500 of them are multi-brand users whom Simple shares with other banks.

Of 20,000 potential new customers in the banking category last year (mostly young people with enough financial assets to buy some banking products), 2,000 entered the category and Simple Bank captured just its fair share, or 5%. New customers purchased one banking product each, generating an average revenue of $760.

Simple Bank also had some competitive conversions last year; it was able to take 0.5% of customers from the competition, mostly from Large Bank. Simple's multi-brand customers spend $500 on average with the bank every year; their retention rate is 90%.

In the bucks column, we can see that the primary source of revenue is retention/stimulate demand. The bank is currently not getting a significant amount of its sales from new customers to the category or from competitive conversions. By adding the bucks cells, we can see that the bank is currently generating $16 million in revenue.

Marketing Tool #2: Selecting a Strategic Focus

The Strategic Focus decision must be informed by the company's recent sales history, and its current sources of volume. However, here is where the marketing team considers how the future might be different from the present based on purposeful planning and execution.

Our overall objective is to select the Strategic Focus quadrant that offers the largest and most sustainable growth opportunity based on how we are doing today, given current sources of volume, and the on degree of our competitive opportunity. By sustainable, we mean an opportunity that can be repeated because it fits well with our core competence and customer definition, fits the market opportunity, and also integrates with the rest of our strategy.

Because the choice of Strategic Focus has very significant executional implications, we must be ready to revise our estimates as we progress through the framework and change some of the fundamental assumptions that drive them. For example, the way we choose to segment our markets, whom we target, and the types and amounts of resources we allocate to reaching our targets will naturally affect our bodies, beliefs, behaviors, and bucks estimates. At this stage, we will select a strategic quadrant by choosing the customer group we feel will help us generate the greatest return on our marketing investment. In this way, the 4 Bs exercise is helpful in forcing a great deal of focus in our organization.

Just as our choice of Marketing Objective (retention or acquisition) is highly dependent on the way we define our customer, so our choice of Strategic Focus quadrant is highly dependent on the way we define our business category.

The steps we take in completing the Incremental Opportunity Assessment are:

1. **Estimate the number of target bodies:**
   (a) **Acquisition/stimulate demand.** Define the category and calculate the number of customers (bodies) in the category and the number of potential customers outside the category (non-users). Non-users are potential customers who fit the demographic profile of customers in the category but who have some objection to purchasing from the category.
   (b) **Retention/stimulate demand.** These are our current customers who fit our customer definition. We will target them to increase their number of purchases (volume) or to convince them to increase the value of what they purchase (value) with our firm.
   (c) **Acquisition /earn share.** These are the customers of the competitor we would target, generally the category leader.
   (d) **Retention/earn share.** These are our multi-brand customers, and we would target them to increase their purchases with us at the expense of our competitors.

2. **Estimate beliefs and belief conversions.** Think of the primary belief each group of bodies holds and how it would need to change in order for those customers to be willing to change their behavior. Write down the "before" and "after" beliefs and the estimated conversion probability.

3. **Estimate behavior and behavior conversions.** Write down the behavior we expect from each group and estimate the percentage of customers or potential customers who will engage in that behavior. Notice that we are interested in incremental changes in behaviors, so for the retention quadrants we have excluded retention rates from this analysis; instead, we focus on the number of new purchases by existing customers, and the incremental value from each purchase. For acquisition/ earn share we estimate the maximum number of competitive customers (from a specific company or market segment) we would be able to convert to our brand.

4. Finally, we multiply the number of units we have calculated by the price per unit. In the case of retention/stimulate demand value, price will be the incremental price paid for the upgraded product or service.

☐ EXAMPLE

Table 4A.2 shows the completed 4 Bs example for Simple Bank.

Note that in working through the opportunity estimate by quadrant, we are making a series of assumptions about how many current and potential customers we can reach, what they believe, and what they will do as a result. Here, for instance, we have completed the analysis for a bank that is positioning itself on the benefit of simplicity. We have assumed we have been able to successfully redefine the banking category from traditional to simple. We cannot always assume a company will be able to redefine a business category, but this is how innovative companies like Starbucks and Zipcar generally succeed.

As we redefine the category in the banking example, the non-users now include customers from the current category (50,000 of the 100,000 in the Traditional category become non-users). Also note that the "before" values largely correspond to the behaviors we had already calculated in the current sources of volume estimates (Table 4A.1). Finally, the Retention/Stimulate Demand quadrants now both show the same number of bodies, current customers, who could bring additional revenue by increasing the number of products they purchase (volume) or paying more for better service (value). The conversion rates represent the percentage of customers who, we estimate, will engage in the purchase behavior we will encourage through our marketing efforts. Note that the "bodies" in the acquisition/earn share quadrant are the customers of a specific company or segment, in this case Large Bank, whom we will target with our strategy.

The purpose of conducting this exercise is to select a strategic quadrant. We can assume we have a fixed amount of investment or budget, and we will estimate conversion probabilities by keeping the cost of conversion fixed across all quadrants as a way to select the most efficient strategic choice. In this case, it seems that retention/stimulate demand is the best strategic focus, particularly if we can execute our volume and value strategies concurrently. Ideally, we will collect some market research data to estimate conversion probabilities.

Even in the absence of pilot data or data about customers' behavioral intentions, this type of exercise can be very helpful because it forces us to think about the customer perspective. In particular, in calculating potential sources of volume, we integrate our inside perspective

Table 4A.2 The 4 Bs: Calculating Incremental Opportunity: Bodies and Beliefs

Marketing Objective	Source of Volume	Category	Main Competitors	Bodies	Beliefs		
					Before	% Converted	After
Acquisition (1)	Stimulate Demand	Simple banking	Small Tech Bank	50,000	Banking is a necessary evil ⟶	20.0%	There is a simpler way to bank
Retention (2)	Stimulate Demand/ Volume	Simple banking	Small Tech Bank	5,000	Simple Bank offers a simplified banking experience ⟶	80.0%	I can use simplicity in my loans too
Retention (2)	Stimulate Demand/ Value	Simple banking	Small Tech Bank	5,000	Simple Bank offers a simplified banking experience ⟶	75.0%	I can make my life simpler by upgrading my banking services
Acquisition (3)	Earn Share	Traditional banking	Large Bank Co	25,000	I choose my bank based on convenience ⟶	40.0%	Simplicity is more important than convenience
Retention (4)	Earn Share	Traditional banking	Large Bank Co	500	Working with several banks is most secure	45.0%	Simplicity is the most important aspect of banking

Table 4A.2 (continued) The 4 Bs: Calculating Incremental Opportunity (Behaviors and Bucks)

	Behaviors					Bucks		
Before							Key Strategic Metrics	(Incremental)
before behavior	purchases/ year	% acquisition/ % Converted	Mkt share (fair share)	incremental purchases/ year	after behavior	Incremental Price / purchase		year 1
"I don't purchase"	0	50.0%	5.0%	1	"I will try it"	$ 760	$ sales, # customers, category growth	$ 190,000
I have a checking and savings account with Simple Bank	2	30.0%		1	I will add a loan product	$1,500	CLV, accounts/ client, $/client	$1,800,000
I have a checking and savings account with Simple Bank	2	20.0%		1	I will become a Private Banking Client	$2,000	CLV, accounts/ client, $/client	$1,500,000
I have all my accounts at Large Bank	0	5.0%		2	I will move some of my accounts to Simple Bank	$1,500	Unit Share	$1,500,000
I have a checking acct with Simple Bank and everything else at Large Bank Co	1	65.0%		1	I will switch some more of my banking to Simple Bank	$1,000	Wallet or Revenue Share	$ 146,250

on capabilities and brand positioning with our external perspective regarding the changes in beliefs and behaviors we need to effect in our customers.

☐ RESOURCES

Coyne, Kevin and Somu Subramaniam. "Bringing discipline to strategy," *The McKinsey Quarterly* 4, (1996): 14–25.

Dolan, Robert. "Basic quantitative analysis for marketing," Harvard Business School Publishing, Boston, 1984 (rev. 1986), 1–8.

French, Tom, Laura La Berge, and Paul Magill. "We're all marketers now." *The McKinsey Quarterly* 25, (2011): 26–34.

Porter, M. E. "On competition." Harvard Business School Publishing, Boston, 1988.

Porter, Michael E. *Competitive advantage of nations: Creating and sustaining superior performance.* New York: Free Press, 2011.

Tellis, Gerard, and Peter Golder. "First to market, first to fail? Real causes of enduring market leadership." *MIT Sloan Management Review* 37.2 (1996): 65–75.

chapter five

> "Understand the Differences;
> act on the commonalities."
>
> **—Andrew Masondo, African
> National Congress**

SEGMENTATION

After studying this chapter you should be able to:

1. *Describe the role segmentation plays in marketing strategy*

2. *Describe the types of segmentation variables and how to use them*

3. *Compare the concepts of Main and Dynamic Benefit*

4. *Explain the key criteria in segmenting a market*

5. *Select the main and dynamic benefit*

6. *Describe the steps in the segmentation process*

7. *Integrate segmentation with other elements of the Big Picture*

I n 2006 Best Buy, the largest U.S. electronics retailer, announced a sweeping customer-centricity project designed to improve the growth and efficiency of its business. At the time, Best Buy accounted for close to 20% of the consumer electronics retail market in the United States and Canada. The firm was also the darling of equity analysts, having delivered steady earnings per share growth, with returns superior to those of Microsoft and Intel throughout the 1990s.

Since becoming CEO in June 2002, Brad Anderson had made bold moves to continue the growth trajectory of the 1990s. These moves included Best Buy's effort to shift its emphasis from customer acquisition through new store openings to customer retention by adding services and carefully examining the product mix and the stores' customer focus. In October 2002 the company bought a small company called Geek Squad, which hired and trained technical advisors. Best Buy expanded the Geek Squad concept and by 2007 had close to 20,000 "Geeks" throughout its stores to serve its small-business customers who needed help setting up small network environments in their homes and offices. The purchase of Geek Squad and its foray into services was part of a larger transformation in Best Buy's business model.

Best Buy implemented the customer-centricity project deeply, sifting through its data to figure out which customers made the most money ("Angels") and which were unprofitable ("Demons").[1] The company then sought to realign its stores to better serve Angels and marginalize Demons by implementing restocking fees on product returns and a series of other initiatives. The company went further to cater to Angels by segmenting them into five archetypical core groups: Barry, Jill, Buzz, Ray, and Mr. Storefront. Barry is an affluent tech enthusiast; Jill, a busy suburban mom; Buzz, a young gadget fiend; Ray, a price-conscious family guy; and Mr. Storefront a small-business owner. Other segments interest Best Buy too, like young single women (Carrie) and empty-nesters (Helen and Charlie), but the company placed primary focus on the core five.

Tim Boyle/Getty Images

In implementing the segmentation project, Best Buy made sweeping changes in its stores to better align the store environment, product assortment, and service levels and type to targeting a particular segment. Nearly 40% of the 300 stores in 2007 were redone to aim at Barry—these stores were reorganized to include home-theater systems, expert salespeople, and specialists in mobile electronics. Jill stores featured personal shopping assistants (PSAs) and included brighter colors and more attention to the store ambiance. Buzz stores had broad assortments of video games. Some stores targeted more than one segment—Jill and Barry departments often share a location—and a handful of Best Buys, like the one in the Dallas suburb of Frisco, targeted all five.

Centrizing a store is a big investment—a typical Barry department alone requires as much as $600,000 for lighting and fixtures. And specialized salespeople, such as home-theater experts, get additional training that may last weeks. The question is: Did Best-Buy's investment pay off?

Answering that question is made difficult by the confounding effects of market conditions. Since the implementation of the program Best Buy has had to contend with a very difficult economic climate, including the world-

---

[1]http://bits.blogs.nytimes.com/2009/09/21/netflix-awards-1-million-prize-and-starts-a-new-contest/?_r=0 accessed 8/17/2013.

wide recession that began in 2008. The firm has also faced increased competition from big-box retailers Walmart and Costco, which have come in to fill the void left by traditional Best Buy competitors that failed, like Circuit City. In the 2006–2011 period, Best Buy's stock lost 41% of its value, while Costco's gained 50% and Walmart's 15.76%; over the same span the S&P stock index (a leading market indicator) advanced only 3.89%.

Segmentation is a process by which we seek to identify specific groups of customers who, we hypothesize, will be most receptive to our marketing messages. A key reason to undertake segmentation is to improve the efficiency of our marketing operations. In developing and implementing a segmentation initiative we must not let go of the strategic decisions made to this point in the Big Picture, particularly about our fundamental entity and core competence. If catering to multiple segments requires multiple core competencies, we might find it difficult to preserve the efficiency of our marketing efforts as we target and serve segments with divergent needs.

Sources: McWilliams, Gary, "Analyzing customers, Best Buy realizes not all are welcome." *The Wall Street Journal* 8, November 2004.

Boyle, Matthew, "Best Buy's giant gamble." *Fortune Magazine*. March 29, 2006. http://money.cnn.com/magazines/fortune/fortune_archive/2006/04/03/8373034/. Accessed March 12, 2012.

"Google Finance five-year price comparison of Walmart, Costco, and Best Buy." https://www.google.com/finance?q=wmt&ei=yFBtUdC OKsW3qgH8vwE. Accessed April 16,2013.

SEGMENTATION: FROM STRATEGY TO EXECUTION

The first three elements of the Big Picture framework that we've introduced deal with strategic questions regarding our firm, our competition, and our market potential. The final four elements are executional in nature, concerned with pricing, communications, product, and distribution decisions. The crucial link between these strategic and executional elements is the process of segmentation, targeting, and positioning. It is here that we take our strategic work and translate it into marketing activities that directly influence consumers. The process of segmentation requires us to develop a deeper understanding of consumer attitudes, behaviors, and characteristics. If we develop a strategic research strategy, this work will produce a focused, efficient segmentation and execution. Our overarching goal for segmentation, therefore, is to build our execution on the strategic foundations we have already developed.

This chapter formally discusses **segmentation,** the process of identifying a group of customers who share at least one characteristic that will make them more responsive to our marketing message. Notice that we have already engaged in the segmentation process earlier in the framework. In our discussion of Marketing Objective/ Customer Focus, we segmented the market into new and existing customers. We continued this process with our competitive analysis, dividing the market into competitive users and non-users. Finally, in our 4 B's analysis, we also laid the foundation for *attitudinal* segmentation by starting to link attitudes with behaviors. That early work is the groundwork for the segmentation we will discuss here.

Segmentation. The process of identifying a group of customers who share at least one characteristic that will make them more responsive to our marketing message.

Proper segmentation can mean the difference between success and failure. Consider MySpace, initially the dominant name in social networking. Its lack of segmentation eventually allowed its popularity to fall. The MySpace network was inhabited by kids, adults, artists, musicians, companies, and other users who all were able to customize the look of their profiles, providing great personalization, but resulting in a lack of coherence on the site. By contrast, Facebook was started in a university setting and first built an audience among college students. Next it moved to high schools, building on the interest younger people have in belonging to a college club.

Facebook successfully overtakes MySpace thanks to effective segmentation.

Facebook opened its doors to adults only after high school and college users were in place.

Consider the example of a commercial airline. If the firm has chosen to implement an acquisition/earn share strategy and has identified the category as business travel, its marketers already know the target audience consists of users of a competitive brand (behavioral) who are employed full time (demographic) and who travel for business (behavioral). Because they have narrowed the target audience with these definitions, they are already engaged in the initial process of segmentation. Demographic and behavioral segmentation are just the beginning, however; in this chapter we will deepen our analysis by further examining attitudinal segmentation variables. This additional segmentation will allow us to add value to our strategic choices, and to come to a specific description of our target customer.

The process of segmentation, targeting, and positioning is commonly referred to as STP, a familiar acronym that reflects the tight interrelationship between the steps in this process. While their interrelationships are key, we want to avoid blurring the steps. Segmentation, targeting, and positioning are distinct, sequential activities; each is dependent on the preceding one, and each adds incremental value to our market knowledge. As is true throughout the Big Picture framework, a bad choice in initial stages will likely lead to less than optimal choices in subsequent stages. Very often what appears to be a poor targeting or positioning strategy is actually a symptom of an earlier incorrect choice, possibly of our marketing objective or segmentation variables. Thus, as we focus on the segmentation decision throughout this chapter, we should think ahead, considering how each segmentation choice might be manifested in customer targeting and the positioning of our offering. Likewise, as we progress into the targeting and positioning phases of the Big Picture framework, we may wish to revisit our segmentation choices and update or revise as appropriate.

Our end goal for the STP process in any market is for our consumers, upon hearing our brand, to play back *one word: for example,* McDonald's: convenience. Wal-Mart: low price. BMW: performance. This goal represents not naïve simplicity, but rather *profound* simplicity that comes from a distillation of our work into a focused strategy. That simplicity is necessary if our message is going to break through the cluttered environment our consumers face and gain a foothold in their consciousness. Unlike us, our consumers are not thinking about our brands night and day. They do not work to remember our value proposition. It is our task to get them to remember it.

Why Segment a Market?

In most cases the best market is the biggest market, the one with the most potential customers. By definition, however, segmentation shrinks our potential audience, so the decision to do it should not be made without careful consideration if we segment effectively, then even as the size of our target population decreases, our probability of converting the members of this smaller population should increase. Thus, there is a trade-off between population size and the conversion rate of this population, based on the effectiveness of the marketing message. The segmentation process will enable us to strike the optimal balance between market size and market specificity, that is, to find the combination of the two that gives us the greatest return on our marketing investment.

As we go through the process of segmentation and then targeting, we will naturally enhance our understanding of customer needs and the links between these needs (addressed in Chapter 6) as well as our sense of the core competencies of the firm. The processes of segmentation and targeting include developing hypotheses about the fit between customer needs and company core competencies and conducting research to test these hypotheses. Letting strategy drive our research plan will give us the best return on our market research dollar. By utilizing the Big Picture framework and our own good sense, we can generate a goal-based plan based on sound strategic analysis that can substantially improve our understanding and confidence about our STP choices.

SEGMENTATION VARIABLES

In undertaking the process of segmentation, marketers generally consider four basic types of segmentation variables: demographic, behavioral, attitudinal, and aspirational. In selecting the variables that we will use to segment our market, we must trade off the ease with which we can collect information about a type of variable and the competitive advantage that variable affords (see Fig. 5.1). For example, information about a demographic variable, such as age, is relatively easy to obtain; however, if we experience success using this variable, it is highly probable that our competitors will be able to quickly and easily recognize and imitate our strategy. Thus, the more insightful we make our segmentation approach, the more defensible it will be.

Specifically, we are seeking to identify variables that will allow us to (1) continue to improve our understanding of and relationship with our customer base, and (2) continue to improve the accuracy of our predictions regarding likely responses to our marketing efforts. The discussion below outlines the four basic types of segmentation variables and their potential for helping us achieve our segmentation and marketing goals.

Demographic Variables

Demographic variables are those we can physically observe and measure. They include personal characteristics like age, gender, educational status, household size, income, marital status, and a few others. Also included here is geographic information like country of origin and population density of hometown.

Sometimes, the customized approach a company takes to customers of a particular geographic region is singled out as geographic segmentation. For example, global companies like McDonalds, Coke, Hilton, P&G, and others will adapt their offerings to fit the tastes, customs, weather patterns, income levels or other characteristics of

Demographic variables. Those variables that we can physically observe and measure such as age, gender, educational status, household size, income, marital status, and geographic information like country of origin, population income, and population density.

Figure 5.1 Relationship between type of segmentation variable and reliability and competitive advantage.

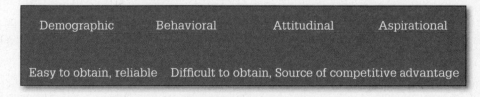

| Demographic | Behavioral | Attitudinal | Aspirational |

Easy to obtain, reliable   Difficult to obtain, Source of competitive advantage

a particular population given their geographic location. McDonald's varies its menus in different countries adapting them to local tastes; it serves vegemite in Australia, carries shrimp hamburgers in Japan (EBI Fillet-o), and serves porridge at breakfast time in Malaysia and Singapore. Especially for consumer products, it might make sense for companies to group its markets into geographic regions if potential consumers in those regions have specific requirements or expectations requiring different company skills to adapt the product offering and marketing messaging.

Demographic variables can be continuous or categorical. An example of a continuous variable is age: you can plot the age of your population along a vector ranging from 0 to 100 years, and you know that age 80 is older than age 20. An example of a categorical variable is gender: your population can be divided into one of two categories, male and female. Neither category represents a quantity, simply a characteristic. As we will see later in the chapter, most attitudinal and aspirational variables can be represented as continuous variables; some behavioral and demographic variables can be expressed only categorically.

Historically, demographic variables have served as default segmentation variables for several reasons. First, demographic information is readily available, quite often in the public sector. Second, because they are physical variables, demographics are quite reliable. This means we can use them to predict the future; if the segment of 50- to 60-year-olds is quite large this year, it is reasonable to predict that the segment of 60- to 70-year-olds will become larger over the next 10 years. Finally, these variables are also high in validity; it is relatively easy to verify their accuracy compared to that of other types of variables.

social**media**

Social Media and the End of Demographic Segmentation Based on Gender

Media and advertising companies have used basic demographic information, such as age and gender, to categorize viewers and target them with programming. However, media researcher Johanna Blakley has found that consumers in online "taste communities" do not cluster around traditional demographics. Taste communities, groups of people who watch the same shows and like the same things, are incredibly diverse in their gender and age.

Dr. Blakley hopes the study of social media trends will help remove stereotypes that advertisers and media companies have used ineffectively for years. Instead, as social media starts outweighing traditional media, companies can start using tastes and preferences to develop more subtle and appropriate programming that meets audience preferences, rather than relying on crude characterizations that ultimately please no one and perpetuate stereotypes.

Michael Loccisano/ Getty Images

Sources: Blakley, Johanna. "Social media and the end of gender," *TED.com*, February 2, 2011. http://www.ted.com/talks/johanna_blakley_social_media_and_the_end_of_gender.html. Accessed April 12, 2012; Blakley, Johanna. "Media in our image," *Blogpost*, June 18, 2011. http://johannablakley.wordpress.com/2012/06/18/media-in-our-image/. Accessed April 12, 2012.

All these factors make using demographic variables to segment a market quite appealing. In fact, most first attempts at market segmentation are based on demographics. Demographic information is quite useful for initial market sizing, but it is not sufficient for truly strategic segmentation for several reasons. First, while we can *react* to demographic information, we cannot *influence* demographics with marketing tools. Thus, relying exclusively on demographics reduces our strategic power. Second, excessive reliance on demographics can sometimes unnecessarily limit the size of our potential target audience. For example, when war-themed online role-playing video games such as World of Warcraft were first introduced, many marketers assumed most players would be male; however, as the gaming industry matured it became clear that both men and women were equally likely to play these games. Segmenting by demographics can thus lead to **stereotyping**, a practice that could be damaging to the brand franchise in the long run. Finally, segmentation strategies based solely on demographics are easy for competitors to duplicate. For example, Pepsico introduced Pepsi Max, a diet cola aimed at men, into U.S. markets in 2007. In response, Coca Cola modified the packaging of Coke Zero, changing it from white to black, observing that black was more appealing to men. Coke Zero quickly overtook Pepsi Max in the United States, capitalizing on its popularity among male drinkers. In summary, reliance solely on demographics will not provide us a sustainable competitive advantage. In order to achieve this, we must consider behavioral and attitudinal segmentation variables as well.

Behavioral Variables

Behavioral segmentation variables describe the specific actions of consumers or potential consumers. Behavioral segmentation generally starts with analysis of product and category usage; for example, it is very common for companies to segment markets into heavy and light users and then target a subset of these users. In addition, other behaviors may also prove useful for segmentation. For example, by segmenting the commuter population according to usage occasion, a newspaper publisher might find that drivers and train riders have significantly different needs and desires for their newspapers; this segmentation could help the publisher improve its layout and distribution scheme, and possibly even the type of coverage it provides.

Further, we can apply information about behavior in one category to help predict attitudes and behaviors about another category: a person who purchases alternative music may be more likely to adopt a new high-tech device; a procurement manager who selects a company car based on safety features may prefer to purchase computers from a supplier that provides strong warranties and after-sale service. Often we can leverage available behavioral data from existing, mature product and service categories to predict future behavior in emerging categories.

While we most often seek to link behaviors to attitudes, sometimes we can use frequent past behavior to predict future preferences without considering attitude. This ability is the basis for Amazon and Netflix's algorithms for making purchase recommendations to existing customers. In essence, when a customer purchases a particular book, Amazon does not need to ask that customer *why* in order to make other recommendations; the program simply searches for other users who have purchased that book, looks at the other purchases this customer made, and recommends items to the current buyer. Of course, the algorithm is substantially more complex than this,

Mary Ann Price/JohnWiley & Sons

Pepsi Max and Coke Zero are diet Colas primarily aimed at men. Coke Zero was highly successful with both men and women who wanted a taste closer to the original Coca-Cola product.

Stereotyping. The practice of considering any individual in a segment or population as a representative of the population as a whole by emphasizing physical or demographic variables to draw unrealistic and potentially offensive conclusions regarding attitudes and behaviors.

Behavioral segmentation variables. Variables that describe the specific actions of consumers or potential consumers.

socialmedia

Netflix's Use of Behavioral Data and the Power of Crowd Sourcing

Netflix, a subscription-based movie rental and streaming company, launched its first algorithm challenge at the end of 2006. For a $1 million prize, it invited the public to come up with recommendation software that could do a better job of predicting the movies Netflix's customers would like than its existing in-house software, Cinematch. To qualify for the prize, entries had to be at least 10% better than Cinematch.

The winner was a seven-person team of statisticians, machine-learning experts, and computer engineers from the United States, Austria, Canada, and Israel that called itself BellKor's Pragmatic Chaos. The group—a merger of teams—was the longtime front-runner in the contest, and in late June 2007 it finally passed the 10% barrier. Under the rules of the contest, that set off a 30-day period in which other teams could try to beat those results.

The final stage in the competition prompted a wave of mergers among competing teams, who joined forces at the last minute to try to top the leader. In late July 2007 Netflix declared the contest over and said two teams had passed the 10% threshold, BellKor and the Ensemble, a global alliance with some 30 members. The BellKor team had presented its final submission 20 minutes before the final deadline. Then, just before time ran out, the Ensemble team had made its last entry. The two were a dead tie mathematically, but under contest rules, in case of a tie,

The winning team in the Netflix crowd sourcing project was BellKor's Pragmatic Chaosteam, which beat Netflix's own algorithm for predicting ratings by 10% and won $1 million in the process.

Paul Sakuma/AP Images

the first team past the post wins. "That 20 minutes was worth $1 million," said Reed Hastings, Netflix CEO.[1]

The data set for the contest was 100 million movie ratings with personal identifying information stripped off. Contestants worked with the data to try to predict what movies particular customers would prefer, and their predictions were compared with how the customers actually did rate those movies later on a scale of one to five stars. Encouraged by the success of the first contest, Netflix launched a second challenge in August 2009. Although the data sets were changed to preserve customer privacy, two researchers from the University of Texas were able to identify individual users by matching the data sets with film ratings on the Internet Movie Database. By March 2010 Netflix had cancelled the contest due to a lawsuit and Federal Trade Commission privacy concerns.

The Netflix contest was widely followed because its lessons could extend well beyond improving movie picks. The way teams came together, especially late in the contest, and the improved results that were achieved suggest that this kind of Internet-enabled approach, called *crowd sourcing, can be successfully applied to complex scientific and business challenges*. However, in mining large data sets for segmentation and targeting, we are reminded of the delicate balance between marketing efficiency and respect for customers' privacy.

Sources: http://www.wired.com/science/discoveries/news/2007/03/72963. "Rise of the Netflix Hackers," Dave Demerjian; http://www.wired.com/threatlevel/2009/12/netflix-privacy-lawsuit/. "Netflix Spilled Your Brokeback Mountain Secret, Lawsuit Claims," Ryan Singel; http://bits.blogs.nytimes.com/2009/09/21/netflix-awards-1-million-prize-and-starts-a-new-contest/. "Netflix Awards $1 Million Prize and Starts a New Contest," Steve Lohr.

[1]http://bits.blogs.nytimes.com/2009/09/21/netflix-awards-1-million-prize-and-starts-a-new-contest/?_r=0 accessed 8/17/2013 .

but the key to its success is the fact that it leverages the substantial behavioral database Amazon owns.

How do behavioral segmentation variables stack up against their demographic counterparts? Behavioral information is a bit more difficult to collect than demographic information. Technological advances have significantly decreased its cost and

NEW PRODUCTS/INNOVATION

LEVERAGING TECHNOLOGY TO UNDERSTAND CONSUMER BEHAVIOR

Radio-Frequency Identification (RFID) technology is a tracking technology originally developed for tracking large pieces of expensive equipment. Soon, however, use of RFID expanded to the retail sector, led by discount giant Walmart. RFID tags were considered state-of-the-art tools for tracking inventory and ensuring that products were in stock.

In 2010, however, Walmart made another industry-leading move, rolling out new "smart tags" for use on garments. These tags are easier to scan and can collect data in a large space, making inventory control even more efficient. This next-generation technology has even more wide-reaching implications, however, because it can't be turned off. Theoretically, marketers might be able to "drive by consumers' homes and scan their garbage to discover what they have recently bought."

RFID radio technology is also being used in some personal ID cards, including enhanced driver's licenses in certain states. Could this personal data somehow be combined with the information from products to create a complete picture of what a specific consumer has purchased, all without his or her knowledge?

While privacy issues loom large, the prospect of being able to quickly and efficiently understand what consumers have purchased is a powerful one for marketers. Access to this information will likely increase their ability to use behavioral information for segmentation purposes. ■

Sources: Want, R. "An introduction to RFID technology," *Pervasive Computing, IEEE*, January–March, 2006, 25–33; Bustillo, Miguel. "Wal-Mart radio tags to track clothing," *The Wall Street Journal*, July 23, 2010.

---

increased its reliability, but behavioral data is still generally more expensive to obtain than demographic data. Collecting it requires either customized research or expensive secondary sources such as Nielsen (http://www.nielsen.com/us/en.html). The good news is that this type of information may give us a better chance of creating a sustainable competitive advantage that is not easily duplicated by competitors. The skills we develop in identifying and leveraging behavioral data to target lucrative customer segments are therefore a potential core competence.

While data is not a panacea, behavioral data is increasingly available and holds great potential for behavioral segmentation. However, the amount of truly useful information generated as a percentage of total data collected can actually be quite low if companies are not using these data strategically. Thus in exploring behavioral data, we want to avoid becoming enamored of these technologies and the mountains of data they generate. Instead, we should evaluate possible data sources based on the quality (not the quantity) of *actionable information* they provide in helping to answer specific research questions.

Attitudinal Variables

Attitudinal variables describe the thoughts, feelings, and beliefs of consumers. Marketers have implicitly used attitudinal segmentation strategies for years by appealing to consumers' needs for safety, self-esteem, or to be "hip" or "cool." The use of attitudinal variables for segmentation purposes is based on a crucial assumption that attitudes drive behaviors. This may seem obvious: a person who reports disliking the taste of beer is not likely to purchase beer. In some cases, however, reported attitudes are really more like wishes. For example, in the 1980s a growing percentage of U.S. adults agreed with the statement, "I believe it is important to eat right and exercise." At the same time, per-capita consumption of salty snacks and dessert items in the United States grew dramatically, even among those groups claiming an

Attitudinal variables.
Variables that describe the thoughts, feelings, and beliefs of consumers. Marketers have implicitly used attitudinal segmentation strategies for years by appealing to consumers' needs for safety or self-esteem or desire to be "hip" or "cool."

interest in healthy lifestyles. Obviously, certain attitudes are *related* to behaviors; a key challenge for a marketer to determine the strength and nature of the relationship between attitudes and behaviors. In order to accomplish this, we must gain access to these beliefs and attitudes. While a variety of research tools are available to help us accomplish this task, such as surveys, focus groups, and observational techniques, it is nonetheless a quite difficult task. Unlike demographic data, collected attitudinal data often fails to meet researchers' standards of *reliability* and *validity*.

Attitudinal data can be *invalid* for a variety of reasons. Consumers may be tempted to lie about their own attitudes, especially if they believe their true feelings may be embarrassing in some way. For example, people commonly overstate how much money they would be willing to give to charity. In other cases they may not really know their true feelings about a certain issue, perhaps because they have not thought about it deeply. In either of these cases, the attitudinal information we collect may not be valid.

Attitudinal data can be *unreliable* because attitudes are inherently dynamic. Feelings and beliefs can change; in many cases we, as marketers, are the ones who bring about this change. While we can reliably predict that a consumer who is 29 years old this year will be 30 years old next year, we cannot predict that a consumer who believes eating fiber is the best way to lose weight this year will continue to believe this next year, or even next month. Observers of focus groups regularly note how one person can influence or even reverse the opinion of other group members, regardless of how strongly held that opinion was at the outset.

All this seems to make the prospect of segmenting on attitudinal variables quite dim. But the bad news can also be the good news: however difficult attitude-behavior relationships are for us to uncover, they are difficult for our competitors to find. Therefore, to the extent that we are able to develop skills or insights in the area of attitudinal segmentation, we will likely realize a sustainable competitive advantage. Furthermore, the fact that attitudes are dynamic means that we, as marketers, can influence them. We cannot, through our marketing efforts, change the number of 20- to 30-year-olds in a certain region. We can, however, change their *attitudes* about our product or service. In the end, this ability is the foundation of marketing: identifying key attitude-behavior linkages and then seeking to change behaviors by changing attitudes.

Brands such as Apple, Coca-Cola, and Harley Davidson (among many others) have realized significant profits by developing and leveraging skills at segmenting based on attitudes (see the Customer Focus box in this chapter). Nike's long-running "Just do it" campaign reflected the company's understanding of its target customers' attitudes not only toward sports, but also toward life in general. By segmenting on this attitude toward life, Nike was able to create a differentiated image in consumers' minds. It is this practice to segmentation, leveraging both behaviors and attitudes, that defines the truly strategic marketer.

Aspirational Variables

Aspirational variables. Variables that reflect beliefs and attitudes about the future: the wishes, hopes, and dreams of our target audience.

Unlike attitudinal variables, which describe attitudes about right now, **aspirational variables** describe attitudes and beliefs—even wishes, hopes, and dreams—about the future. For that reason, and because a significant portion of positioning work is done

CUSTOMER FOCUS

THE VALUE OF STRATEGIC CUSTOMER DATA: HARLEY-DAVIDSON FINANCIAL SERVICES

The U.S. motorcycle manufacturer, Harley-Davidson, is legendary for the way it fosters fervent loyalty in its customers. The company does so by openly stating that it sells an experience, not just motorcycles. Harley-Davidson also leverages community-building tactics and technology tools to foster loyalty and customer intimacy. Harley's segmentation variable is not "need for speed" or another functional benefit related to motorcycling, but rather an emotional benefit related to the Harley-Davidson lifestyle. Harley sponsors The Harley Owners Group, aka "H.O.G.," online which has more than 1 million members and offers motorcycle owners a variety of membership benefits, including roadside assistance, a members' magazine, and access to events and local chapter meetings. The HOG community allows Harley customers to share in their passion for the Harley brand, exchanging stories and finding friends.

© Johnrob/iStockphoto

From a company perspective, the community also offers a rich data source as Harley seeks to develop more intimate relationships with its customers in an effort to develop customer-appropriate products and services.

From an Information Technology perspective, Harley focuses on obtaining customer data and making it available throughout the firm so it can be accessed by cross-functional teams that combine sales, marketing, operations, and finance functions. The company uses technology partners, such as SAP, to stay abreast of advances in data sharing and social networking tools for its customers, dealers, and employees. For example, Harley dealers enter new customer data in a shared SAP CRM system, and other dealers in the network and corporate employees can access that data to perform analyses including credit underwriting for specific customers.

The technology-enabled communities that Harley has built allow the company to stay close to its customers and customize product offerings and services to their needs. Harley-Davidson Financial Services (HDFS), the company's financing arm, extends loans to buyers of Harley motorcycles. These loans sometimes exceed the cost of the motorcycle, allowing customers to finance accessories and customization options. In assessing creditworthiness, HDFS is able to extend financing to some customers who might have been rejected by more traditional financial institutions. HDFS can do this by relying on the relationship databases Harley maintains, containing millions of transaction and payment data points on its customers. Many customers who hold HDFS debt would rather default on their mortgage or utility payments than risk losing their motorcycles. That makes HDFS comfortable extending credit even in the absence of very high credit scores or other more traditional information generally used by other lenders. ∎

Source: Harley-Davidson Company website. http://www.harley-davidson.com/en_US/Content/Pages/home.html. Accessed April 12, 2012.

Clark, Tim. "Harley-Davidson goes whole hog with customer insight," June 29, 2011. *Forbes Magazine*. http://www.forbes.com/sites/sap/2011/06/29/harley-davidson-goes-whole-hog-with-customer-insight/0).

---

against segments identified by targets' aspirations, we consider these variables separately here.

The future in this context can be either real or imagined. A young student may aspire to graduate and become more mature and sophisticated. As a result of this attitude, he may consider switching from the can of beer he drank in college to scotch in a heavy glass. As marketers we refer to this as a *reality* or **life-stage** aspiration; it is quite likely that this student's dreams of graduation will be realized, and his attitudinal and behavioral shift from beer to scotch could likely be realized as well. In fact, drinking scotch may give him the appearance and feeling of sophistication he is seeking. The term life-stage marketing more generally refers to the practice of adapting marketing messages and offerings to customers' specific life phases. Marketers have identified that key events in a person's life (e.g., expecting a child, being a new parent, getting a new job, moving) drive changes in her needs and therefore make him or her

Life-stage marketing.
More generally refers to the practice of adapting marketing messages and offerings to customers' specific life phases.

Jennifer Aniston for Smart Water

open to changing product and service providers. Tracking customers' or potential customers' life stages can help marketers identify consumers when they are most receptive.

The same beer-drinking student may wish he could spend his days and nights living by the beach, partying with friends while drinking his beer. This is a *fantasy* or *escape* aspiration; it is not likely that his life will unfold in this manner. Nonetheless, he may associate a particular brand of beer with this fantasy aspiration, and he may find that drinking this beer evokes the feeling he is seeking.

The archetypical example of aspirational segmentation is Gatorade's "I want to be like Mike" campaign, which targeted the aspirations of kids in the 1990s with images of Michael Jordan, then at the height of his pro basketball career.

A more recent example is Jennifer Aniston's promotion of Smart Water. Smart Water is a brand of Glacéau, a subsidiary of the Coca-Cola Company. Smart Water claims that because it is enhanced with electrolytes, it is absorbed by the body faster than regular water and thus provides more hydration, especially during exercise. Aniston says "My Secret Revealed" in a series of commercials and print advertisements, implying that Smart Water is the reason for her youthful appearance.

Firms often use reality aspirational variables to influence consumers as they make key transitions, such as graduating from college, getting married, having children, or retiring. Financial services marketers often develop a deep understanding of these transitions in order to market products such as credit cards, mortgages, life insurance, and retirement planning. These firms are often more focused on retention strategies because they are interested in maintaining a relationship with their customers through these transitions. In contrast, firms leveraging fantasy aspirational variables will often target several segments, with different brands representing different fantasy aspirations.

▸ Service fees are so last millennium.

INGDIRECT.CA   ING ▧ DIRECT
forward banking™

ING's My Financial Life website illustrates a retention-focused life-stage campaign that uses aspirational images to encourage ING customers to plan their financial life around the company.

Psychographics

Marketers sometimes combine demographics, behaviors, and attitudes to characterize a market segment using **psychographics**, variables that relate to personality, values, attitudes, interests, and lifestyles. Psychographics became popular in the 1980s, following work by social scientist Arnold Mitchell. Mitchell created an instrument he called **VALs**, or Values, Attitudes, and Lifestyles. **VALs** is a survey that contains 35 questions including demographics and attitudes (beliefs). Responses to the questionnaire are compared to the responses of thousands of other U.S. consumers, and respondents are placed in a segment with people who have answered the survey similarly. Although **VALs** has lost some popularity, it is still used by some consumer companies. Another well-known use of psychographics is the segmentation of consumers by generational group. For example, some marketers refer to psychographic groups such as the **millennials**, people born between 1981 and 2000. Millennials are characterized as being readily comfortable with technology, including tweeting, texting, and inhabiting websites like Facebook, YouTube, Google, and Wikipedia. They are said to be relatively progressive and liberal (55% of them voted Democratic in the 2012 election[1]), and they respect institutions more than their predecessors, the members of the X and Y Generations.

A danger with grouping customers psychographically, however, is falling into incorrect generalizations. For example, while many millennials are liberal and text obsessively, that does not describe *everyone* born between 1980 and 2000. Baby boomers text obsessively as well. Several research studies have shown that older adults are as likely to text while driving as younger adults.[2] As we group customers, we must take care not to develop stereotypes about them (more about this later in the chapter).

Psychographic variables. Variables that combine demographics, personality, values, attitudes, interests, and lifestyles of consumers for segmentation purposes.

VALs. Acronym for Values, Attitudes, and Lifestyles. VALs is a system for grouping consumers according to certain attitudes and demographics (together known as psychographics) in order to predict their response to marketing and advertising initiatives.

Millennials. The generation born between 1980 and 2000 (approximately). Millennials are sometimes referred to in the media as "Generation Y."

SEGMENTATION: MAIN AND DYNAMIC BENEFIT

A common approach to market segmentation is to define a segment based on a large number of variables, often with the use of analytical tools such as **cluster analysis** that help identify natural groupings of customers by sorting them in ways that emphasize customer differences across groups and minimize them within groups. Cluster analysis is thus very useful for finding natural segments within our target market. However, sometimes marketers describe many segments in detail and then develop differentiated value propositions for each. In order to avoid this problem, it is best to use research to *prioritize* segmentation variables and customers. The goal of segmentation is to help us most efficiently direct scarce resources to our most profitable prospects. We should think of segmentation tools as helping us identify similarities between customers, bringing customers together toward our brand rather than breaking them apart.

To illustrate an important difference between segmentation and fragmentation, consider the example of a fictitious grocery store; let's call it Fresh Grocer. This company has decided to implement a retention/stimulate demand strategy because it is the market leader in its geographic area. It wishes to grow by increasing purchases per

[1] Hoover, Margaret. "Opinion: Failure to attract millennials is sinking the GOP." *Cnn.Com.* November 14, 2012. www.cnn.co/2012/11/14/living/millennials-gop-vote. Accessed April 13, 2013.

[2] Halsey, Ashley. "Teen drivers are texting, just like their parents." *Pew Internet.* May 13, 2012. http://pewinternet.org/Media-Mentions/2012/Teen-drivers-are-texting-just-like-their-parents.aspx. Accessed April 13, 2013.

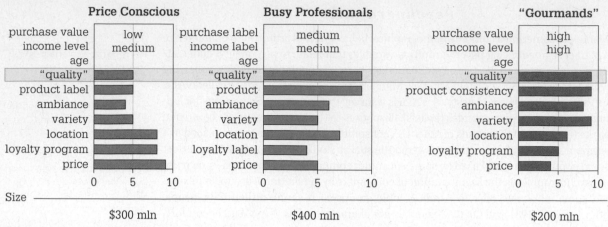

Price Conscious	Busy Professionals	"Gourmands"

Figure 5.2 Fresh Grocer customer segments.

customer. Thanks in part to its loyalty program, Fresh Grocer was able to collect some demographic information (e.g., age, address, income bracket, average purchase in dollars/month) and behavioral information (frequency and value of purchases per household) about its customers and combine it with some attitudinal information arrayed on a scale of 1 to 10. It then used cluster analysis to group customers into segments.

Fresh Grocer identified the importance to its customers of the following needs: product quality, product consistency, product variety, store ambiance, store location, the customer loyalty program, and price. The cluster analysis ranged the respondents to the survey into three groups, shown in Figure 5.2. Households in each group have similar purchase and income levels and similar preferences. The marketing team also calculated the size of each segment by adding the revenue each group represents, as shown at the bottom of the figure.

As most marketing teams do in reviewing cluster analysis data, Fresh Grocer's marketers decided to label the clusters so others in the company could make some assumptions about the types of people who belong to each one. Current customers with lower income levels, slightly lower purchase values, and slightly lower importance ratings for product quality, product variety, store location, and ambiance who really value low price are called Price Conscious; the team assumes this segment will be willing to trade product quality and variety and convenience to get lower prices. In a higher-income and more demanding group are customers who seek an easy and efficient shopping experience, are less price sensitive, and are not that concerned about store ambiance. The marketing team calls this the "Busy Professionals" segment. Finally, those who account for the highest per-household spending, highly value ambiance and product variety, and have the highest average incomes in the customer base are called the "Gourmand" segment.

Even when the data apparently justifies these labels, a danger we run in using them is that we can make implicit assumptions that go beyond the data, leading us into generalizations and sometimes erroneous and possibly unethical stereotypes (see below for more about stereotypes). Labeling also seems to imply that customer preferences are static when, in reality, people change all the time, and if we do a good job as marketers, they will change in a way that is consistent with our strategy. For example, before Walmart became very successful in the late 1980s, U.S. consumers did not care as much about the price of the products they purchased as they do today.[3]

Beyond these common pitfalls, a huge issue in segmentation studies arises when marketing teams leverage the same fundamental entity, core competence, and strategic assets to simultaneously pursue several segments with different value propositions for each. Fresh Grocer would be challenged to design a store that appeals equally to the three customer segments it has defined. The Gourmand and Price Conscious segments would require different merchandising and product portfolios. The Busy Professionals would probably be best served by stores located in very busy urban areas, where the price of real estate could make it difficult to serve Price Conscious customers equally well. Given such challenges, the company might be better off selecting one segment than trying to serve all three.

Alternately Fresh Grocer can select a need that runs across all three segments, such as product quality. Ideally this need fits well with the company's core competence. It could then differentiate itself by delivering the freshest and highest-quality products in its market, attracting customers from one or two of the segments described by the cluster analysis and losing some who are seeking different benefits and would probably be happier shopping elsewhere. Along the way, the importance of product freshness will probably go up in the market overall, limiting the loss of current customers and helping the company acquire some new ones.

We use segmentation to identify the key variables, generally expressed as benefits, that can attract a substantial segment of customers to our brand, and that we can use to differentiate our product or service versus the competition. The **main benefit,** simply put, is the primary benefit consumers are seeking in a category, and therefore the cost of entry for any firm wishing to compete in that category. For example, the main benefit in the fast-food category is convenience. Any company seeking to compete in this category must be able to deliver on this variable, because this is a key reason consumers are purchasing these products.

The main benefit generally is the benefit on which the category leader is differentiated. While all competitors are expected to deliver some acceptable level of this benefit, those seeking to earn share from the market leader most often will emphasize a variable *other* than the main benefit. This **dynamic benefit** is a variable on which the competition believes it can outperform the category leader, thereby convincing some percentage of consumers to trade a lower level of the main benefit for more of the dynamic benefit. For example, some consumers are willing to trade off McDonald's convenience for Subway's fresher, lower-calorie offerings.

Regardless of whether we are the category leader seeking to stimulate demand or a competitive entrant seeking to earn share, our main and/or dynamic benefit must be supported by our core competence. In the fast-food category, variables such as taste (Wendy's), freshness/low fat (Subway), and customization (Burger King) all have been emphasized as dynamic benefits against McDonald's. All these companies, of course, have to also deliver on the convenience variable, but they do not emphasize this in their communications. Instead, they rely on McDonald's to attract consumers to the

Main benefit. The primary benefit provided by the category and that differentiates the category leader.

Dynamic benefit. The benefit used by a competitor to take share from the category leader.

---

[3]Fishman, Charles. *The Wal-Mart Effect: How the World's Most Powerful Company Really Works—and How It's Transforming the American Economy*. Penguin Books, 2006.

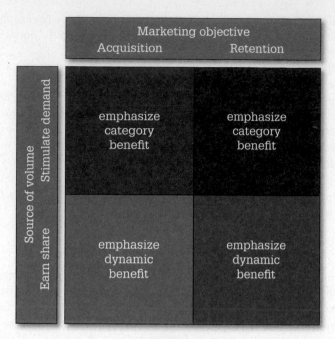

Figure 5.3 Segmentation and the main and dynamic benefit.

category based on their need for convenience, and then they seek to earn some of McDonald's share by emphasizing another important benefit.

As marketers we make the decision whether to emphasize the main or a dynamic benefit when we select our source of volume (see Fig. 5.3). If we are the category leader, we are differentiated on the main benefit for that category. If we chose an earn share source of volume, we will emphasize a dynamic benefit on which we can dominate the competitor from which we chose to earn share.

Our choice of which dynamic benefit to emphasize will be based on (1) our assessment of customer needs, and (2) our core competencies in delivering on those needs. When we compare our brand to the category leader, we anticipate that consumers will infer that we are "within range" on the main benefit; Subway may not be as convenient as McDonald's, but it is convenient enough for some consumers to choose to trade a bit of convenience for fresher fast food.

The relationship between competitors is not static; relative share may shift as consumers change their evaluation of competitive performance on benefits or adjust the relative importance they attach to these benefits, based on factors such as price and their experience with the brands. In some cases, a competitor seeking to earn share may be so successful that an entirely new segment is formed. For example, when Toyota first entered the U.S. auto market it sought to earn share from U.S. brands based on the dynamic benefit of low price. Toyota was so successful that U.S. automakers were forced to respond, and very quickly an "economy segment" was formed in the auto industry. In this new segment, the main benefit is low price, and entering competitors will seek to earn share based on other benefits.

If we choose a stimulate demand strategy, emphasizing the main or category benefit, our focus is on keeping this benefit salient for consumers. At the same time, it is up to the category leader to continue to explore possible new category benefits, in case it loses the ability to differentiate on the current main benefit. For example, FedEx first entered and built the overnight delivery industry by emphasizing the main benefit of reliability ("When it absolutely, positively, has to be there overnight"). However, over time other competitors, notably UPS and DHL, were able to increase perceptions of their product performance to the point at which consumers did not see a great difference between the different brands on this main benefit. FedEx now had three choices: (1) invest to further increase the *importance* of reliability such that even small perceived differences would still drive consumer preferences, (2) invest to increase the distance between itself and the competition on *perceived* reliability, or (3) select a *new* dynamic benefit to emphasize, acknowledging that reliability was now commoditized and no longer a possible point of differentiation. In the end FedEx chose a new benefit, ease of use.

SEGMENTATION CRITERIA

How do we choose the appropriate segmentation variable? Of course, we will make use of whatever consumer research is available to us in order to begin to identify benefits sought in our category. As stated above, our goal is to prioritize these benefits in order to determine which ones we will focus on. In doing so, we should consider issues related to the type of segmentation variable and benefit, consumer perceptions, and our own capabilities.

Characteristics of the Segmentation Variable

Several characteristics of the segmentation variable itself are important during the selection process. First, it is important that we are able to *measure* attitudes related to this variable fairly readily. Increasingly sophisticated market research tools allow us to access and track consumer attitudes more and more easily. As we will discuss below, we gain the most value from attitudinal information when we measure *trends*: changes in these attitudes over time. Second, the variables should describe a target audience that we reasonably believe can be *accessed*. Some benefit segments, such as people who value privacy, might be quite difficult to communicate with, especially if we are trying to acquire them as new customers. Finally, the benefit should generate a reasonably *substantial* potential target audience. If there are not enough consumers who do or could value the benefit we are considering promoting, we cannot make a business case for using this variable.

Consumer Perceptions

Of course, we also must take into account the perceptions of the consumer as we select our potential segmentation variables. Consumer perceptions do not remain fixed; what we are interested in here is not only how consumers perceive our brand right now, but also how they *might* perceive it in the future. In order to fully understand this dynamic, we must gauge perceptions at the outset and also monitor them on an ongoing basis in order to assess the effectiveness of our campaign. Consumers tend to be highly adaptive; their desires quickly change to expectations as product categories mature. When laptop computers were first introduced, the dynamic benefit of need for portability reflected the desires of consumers at that time. Quickly, however, portability became an expected feature of the product, and need for portability became a less-compelling segmentation variable. (This distinction between expectations and desires is crucial. Expected features are those generally available, usually offered by two or more competitors. Desired features or benefits are those that may still differentiate a particular competitor as they have not become generally available.

Company Capabilities

Finally, and most importantly, we must take company capabilities into account when selecting segmentation variables. There must be a fit between the benefits sought by the target and the core competence of the company. This aspect of segmentation is the most crucial and most overlooked piece of the process. All too often firms choose to position their products based on benefits that consumers seek, but that the company cannot deliver on in a sustainable fashion. If we are successful in promoting a benefit that we cannot deliver on, we are simply acting as a market research firm for our competition, demonstrating demand for a benefit that we cannot provide. For example, we may have identified *need for innovation* as a potential segmentation benefit. However, if our company does not possess the skills necessary to establish a competitive advantage on this benefit, then another firm that does have capabilities in this area might fill this demand. Wal-Mart selected low prices as a main benefit not only because consumers desired lower prices, but also because the firm had developed a core competence in logistics and sourcing that enabled it to consistently deliver lower prices. Without this core competence the firm would not have been able to succeed

GLOBALMARKETING

HEINZ KETCHUP IN THE CZECH REPUBLIC

Ketchup is an essential condiment in the United States, and individuals have preconceived expectations of the product. In many countries, however, ketchup is a commodity with minimal differentiation among the various brands, and consumers expect little of it. Entering the Czech Republic in 1997, Heinz understood that the local market was driven by low-quality producers and wanted to create an ad addressing the customer's needs. Heinz created an ad with the tag line, "Ordinary Things, Extraordinary Taste." Heinz's offered a new benefit—distinctive taste—intended to help reshape the category in the Czech Republic, setting itself apart from less differentiated local producers.

Used by permission of MARK BBDO and Heinz

Since the late 1990s, the company has established itself as a market leader in the Czech Republic and introduced a number of product innovations—through both new formulations and packaging—that are aligned to its premium positioning. For example, in 2008 Heinz rolled out its Ketchup Top Down bottle with a more iconic and premium look. The company has also introduced locally appropriate products such as Granny tartar sauce and mayonnaise; these distinguish themselves from competitors as the only products in the market without preservatives. The entry and subsequent growth of ketchup in the Czech Republic illustrates how a company re-created what seemed like an established and undifferentiated category by emphasizing a new variable.

Source: http://www.advertolog.com/heinz/print-outdoor/decorations-11067705/ *Blogpost.* Accessed April 10, 2010; Company website: http://www.heinz.cz/heinz-czech.htm. Accessed April 12, 2012.

with this positioning. This is why it is crucial that our segmentation variables relate to a clearly identified core competence in our firm.

Thus, in looking for our ideal main or dynamic benefit we simultaneously must satisfy a number of conditions—our company should have a competitive advantage in delivering this benefit; the benefit should be measurable; there must be a group of customers that cares enough about this benefit to purchase our offering; this group must be large enough to enable us to reach our business objective; and we must have some way to inform these customers of the benefit we provide. This is a tall order; however, if we are able to satisfy these criteria we will radically improve our chances of establishing a sustainable competitive advantage.

SEGMENTATION VS. STEREOTYPING

While segmentation is a legitimate and important marketing activity, stereotyping is an unethical and destructive social practice. Segmentation is *not* stereotyping. If we appropriately employ the Big Picture framework, proper segmentation will actually *reduce* our risk of stereotyping. Before we can do this, however, we must clearly understand the important differences between segmentation and stereotyping.

Stereotyping is based primarily on *physical* characteristics—demographics. While we will obviously utilize demographics to inform our estimates of market potential, we should avoid drawing inappropriate and often offensive conclusions about our target audience based on physical characteristics such as age, gender, or ethnic origin. Even if a majority of a particular demographic group shares a certain attitudinal characteristic, this does not mean everyone in this group shares this characteristic, nor does it mean that people outside this group do not share this characteristic.

For example, if we are selling a home security product and seeking to target people who are risk averse, we might discover that a higher percentage of elderly people are risk averse and decide to target all our efforts against this demographic group. We may decide to leverage a fear appeal in our communications in order to increase this feeling of risk aversion. In doing so we have created a campaign arguably designed to engender fear among the elderly. Further, because not all elderly people are risk averse, we are using our marketing dollars inefficiently. Finally, because many people who are risk averse are not elderly, we are missing these people entirely.

Instead of inferring attitudes based on demographics, we can much more efficiently and effectively infer attitudes based on behaviors. That is, we can collect information about attitudes via market research, evaluate and synthesize this information in combination with information about behaviors, and then segment the market efficiently and effectively. In the example above, we might survey homeowners about their interest in security and also collect information about what other safety-conscious behaviors they engage in (such as wearing seatbelts, buying life insurance, or using a hotel safe). The answers to these questions will help us to form a much more accurate and appropriate picture of our target audience.

Except for obvious physical characteristics, demographic segmentation variables also do not predict behavior nearly as well as attitudes do. It is fairly obvious that if we are selling retirement products, we will target people of a certain age. This information is obvious to our competitors and us alike, and alone it does not afford us an opportunity to differentiate and establish a competitive advantage. More detailed

Advertising Archive/Everett Collection, Inc.

Stereotypes about women in advertising.

Women (and men) have long been the subject of stereotypes in commercials. Holly Buchanan, author of *The Soccer Mom Myth*, developed a test to identify whether a commercial presents women in a stereotypical role. To pass the Buchanan test, commercials must meet three criteria.

1. Feature a woman outside her home
2. In a role other than being a mother
3. Not doing yoga

Source: Willard Cross, Amy. "The one test that popular commercials keep failing." *VitaminW.Blog Post.* March 7, 2013. http://vitaminw.co/interview/one-test-popular-commercials-keep-failing. Accessed April 30, 2013.

Blogpost. http://marketingtowomenonline.typepad.com/blog/. Accessed April 30, 2013.

demographic information—for example, how many children our potential customers have or how much money they make—may be somewhat interesting, but not nearly as interesting as their attitudes and behaviors around saving money and planning for the future. Thus, beyond collecting the obvious market-sizing demographic data, we are better off spending our market research dollar uncovering behavioral and attitudinal information.

Another unfortunate aspect of stereotyping is that it presumes all members of a particular group are exactly alike: that our target audience is *homogeneous* and *static*. This is, of course false, and leads to two important problems. First, the assumption that our audience is homogeneous leads us to rely on averages, and we thus end up targeting a consumer who doesn't exist. There is no U.S. family with 2.2 children. Drawing conclusions based on averages may be of interest to certain types of journalists or demographers, but it has little value for marketing strategists seeking to make a genuine connection with specific consumers. Second, by definition, a target audience that is static holds less interest to marketers seeking to differentiate a product or service. The job of a modern marketer is more than simply to identify static demographic classes of people and try to fill their needs. This is really a cost of entry—all marketers must do this assessment. *We cannot change the demographics of our potential target audience; we can only aspire to change their attitudes.* Hence, a demographic-bound, stereotypical target audience is not what we are targeting as marketers seeking to create a sustainable competitive advantage.

Finally, those who think in stereotypical and prejudicial ways believe they can draw complete conclusions regarding an individual's personality based on one or two physical attributes. Recall that our definition of segmentation focuses on "consumers sharing *at least one* characteristic." Ideally, this one characteristic is an *attitude* or benefit consumers seek and one that we can provide, such as convenience or reliability. Sound segmentation strategies thus focus on one or two key attitudes and make no assumptions about other characteristics, particularly physical ones that may have no bearing on product-related behaviors. The approach to segmentation we propose here requires gaining a deep understanding of one or two key attitudes or benefits sought. All resources devoted to segmentation will focus on these attitudes and our ability to respond to them from a marketing perspective.

In summary, from an ethical standpoint, the practice of stereotyping is unacceptable. From a professional standpoint, it is an inefficient and inevitably incorrect practice that will, in the long run, have damaging effects on our brand and corporation.

SEGMENTATION: STEPS IN THE PROCESS

We've seen that segmentation is the first in a three-step process aimed at developing a detailed target audience description and positioning statement (targeting and positioning are the other two). Our goal in segmentation is to identify the main and dynamic benefit upon which we will base our marketing strategy. These are expressed as benefits because they represent the attitudinal or aspirational desire of our consumers, as opposed to simply their demographic or behavior characteristics. An example of a benefit, therefore, might be an attitude such as the need for convenience or ease of use, or an aspiration such as a need to feel hip or smart.

To specify which benefit we will eventually use as the core of our value proposition, we *first generate a set of potential benefits from which to choose.* Firms may generate this initial list in many different ways, but all include using information about what benefits consumers consider important, and their perception of how well competitors deliver these benefits.

After generating an extensive list of potential benefits, we then need to *select the key benefit to emphasize.* If we are the market leader, we will be selecting the main benefit. The main benefit is the benefit that differentiates us as market leader and is the primary reason we dominate the market. For example, Nike is the market leader in the running shoe category, and it positions its brand by promoting the main benefit of performance. The company is differentiated on this benefit and it is the primary reason it enjoys a #1 share position. Tabasco, the leader in the hot sauce category, will continue to promote the main benefit of "hot."

In existing categories where there is a clear market leader, it is usually quite easy to identify the main benefit of that competitor. If, on the other hand, we are competing in a category with no clear leader, or if we are attempting to build a new segment or category that we hope to dominate, our first task is to identify the main benefit we believe will emerge for that category. For example, when TiVo introduced the first interactive digital video recording device (DVR), the firm had to choose from among a variety of potential benefits ranging from ease of use to customization to enhanced entertainment.

Why must we select only *one* main benefit? Of course we must deliver a variety of benefits at an acceptable level to remain competitive in the category, but we will choose to emphasize only one for brand differentiation purposes. If we promote multiple benefits, we run the risk of confusing our customers and ourselves. This "more is more" approach seems appealing at first, but it will inevitably lead to an ineffective marketing strategy that lacks focus. A single main benefit enables us to support one clear strategy with sufficient resources to break through the clutter and present a convincing argument. With multiple benefits, we end up spreading our resources across multiple messages, none of which receives sufficient support to have an impact in the marketplace. As the amount of competition and clutter in the marketplace increases, the importance of focus increases as well. Thus, we must prioritize our segmentation, targeting, and positioning and direct one clear, single-minded message toward a well-defined group of customers.

If we are not the market leader then we do not have the privilege of selecting the main benefit. That decision has been made already by the #1 brand in the segment or category. Our task is to identify the *dynamic benefit,* that is, the benefit we believe will help us to lure customers away from the market leader. For example, New Balance emphasizes the benefit of "fit" in marketing its running shoes as it attempts to gain share from market leader Nike. While New Balance shoes must deliver an acceptable level of performance, the company recognizes that Nike "owns" this positioning, because it promotes a set of core competencies tied to it. By choosing a different benefit, one that is tied to the core competence of New Balance, the firm seeks to convert customers from Nike to its brand.

Any firm seeking to enter this category will likely choose a benefit other than performance on which to compete, unless it has developed a core competence that enables it to dominate on the main benefit. For example, if my firm has developed a particular competence in product design, enabling us to deliver shoes that consistently deliver higher performance, I may go after Nike head-on. In most cases, however, there is a reason why the category leader *is* the category leader. More often than not, a challenging firm will need to pick another benefit to emphasize.

Thus, the market leader will select the main benefit, and all other competitors will select a unique dynamic benefit to emphasize. This decision will direct our targeting and positioning for our brand and is therefore crucial. The key question here is, of course, how to decide which specific benefit to choose? Why does New Balance promote fit instead of, say, reliability or style? Our choice of segmentation benefit should be driven by two key questions:

1. Is the benefit important to a large enough segment of potential and/or current customers? Or, if not, do we believe we can use marketing tools to increase the importance of this benefit?

2. Is the benefit tied to our core competence? Do we have the appropriate skills and strategic assets to be able to deliver this benefit *better* than our competitors?

The answers to these two questions will drive our choice of specific main or dynamic benefit. To resolve them we must rely on consumer information. The Big Picture toolkit at the end of this chapter presents an approach to collecting and analyzing consumer data for use in segmentation, targeting, and positioning. As we engage in this process, bear three facts in mind:

1. *We are concerned with consumer perceptions, as opposed to reality:* Toyota may, in fact, manufacture the safest car on the planet, but if consumers currently believe Volvo is safer, that is the landscape we must consider. Of course, reality does have some influence on perception, at least in the long run. If our firm has a reputation for reliability but we experience a number of product failures over a period of time, our reputation will eventually suffer. Nonetheless, it is consumer perception, not reality, that drives product sales.

2. *We must let our strategy drive our data collection:* Our choice of strategic quadrant is the foundation for our consumer research. If we have selected an acquisition/stimulate demand strategy, we should be talking to consumers currently *outside* the category; for retention/earn share we are interested in surveying multi-brand users. Both the sample and the questions we ask will vary depending on which quadrant we are in.

3. *We are interested in current and potential perceptions:* We must always remind ourselves that we are in the business not simply of identifying beliefs, but also of changing them where we can. If we find that our brand perception is low on a particular benefit, we should consider whether we might be able to lift that perception, and the potential business impact of such a lift. Our job as marketers is to change beliefs, not simply to identify and react to them.

These three points should serve as a guiding philosophy for our segmentation research and decision-making. They will ensure that our research is strategic and yields results efficiently.

INTEGRATION: SEGMENTATION AND THE BIG PICTURE

We've seen in this chapter that the different types of variables have different degrees of value for segmentation. While many traditional marketing segmentation studies have tended to rely heavily on demographic and behavioral variables, the true added value of a good analysis stems from our understanding of attitudinal and aspirational variables.

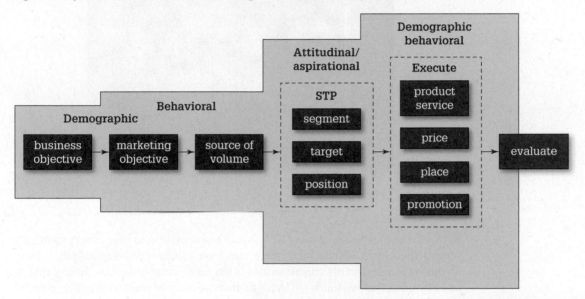

Figure 5.4 Segmentation and the Big Picture.

The relationship between different types of segmentation variables and the Big Picture framework.

This is not to say that demographic and behavioral variables are not important: within the framework, we leverage demographic and behavioral information early as a means for assessing market opportunity (see Fig. 5.4). For example, in our business objective we identify what business we are in; in this process we identify obvious demographic variables (for instance, we segment by gender to enter the feminine protection market). Moving through the framework, if we have decided to implement an acquisition/earn share strategy, we are segmenting based on a behavioral variable (competitive product usage) and may also consider certain demographic characteristics that define these competitive users, such as age or income. At the STP stage, we must build on this information by layering on our understanding of attitudes and aspirations. It is at this point in the process that we truly add value to the analysis.

The primary purpose of segmentation is to help us prioritize our opportunities. When we consider the purpose of segmentation in the context of the strategic quadrants, we can see that segmentation analysis will take a slightly different emphasis depending on our choice of quadrant (see Fig. 5.5):

■ In *acquisition/stimulate demand* we leverage segmentation to help prioritize non-users. Here we will use segmentation to group non-users by their primary objection to purchase, and then we will prioritize those non-users by likelihood of trial of the category.

Figure 5.5 Primary goals of segmentation by strategic focus.

Primary goals of segmentation by strategic focus:

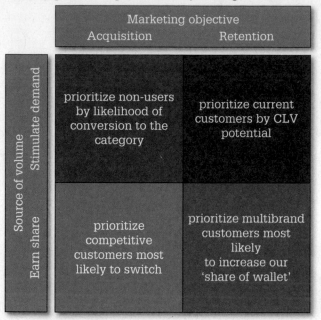

In *retention/stimulate demand* we leverage segmentation to prioritize current customers by our hypothesized incremental customer-lifetime value opportunity. We will do this by focusing on the characteristics of our customers (behaviors, demographics, and attitudes) that we think will make them most likely to want to upgrade to a new version of the product or to purchase more.

In *acquisition/earn share* we use segmentation to identify competitive customers who are most likely to defect from the competition.

In *retention/earn share* we use segmentation to identify multi-brand customers who are most likely to be persuaded to switch some of their consumption to our company (becoming more loyal).

After we have selected our segmentation benefits, we will move to plotting the market (targeting) and writing a positioning statement. While in this book we must necessarily work through the processes of segmentation, targeting, and positioning in sequence, in reality this as an iterative process. We may select two benefits and "try them out," by plotting them and considering possible positioning statements. At any stage in the process, we might decide to go back and choose different benefits before proceeding. Furthermore, going through the process of choosing segmentation variables and plotting the market may lead us to consider changing other strategic choices, such as marketing objective or source of volume. These are perfectly reasonable actions to consider. By combining a systematic approach to the framework as a whole with the flexibility that these iterations provide, we will optimize our chance of developing an effective strategy.

☐ SUMMARY

1. Describe the role segmentation plays in marketing strategy

Segmentation is the process by which we identify current or potential users most likely to be receptive to our marketing message. Segmentation increases efficiency and combines an understanding of the market we are trying to penetrate with a deep understanding of the capabilities of our organization. With these we can direct our efforts to the customers or potential customers with whom we are most likely to succeed.

2. Describe the types of segmentation variables and how to use them

Variables used for segmentation purposes include demographics, behaviors, attitudes, and aspirations. Psychographics combine demographics, personality, values, attitudes, interests, and lifestyles. While generally less strategic than proprietary information about attitudes and purchase patterns, demographic and generic behavioral data are useful for categorizing and sizing the market. However, true strategic segmentation requires that we understand customer attitudes and the relationship between attitudes and behaviors toward our brands.

3. Compare the concepts of Main and Dynamic Benefit

We segment our markets by focusing primarily on two variables: the main variable and the dynamic variable. The main variable is the principal benefit customers seek when purchasing a product or service; and the dynamic variable is the benefit that differentiates it versus the category leader. If the firm elects to pursue a stimulate demand strategy, it will emphasize the main variable; if it implements a steal share strategy, it will build its execution around the dynamic variable.

4. Explain the key criteria in segmenting a market

In performing a segmentation analysis we must select segmentation variables that are measurable and that result in accessible and substantial segments. Once we have identified relevant segments in our market, we must turn to an internal analysis of our capabilities to assess the attractiveness of the segments we have found. A common mistake companies make is to skip this important step and pursue segments just because they are large, even if the firm has no particular advantage with them.

5. Select the main and dynamic benefit

Our goal in this step is to identify the main and dynamic benefits upon which we will base our marketing strategy. To achieve this goal, we first generate a set of potential benefits from which to choose. Firms may generate this initial list in many different ways, but all include leveraging information about what benefits consumers consider important, and their perception of how well competitors deliver these benefits. After generating an extensive list of potential benefits, we will identify a key benefit, either main or dynamic depending on our market position. We choose this benefit by considering customer insights and our capability assessment.

6. Describe the steps in the segmentation process

Our goal in segmentation is to identify the main and dynamic benefit upon which we will base our marketing strategy. The market leader will select the main benefit, and all other competitors will select a unique dynamic benefit to emphasize. Our choice of segmentation benefit should be driven by two key questions: (1) Is the benefit important to a large enough segment of potential and/or current customers? (2) Is the benefit tied to our core competence? The answers to these two questions will also drive our targeting and positioning choices. As we engage in this process, bear three facts in mind: (1) We are concerned with consumer perceptions, as opposed to reality. (2) We must let our strategy drive our data collection. (3) We are interested in current and potential perceptions.

7. Integrate segmentation with other elements of the Big Picture

While many traditional marketing segmentation studies have tended to rely heavily on demographic and behavioral variables, the true added value of a good analysis stems from our understanding of attitudinal and aspirational variables. As we undertake our segmentation efforts, it is critical that we retain the strategic focus developed earlier in the Big Picture framework and avoid trading efficiency for exhaustiveness.

☐ KEY TERMS

Aspirational variables. (p.144) Variables that reflect beliefs and attitudes about the future: the wishes, hopes, and dreams of our target audience.

Attitudinal variables. (p.143) Variables that describe the thoughts, feelings, and beliefs of consumers. Marketers have implicitly used attitudinal segmentation strategies for years by appealing to consumers' need for safety or self-esteem or desire to be "hip" or "cool."

Behavioral segmentation variables. (p.141) Variables that describe the specific actions of consumers or potential consumers.

Categorical variables. (p.140) A categorical variable like gender, occupation, or marital status that is used to represent discreet types, or categories, or numerical categories on a scale.

Continuous variables. (p.140) Variables that can take any value within the scale used to measure them (not simply the whole numbers on the scales, but including fractions).

Demographic variables. (p.139) Those variables that we can physically observe and measure such as age, gender, educational status, household size, income, marital status, and geographic information like country of origin, population income, and population density.

Dynamic benefit. (p.149) The benefit used by a competitor to take share from the category leader.

Life-stage marketing. (p.145) Life-stage marketing more generally refers to the practice of adapting marketing messages and offerings to customers' specific life phases.

Main benefit. (p.149) The primary benefit provided by the category and that differentiates the category leader.

Millennials. (p.147) The generation born between 1980 and 2000 (approximately). Millennials are sometimes referred to in the media as "Generation Y."

Psychographic variables. (p.147) Variables that combine demographics, personality, values, attitudes, interests, and lifestyles of consumers for segmentation purposes.

Segmentation. (p.137) The process of identifying a group of customers who share at least one characteristic that will make them more responsive to our marketing message.

Stereotyping. (p.141) The practice of considering any individual in a segment or population as a representative of the population as a whole by emphasizing physical or demographic variables to draw unrealistic and potentially offensive conclusions regarding attitudes and behaviors.

VALs. (p.147) Acronym for Values, Attitudes, and Lifestyles. VALs is a system for grouping consumers according to certain attitudes and demographics (together known as psychographics) in order to predict their response to marketing and advertising initiatives.

☐ REVIEW AND DISCUSSION QUESTIONS

1. Think about the global hybrid car category.
   (a) Provide a list of potential segmentation variables that might help Toyota plot the category. Include demographics, behaviors, attitudes, and aspirations.
   (b) Now build a feature-benefit-value ladder for "Toyota Hybrid Cars." How might the list of variables you have compiled change if you were interested in segmenting the market from the perspective of BMW's hybrid cars rather than Toyota?
   (c) Build a value ladder for BMW assuming BMW is a newer entrant into the category and is considering earning share from Toyota in this category.
2. What is the primary segmentation variable for Toyota? What is the primary segmentation variable for BMW? Assume that BMW is not the market leader in the hybrid sedan category, and it is attempting to earn share away from Toyota. How might BMW use segmentation tools to achieve its market share goals?

3. Go to the P&G website and select one of its business categories. Now answer the following questions.

    (a) For the category you have selected, how does P&G segment consumers?

    (b) What segments does P&G currently serve?

    (c) What benefits do P&G's brands offer for each of the segments in which they participate?

    (d) For the category you have selected, are there any segments P&G is currently not serving? Why might this be the case?

☐ APPENDIX: MARKETING ANALYSIS AND PLANNING

The STP Process: Define the Segmentation Variables

Segmentation, Targeting, and Positioning require six sequential marketing activities as follows:

1. Define segmentation variables
2. Select segmentation variables
3. Plot the market
4. Select target
5. Create positioning statement
6. Articulate the value proposition

At this first stage in the STP process, we will (1) define segmentation variables, and (2) select potential segmentation variables for further consideration.

Defining the Segmentation Variables

Strategic segmentation variables are those that drive brand choice and purchase decisions generally in the category, and more specifically for our brand. Sometimes, segmentation variables are called "bases" because they help us split the market into groups of current or potential customers who are likely to have similar needs with respect to our product or service category.

The most direct way to define segmentation variables is to simply ask customers: "What are the primary benefits you seek from the brands in the category?" Unfortunately, when we use open questions like these, we are unlikely to get a nicely ordered list of variables. For this reason, it is useful to rely on qualitative interviewing techniques as a way to generate variables. Another way to generate potential variables, particularly for established brands, is to conduct a feature-benefit-value ladder exercise. We cover these two methods in turn.

(a) Conducting Semi-Structured Qualitative Interviews

In a *semi-structured qualitative interview*, we ask customers to follow an interview protocol only generally, allowing them to spend more time and add specificity in the areas that most appeal to them. Successive interviews allow us to obtain a deep understanding of all areas of the semi-structured interview questionnaire.

We find the critical incident interview very helpful in revealing potential segmentation variables for customers already in the category. In it we ask customers to review the customer experience process steps in the category[4] step-by-step and to tell us about experiences that were either extremely positive or extremely negative. By asking 10 to 12 customers about their extreme experiences, we can uncover needs that are important; these needs are either currently being satisfied by a competitor or are not being met and are therefore opportunities to segment the market and, if we can successfully meet them, position our brand.

(b) Using a Feature-Benefit-Value Ladder

Sometimes, in markets that are not going through very rapid change or in which successful companies market equivalent products, we can look at the brands in the market—ours and

---

[4]See the Marketing Tool on Purchase Process elsewhere in this book for a more detailed explanation of purchase process analyses.

the competitors'—and think about the benefits our products provide as a way to develop potential groupings of customers in that market.

In constructing a *feature-benefit-value ladder,* we hypothesize which features, benefits, and values of our brand are most differentiating in the eyes of our target customers. A feature-benefit-value ladder is an inside-out look at the brand. We build feature-benefit-value ladders by first listing the most important brand features, and then listing their connected benefits and values. A well-constructed ladder will contain a fairly complete list of potential attitudinal and aspirational variables to be used for segmentation. Let's first define the terms *features*, *benefits*, and *values*.

> **Features:** A feature is an inherent physical or functional attribute of a product or service. For example, the physical features of this book include the type of paper it is printed on, the editorial elements of the book—learning objectives, chapter structure, and marketing toolkit sections—while functional features include the fact that it is offered in a digital as well as paper edition.

> **Benefits:** A benefit describes what the customer stands to gain from using the product or service. Benefits are directly linked to features. So, for example, if this book is available in digital form (feature), it will be easy to access (benefit). Its marketing tools section (feature) might make the book more practical (benefit).

> Benefits can be *functional*, *economic*, or *psychological/emotional*. Functional benefits arise directly from the way the product works or functions; examples include ease of use, speed, durability, and performance. Economic benefits are the financial impacts of features or functional benefits. For example, a knife made of stainless steel (feature) is long-lasting (functional benefit); because it is long-lasting it will also have lower cost of ownership (economic benefit). A product that is small (feature) will take up less space in inventory (functional benefit), and business customers will save on inventory costs (economic benefit). Psychological/Emotional benefits are thoughts, feelings, emotions, and subjective evaluations (happy, sad, taste, safety, trust).

> **Values:** Values are high-level attitudes or aspirations that help describe the status or image conferred to the user of the product by virtue of his or her choice ("I am an innovator," "I am sophisticated," "..."). Values are subjective because they reflect the relationship between the emotional product and the individual; for example, I may believe that I am a more efficient person because I use an easy-to-access digital edition of the book.

To develop a feature-benefit-value ladder, we take the following steps:

1. *Identify all relevant features of the product or service.* Here we are particularly interested in features that are relevant, depending on our strategy. For example, when working within the acquisition/earn share quadrant, we should list features that offer potential for differentiation from the competition. When working within retention/stimulate demand, we will place particular emphasis on the features that lead to benefits our current customers might enjoy.

   As we go through this process we will likely identify component features. For example, a pen may have a roller-ball ink delivery system made up of particularly smooth-flowing ink and a precisely machined ball-bearing.

2. *Build up to benefits.* For each feature we have listed, ask: "Why would a customer care?" Customers care about the benefits of the features, not about the features themselves. A roller-ball ink delivery system may confer the benefit of easier writing and cleaner lines. One feature may ladder up to several different benefits. For example, Huggies diapers with Ultrathin design have a benefit of comfort (functional/psychological), and due to their comfort they can be worn for longer periods (functional), so Mom or Dad can save time (economic).

3. *Build up to values.* Values are terminal benefits, the highest-level benefit that our customer experiences when using our product or service. These are generally psychological or emotional responses to the product and therefore refer more to the customer than to the

product. For this reason it is often helpful to express them in a first-person statement; for example, "I am a caring mother because I use Johnson's Baby Shampoo," or "I am a high-status person because I drink Dewar's 12 Year Old Special Reserve Scotch Whisky."

4. **Note the connections between features, benefits, and values.** As we work through the ladder, we will graphically link features, benefits, and values with arrows to help visualize the logical connections between them. Benefits that have many feature arrows leading to them are well-supported claims about our brand or product; these benefits might become critical to our positioning later on. Conversely, benefits that are not linked to any features may represent unsubstantiated claims; we will consider de-prioritizing these. If these benefits become critical to the brand's positioning, we should consider investing to substantiate them by developing additional features. Finally, features connected to important benefits may be critical to making the value propositioning believable.

5. **Consolidate and complete the feature-benefit-value ladder.** Delete redundant features or benefits and organize similar benefits together. Remove weak benefits.

6. **Select a vertical and horizontal message orientation.** Once we have a complete feature-benefit-ladder, we select a *vertical* message orientation; this is a grouping of features and benefits we think our brand or product might want to focus on for segmentation, targeting, and positioning purposes. We will also identify a *horizontal* message orientation that signals how high on the ladder we wish to focus. In general, for retention strategies and heart loyalty we will focus higher; for acquisition strategies and head loyalty we will orient ourselves lower in the ladder.

7. **Reality check.** At the end of every process we should double-check to be sure the benefits on which we are focusing are linked to and supported by our core competence. What skills will be necessary for us to consistently deliver this benefit in a way that differentiates our brand?

Example: Michelin Tires

In 1987 Michelin coined and trademarked the tag line: "Because so much is riding on your tires." These words positioned the company as a premium tire maker focused on safety. We can build a feature-benefit-value ladder based on the most notable features of a Michelin tire: the steel and rubber materials and the surface area of the tire (see Fig. 5A.1).

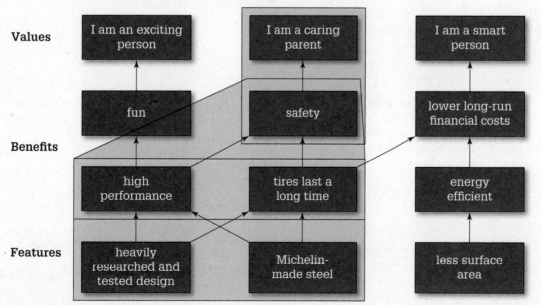

Figure 5A.1 Feature-benefit-value ladder for Michelin tires.

© Regis Duvignau/Reuters/Corbis

Michelin could generate potential segmentation variables by listing the differentiating features of its tires (heavily researched and tested, Michelin-made steel, smaller surface area) and then simply looking at the functional benefits (long life, high performance, energy efficiency) that arise from those features, as well as the economic and psychological ones (lower long-run financial costs and fun and safety, respectively). From these benefits we derive higher level values that relate to how the customer feels when they use the product. In this example the customer may think of himself as exciting because the tire is fun, or smart because the tire costs less to own, or caring because the tire is safe. Ultimately, Michelin positioned its brand on safety, as evidenced by its tagline.

Selecting the Segmentation Variables

After generating a list of potential variables through interviews or feature-benefit-value ladders, we select from the list those variables that are most promising from a segmentation standpoint. Variables that make it to our segmentation short list:

(a) Are most important to the customers in the category.

(b) Have the potential to differentiate our brand in the category.

(c) Have the potential to differentiate our primary competitors in the category.

The process by which we generate the list is iterative: we can try variables on by drawing market plots, by thinking about how many levels of benefits we need in the list, and by obtaining additional customer feedback. For example, after building its feature-benefit-value map, Michelin might have generated the following list:

- Tire longevity
- Tire driving performance
- Steel characteristics
- Price
- Energy efficiency
- Long-run cost of ownership
- Surface area
- Fun
- Safety

Later, the company might decide that customers don't associate "fun" with tires and might decide to drop "fun" and keep only "driving performance" in the same vertical ladder.

Once we have generated a shortlist of potential segmentation variables we plot the market to further pair down the list of variables. See Chapter 6 on targeting.

☐ RESOURCES

Singleton, Dave. "Segmentation reexamined," *Marketing Management*, a Publication of the American Marketing Association (Winter 2010), 20–25.

"Actionable consumer segmentation tools and practices for ensuring high-return efforts," *Marketing Leadership Council Research Brief*, June 2004, i–30.

Wilcox, Ronald T. "A Practical Guide to Conjoint Analysis," University of Virginia, Darden School of Business, Charlottesville, VA. Darden Publishing Note Number UV0406 (2003).

Kim, W. Chan and Renée Mauborgne, "Creating new market space," *Harvard Business Review*, January–February 1999, 83–93.

Collins, Sean R., Peter W. Dahlström, and Marc Singer, "Managing your business as if customer segments matter," *The McKinsey Quarterly*, August 2006, 85–95.

Arjona, Luis D., Rajesh Shah, Alejandro Tinivelli, and Adam Weiss, "Marketing to the Hispanic consumer," *The McKinsey Quarterly*(3): 1998, 106–114.

Yankelovich, Daniel and David Meer, "Rediscovering market segmentation," *Harvard Business Review*, February 2006, 1–12.

Hütt, Eduardo, Robert Le Brun, and Thilo Mannhardt, "Simplifying Web segmentation," *The McKinsey Quarterly*(3): 2001,12–14.

chapter six

"... and moreover conjure
you by that object which of
all others in this life you have
most loved, or are most in
love with, to tell me who you
are ..."

Cervantes Saavedra, M. de. (1793).

*The History and Adventures of the Renowned
Don Quixote, 6th ed. corr. London: Printed
for A. Law, W. Miller, and R. Cater.Vol.1, p.169.*

TARGETING

After studying this chapter you should be able to:

1. *Explain the benefits of understanding the target audience*

2. *Create benefit plots to identify areas of strategic opportunity*

3. *Describe the purpose of the target audience description*

4. *Draft a complete target audience description*

5. *Integrate targeting with other strategic decisions of the firm*

Target Stores: Increased Profitability through Accurate Targeting

Most of our consumer-products purchases are driven by routine rather than conscious choice. Such accurate targeting of us during the brief periods when we may change our habits can lead to a gold mine for marketers. Researchers have found that key periods of cognitive awareness occur around big life changes, among which perhaps none is more important than the arrival of a new baby. Tired new parents look for easy ways to consolidate tasks, and for a "one-stop-shop" retailer like Target, calculating how to capture this population can mean attracting a whole new group of people who might flock to Target for years to come.

Tom Starkweather/Bloomberg/Getty Images

To reach this goal, Target assigns every shopper a "Guest ID" number linked to the shopper's credit card, and if a guest fills out a survey, mails in a refund, visits the website, uses a coupon, or opens an email from the company, that information is stored as well. Target can also buy other consumer data such as job history, number of cars owned, magazines subscribed to, college attended, and bankruptcy history and add that to a person's Guest ID. With this background, the store can analyze purchases, and if a female shopper begins to buy from a specific list of around 25 items (including unscented lotion, large packs of cotton balls, and multivitamins), she is assigned a "pregnancy prediction" score, complete with a very accurate estimate of her due date. Target then sends her coupons timed to specific stages of her pregnancy, mixed with non-pregnancy-related items like lawn mowers and wine glasses because consumers are less likely to use the coupons if they feel they are being spied upon.

From the time the program began in 2002 until 2010, Target's revenues rose from $44 billion to $67 billion, and Target's president attributed some of the increase to a "heightened focus on items and categories that appeal to specific guest segments such as mom and baby" (the company does not break out profits for specific divisions). Target has become very successful by being able to precisely target customers who might need what the retailer has to offer. It achieves great targeting precision by integrating predictive statistical models and research about how humans develop routines and how those routines become self-perpetuating. ■

Sources: Dale, Sean. "Target's predictive analytics misfires again!," *Retailnet Group: In-Store Trends.* http://www.instoretrends.com/index.php/2012/04/17/target-marketing-wedding-misfire-blunder/. Accessed March 12, 2012.

Duhigg, Charles. "How companies learn your secrets," *The New York Times.* February 16, 2012. http://www.nytimes.com/2012/02/19/magazine/shopping-habits.html?_r=2&pagewanted=1&hp.

TARGETING: THE VALUE OF UNDERSTANDING THE TARGET AUDIENCE

Target is not alone in its use of consumer data to tailor the retail experience, and the explosion of social media and new technology for mining this data has transformed the marketing industry. Consumers are usually aware that the websites they visit, the information they post on Facebook, and their Twitter accounts are readily accessible to companies. New technologies are growing rapidly offline as well, however, as the positive results of specifically tailored marketing strategies become more apparent.

In Chapter 5 we introduced a three-step process for translating strategy into execution: segmentation, targeting, and positioning (STP). The focus of this chapter is on the second activity—**targeting.** Targeting is distinct from segmentation. When we segment the market, we describe the general space in which we will be competing based on the key benefits we believe consumers are seeking, and that we can deliver. In the targeting step, however, we focus this analysis into a more detailed understanding of *where* in this space we plan on competing, and specifically *who* might respond positively to our appeal. We will illustrate this understanding with a detailed description of our target audience in terms of his or her attitudes and behaviors. By plotting our market space and developing this **target audience description,** we gain a rich understanding of our target customers and their perceptions of our brand, setting the stage for assembling a value proposition, which we address in Chapter 7, and preparing for execution.

To ensure that this process is integrated with our earlier strategic work, we will first consider our target audience in the competitive context, by illustrating customer perceptions of our brand and of competitive brands, so we can understand where we are and where we wish to move in this space. This illustration, in combination with our detailed target audience description, will serve as the foundation for our positioning statement in this chapter. Keep in mind that the process of visualizing the market and selecting our desired position within it is *iterative;* that is, we are free at any step to move back and make changes to earlier decisions in order to ensure our strategy is optimal and integrated.

PLOTTING THE MARKET: CREATING AND INTERPRETING BENEFIT PLOTS

In the segmentation phase of the STP process, we identified the main and/or dynamic benefit for the category, which will form the basis of our **benefit plot.** Also called a **competitive plot,** a *perceptual map,* or a *market plot,* the benefit plot is a chart that helps us visualize customer perceptions of our brand relative to competitive brands. In order to generate perceptual benefit plots, we can use sophisticated analysis tools such as multidimensional scaling, factor analysis, discriminant analysis, or cluster analysis to plot multiple benefits along different vectors and then place the brands in the market space within the map. These statistical tools can be quite effective, although their details are beyond the scope of our discussion here, but they can also sometimes obscure simpler, more basic truths about the needs of our target audience and what we might do to satisfy them.

For simplicity's sake and to stay true to the strategic analysis, we first review a simple way to plot the entire market set and then draw a benefit plot with just two axes. We will call the first type of plot, used to visualize the entire market, a **perception and importance benefit plot.** We then review another type of benefit plot, the **main and dynamic benefit plot,** which we use to link our core competence to the benefit that is or could be valued by a substantial group of consumers.

Targeting. The process by which we locate and describe specific groups of customers who we hypothesize are most likely to be interested in obtaining the benefits we offer through products and services.

Target audience description. A rich description of a member of the market segment we are pursuing, leveraging demographic, behavioral, and attitudinal characteristics.

Benefit plot. A graphic showing importance and perception ratings. Sometimes these plots are also called perceptual plots.

Competitive plot. A plot of just a couple of benefits that define our specific market space and help us locate brands in that space.

Perception and importance plot. A benefit plot that illustrates the relative importance of the key benefits in the market space and how customers perceive each of the brands' performance on those key benefits.

Main and dynamic benefit plot. A benefit plot that illustrates the basis of competition in a particular market space by showing target customers' perceptions of the different brands' performance of the main and dynamic variable.

In the segmentation chapter (Chapter 5), we described the main and dynamic benefit and also introduced a tool to qualitatively develop potential segmentation variables, thus helping us organize our foundational data collection efforts (see the Marketing Analysis and Planning feature at the end of Chapter 5). To now draw benefit plots, we must be able to measure the value of service and product attributes and customers' perceptions of each brand's performance; in other words, we will select some of the segmentation variables we generated earlier and collect perception and importance ratings. Plotting the market allows us to identify benefits for which our brand holds a unique advantage over competitors; this method also allows us to identify areas of potential weakness—important benefits on which our customers perceive our brand to perform poorly compared with other companies in the market.

Measuring importance and perception regularly is valuable both for understanding our market and for managing our company's performance for our customers. The simplest way to collect the data is to run a short survey with our target customers and simply ask how well the firms in the category deliver on a specific benefit (e.g., "On a scale of 1 to 10 where 10 is best and 1 is worst, how well does McDonald's deliver convenience?"), and how important that benefit is (e.g., "When you are selecting a fast-food restaurant, how important is convenience on a scale of 1 to 10?"). At the end of this chapter, in the Marketing Analysis and Planning Section, we discuss alternative methods for obtaining consumers' rated importance for key benefits, as well as their perceptions of how well we and our identified competitors deliver these benefits.

The purpose of this plotting effort is to describe the market as it is right now, in order to consider what it might become. Marketing, at its core, is a dynamic process; our goal is to use benefit plots to identify where and how we can change key beliefs. This decision is arguably one of the most important we will make in the marketing process. We make it by (1) plotting all the brands and the most important benefits provided to customers within our business category, and (2) choosing where in the competitive space we will stake our claim by selecting a main and dynamic benefit.

The Perception and Importance Plot

The perception and importance plot contains the brands within our market space and the key benefits or segmentation bases that are most critical to customers' brand choice. Assume we have been able to collect importance ratings for the benefits, and perception ratings of the performance of each brand on each benefit. For example, consider the data presented in Figure 6.1 that compares perception and importance data for companies in the personal computing market. This perception and importance benefit plot shows customer perceptions of each brand in the market space, designated as "Our Brand" and "Competitors A through C," using a scale of 1 to 10, and customers' importance ratings of different key benefits for the category (good price, ease of use, customization, availability, and convenience) using a solid black line. In looking at this data we want to identify four types of relationships between perception and importance:

- **Rated importance exceeds our brand perception.** If customers value a particular benefit more highly than they perceive how our product offers it, we are under-delivering on this benefit. In Figure 6.1 this is the case for our brand on the convenience benefit. This may be an opportunity for us, if we have or could develop a core competence to deliver this benefit.

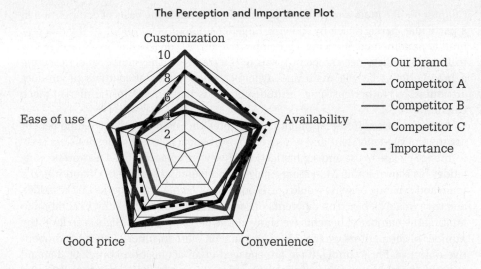

The Perception and Importance Plot

— Our brand
— Competitor A
— Competitor B
— Competitor C
- - - Importance

Figure 6.1 The perception and importance plot illustrates the relative importance of the key benefits in the market space and how customers perceive the performance of each of the brands on those key benefits.

- **Our brand perception exceeds rated importance.** In this scenario, we are over-delivering, as in Figure 6.1, for ease of use. Ideally we would invest marketing dollars to increase customers' rated importance for this benefit. If this is not a viable option, we should consider reducing investment in competencies tied to this benefit.

- **Perception of our brand is similar to that of our competitors.** This is the case in Figure 6.1 for the availability benefit. Since importance of this benefit is relatively high, our brand could experience gains if we were able to enhance our customers' perception of it. Again, we must believe we have a competence that will allow us to deliver on our promise on this benefit.

- **Perception of our brand is lower than perception of our competitors.** In Figure 6.1 our product is poorly perceived on convenience relative to the competition. In addition, importance is higher than our perception rating. While we may choose not to differentiate on this benefit, we might have to shore up our actual and perceived performance in order to compete successfully. This data is a red flag for us in terms of our brand performance.

A careful analysis of the perception and importance plot will thus help us to (1) identify areas where we may be under- or overspending, and (2) most importantly, select a benefit for targeting and positioning purposes. The selection of our positioning benefit really starts in segmentation, when we discover customer needs through qualitative research methods and feature-benefit-value laddering (see the Marketing Analysis and Planning section in Chapter 5) and refine those needs through rounds of qualitative interviews. It continues when we plot the customer data into benefit plots and analyze it, selecting potential variables and focusing on benefits for positioning purposes. Our results are further confirmed and refined in the main and dynamic benefit plot.

The Main and Dynamic Benefit Plot

During the next step in our analysis, we focus our attention on two key benefits, the main and dynamic benefits, as already discussed in the Segmentation chapter (see

Chapter 5). The main and dynamic benefit plot illustrates the basis of competition in a particular market space by showing target customers' perceptions of the different brands' performance. Focusing our competitive analysis on two key benefits allows us to frame the customer choice in terms of the trade-offs they make when selecting a brand. Note that the main and dynamic benefits are not features or product attributes, but rather customer attitudes or needs that brands in the market place can fulfill.

As we discussed in the Segmentation chapter, the main and the dynamic benefit are mutually independent and non-overlapping benefits, for example, price and performance or ease of use and sophistication. If we were constructing a feature-benefit-ladder (as shown in the Marketing Analysis and Planning section of Chapter 5), the main and dynamic benefits would correspond to different vertical paths on the ladder, and they would be based on different core competencies. For simplicity, in addition to limiting the number of benefits we show in this benefit plot, we might also limit the number of competitors we include, depending on our consumer focus and competitive objective. For example, if we are engaged in an acquisition/stimulate demand strategy, the relative position of competitors is less important; we may choose to plot only the #2 brand to keep an eye on its position relative to ours. Because each competitor in the market will likely be implementing a different strategy with different main and dynamic benefits, each will actually be developing a different plot. This is the basis of a truly differentiated market: each competitor works to position its brand based on its own core competencies and linked benefits.

Figure 6.2 represents a typical main and dynamic benefit plot. In addition to placing each brand within the perceptual benefit map, we size each of the bubbles to illustrate the relative market share of each brand in the category. The bubble size for each brand might indicate the total number of units sold by that brand, its **unit market share,** or its **revenue market share.** Unit market share is the number of units sold in a category by our brand divided by the total number of units sold in a category within a specific time frame, while revenue market share is the revenue of our brand divided by the total revenue corresponding to all brands in a category within a specific time period.

Unit market share. The number of units sold by our brand divided by the total number of units sold in a category within a specific time frame.

Revenue market share. The revenue of our brand divided by the total revenue corresponding to all brands in a category within a specific time frame.

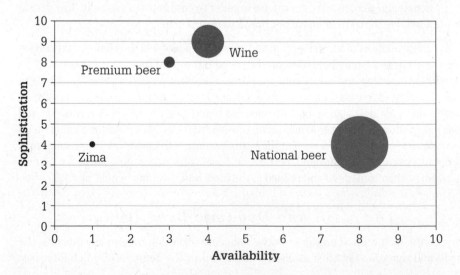

Figure 6.2 The Main and Dynamic Benefit Plot helps us understand the trade-offs customers make in selecting a brand within the category. The sizes of the circles in this sample show how the market leader dominates on the main benefit in the alcoholic beverages category.

CHAPTER SIX TARGETING

The main and dynamic benefit plot shown in Figure 6.2 is drawn from the perspective of National Beer, which appears to be the category leader in this market of alcoholic beverages. Each bubble represents market size, and the competitors are plotted based on current market perception. National Beer is perceived as strong on delivering the benefit of availability, and based on market share this benefit appears to be the main one for the category. If a category is well established and all major brands are relatively well distributed, the easiest way to identify the main benefit is to look at perception and share data for the market leader. The reason is that market share in a developed category basically reveals the value consumers place on each benefit.

In a stable category, the main benefit is essentially "owned" by the category leader. This means that any other brand seeking to enter and compete in this category must deliver some acceptable level of this benefit and then identify another dynamic benefit it might leverage to earn share from this competitor. In Figure 6.2, for example, Wine would attempt to earn share from National Beer by increasing either the perception or the importance of sophistication.

Benefit Plotting and Strategic Choice

Recall from the Source of Volume chapter (see Chapter 4) that to a certain extent we can choose the category in which we compete. For example, Premium Beer might elect to define the category as "Premium Alcoholic Beverages," in which case it would plot only premium beer and wine. This flexibility in considering different category definitions, competitors, and benefits to try out different market plots is an extremely valuable quality of STP process. It enables us to visualize where we are right now and where we would like to be. And, as always, we must keep core competence in mind: our choice of segmentation benefits and our desired location must be realistic given the skills our firm possesses or plans to develop. When we are confident about the accuracy of this market plot, we will proceed to the target audience description.

Of course, in collecting customer perceptions through a survey, plotting those perceptions, interpreting those plots, and selecting a main and dynamic benefit, we face considerable uncertainty. Even assuming we can collect good data, which represents the true beliefs or our target audience, and that we have analyzed it correctly, we will never be able to predict future attitudes and behaviors with 100% confidence. Decision-making under uncertainty is obviously difficult and uncomfortable. For this reason many marketers choose to hedge their bets by selecting a large number of benefits to talk about and an equally large number of competitors to target. Unfortunately, this approach results in a lack of focus in our marketing campaign and an inefficient spreading of resources that will inevitably lead to consumer confusion about our brand. In general, confused consumers tend to rely more heavily on price information, or they may exit the market if they can. Consumer confusion is bad for our brand and bad for the industry.

Instead, we must seek to differentiate our brand, building on a disciplined decision based on feedback about our potential consumers and our company's competencies. We may choose to invest in order to either realign our competencies to deliver a benefit consumers are seeking, or to realign consumer attitudes so the market values more highly the benefit we can deliver. The perception and importance plot and the main and dynamic benefit plot will guide us in this decision.

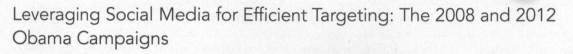

social**media**

Leveraging Social Media for Efficient Targeting: The 2008 and 2012 Obama Campaigns

© Juan Camilo Bernal/Shutterstock.com

Barack Obama's 2008 campaign was a grassroots effort spearheaded by skilled marketers who were able to effectively tap into Obama's target audience: a generally younger demographic that communicates primarily through the Internet. Innovative strategies like showcasing the candidate's 75,000 donors on the blog and offering a chance to win seats at a dinner with Obama to donors of any amount—a prize normally reserved for elite donors—resonated with "everyday Americans." The campaign also uploaded over 1,800 videos on YouTube, which were viewed millions of times and would have cost $47 million to run on television.

Obama's external online director Scott Goodstein cited the campaign's encouraging young people to engage with it and its ability to "move with the marketplace" as two key factors in its success. Goodstein created an iPhone app that allowed supporters to easily access Obama news and videos; he also mapped out the location of local campaign offices, bringing eager new volunteers to those offices ready to help, iPhones in hand.

In 2008, Obama gathered 5 million supporters through social networks; his Facebook page alone boasted around 2.5 million friends, nearly four times as many as rival John McCain. Obama's lead over the Republican candidates in the use of social media continued into the 2012 electoral campaign. This time around, Obama had over 29 million likes on Facebook, compared with 7.9 million for Mitt Romney. And by 2012, Twitter had 10 times more users than it had in 2008. The two candidates used Twitter extensively to comment on specific issues, to react to comments made by the opposition, and even to ask for donations. Here, too, Obama had a great lead over the Republican candidate, with over 20 million followers vs. over 1 million for Romney.

By targeting segments of the population with historically low voter turnout through popular and easily accessible tools like Facebook and Twitter, as well as through person-to-person interactions, Obama's campaign effectively harnessed the power of social media to turn a relatively new political actor into a formidable presidential candidate, and to then continue his leadership into a successful reelection effort in 2012, tapping into the strengths of his young, enthusiastic, and tech-savvy constituency.

Sources: Worthan, Jenna. "The presidential campaign on social media," *The New York Times*. October 8, 2012. http://www.nytimes.com/interactive/2012/10/08/technology/campaign-social-media.html?_r=0. Accessed March 12, 2013.

"How Obama used social networking tools to win," *Blog post*. July 10, 2009.
http://knowledge.insead.edu/contents/HowObamausedsocialnetworkingtowin090709.cfm. Accessed March 12, 2012.

Understanding the Target Customer

In Chapter 5 we identified a main or dynamic benefit that was measurable, linked to our core competence, and important to a significant number of "reachable" consumers. Now we've further refined this process by developing a competitive plot. The next step is to develop a deeper understanding of who our target consumer is. It is not enough to know that our offering will appeal to a sizeable number of customers; we must fully appreciate who these customers are, what their needs are with respect to the main and dynamic benefit, and how we might be able to influence their beliefs and behaviors.

Qualitative research helps us uncover what is most important to customers or potential customers, that is, potential segmentation benefits. Qualitative research is simply in-depth research, typically with either an individual or a smaller group of consumers, in which we explore the thoughts and feelings of our target audience in a more unstructured, open-ended way. Our research might be unstructured in that we don't ask predetermined questions in a predetermined order, but it is not unfocused: we are seeking to deepen our understanding in a very specific way. Here we come back to using qualitative research to deepen our understanding of the target customers we have selected and the main or dynamic benefit around which we will seek to differentiate our brand.

Ideally our observations in this stage should extend to a variety of contexts in which the consumer interacts with our product or service—the customer "touch points." These might include occasions when the consumer evaluates a communication about our brand, interacts with friends and family about the brand, researches our products in stores or on the Internet, or engages with customer service or sales, and of course when the consumer uses our product. A very helpful tool in organizing this inquiry is the **customer experience process map,** a tool that reviews the stages in the customer's experience with a particular brand or an entire product category and the factors that influence that experience. Figure 6.3 shows a typical customer experience map.

Marketers often claim to be "customer-focused" or "customer-oriented." It is one thing, however, to attempt to respond to any and all customer demands at the point of product purchase and sale; it is an entirely different matter to develop a deep understanding of the complete process of engagement with our customers, which begins long before purchase and extends forward in time to our new-product development efforts. Mapping the customer experience helps us develop a rich and deep understanding of the current experience customers have with our product or service, including:

(a) How they come to recognize that they have a need, whether latent or explicit. Customers will recognize basic needs on their own (food, clothing, health care) but for most of their needs, recognition will arise because they are dissatisfied with a current product or service or because a company has created a sense of need. For our target audience and with respect to our main and dynamic variable, we need to understand whether the need is latent or explicit and the type of need recognition process that is most common.

(b) How customers gather and evaluate information about potential solutions to that need. Here, we would like to know what solutions consumers are aware of and what criteria they use to form a consideration set. We would also like to know how and where they gather information.

(c) How they go about comparing the potential solutions in their consideration set. We would like to know what criteria consumers use to evaluate the alternatives in their consideration set. What factors weigh most heavily? What is the perception and importance rating for the main or dynamic variable?

(d) How customers purchase, and what is their purchase experience. Again, what considerations go into making the purchase decision? How does emotion, impulse, and rational decision-making play into the purchase decision?

(e) How customers use and evaluate the product after purchase. The post-purchase and use experience will affect future purchases and the opinions customers have about the brand and the category. Customers evaluate their purchases by assessing product and service performance against their expectations. Here, too,

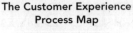

The Customer Experience Process Map

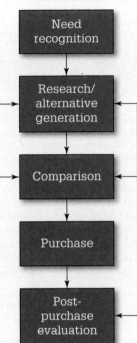

Figure 6.3 The customer experience process map organizes the research we conduct to understand our target audience.

Customer experience process map. A tool that reviews the customer experience with a particular brand or an entire product category and the factors which influence that experience.

GLOBALMARKETING

GLOBAL ISSUES: ICE BEER TARGETING

Ice beer, first introduced in the United States by Molson Breweries of Canada, is made by lowering the temperature of the already fermented beer enough so that ice crystals will form, and then filtering the liquid. Because water has a higher freezing point than alcohol, this process removes some of the water and yields a higher alcohol content than regular beer has. The average ice beer in the United States has between 5.0 and 6.5% alcohol content, whereas U.S. lagers average between 4.5 and 5.0% alcohol. Ice beers sold in the United States target customers seeking more alcohol per can. However, things in Japan are different. One of Japan's leading beer companies, Kirin, has developed an

By including graphical instructions of use on its cans, Kirin supports its targeting effort to attract consumers who want to use beer as a refreshment served over ice.

David Pursehouse/CCPL 2.0

interesting twist on the ice beer concept by introducing Ice+Beer, designed to be consumed over ice to maximize its refreshing quality. Because the beer becomes diluted over ice, its alcohol content when consumed is lower than that of regular beer. With a similar-sounding product, Kirin targets a different set of customers seeking a lower alcohol content than regular beer drinkers. ■

Sources: Alt, Matt. "Beer popsicle alert as ice beer hits Japan," *CNN Travel*, August 3, 2011.http://travel.cnn.com/tokyo/drink/beer-popsicle-alert-ice-beer-hits-japan-518118. Accessed November 20, 2012.

Elliot, Stuart. "THING; Ice Beer," *New York Times Style Magazine*. September 19, 1993.

outside influences—social issues, changes in the environment—can change the customer perception. For example, high-end blender manufacturers or espresso machine manufactures, like Vitamix or Jura, realize that the first few uses in the life of a high-end appliance are critical to customers' long-term opinion of the brand. If customers are able to operate the appliance easily and successfully, they will incorporate it into their daily routines. If not, they might return it—or keep it but become highly dissatisfied.

Continually engaging in deep, proactive research is the only way to truly forge a link between our competencies and our customer needs. As firms have become increasingly interested in enhancing their customer knowledge, they have developed a number of tools to accomplish this goal. For example, Total Quality Management (TQM) and Six Sigma emphasize the need for extensive Voice of the Customer (VOC) research. These tools can be extremely useful for establishing a baseline picture of the customer, identifying consumer preferences, and finding latent needs that consumers may not be able to immediately articulate. However, if we use such tools blindly, without careful adaptation to the particular needs and strategic focus of our brand, we might not collect customer insights that lead to differentiation.

Some VOC is necessary because this type of data can quickly and efficiently yield a "snapshot" of the consumer landscape. However, these tools are not sufficient for differentiation because (1) they are generally in use by many competitors in a particular industry, so the knowledge they produce is somewhat commoditized; and (2) they are not generally customized to reflect the strategic approach of specific firms. The firm's competence, customer focus, and competitive focus should drive detailed consumer research. A firm seeking to stimulate demand, for example, will be far more interested in exploring latent needs of the category non-users, as well as possible reasons why these consumers are reluctant to enter the category. In contrast, a company seeking to earn share from a key competitor will be far more interested in existing users, their habits, and their purchase drivers.

Even more important, any firm seeking to establish a sustainable competitive advantage must have a deep understanding of the relationship between its core competence and consumer needs. A firm with a core competence in industrial design will spend far more time observing customers interacting with a product, while one with a core competence in service operations might invest in observing the customer/customer service exchange. Using panel data (see Global Issues box below) or efficiently gathering their own data, firms that use marketing strategy to drive consumer research will deepen their knowledge in specific ways that are difficult for competitors to replicate. This knowledge is what we call **strategic customer insights:** information about customers or potential customers that holds special value to our firm given our capabilities and marketing strategy. Use of the marketing strategy to drive its customer research is a sign that the firm has developed a true competence in customer research.

Strategic customer insights. Information about customers or potential customers that holds special value to our firm given our capabilities and marketing strategy.

Panel data. Information regarding customers' behavior and attitudes toward products and services that is collected from a group of consumers (a panel) over time. This enables the researcher to track trends among a group of consumers.

GLOBALMARKETING

GLOBAL ISSUES: PANEL DATA

Panel data is consumer research data gathered from groups of people surveyed over time. For years, this type of data has been critical to understanding consumer trends and is particularly useful for companies with mass-distribution strategies. As consumer activity has moved online, so have panel data gathering efforts. However, data availability varies greatly across countries.

Nielsen, for instance, tracks responses on over 30,000 websites for more than 200,000 U.S. Internet users, for more than 250,000 households in 25 countries worldwide, and across a variety of devices, including tablets, smartphones, and computers. The company recruits an online panel following strict calibration methods to ensure it is representative of the online consumer population. YouGov and Europanel are other large panel data providers. Europanel uses a variety of collection techniques including Internet technology, scanners, telephone, paper diaries, and receipts to assess items purchased by households and individual panel members. This in-depth analysis gives an idea of exactly what was bought, when, where, and in what quantity.

Europanel delivers its information to companies to serve as feedback about whether they are accurately reaching their target market, how their brand's strengths compare to those of competitors, and whether their market share is changing. Europanel is active across Europe, the United

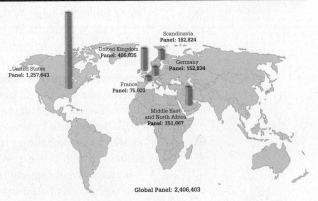

Market research firms are increasingly focused on gathering global data. As of 2013, the firm YouGov was maintaining a global panel with over 2 million people, although more than half these consumers are located in the United States.

States, and most of South America and Asia; however, data is largely unavailable for African and Middle Eastern countries outside Saudi Arabia. This limitation can be frustrating to marketers; however, a well-directed research effort can efficiently uncover customer insights in less-developed consumer marketers as well. In fact, it is in those countries where data is least available that it becomes most valuable. ■

Sources: Nielsen Company website. "Online Measurement." http://www.nielsen.com/us/en/measurement/online-measurement.html. Accessed May 8, 2012. http://www.princeton.edu/~deaton/downloads/Collecting_Panel_Data_in_Developing_Countries.pdf.
http://www.europanel.com/.
http://www.gmi-mr.com/global-panel/demographic-profiles.php.

THE PURPOSE OF THE TARGET AUDIENCE DESCRIPTION

After we have applied our qualitative research tools to develop a detailed understanding of our customer, we are ready to share this information throughout our firm and with our marketing partners, usually in the form of a detailed description of our target audience. Traditionally, this description has been considered important only when a consumer advertising campaign is being developed. Within the Big Picture framework, however, the target audience description represents a crucial link between corporate strategy and execution. If it has been carefully developed, it will serve to focus the firm in a way that a vision statement or strategic plan cannot. Everyone in the firm must be unified around a single conception of who the customer is, and the target audience description is our means of conveying this vision.

Unlike the other parts of the Big Picture framework, this profile will not be a succinct two- or three-word statement. Instead, we will develop a rich and detailed description of our target, sufficient to generate a mental picture in the minds of everyone who develops and delivers services or products to our customers. It is not intended to represent all our target consumers, nor is it an average or amalgam of this group. Instead, we will, in essence, pluck a person from the pool of people who make up our potential customer base and describe this person in substantial detail. We are attempting to bring this person to life for the people charged with creating value for him or her.

Let's look in a little more detail at how our creative teams will use this target audience description to create messages tailored to our customers. This team will need a clear, vivid picture of its intended audience, a sort of "muse." If the target audience description we provide consists of vague characterizations, stereotypes, or averages instead of a specific picture of a potential customer, the team will have to fill in the blanks themselves, and the results might not be ideal.

To develop the target audience description we rely on our intensive strategic work as well as the consumer insights we developed during our brainstorming and consumer research process. We refer back to our earlier strategic analysis and purchase process analysis, tapping information about the demographics, behaviors, attitudes, and aspirations of our target consumer and even what he or she does outside the category. For example, the potential Range Rover consumer likely goes out to eat at a nice restaurant two or three times per month. He or she probably believes paying a little more is a good way to ensure getting the best quality, whether for clothing, cars, or furniture. He or she owns a dog, and it is a purebred; a watch, and it is a Cartier; and has a bottle of Pol Roger champagne chilling in a Sub-Zero refrigerator (just in case).

This approach to writing a target audience description stands in stark contrast to a more traditional approach that describes the target in terms of ranges and averages: "The target is women 25–35 with above-average income." This type of description fails to capture and convey a deeper understanding of the customer. In the end, products and services are consumed not by generic consumers but by living, breathing individuals. Creative people charged with the task of communicating and persuading customers know this; it is important that everyone else in the firm understands it as well. We must develop a vivid target audience description because it will be passed on to our creative team, our product development team, our customer service team, and the many other people critical to creating, conveying, and delivering the offering we intend to provide.

Does this mean every member of our target audience looks and behaves exactly like the one in our description? Of course not, but when we bring one member of our target audience to life, we lay the foundation for the development of a marketing program that also will come to life. A well-developed and detailed target audience description will ensure the quality of the final product of the STP process, the positioning statement.

A question that often arises at this stage is whether we can go after more than one target segment at one time. To answer, we must consider several issues. First, do we have an adequate budget to target distinct consumer groups? We should engage in a careful analysis of the cost of targeting multiple groups compared to our budget. It is not appropriate to simply divide a budget in half in order to reach two groups. Second, we must consider whether the messages intended for the two audiences conflict with one another, which may lead to significant target confusion, unless we are able to carefully segregate these targets. Third, we must ensure that the two (or more) messages we are considering are all linked to our core competence. Finally, we should consider whether these various targets imply different overall strategies, such as a different marketing objective and source of volume. If that is the case, we may want to develop a distinct Big Picture analysis and framework for each one.

social**media**

Zipcar Targets Computer-Savvy People Who Hate Cars

When it was founded in 2000, Zipcar, the U.S. membership-based car rental company, created a new business category: car sharing. Members can reserve Zipcars online or by phone at any time, immediately or up to a year in advance, although most reservations are for immediate and short-term use. Zipcars have become very popular in major metropolitan areas where people now do not need to own a car but might want to use one occasionally. Zipcar does not use traditional advertising but instead parks its cars in public places and highly visible parking lots, where it also distributes membership application materials. Its nontraditional promotional methods align with its customer targeting, which seeks highly tech-friendly customers and therefore uses technology extensively. For example, the membership cards work as access cards to unlock the car doors; members find the keys inside. Zipcar also offers iPhone, web, and Android apps that allow members to locate cars available within walking distance of their location in real

Zipcar does not do mass-media advertising and instead places its cars in highly visible spots where the company's target audience is likely to see them.

Andrew Harrer/Bloomberg/ Getty Images

time. Because the company's customers are tech-savvy, traditional advertising channels not only are unnecessary but would also be ineffective.

Source: Zipcar Company website. http://www.zipcar.com/how. Accessed November 20, 2012.

ELEMENTS OF THE TARGET AUDIENCE DESCRIPTION

While the specifics of each target audience description may vary widely, most good descriptions have a number of features in common, including the following:

- **A name:** The presence of a specific customer name, as opposed to a generic category description, is key to an effective target audience description. If chosen carefully, this name will automatically communicate important nuances about the target that might not be conveyed otherwise. Very often this name becomes a live point of reference for people throughout the organization when they are making key executional decisions, such as "What would Jamie Lee Thurston think of this packaging?"

- **A habitat:** It is important to construct a clear picture of where our target lives and works; the more revealing details the better. For example, a description of a

CUSTOMERFOCUS

IN LIGHTHOUSE'S INTERNATIONAL COMPETITION, SIZE MATTERS

In 2001 Lighthouse International Sight, a nonprofit organization focused on improving vision, created an unusual advertising exhibit, "Size Matters," which centered on a Readable Type Competition. Rather than scoring the advertisements on typical criteria, such as originality, judges simply determined whether or not the target audience—consumers over the age of 45—could actually read the message. Many blue-chip companies whose ads appear in U.S. magazines were part of the exhibit. From Depends™ to Viagra®, many ads were deemed illegible; the companies had ignored the realities of their target audience.

Jerry Della Femina, chair of Della Femina Rothschild Jeary & Partners, said, "The problem is that art directors are young and have great eyesight, so consequently they design for themselves and not for the over-45 age group." It is thus critical to establish a target audience description that details every nuance, including that the audience may need glasses, to ensure the creative team designs ads that are actually readable.

These are some of the guidelines that Lighthouse International offer to increase text legibility:

Lighthouse International competition lends emphasis to the importance of readable type.

(1) **Contrast.** Text should be printed with the highest possible contrast. There is good evidence that for many readers who are older or partially sighted, light (white or light yellow) letters on a dark (black) background are more readable than dark letters on a light background.

(2) **Type Color.** Very high contrasts are difficult to achieve with color combinations other than black and white. Printed material, generally, is most readable in black and white.

(3) **Point Size.** Type should be large, preferably at least 16 to 18 points.

(4) **Leading.** Leading, or spacing between lines of text, should be at least 25 to 30 percent of the point size. This is because many people with partial sight have difficulty finding the beginning of the next line while reading.

(5) **Font Family.** Avoid complicated, decorative, or cursive fonts and, when they must be used, reserve them for emphasis only. Standard serif or sans-serif fonts, with familiar, easily recognizable characters are best. Also, there is some evidence that sans-serif fonts are more legible when character size is small relative to the reader's visual acuity. ■

Sources: Lighthouse International website post. http://www.lighthouse.org/accessibility/design/accessible-print-design/making-text-legible. Accessed March 12, 2012.

Crain, Rance. "Advertising's vision problem: Ignoring the sight impaired," *Adage.* February 26, 2001. http://adage.com/article/viewpoint/advertising-s-vision-problem-ignoring-sight-impaired/55412/. Accessed 8/12/2013.

Mariana Rivera is married, 35 years old, with two children, 5 and 13. She lives in Brisas, in a brick house, and has one dog and two cars. She and her husband work full time, have credit cards, part-time maid, mortgage, and a loan. She cooks on the weekends, and the maid cooks during the week. Her family's income is $1,900 per month. She cares about how she looks and she goes to the hairdresser. She buys at "Fresh Supermarkets" once a week and her maid/kids go to the "ethnic convenience store" during the week for milk, bread, or candy. Sometimes she goes to "99 Supermarkets" to buy in bulk or "The House of Delicatessen" for luxury items. She buys lottery tickets; she also buys expensive things in installments. She sends her laundry to the cleaners. She cooks from scratch; her family takes her good cooking for granted and they don't entertain except on holidays. She worries if her children don't finish the food on their plate. She is more and more stressed about taking care of her family's needs every day—bills, maid, kids' clothes, food, and groceries. She appreciates value, but if something she buys is not good she goes back to the store to complain; when that happens she gets very upset. She has to drive to work every day and feels that traffic gets worse and worse every year. The family does not eat lunch at home but they get together for dinner every night.

Mini-Cooper customer might reveal that her refrigerator is covered with pieces from a magnetic poetry kit, whereas the Ford Explorer customer has a refrigerator covered with artwork created by her three children.

- **Revealing behaviors:** Does she walk the dog or simply let it out in the backyard? Does he keep and file his utility bills or throw them out after paying them? These types of specific behaviors say a great deal about the type of customer we are targeting.

- **Consumption habits:** The products and services that our target customer already consumes provide another set of insights into his or her character. Does she own a hybrid or a Hummer? Does he have a Mac or a Dell?

A detailed target audience description doesn't necessarily have to be long. In fact, by carefully choosing a few key elements from each of the categories above, the firm can develop an incredibly efficient instrument that offers us a deep understanding of the target audience. Figures 6.5 and 6. 6 illustrate two target audience descriptions for different companies with different strategic objectives.

The Perez family, Jose (32), Monica (28) and their sons Jose Junior (5) and Jaime (3) live in a rental apartment; it is small now that they have Jaime so they have been thinking about buying a house. On the weekends, they look at the real estate ads in the newspaper. The apartment is in Parque Lefebre. Both Jose and Monica work; he is a technician, and she is a secretary for the government. They have one car (a Toyota Corolla '98). They have basic furniture and appliances. Their family's monthly income is $1,000 approximately. They have almost no savings. Over the last few months, on Sunday mornings, everyone gets in the car and goes to see the developments advertised in the newspaper that are nearby. Several of their friends just recently moved from apartments to houses and have talked to them about the different areas and houses. They have heard the name Villa Luces and they have planned to visit a house there. When they go to see the different developments, they want to understand what types of people are moving in, and will spend a fair amount of time walking around and getting to know the neighborhood. After visiting at least six or seven different areas, they will probably narrow their decision to between three and four houses, and will make their final decision from two alternatives. They will visit the same house two or three times and will invite extended family to visit it once they are almost certain they will buy it. The purchase process will extend over a period of six months. They will finance the purchase.

Integration: Targeting and the Big Picture

Like all chapters in the framework, targeting must be considered in light of the overall strategy. The most important point here is that we are moving people from one state to another, and exactly what this move will be is determined by our marketing objective and source of volume.

If we are pursuing an acquisition/stimulate demand strategy, our target audience *potential* users of the category. We want to move them to become users of the category (and ideally of our brand). We are in essence inviting consumers in and introducing them to the benefits of our category and our brand.

For an acquisition/earn share strategy, our target audience is already in the category but using another brand, product, or service type within it. Our challenge is to move them from this state to one in which they choose our brand instead of the competitor's. This may be a much more difficult task, particularly if these consumers are content with their current brand.

For retention/earn share, our target audience is people who are using our brand and another brand or brands. We must move them from this state of variety-seeking to one in which they actively decide to use our brand more often and, ideally, exclusively. As usage increases, we will likely move to a retention/stimulate demand strategy.

Finally, for retention/stimulate demand, our target audience is our current customers, and we wish to move them to a state of deeper commitment to our brand. For many firms this is the ultimate goal of all marketing efforts; ideally, the majority of their current customers live in this state.

With the target audience description in hand, we now have a deep understanding of how we will segment that market and to whom we will talk. We can move on to the final stage of STP, in which we determine what we wish to say to them.

☐ SUMMARY

1. Explain the benefits of understanding the target audience

The targeting process helps us define where in the market space we will focus and which customers are most likely to respond to the value proposition we are beginning to assemble through segmentation and positioning. Understanding our target audience will help us determine specifically how to articulate our value proposition, how to prioritize customers, and what channels of communication and distribution to use.

2. Create benefit plots to identify areas of strategic opportunity

Benefit plots are a graphical representation of customer perceptions about the relative importance of benefits in a category and the performance of the brands in the category on those benefits. We use benefit plots in two ways: (1) to assess whether we might be under- or overspending through our executional effort; and (2) to select benefits on which we want to focus for differentiation purposes. Perception and importance plots contain the brands within our market space and the key benefits or segmentation bases most critical to the customers' brand choice. The main and dynamic benefit plot shows customer perceptions of two or more brands' performance in the category.

3. Describe the purpose of the target audience description

The target audience description is rich and detailed and specific enough to generate a mental picture of the target audience. It should be shared and validated with all those charged with execution, including communications, product development, and sales.

4. Draft a complete target audience description

To write a target audience description we will, in essence, pluck a person from the pool that makes up our potential market and describe this person in substantial detail. To bring this person to life for the people who are charged with creating value for him or her, we will include a name, a habitat, revealing behaviors, and consumption habits.

5. Integrate targeting to other strategic decisions of the firm

When we are executing an acquisition/stimulate demand strategy, we are dealing with a heterogeneous group of customers who might never have considered the benefit we are trying to commercialize. In retention/ stimulate demand we are describing our own customers and seeking an opportunity for cross-selling or upgrading their use of our brand. In acquisition/ earn share we are describing competitive customers, the toughest target audiences to reach and understand. Here it is critical that we develop realistic descriptions and estimates of our ability to influence them. Finally, in retention/earn share we seek to increase the importance of our dynamic benefit so our least loyal customer will experience our brand a little differently and will be open to changing his or her usage patterns.

☐ KEY TERMS

Benefit plot. (p.169) A graphic showing importance and perception ratings. Sometimes these plots are also called perceptual plots.

Competitive plot. (p.169) A plot of just a couple of benefits that define our specific market space and help us locate brands in that space.

Customer experience map. (p.175) A tool that reviews the customer experience with a particular brand or an entire product category and the factors which influence that experience.

Derived importance. (p.186) Also called "revealed" importance as the researcher uses statistics methods to estimate importance indirectly, based on answers to other questions rather than by asking directly.

Main and dynamic benefit plot. (p.169) A benefit plot that illustrates the basis of competition in a particular market space by showing target customers' perceptions of the different brands' performance of the main and dynamic variable.

Panel Data. (p.177) Information regarding customers' behavior and attitudes toward products and services that is collected from a group of consumers (a panel) over time. This enables the researcher to track trends among a group of consumers.

Perception and importance plot. (p.169) A benefit plot that illustrates the relative importance of the key benefits in the market space and how customers perceive each of the brands' performance on those key benefits.

Revenue market share. (p.172) The revenue of our brand divided by the total revenue corresponding to all brands in a category within a specific time frame.

Stated importance. (p.186) Perceptual estimate obtained from a survey in which customers are asked directly to rate the importance of a benefit or product attribute.

Strategic customer insights. (p.177) Information about customers or potential customers that holds special value to our firm given our capabilities and marketing strategy.

Target audience description. (p.169) A rich description of a member of the market segment we are pursuing, leveraging demographic, behavioral, and attitudinal characteristics.

Targeting. (p.169) The process by which we locate and describe specific groups of customers who we hypothesize are most likely to be interested in obtaining the benefits we offer through products and services.

Unit market share. (p.172) The number of units sold by our brand divided by the total number of units sold in a category within a specific time frame.

☐ REVIEW AND DISCUSSION QUESTIONS

1. Describe how to use targeting tools to improve the accuracy and usefulness of the estimates of opportunity calculated using the 4Bs template (introduced in Chapter 4).

2. Read the following article about Piano Tuning:

   Chicago Piano Tunes Ltd. is a fictitious piano sales and repair company located in the heart of the Loop, in Chicago. The company has been in business for over 100 years and offers a range of pianos from a variety of brands, both new and used. The company also has a repair and tuning department, which offers solid service and has some loyal clients; however, in recent years the repair and tuning department has experienced a slow yet steady decline in its business. The new manager of the repair department has worked to assemble a list with the names and addresses of Chicago Piano Tunes's customers—anyone who has purchased a piano or other services in the last three years from the company. The manager has also been able to cobble up a list of other piano owners in Chicago through a few disparate sources. The manager feels that part of the reason for the decline in sales might have to do with the lack of a clear value proposition for his department, and perhaps for Chicago Piano Tunes more generally. He is looking to change that, and to develop a clear value proposition.

   (a) What information should the manager obtain in order to make a fact-based strategic decision about segmentation and targeting?

   (b) Assume the manager wants to do some research on its customers. What roles should quantitative and qualitative research play in the manager's investigative efforts?

3. Referring to question 2, assume the manager has done all his homework and has identified two large market segments. One is cost-conscious and is generally made up of occasional piano users. The other is made up of serious, mostly professional piano users and tends to be more concerned about sound quality and less about cost. Write two separate target audience descriptions:
   - One for the cost-conscious segment
   - One for the sound-conscious segment

   In writing your target audience descriptions be sure to include demographic characteristics (income level, family size, etc.) as well as attitudes and behaviors toward pianos.

4. Referring to question 2, write a target audience description corresponding to a piano tuning company that looks for families who are risk-averse and might be interested in piano tuning to avoid problems.

5. Referring to question 2, write a target audience description corresponding to a piano tuning company that targets families who are frequent users of its service, use it very frequently, and want their piano to always sound as good as it can.

6. Take a look at the following competitive plots. Comment on the competitive position of the three companies depicted. Comment on what might be happening in the category in terms of customer perceptions.

Competitive Plot #1

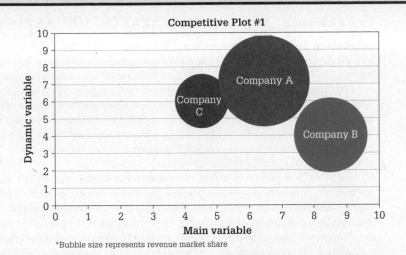

*Bubble size represents revenue market share

Competitive Plot #2

*Bubble size represents revenue market share

Competitive Plot #3

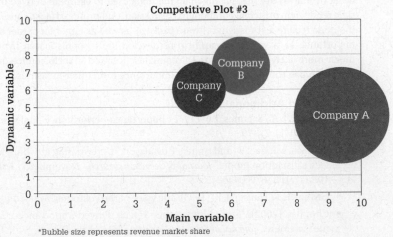

*Bubble size represents revenue market share

☐ APPENDIX: MARKETING RESEARCH AND ANALYSIS TOOLS

Marketing Tool #6.1: Measuring the Stated Importance of Attributes

In this chapter we described a simple survey question that asks customers to rate importance using a 1 to 10 scale. This type of survey item is known as a *scale-rating* question. Researchers use two other types of questions to ask about importance: *point allocation* and *paired comparisons*. In a point allocation question, customers must allocate a fixed number of points, generally 100, among a group of benefits. In a *constant-sum scale*, customers allocate 100 points among a set of benefits, being asked to allocate more points to the most important benefits and fewer points to other less important benefits. The researcher then translates the point allocation to importance weights for the different benefits.

In a paired comparison question, the researcher arranges benefit pairs and the customer must select one benefit in each pair. For example, if we are asking about the relative importance of price, performance, and convenience, we would present respondents with the following pairs: price-performance, price-convenience, and performance-convenience. The researcher then derives importance ratings by comparing the number of times customers selected each benefit.

Rating scale, point allocation, and paired comparison questions are all examples of **stated importance** measures, questions in which we simply ask customers for their opinion about what is most important. The great advantage of stated importance metrics is that they are easy to use, to plot, and to interpret; anyone in the company will understand this type of data. However, there are a few drawbacks.

One problem is that customers tend to rate many benefits as very important, so the researcher ends up with very high values (mostly 9's and 10's in a 10-point scale) and little differentiation among benefits. Also, when asked directly customers might also not be very good at distinguishing between benefits that affect their brand loyalty a lot and those that have only a small effect. Another practical issue is that asking customers to respond to both importance and perception questions might seem repetitive and might lengthen the survey. This is especially true if we have used paired comparison questions. A long survey results in low response rates if we have many benefits and several competitors. Finally, depending on what we are asking, direct questioning might result in socially acceptable answers that are not truly representative of how people act (e.g., if we asked a surgeon to rate the importance of patient safety, they might rate it higher than it actually is). For these reasons, some researchers use derived importance where they need precise estimates.

Derived importance calculations can help us reveal the degree to which a change in our company's performance on a particular benefit would improve overall satisfaction or some other overall loyalty metric. The main methods used to estimate derived importance are multiple regression, principal components regression, and principal least-squares regression. These methods require a statistical software package, as well as larger customer samples than stated importance. However, they can help us develop more sophisticated hypotheses about how much more likely customers are to repurchase a brand if performance on some benefit improves; that is, they can help us derive importance from other measures.

Sources and Additional Readings

- Martilla, J. A., & James, J. C. (1977). Importance-performance analysis. *The Journal of Marketing* 41(1): 77–79.
- Johnson, Michael D. and Anders Gustafsson. "Determining attribute importance in a service satisfaction model," *Journal of Service Research*, November 7, 2004, pp. 124–141, doi: 10.1177/1094670504268453.
- Griffin, A., & Hauser, J. R. (1993). The voice of the customer. *Marketing science, 12*(1), 1-27.
- Chu, Ray (2002). "Stated-importance versus derived-importance customer satisfaction measurement," *Journal of Services Marketing* 16(4): 285–301.

Stated importance. Perceptual estimate obtained from a survey in which customers are asked directly to rate the importance of a benefit or product attribute.

Derived importance. Also called "revealed" importance as the researcher uses statistics methods to estimate importance indirectly, based on answers to other questions rather than by asking directly.

Marketing Tool #6.2: Tracking Customer Attitudes: Key Questions

Tracking customer attitudes around the main benefits customers seek in our category is critical to understanding the effectiveness of our marketing efforts. This chapter discussed how to ask perception and importance questions. In building this type of questionnaire, we should also include an open-ended question to let consumers explain in their own words what motivates their purchases in the category. Finally, it is always available to track perceived value and overall satisfaction. Including all these factors will yield a short questionnaire that helps us track our customers' perceptions over time. We include a sample questionnaire below:

Sample Benefit Tracking Questionnaire

I would like to ask you a few questions regarding your opinion of *<product category>*. Your answers will be used to improve our service and the quality of our products, and they will otherwise be maintained in strict confidence. This questionnaire will take no longer than five minutes to complete. May I please continue?

1. Please provide the primary reasons (up to three) why you use (or purchase) *<insert brand A><product category>* most often (collect at least three).

2. We would like you to rate *<product category>* brands on a series of factors using a 10-point scale, where 1 is poor and 10 is excellent. It is important to stress that there are no right or wrong answers; we just want your opinion. As you consider these questions, please be sure to base your answer on your perception of the Brand.

	Brand A	Brand B	Brand C
Benefit 1			
Benefit 2			
Benefit 3			
. . .			
Represents good value for the price			

3. Now we would like you to rate the importance of the attributes generally considered when making a <product category> purchase decisions. We will be using a 10-point scale, where 1 means something is not at all important in driving your <product category> purchase decisions and 10 means the attribute is extremely important in driving your <product category> purchase decisions. There are no right or wrong answers; we just want your opinion.

	Brand A	Brand B	Brand C
Benefit 1			
Benefit 2			
Benefit 3			
. . .			
Represents good value for the price			

4. Based on your entire experience with <**Brand A**> to date, please rate your agreement with this sentence: "Brand A provides good value for the cost." Please indicate your response on a scale of "1" to "10," where "1" means you completely disagree and 10 means that you completely agree with that sentence.

5. Based on your entire experience with <**Brand A**> to date, please rate your overall satisfaction with <**Brand A**>. Please indicate your response on a scale of "1" to "10," where "1" is *very dissatisfied* and "10" is *very satisfied*."

6. Given your experience to date with <**Brand A**>, how likely would you be to increase, decrease, or maintain your current usage level of <**Brand A**>'s products? Now please use a 5-point scale as follows:

   1. Very likely to decrease usage of Brand A's products
   2. Likely to decrease usage of Brand A's products
   3. I am not planning to change my usage of Brand A's products
   4. I am likely to increase my usage of Brand A's products
   5. I am very likely to increase my usage of Brand A's products

Thank you very much for your feedback today.

Marketing Tool #6.3: Benefit Plots

Chapter 6 covered some simplified ways to track customer perceptions of our products and services. Using a questionnaire like the *benefit tracking questionnaire* shown above, we can obtain the perception and importance ratings that we will use to construct benefit plots. We can use a tool like MS Excel to draw the Perception and Importance and the Main and Dynamic variable plots discussed in this chapter.

Perception and Importance Plots

Strategic Focus	Focus of the Perception and Importance Plot
Acquisition / Stimulate Demand	**Identify the Main benefit.** New benefit which satisfies need not currently provided in the category.
Retention/ Stimulate Demand	**Monitor the Main benefit.** Here the main variable is an existing benefit already provided by the market leader.
Acquisition / Earn Share	**Identify Dynamic benefit.** We plot a benefit which competitive users are currently not receiving or (a) where market leader is perceived to be inferior (perception opportunity); or (b) competitive customers do not value but could value.
Retention/ Earn Share	**Monitor Dynamic benefit.** We track our brand's ability to cause multi-brand customers to become more loyal.

Main and Dynamic Benefit Plots

Strategic Focus	Objective of the Main and Dynamic Benefit Plot
Acquisition / Stimulate Demand	**Main benefit.** We plot a new benefit and reflect on whether it is or could be significant enough to establish a new category.
Retention/ Stimulate Demand	**Main benefit.** Multiple plots showing the main benefit against different dynamic benefits may be drawn to analyze alternate competitors trying to earn share from the market leader.
Acquisition / Earn Share	**Dynamic benefit.** We plot the main and potential dynamic benefits. The ideal dynamic benefit is one that: (a) competitive users are currently not receiving; or (b) where market leader is perceived to be inferior (perception opportunity); or (c) competitive customers do not value but could value.
Retention/ Earn Share	**Dynamic benefit.** We plot the dynamic benefit and the main benefit and reflect on how to leverage the dynamic benefit to increase multi-brand user purchases.

☐ RESOURCES

Kim, Yong Seog and W. Nick Street "An intelligent system for customer targeting: A data mining approach." *Management Sciences*, University of Iowa, Iowa City, IA. Received August 1, 2002. Accepted December 1, 2002. Available online February 15, 2003.

Mitchell, V. W. (1994). "How to identify psychographic segments," *Marketing Intelligence and Planning* 12 (7): 4–10.

Park, C. H. and Y. G. Kim (2003). "A framework of dynamic CRM: Linking marketing with information strategy," *Business Process Management Journal* 9(5): 652–671.

Peltier, J. W. and J. A. Schribrowsky (1997).The use of need-based segmentation for developing segment-specific direct marketing strategies," *Journal of Direct Marketing* 11(4): 53–62.

Woo, J. Y., S. M. Bae, and S. C. Park (2005). "Visualization method for customer targeting using customer map," *Expert Systems with Applications* 24(4): 763–772.

Martilla, J. A. and J. C. James (1977). "Importance-performance analysis," *The Journal of Marketing*, 77–79.

Gustafsson, A. and M. D. Johnson (2004). "Determining attribute importance in a service satisfaction model," *Journal of Service Research*, *7*(2), 124–141.

Griffin, A. and J. R. Hauser (1993). "The voice of the customer," *Marketing Science*, *12*(1), 1–27.

Chu, Ray (2002)."Stated-importance versus derived-importance customer satisfaction measurement," *Journal of Services Marketing* 16 (4): 285–301.

chapter seven

"... let us put into action what
I have proposed."

**Cervantes; Montgomery, James H.;
and Quint, David (1/21/211).**

*Don Quixote (Translated & Annotated) (p. 740).
Hackett Publishing. Kindle Edition.*

POSITIONING

After studying this chapter you should be able to:

1. *Describe the positioning process*

2. *Evaluate marketing communications campaigns by assessing the fit of the positioning statement with the rest of the brand execution*

3. *Construct an effective positioning statement using the five-box tool*

4. *Write an effective value proposition for business markets*

5. *Integrate positioning with other strategic decisions of the firm*

McDonald's and the Evolution of Its Convenience Promise Around the World

When McDonald's Corporation first began to set up franchises in the 1950s, founder Ray Kroc flew his helicopter across the United States looking for the best spots to open restaurants. Today Kroc's focus on convenience continues to guide the company's commercial operations, but as McDonald's has grown across the country and the world, the execution of its convenience promise has varied greatly in a fascinating balancing act between global positioning and local flexibility. In the United States, the tradition of placing franchises in the heart of communities is still strong, but now the restaurants are also found in universities, shopping centers, airports, and along many highways. In other countries, franchise location and food operations are all adapted to the habits and preferences of local customers so the company can still lead each market with a differentiated convenience promise.

Easy-to-access locations are just one of the many ways in which McDonald's delivers on its convenience promise. Over the years it has also made major advances in food operations, technology, and employee training, including a switch from fresh to frozen French fries in 1966. Instead of peeling, cutting, and frying pounds of French fries every day at each location, McDonald's opted to manufacture frozen fries at a central facility capable of producing 2 million pounds of fries a day. Also in the 1960s, employees were trained to carry out individualized tasks, which promoted production-line efficiency. Later, automated machines were added to eliminate the need for extra workers to dispense drinks and fries or assemble sandwiches.

Recent advances in technology have reduced customers' waiting time, thanks to increased accuracy in digital displays along drive-through windows that allow customers to view their orders after placing them. Some restaurants have even outsourced their order-taking to call centers, which then match drivers to their orders at the window via cameras hidden in the drive-through menus.

© Holger Mette/iStockphoto

McDonalds's convenience promise is no less central to operations outside the United States. In India, the company has opened many franchise locations along major highways and in bus and train depots and has partnered with India's state-owned oil company to open restaurants in its gas stations. McDonald's is particularly focused on Indian shopping malls, like Crossroads, a mall in Mumbai catering to budget-conscious window shoppers.

In large cities in Asia where consumers rely heavily on public transportation and retail space is very expensive, McDonald's offers convenience by delivering for a low price (in parts of China, delivery fees are approximately $1). Delivery has boasted double-digit growth in all 15 countries offering it. Most countries still take delivery orders over the phone, but Singapore and Turkey have begun taking orders online.

Technology in Japan has taken the convenience of McDonald's a step further by linking the ability to order food to the ITS, Japan's wireless traffic news network. When a car enters the vicinity of a McDonald's, its occupants can access the menu via the car's GPS touch screen. Once the order has been placed and paid for, the driver is

continued

directed to the nearby franchise location for pickup. Since its founding, McDonald's has maintained a single-minded focus on developing internal capabilities to deliver convenient food. In the marketing-driven organization, positioning and execution are tightly aligned and the company positioning helps prioritize operational investments. ∎

Sources: Jargon, Julie. "Asia delivers for McDonalds," *The Wall Street Journal*. December 13, 2011. http://online.wsj.com/article/SB10001424052970204397704577074982151549316.html. Accessed April 12, 2012.

McGrath, Jane. "How McDonald's works." *How Stuff Works*. http://money.howstuffworks.com/mcdonalds7.htm.

Scharwath, Kara. "Are McDonalds golden arches losing their luster?," *Triple Pundit Blog Post*. February 27, 2012. http://www.triplepundit.com/2012/02/mcdonalds-golden-arches-losing-luster/. Accessed November 25, 2012.

Sources: http://www.bfeedme.com/mcdonalds-delivery-2/. http://blog.wakeforesthomes.com/2012/02/16/heritage-wake-forest-mcdonalds/.

POSITIONING: WHAT IS OUR MESSAGE?

It is in the **positioning statement** that all elements of the marketing strategy coalesce into a single, focused idea. This statement will marry our entity's core competence, strategic intent, and understanding of the target consumer; it will direct us as we attempt to communicate the value we deliver to our target customer in a compelling way. Positioning is the last stage in the segmentation, targeting, and positioning (STP) process. Segmentation informs us *how* we will define our market; targeting describes very specifically *whom* we will attempt to reach; our positioning statement outlines *what* we will say to them.

Historically, positioning statements were used in a very specific context in which an advertiser, working in a traditional relationship with an agency, developed a strategic statement to direct the creative efforts. This statement was used only for advertising development, not for other consumer communications such as consumer

Positioning statement. This statement will marry our entity's core competence, strategic intent, and understanding of the target consumer.

GLOBALMARKETING

HAITI TOURISM: LOOKING FOR A BETTER WAY OUT OF POVERTY

Since a disastrous earthquake hit Port au Prince, the Haitian capital, in 2010, killing over 200,000 people and destroying much of the country's already frail infrastructure, the international community has invested billions of dollars in rebuilding the country. Yet progress has been slow, and more than 400,000 Haitians displaced by the earthquake are still living in tents. Thus in 2012, the Haitian government began a major effort to try to reposition Haiti, not just as a destination for charitable donations but as a tourist attraction. The ministry of tourism launched a

Dieu Nalio Chery/AP Images

crowd sourcing contest for a new logo to represent the country's tourism appeal (the winner, designed by Xaver Delatour, is shown here). The ministry has also worked to attract hotel investment and customers to the country's beaches and other attractions. In 2011, Haiti had fewer than 1,000 hotel rooms, a very small number compared to its neighbor, the Dominican Republic, with more than 50,000. If the government's efforts to reposition Haiti's appeal are successful, the tourism industry may offer Haitians a sustainable way out of homelessness. ∎

Sources: Alcindor, Yamiche. "Haiti's tourism makeover: From devastation to destination," *USA Today*. June 8, 2012. http://travel.usatoday.com/destinations/story/2012-06-10/Haitis-tourism-makeover-From-devastation-to-destination/55471968/1. Fieser, Ezra. "The buzz about Haiti—As a tourist destination?," *The Christian Science Monitor*. August 6, 2012. http://www.csmonitor.com/World/Americas/2012/0806/The-buzz-about-Haiti-as-a-tourist-destination.

promotions, sales materials, and business identity pieces, nor for any other functions in the firm such as customer service or new product development or sales, even though the individuals performing those functions are also charged with communicating value.

For a firm to develop a truly integrated brand image, however, positioning statements should serve a broader purpose. *Every* company engaged in either consumer or business-to-business marketing should have a carefully specified target audience description, regardless of whether traditional advertising is part of the development or delivery of the product or service. Any person charged with influencing a consumer touch point should clearly understand the objective of our communications. Hence, the positioning statement is much more than a simple hand-off to the communications agency; it is the final step on the bridge between strategy and execution.

EVALUATING EXISTING CAMPAIGNS

One excellent way to establish a baseline understanding of positioning statements is to look at communications such as advertisements, sales materials, and product packaging from various firms. If a particular campaign is well executed, we will have no trouble discerning the positioning strategy on which it is based. In essence, we should be able to reverse-engineer the positioning strategy by dissecting the materials that were developed based on that strategy. In a good marketing campaign, the brand's positioning should leap off the page; in a not-so-good campaign, it may be more difficult to identify the positioning of the offering, and this may be an indication of an executional or strategic weakness.

The ability to evaluate advertising and other promotional materials to discern product positioning is an important skill to develop because it will help us keep tabs on competitors in our category. If we are able to distinguish the strategic intent behind a campaign as we see it, we will quickly be able to assess our own product's positioning more effectively. This evaluation skill is one of the most effective tools for competitive analysis.

The first clue to look for in an advertisement is the **tag line**, the closing, signature line, or slogan usually found at the end of a TV or radio ad, or as a closing line or the *headline* in a print ad or billboard (often printed in large typeface to be eye-catching). This line summarizes the intended communication of the company, and as such it should give a clear indication of the intended strategy for the campaign. The tag line "Have You Driven a Ford . . . Lately?" is clearly intended to suggest to former Ford owners that Ford has improved the quality of its product line. FedEx® conveys an ease-of-use strategy with the long-running tag: "Relax . . . it's FedEx." In well-executed campaigns these lines are more than just empty promises; they are supported fully by the firm's product, pricing, and distribution strategy.

As we develop skill at evaluating campaigns, we begin to see subtle but important differences between positionings. Consider the ads presented in the following two photos. These are examples of two different positioning strategies, with two different target audiences, for the same product. In 1952, Dial® soap was targeted at women

Tag line. A short statement that is meant to capture the essence of the brand positioning, accompanies the brand logo and is an integral part of the brand identity of the firm.

and positioned as providing the benefit of a better complexion. In 1960, the same soap was targeted at men and positioned as providing the benefit of reducing body odor. This second positioning statement resulted in the long-running (and ultimately quite successful) tag line: "Aren't you glad you use Dial®? (Don't you wish everybody did?)." Both ads mention the same product feature, antibacterial AT-7. However, while the antibacterial *feature* of the product is the same, the *benefit* of this feature that is emphasized differs.

Through this detailed analysis we should be able to infer the segmentation variables, source of volume, and marketing objective as well. The Dial 1952 ad represents the "need for good complexion" as the main variable, whereas the 1960 ad represents "need to prevent body odor" as the main variable. Because neither ad invokes a comparison to any specific brand, they both arguably represent stimulate demand strategies where the main or category benefit is emphasized. The 1960 ad is designed to promote Dial soap in a then newly forming segment of deodorant soaps, whereas the 1952 ad promotes Dial in the face-soap category, where it is presumably a category leader. Thus, by carefully evaluating existing communications, we can infer not only the positioning statement, but also the source of volume and marketing objective being pursued by a firm.

Distinguishing Between Strategy and Execution

It is important to note the difference between the *positioning strategy*, which is part of our marketing strategy, and executional elements such as the tag line and other advertising elements. The positioning strategy is the input; the tag line and other advertising copy are the outputs. A firm develops a positioning statement as part of the marketing plan and then reflects the strategy inherent in that statement in its subsequent communications with the consumer. The positioning statement is thus a strategic document intended to communicate the key focus of our communications, and ideally it will drive our product, pricing, and distribution as well: all elements of the marketing execution. It is not our job at this stage to develop an artfully worded tag line; rather, we are concerned here with developing a compelling, focused positioning statement that the creative team will then transform into an appealing phrase (or image).

The distinction between strategic and executional elements is very important, particularly when we face challenges in developing communication materials. Consider, for example, the ad presented in the following photos for Red Bull. The tag line "Red Bull Gives You Wings" is pervasive throughout this campaign, reflecting the company's energy strategy. The two different executions, however, convey quite different images for the brand. The use of Albert Einstein implies that Red Bull's energy will be leveraged for intellectual performance, while the skydiving execution suggests it can be used for adventure activities. The same strategy can thus generate a variety of executions.

Furthermore, regardless of how appealing the execution may be, we must always take a step back and ensure that we are objectively evaluating the strategy. For Red Bull, we must compare the energy strategy to other potential strategic approaches,

The skydiving execution implies the energy from Red Bull might be used for adventurous activity.

such as a *hip/cool* positioning, a *refreshment* positioning, or perhaps a *performance* strategy. All these strategies might yield equally appealing executions; however, they may not be appropriate because either (1) another competitor already "owns" the positioning, or (2) we do not have a core competence that enables us to deliver on the promise of this benefit. If we have done a thorough analysis up to this point, we will avoid strategic pitfalls and develop a clear, focused foundation for the development of a compelling and effective execution. We can accomplish this only if we understand the difference between strategy and executiovan.

CONSTRUCTING THE POSITIONING STATEMENT

Now that we have a general sense of how positioning statements are manifested in marketing communications, we will begin the process of actually constructing a statement. A wide variety of these documents is currently in use by different companies around the world under many different names; however, the primary building blocks are generally the same. Most include some form of *target audience description*, a *communication objective*, and *supporting information* or *permission to believe*. Many also include extensive background information regarding the consumer and competitors. All too often, however, as these documents grow in size they decline in value. Remember that our purpose here is to maintain *focus* and *clarity* in the positioning statement. We pursue this goal for two crucial reasons, (1) to maintain a clear, understandable connection between our firm's competence and the consumer benefit, and (2) to ensure we create understanding, as opposed to confusion, among our target audience. The best way to accomplish this is with a simple, elegant document, ideally one whose key idea can be easily understood and remembered.

Steps in the Process

Of the various positioning tools that have been developed over the years, one stands out in terms of its ability to help us achieve the objectives of clarity and focus. A team at Leo Burnett Advertising led by Robert Shen developed the first version in the late 1980s. We present a modified version of this five-box positioning statement in Figure 7.1.

We complete these five boxes in the following sequence:

- **Current Do:** What key behaviors are our target customers engaging in right now that we want to change? For example, if we are promoting the Kindle Fire

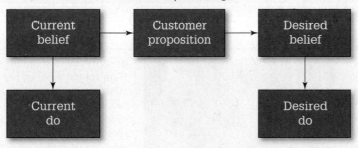

The five-box positioning tool.

Figure 7.1 The five-box positioning tool helps us focus on the key customer insights upon which we are building the entire marketing strategy. In forcing us to simply state the value proposition and to relate it to customer beliefs and behaviors, this positioning tool exposes our logic and therefore allows us to see any potential flaws in our reasoning.
Source: Adapted from the work of Robert Shen at Leo Burnett, circa 1980.

and seeking to earn share, our target customers may currently be using a Barnes and Noble Nook. If we wish to pursue an acquisition/stimulate demand strategy, our customers are those who are not using an e-reader. All "do" and "believe" statements are written in the first person, from the perspective of our target audience.

■ **Current Belief:** We next ask *why* we believe our audience is doing what they are doing. Of course there are likely many reasons; however, ideally we present what we believe to be the most important reason here. For example, they may be using the Nook because they believe it is easier to use. If they are not using any e-reader, they may think the devices are too complicated.

■ **Desired Do:** What do we want our target customers to do? We want them to *switch* to the Kindle from the Nook in the case of earn share, or *try* the Kindle for acquisition/stimulate demand.

■ **Desired Belief:** What attitude might drive our target audience to do what we want them to do? Perhaps they might switch to a Kindle Fire because we convince them that it is even easier to use than a Nook, or that the access to content it provides is more important than ease of use. For acquisition/stimulate demand, we simply need to convince our audience that the Kindle Fire is *not* too complicated.

■ **Customer Proposition:** Most importantly, we will identify a simply persuasive sentence that we hope will move our target from the current belief to the desired belief, and therefore from the current do to the desired do. This sentence is written in the company's voice, as it is a persuasive appeal from the firm to the consumer. Continuing the example above, we might say, "The Kindle Fire provides instant access to more books than the Nook." Or, "The Kindle Fire is specifically designed so that anyone can use it."

Finally, we may want to include additional facts, logic, and data that provide further support for our argument. A specific, side-by-side comparison of the number of books the Kindle can download vs. the number for the Nook is an example of a support point.

Five-Box Positioning Tool: A connected set of boxes that outline our positioning statement. These include the five descriptions listed below:
Current belief. Focused description of the single-most significant belief held by the target audience that most directly impacts the current customer behavior we are attempting to change with our marketing effort.
Desired belief. Focused description of the future belief that, if held by the target audience, will result in the specific behavioral change we are attempting to create with our marketing effort.
Current do. Single-minded description of the primary behavior of the target audience that we are trying to change with our marketing effort.
Desired do. Singled-minded description of the future behavior that will be exhibited by our target audience once the desired belief is achieved.
Customer proposition. A singled-minded statement that contains the essence of the value proposition to our target audience. The customer proposition is designed to achieve a belief change from current to the desired belief such that the target audience will change their behavior, moving from the current to the desired do.

NEW PRODUCTS/INNOVATION

NIKE AND "JUST DO IT" TECHNOLOGY

Nike CEO Phil Knight revolutionized marketing in the 1980s with the brand's "Just Do It" tag line and accompanying blitz. By pairing the high status of U.S. athletic figures with the Nike name, he did more than just position the company's athletic shoes—he promised empowerment and self-realization. The ideal of a better self and a better community resonated strongly with urban black youth, who idolized larger-than-life athletes like Michael Jordan and Bo Jackson. In Nike advertisements the charismatic spokesperson featured prominently with the iconic Nike "swoosh," while the brand name was barely mentioned, if at all. Even non-celebrity spokespeople like 80-year-old runner Walt Stack, who traversed the Golden Gate Bridge as part of his morning workout, embodied the brand's can-do attitude. Youthful idealists and dreamers of all ages flocked to Nike. Nike stands for self-empowerment, and the product being sold is a mere access point to that intangible quality. The broad emotionally rich positioning chosen by Nike, allows the brand to sell a very broad product platform.

Technology has opened new pathways for Nike and its motivational battle cry. Nike+ was a revolutionary feature that allowed users to track their runs. Now the line features the Nike+ Training and Nike+ Basketball programs, which use

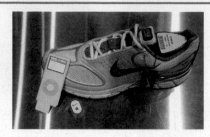

Richard Clement/Zumapress.com/Newscom

pressure sensors in the wearer's shoe to track his or her workout stats and feed them directly to a mobile phone. Users can measure quickness and vertical jump and receive personal training tips and workout regimens from top Nike athletes.

With the Nike+ Sports Kit, the brand teamed up with Apple to feed running data to the user's iPod, which interjects voice notifications to let runners know how far they have gone and their speed. The data can then be transferred to the Nike+ website, where the user can view charts that keep track of previous and planned runs. The site also helps users set goals and measure progress. The integration of social media apps like Gowalla and SCVNGR allows athletes to take their workouts a step further by encouraging friends to get involved. A leader board tracks how users stack up against others and lets them broadcast their scores to Facebook and Twitter.

Nike began with a big dream, challenging people to see the potential in themselves and aspire to their personal best. This broad and emotionally charged brand positioning has the potential to speak to the dreamer in everyone, integrating itself into community life and modern culture. ■

Sources: Sim, Booker. "The 90s marketing frenzy," *Booker Sim,* March 31, 2007. http://www.bookersim.com/articles/inspirational-urban-branding-part-2-nike. Accessed March 12, 2012.

Krentzman, Jackie. "The Force behind the Nike empire." *Stanford Alumni Magazine,* January/February 1997. http://alumni.stanford.edu/get/page/magazine/article/?article_id=43087 accessed 8/12/2013.

1rick and Calow, Rhonda "Nike plus iPod sports kit: For geeks who want to run," *Bright Hub.* May 19, 2011. http://www.brighthub.com/electronics/mp3/articles/23647.aspx. Accessed March 12, 2012.

Akitunde, Anthonia (May 2012). "New Nike+ is iPhone centered, offering you a personal training and workout tracking." *Fast Company. Co Design.* http://www.fastcodesign.com/1669109/new-nike-is-iphone-centered-offering-you-a-personal-trainer-and-workout-tracking. Accessed May 12, 2012.

While it is advisable to follow this sequence when developing the five-box positioning statement, it is an iterative process. We may move back and forth between the boxes, making adjustments to ensure that our positioning statement is cohesive and effective. We will discuss specific techniques for improving our positioning statement in subsequent sections.

Why the Five-Box Positioning Tool?

While any positioning statement that contains a good target audience description and communication objective will generally suffice for copy development, the five-box format is a particularly useful technique within the Big Picture framework for several reasons.

First, the five-box positioning tool is a concise summary of our strategic work. The *current do* reflects our marketing objective and source of volume, the *desired do* links out to our business objective, and the *current belief, consumer proposition, and desired belief* should illustrate our main and/or dynamic segmentation benefits.

Second, the five-box positioning tool helps us to think clearly about the difference between *beliefs* and *behaviors*. As marketers, we are charged with identifying the links between beliefs and behaviors, then leveraging the tools available to us to change beliefs, thereby changing behaviors. Any marketer who ignores this crucial belief-behavior linkage runs the risk of simply taking pricing and promotion actions that are short-term, un-strategic, and ultimately un-sustainable. For example, starting in the late 1980s, U.S. automakers became increasingly reliant on rebates and financing incentives to stimulate new car sales. Essentially, they were lowering the price in an effort to change behaviors, with no real thought about beliefs. Consumers responded,

GLOBALMARKETING

BUICK POSITIONED AS A LUXURY BRAND IN CHINA

While McDonald's and many other brands operating in multiple countries aspire to a fairly homogenous global brand meaning, sometimes brands that are marketed and consumed locally can take advantage of specific market conditions to position themselves. The motivations behind consumer behavior in China are fundamentally different from those of any other nationality, according to the chief executive of the Chinese advertising agency JWT, Tom Doctoroff. The Chinese value order is heavily influenced by Confucian notions of the circularity of history, and while placing individual ambition above the welfare of society is discouraged, personal desire for wealth is encouraged because it benefits society as a whole. These nuances sometimes express themselves in unexpected ways; for example, while Buick cars in the United States suffer from the perception that they are primarily sought after by older consumers, in China "Buick" projects an image of financial ambition and social status, and the brand has enjoyed great success among younger generations.

© Imaginechina/Corbis

Buick has a long history in China; the last emperor, Emperor P'u-i, imported two of the cars in 1924, making them the first automobiles to enter the country. With his endorsement, by 1930, Buicks accounted for one-sixth of all cars in China, and their illustrious history still holds much sway in China's traditional culture. Buick is the brand of choice among Chinese businessmen, upscale travelers, and executives and bureaucrats, who often have drivers and represent a large portion of the Chinese market. Buick has taken note

and positions its cars differently in China than it does in the United States to better target these youthful, sophisticated consumers. The brand has created eight car models exclusive to the Chinese market, many of which feature luxurious rear seat areas, where professionals can control the stereo and air conditioning and enjoy ample legroom. Further, the minivan in China is not a symbol of middle-class suburban families, thanks to the country's one-child birth policy, and is instead seen as a comfortable corporate vehicle. As a result, motivated, upwardly mobile young Chinese professionals have elected to buy Buicks, which reflect their social aspirations and the lives they hope to lead. ∎

Sources: Petersen, Barry. "In China, buy American still resonates," *CBS Evening News.* May 21, 2009. http://www.cbsnews.com/2100-18563_162-4932683.html. Accessed March 12, 2012.

Gross, Daniel. "Why Buick is big in Beijing – and elsewhere in China," *Yahoo Finance Blog Post.* November 9, 2011. http://finance.yahoo.com/blogs/daniel-gross/why-buick-big-beijing-elsewhere-china-175445476.html. Accessed March 12, 2012.

taking advantage of the lower prices. However, the automakers had done nothing to enhance or change consumers' beliefs about the value of U.S. autos. In fact, it is quite likely that these lower prices had a negative impact on perceived value. Very quickly automakers saw a drop in revenues. Consumers had essentially responded to the lower prices by buying cars *sooner* than they might have, but not *more often.*

Third, the five-box positioning tool enables us to consider visually just how far in "belief space" we are asking our target audience to move. This gives us a chance to do a reality check on our strategy. It may feel quite realistic to move people from believing a Barnes and Noble Nook is easier to use than a Kindle Fire to believing the Fire is easier than the Nook. However, for consumers who have never used an e-reader (and who might actually be afraid of technology), the idea that they are easy to use might be too much of a leap.

What Makes a Good Five-Box Tool?

The five-box positioning tool is designed to be as simple and straightforward as possible. While it is simple, it is in no way simplistic. The best five-box tool is an elegantly crafted, cohesive, and ultimately inspiring articulation of our communications strategy. In order to achieve this level we need to pay attention to the following key questions.

- ◼ Are the statements clear and concise? Our goal is not to present every idea here, or even several. Our goal is to prioritize and select what we believe to be the most important idea. Ideally, each box will contain one sentence that reflects this prioritization.

- ◼ Are behaviors and beliefs clearly distinguished? Very often we confuse belief and behavior statements. A behavior is an *action*, in this case usually with regard to a product: purchase, trial, switching. A belief is an *attitude*, such as whether a consumer values a certain benefit, or whether he or she believes a product delivers a certain benefit.

- ◼ Are behaviors linked to beliefs? If a consumer believes all products are basically the same, she might switch back and forth or buy on price. If our target audience believes hybrid cars are not reliable, they may currently own a gasoline car that gets good mileage.

- ◼ Are the current and desired statements linked? If the current belief is that hybrid cars are not reliable, the desired belief should refer to reliability as well; if the current do is using the competitor, the desired do is switching from the competitor to our brand.

- ◼ Finally, is the five-box positioning tool a clear representation of our strategy? We should be able to determine marketing objective, source of volume, and segmentation benefits from the five-box positioning tool. As a rule of thumb, for example, virtually all earn share five-boxes positioning tools will include the word "switch" in the desired do.

If we use these criteria in a disciplined fashion, our five-box positioning will be clear, concise, and ultimately *useful,* not only as a document which drives our communications, but also as a crucial connection between execution and strategy. The brand positioning thus captures customer insights and represents the target audience we are trying to reach, while also guiding our organization to execute well.

Converting Beliefs and Behaviors

Recall that in the targeting module we began to consider the idea that we are moving people *from* one belief/behavior state *to* another. This concept is further developed with the move in the five-box positioning tool from current belief to desired belief. As we use this tool to create a positioning statement, we are of course concerned with creating a successful strategy; whether we will actually be able to move our target audiences' beliefs is the *probability of conversion* we presented as the 4B's tool in module 4. As we create the positioning statement, we can refine our conversion estimates in this tool, because we now have more information that will strengthen our confidence in this guess:

- **Target audience specificity:** The more clearly and specifically we describe our target audience, the greater our chances of achieving a belief change. In a sense, we are framing an argument, and the strength of this argument depends on how well we know our audience.

- **Target audience access:** Obviously, it is easier to convince our target audience if we can reach them. This is more likely if we have a retention objective, because then we are targeting our current customers. It is usually more difficult to access non-customers, as in customer acquisition.

- **Distance between current and desired state:** How far do we need to move our target? Convincing a potential consumer that an electric razor is more effective than a manual razor is a daunting task; convincing someone that a large order of popcorn is worth 25 cents more will be more satisfying is probably a bit easier.

- **Support for our argument:** No argument is convincing without support. For example, if we demonstrate the effectiveness of an electric razor with a side-by-side comparison, our probability of conversion will likely be higher.

GLOBALMARKETING

BEER BRANDS AND NATIONAL PRIDE: CAN BRAND POSITIONING AND OWNERSHIP INTERESTS DIVERGE?

Consumer preferences and national feeling often combine to ensure that a country or region has an iconic beer—Budweiser, Coors, and Miller in the United States; Estrella, Mahou, and San Miguel in Spain; Singha and Chang in Thailand; and Sapporo and Kirin in Japan. Beer advertising often reflects the local pride these brands inspire. However, economics of scale in production and distribution mean that global companies can more efficiently manage local beer brands than local companies can. This creates a paradoxical situation. For example,

Chris Ratcliffe/Bloomberg/Getty Images

Budweiser is an iconic U.S. brand owned by AB-InBev, the largest beer company in the world and headquartered in Belgium. Miller is owned by SAB Miller, a South African conglomerate. Despite their foreign ownership, these brands are still positioned to reflect a distinctly U.S. spirit, but since Budweiser's acquisition by In-Bev, a number of consumers and media voices have called the beer "Anti-American," raising questions about the brand's long-term viability. ■

Sources: "The top 20 selling domestic beers," *The Huffington Post.* September 3, 2012. http://www.huffingtonpost.com/2012/09/03/top-selling-domestic-beers_n_1846582.html#slide=14 56387. Accessed 8/12/2013.

Tuttle, Brad. "How to support America and drink beer in the same gulp," *Time Magazine: Business and Money.* August 2, 2012. http://business.time.com/2012/08/02/how-to-support-america-and-drink-beer-in-the-same-gulp/. Accessed 8/12/2013.

For existing campaigns we can evaluate these three elements to predict the probability of success, and for campaigns in development these represent our levers for ensuring our future success. We may also use this information to estimate how much resource we may need to commit to our campaign in order to ensure its success.

Articulating Our Positioning

The five-box positioning method is designed to express the marketing strategy in a single, crisp consumer proposition. This message is sometimes called a "brand promise" or "unique selling proposition." Whatever the term, it is the core concept that will

CUSTOMERFOCUS

MARKETING PINARELLO KIDS' BIKES TO PARENTS

Pinarello, the Italian road bicycle manufacturer, holds an enviable market position among elite road cyclists. The lightweight design, component quality, and aesthetics of its bicycles appeal to avid cyclists who are interested in gliding on and off road at high speeds. Pinarello also manufactures a few bikes for children featuring the same streamlined design. At prices nearing $1,000, however, these bikes are not targeted at the average child. They are positioned as top-choice bikes for parents who love biking and wish to transfer that passion to their children. This is how a high-end bike retailer, Real Cyclist (http://www.realcyclist.com/), positions the Pinarello kids bike to prospective parent buyers:

©Gilles Rolle/REA/Redux Pictures

". . . Once you make the discovery (conscious or not) that, by God, life is unlivable if you don't view yourself—at your essential core—as a bike racer, seemingly nothing will interfere with your daily rendezvous with pain-on-two-wheels. . . . When kids hit 6 or 7. . . that's when everything changes. Daddy, your kids are true little humans by then. It's full-on interaction, and they need you as Dad in a way that goes beyond your paycheck or your ability to make their breakfast . . . The fact that you're riding together – sharing the act that for so long defined your sense of self-hood—it's an act of love like little else. Given its power, don't blow it by letting your child ride knobby-tired trash."

Parents are the ones holding the purse strings and are likely to better appreciate the myriad features of a Pinarello bike than their young children, so convincing parents to spend $1,000 on a bike for their child is key. Of course, the experience of the end consumer must align with the appeal to the buyer, and children do enjoy the easy-to-use, fast, and lightweight bike. Positioning the bike as a trusted friend for the whole family, one that allows parents to feel they are delivering qualities a child will grow to appreciate, is integral to the brand's success.

When the user and the buyer of a product or service are different, some companies choose to target the user or the buyer exclusively. However, while directing communications to the party most directly interested in the product might seem to hold some logic, ignoring other stakeholders exposes the marketer to the risk that they might later influence or even veto the purchase; also, over time, the power of the different stakeholders in the purchase decision tends to change, leaving the marketer to develop new relationships from scratch. Sustainable marketing campaigns speak to all stakeholders by emphasizing a brand benefit that can powerfully align their seemingly diverse interests. In marketing to parents and kids, Pinarello faces a challenge not unlike that confronting B2B marketers who everyday must understand and align the diverse needs of stakeholders. ■

Sources: December 28, 2011. "Pinarello bikes take the market by storm," author: Bikelover, November 5, 2011 *http://bestvintagebikestore.com/bicycles/pinarello-bikes-take-the-market-by-storm*. Accessed 8/12/2013.

Pinarello FP O Kid's Complete Bike. http://www.competitivecyclist.com/frame/2012-Pinarello-fp-0-kid%27s-complete-bike-10126.html. Accessed 8/12/2013.

Lagorio, Christine (February 11, 2011). "Resources: Marketing to kids," *CBS News BlogPost.* http://www.cbsnews.com/2100-500823_162-2798401.html. Accessed March 12, 2012.

drive all the tactical marketing decisions we will be making. The five-box method encourages us to (1) take into account the current attitudinal and behavioral state of the customer, (2) describe the potential future state, and then (3) illustrate what must be done to build a bridge between these two states.

As we discussed above, many firms utilize their own positioning statements, many of which share similar elements with the five-box. Regardless of the specific format a firm chooses, it is worthwhile to go through the process of developing a five-box as a foundation for other positioning statements. In addition, the strategic nature of the five-box means that it can and should be used as a key strategic driver for pricing, product development, and channel strategy as well.

THE VALUE PROPOSITION IN BUSINESS MARKETS

Many classic and innovative examples of the value proposition center on business-to-consumer (B2C) marketing. But focused, strategic positioning statements are in some ways even more important for B2B than for B2C. The constraints of traditional advertising (a 30-second commercial, a print ad) tend to force the B2C marketer to create a focused message that fits the medium. In contrast, it is quite a challenge to marshal a B2B sales force to deliver one clear message. Instead, salespeople are usually trained to identify the needs of each specific customer and then satisfy those needs, regardless of whether they are linked to our competencies or overall marketing plan. For the B2B firm, then, a clear, concise value proposition represents a driver toward strategic marketing and sustainable growth.

Marketing to Diverse Stakeholders

The key challenge for marketers in business-to-business markets is complexity; instead of one end consumer, the B2B marketer must communicate with several stakeholders along the supply chain. For example, a manufacturer of medical devices might have to consider a distributor, the hospital purchasing agent, nurses, surgeons, insurers, and, ultimately, the patient. Each generally has different needs, and traditionally firms have striven to meet all of them, regardless of how diverse they are. For example, the hospital buyer may seek low price, whereas the surgeon may value instrument ease of use and short-term outcomes related to the procedure, the materials manager may value efficiency and lowering costs, and the patient of course cares most about long-term outcomes and safety. Some stakeholders may also share some common values, as you can see in Figure 7.2, but they place different priorities on them.

In our marketing dreams, all stakeholders would value the same benefit, and that benefit would be the one tied to our core competence. In this dream we enjoy sustainable growth based on one clear, differentiated value proposition and continued investment in one or two key competencies. Unfortunately, we cannot realistically expect these dreams to come true. We can, however, leverage the tools of marketing to move ourselves closer to, as opposed to farther away from, this state.

Consider the situation discussed above, in which the B2B marketing and sales team attempts to meet the needs of any and all customer requests. From the firm's perspective this effort would realistically include investment in a broad array of "core"

Aligning diverse stakeholders through consistent positioning: The role of evidence.

Channel Member	Key Benefits Sought/Motivations	Potential Challenges	Alignment Actions / Role of Evidence (Training, Incentives)
Governments/ Payers	• Broad healthcare metric improvements • Efficiency	• Resource constraints/lack of funding for innovation	• Link individual patient outcomes to societal benefits
Hospital Administration	• Competitive differentiation/ brand reputation • Safety	• Reluctant to make cost/ outcome trade offs	• Provide evidence linking patient outcomes to reputation and competitive differentiation
OR Management	• Efficiency • Cost and throughput • Safety	• Reluctant to make cost/ outcome trade offs	• Link patient outcomes to operational efficiency/avoiding rework
Clinician	• Ease of use • Short-term procedural outcomes	• Lack of long-term orientation	• Link patient outcomes to reputational benefits and procedural outcomes
Patient	• Long-term outcomes • Safety	• Lack of information awareness/expertise	• Consider increasing patient awareness through education

Figure 7.2 A medical device company seeking to align diverse stakeholders in the healthcare supply chain will try to identify positional benefits that have a positive impact on patients, because they are the ultimate end-users of the product or service. While the primary motivations of the intermediaries in the healthcare supply chain are not naturally aligned to patient benefits in all cases, the device company can improve that alignment by developing evidence that links its product's patient outcomes to the benefits each channel member seeks.

competencies: to deliver low price we will likely invest in operational efficiency and sourcing; to deliver ergonomics we must spend on R&D; for outcomes we might need to allocate our resources toward surgeon training and clinical evidence generation. As many firms now realize, this spreading of resources opens us up to competitive attack from firms that are more strategic and focused in their resource allocation.

On the marketing side, by talking about a different benefit to each stakeholder we likewise spread resources and risk creating confusion in the marketplace. Perhaps more importantly, the fragmentation of our message leads to a vicious cycle in which these efforts further fragment the needs of our value chain, thus increasing pressure on our firm to spread our resources across too many competencies and benefits. This cycle is the result of traditional marketing thinking which leads us to try to simply identify needs and fill them. Today's marketer must act on a different and ultimately more optimistic way of thinking.

The modern marketer must consider both what our stakeholders want today as well as *what they might want* after exposure to our marketing efforts. From this perspective we can consider our marketing strategy in the face of diverse stakeholder needs in an entirely different way. Instead of letting our actions further fragment the value chain, it is our responsibility as B2B marketers to attempt to align the value chain. For example, while hospital buyers may report that they value price most of all, it is quite plausible that they could be persuaded to value patient outcomes, in part because this is the final purpose of the healthcare value chain, and ultimately because if the channel members are aligned in delivering patient outcomes, the overall value created by the channel will likely increase, and likewise the profitability of the various stakeholders. Thus, as marketers in business-to-business markets, we should leverage the value proposition to help us move toward *channel alignment*.

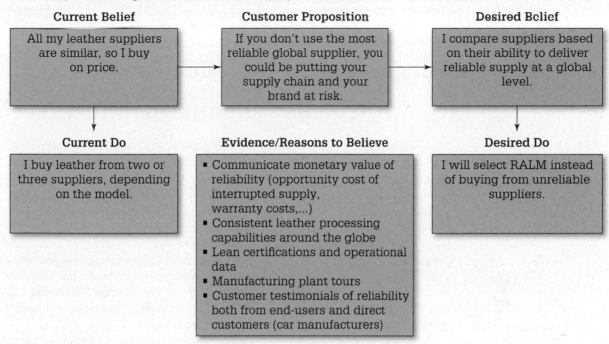

Sample Positioning Statement for a B2B Company: The Reliable Automotive Leather Manufacturer (RALM)

Current Belief

All my leather suppliers are similar, so I buy on price.

Customer Proposition

If you don't use the most reliable global supplier, you could be putting your supply chain and your brand at risk.

Desired Belief

I compare suppliers based on their ability to deliver reliable supply at a global level.

Current Do

I buy leather from two or three suppliers, depending on the model.

Evidence/Reasons to Believe

- Communicate monetary value of reliability (opportunity cost of interrupted supply, warranty costs,...)
- Consistent leather processing capabilities around the globe
- Lean certifications and operational data
- Manufacturing plant tours
- Customer testimonials of reliability both from end-users and direct customers (car manufacturers)

Desired Do

I will select RALM instead of buying from unreliable suppliers.

Figure 7.3 RALM, a manufacturer of automotive leather coverings for cars, is positioning itself as the market leader in its sector and trying to create brand differentiation around reliability. It faces the challenge of translating reliability to car manufacturers that are currently buying primarily on price. In this B2B marketing example, the role of evidence will be critical in generating believability around the statement in the customer proposition.

The Role of Evidence in Positioning

In B2B marketing, support for our claims also plays a different role; our customers have a different standard in this arena. Customers choosing aircraft engines, for example, have somewhat higher stakes than those selecting between brands of cookies. The Keebler Elves's claim that their cookies are "uncommonly good" is supported by the "fact" that they are "made by elves;" Trident sugarless gum is better because it is preferred by "4 out of 5 dentists who let their patients chew gum." These types of support points simply lack the strength to justify purchase of office software or an electric generator. In B2B markets, customers generally require data regarding product performance, market acceptance, product specifications, and the like. Hence, when developing the five-box positioning tool for B2B marketing, we include a crucial sixth box that must contain this evidence-based support, as shown in Figure 7.3.

The Influence of Positioning on Subsequent Decisions

Once the consumer proposition is in place, our challenge is to leverage our strategic work in a disciplined fashion in all aspects of execution. An effective marketing campaign is one in which all marketing elements, not just the advertising, align with the positioning. For example, if we have chosen to position Range Rover as a high-status vehicle, we should not participate in price promotions that might work against this positioning. We will exercise strict control over our distribution so the buying experience reinforces a feeling of luxury, and our product development will of course be focused on product features and attributes that also deliver this experience. While we discuss these elements in distinct chapters that follow, keep in mind that they are four elements of what must be a *unified* strategic plan.

POSITIONING AND THE BIG PICTURE

As shown in Figure 7.4, segmentation, targeting, and positioning are the final strategic stages in the Big Picture framework. As we advance through the framework and proceed to execution, we add detail to our strategy. A well-executed positioning statement will reflect our strategic work and bring clarity and efficiency to our decision-making process in the executional stages. This is the payoff to the hard work we have dedicated to our strategic development; the difficult decisions we have made thus far will make the multitude of executional decisions we face much easier. In an increasingly dynamic environment, the number of decisions a marketing manager must make has increased exponentially; we must identify ways to make our decision-making more efficient without losing consistency and effectiveness. We should thus seek to leverage our strategy in a disciplined fashion to direct our execution, always checking to ensure that strategy and execution are linked.

As Figure 7.5 shows, the strategic quadrant decision we made earlier in the framework will dictate the general customer group we target for segmentation research and for our positioning. In the segmentation chapter, Chapter 6, we discussed the main and dynamic variables as strategic customer insights, or knowledge about our target

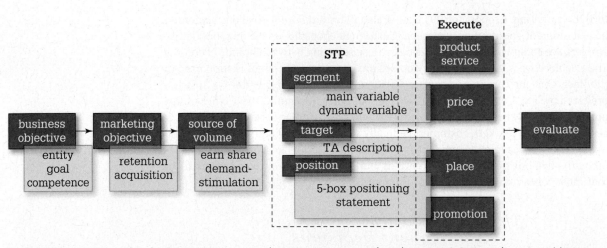

Figure 7.4 Positioning within the Big Picture Framework. As it serves to translate the strategic into a value proposition to a current or potential customer, positioning also acts as the crucial lynchpin between strategy and execution. A well-developed positioning statement will help us greatly simplify our executional decision-making downstream.

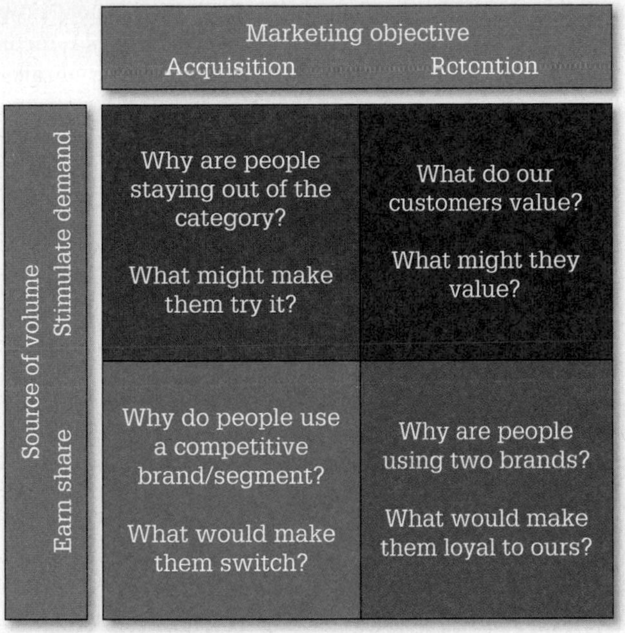

Figure 7.5 Key strategic insights required for effective positioning by framework strategic quadrant

The figure is a matrix. Top header: **Marketing objective** with columns **Acquisition** and **Retention**. Left side header: **Source of volume** with rows **Stimulate demand** and **Earn share**.

	Acquisition	Retention
Stimulate demand	Why are people staying out of the category? / What might make them try it?	What do our customers value? / What might they value?
Earn share	Why do people use a competitive brand/segment? / What would make them switch?	Why are people using two brands? / What would make them loyal to ours?

customers that meets two criteria: (1) it taps into a current or latent customer need and therefore has the potential to motivate behavior, and (2) it is more actionable for us than for our competition due to the nature of our core competence. From this perspective, the main or dynamic variable represents objections to purchase that we can overcome (for acquisition/stimulate demand), sources of current and future value for our customers (for retention/stimulate demand), or competitors' customer needs that will cause customers to switch to our brand if we can fulfill them (for acquisition and retention earn share).

The work we've done earlier in the framework to uncover these strategic customer insights will now help us focus, and these insights dictate how we complete the current and desired belief part of the five-box tool. For acquisition/stimulate demand, the current belief and the desired belief corresponds to a strategic insight that answers the following questions: "Why are people staying out of the category?" and "What might make them switch?" For retention/stimulate demand, these insights inform the current belief, "What do our customers value?" and the desired belief, "What might they value?" For acquisition/earn share they inform the current belief, "Why do people use a competitive brand?" and "What would make them switch?" And for retention/earn share we can address the current belief, "Why are people using two brands?" and the desired belief "What might make them more loyal?"

As we move into execution, we may be tempted to diverge from our strategy. For example, consider a firm that has decided on a retention/stimulate demand strategy promoting status benefit for positioning. We would expect this firm to price at a premium and offer the product in limited distribution. However, what if it is approached by a mass-market retailer whose brand image is inconsistent with the firm's positioning but promises huge short-term increases in sales among new customers? The lure of short-term gains, even at the potential cost of long-term sustainability, is strong. We therefore must have a clearly developed and articulated strategy that helps us to understand the long-term costs and benefits of certain executional decisions.

☐ SUMMARY

1. Describe the positioning process

Positioning is the last stage in the segmentation, targeting, and positioning (STP) process. Segmentation informs us *how* we will define our market. Targeting describes very specifically *whom* we will attempt to reach. Our positioning statement outlines *what* we will say to them. Articulating the firm's positioning in a concise and focused way is key to maintaining the alignment between strategy and execution.

2. Evaluate marketing communications campaigns by assessing the fit of the positioning statement with the rest of the brand execution

To evaluate campaigns, we should aim to backward-engineer the strategy from our positioning. A good campaign stems from a clear and focused positioning statement born from the strategy. If the positioning statement reflects the strategy, it makes sense that we should be able to look at the positioning statement and infer what strategic decisions were made, including segmentation variables, marketing objective, and source of volume.

3. Construct an effective positioning statement using the five-box tool

The elements of the five-box tool—current belief, current do, desired belief, desired do, and customer proposition—isolate the key beliefs that drive customer behaviors for our target audience and help us develop strategies for changing them. Successfully positioning our brands begins with a detailed understanding of the *target audience*. Positioning statements are also *realistic*, meaning that the distance between the current do and the desired do is achievable with the resources and within the timeframe we have earmarked for this effort. Equally important is the strength of the support for our argument.

4. Write an effective value proposition for business markets

In business markets, positioning presents additional challenges. We must: (1) articulate our message to stakeholder groups with diverse needs and motivations, and (2) present proof of a value proposition to change beliefs. B2B marketers face these challenges by aligning stakeholder interests on positioning benefits that create value for end-users of the product or service being created by the entire supply chain. B2B marketers must be adept at developing appropriate evidence that links individual stakeholder motivations to the end-user value.

5. **Integrate positioning with other strategic decisions of the firm**

The role of positioning varies according to the strategic quadrant we chose earlier in the framework. The strategic quadrants are most helpful here as a guide for the type of strategic insights we require from our target customers. In an increasingly dynamic environment, the number of decisions a marketing manager must make has increased exponentially; we must identify ways to make our decision-making more efficient without losing consistency and effectiveness. We should thus seek to leverage our strategy in a disciplined fashion to direct our execution, always checking to ensure that strategy and execution are linked.

☐ KEY TERMS

Five-Box Positioning Tool. (p.197) A connected set of boxes that outline our positioning statement. These include the five descriptions listed below:

Current belief. (p.197) Focused description of the single-most significant belief held by the target audience that most directly impacts the current customer behavior we are attempting to change with our marketing effort.

Desired belief. (p.197) Focused description of the future belief that, if held by the target audience, will result in the specific behavioral change we are attempting to create with our marketing effort.

Current do. (p.197) Single-minded description of the primary behavior of the target audience that we are trying to change with our marketing effort.

Desired do. (p.197) Single-minded description of the future behavior that will be exhibited by our target audience once the desired belief is achieved.

Customer proposition. (p.197) A single-minded statement that contains the essence of the value proposition to our target audience. The customer proposition is designed to achieve a belief change from the current to the desired belief such that the target audience will change their behavior, moving from the current to the desired do.

Positioning statement. (p.193) This statement will marry our entity's core competence, strategic intent, and understanding of the target consumer.

Tag line. (p.194) A short statement that is meant to capture the essence of the brand positioning, accompanies the brand logo, and is an integral part of the brand identity of the firm.

☐ REVIEW AND DISCUSSION QUESTIONS

1. Discuss how positioning is linked to segmentation and targeting.

2. Consider two major metropolitan restaurants. One offers hamburgers and other fast food and wishes to position itself as a healthy alternative to McDonald's; let's call this quick service restaurant Healthy Burger Co. The other restaurant is a French-styled bistro serving traditional French cuisine such as escargots and coq-au-vin and wishes to position itself as the most authentic French food establishment in the city. Let's call this restaurant "Les Amis." Currently, there are two other French restaurants in the city, but both offer less-authentic French food.

   (a) For each restaurant, create a Big Picture diagram through Positioning, create a list of potential segmentation variables, draw a market plot, and select one to position each of these restaurants. In creating your Big Picture diagram,

be sure to identify a core competence, strategic asset, and benefit list for each of these.

   (b) Now write a positioning statement for each of these restaurants.

   (c) Write a list of five key business priorities for each of these restaurants. How does the positioning relate to the operational priorities of these businesses?

3. Look at these print ads used by Microsoft when it launched the Windows 7 Operating System in 2010. Then draft a positioning statement for Windows 7.

   • What is Windows 7's Marketing Objective and Source of Volume decision? In other words, from which quadrant is Microsoft executing its strategy?

   • What is its segmentation variable? What is the behavioral change it is attempting to cause in its target audience?

"Simplify My PC"

Daniel Acker/Bloomberg/GettyImages

☐ APPENDIX: MARKETING PLANNING AND ANALYSIS

Marketing Tool #7.1: The Five-Box Positioning Tool

A Short Guide to Writing Your Positioning Statement

Current and Desired Belief

- This is a statement written from the customer's perspective and must begin with "I."
- For an acquisition/steal share strategy, the current belief will reference the main variable for the category and the desired belief will contain the dynamic variable.
- For an acquisition/stimulate demand strategy, the current belief may reference several objections to purchase. The desired belief will emphasize the main variable.
- For a retention/stimulate demand or retention/steal share strategy, the current/desired belief will reflect a rebalancing of priorities to make your main/dynamic variable more salient in the customers' mind.

Current Do

- The current do describes a key customer or target customer behavior that our strategy is seeking to change.
- For an acquisition/stimulate demand, the current customer behavior can generally be summarized as "I don't purchase. . . ."
- For an acquisition/steal share case, the current behavior is to purchase your competitors' products.
- When we are in retention/stimulate demand, the current behavior is to purchase our FE's products at lower volumes or with lower value than we wish.
- For a retention/steal share case, the behavior is "I sometimes purchase the FE and sometimes purchase the competitive brand."

Desired Do

- Describe the desired do.
- Carefully consider the distance between the current and desired states, to identify how expensive and difficult it may be to implement your entire strategy. For example, it may be very expensive or even unrealistic to get a customer who currently is exclusively purchasing a competitive product to exclusively purchase yours.

Customer Proposition

- The key to figuring out whether a behavior change is realistic, expensive, or unrealistic lies in having a deep understanding of the customer attitudes (Current Belief) that underlie current behaviors.

- The customer proposition is written in the second person as a statement from the Fundamental Entity to the target customer.
- It contains the main or dynamic variable but will never have an "and" because it will never reference both simultaneously.
- For steal share strategy, reference the steal share target to invoke the main variable.
- A key difference between the customer proposition and the desired belief is that the customer proposition contains a reason to believe. Commonly, reasons to believe include data providing evidence of performance or effectiveness, end-user or expert testimonials, market data (how many customers the FE has, its market share), and process or feature details (a Dyson vacuum cleaner utilizes 100 times the force of gravity, Fiji water is sourced from an artesian well in the Fiji Islands).

chapter eight

"...but as their pieces are made for sale, they say, and it is very true, that the players would not purchase them, if they were of any other stamp: so that the author is fain to accommodate himself to the demand of the actor, who pays him for his work."

Cervantes, Saavedra, M. de. (1793).

The history and adventures of the renowned Don Quixote. 6th ed. corr. London: Printed for A. Law, W. Miller, and R. Cater. Vol. 1, p. 400.

PRODUCT

After studying this chapter you should be able to:

1. *Describe where product fits within the executional plan*

2. *Differentiate between products and brands*

3. *Describe the product and brand life cycle*

4. *Define the most important aspects of the product portfolio*

5. *Describe how to use product attributes to establish brand value*

6. *Integrate product with other elements of the Big Picture*

The Impact of Product Performance on Brand Perceptions

Major product failure can have a significant negative impact on the associated umbrella brand or brands. Consumers usually form immediate negative associations with the salient brand name, regardless of whether that company actually contributed to the failure. Once that damage has been done, information that tries to correct any misunderstanding is often ineffective, particularly if the true culprit is obscured by a more heavily branded component. Two recent examples illustrate.

Toyota, the global automaker based in Japan, recalled 7.7 million vehicles around the world in 2009 and 2010 for a problem with faulty brakes. The flaw was eventually traced back to a supplier called CTS, but Toyota bore the brunt of the consumer backlash. Subsequent investigation by the U.S. Department of Transportation revealed that the majority of crashes were actually caused by driver error, a finding that did little to ease the public's need for a visible scapegoat or repair the damage to Toyota's finances and reputation. Toyota was the only well-known brand in this case and it received all the blame.

Matthew Staver/Bloomberg/GettyImages

When exploding Firestone tires led Ford Explorers to roll over in 2000, consumers' wrath was immediately directed toward the Bridgestone Firestone Company, the visible brand most closely associated with the problem. Subsequent tests revealed that Ford's top-heavy car design had a dangerous propensity for flipping on its own, and that Ford, which encouraged driving of overloaded cars on under-inflated tires, may actually have been the true culprit. The image of exploding tires and high-speed crashes created stronger emotions in the minds of consumers, however, and contrary data methodically gathered months after the accidents did little to absolve Firestone of blame.

In Chapter 2 we discussed how the brand helps support the products under it. Now we will expand on that discussion to talk about how, once the brand positioning has been established, the product articulates the positioning of the company by delivering benefits to consumers. Our success (or failure) in managing our products will determine the success of our brands. ■

Sources: Viele, Lawrence. "Bridgestone settles Firestone tire case." *Los Angeles Times*, January 12, 2002. "Toyota issues global recall," *WSJ*, October 10, 2012. http://online.wsj.com/article/SB10000872396390444799904578047700401681438.html.

Su, Wanru, Yuan-Ze University. Michael J. Tippins, University of Nebraska-Lincoln. "Consumer attributions of product failure to channel members and self: The impacts of situational cues," *Advances in Consumer Research* 25, 1998: 139–145.

PRODUCT: FROM STRATEGY TO EXECUTION

In the course of developing strategies and segmenting our markets, we identify individuals or companies with common behaviors and common aspirations and establish goals for reaching them. With this strategy defined, we must now create a set of coordinated tactics, including product, price, distribution, and promotional elements, to execute it. This chapter plucks one of these tactical decisions from among the rest—it focuses on how to design and manage a product and brand to effectively implement the strategy we have created in the seven preceding chapters. This chapter represents a key transition point in the Big Picture—we will now turn from planning our strategy to putting our plan into action.

A fundamental tenet of the Big Picture is that our strategy *must* drive our executional decisions; our success depends on the discipline of matching actions with strategic intent. The fact that we have already done the difficult strategic work will make these myriad executional decisions much easier. If, on the other hand, we have not taken the time to fully develop our strategy, or we do not really have confidence in our strategic plan, we quickly will become mired in executional details going forward. Too many companies and business managers fall prey to tactical tunnel vision—they get sucked into devoting all their focus to the day-to-day planning of tactical programs and policies without stepping back to ensure that these tactics align with a consistent strategy, or even whether the legacy strategy is a good one. This is a fatal error and perhaps the biggest cause of marketing underperformance in many firms.

If we find ourselves making executional decisions that do not align with our strategy, we must stop and ask why. A disconnect between strategy and execution is a sign that we either don't have the discipline to execute our strategy, or, more likely, we don't really believe in the strategic decisions we made. Either way, it is important to stop and determine how to realign strategy and execution.

There are four basic categories of tactical decisions in a marketing plan: (1) product, (2) pricing, (3) distribution (place), and (4) promotion, commonly known as the 4 P's. Each of these elements flows naturally from the STP (segmentation, targeting, and positioning) work we have just completed. Equally important, however, is the link between these elements and the other boxes in the Big Picture. For example, if our business objective has an extremely short time frame, then our promotional focus will likely be on short-term consumer or trade promotions rather than on image-building advertising. If, on the other hand, we have a longer-term objective of earning share from a key competitor, we will need to focus on developing products that support our positioning with regard to this competitor. Thus the strategic decisions we made earlier in the framework will drive every choice we make in execution. This ensures the integration of execution and strategy.

PRODUCT VS. BRAND

In order to execute effectively, we must clearly understand the difference between a *product* and a *brand*. These terms are often used interchangeably, even though they represent very different concepts. We commonly think of a product as a tangible object: a can of Coke, a Viagra® tablet, or a Chevy Camaro. Let's pause here, however, to consider the *concept* of product and how it fits into our overall marketing plan.

Brand Defined

The standard definition of a **brand** is "a name, sign, symbol, or design intended to identify the products or services of one seller and to differentiate them from those of competitors."[1] On one hand, this definition makes the brand seem like something intangible, simply a logo on a package. On the other hand, however, we know the brand is the repository for virtually all the value we create in our firm. While it may be difficult to precisely assess what this value is, it is clear that in well-managed firms it is

---

[1] American Marketing Association.

extremely high. Our basic goal as marketers is to build and maintain this value; we accomplish that by clearly understanding the basic functions of a brand.

- At the most basic level, a brand serves as a *memory aid,* enabling consumers to identify a product they may have used successfully in the past. Here the brand signifies nothing more than an acceptable level of performance. For example, the Morton® Salt logo and packaging is recognized easily by consumers. Presumably, most consumers do not spend a lot of time and energy evaluating different salts; instead they simply rely on their past experience and memory to consistently choose a product that works. A brand name will also help consumers remember which products to *avoid,* when a particular product fails to perform as promised.

- In many cases, a brand name can be leveraged to signal *superior product quality.* Here it signals not just that the product is good enough, but rather that it is better in some general way than the competition. A first-time computer buyer, for example, is more likely to buy a laptop with an Intel chip than with an AMD Athlon™ chip, regardless of the objective performance of the two chips, simply because he presumes the more familiar brand name is associated with a better-quality product. This type of reliance on brand name can tend to diminish as customer expertise increases and customers begin to leverage available information.

- While perceived product quality was an important purchase driver at the end of the 20th century, the source of sustainable growth for a brand in the 21st century is *differentiation.* Many marketers, unfortunately, fail to distinguish between perception of general brand quality and true, distinctive differentiation. Both Singapore Airlines and Southwest Airlines are considered *quality* brands; however, they represent very distinct types of quality. Singapore represents ultimate luxury, whereas Southwest represents consistent, straightforward service and value. In the current competitive environment, a brand must serve as a basis for differentiation, beyond basic quality.

- Finally, a brand should serve as a *locus of emotion.* When a customer has positive feelings during a product consumption experience, the brand acts as a repository for these emotional memories. If the product did not have a brand name, the experiences would essentially be lost. These emotions can transform our consumers' brand relationships from head to heart. For example, the Master-Card "priceless" campaign is aimed at capturing emotional experiences with the credit card brand. As Ruth Ann Marshall, president of MasterCard International's North America division, said in an interview, the goal of the "Priceless" campaign is to get people "to put our cards at the top of the wallet by talking to the heart and giving examples in life of where you might use a card to make a priceless experience for yourself."[2]

Thus, at its core a brand is a simple identifier, but a well-managed brand is much more. In order to fully develop our brand we must deeply consider the strategic implications of the different brand functions. The fact that a brand is a memory aid and an indicator of quality means it cannot add value to the firm if the product does not

---

[2]Powell, Eileen Alt. "Mastercard: 'Priceless' lure," *The Associated Press.* August 25, 2003.

GLOBALMARKETING

CHIQUITA BANANA: FROM BRANDING BANANAS TO EXPANDING GLOBAL SOCIAL RESPONSIBILITY

The power of branding is epitomized by brands like Dole or Chiquita that have been able to create power brands for products we would normally think are relatively undifferentiated, like bananas. The evolution of the Chiquita brand is an interesting example of how a brand can change its key benefit from a simple function alone to a more powerful, emotional benefit. For a long time, Chiquita was simply associated with reliable taste. However, in 2012 the Company adopted an ambitious tag line, "Improving World Nutrition. Because Taste Is Not the Only Thing We Care About."

Chiquita traces its origins to the 120-year-old United Fruit Company, which used possibly questionable business practices in Central America. The new tag line clearly moves the brand to a new positioning based on social responsibility and sustainable farming practices. In fact, in recent years Chiquita has become a world leader in responsibility and sustainable

© Ted Foxx/Alamy

farming; the company has worked collaboratively with the Rainforest Alliance and other environmental groups to ensure the protection of the environments where it operates. "We can do good and do well at the same time," Fernando Aguirre, the firm's chief executive, recently wrote in the company's social responsibility report.

Chiquita has also collaborated with local and international food unions, leading the agricultural industry in adopting sustainable farming techniques and partnering with local environmental groups. After a campaign by a group called Forest Ethics, Chiquita agreed in November 2011 not to use any Canadian tar sands oil, because extracting it is a highly polluting process. Also in 2011, the company announced an effort to promote more women and to prevent sexual harassment on the plantations it owns and buys from. ∎

Sources: "Going bananas. Chiquita has tried hard to be good—and got no credit for it," *The Economist*. March 31, 2012, print edition. http://www.economist.com/node/21551500. http://chiquita.com/The-Chiquita-Difference/Sustainability.aspx.

Chiquita Company website. http://chiquita.com/Home.aspx. Accessed March 12, 2012. *Reliable Plant Blogpost*. http://www.reliableplant.com/Read/24211/Chiquita-outlines-sustainability-efforts. Accessed March 12, 2012.

---

perform *consistently*. Because a brand enables consumers to more easily remember their experiences, *good or bad*, any product failure can serve to accelerate the demise of the brand. For this reason, we should not brand a product until we are sure we can provide consistent performance. While the Chiquita brand and certain advertising were introduced in the United States in the 1940s, for instance, it was not until 1963 that the corporation perfected a method for controlling ripening of the bananas and shipping them with minimal bruising. With an assurance of quality, Chiquita was able to leverage a simple sticker, a memorable jingle, and a terrific advertising campaign to build share for a branded banana.

Customers will also use a brand name to help them remember which products performed poorly in order to avoid purchasing them in the future. The Firestone brand name arguably became a negative asset for the Bridgestone Firestone Corporation in the early 2000s, as the chapter opener described. When product failures of this sort occur, it is a powerful reminder that the communicative benefits of a brand name can operate in either direction, and that rapid and dramatic action must be taken to protect the brand as well as consumers. Customers historically have rewarded firms that acted quickly to correct known problems with their brands. This fast action is a signal to customers that quality remains important to the company, and that failure is a temporary, rare event.

When we consider the function of a brand as a *basis for differentiation,* we begin to get into the real work of marketing. It is no longer enough for a firm to simply establish its products as high quality; in most industries there are usually several competitors that can make this basic claim. Our job as marketers is to establish the specific nature of that quality, to ensure that consumers understand what we have to offer over and above simple consistent performance. BMW, Mercedes, and Lexus all offer luxury-quality automobiles; however, each firm attempts to further differentiate itself beyond the basic quality positioning, BMW on performance, Mercedes on comfort, and Lexus on value. It is this differentiation that today's marketers strive for.

Finally, as a *locus of emotion,* the brand takes us beyond mere product performance and into the realm of brand–consumer relationships. From this perspective the brand reflects upon the consumer who is using it. Are you a Pepsi person or a Coke person? Are you an Apple person or a PC person? At this level we consider the brand a *badge* for the user. Words such as hip, cool, smart, cutting-edge, funky, and alternative are viable positioning terms when the brand functions as a locus of emotion.

Leveraging Product to Build Brand Equity

With a clear understanding of branding, we now turn to products. Simply put, a product is a *tool* for building brand equity. We are not in business to sell products; we are in business to create and capture value. One way to accomplish this is by leveraging our product portfolio. In essence, a product enables us to deliver the key benefits we identified in our strategic work. We will also deliver these benefits via service, communications, distribution, and pricing; however, for most firms, products are the most important tools in our toolkit for building brand equity.

Virtually all consistently successful companies understand this relationship between product performance and brand building. Traditional packaged goods firms such as Procter and Gamble, Unilever, and Johnson and Johnson built grew a loyal customer base by ensuring that each and every product they introduced possessed a certain level of quality, such that customers came to associate the parent company with this characteristic. More recently, Mini Cooper has released a series of automobiles that all embody the brand's positioning of fun. Regardless of whether the specific model has four-wheel drive, a convertible top, or two or four doors, each car represents the essential benefit of the Mini brand and therefore helps to build the brand over time.

By defining a product as a tool for benefit delivery, we establish the consumer as the priority in our strategic thinking. Instead of thinking first about market share and product features, we think first about customer lifetime value and how we can leverage product and features to increase this value. Thus, when we are planning the type of product to develop, or the direction to take the next version of our product, our decisions will be driven by the analysis of customers that we made in the targeting step of the Big Picture. Just as our positioning decisions were driven by our customer understanding, so too should all our subsequent decisions, whether they be product, pricing, promotional, or distribution oriented. The customer, not the product/features, drives this process.

Product as Value Delivery

A product is thus a crucial *point of contact* between the company and the customer. There are obviously many other points of customer contact—customer service, advertising, promotional displays, social media—all of which contribute to the end-users' overall experience and need fulfillment. This contact continues during all stages of the purchase process, beginning with need generation, awareness building, and trial generation and continuing through purchase and post-purchase experience. The product has a particular impact during the post-purchase experience, and this portion of the purchase cycle drives customer retention, the foundation of sustainable growth. During the purchase and post-purchase stage the consumer develops and solidifies opinions regarding our product and brand. Hence, while the product is not the only way we deliver on our promise, it is one of the most powerful tools in our marketing toolkit.

PRODUCT VS. CUSTOMER PERSPECTIVE: "LIFE CYCLE"

Our entire notion of marketing dynamics changes when we change our perspective from product-driven to customer-driven. For example, for many years marketers' decisions were guided by the notion of **product life cycle**. This concept describes the growth, maturity, and eventual decline of a product as if it were a living being. The product life cycle is generally modeled using an upward sloping S-curve (Fig. 8.1) during the product adoption phase, followed by a period of plateau when demand reaches its maximum, followed by a period of decline as the product enters its "twilight years."

This model of product sales is widely known, but over-reliance on it can lead to problems. For instance, what is driving this S-shaped curve? If a firm believes going in

Product life cycle. This concept describes the growth, maturity, and eventual decline of a product as if it were a living being.

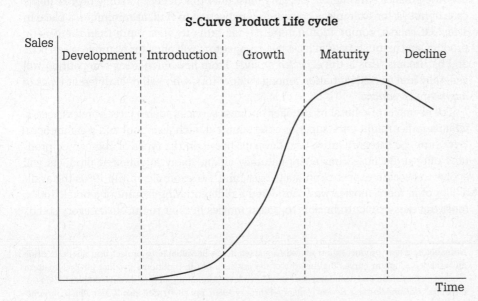

S-Curve Product Life cycle

| Sales | | | | |
| Development | Introduction | Growth | Maturity | Decline |

Time

Figure 8.1 The product life cycle graph, which relates product sales to time since product launch, is helpful in understanding the traditional evolution of products, particularly technology products or others subject to fads in consumer preferences. The life cycle curve suggests that there are certain points of inflection in the life stages of products at which sales accelerate, flatten, or decline. Some products and some brands, like Coca-Cola and baking soda, are not subject to the life cycle at all.

that its product sales will follow this pattern, it will apply a marketing budget that matches its assessment of each product's current level of "maturity." Since sales volume is often closely related to the marketing spend, the question arises: are product sales following the traditional life cycle pattern which then drives marketing spend, or is a life cycle-based marketing plan driving product sales to create a life cycle pattern?

Thus, one limitation of the life cycle model is that it does not necessarily help us to *diagnose* potential marketing issues and opportunities. Although we might observe that prior sales have followed the life cycle pattern to some extent, it is impossible to know how far along in the life cycle our product is, how long the plateau will last, and whether a recent sales decline is a short-term blip or the beginning of long-term sales erosion. Some products seem to remain in the "mature stage" indefinitely—how long has Coca-Cola been on its "plateau?"

The central weakness of the traditional product life cycle approach is that it relies on products and feature sets to drive decisions instead of consumers and benefits. We are really much more interested in how a product helps us deliver on the brand promise. A specific version of a product may mature and decline; however, the product, and more importantly, the brand, may live forever. A better model for managing a product's "life cycle" is one that incorporates the idea of the product as a dynamic set of consumer benefits that, in the end, deliver on our brand promise.[3]

The idea of the product, and ultimately the brand, having a long and dynamic life is better represented in the "bull's eye" diagram illustrated in Figure 8.2. This approach enables us to think about our products and brands as evolving in response to changing consumer needs and market conditions. It is also consistent with our earlier discussion of segmentation, targeting, and positioning, when we considered different possible dynamic benefits with which to earn share as well as the changing nature of the main or category variables.

To map product evolution using the bull's eye, we start from the center and work outwards. A product that offers a core benefit is, in essence, providing a *generic product*. Any product entering the category must offer this benefit to some degree. In the case of hotels, for example, a consumer is expecting to find, at minimum, a place to sleep. Of course, competition naturally leads firms to offer more than the generic product, and in most cases at least two competitors will offer, for example, clean beds and bathrooms. This is the *expected product*. From here, increasing competition will generally lead to differentiation among competitors, who will offer different types of *augmented products*.

For example, one hotel might offer business services such as free wireless access, while another might offer superior entertainment such as a pool and a game room. Over time the category grows and develops based on the types of augmented products offered. Because consumers naturally adapt, many augmented products will evolve to become expected products over time. For example, in the 1980s the availability of in-room movies was considered a differentiating feature of a hotel. Today, most travelers expect to be able to access movies in their room. No category stands

---

[3]Note: before a new product is introduced to market, it can be valuable to project user adoption using an S-shaped adoption curve. The majority of the criticism of the traditional product life cycle pattern focuses on its plateau and decline stages. Levitt, Theodore, "Marketing success through differentiation—of anything," *Harvard Business Review* (January–February 1980), pp. 83–91. See also Kotler, Philip, *A framework for marketing management*, p. 222.

Product Life Cycle: "Bull's Eye" Life Cycle

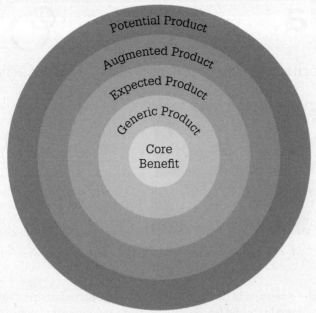

Figure 8.2 This concentric-circle conceptualization of product and brand evolution is helpful in illustrating how companies must continually improve their performance to keep up with rising customer expectations and competitive forces. Successful companies navigate the evolution of products by ensuring that they always provide relevant customer benefits and that, as much as possible, those benefits are based on a unique set of organizational skills or a core competence.

still; competition naturally leads to augmented products, and consumers naturally expect more over time.

The bull's eye also highlights the fact that we can successfully evolve a product in many possible directions. Ideally, each firm is innovating in a particular consistent direction, based on its core competence. For example, a firm competing in the hotel industry with a competence in service will likely innovate with concierge services, room service, and possibly a spa, where as a company that possesses a core competence in operations and technology may provide convenience innovations such as kiosk check-in, easy-access parking, and an app that allows consumers to find the chain's locations quickly and easily. If each company leverages a distinct core competence to continually deliver new benefits associated with that competence, the entire industry will likely thrive and grow.

The dynamic nature of the bull's eye model is related directly to the market dynamics we observed during the segmentation process. As a result, we can map these stages in product category development directly back to the main and dynamic benefit discussed in the STP chapters.

The **expected product** represents the main or category benefit, and the **augmented product** represents a dynamic benefit, that is, a potential direction for innovation in the category. In determining which augmented product (and therefore which dynamic benefit) to promote, marketers evaluate **potential products**. Different potential products may support different dynamic benefits and the marketer must choose which is most aligned to the core competence while creating the greatest consumer demand.

Expected product. The basic product attributes and benefits that customers expect when purchasing a product. Generally all products in the category deliver an expected product.

Augmented product. Product innovation that represents the dynamic benefit.

Potential products. Products with new attributes (and therefore a new dynamic variable) that marketers evaluate in considering innovations.

Furbys: Augmenting Old Products through Digital and Social Media

Furbys are entertaining and interactive robotic friends which were a blockbuster toy introduced by the Hasbro Company in 1998. The toys originally spoke only in their own language, Furbish, and had limited mobility and even battery life. The highly improved 2012 version is much more interactive, can speak English and other languages, and can

Yoshikazu Tsuno/AFP/Getty Images

develop a personality depending on how it's treated. A downloadable iOS or Android app for mobile devices can also increase the functionality of the toy. Hasbro has also turned to social media and uses Facebook and Twitter to allow Furby owners to interact and form communities of interest, further catalyzing passion for the toys.

Consider the evolution of the automobile industry: manufacturers have evaluated a wide variety of products and features that might yield important consumer benefits, beginning with simple transportation, evolving to reliability, speed, safety, efficiency, and so on. While each competitor may have to match others on expected features such as airbags and automatic windows, each is also seeking to identify a bundle of potential features that will differentiate the brand. The question automobile manufacturers ask themselves today is the same question successful marketers always ask: "What benefit can I profitably deliver to my customers?" The answer may change over time, and companies face the constant challenge of adapting to and managing these changes.

THE PRODUCT/FEATURE PORTFOLIO

Our discussion of product life cycle highlights the facts that a product is a bundle of benefits derived from specific features. These products are, in turn, bundled together to build brand equity. Our job as marketers is to create and capture value; brand equity is a key *strategic asset* where we capture and hold this value. By aligning features, and then products, with the promise of our brand, we build this equity efficiently.

Product Portfolio Alignment

Our product portfolio is the collection of products we offer our customers. These products offered by our firm are proof of our brand's promise. If our brand positioning is convenience, our products must be convenient; if we are positioned on customization, our products must be customizable. Thus, our brand positioning should direct our product strategy. A reactive, shortsighted man-

The Tide product portfolio provides solutions for different needs (breadth), and each has a number of offerings (e.g., five different types of detergents).

ager will develop products in response to competitive activity; a strategic manager seeking sustainable competitive advantage will develop products that support a viable positioning strategy, developed based on a clearly understood core competence. The process of portfolio alignment is a step toward accomplishing this goal.

Product Assortment: Positional vs. Supplemental Products

To compete successfully in an industry or segment, we must have sufficient product offerings, or **product assortment**, to satisfy the needs of our customers. Product assortment is the different products within a set that a particular company offers. In classic marketing texts, the terms *product length, depth, breadth,* or *width* typically describe product assortment. Product breadth represents the different types of products in the product line. For example, Tide offers laundry detergent, stain remover, and softener products. Product length is the number of products in each of those product lines. And product depth is the variations by specific product (Tide with Bleach, Tide Coldwater). When a firm extends a brand from one product category to another, it is usually said to be adding breadth or width. Tide Boost Pre-Treat Spray, Tide Scented Lint Roller, Tide Free, and Tide Pods contribute to product breadth or width.

Issues of line length, breadth, and depth may be interesting from an academic standpoint. Of far greater interest, however, is exactly how a specific product contributes to our brand positioning. There are many reasons why a product ends up in our

Product assortment. The different products within a set that a particular company offers.

portfolio, some of them tactical, some strategic. For example, we may introduce a product to match our competitor's offering, or even simply because a major customer asks for it. On the other hand, certain products in our line are critically tied to our brand promise. In any case, it appears that the number of situations that lead to *adding* a product to our portfolio far exceed those that lead to *deleting* a product from our line. These circumstances have encouraged increasing **product proliferation**, a situation in which firms find themselves attempting to manage an unwieldy number of products, including many that may not deserve the time and resources they receive.

To ensure that the mix of products in our portfolio is appropriate, we should consider whether the product mix is relatively *positional* or *supplemental*. A product is more positional if it is better aligned with and therefore provides better support for our brand promise. For example, if we assume BMW is positioned as a performance brand, the M series cars that deliver fast acceleration, higher top speeds, and more aggressive handling are judged to be more positional. In contrast, the BMW X5 sport utility vehicle, though relatively high performing, does not align as well with the performance positioning. The product is nonetheless important to our line because certain of our customers have specific functional needs that it fulfills. Thus, we would consider this a more supplemental product with regard to our branding strategy. Both positional and supplemental products may be necessary in our product mix; our job is to balance this mix appropriately in order to align our portfolio.

The Portfolio Alignment Process

Portfolio alignment is the process of strategically determining our ideal product mix and resource allocation. There are several factors to consider as we make this assessment:

- **Alignment with positioning:** As stated above, a product is positional if it delivers clearly and effectively on our brand promise. **Positionality** is the most important criteria for adding products to our portfolio. A positional product does more than simply create revenues through sales; it also builds brand equity and enhances our relationship with our customers.

- **Consumer needs:** Certain products are in our portfolio simply because our customers ask for or expect them to be a part of our product offerings. For example, until the 1990s families visiting McDonald's found a product selection consisting of hamburgers and French fries. Certain family members were looking for healthier options and would therefore object to McDonald's as a dinner choice, increasingly selecting Subway instead. McDonald's added salads to the menu in order to eliminate this objection. The brand promise of McDonald's is still delivered best with its French Fries and Big Macs, but salad is an important supplemental product.

- **Competitive considerations:** Certain products in our portfolio are there not because they deliver our brand promise, but rather because they enhance our general competitive position. For example, they may have a high-share, legacy brand that enables us to make claims about our market leading position in a particular category. General Electric long dominated the incandescent light bulb category, and GE light bulbs are a symbol of the company's leadership in the lighting category, even as the popularity of incandescents declines. Ideally, of course, such products are also positional; however, as market needs shift we may rely on certain high-share products to maintain competitive advantage as we make necessary adjustments to either our positioning or our portfolio.

Product proliferation. A situation in which firms find themselves attempting to manage an unwieldy number of products, including many that may not deserve the time and resources they receive.

Positionality. The most important criteria for adding products to our portfolio. A positional product does more than simply create revenues through sales; it also builds brand equity and enhances our relationship with our customers.

- **Revenue/profit mix:** Of course, we must also consider the *value capture* side of this equation. At any point in time, certain products, regardless of positioning or competitive considerations, may simply deliver more profit or revenue. Again, in an ideal world these high revenue/profit products should also be strongly aligned with our positioning. In a dynamic environment, however, there will always be times when this alignment is in flux.

Managing our portfolio in a dynamic environment can be the most challenging aspect of portfolio alignment. Profitable products are obviously important as is fulfilling customer needs. We must know whether and when to shift resources to more positional products in order to ensure future, as well as current, financial strength.

CUSTOMERFOCUS

VOLVO AND THE BENEFITS OF RETENTION/STIMULATE DEMAND

For many years Volvo has consistently positioned and augmented its products to support a *safety* benefit positioning. Throughout the 1970s and 1980s Volvo's boxy shapes, safety innovations around technology such as seatbelts, and collision protection inspired a series of highly memorable commercials and print ads focused on safety. These featured such images as an elephant standing on the car, Volvos stacked on top of one another to show how strong the roof structures were, and a truck stacked on top of a Volvo. Other images showed crashed Volvos with the driver's compartment totally intact.

However, the acquisition of the company by Ford in the 1990s and subsequent sale to Zhejiang Geely Holding Group Company Limited in 2010, as well as a number of management changes, are often blamed for a more recent lack of leadership around safety. For example, in 2010, the company suffered public embarrassment when it assembled journalists in Europe to witness its automatic braking system, which detects pedestrians and automatically applies braking to avoid tragic accidents. With cameras rolling, the system failed, and the Volvo sedan crashed into the back of a parked truck that was standing in for a pedestrian. The video was posted on YouTube and viewed millions of times around the world.

Assuming Volvo wishes to continue with its safety positioning, its source of differentiation is its bundle of features and benefits that combine to deliver a perception of superior safety. Even with the recent mishaps, and as many competitors deliver nearly identical safety features such as side air bags, daytime running lights, and superior crash test ratings,

Franck Robichon/EPA/NewsCom

A Volvo display at an auto show uses color-coding to indicate the type of metal reinforcement used to increase the safety of the cars. Grey and silver are standard steel and aluminum, respectively. Blue is high-strength steel, orange is very-high-strength steel, yellow is extra-high-strength steel, and red is ultra-high-strength steel.

retained customers still perceive Volvo as superior on safety. A 2011 Consumer Reports survey reveals that Volvo is the undeniable leader in the minds of consumers in the safety category, with a dramatic 50-point advantage over second-place Ford (70% vs. 20%). Customers who buy on safety continue to think of Volvo first. When a firm applies a disciplined positioning strategy, consumers come to associate the brand with a particular *benefit positioning*, even when similar *features* associated with this positioning are available from other brands. ∎

Source: Kiley, David. *AOL Autos Blog Post.* March 19, 2011. http://autos.aol.com/article/volvo-no-longer-trying-to-be-mr-safe-guy/. Accessed March 12, 2012.

Consumerreports.org Press Release. "Consumer Reports Car Brands Perception Survey: Consumers say Ford leads the pack in factors that matter most," January 5, 2011. http://pressroom.consumerreports.org/pressroom/2011/01/consumer-reports-car-brands-perception-survey-consumers-say-ford-leads-the-pack-in-factors-that-matt.html/. Accessed March 12, 2012.

Assessing Brand Value

Proper portfolio management will help us accomplish our ultimate goal of enhanced brand value. Unfortunately, it is far easier to measure current revenues than it is to assess potential future revenues in terms of brand value. It is this brand value that will ensure the continued success of our firm, however, so although it is more difficult to measure, it is also more important to do so. Historically, marketers have used two approaches for estimating brand value.

- **Asset estimation:** Publicly held corporations often assess brand value by simply adding up the value of all their other tangible assets and then comparing this number to the actual market value of the firm. The difference between tangible asset value and total firm value is presumed to be the value of the brand. Another common tactic is to evaluate the asset value of a corporation before and after a new brand introduction. Unfortunately, these estimates of firm valuation rely on the opinion of market analysts and investors, and these opinions appear to change quite quickly from day to day. Our determination of brand value using this method can therefore be quite uncertain.

- **Customer perceptions/choice:** From a strategic perspective, it is always best to include the consumer directly in our brand value estimation process. We can do this in a variety of ways. For example, the price premium consumers are willing to pay for our brand over other brands in the category is a terrific indicator of brand value. Or we can conduct specific research that examines consumers' preference for a product with and without our brand name. Finally, we can simply estimate how much it might cost to develop a new brand from scratch with an equal market share. Each of these estimate methods likely will yield different results, but by triangulating we may arrive at a best guess of brand value. Approaches that directly consider the consumer are likely to be more accurate, and they may also yield more strategic information.

One reason assessing brand value is so difficult is that it depends on consumer preferences, which are dynamic. These preferences are influenced by our own marketing efforts, and a change in these efforts can substantially change the value of a brand. Perhaps the most famous domestic example is the saga of Snapple brand beverage, a "new-age" noncarbonated beverage the Quaker Oats Company acquired from the Snapple Beverage Corporation in 1994. Quaker did a *discounted cash flow analysis* in which it predicted future sales of Snapple. This first estimate of the potential value of the Snapple brand was based on the assumption that Snapple brand sales would not only continue at the same level but would actually further improve based on Quaker's strength in distribution. This analysis indicated that the value of the brand was far higher than the $1.7 billion Quaker was paying.

Unfortunately Quaker failed to understand all the marketing elements that had contributed to Snapple's success. These included a quirky employee/spokesperson known as Wendy who was leveraged extensively in a popular marketing and brand-building campaign that had built a loyal following for the brand. Quaker missed the importance of this campaign and decided to "fire" Wendy. Negative consumer response was quick and powerful: by 1997 product sales were in a tailspin, and Quaker sold the brand to Triarc Beverage Group for a mere $300 million. Interestingly, Triarc recognized Wendy's importance to the brand and reinstated her and the campaign. Three years later it was

GLOBALMARKETING

THE INTERNATIONAL ORGANIZATION OF STANDARDIZATION (ISO): MAKING STANDARDIZATION A CRITICAL PRODUCT ATTRIBUTE

Most industrialists believe standardization among products is critical to the success of world trade. Thanks to standardization, manufacturing companies are able to more easily switch suppliers or work with several companies simultaneously, reducing their supply risk. Also, standardization makes products easier to maintain. For instance, a repair shop may not have had the right screws to fix any given bicycle, car, or refrigerator. Nations around the world had different manufacturing and safety standards, making it complicated to trade manufactured goods with one another.

Then, in 1947, delegates from 25 countries met and formed the International Organization of Standardization (ISO) to coordinate standardization efforts throughout the world, beginning with 67 projects. Today, ISO has guidelines for thousands of goods, ranging from basic ones like screws and mica to more unconventional items like pigs. Ensuring that products are made according to ISO standards and guidelines has become critical for organizations wanting to be a part of world trade and manufacturing, making standardization a critical attribute. ■

Sources: "World-wide industrial standardization sought; 26 nations start work on tools, parts and tests after Zurich meeting," *Wall Street Journal*, New York City, July 1, 1947: 2 (1 page).

"It requires a world agency to define the sizes of pigs," *New York Times*, New York City, May 14, 1971: 23. ISO website. http://www.iso.org/iso/en/aboutiso/introduction/index.html#eight. Accessed 5/15/2103.

---

able to resell the brand to Cadbury Schweppes at a valuation of $1.45 billion. This example underlines the crucial importance of considering the customer in our calculations of brand value. In essence, Quaker considered bottles instead of customers in developing the brand valuation estimates that drove its strategy.

LEVERAGING PRODUCT ATTRIBUTES TO ESTABLISH BRAND VALUE

In the sections above we considered product portfolio mix as a key driver of brand value. Here we dig deeper to understand how specific product features can be leveraged to drive brand value as well. Just as we align products to our brand promise, so we must align the product features of our products. To do this we must consider two dimensions of the consumer experience: (1) the emotional involvement customers have with our product, and (2) their expectations about the way the product should function. We will refer to these dimensions as **emotional and functional risk of loss**.

Types of Involvement: Emotional and Functional Risk of Loss

Risk of loss is the potential negative outcome the consumer incurs when making a product choice. The consumer's involvement level is driven by this risk of loss, which has emotional and functional components. **Functional risk of loss** is the potential loss a consumer faces if the product fails to perform properly. The most famous product example is a parachute—if it doesn't open when we want it to, we are exposed to a very high functional risk of loss: injury or death. In contrast, **emotional risk of loss** refers to our emotional exposure when a product fails. If we choose the wrong type of wine to

Risk of loss. The potential negative outcome the consumer incurs when making a product choice. Consumer involvement level is driven by this risk of loss, which has emotional and functional components.

Functional risk of loss. A loss incurred when a product fails to perform as promised from a utilitarian perspective.

Emotional risk of loss. A loss incurred when a product fails to perform and causes emotional distress to a customer because that customer felt emotionally involved with the product.

bring to a dinner party, for instance, we do not risk physical harm or loss, but we may be quite embarrassed. Our degree of involvement can be described based on the intensity of our concern with this risk. In the case of parachutes, for example, we are likely highly involved. We consider these involvement levels in three basic categories that map onto our discussion of hand, head, and heart loyalty presented in Chapter 3.

1. *Low involvement:* Some products, like salt and wax paper, generally hold little interest for consumers, and buyer involvement is simply low. Consumers are not interested in dedicating more than a nominal amount of time and effort to thinking about different performance aspects of these products, because the perceived risk of loss, both functional and emotional, is quite low. Low-involved consumers may be likely to be more loyal because they are not interested in searching around; they often simply stick with the same brand as long as it works. We refer to these low-involved consumers who are brand loyal as hand loyals in Chapter 3.

2. *Functional involvement:* The degree to which consumers are engaged in evaluating and considering practical aspects of the product's performance. For example, when consumers consider the gas mileage, safety ratings, or type of sound system in an automobile, they are assessing functional attributes. Functional loss occurs when a product fails to perform in this practical way. Products with extremely high levels of functional risk include pacemakers and parachutes; product failure can result in death. Head loyals, referred to in Chapter 3, tend to be more functionally involved.

3. *Emotional involvement:* This is the degree to which consumers evaluate products based on their emotional needs. A cologne might make someone feel sexy; a car might make someone feel powerful; a bowl of soup might make someone feel caring; homeowner's insurance might make someone feel safe. Consumers with high emotional involvement are essentially experiencing potentially high levels of emotional risk of loss. For example, if a person learns that he has chosen the wrong brand of wine to bring to an important dinner party, he may not necessarily experience any functional loss, but he may suffer a blow to his ego. Consumers who experience high emotional involvement with their brands are heart loyals.

While we have discussed risk of loss in three distinct categories, most brand/product experiences fall on a continuum as illustrated in Figure 8.3. In many industries both functional and emotional risk of loss are possible to differing degrees; specific brands may be plotted anywhere in the space above depending on the nature and extent of this involvement. It certainly is important for a car to possess key functional characteristics, but very few car marketers do not at least consider the emotional elements of the decision. Exactly where our brand falls is determined by the competitive context, consumer attributes, and, importantly by our marketing efforts in emphasizing different types of **product attributes**. A high-end, luxury automobile such as a Jaguar provides far more than functional benefits; the Jaguar driver enjoys emotional feelings of status or power. In contrast, the Ford Focus buyer is predominantly looking for functional attributes—getting from point *a* to point *b* reliably and efficiently. Advertising for these two brands will reflect these differences, with Ford advertising

Functional involvement. The degree to which consumers are engaged in evaluating and considering practical aspects of the product's performance. For example, when consumers consider the gas mileage, safety ratings, or type of sound system in an automobile, they are assessing functional attributes.

Emotional involvement. The degree to which consumers evaluate products based on their emotional needs.

Product attributes. Characteristics of products that drive the way customers learn about them and that we categorize as Search, Experience, and Credence.

emphasizing functional attributes such as gas mileage, and Jaguar emphasizing emotional attributes such as feelings of success.

As marketers, then, we can influence the type and depth of consumer involvement with our products. The extent to which we can exert this influence depends on the product and the consumer. We should avoid making quick assumptions about whether and how we can influence particular products. For example, most people would assume a product category as mundane as table salt would not be a viable option for increasing involvement level. This seemed to be the case for many years when Morton Salt was essentially the only recognized brand name, a product that arguably had mostly hand-loyal customers. It may seem unlikely that Morton® and other basic table salt manufacturers would ever get a critical mass of consumers to start thinking more deeply about the functional attributes of salt or its impact on their self-image. However, sales of high-involvement products in the salt category have proliferated wildly in the past 10 years. These include flavored salts, smoked salts, and salts that must be hand-ground or shaved. In 2012 a consumer could purchase a 4 lb box of Morton salt for $0.11 an ounce or a 6 oz. jar of Das Food French Sea Salt for $1.50 an ounce. This change in involvement level in the salt category is the direct result of increased marketing efforts.

On the other hand, many marketing managers make the mistake of over-estimating the depth of consumer involvement with a particular product or category. Often we mistake our own involvement for consumer involvement. As marketers,

Jaguar vs. Ford Focus: Emotional vs. Functional Products.

These two products, both marketed by Ford, emphasize two different types of benefits, emotional and functional.

GLOBALMARKETING

'MADE IN CHINA' WITH PRIDE

Thanks to China's role as low-cost producer in the world market, products made there are generally perceived to be cheap. However, today China manufactures a range of luxury products, from German sports cars to high-end leather goods to premium violins. These are not based just on non-Chinese designs; Chinese entrepreneurs like Li Yanno, a clothing designer (shown here), are trying to establish their businesses as original Chinese enterprises. But they face serious image barriers, both within and outside China.

In December 2009 the Chinese government launched an international TV advertising campaign, airing in networks with global viewership such as CNN. The Chinese Chamber of Commerce for Import and Export of Light Industrial Products and Arts-Crafts, which created the ad, wants the world to know that China not only manufactures products inexpensively but also designs and creates higher-end products as well. Emphasizing these goods will be the key to successfully repositioning China's business brand. ■

Sources: "Made with pride in China," *Global Times*, January 4, 2011. http://www.globaltimes.cn/beijing/people/2011-01/608587.html.
Zhengfu, Zhang. "'Made in China' ad campaign wins applause in China." December 5, 2009. Xinhua http://news.xinhuanet.com/english/2009-12/05/content_12594805.htm.

we spend our working lives thinking deeply about our brands and products; in most cases, our customers do not. When we think strategically about consumer involvement, we must also think realistically about where our customers are and where we hope to move them.

Product Involvement and the Customer Experience Cycle

We've seen that involvement level is dynamic; the level may change as a result of our efforts or in response to other factors. As they move through different levels of involvement, consumers may learn about the product, develop feelings about it, and, presumably, take action to purchase and use it. Simply put, consumers will *learn, do,* and *feel.* Furthermore, actions can influence feelings and learning, learning can influence actions, and so on. From a marketing perspective, the order in which consumers engage in learning, doing, and feeling will thus have an impact on their later activities. For example, if a consumer has already developed particular feelings about a product, he or she will tend to collect information that supports these feelings. On the other hand, a consumer who has no feelings about a product may collect a broader range of information and might assess it more objectively. These different paths toward involvement are described in Figure 8.3.

Learn-Do-Feel: For products with a high functional risk of loss, consumers generally engage in relatively more research prior to purchase. Hence the consumer relationship begins with learning, followed by a purchase behavior (do). Over time, if experience with the product is positive, the consumer may develop a more emotional relationship with the product and brand (feel). For example, a father purchasing diapers for his first baby might engage in relatively extensive research regarding the price and performance characteristics of the different products available (absorbency, fit, ease of use). After he has chosen the specific brand, the

Figure 8.3 When making a purchase, consumers consider both emotional and functional performance in terms of "risk of loss."

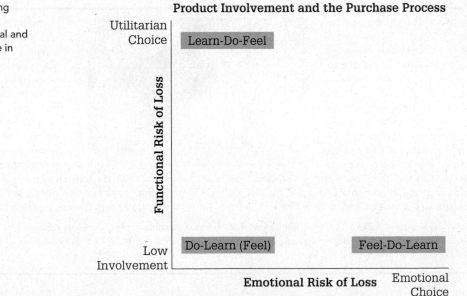

CHAPTER EIGHT   PRODUCT

product becomes part of the routine of caring for the baby. It is during this period that feelings toward the brand tend to develop based on research and experience.

Feel-Do-Learn: In product categories with more ego-related attributes, the consumer may not engage in the kind of objective research described above. Instead, after exposure to advertising or interaction with other users, the consumer may develop feelings about the product and decide to either find out more about the product (learn) or simply purchase the product (do). In this situation, much of the learning the consumer experiences occurs *after,* as opposed to *before*, the purchase, and this changes the nature of that learning. A consumer may have chosen a particular brand of jeans, for example, because she has learned that a famous actor prefers this brand. After purchase, she may "learn" that they fit well and soften nicely with repeated washings. In this example she is collecting information to support, as opposed to change, her feelings.

Do-Learn-(Feel): For low-involvement products, the consumer may never develop feelings about the brand and remains uninterested in spending significant time researching it. He simply tries it. The learning that does occur is very basic, generally whether the product works or not. Consider the college student faced with doing his own laundry for the first time. When he goes to purchase detergent, he will quite possibly choose the brand he recognizes from home, since this takes the least amount of mental effort. As long as the product works, it is quite likely he will continue to purchase this brand, based on the fact that he doesn't want to bother rethinking his original decision.

Obviously, these linkages between actions, attitudes, and emotions will vary from consumer to consumer and product to product. The marketing actions in which we will engage will change depending on the nature of this cycle. For consumers seeking out information prior to purchase, we must ensure that our product is perceived favorably versus the competition during the research phase, and that we are able to encourage emotional development after purchase. On the other hand, for emotional products we will likely concentrate on directing consumer learning *after*, as opposed to *before*, learning. Finally, for low-involvement products we care most about simply getting the product into the hands of our potential consumers, on the assumption that once they try it and find it acceptable, they are unlikely to search for alternatives. As we consider these different actions, we must consider what specific aspects of the product we might emphasize to ensure our success.

Product Involvement and Product Attributes

All products, regardless of category or customer involvement level, have specific **attributes** on which we can capitalize to achieve different marketing goals based on the processes described above. We can characterize these attributes as follows:

- A *search attribute* is an aspect of the product that can be evaluated *prior* to product purchase and consumption. Observable attributes in this category include price, package size, performance attributes such as EPA ratings or miles per gallon, and guarantees or warranties. Search attributes are particularly important for engaging with consumers who follow a *learn-do-feel* experience process. Search attributes enable learning, and we can leverage these attributes to help position our product in consumers' minds.

GLOBALMARKETING

EXPORTING TV SHOWS: PRODUCT FORM VS. SUBSTANCE

The United States is the biggest exporter of TV programming to the rest of the world, although not the only one. As early as the 1970s, U.S. TV shows like Dallas, Moonlighting, Knight Rider, and others were widely popular around the world. Sometimes shows that work well in the U.S. market work even better in another market. "House," a medical drama about an eccentric but highly effective diagnostician, was viewed by almost 10 million people per episode in France in 2011, whereas its highest U.S. ratings were for season 3 which reached fewer than 20 million people per episode (the U.S. population is 330 million whereas France's is about 65 million).

TV show producers and content managers have the tough job of predicting what will work where and how well. They also must decide whether to export as how intact and dub or subtitle it, or export just the format and recreate it with local actors. For example, U.S. audiences like British shows that capture the essence of British culture, such as the highly popular Downton Abbey,

PBS/Photofest

Fox/Getty Images

which offers a window into the lives of the restrained and proper English aristocracy in the WWI era. Viewers in the UK, on the other hand, can enjoy "Law and Order UK," fashioned after the popular U.S. show, "Law and Order" but with slightly more polite detectives. Other popular shows, like "Top Chef" and "American Idol," are imports that have been adapted for the U.S. market. Decisions about what shows to export and how must take into consideration local tastes, product content, costs, and regulatory issues. ◼

Sources: Mitchell, Kerrie. "The world's most popular TV show is … 'House?,'" *PopWatchfrom Entertainment Weekly.* June 12, 2009. EW.com.http://popwatch.ew.com/2009/06/12/house-worlds-most-popular-show/. Accessed March 12, 2012.

Yentz, Amanda. "The effects of France's language protection laws on French media," working paper. Northwestern University, IES Nantes, June 7, 2007.

Experience attributes.
Attributes we can assess only after the product has been consumed (taste, performance, durability).

◼ An **experience attribute** is an aspect of a product that only can be evaluated *after* consumption. The classic example of a product high in experience attributes is canned tuna: you must open the can and put the tuna in your mouth before you can evaluate it. Other examples of experience attributes include *actual* (as opposed to predicted) fuel efficiency, cleaning ability of detergents, and shoe comfort. Experience attributes are most important to consumers who engage in a *do-learn-feel* process; essentially, they need to try the product in order to begin their relationship with it and the brand. If our product has powerful experience attributes, we will be interested in getting potential consumers to try it.

Credence attributes.
Attributes that we cannot assess even after consumption (air line safety, beauty claims).

◼ A **credence attribute** is one that we cannot evaluate, even *after* consuming the product. At first glance this might seem quite strange, but many products are marketed based on their credence attributes. Vitamins and other health-related products tend to be high in credence attributes; it is impossible for a consumer to tell whether she is smarter because she ingested large quantities of Ginko Biloba or whether she is generally healthier because she takes a multivitamin every morning. The essential point here is that it is impossible to objectively compare two products based on credence attributes—you *can* do a side-by-side taste test to evaluate experience attributes, but you cannot get two appendectomies to evaluate the quality of a surgeon. Credence attributes are most important when customers have high ego involvement in a category—when they are following a *feel-do-learn* process with regard to the product.

All products possess some search, experience, and credence attributes. The key question is, given our marketing strategy, which attributes should we emphasize? Once we have answered this question, our marketing execution will be more efficient and effective.

social**media**

Red Bull: Lessons in Marketing Experience and Credence Attributes

Red Bull's CEO, Dietrich Mateschitz, stumbled upon the precursor to Red Bull during a trip to Thailand in 1982. Curious to know what drew the locals to a "tonic" beverage called Krating Deng ("water buffalo" in Thai), he tried it and noticed his jetlag immediately disappeared. He took it to a friend at an ad agency in Frankfurt, and they developed the slogan "Red Bull gives you wings" to evoke the experience that has endured with the brand— that the drink lifts you up physically and emotionally.

Red Bull has many search attributes: the 12 oz can contains 80 mg of caffeine (the equivalent of a cup of coffee), the amino acid taurine, and sugar. However, its promotional efforts have always focused on credence rather than search attributes. These are bolstered primarily through subtle branding and promotion of sporting events like the X-games and sponsorship of athletes deemed a bit anti-establishment. Red Bull counts over 250 agreements with top athletes but no written contracts; it simply treats its spokespeople as friends. Consumers may see a YouTube video of skateboarder Shaun White's private training on a Red Bull half-pipe, attend a global brand event like LA's Red Bull soapbox race, or participate in one of nearly 100 Red Bull Flugtag events held around the world. At the Flugtag show, Red Bull challenges innovative individuals to design and build their own flying machines and launch them off a 30-ft flight deck. The show attracts curious and thrill-seeking spectators, generating positive hype around the irreverent Red Bull brand.

Red Bull's marketing tactics have avoided traditional techniques from the beginning. In addition to letting rumors of the drink's mysteriously derived powers run rampant (including hosting a dedicated page of user-generated content on the brand's website), Red Bull refused to pay top prices to run Super Bowl ads, banner ads, or billboards. It

The "original" Red Bull drink, first developed in Thailand in the 1970s and the Global Red Bull product sold by Red Bull GmbH launched in Austria in 1987.

has not done a single web-marketing campaign. Instead, it relies on a core team of dedicated users to generate ground-level buzz among their friends and family. The brand recruits student brand managers, who receive free cases of the drink and are encouraged to throw parties. Another group of paid "consumer educators," motivated and well-educated professionals, drive around in silver Minis with cans of Red Bull strapped to the back, seeking out people in need of a boost and giving them a cold can of Red Bull.

Social media has played an integral role in the forward-thinking brand's marketing strategy as well. Red Bull has over 8 million Facebook fans, which it attracts with content on extreme sports, a "procrastination station," and social games. Red Bull Media House generates material for television, DVD, and the Internet for the brand's cult following. Combining social media with real person-to-person buzz reinforces the social mystique and fan base of the edgy drink. The fact that it keeps you awake long enough to study for tests is never mentioned.

Sources: "Red Bull's adrenaline marketing mastermind pushes into media," *Bloomberg Blog Post*, May 19, 2011. http://www.bloomberg.com/news/2011-05-19/red-bull-s-adrenaline-marketing-billionaire-mastermind.html. Accessed March 11, 2012.

Rodgers, Anni Layne. "It's a (Red) Bull market after all," *Fast Company*, October 2010. http://www.fastcompany.com/articles/2001/10/redbull.html. Accessed March 11, 2012.

PRODUCT, BRAND, AND THE BIG PICTURE

As we move into execution, we start to use the strategic decisions we've already made to set a course (Figure 8.4). The strategic quadrants do not dictate what our execution must be, but they do point us in the right direction. In the case of product, our choice of strategic quadrant provides information about which attributes need to be relied on first. The relationship between Marketing Objective, Source of Volume, and Product Attributes is illustrated in Figure 8.5.

- If we are implementing an *acquisition/stimulate demand* strategy in which we are attempting to attract new users to the category, we likely will emphasize *search* attributes, because these most clearly reduce the uncertainty consumers may be feeling as they consider entering a new category. If possible, we will also try to leverage any viable experience attributes to convince consumers to enter the category; this is generally accomplished via product sampling.

- For an *acquisition/earn share strategy,* we will try to emphasize *search* attributes that highlight our product point of difference vs. the competitor or segment from which we are attempting to earn share. Also, if possible, we will try to identify potential *experience* attributes of our product that might demonstrate our point of difference vs. the competition.

- For a *retention/stimulate demand* strategy, we will try to promote and solidify our brand position by emphasizing *credence* attributes of the product. This means we deliberately move our communications away from search and experience attributes and instead emphasize the higher-level benefit of our product (like safety and reliability). This move is intended to discourage our current customers from considering search attributes of competitive products.

- Finally, for a *retention/earn share* strategy, we will try to emphasize *experience* attributes of our products that emphasize our superiority over the competitor. Recall that in this quadrant we are speaking to multi-brand users who have access to both our product and the competitors'. Our goal is to encourage our

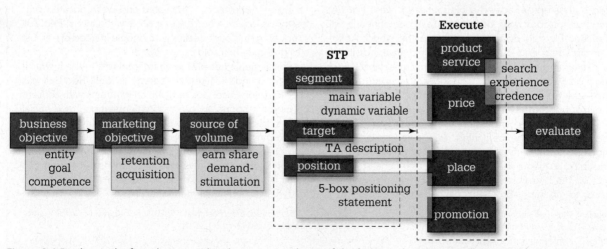

Figure 8.4 Product is the first element within the executional part of the framework and is critically important to articulating the positioning to our target market.

target audience to evaluate our product against the competition on an attribute where our performance is superior. Or we may consider emphasizing a credence attribute to attempt to move our customers from this quadrant into the retention-stimulate quadrant, where they will be heart loyal, exclusive users. This strategy will generally require a substantial investment.

Just as in other areas of the Big Picture, our choice to emphasize one type of product attribute does not mean we will not be concerned with the others. It does mean, however, that our primary focus will be on a particular type of attribute. By maintaining this focus, we can ensure that our product-related efforts, as well as other executional efforts, are as efficient and effective as possible. Our approach to marketing a specific product should be driven by a deep understanding of our strategic approach, our brand positioning, and, most importantly, our understanding of the customer–product interaction. By understanding this relationship, we can begin not only to market a product, but also to build a brand (see Fig. 8.5).

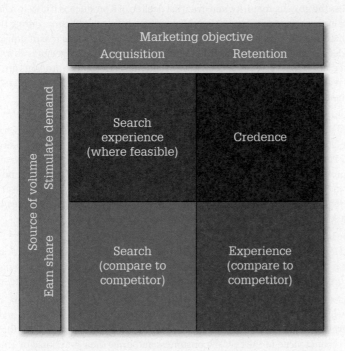

Figure 8.5 Key Product Attribute by Strategic Focus Quadrant

□ SUMMARY

1. Understand where product fits within the executional plan

Each element of execution must efficiently and effectively articulate the positioning of the company. Also, if we are to integrate strategy and execution, the tactical elements of our plan must integrate to the strategic focus chosen by the company. Products play a critical role in helping articulate the strategy of the company as they convey our brand benefits to our customers.

2. Differentiate between products and brands

Products are a main point of contact between the brand and customers. A brand is essentially a promise of an experience, and products are the concrete elements that deliver that experience on behalf of the brand. Brands function as a memory aid, as an indicator of quality, and as a source of differentiation for the company, and as a locus of emotion. Because a brand enables consumers to more easily remember their experiences, *good or bad*, any product failure can serve to accelerate the demise of the brand.

3. Describe the product and brand life cycle

For many years, marketers' decisions were guided by the notion of **product life cycle**. This concept describes the growth, maturity, and eventual decline of a product as if it were a living being. The product life cycle is generally modeled using an upward sloping S-curve during the product adoption phase, followed by a plateau period when demand reaches its maximum, followed by a period of decline as the product enters its "twilight years." Well-managed brands are strengthened with the launch of successful products, and hold their value as the products are eventually retired and replaced by newer versions. Therefore, a bull's-eye diagram, illustrating their evolution over time, better represents their life cycles.

4. Define the most important aspects of the product portfolio

The group of products offered under a brand name is called a product portfolio. Product portfolios generally contain products that are very aligned to the positioning of the brand, that are "positional." Positional products are very representative of the brand benefit. Conversely, non-positional products also play an important role as they complement the brand portfolio and help the brand overcome potential objections to purchase. They might be necessary for competitive reasons or because customers demand that we offer a full portfolio but are not differentiating vis-à -vis our competitors. We refer to these products as "supplemental."

5. Describe how to use product attributes to establish brand value

At a product level, we can conceptualize the value of the brand as the difference in price between products that offer the same performance attributes and only differ in the brand name. Doing this in practice requires the use of choice models and other advanced statistical techniques.

We distinguish search attributes, which we can assess prior to consumption, experience attributes, which we can assess only after we sample or consume the product, and credence attributes, which we cannot assess even after we consume the product. Product attributes are a source of product value in the eyes of consumers and drive their functional or emotional involvement or commitment to products. In order to align attributes to customer loyalty, we must consider customers' emotional involvement and their functional involvement, based on their expectations about how the product should function. Marketers can create new attributes and change the salience of existing attributes by emphasizing or deemphasizing them depending on the strategic objectives.

6. Integrate product with other elements of the Big Picture

In the case of product, our choice of strategic quadrant provides information about which attributes to consider leveraging first. For acquisition/stimulate demand strategy, when we are attempting to attract new users to the category, we likely will emphasize search attributes because these most clearly reduce the uncertainty consumers may be feeling as they consider entering a new category.

For an acquisition/earn share strategy, we will try to emphasize search attributes that highlight our product point of difference vs. the competitor or segment from which we are attempting to earn share. For a retention/stimulate demand strategy, we will try to promote and solidify our brand position by emphasizing credence attributes of the product. For a retention/earn share strategy, we will try to emphasize experience attributes of our products that emphasize our superiority over the competitor.

☐ KEY TERMS

Augmented product. (p.221) Product innovation that represents the dynamic benefit.

Credence attributes. (p.232) Attributes that we cannot assess even after consumption (air line safety, beauty claims).

Emotional involvement. (p.228) The degree to which consumers evaluate products based on their emotional needs.

Emotional risk of loss. (p.227) A loss incurred when a product fails to perform and causes emotional distress to a customer because that customer felt emotionally involved with the product.

Expected product. (p.221) The basic product attributes and benefits that customers expect when purchasing a product. Generally all products in the category deliver an expected product.

Experience attributes. (p.232) Attributes we can assess only after the product has been consumed (taste, performance, durability).

Functional involvement. (p.228) The degree to which consumers are engaged in evaluating and considering practical aspects of the product's performance. For example, when consumers consider the gas mileage, safety ratings, or type of sound system in an automobile, they are assessing functional attributes.

Functional risk of loss. (p.227) A loss incurred when a product fails to perform as promised from a utilitarian perspective.

Positionality. (p.224) The most important criteria for adding products to our portfolio. A positional product does more than simply create revenues through sales; it also builds brand equity and enhances our relationship with our customers.

Potential products. (p.221) Products with new attributes (and therefore a new dynamic variable) that marketers evaluate in considering innovations.

Product assortment. (p.223) The different products within a set that a particular company offers.

Product attributes. (p.228) Characteristics of products that drive the way customers learn about them and that we categorize as Search, Experience, and Credence.

Product life cycle. (p.219) This concept describes the growth, maturity, and eventual decline of a product as if it were a living being.

Product proliferation. (p.224) A situation in which firms find themselves attempting to manage an unwieldy number of products, including many that may not deserve the time and resource they receive.

Risk of loss. (p.227) The potential negative outcome the consumer incurs when making a product choice. Consumer involvement level is driven by this risk of loss, which has emotional and functional components.

Search attributes. (p.231) Attributes we can evaluate prior to consumption (price, physical product characteristics).

☐ REVIEW AND DISCUSSION QUESTIONS

1. Aligning product attributes to the positioning: **Fiji Water**

   Read the description of Fiji water obtained from the company's website. Now complete a Search, Experience, and Credence Product Alignment Exercise (see Marketing Tool #8.1) for two different positionings: (1) sophistication and (2) sustainability, and assuming an acquisition/stimulate demand strategy. Which positioning is better suited for Fiji, and why?

2. Identify three search, three experience, and three credence attributes for the following products:

   (a) An Apple iphone

   (b) Channel No. 5 perfume

   (c) An AMD computer

   (d) A meal at McDonald's

   (e) A GE aircraft engine

3. Imagine that you are establishing your own fast food company in a city where McDonald's is the clear market leader. Explain how you would promote your product to: (1) earn share from McDonald's, and (2) stimulate demand for organic locally sourced fast food.

Marketing Tool #8.1: Product Attribute Strategic Alignment

Product attributes were first discussed by Bauer in 1960 and have guided much of the research around product advertising and communications. The U.S. Federal Trade Commission (FTC) even uses them to regulate advertising. In the Marketing Framework we use these concepts to align both product development efforts and product communication efforts to the strategic priorities of the company. To identify key product development and communication priorities for the product that are linked to the strategy, we follow these steps:

1. List all attributes of the product, categorizing them into search, experience, and credence attributes.

2. Select the most powerful attributes, those that are (a) most aligned to the positioning; and (b) most compelling to customers.

3. Highlight the power attributes that also correspond to our strategic focus (search for acquisition/stimulate demand; credence for retention/stimulate demand; search relative to competition for acquisition/earn share and experience for retention/earn share).

Product Name	Search Attributes	Experience Attributes	Credence Attributes

Marketing Tool #8.2: Product Portfolio Alignment

As discussed earlier in the chapter, product portfolios contain both positional products and supplemental products. The products in the first category are highly aligned to the brand strategy and are most helpful in articulating the positioning of the brand; they are, therefore, at the heart of the brand's competitive advantage. The second type of product, supplemental products, plays an important role in that they round out the product portfolio and thus can help us overcome potential objections to purchase. We need them to be competitive, but they are not the ones we will use to differentiate our brand vis-à -vis our competitors. This exercise can be used to align the product portfolio to the positioning of the brand, helping us distinguish between positional and strategic products and also helping us tie each product to our overall marketing objective of customer acquisition or customer retention. We also use this exercise to identify changes or adjustments that are needed in the product portfolio to better align the product line-up to the brand strategy and positioning. For example, if we choose reliability as the positioning variable, we may find that some products within the portfolio will articulate this benefit better than others. As a result, we may need to emphasize some and deemphasize others.

List the products in the brand portfolio and for each, answer the questions below:

Enter the Fundamental Entity (FE) Brand:

	Articulate Positioning (1–5)	Acquisition/ Retention	Degree of Competitive Differentiation (1–5)	Relative Sales (%)	Ideal Resource Allocation (%)
Product A					
Product B					
Product C					
Product D					

- What is the product's relative fit with the company positioning? We can perform a conceptual assessment and score the product using a scale of 1 to 5, with 5 indicating that the product is an excellent fit and 1 indicating a poor fit.
- Is this an acquisition or a retention product?
- How differentiated is this product relative to the competition? We can use the same 1 (low) to 5 (high) scale to indicate relative degree of competitive differentiation.
- What are the relative sales (or operating profit) of this product? Here we take the total sales of the FE and allocate them by product to get a sense of the relative contribution of each product to the portfolio. If available, we would prefer to use profit or revenue information rather than sales to account for the fact that some products may have low sales volume but high price or margin.
- Should resources be allocated differently to promote each of the products in the portfolio based on this exercise?

Now:

1. Think through how you might better align your product offerings to the strategy. You may accomplish this by reallocating resources to the products that (1) best represent your FE's positioning to the market place, and (2) fit your customer objective (acquisition or retention).

2. Does your current resource allocation by product relate to your product's contribution to your overall sales? If not, why not?

☐ RESOURCES

Bauer, R. A. "Consumer behavior as risk taking," *Dynamic Marketing for a Changing World*, R. S. Hancock, (Ed), American Marketing Association, 1960.

Nelson, P. "Information and consumer behavior," *The Journal of Political Economy* 78(2), 1970: 311–329.

Day, G. "The product life cycle: Analysis and applications issues," *Journal of Marketing* 45, Autumn 1981: 60–67.

Levitt, T. "Exploit the product life cycle," *Harvard Business Review* 43, November–December 1965: 81–94.

chapter nine

"Nothing is so reasonable and cheap as good manners."

Cervantes, Saavedra, M. de. (1786).

The history and adventures of the renowned Don Quixote. Translated by T. Smollet and Francis Hayman. Printed for W. Strahan, J. and F. Rivington, W. Johnston, R. Baldwin, T. Longman, Hawes and Co., London. Vol. 3, p. 379.

SERVICE AS PRODUCT

After studying this chapter you should be able to:

1. *Contrast products and services*

2. *Describe the characteristics of services*

3. *Map the customer service experience*

4. *Explain how to manage the concept of Zone of Tolerance for customer satisfaction*

5. *Describe the relationship between customer service and customer satisfaction*

6. *Integrate services with other elements of the Big Picture framework*

IBM's Transition from Computers to Software and Services

When Louis Gerstner took over as CEO of IBM in 1993, he observed that its customers increasingly required not just help with technology products, but also a partner to integrate the various platforms and align them to their business processes to obtain more intelligence from their information. For IBM to play that role, and to fulfill its goal of becoming a "world-class services company," Gerstner believed it needed to be better integrated internally. He brought together multiple internal networks under IBM Global Network in 1994 and in 1995 created the IBM Global Services unit, which by the late 1990s was organized around lines of business that corresponded to customer needs. The unit had dedicated groups to address integration and innovation issues, support of technology infrastructure, and strategic outsourcing to meet demand for technology outsourcing services. By the mid-2000s, IBM Global Services was organized into 16 industry groups structured into five sectors.

IBM's 2011 annual report highlights the company's efforts to continue expanding in services and software, which now drive hardware sales rather than complementing them. The company's growth initiatives include cloud computing services, business analytics, and intelligent-software platform integration, branded "Smarter Planet." The business analytics unit helps companies turn unstructured data into actionable information. The Cloud unit delivers software and services over the Internet to clients as well as building client-owned cloud capabilities, so companies and governments can tap into private networks and software. The Smarter Planet services unit had served more than 2000 cities by the end of 2011, helping them improve rapid-response systems and predict where emergencies might occur based on historical data.

While the IBM story illustrates a successful transition to services from products, companies seeking to make a similar transition should not underestimate the time, effort, and

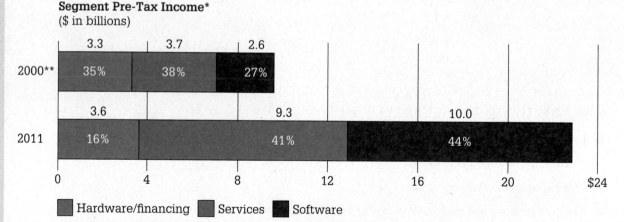

Segment Pre-Tax Income*
($ in billions)

Legend: Hardware/financing · Services · Software

*Sum of external segment pre-tax income not equal to IBM pre-tax income.
**Excludes enterprise investments and not restated for stock-based compensation. 2000 segment PTI is reclassified to conform with 2011 presentation.

This bar chart illustrates the very significant shift IBM has made from selling products to selling services and software.

Source: 2011 IBM Annual Report. http://www.ibm.com/annualreport/2011/bin/assets/2011_ibm_higher_value.pdf
http://www.businessinsider.com/ibm-software-company-2012-8.

competency enhancements to do so successfully. Services are intangible and harder to deliver consistently than products. Thus successful service delivery requires different skills, processes, pricing models, and metrics than delivering products. ■

Sources: Blodget, Henry. "IBM's a software company now," *Business Insider*. August 21, 2012. www.businessinsider.com. Accessed March 30, 2012. 2011 IBM Annual Report. http://www.ibm.com/annualreport/2011/.

Cusumano, Michael. "The changing software business: Moving from products to services." Institute of Technology. *The IEEE Computer Society*. 0018-9162, 2008. http://www.iae.univ-lille1.fr/SitesProjects/bmcommunity/Research/cusumano.pdf. Accessed March 12, 2013.

SERVICE AS PRODUCT: DIFFERENCES AND SIMILARITIES

The focus of this chapter is on services—how to manage service offerings and how to augment products with services. Today, there are very few companies that only sell products; even consumer packaged goods and food giants like Procter & Gamble and Kraft augment their product offerings with services like category management (offered to large retailers like Walmart) and product usage advice. An increasing number of new marketing graduates begin their careers each year in service industries, and even those who choose to work in "product" industries are likely to deal with aspects of bundled product–service offerings. One reason is that many traditional hard goods manufacturers in mature markets are adding service components in order to sustain their competitive advantage. Furthermore, services are becoming a key component of retention activities—crucial contributors to the sustainable competitive advantage of the firm. These facts demonstrate the crucial importance of services marketing.

Because of the importance of services, we devote a distinct chapter to the topic. Where we can treat services in the same way as other products we will apply the same general framework, considering a marketing question for a service as we would any other product/branding marketing challenge. However, there are certain differences between services and hard goods we must consider as we engage in marketing planning and execution; here we consider those differences.

When we assess services through the lens of consumer involvement, we see that a higher percentage of service products are high-involvement credence products, because services are quite difficult to evaluate even after they have been consumed. Consider a patient visiting a doctor for a simple check-up. Even if we go through a careful selection process, considering references, education, and other qualifications and then have what we consider to be a positive experience with the doctor, we still cannot say with objective certainty that our doctor has provided us with better health care than another one down the hall. In the case of a service, whether it be a haircut or a legal consultation, it is usually quite difficult to conduct a side-by-side comparison, as we can with hard goods.

When consumers are unable to depend on objective measures of quality, many other factors may influence their judgments, some within our control and some outside it. Hence, from a marketer's perspective, it is not enough to simply attempt to control the quality of the specific service being provided. We must carefully coordinate all aspects of the experience before, during, and after service delivery to maximize the effectiveness of our marketing efforts. We first consider when and how to treat a service differently from a traditional product.

IDENTIFYING THE CHARACTERISTICS OF SERVICES

Productization of services. Transforming services offerings so they resemble tangible products. This is accomplished, for example, by creating a name/logo/identity for the service and marketing it as similarly to a traditional tangible product as possible.

Why should we consider services distinct from hard goods? At the end of the 20th century there was a strong trend toward **productization of services**, in which managers attempted to treat services as products in order to capture more brand equity. This move, observed particularly in the financial services and consulting industries, helped to underline the importance of traditional marketing principles and strategic discipline in industries where it often has been in short supply. Productizing services has generally increased the profitability of service organizations. By standardizing services, a company avoids reinventing the wheel every time a service is performed, thus reducing costs and increasing margins. The other key benefit of standardizing services into modularized "products" is that it increases the ability of the service organization to maintain consistent performance quality across customers and projects. As we pointed out above, consistency is critical to the successful sale of services.

While productization of services has been a growing and important trend, there are still a number of ways in which services are distinct from hard goods, and implications that arise from these differences. Hence, as we consider services within the traditional framework of the Big Picture, we also should recognize where products and services diverge, and what we can do about it.

social**media**

It's a book, it's a product, it's a service!

Although you may think providers of ebooks and downloadable audio books are competitors, as has happened in other industries, the lines between competition and collaboration are being blurred through licensing agreements. Amazon, maker of the Kindle and the largest retailer of ebooks in the world, has partnered with Audible.com, the largest provider of downloadable audio books, to offer a seamless audio +text experience to customers of both companies. If successful, the combined service might not only increase business for both firms but also attract entirely new users (such as kids learning to read), thus bolstering both acquisition and retention efforts.

Amazon/AP Images

Sources: Audible.com Company website. www.audible.com/t1/kindletrial. Accessed on March 12, 2013.

Intangibility

First, services are **intangible**: we cannot see or touch them.[1] This makes brand-building much more difficult. A consumer wearing a new pair of blue jeans not only will be able to see herself in them, she also will be able to feel how comfortable they are and receive comments from friends and associates about how good they look. The brand and product are physically present to both generate and capture positive brand emotions. In contrast, a consumer who receives excellent brokerage advice over the phone or online may feel quite satisfied, but those feelings will most likely be associated with the specific investment advisor rather than with the firm. Further, since there is no physical presence, the likelihood of continued positive brand associations is lower. The physical presence of hard goods is therefore an important marketing advantage that services lack.

The fact that services are not physical means that logos, tag lines, and other memory aids are even more important than they are for products. These are critical for services because they help make the intangible *tangible*. Prudential Life insurance is an intangible product; its tag line, "Own a piece of the rock," and rock logo are great examples of the use of a highly tangible object for a service product. Other examples of powerful logos in the service sector include NASA, FedEx, and UPS. Of course, there are many brilliant examples of logos in the hard goods sector as well, but these designs must be judged by a different standard because they benefit from the fact that *they are living on a product*. Service-sector logos do not have this advantage. They may appear on a truck, envelope, or business card, but they are not constantly present during the product consumption experience. Hence, the development of a strong brand identity for service-sector products is both more difficult and more important for services than it is for hard goods.

While visual logos are one way to increase the tangibility of a service, other methods are also viable. Taglines, words, and even sounds, supported by strong advertising, can occupy significant real estate in consumers' brains. Lines such as "You're in good hands with Allstate," "Fly the friendly skies," and "We try harder" help to establish service sector brands without depending on a visual representation. Many consumers in the United States, whether they like it or not, are able to recite the phone number for Empire Carpet; Bostonians know the jingle for Giant Glass equally well. In recent years, "earcons" have become more popular. The Intel sound and the ubiquitous Microsoft "startup sound" (crafted in part by Brian Eno) are firmly embedded in virtually every PC user's memory. Again, these marketing tactics are certainly important for hard goods as well, but they are crucial for service products.

Other promotional tactics serve this purpose on a smaller scale. The tiny chocolate mints left on our pillow by the turndown service at the Hyatt Hotels are an effort to increase the tangibility of a service (the mint reminds us that we have been given service), as are the little plastic wings given to your child by the Delta Airlines flight attendant. These seemingly minor tactical moves can significantly increase a company's ability to capture value created by good service.

Intangible. A characteristic of services that means they cannot be touched or felt.

---

[1] See Levitt, Theodore. "Marketing intangible products and product intangibles," *Harvard Business Review,* May–June 1981: 94–100.

Another area to which marketers in the service sector must pay particular attention is word-of-mouth. In the absence of a physical product and associated cues such as packaging and logo, word-of-mouth becomes a crucially important factor. With the rise of social media, the rate at which this information moves has increased exponentially. Consumers are consistently asked to provide ratings of everything from hotels, to restaurants, to contractors and landscapers. Marketers of services must be vigilant about managing their digital reputation, emphasizing positive experiences and dealing quickly and effectively with negative reports. Even before this new wave of social media, the general rule of thumb was that every customer who has an extreme service encounter, positive or negative, tells ten other people. In the digital age this number is likely so large that it defies measurement.

Inventory Issues

Services cannot be inventoried. This has crucial implications for both quality control and operations. A physical product that can be inventoried can be inspected prior to sale, thus ensuring consistent quality. In contrast, if a service offering fails, it generally fails in the field. This, of course, is the absolute worst place for a product to fail because it offers the least opportunity for recovery. Furthermore, if we cannot hold inventory, we cannot be prepared for fluctuations in demand. When demand for soft drinks increases in the summertime, we can produce a stockpile to cover our requirements. In contrast, when demand for accounting services goes up at tax time, we can't go to our warehouse and pull out the extra accountants we have stored there. Hence, the fact that services cannot be inventoried is a crucial issue to deal with.

In order to deal with the unique inventory challenges of services, we must change our thinking. Unfortunately, our tendency to adopt the produce-then-inspect model is strong; this generally means that we fail to allocate sufficient resources to *advanced planning*. In the case of services, since we can't correct product problems after production, we must try to anticipate them in advance. This calls for an entirely different approach and mindset; in essence we must imagine all the things that *might* go wrong and then develop strategies and tactics for dealing with these potential events. While we can't plan for everything, we can reduce the frequency and impact of service failures with this approach.

The cost of failing to plan can quickly exceed the cost of planning and allocating resources in a proactive manner. When we don't commit necessary resources and a service failure occurs, we must spend additional resources to fix the problem. Over time, as we shift resources from prevention to remediation, we fall into a "death spiral" in which increasing service failures leave us less able to prevent new ones. Simple budget tracking, with customer service expenditures properly allocated, will help us spot this situation and correct it.

Because inspection is not possible, operations excellence is a necessary core competence for any company wishing to create a sustainable competitive advantage on a service dimension. Without the operations excellence necessary for consistent service quality, aggressive marketing and sales teams actually will help to drive a service organization out of business *more* quickly, by creating expectations that cannot be met. Operations excellence and planning will enhance service quality, and, ideally, increase our ability to meet fluctuating demand.

We can also leverage other marketing tools to attempt to smooth demand fluctuations. To accomplish this we need to either (1) offload demand during peak periods, or (2) boost low-period demand sufficiently to support the fixed and labor costs necessary to meet peak demand. A restaurant bar is a classic example of offloading: customers are more willing to wait to sit down to dinner at 9:30 P.M. instead of 8 P.M. if they are provided a comfortable bar and lounge area in which to socialize while waiting. The same restaurant may also offer a 5 P.M. dinner special or happy hour to generate increased revenues during a commonly slow period. These same basic principles can be applied in virtually every service industry—we can smooth peak loads by creating promotional strategies to shift demand to other periods or increase the acceptable waiting time.

CUSTOMERFOCUS

VISA CREDIT CARD SERVICES

After 20 years, Visa retired its iconic "Visa: it's everywhere you want to be" marketing campaign in favor of a new positioning for its portfolio of products and services, expanded to include commercial, debit, and prepaid cards. The new "Life takes Visa" slogan was designed to convey that Visa is the most widely accepted credit card in the world. The campaign empowers consumers, encouraging them to enjoy life's experiences on their own terms with the freedom and convenience Visa offers.

Visa's earlier tag line was built upon the benefit of acceptance; the card was accepted not literally everywhere, but rather "everywhere you want to be." Recently, however, reliability and security have increased in relevance, and other credit cards have caught up in terms of acceptance. The new positioning plays on emotional as well as rational drivers by implying that using Visa is essential to life, just like intangible traits such as courage and determination.

The new campaign debuted during the 2006 Winter Olympics, and as the only credit card sponsor of the event, Visa linked its universal acceptance and convenience to the spirit and hope of the games. Within two months, the new tag line had already garnered an incredible 45% aided awareness.

Continuing with the inspirational theme, LifeTakesVisa. com features a number of different video spots depicting regular people doing things from the commonplace to the extraordinary, narrated with descriptions of the qualities

© PeterPhoto/Istockphoto

necessary for these tasks, including spontaneity, ambition, and practice. The commercials conclude with the statement that "no matter what it takes, life takes Visa." Viewer response was extraordinary, with some videos getting over 300,000 views in the first month.

In a positioning move designed to further integrate Visa into the lives and experiences of consumers, now *Life* literally takes Visa. The newest edition of Hasbro's *Game of Life: Twists and Turns* edition has replaced cash with plastic credit cards. Co-branding with the board game fits Visa's new slogan perfectly and encourages parents to discuss money management and debt with their children. In the latest edition, the winner of the game is not the one with the most money, but rather the one who collects the most "life points," which are a mixture of wealth and life experiences. ■

Sources: Zabin, Jeff. "Visa: Life takes rebranding." *Chief Marketer Blog Post.* April 6, 2006. http://chiefmarketer.com/disciplines/branding/Visa_rebranding_04242006. Accessed April 11, 2012.

Horovitz, Bruce. "Marketing play: Game of life really does take Visa." *USA Today.* March 8, 2007. http://www.usatoday.com/money/advertising/2007-03-07-visa-game-usat_N.htm. Accessed April 11, 2012.

Performance Aspects

Services are generally produced and consumed at the same time. This means that there is a performance element to services that is not present for hard goods. Further, the consumer is generally intimately involved in establishing the quality of the final product. A cooperative patient helps to produce a better medical examination; a responsible client can help a lawyer achieve a favorable decision. In essence, we should think of services as being *coproduced* by the service provider and the consumer.

The performance element in services is another challenge we must meet with the help of operations. The key to truly exceptional service delivery is tight integration of operations and marketing. Without this integration, marketing will continue to over-promise delivery time and product performance, and operations will continue to under-deliver. Both functions need to be in sync so marketing will create expectations that match the company's delivery capabilities. In this way, expectations are always appropriately set and met.

The success of Zappos, the online clothing retailer, illustrates some of the keys to building a service core competence (see the following Customer Focus box): create a culture where individual employees are empowered to grow professionally and are given autonomy within well-established broad parameters; add concrete elements to the brand to make it tangible to customers; create customer expectations that match the reality of the customer experience; deliver consistently on that experience; and price accordingly.

Humans and Service Delivery

Humans typically perform services. We saw above that consistency is crucial for competitive success, and it is paramount for service marketers. Historically, our answer to the challenge of producing consistently has been to simply replace humans with machines and technology wherever possible. Consumers are increasingly comfortable with technology, which continues to improve to meet specific needs. Often this strategy enhances consistency and also can lower costs; however, there is a limit to its effectiveness. We cannot always replace human service in a cost-effective way that enables us to maintain our service differentiation. An ATM is a terrific way to deliver cash to bank customers; it is a bit more difficult to provide estate planning services entirely via machine.

So we must ask *whether* and *when* we should mechanize or automate services. This is a dynamic question; consumer acceptance of technology and our skill at leveraging technology to deliver service is constantly changing. Cost is a key consideration: as the cost if automation and technology continue to decline we would likely fulfill more and more service needs in this way, nonetheless, there will likely always be situations in which we prefer to deliver services with humans.

Thus, in our effort to provide superior service, we must determine which strategy will be more profitable for our firm. Figure 9.1 provides an approach for addressing this issue by considering two aspects of service performance: whether the service is delivered *front office* or *backstage*, and whether the service is *custom* or *standard*. A service performed in the front office is performed in front of the consumer, for example, taking a credit card payment or checking in at a hospital. In contrast, a *backstage*

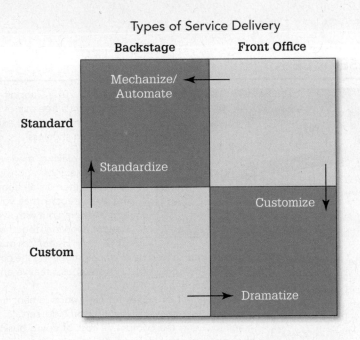

Types of Service Delivery

Backstage   **Front Office**

Mechanize/Automate

Standard

Standardize

Customize

Custom

Dramatize

service is one that is performed out of view of the consumer, for example, performing a lab test or searching for a bag lost by an airline. The custom/standard distinction addresses whether the service is customized for each consumer or not. A doctor taking a patient history is performing a custom service, whereas a customer checking into a hotel experiences a relatively standardized service.

The key trouble spots in this framework are in the lower-left and upper-right cells. When a custom service is performed backstage, the customer does not have an opportunity to observe the specialized work being performed, and any perceived value that might be generated by customization is lost. In this situation we must either perform the service directly in front of our customers, so they recognize the value of the customization, or attempt to standardize the service and reduce its cost.

The other area of opportunity is a standard/front-stage service, which we perform over and over in front of our customers. Because it is a standardized service, there is little differentiation, and therefore little opportunity to create consumer surplus. Furthermore, for the service provider, boredom and lack of challenge can increase the possibility of errors or service failures. Front-stage failures occur right in front of the customer and also may be observed by other customers, increasing their potential negative impact. We need to clear this quadrant by either customizing our service delivery or moving the activities backstage. For example, in moving from personal tellers to ATM's, banks have taken the standardized service of recording customer deposits from front stage to backstage. An analysis of frontstage/backstage and custom/standard can thus significantly enhance the efficiency and effectiveness of our service delivery.

CUSTOMERFOCUS

ZAPPOS AND CUSTOMER SERVICE

Online retailer Zappos has built its business model around providing excellent customer service. The effort has paid off; Amazon purchased the company in 2009 for $1.2 billion, and Zappos continues to enjoy the reputation of a premier high-service retailer in the United States. The company is headquartered in Las Vegas, where 500 employees are dedicated to providing customer service full time; however, everyone at the company goes through four weeks of customer-service training.

Karen Bleier/AFP/Getty Images

Zappos places great value on authenticity; its advertising campaigns regularly feature real customer calls. The 2010 advertising campaign was titled "Happy People Making People Happy" and was designed to illustrate Zappos's 3 Cs: clothing, customer service, and culture (the company has since added a fourth C for community). The company has been called "insane" and "fanatical" for doing anything to please its customers. It publicizes stories like these:

- In 2011, Zappos sent flowers to a woman who ordered six different pairs of shoes because her feet were damaged by harsh medical treatments.
- In March 2012, a customer service rep went to a rival store to get a specific pair of shoes for a hotel guest in Vegas when Zappos ran out of stock.

- Also in 2012, Zappos shipped overnight a free pair of shoes to a best man who had arrived at a wedding shoeless.

"Take making money out as part of the motivation or equation, and then it's all about working with people that you would enjoy hanging out with even if you weren't working together," says CEO Tony Hsieh. Zappos's management tries to lead by example, modeling the company's values of "being humble, adventurous, creative and open-minded."

One benefit of achieving high engagement from customers is that they will happily provide service to each other, lowering the company's cost of doing business and also adding value from authenticity. Customer reviews help Zappos customers with purchases that have rapidly expanded from shoes to clothing, cosmetics, housewares, and even sporting goods. A company official says, "The one constant is that we are a service company that happens to sell _____ (fill in the blank). Our biggest efforts revolve around building likeability around our brand so that consumers turn to a brand that they trust, find reliable, and have an emotional connection with. That's where service comes in!" ■

Sources: Edwards, Jim. "Check out the insane lengths Zappos customer service reps will go to," *Business Insider*, January 9, 2012. http://articles. businessinsider.com/2012-01-09/news/30606433_1_customer-service-zappos-center-services#ixzz2F3M1Tt00.

Wauters, Robin. Techcrunch. November 2009. http://techcrunch.com/2009/11/02/amazon-closes-zappos-deal-ends-up-paying-1-2-billion/.

Hsieh, Tony. "Four lessons on culture and customer service from Zappos CEO," *HBR Blog Network*, July 14, 2010. http://blogs.hbr.org/tjan/2010/07/four-lessons-on-culture-and-cu.html.

MAPPING THE CUSTOMER SERVICE EXPERIENCE

One approach to clearing the frontstage/standard and backstage/custom quadrants is to map the customer experience, outlining all the points at which we develop or deliver services for our customers. These touch-points represent our opportunities to either strengthen or weaken a valuable customer relationship.[2] Some come easily to mind—an interaction with a customer service representative, salesperson, or

---

[2]This phrase was coined by Patricia Seybold in her article by the same name. Op. cit. 3.

website—while others are more mundane and less public activities, such as billing, extension of credit, management of returns, and telephone and e-mail support. Mapping a detailed description of the entire customer experience allows us to identify all the opportunities to maximize the value of our service offerings.

An example from the hotel industry appears in Figure 9.2. Recall the customer experience process phases reviewed in Chapter 6; we now apply them to a specific service setting. For example, as shown in Figure 9.2, mapping the customer experience of a hotel guest starts the exercise by identifying the first interaction a potential customer has with our firm or brand—perhaps it is an advertisement or a recommendation from a friend. Then we define every point in the burgeoning relationship with that customer: how the customer gathers information about our offering, how she evaluates it, how she uses it. We work our way through the purchase, the consumption, the post-consumption evaluation, and the consideration of repurchase.

Mapping the Customer Experience

Booking and Staying in a Hotel Room

This example lists all the myriad steps a consumer could actually go through in the seemingly simple act of booking and staying in a hotel room. At each step, it is clear that there are vast possibilities for fulfilling customers needs.

Choose Hotel
- Awareness and familiarity: recall
- Competitive advantage: ex. price
- Quality

→ **Make Reservation**
- Availability
- Flexible pricing
- Telephone customer service
- On-line access

Greeting
- Friendly, casual
- Cordial, professional
- Discreet

← **Enter Lobby**
- Physical environment

← **Park Rental Car**
- Clear, not confusing

← **Travel to Hotel**
- Easy access
- Convenient site location
- Access any time of day

Bellboy Carries Luggage
- Attentive employees
- Festive, informal impression
- Sedate, formal impression

→ **Check-in**
- Fast, efficient service

→ **Go to Room**
- Sensible layout of rooms
- Nice ambience
- Plush surroundings, generous amenities

→ **Require Assistance of Hotel Employee**
- Quick attention to major and minor problems
- Customized service

Breakfast
- Room service

← **Use Shower**
- Good shower design
- Reliable plumbing maintenance

← **Workout**
- Location and range of equipment

← **Call Home**
- Fast, friendly hotel-operator assistance
- Smooth call-center management

Checkout
- Quick, seamless departure

→ **Follow Up**
- Satisfaction guarantee
- Effective handling of dissatisfaction
- Tracking preferences, direct marketing

Figure 9.2 Executing great customer service requires detailed operational maps of the customer service experience including all customer–company interactions.

Source: Iacobucci, Dawn and Christie Nordhielm, "Creative benchmarking," *Harvard Business Review*, November–December 2000. See also Shapiro, Benson P., V. KasturiRangan, and John J. Sviokla, "Staple yourself to an order," *Harvard Business Review* 70 (4), July/August 1992: 113.

Again, the services we create backstage are as important as those delivered in the presence of our customer.

Our consumers will often take more than one path in their experience with our product. For example, not every airline passenger has his or her bags misplaced, but we must map this potential path. Our ultimate objective is to have a complete visual illustration of all potential touch-points. After we have identified each point of interaction with the customer—each step in the process-flow that makes up our customer relationship—we place them into the appropriate quadrant in the frontstage–backstage/custom-standard grid. We then consider whether and how we can clear the lower-left and upper-right quadrants.

NEW PRODUCTS/INNOVATION

MEDICAL TOURISM AND THE IMPORTATION OF SERVICES

The very high cost of medical care in the United States has created an incentive for as many as perhaps 2 million patients each year to seek those services in other countries like Mexico, Costa Rica, India, and Thailand, a phenomenon called "medical tourism." Like all services, however, medical care is characterized by intangibility, because it is rich in experience and credence attributes and naturally lacking in search attributes. This makes assessing service providers difficult, never more so than when we literally entrust our life to someone we don't know, and with whom we might not be able to communicate. Bumrungrad Hospital in Bangkok, Thailand goes out of its way to address this risk, adding many elements of tangibility to its offering and creating trust. Here are some of the ways.

The physical environment: The immaculate hospital lobby showcases a sense of order and calm, resembling the lobby of a fancy hotel. The waiting lounges feature a Starbucks Café and Wi-Fi-access.

Process discipline: The hospital environment offers a fully automated service. From admission to discharge, all processes are centrally linked to the patient's records and care delivery, and support services are delivered and monitored at the patient level. The hospital also integrates clinical care with support services, including travel, accommodations, transport within Bangkok, and billing and post-procedure follow-up.

Clinical excellence: Many of Bumrungrad's doctors are board certified in the United States as well as in Thailand. Bumrungrad is also accredited by an independent certification agency, the Joint Commission International. The hospital also makes public a series of outcome metrics, formatted for comparison to U.S. and E.U. hospitals. For example, its patient-satisfaction statistics place it in the 90th percentile of comparable U.S. and European hospitals.

Use of IT for patient care: The hospital's patient information portal lets individuals monitor their own electronic health records (EHR) while in Thailand and later, when they need to schedule check-ups in their home country. These EHRs integrate diagnostic information, clinical information (tests, labs, nurses, and clinical support services), and patient case history, helping to minimize medical errors and allowing doctors to monitor patients and their progress in fine-grained detail.

Finally, Bumrungrad uses web-based channels extensively, not just for engaging with customers but also for outbound marketing. A cost simulation lets a potential patient enter details of his or her condition and estimate the potential costs of treatment, for instance. This electronic estimate is based on actual costs of past patients and it is constantly updated from the hospital's database, just another example of the way the hospital tries to decrease the perceived risk of purchasing its services. ■

Sources: Aron, Ravi. "No other choice: Why medical tourism continues to thrive." In *India Knowledge@Wharton*, June 2, 2011. Mack Center for Technological Innovation at the University of Pennsylvania. Accessed 8/29/13. Hamilton, Jon. NPR.org. "Medical tourism creates Thai doctor shortage," November 29, 2007, 12:06 pm. http://www.npr.org/templates/story/story.php?storyId=16735157. Accessed 9/3/2013.

Levin, Matt. "What Obama's Affordable Care Act means for the world's hospitals," *The Global Post.* October 3, 2012. http://www.globalpost.com/dispatch/news/regions/americas/costa-rica/120923/obamacare-health-care-reform-medical-tourism. Accessed 9/3/2013.

To clear the frontstage/standard quadrant, we may choose to simply mechanize standard procedures. Many firms have already done much of this work: ATM's, self-checkout, and airline kiosks are familiar examples, and advancing technology will create opportunities for more. The lure of mechanization often distracts us from another option for clearing this quadrant, however: we can elect to *customize* standard procedures. For example, instead of replacing a bank teller with a machine, we might leverage IT to provide our tellers with instant information that enables them to have more individualized conversations with their customers. Mechanization is most helpful and cost effective for standardizing procedures, while a live human is better at dramatizing and customizing services. The decision about where to stage a specific activity should be a function of the firm's overall marketing strategy and core competence. For example, a firm targeting highly involved customers with low time demands (such as retirees) may elect to customize and dramatize many services, whereas a firm targeting high need-for-convenience time-constrained customers likely will elect to move services into the backstage/standard quadrant.

CUSTOMER SATISFACTION: THE ZONE OF TOLERANCE

Controlling all aspects of service delivery may seem like a daunting task. The good news is that our consumer can actually be quite forgiving, within certain bounds that define the **zone of tolerance**.[3] The zone of tolerance is a range of expected and acceptable outcomes of a service experience. If customers perceive their experience to be within this range, they report satisfaction with the product, even though service delivery may vary. Essentially, all experiences within the zone of tolerance are perceived to be similar. This is good news when consumers give us credit for a quality of service level that we did not quite achieve, and not so good when we slightly exceed expectations within the zone of tolerance but do not fully reap the fruits of our labors. In either case, as long as our service levels fall within this zone of tolerance, we generally have satisfied our customers.

On the other hand, we observe a different dynamic when our service delivery falls outside the zone of tolerance (Figure 9.3). There is some lower bound of expected service delivery, and if we fall below that line, however slightly, our customers' reported level of dissatisfaction likely will be much worse than their actual experience. Hence, we do not find a one-to-one correspondence between *actual* performance and *reported* performance. Within the zone of tolerance, perceptions and reports of performance tend to regress toward expectations; below the zone of tolerance, perceptions tend to fall precipitously.

Customer satisfaction. The gap between the customer's expectation of company performance and the perceived experience of performance.

Zone of tolerance. The range of acceptable or expected outcomes in a service experience.

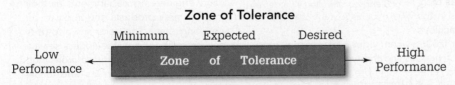

Figure 9.3 The Zone of Tolerance is a range of customer expectations within which customers interpret service as adequate. When service performance falls outside the zone, customer expectations will shift, which can affect customer satisfaction.

---

[3]See Zeithaml, Valarie, Leonard L. Berry, and A. Parasuraman (1993), "The nature and determinants of customer expectations of service," *Journal of the Academy of Marketing Science* 21(1): 1–12.

What happens when we exceed expectations, rising above the upward bound of the zone of tolerance? In many companies employees are constantly exhorted to exceed expectations. However, we should consider the logical consequences of these types of efforts. Consumers are extremely adaptive. When our customers first have a positive service or product experience, they are certainly delighted and may share information about their experience with others. Unfortunately, they will also likely adjust their expectations upward, anticipating that the next service experience will be equal to or even better than the last. If the company cannot continually (and profitably) meet these rising expectations, customers will eventually be disappointed, more than they might have been if we had simply performed at a lower but more consistent level. Furthermore, each customer has a different set of

social**media**

Blendtec Uses Social Media to Deliver Value-Added Services

Social media like Facebook and Google Plus offer companies a chance to have two-way conversations with customers and also to listen in on what the company's most engaged customers tell each other about products and services. Some companies go even further and use social media to deliver value-added services. Blendtec, a manufacturer of high-powered blenders based in Utah, has made great use of social media.

The company was founded in the 1980s by Tom Dickson, an engineer and inventor who designed a high-powered wheat mill and a revolutionary high-powered blender, The Total Blender. Although its product was technically superior to most blenders in the market, the company did not achieve widespread fame until October 2006, when videos of Dickson blending an iPhone went viral around the world. (The blended phone actually sold on eBay for more than a new phone.) Since then, Dickson's many "Will It Blend" videos have made Blendtec an Internet sensation, both

Tom Dickson, CEO and Founder of Blendtec, blending a gardening rake for his Youtube channel.

on its website, willitblend.com, and on its YouTube channel. Dickson has been featured on many local and national news and entertainment programs, newspapers, magazines, and blogs. The company credits its viral marketing efforts with helping it increase sales by more than 600%.

Social media is more than a marketing channel for Blendtec. The marketing force regularly uses social media to survey customers and the features of the product they like or dislike, the way they use the product, and the type of improvements they would like to see. This information circulates through the organization and helps the production and engineering departments as they design new products and improve on existing ones. The company also uses social media to deliver recipes, a value-added service that enhances the value of the product to the more than 100,000 customers and would-be customers who follow Blendtec on Facebook.

Sources: Bolton, Stephanie. "BlendTec's recipe for online video success," *Skeleton Productions Blog.* July 9, 2010. http://www.skeletonproductions.com/blog/video-production-tips/blendtecs-recipe-for-online-video-success/. Accessed March 12, 2012.

Company website. Blendtec.com. Accessed March 12, 2012.

expectations, some of which might lead our firm down a path not linked to our competence.

It is somewhat counterintuitive but ultimately crucial to understand that, when it comes to service delivery, the firm must achieve *consistency* before *brilliance*. Certainly the firm should seek to improve services in order to profitably compete and differentiate; however, the path this improvement takes should be systematic rather than irregular. Exceeding expectations is *not* a recipe for sustainable growth. Instead we should seek to consistently deliver services and benefits based on the foundation of our core competence, and constantly strive to improve our overall level of service delivery within this framework.

CUSTOMER SATISFACTION AND CUSTOMER SERVICE

Firms invest in customer service because they believe that if service improves, then satisfaction, loyalty, and ultimately profitability will follow. The relationship between service and these elements, however, is complex; a simple increase in our investment in service does not in any way guarantee enhanced satisfaction. Furthermore, evidence is mixed as to whether increased satisfaction leads directly to increased loyalty. Finally, the assumption that increased satisfaction will lead to automatic increases in profitability has not always proven to be true.

In fact, the strength of the links between improved service, improved satisfaction and loyalty, and improved profitability rely on more than simple investment increases. Furthermore, it is quite possible that blind investment in customer service (without sufficient regard to the way customers are responding to this service) can lead eventually to a *decline* in satisfaction and profitability because customers' expectations are *dynamic*, changing over time in response to a number of factors. As we discussed above, if we commit resources with the goal of exceeding customer expectations, we will eventually find that consumers have adapted to this new level of service and come to expect it from your organization. This dangerous cycle is represented in Figure 9.4, where customer expectations are met, then consumers adapt upward to the point where we either fail to meet them or fail to achieve profitability. This situation arises when we fail to approach customer service in a strategic manner, as a part of our overall marketing approach, and simply set a vague goal of improving customer service in a general way.

To avoid such an outcome, we must evaluate and execute our customer service strategy as an integral part of our overall strategy. First and foremost, we must refer to our core competence in determining whether and how to improve customer service. Southwest Airlines's success in the 1990s can be traced to the company's core competence in human resources, which in turned allowed it to deliver consistent, if basic, service at a low price. This competence was clearly understood by Southwest management and, perhaps more importantly, by Southwest employees. Armed with this knowledge, employees could manage customer expectations and consistently (and profitably) deliver on them. Essentially, they possessed **corporate self-esteem**: they clearly understood that they were empowered to deliver certain services (such as prompt, efficient boarding processes) and were unapologetic about *not* delivering

Corporate self-esteem. The organizational confidence that arises from a shared understanding of the company's purpose and core competence.

Customer Satisfaction and Profitability

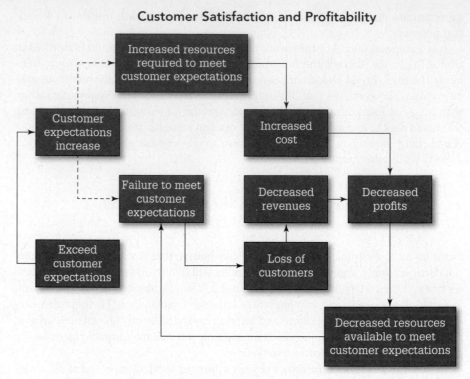

others (such as hot towels and three-course meals). We can summarize the lessons of Southwest and a number of other companies that have made the connection between investment in customer service and profitability as follows:

1. **Manage expectations:** Instead of promising the world, we should ensure that our organization works hard to define expectations within the limits of our expertise. The objective here should be to never make a promise we cannot keep. A marketing department might balk at this objective because it limits its ability to compete against escalating competitive claims about product performance. In the long run, however, it is not the companies that make the biggest promises that succeed, but those that consistently deliver on the promises they make. By realistically assessing our abilities at this stage, we will avoid near-certain failures at the next stage.

2. **Manage production:** The call to action here is *consistency before brilliance*. While many companies reward outstanding service providers (e.g., with "employee of the month" awards), these employees may actually be doing the organization a disservice by raising consumer expectations beyond the point at which the company can consistently meet them. Of course, in the long run we do want to provide exceptional service, but only when we can do it all the time. If we have exceptional performers, we should take them off the front line as quickly as possible and find a way for them to transfer their skills and knowledge to other service providers within the organization. This will enable them to increase the overall brilliance of the organization instead of just their own personal equity.

SHORT EXAMPLE/CAPTION
DIFFERENTIATING A BRAND THROUGH CUSTOMIZATION AND RELIABLE SERVICE

Thriving in the aluminum extrusion business is really tough. A perception that the product is a commodity, a glut of cheap exports, and the rising prices have made it difficult for many U.S. extruders to survive. And even though aluminum extrusions (die-shaped components) are often just a small part of end products like trucks and solar panels, having an unreliable supply can disrupt an entire manufacturing line at a cost of millions of dollars. Futura Industries, a privately held company in Utah, is hardly closing its doors; it actually has been expanding its business. In what might seem like a counterintuitive business model, the company manufactures small batches and targets customers who require high operational flexibility. Futura therefore segments its customers not by industry but rather by their needs for responsiveness and reliable service. Its customers recognize the value of excellent service and partner with Futura even though cheaper imported extrusions exist. ∎

Source: Futura.com; Expert Interviews. November 14, 2012.

3. **Manage the memory:** Because services are high in credence attributes, consumers' opinion of their service encounter can be influenced even after the encounter. We should seek to emphasize successes, reminding our customers of what we have delivered. In addition, we should evaluate what constitutes failure. Consider two grocery stores, one positioned to deliver fresh products and the other claiming to be more convenient. The first store may actually choose not to stock a certain produce item if it is not fresh, while the second store might be willing to stock a slightly older product so the consumer will not be inconvenienced. It is up to the firm to define and communicate success and failure.

SERVICES AND THE BIG PICTURE

Managers love to talk about superior service, marketers love to promise it, and operations people wish they could deliver it. As consumers, we all have our own sad story of a bad service encounter; we all dream of having those wrongs righted and of being treated with respect and intelligence each time we receive service. The inherently emotional aspects of service encounters, coupled with the challenges in delivering service, make this area of marketing highly volatile and therefore difficult to treat strategically. For this reason, it is crucial to maintain discipline and take a systematic approach to service issues.

At the *Business Objective* stage, we may choose to redefine the business we are in to include service aspects. For example, instead of being in the home-alarm business, we may be in the home safety business—many more services must be leveraged to deliver home safety than just installing a home alarm. The home safety business may sound grander and more appealing, but we should also consider the additional costs of providing the services necessary to compete in this category.

As service marketers, we need a clear understanding of our core competence. We must be brutally realistic about what we are able to deliver on a consistent basis, and be careful not to promise more than this to our customers. We must also value our core competence and be able to communicate this value to our customers. Very often, a demanding customer is asking us to deliver something outside our area of competence. Companies often reward employees as heroes for delivering services that fall outside the defined scope of competence for the corporation. In the short run, these employees increase customer satisfaction. However, if the company is not able to deliver these services consistently, our actions will lead us down a path of inconsistency in both service provision and resource allocation. Hence, we must clearly understand and communicate both the value and the limit of our competencies.

When we determine our *Marketing Objective,* we should clearly understand the different nature of the services needed for customer retention as opposed to acquisition. A company with a large installed base of customers will likely field customer service calls from people with a high level of experience and expertise with the product and category. Its customer service representatives must be able to match that high level of knowledge to meet callers' needs efficiently and effectively. On the other hand, a company emphasizing acquisition may need service providers who can teach and reassure potential customers. Services play the greatest role in customer retention, however, so it is here that we should see the greatest concentration of expenditures on retention.

Of course, at the *Source of Growth stage,* we may elect to leverage a service attribute in order to earn share from our competitors or stimulate primary demand in a new category. In order to do this, we must be able to *profitably* dominate on that attribute. We need to avoid wishful marketing at this stage of the process; in the absence of any substantive product points of difference, we may be tempted simply to convince ourselves that we can dominate on some service attribute. This is easier to think than to do, because the intangibility of services makes it difficult to disprove our claims of having an advantage in this area. However, we will have a competitive advantage in providing a service only if we have a core competence in providing that service.

This thinking must follow through to the *STP* stage. If we elect to segment on service variables, we must be sure that the need for (and the readiness to pay for) these services exists among enough people to justify such a strategy. Furthermore, we must effectively position ourselves on a service (credence) attribute.

In summary, even a packaged goods manufacturer must provide some services to his or her customer, and much of the product differentiation occurring in mature industries is essentially the addition of service attributes. Marketing services is increasingly important, and therefore we must clearly understand the differences between goods and services to ensure proper strategy and execution.

☐ SUMMARY

1. Describe the major differences and similarities between products and services

Services have become a critical part of most product companies' portfolio of offerings and of their retention activities, making crucial contributions to the sustainable competitive advantage of the firm. In marketing services we must remind ourselves just how different from products they are and what those differences imply for our efforts.

2. Describe the characteristics of services

First, services are intangible. They cannot be evaluated prior to consumption, which puts them to the right on the search-experience-credence continuum. Customers therefore generally perceive a greater risk of loss associated with trying new services or new providers. Second, services cannot be inventoried; they are perishable. This creates a natural problem for service providers when trying to cope with fluctuating demand. Third, services are coproduced with customers; they are performed rather than manufactured. This means that well-informed customers will receive better service than uninformed customers, or customers whose expectations have been set too high or too low. Fourth, services are naturally heterogeneous, because they are provided by humans and humans are notoriously poor at performing standardized tasks. Providing great service therefore requires planning every detail of the customer experience and preparing for any eventuality that might arise as the service is being coproduced.

3. Map the customer service experience

Our ultimate objective is to have a complete visual illustration of all potential touch-points. After we have identified each point of interaction with the customer—each step in the process-flow that makes up our customer relationship—we place these into the appropriate quadrant in the front stage–backstage/custom-standard grid. We then consider whether and how we can clear the lower-left and upper-right quadrants.

4. Explain how to manage the concept of Zone of Tolerance for customer satisfaction

Customer satisfaction is the gap between expectations and perceived performance. Expectations fall within a range of what the customer considers acceptable service; this range is called the Zone of Tolerance. If consumers perceive their experience to be within this range, they report satisfaction with the product, but performance outside this range will drastically shift expectations positively or negatively.

5. Describe the relationship between customer service and customer satisfaction

Setting and meeting expectations is particularly critical for services because although humans are poor at managing processes for consistency, we require consistent service to be satisfied. Great service providers excel at: (a) setting expectations, (b) managing production for consistency, (c) managing memory by emphasizing and globalizing successes and de-emphasizing and localizing failures.

6. Integrate services with other elements of the Big Picture framework

Given the inherent variability to services, companies entering the service space must do so in a very disciplined manner. This discipline starts in Business Objective, ensuring that we have clear goals within the organization and understand the competency requirements of offering services. Services management requires different skills and training for our sales forces, different production and quality assurance methods, different pricing models, and different communications tactics. Companies that underestimate this effort will put their competitiveness at risk as services become increasingly critical in differentiating our offerings and retaining customers.

☐ KEY TERMS

Corporate self-esteem. (p.255) The organizational confidence that arises from a shared understanding of the company's purpose and core competence.

Customer satisfaction. (p.253) The gap between the customer's expectation of company performance and the perceived experience of performance.

Intangible. (p.245) A characteristic of services that means they cannot be touched or felt.

Productization of services. (p.244) Transforming services offerings so they resemble tangible products. This is accomplished, for example, by creating a name/logo/identity for the service and marketing it as similarly to a traditional tangible product as possible.

Zone of tolerance. (p.253) The range of acceptable or expected outcomes in a service experience.

☐ REVIEW AND DISCUSSION QUESTIONS

1. Write a short paragraph discussing why companies are adding services to their product portfolios. Provide an example of how a medical equipment manufacturer can add services to its product portfolio and discuss the implications for its business.

2. What are the four major differences between products and services from a marketing perspective? How should companies adapt their marketing and operations to account for these differences?

3. What is the zone of tolerance?
   (a) Explain the effect of over-promising and under-delivering services.
   (b) Explain the effect of under-promising and over-delivering.
   (c) Provide one example of (a) and (b) from your personal experience.

4. Identify three companies you think deliver great service (e.g., Zappos, The Four Seasons Hotels and Resorts, American Express, Amazon). Visit their websites.
   (a) What service promises do they make?
   (b) How do they set expectations and what are the expectations they set?
   (c) How does the design of each of their websites contribute to the service expectations the firms are trying to create?

☐ APPENDIX: MARKETING ANALYSIS AND PLANNING

Marketing Tool #9.1: Front Stage and Backstage Service Marketing

This tool is helpful in increasing the perceived value to our customers by moving customized activities front stage. It can also help increase the profitability of service activities by moving certain less-value added activities backstage and automating or standardizing them.

Process steps:

1. Through customer process mapping (see Fig. 9.5) or brainstorming, list all the service activities your organization performs for customers. Be sure to include not just the activities that the customer sees but also activities that happen backstage—service activities the organization performs on behalf of customers but that are not obvious to them (back-office processes, manual problem resolution, quality assurance, planning, service preparedness, etc.).

2. Place the activities in the 2 x 2 chart shown on the next page by categorizing them first by whether they are performed in front of customers (front stage) or behind closed doors (backstage) and then by whether they are customized for each customer or standardized—always more or less the same regardless of the customer.

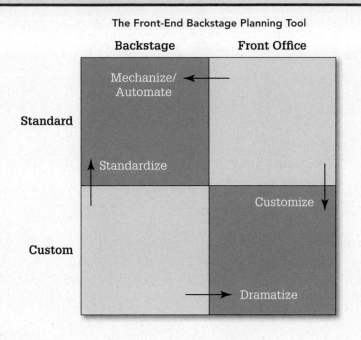

The Front-End Backstage Planning Tool

Figure 9.5 We can use the Front stage and Backstage tool to map current service activities and identified desired changes.

3. Identify opportunities to:
   (a) Move activities backstage: by standardizing or automating, thus lowering the variable cost of providing them.
   (b) Move activities front stage: and dramatize or customize to demonstrate value to the customer, thus increasing willingness to pay and pricing accordingly.

☐ RESOURCES

Berry, Leonard L. and A. Parasuraman (1991). *Marketing Services: Competing Through Quality*. New York: Free Press. ISBN 978-0-02-903079-0.

Zeithaml, Valarie A. (1981). "How consumer evaluation processes differ between goods and services," in Donnelly and George, eds., *Marketing of Services*, American Marketing Association, Chicago, pp. 186–190.

Parasuraman, A., V. A. Zeithaml, et al. (1988). "Servqual," *Journal of Retailing* 64(1): 12–37.

Zeithaml, Valarie A., A. Parasuraman, and Leonard L. Berry (Spring1985). "Problems and strategies in services marketing," *The Journal of Marketing* 49(2): pp. 33–46. Published by: American Marketing Association Stable URL: http://www.jstor.org/stable/1251563.

Oliva, Rogelio and Robert Kallenberg (2003). "Managing the transition from products to services," *International Journal of Service Industry Management* 14 (2): 160–172.

chapter ten

*". . . she explained her
meaning by signs oftner than
by words."*

Cervantes, Saavedra, M. de. (1793).

*The history and adventures of the renowned Don
Quixote. 6th ed. corr. London: Printed for A. Law,
W. Miller, and R. Cater. Vol. 1, page 338.*

MARKETING COMMUNICATIONS

After studying this chapter you should be able to:

1. *Integrate communications into the strategy of the firm*

2. *Define the primary objectives of marketing communications*

3. *Discuss the planning and evaluation of marketing communications*

4. *Integrate marketing communications with other elements of the Big Picture framework*

Integrating Communications throughout Execution

American Express knows how to integrate communications into its strategy execution. Since its reputation for excellent customer service is a major draw to potential new customers, the company trains and organizes its service operations department in the delivery of that promise. During and after each service encounter it reminds customers that they are part of a unique and high-status club, creating a psychological link between a customer request and the company's response in a way that earns it a loyal following and satisfied customer base. It hires employees with prior hospitality-industry experience for call center work and creates an internal environment of care and personalized service for its employees, which they project outward to customers.

Spencer Platt/Getty Images

Reinforcing its commitment to customer satisfaction through directed communications generates big financial rewards for American Express while costing relatively little. For example, when delivering on its promise to replace a lost credit card within 24 hours, the company includes a note with the replacement card to remind the relieved customer that the company met its goal. American Express wrote to customers affected by Hurricane Sandy, the devastating East Coast storm of October 2012, reassuring them of help in case of an emergency. It also chose not to charge merchants the standard commission for any charitable contributions made to nonprofit hurricane relief organizations with an American Express Card. ∎

Sources: French, Tom, Laura LaBerge, and Paul Magill. "We're all marketers now." *McKinsey Quarterly*. McKinsey & Company, July 2011. http://www.mckinsey.com/insights/marketing_sales/were_all_marketers_now. Accessed December 31, 2012.

Colvin, Geoff. " AmEx customer service in action." *CNN Money. Fortune*, April 19, 2012. http://management.fortune.cnn.com/2012/04/19/amex-customer-service-reps/. Accessed December 31, 2012.

Glagowski, Elizabeth. "American Express' Customer Service Makeover." *Think Customers: The 1to1 Blog. 1to1 Media*, April 19, 2010. http://www.1to1media.com/weblog/2010/04/american_express_customer_serv.html. Accessed December 31, 2012.

COMMUNICATIONS: STRATEGY AND EXECUTION

The scope of marketing communications extends far beyond television, print, and online advertising to include all contacts between the brand and the consumer. Any time the consumer or any member of the value chain comes in contact with the brand, marketing communication can take place. Opportunities for brand contacts include corporate/public relations, communications, customer service encounters, packaging elements, pricing communications, social media, event promotions, sponsorships, trade promotions, sales materials, sales presentations, consumer promotions, and, of course, advertising.[1] Because marketing communications pervade all elements of our marketing plan, we need to take a systematic approach to them. In particular, we need to (1) ensure we deliver a consistent message across all promotional elements, and (2) enhance the efficiency of these communications by aligning our activities across all communications components.

Perhaps the most challenging communications issue is measurement and accountability. Marketing communications, of course, have a creative element; if not, it is unlikely they would compel consumers to change their attitudes or behaviors. And as legendary ad executive Leo Burnett once said, "You cannot bore someone into buying something."[2] Persuasion is accomplished through some combination of rational argument, emotional appeal, and dramatic presentation. But just because communications need to be creative doesn't mean we can discount measurement and accountability. Successful marketing communications campaigns are built from expertise in a variety of functional areas. As marketing managers, we will use our strategic skills to develop and assess marketing communications plans that make the most of both art and science to persuade effectively and efficiently.

There are two keys to ensuring successful communications. First, we must exhibit exceptional discipline in adhering to a single-minded strategic plan. If, for example, we have elected to pursue an earn share strategy on the dynamic benefit of convenience, all our marketing communications developed to support this strategy must invoke a comparison to our key competitor and emphasize this benefit. It is this alignment between strategy and execution that will maximize our chances for success. In addition, if our outcome is negative, the fact that we consistently executed against our strategy means that we can learn from this experience. We have learned that the strategy, not just the execution, is not working. If, on the other hand, we are inconsistent in our execution of the strategy and we have bad results, we can't know whether this failure was the result of a bad strategy or simply bad execution.

Second, we must identify and understand the elements of our marketing communications that are *strategic*, and those that are *executional*. A great execution built on a bad strategy will run us into trouble faster than if we had done nothing at all. If, on the other hand, we have done our work thus far in the framework, we will have a solid strategic foundation from which to launch our execution. Likewise, when we are looking to make adjustments and improvements to our plan, we must first determine whether the improvements we need are in the area of execution or strategy. This will ensure that the person best suited for the job is doing the work. The simple act of allocating responsibility along these lines will greatly enhance both the efficiency and the effectiveness of our marketing efforts.

One final note of caution: marketing communications are among the easier elements of the marketing mix to change; a new brochure or an idea for a print or TV campaign can theoretically be developed in a matter of hours, whereas to change channel strategy or product design is a more time-consuming process. Because judging marketing communications materials is an inherently subjective process, these decisions can sometimes be more emotional than logical. This situation leads firms to

---

[1] Pricing-related promotional objectives (trial and repeat) are treated in Chapter 11.

[2] Leo Burnett: Communications of an Advertising Man, 1961, Private Corporate Publication, The Leo Burnett Company, Chicago, Illinois.

NEW PRODUCTS/INNOVATION

MICROSOFT USES FACEBOOK TO ALIGN EXECUTION AND STRATEGY

For years, Microsoft has tried to compete with Google, most recently by positioning one of its brands, Big, as a decision engine rather than only a search engine. Microsoft's efforts have vaulted Bing to second place in the search engine category, behind Google. And yet Bing's success has come at the expense of Google's competitors, not of Google itself.

imago stock&people/NewsCom

While search results obtained through both sites are remarkably similar, Bing hopes to attract consumers through cosmetic upgrades, like pop-up balloons that preview the first few paragraphs of text or the first seven seconds of video from the individual links and colorful, full-page background photographs featuring icons about the item or place being searched for. A left-hand panel displays helpful links related to the search topic, suggests related searches the consumer may find useful, and maintains the search history. Unlike Google's page, the Bing page scrolls continuously, featuring evermore photos (image information is hidden until you roll over a thumbnail). Through partnerships with companies like Expedia and Open Table, Bing allows consumers to book flights and make restaurant reservations without having to exit the search page.

Still, Microsoft needed to find the next big thing to really break into Google's share of the market. Microsoft owns shares of Facebook, and since Facebook competes with Google +, the two companies teamed up to battle a common enemy. Pairing with Facebook allowed Bing to tap into a powerful network of almost 1 billion people, vastly outnumbering the approximately 170 million on Google + in 2012. Relying upon the advice of friends takes away the uncertainty of sifting through a number of sites that may or may not be reliable, and Bing now features a search column that allows people to see friends who may know something about the specific query and ask them for advice through a pop-up box without having to go through the Facebook page. This social search feature also taps into public posts on other sites like Twitter and even Google+. ■

Sources: Thompson, Derek. "Is Microsoft Bing really better than Google?" *The Atlantic.* July 9, 2009. http://www.theatlantic.com/business/archive/2009/07/is-microsoft-bing-really-better-than-google/20963/. Accessed December 31, 2012.

Louttit Meghan, Brustein Joshua, "A search engine match up: How different are Google and Bing?." *The New York Times.* July 30, 2011. http://www.nytimes.com/interactive/2011/07/30/technology/bing-versus-google.html. Accessed December 31, 2012.

---

change communications campaigns (and the agencies that create them) much more often than is probably wise or necessary. But just because we *can* change the communication doesn't mean we *should*. In fact, just the opposite is true: virtually all the most successful marketing communications campaigns are also the ones that have remained the most consistent, relying on brand equity to efficiently build or maintain awareness and attitudes. Thus the fact that we can change the advertising means we need to be extremely cautious when considering whether we should.

COMMUNICATIONS OBJECTIVES

Communications objective. The type of change in beliefs or, in some cases, behavior we wish to accomplish through communications.

With the above in mind, the first step in the communications process is to clearly identify our **communications objective**, that is, the primary attitudinal or behavioral goal of the communications execution. This step helps us separate the goals of communications from the goals of marketing in general.

Above all we should avoid assuming that the objective of every marketing communications campaign is to sell something. Of course as marketers we wish to sell something, and we accomplish this marketing objective by setting and meeting sub-objectives for each of the four P's. But while the objective of marketing is usually to change behaviors, the objective of marketing communications is generally to accomplish an intermediate step in that process such as an increase in awareness or a change in attitude. These changes, coupled with our effective work in product, place, and price, will result in a change in behavior.

In communications, as in other chapters of the Big Picture, we will seek to identify a primary objective—the most important goal for our marketing communications to accomplish. This goal stands out from both a creative and a media standpoint; it will direct our creative development, media, and promotion planning. In executing a campaign, we will evaluate all possible communications tools and choose those we believe will most effectively achieve one of five possible objectives: basic awareness, top-of-mind awareness, information delivery, image or attitude change, or behavioral change. Let's look at each of these.

Basic Awareness Objective

A brand newly introduced to the market will generally pursue a **basic awareness** objective. The objective of a basic or unaided awareness campaign is simply to increase brand recognition, the chance that a potential consumer, presented with the brand name or logo, will acknowledge that he or she has seen it before. To achieve basic awareness we must do two things:

First, we must capture the attention of our target consumers. In this particular case our potential customers do not know and likely do not yet care about our brand; hence, we must capture their attention before we can hope to achieve awareness. This is a creative challenge; we must break through the clutter to which consumers are exposed on a daily basis, and the most efficient way to accomplish this is with an interesting, differentiated execution.

Second, basic awareness campaigns will emphasize the brand name either by featuring the brand as "hero" in a communication or simply by repeating the brand name as many times as possible. As we all know, repetition can often lead to irritation, and an irritated consumer is not what we are seeking to create. Meeting this challenge is critical for basic awareness; communications meant to introduce new brands must be inherently entertaining so consumers will tolerate repetition.

We can measure our success at achieving basic awareness quite simply, with a survey that presents consumers with a list of brands to confirm whether they recognize ours. Very often, however, a certain percent of consumers will claim to recognize almost any brand, regardless of whether it is on the market. For this reason we must take a baseline measure of awareness before launching our campaign.

> **Basic awareness** (also called aided recognition). Consumer's ability, when presented with the brand name or logo, to acknowledge that he or she has seen it before.

Top-of-Mind Awareness Objective

A basic awareness objective may be an obvious first step for any new product or company; however, this is generally just the start of a longer process. The product or brand will very quickly need to move beyond basic awareness. Many companies, notably beer and soft drink marketers, appear to be advertising nothing more than their brand name even though it is clear they have already achieved nearly 100 percent brand recognition. These are examples of firms with a **top-of-mind awareness** objective. They do not just want to be recognized; they want to be foremost in the minds

> **Top-of-mind** (or **unaided**) **awareness.** Customers' ability to identify the brand or product with the business category.

of consumers making a brand choice. From a creative perspective this type of awareness objective presents a challenge quite distinct from that of basic awareness: if consumers are already aware of our brand name, there is a chance they may tune out when exposed to our communications. Repeating the name over and over may not be necessary, but we must still capture attention in a dramatic way.

It is generally easy to do so by simply reminding consumers of a brand they already know. Unfortunately, this type of awareness can decline quite easily as well. This means we must either (1) continually spend money on communications, or (2) leverage creative and/or social media tools in order to gain additional unpaid exposure through word-of-mouth. YouTube, Facebook, Twitter, and other social networking sites are among the newer ways to use this second option for creating "buzz" around a brand. But firms have been leveraging word-of-mouth, or *network effects,* for many years, usually by developing catchy slogans, phrases, or songs that consumers enjoy repeating among themselves. In 1971 the Coca-Cola Company launched an ad campaign featuring a song titled "I'd like to buy the world a Coke." This song became so popular that a well-known singing group, The New Seekers, recorded it and it eventually became a top-10 hit. Each time listeners heard the song they were reminded of the brand, at no additional cost to Coca-Cola. Whether achieved through new social media or good old-fashioned song writing, this effect is crucial for building and maintaining top-of-mind awareness. Firms with this type of marketing communications objective might also explore "below the line" communications strategies such as product placement or public relations programs.

Top-of-mind awareness is distinct from basic awareness in that with it consumers don't just *recognize* our brand; they can *recall* it. We measure this awareness by collecting *first mentions:* we survey consumers and ask them to tell us, for example, the first three brands of beer that come to mind. If our campaign is successful, we will see an increase in the percentage of first mentions among our target; if our strategy is successful, this increase will also result in an increase in sales.

Information objective. Communications intended to provide specific information about the brand; the information must be focused on the positioning.

Information Objective

Another common communication objective is to deliver specific **information objectives** about the product or service. Southwest Airlines has the lowest prices; Kinko's is open 24 hours; Subaru has 4-wheel drive. Ideally there is only one piece of information; this is how a single-minded campaign is developed. If we have done the difficult strategic work leading up to this chapter, we can presume the information in this single thought is of interest to consumers and is a benefit differentiating us from the competition.

The inherent appeal of this benefit will help to drive the effectiveness of our communications; however, it is important that the appeal of the benefit doesn't outstrip the appeal of the brand. For example, if we are launching a product with an exciting new feature such as 4G Internet access, speech recognition, or a superior sound system, we may become so enamored of the benefit that we fail to appropriately promote our brand. Then our potential consumers may remember

Coca-Cola's TV commercials have often featured images from all over the world.

social**media**

Social Media Amplifies Communications

For marketers, the dark side of social media is that they amplify negative buzz that used to be communicated between one consumer and another. Now the story of one consumer's bad experience can snowball, overpowering the brand's publicity.

The W Hotel's "Whatever, Whenever" promise has been distorted through social media. The slogan was originally intended to represent a unique promise of excellent customer service—"Whatever you want, whenever you want it"—but unhappy clients say it means "Whatever management feels like, whenever they feel like it."

However, one W Hotel customer posted on a blog: "On Friday evening I wanted to order some room service. The first time I called the whatever/whenever line I let it ring 20 times. I waited 10 minutes and called the whatever/whenever line again and let it ring another 20 times. Then I went to the sushi bar up the street. Whatever."

The ability to have whatever you want, delivered immediately, should be enough to create many brand devotees, even at several hundred dollars per night for a room. Failure to deliver on the "Whatever/Whenever" guarantee, however, inflates and then deflates customer expectations and can be worse than offering no guarantee at all. Making grand promises is an excellent way to distinguish your firm from competitors, but integral to that strategy is the commitment and the ability to fulfill those promises.

Airlines and banks are so important to the everyday lives of customers that both face heavy competition and seek ways to make themselves more attractive, but firms

© Roma/iStockphoto

in both industries are often called to task on social media for their failures. Problems at airports rank among the most difficult for consumers, and Internet forums provide a haven for people eager to discuss the other side of the story. Customers also demand great service from banks and immediate resolutions to problems. In an attempt to reach out to customers, Bank of America created its own Facebook page and quickly witnessed how social media empowers consumers at the cost of company control. The page has become a place where dissatisfied customers regularly commiserate over negative experiences with the bank. While the bank may elect to remove the page, this step would likely have a negative impact on the firm's credibility in the social media world.

Sources: Post by "Jumpgate:" "Whatever/whenever failure at the W City Center." *FlyerTalk*.N.p., January 27, 2009. http://www.flyertalk.com/forum/starwood-preferred-guest/914142-whatever-whenever-failure-w-city-center-chicago.html. Accessed December 31, 2012.

Thompson, Avni P. "W Hotels: The perils of promising 'Whatever, Whenever'" brand sundae. N.p., May 5, 2010. http://www.brandsundae.com/blog/2010/05/w-hotels-the-perils-of-promising-whatever-whenever-.html. Accessed December 31, 2012.

Bank of America Facebook Page. Facebook.com, https://www.facebook.com/BankofAmerica. Accessed December 31, 2012.

I HATE Bank of America Facebook Page. Facebook.com. https://www.facebook.com/pages/I-HATE-Bank-of-America/335801912634. Accessed December 31, 2012.

only the feature or benefit and not who offers it. The challenge for the creative team is to tightly tie our brand to the information, so the brand and the benefit are recalled together.

From a measurement perspective, we must consider that our campaign may have a dual objective: we are seeking to convey information, but also to enhance the perceived importance of that information. We are doing more than simply dis-

Walmart's logo includes its concise informational tagline, *Always Low Prices, Always,* which has become a company promise to its customers and a decision aid to its employees.

seminating information; we are also attempting to shape the market. For example, Walmart has supported the tagline "Always Low Prices" for so many years that the whole target audience is likely aware of this information. By continuing to support it, however, Walmart has had an even greater impact on the market: not only do consumers believe it has low prices, but also more of them across all economic segments have begun to believe it is important to shop based on price because the quality is about the same.[3] In other words, the importance of the variable has been increased, and this increase has fueled Walmart's continued growth. To gauge the success of informational campaigns, we will therefore collect two pieces of information: first, whether there has been an increase in consumer knowledge of the information we are trying to convey, and second, whether there has been an increase in the importance of this information.

Image/Attitude Objective

Image objective.
Communication created to capture share of heart, evoking an emotional response in consumers. The focus of an image objective is the *person* in the target audience, as opposed to the *brand.*

The primary objective of most communications campaigns is to change an attitude toward or image of our brand. Whereas awareness and information campaigns are seeking to capture share of mind, image campaigns seek to capture share of heart, evoking an emotional response in consumers. Most advertising for credence products, products that tend to have more subjective, emotional benefits such as perfume and luxury watches, has **image objective.**[4] Many mature brands, in attempting to solidify their position in the marketplace and protect against competitive entry, will try to shift their communications objective from information or awareness objective to image/attitude. The focus of an image objective is the person in the target audience, as opposed to the brand. For example, Volvo initially focused on communicating information about its brand by emphasizing product features such as daytime running lights and driver's side airbags: *Volvo cars are safe cars.* As the brand matured, Volvo campaigns began to emphasize the Volvo driver: *Volvo drivers care about the safety of their family.* These two campaigns both focused on a target audience with a high need for safety and likely represent highly similar positioning strategies. However, they have distinct communications objectives; the first was about information, and the second was about attitude/image.

The Volvo brand has consistently projected a safety image, first by featuring safety features for acquisition, and later by reinforcing its customers for making safe choices.

When it comes to creative execution, the challenges of accomplishing an image objective loom large. How can a brand

---

[3]"Retail: The Wal-Mart effect." *McKinsey Quarterly*, 2002, Number 2, pp. 40–43.
[4]A discussion of credence products is presented in Chapter 9.

convince consumers that it is "cool," for example? Sophisticated consumers might view a traditional television commercial about coolness with skepticism about its credibility; we are much more likely to believe a friend or relative who says a brand is cool.[5] From a communications execution perspective, therefore, we may try to accomplish this by using social media to generate positive ratings of our products among groups of friends on Facebook or Twitter. If not, it is still best to find a way to

CUSTOMERFOCUS
THE DOVE REAL BEAUTY CAMPAIGN

To find out what women think about beauty and beauty products, and to transform its Dove brand to reflect those views and fill gaps in the market, Unilever consulted two renowned psychologists and distributed 3,000 surveys to women in 10 different countries. Fewer than 10% believed themselves to be "attractive," and more than 0% responded that the beauty industry's idea of beauty was unattainable.

Unilever responded with Dove's "Real Beauty Campaign," declaring it Dove's mission "to make more women feel beautiful every day by broadening the narrow definition of beauty and inspiring them to take great care of themselves." This image campaign was very successful and relied on billboards, magazine print ads, and social media to execute a number of different stories articulating one positioning message: every woman is beautiful. Unilever used real women instead of models in advertisements and invited consumers to engage with the brand by providing forums and questions to provoke thought and discussion on societal values and modern standards of beauty. It targeted a younger demographic and linked mothers and their daughters by encouraging moms to talk to their daughters "before the beauty industry does." Dove also partnered with organizations like the Girl Scouts of America to promote its Uniquely ME! and It's Your Story-Tell It! Journey Series of multidisciplinary training and self-esteem building programs, as well as the National Eating Disorder Information Centre. The Dove Self-Esteem Fund fosters positive self-image in women of all ages and has engaged over 3 million people since its inception in 2006.

New Dove Firming. As tested on real curves.

© Lee Snider/The Image Works

Unilever also created several provocative advertisements, the most famous of which was a short time-lapse video called "Evolution," which shows makeup artists spending hours altering a woman's appearance, then photo shopping until an unrealistically glamorous finished product is plastered on a billboard with the line "No wonder we have a distorted perception of beauty." The video aired on Good Morning America and has garnered over 12 million views on YouTube. Another video, "True Colours," depicts young girls from different ethnicities who all wish they could change things about themselves to become 'beautiful' and calls upon the public to affirm their unique kinds of beauty. The Dove "Real Beauty" campaign was a huge success, bringing in $3 of product sales for every $1 spent on advertising. ■

Source: Eppright, Margaret. "Only sixty beautify women," *Journal of International Management. Blog Post.* May 11, 2011. http://www.unileverusa.com/brands/personalcarebrands/dove/index.aspx. Accessed December 2012.

"Preferred Perfect. how women perceive beauty in advertising," *BlogPost.* http://com215.wordpress.com/history-of-dove-advertising/. Accessed December 30, 2012.

Rappaport, Stephen D. *Listen First!: Turning Social Media Conversations Into Business Advantage.* Hoboken: John Wiley and Sons, Inc., 2011.

---

[5]Salwen, Michael Brian. "An integrated approach to communication theory and research." *Taylor & Francis,* 2009. pp. 424–452.

communicate our message through indirect communications channels such as product placement or testimonials. In short, we would like our image message to seem as if it comes from someplace other than our firm.

It is of course quite difficult to measure directly the degree to which consumers perceive a brand to be "cool" or "smart" or "safe." Qualitative research is generally more useful than quantitative research here; we may simply show consumers our execution and then ask them what thoughts or associations it evokes. Another tactic is to use *surrogates,* other brands or objects that represent the same image we are trying to achieve with our brand, and ask consumers to assess similarity between our brand and the surrogates.

Behavioral Objective

Behavioral objective. Communication with a goal to cause an action or specific behavior in our target audience.

Communications campaigns with a strict **behavioral objective** are quite rare. Their key distinguishing characteristic is that there are no intervening marketing variables between exposure to the communication and the intended behavior. An "infomercial," a long-form advertisement that constantly entreats consumers to call and place an order, is an excellent illustration of this point. The objective of an infomercial's call to action is behavioral: pick up the phone and call. There are no additional steps between exposure to the ad and the intended behavior.

Infomercials also provide insight into the nature of our creative execution for a behavioral objective. Consider how marketers use most long-form communications with a behavioral objective: do they make several different points or make the same point several times? The answer is the latter: to achieve a behavioral objective, we repeat the call to action as often as possible. The creative challenge is to accomplish this level of repetition without driving our potential customers away because they are irritated.

The good news is that measurement of a behavioral objective is quite straightforward. We simply assess whether the behavior we are seeking occurs as a result of exposure to our marketing communications. By evaluating the cause and effect relationship between our communications execution and the behavioral response, we can fine-tune our executions to a much greater extent than we can with the other communications objectives.

EXECUTING COMUNICATIONS: PLANNING AND COPY DEVELOPMENT

Creatives. Writers and designers responsible for bringing a copy strategy to life, transforming it from a simple set of words in five boxes of the positioning statement.

Once we have established our communications objective, we must develop our communications materials and determine how, and how much, we will spend on media. If we have identified our objective clearly, and it is linked to our overall strategy, these tasks will be significantly easier. Generally, executions are not created directly by the brand manager or account executive; the actual commercials, print ads, point-of-purchase displays, brochures, and websites are usually developed by a communications firm such as an advertising or PR agency. The agency's **creatives** are the writers and designers responsible for bringing a copy strategy to life, transforming it from a simple set of words in five boxes from the positioning statement (Chapter 7), to a dramatic execution that captures and holds consumers' attention.

MEDIA PLANNING AND BUYING

In traditional marketing models, media planning and buying was a distinct task with little consideration of the specific copy that had been developed. In the current marketing environment, however, it is unrealistic to consider copy development and media purchase as separate undertakings. The choice of media drives the creative work and vice versa; therefore, it is preferable that media strategy be developed side by side with creative strategy.

In addition, radical changes in communications over the past years have called traditional media models into question. We are no longer simply allocating our advertising spending between a few different outlets such as TV, print, and radio. Instead, we must consider all the possible ways of reaching our customers, including social networking, product placement, word-of-mouth referrals, broadcast e-mails, on-site events, cable, Internet and broadcast TV, and satellite radio.

The variety of media choices we face is daunting, but our choices will be more efficient and effective if we take a strategic approach to media buying rather than adopting a new media approach simply because it is new. No brand today can compete without a webpage; for most firms it is a cost of entry instead of a differentiator. The same often holds true for a presence on Facebook, Twitter, RSS feeds, blogs, and so on. However, the vast array of media choices remains a set of tools for achieving goals, not goals in and of themselves.

Consider, for example, one manager with a top-of-mind objective and another with an information objective. To achieve top-of-mind awareness efficiently, the first manager might elect to develop a social media campaign in order to generate word-of-mouth buzz about the product. In contrast, the manager with the information objective might select print and web-based communications, because these are more effective for delivering basic information to potential consumers who are already interested in finding out more about the product. The bottom line is that our strategy should drive our choice of media tools; we should never let media tools drive our strategy.

In addition to determining where to place our resources in terms of communications spending, we must decide just how much to spend. Very often media spending levels are based on historical criteria that do not necessarily result in sound spending decisions. For example, a common rule of thumb is to take a historical industry standard for communications spending and apply it to future spending for our brand. Unfortunately, this backward-looking approach can have perverse results. Communication spending as a percent of sales is an excellent way to evaluate the overall efficiency of our media spending; however, as a decision rule for future spending it may lock us into some dangerous spending plans.

Consider, for example, a scenario in which our sales are increasing because the market is growing. In this case, the percent-of-sales formula would tell us to increase our communications spending, but if we did so we would likely be spending too much, because demand is already there and does not need to be stimulated by promotions.

Conversely, if the market is shrinking, our formula would tell us to spend less promoting our product. In this case, however, we may actually need to spend more, to defend our share against competitors fighting for a piece of a shrinking pie. Likewise, if we are introducing a large number of new products, we probably need to spend more as a percent of sales, and if we have a large number of established products we can spend relatively less. Hence, blindly following the percent-of-sales approach can quickly lead us off course.

Of course, we do want to track levels of competitive and historical spending in the marketplace so we can assess the general relationship between spending and sales. However, we cannot rely on this information alone to set spending levels, because it does not take into account the dynamic nature of the marketplace, where the number of competitors and new product introductions can change drastically from year to year.

Finally, an alarming number of firms use the "what's left over" method of ad budgeting. Such firms first allocate resources to "hard" expenses such as labor, plant, and equipment and then apportion to advertising any funds that are left over. This is perhaps the most dangerous strategy for ad budgeting, primarily because failure to properly support the brand consistently may result in declines in demand that can quickly threaten the viability of the firm.

Zero-based communications budgeting. The practice of building communications budgets by starting from zero and considering the size of the target audience, the positioning message, and the communication objective and then selecting the most appropriate media channel and number of exposures to arrive at a total budget.

The appropriate way to set media spending levels is through a **zero-based**, objective-driven budgeting process (Figure 10.1). In this approach we literally start from zero and build a budget based on the objectives and strategies we have derived from the Big Picture framework. In particular, we have already identified our target audience description, target audience size, positioning strategy, and communication objective. Ideally we also know the specifics of our campaign, including creative and media. With this information we can estimate how many exposures we need to achieve to achieve our objectives. For example, fewer exposures may be necessary to achieve a basic awareness objective than to accomplish an image objective. A seasoned media planner can help estimate appropriate spending levels.

Advertising Spending: Zero-based Approach

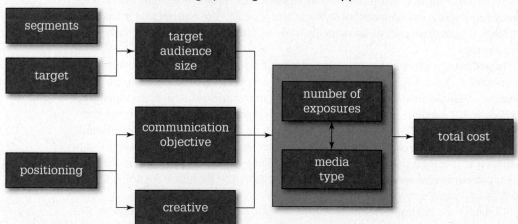

Figure 10.1 Advertising spending should be budgeted taking into consideration the number of exposures we require, the number of customers we need to reach, the communications objective, and the media type.

NEW PRODUCTS/INNOVATION

FROM COST PER THOUSAND TO PAY PER CLICK

Traditionally, mass media advertising rates were based on cost-per-thousand (CPM), a metric used widely in radio, television, newspaper, outdoor, and magazine advertising. CPM is generally defined as the cost of using media to reach 1,000 people or households. The move to a digital environment has meant that advertisers

Bloomberg/Getty Images

can now measure not just exposure to ads but response, captured in viewer's click-through actions as a result of an ad. The metric used for this purpose is **pay per click (PPC)**. ■

Evaluating Creative Execution

In the case of trade or consumer advertising, identity work, logos, or packaging, advertising, or social media campaigns, the first stage of the creative process is generally the development of TV storyboards, print layouts, or some other pen-and-ink representations of the envisioned communication and concepts. One of the most difficult tasks a marketing manager faces in the communications arena is assessing the quality and appropriateness of copy execution. While there is no magic formula for commenting on creative work, a few basic rules make the task easier.

First, remember that the marketing manager is the guardian of the strategy. His or her first task is to determine whether the copy piece accurately communicates the agreed-upon strategy. If the piece is not on strategy, take a step back and ask a few key questions: First, what other strategy does the work represent? Second, is this different strategy better than the one the marketing manager originally developed? If the answer is "no," the creative team will need to go back to the drawing board and develop an execution built on the correct, original strategy.

If, on the other hand, the strategy the creative team developed and executed on is superior, this suggests that they are better at developing strategy than our marketing manager. In this case we should fire our marketing manager and let our creatives do the strategic work as well!

The second possibility is that the execution *does* represent our strategy. Then, and only then, we can evaluate the execution. Here, as in all other elements of the Big Picture framework, we check that strategy and execution are aligned, and if they are not, we change elements of either to integrate the two. The Innovation box (earlier in the chapter) described a successful communications campaign that was not fully aligned to the original strategic intent of the parent company, Microsoft. In evaluating creative execution, even while the task is clear, it is also inherently subjective. Marketing communications are part art and part science; the science part is a product of the process of STP, segmentation, targeting, and positioning. Art is what determines whether our customers will: (1) pay attention, and (2) respond in the way we want them to. We rely heavily on the creatives here, because their expertise should lie in knowing exactly how to accomplish this. If we do have concerns with the execution and they are not strategic in nature, we need to be able to clearly articulate them.

Pay per click (PPC). A method of paying for Internet advertising in which the advertiser does not pay for the placement of the ad, but rather pays each time a consumer clicks on the ad to view more information or place an order.

GLOBALMARKETING

UNILEVER'S "FAIR AND LOVELY" JEOPARDIZES THE COMPANY'S REAL BEAUTY MESSAGING

A global economy offers opportunities for brands but also presents risks if the brand message is inconsistent across countries. International companies adjust their product benefits to the local needs of their target customers, of course, but to maintain successful marketing and public relations campaigns, they must keep their core values consistent. The backlash for failure can be severe, as Unilever experienced after releasing its Dove Real Beauty Campaign in the United States (see the preceding Customer Focus box) while promoting a competing value set through its Fair and Lovely skin-lightening products in India.

The Real Beauty campaign was aimed at boosting women's self-esteem by encouraging them to embrace their bodies as they are. However, the lightening creams in India were sold with a message that women with dark skin are not attractive or desirable but can become so by changing the color of their skin. Unilever came under heavy fire for the inconsistency. Even though its distinct brand structure provided some protection because many U.S. consumers do not associate Dove with Fair and Lovely, news sources such as *The Guardian* newspaper in the United Kingdom publicized the conflicting messages, chipping away at Unilever's credibility and customer equity. Companies can reap huge benefits by expanding into new markets, but they must maintain a cohesive brand message; compromising authenticity for the sake of the bottom line can jeopardize both profits and brand reputation. ∎

The Fair and Lovely product for sale in India sends a very different message to women from that of the Dove Real Beauty campaign.

Sources: Sayeed, Layla. "Stand up to Unilever's hypocrisy over skin-lightening." *The Guardian. Guardian News and Media*, July 16, 2010. http://www.guardian.co.uk/commentisfree/2010/jul/16/unilever-hypocritical-promoting-skin-lightening. Accessed December 31, 2012.

Stewart, Dodai. "'White Beauty' has an ugly message." *Jezebel. N.p.*, July 10, 2008. http://jezebel.com/5023789/white-beauty-has-an-ugly-message. Accessed December 31, 2012.

BUMP. Mnemonic for assessing marketing communications execution. This acronym stands for *Believable, Unique, Memorable, and Pertinent.*

One approach to evaluating execution is to do a **BUMP** analysis that asks whether the creative work is *believable, unique, memorable,* and *pertinent.*

Believable: Is the execution believable? Does the dramatization sufficiently suspend the disbelief of consumers, or will they be watching the ad and saying, "That's silly, that would never happen"?

Unique: Is the execution unique, or have we seen the same storyline in other product categories? Do we think the target audience will see it as boring or interesting?

Memorable: Memorability goes hand in hand with uniqueness; the more unique a spot is, the more memorable. However, if an execution is too unique, it may lose credibility and consumers may dismiss it.

Pertinent: Is the execution relevant to the target audience? Is the dramatization something that will resonate with this group? Can we imagine the target identifying with the characters in the commercial, or finding them entertain-

GLOBALMARKETING

DIGITAL CONTENT DISTRIBUTION REQUIREMENTS IN FRANCE: PARLEZ-VOUS FRANÇAIS?

A major advantage of running an online business is that distribution costs are lower than those faced by brick and mortar companies, making it infinitely cheaper to expand geographically, at least in terms of buildings and physical requirements. It is not necessarily cheaper with regards to legal requirements and regulations. France's commitment to defending its cultural sovereignty and language has driven the country to develop regulations to support the use of French over foreign languages. For example, French radio stations must play at least 40% French songs, and media companies and advertisers must conduct business in French and are prohibited from broadcasting using English words if French equivalents exist. Operating in France might not require buildings, but it certainly requires translating all content to French. ■

Sources: Yentz, Amanda. "The effects of France's language protection laws on French media." June 7, 2007. Northwestern University IES Nantes. Working Paper.

---

ing in some way? Does the execution reflect the culture of the target audience? Companies that target customers internationally must be particularly careful to also comply with any language requirements in their target market (see the box above about digital content distribution requirements in France), while preserving the essence of their message and brand meaning.

Remember that this is an analysis of the *execution*, not the *strategy*. We should already have done a similar analysis on the copy strategy during the development of our positioning statement before moving to the copy development stage.

MARKETING COMMUNICATIONS AND THE BIG PICTURE

This marketing communications chapter completes the executional elements of the Big Picture framework (Figure 10.2). We define marketing communications very broadly and consider any brand contact with a current or potential customer to be a communications event. All communication events give voice to our strategy and are opportunities for us to articulate the positioning of the firm to the target audience.

Like our choices regarding other executional elements, our decisions about marketing communications can be guided by decisions we have already made in the Big Picture framework as illustrated in Figure 10.3.

For *acquisition/stimulate demand*, we are seeking to bring new users to the category and the brand. To accomplish this we must first pursue an awareness objective. We then pursue an information objective, in this case promoting the category benefit where it is tied to our brand.

For *acquisition/earn share recall*, we want to compare ourselves to a key competitor or segment. We will therefore pursue an informational objective to communicate our benefits vs. the competition's, or a behavioral objective to encourage consumers to try our product and compare it with their current brand.

The Big Picture Framework Including Communications (Promotion).

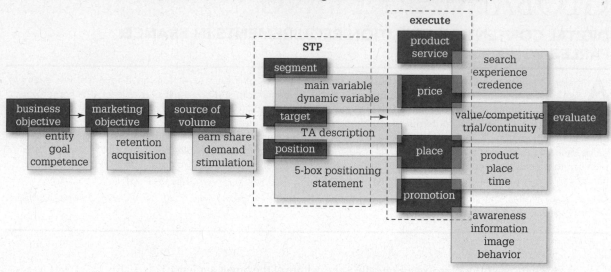

Figure 10.2 Communications is the final element of execution within the Big Picture framework.

In the case of a *retention/stimulate demand* strategy, we are speaking to our current customers and seeking to deepen our relationship with them by pursuing an image objective. Or we may simply want to encourage our customers to use more of our product or use it in different situations. In this case we will pursue a behavioral objective.

Figure 10.3 Communication objectives for each of the Big Picture strategic quadrants.

Marketing Communications: Summary Promotion

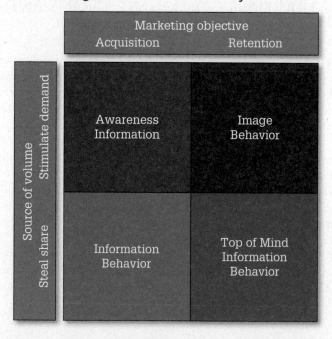

Finally, for a *retention/earn share* strategy, we are speaking to customers who are using our brand as well as a competitive brand. In some cases we will pursue an informational or behavior objective, to encourage consumers to compare and reconsider why they are using two brands instead of just ours. Our goal in this case is to convert them from multi-brand users to exclusive users. In some cases our customers in this quadrant value the variety they enjoy from using two or more brands. For example, it is unlikely we will convince customers to eat the same brand of cereal or drink the same brand of beer every single day. In this situation we simply want to increase the frequency with which our customers choose us instead of the competitor by trying to maintain top-of-mind awareness.

Marketing communications is where our marketing strategy finds its expression. Whether that takes the form of trade brochures or an ad during the Super Bowl, the same philosophy should apply: establish clear, focused strategic objectives and ensure that our executions align with them. This approach will ensure that our marketing communications serve their purpose in the overall marketing plan.

☐ SUMMARY

1. Integrate communications into the strategy of the firm
To successfully execute our communications, we must follow two broad guidelines. First, we must adhere to our communications to a single-minded strategic plan; this increases our chance of success and also enables organizational learning as the communications execution tests our positioning strategy. Second, we must distinguish *strategic* from *executional* marketing communications efforts. Assessing marketing communications should be a two-step process, we must first assess whether the execution follows the marketing strategy; and separately judge its creative merits.

2. Define the primary objectives of marketing communications
There are five types of strategic communication objectives. We can think of them along a continuum, from lowest to highest customer involvement and from lowest to highest cost. At the left (low) end of the continuum, we seek simply to obtain recognition of our brand or product; we will then seek to transmit specific information about our brand. Sometimes we also need unaided recognition, called top-of-mind awareness, particularly when our product is in distribution next to competitive brands and customers buy the first brand that comes to mind. Sometimes we seek to change behavior through communications; in these cases our communications execution should contain a call to action. Finally, some communications seek to reflect the consumer who chooses that brand, with an image goal.

3. Discuss the planning and evaluation of marketing communications
In assessing a communications campaign we must be careful to judge strategy and execution separately. We will assess the strategic fit of the communications by judging its fit to the strategic communications objective as established by our brand needs and strategic focus—awareness and information for acquisition/stimulate demand; image and behavior

for retention/stimulate demand; awareness and behavior vs. the competitor for acquisition/earn share; and top-of-mind awareness and behavior for retention/earn share. We will assess the execution of the communications by judging its adherence to the BUMP rule. BUMP stands for believable, unique, memorable, and pertinent.

Communications budgeting should follow a zero-based process, meaning that we build budgets by estimating how many people we need to reach based on our strategy and then estimate the number of exposures based on the communications objective, media channel, and specific execution. Integrating communications into the company's strategy is key.

4. Integrate marketing communications with other elements of the Big Picture framework
For *acquisition/stimulate demand,* we pursue an awareness objective. For *acquisition/earn share* recall, we will therefore pursue an informational objective to communicate our benefits vs. the competition's, or a behavioral objective to encourage consumers to try our product and compare it with their current brand. In the case of a *retention/stimulate demand* strategy, we may simply want to encourage our customers to use more of our product or use it in different situations and will pursue a behavioral objective. Finally, for a *retention/earn share* strategy, we will pursue an informational or behavior objective, to encourage consumers to compare and reconsider why they are using two brands instead of just ours.

☐ KEY TERMS

Basic awareness (also called aided recognition). (p. 267) Consumer's ability, when presented with the brand name or logo, to acknowledge that he or she has seen it before.

Behavioral objective. (p. 272) Communication with a goal to cause an action or specific behavior in our target audience.

BUMP. (p. 276) Mnemonic for assessing marketing communications execution. This acronym stands for *Believable, Unique, Memorable, and Pertinent.*

Communications objective. (p. 266) The type of change in beliefs or, in some cases, behavior we wish to accomplish through communications.

Creatives. (p. 272) Writers and designers responsible for bringing a copy strategy to life, transforming it from a simple set of words in five boxes of the positioning statement.

Image objective. (p. 270) Communication created to capture share of heart, evoking an emotional response in consumers. The focus of an image objective is the *person* in the target audience, as opposed to the *brand*.

Information objective. (p. 268) Communications intended to provide specific information about the brand; the information must be focused on the positioning.

Pay per click (PPC). (p. 275) A method of paying for Internet advertising in which the advertiser does not pay for the placement of the ad, but rather pays each time a consumer clicks on the ad to view more information or place an order.

Top-of-mind (or **unaided**) **awareness.** (p. 267) Customers' ability to identify the brand or product with the business category.

Zero-based communications budgeting. (p. 274) The practice of building communications budgets by starting from zero and considering the size of the target audience, the positioning message, and the communication objective and then selecting the most appropriate media channel and number of exposures to arrive at a total budget.

☐ REVIEW AND DISCUSSION QUESTIONS

1. Identify and describe the five communications objectives, fit them to the strategic quadrants of the Big Picture framework, and explain the placement of each.

2. Explain why top-of-mind awareness may be particularly necessary when your target customers are multi-brand users (as opposed to brand loyalists).

3. Conduct a web search for communications examples of:

   (a) Information

   (b) Image

   (c) Behavior

   For each of the examples you have selected, discuss the likely strategic quadrant of the company, and whether you think its communications objective is sensible in the context of the company's overall marketing strategy.

   Finally, in each case discuss how the ad would need to change if the company changed its strategy from stimulate demand to earn share or vice versa.

☐ APPENDIX: MARKETING ANALYSIS AND PLANNING

Marketing Tool #3.1: Aligning Communications to the Strategic Objective

In this exercise, we use the customer experience analysis tool as a way to help us brainstorm communications interventions at the most appropriate time, through the most appropriate channel, and to the most appropriate stakeholder in our target audience.

Follow these steps:

1. Determine the overall communication objective given your strategic quadrant.

2. Detail the purchase process steps for your product or service and list the stakeholders active in each process step (those who might influence, veto, specify purchase requirements, and so on). See Figure 10.4.

3. Where in the purchase process does it make sense to intervene with communications?

   (a) **Actions:** Brainstorm and list specific communication ideas that fit within our communication objective and would be most appropriate, given the stakeholder we need to reach at each step of the customer experience cycle. Define the specific communication actions you should take in each purchase process stage and the stakeholders you will reach. Sample actions include: publishing data or evidence of use, promoting product process or ingredients, publicizing end-user or expert testimonials, publishing product FAQs, creating product or service brochures, promoting the brand name, and so on.

Customer Experience/ Stakeholder	Need Recognition	Research Alternatives	Purchase	Use	Post Use / Evaluation
Purchaser	action: channel:	action: channel:	action: channel:	action: channel:	action: channel:
Direct user	action: channel:	action: channel:	action: channel:	action: channel:	action: channel:
Influencer	action: channel:	action: channel:	action: channel:	action: channel:	action: channel:
End-user	action: channel:	action: channel:	action: channel:	action: channel:	action: channel:
Other	action: channel:	action: channel:	action: channel:	action: channel:	action: channel:

Figure 10.4 Listing the major stakeholders in the purchase decision and our activities by phase of the customer experience can help us develop an effective and comprehensive communications plan.

(b) **Channels:** Specify the channels you will use to act on your communication objective. Channels might include: social media, web, TV ad, or product placement, print, press release/white paper, convention/ trade show, direct mail/email, sales force/direct communications, and so on.

Marketing Tool #10.2: Evaluating Communications Efficiency

Table 10.1 can serve to broadly evaluate and summarize the communications actions planned for your target audience by channel, considering strategic fit and relative costs. We list the communications actions brainstormed in Marketing Tool 10.1 by channel and estimate the costs per contact. We can use a scale from 1 to 5, where 1 is the lowest rating, to assess fit with advertising objective, fit with creative concept, and net reach (measured as percent of target).

Follow these steps:

1. Using the list you assembled in Tool 10.1, summarize the communications actions by channel to get a sense of the total effort required for each.

2. Estimate the number of stakeholders and therefore contacts or exposures you need, depending on the specific execution. You will need fewer exposure for direct channels (like a sales force), and more for indirect channels (e.g., banner ads, print ads, and so on).

3. Estimate the total cost per channel by thinking through the cost per exposure. If you cannot easily estimate cost numbers, rate the channels from lowest cost or most inexpensive (score of 5) to highest cost and therefore most expensive (score of 1).

4. Rate the strategic fit of the actions planned for each channel by considering its alignment to the strategic communications objective (awareness, information, top-of-mind awareness, behavior, or image).

5. Rate each channel by the degree to which it will influence your target audience by helping the brand stand out from the competition.

Table 10.1*

Communications Channel	Size of Target Audience/ Number of Exposures	Cost/Exposure and Total Cost ($ or rating, 1 low to 5 high)	Strategic Fit (1 low to 5 high)	Qualitative Impact of Action (1 low to 5 high)

*A table like this one can be very helpful in communications budget planning.

☐ FURTHER RESOURCES

Ogilvy, David and Ray Atherton. *Confessions of an advertising man*. New York: Atheneum, 1963.

Lavidge, Robert J. and Gary A. Steiner." A model for predictive measurements of advertising effectiveness." *The Journal of Marketing* (1961): 59–62.

Schultz, Don E. "Integrated marketing communications." *Journal of Promotion Management* 1.1 (1992): 99–104.

George, Belch, and Michael Belch. *Advertising and promotion: An integrated marketing communications perspective*. 9th Edition. New York: McGraw-Hill/Irwin, (2011).

Mela, Carl F., Sunil Gupta, and Donald R. Lehmann. "The long-term impact of promotion and advertising on consumer brand choice." *Journal of Marketing Research* (1997): 248–261.

chapter eleven

"That which is easily got is little valued."

Cervantes, Saavedra, M. de. (1793).

The History and Adventures of the Renowned Don Quixote. 6th ed. corr. London: Printed for A. Law, W. Miller, and R. Cater. Volume 1, page 277.

PRICING

After studying this chapter you should be able to:

1. *Identify the multidimensional aspects of pricing*

2. *Explain how companies commonly set prices*

3. *Describe the logic of cost–based pricing*

4. *Describe competitive–based pricing*

5. *Explain customer value–based pricing*

6. *Discuss how to align pricing to the firm strategy*

7. *Integrate pricing with other elements of the Big Picture framework*

Google's "Free" Pricing Model

As of December 2012, Google operated over 1 million servers in data centers around the world, processing billions of search requests per day. Google's services allow us to intelligently search information posted by billions of people around the world, including over a million books and scholarly articles; to view a satellite image of virtually any address anywhere in the world; to organize, store, and share our photos and images with our friends; to talk and view anyone in the world in real-time over the Internet; to translate content in seconds to virtually any language. Google doesn't charge consumers to do any of these things. Yet its market capitalization at the end of 2012 was over $240 billion, making it one of the most valuable companies in the world. How does Google make money? In 2012, more than 90 percent of its revenue came from advertising.

Traditionally advertising channels charged advertisers by the length of the ad and the number of times the ad ran in a particular channel. The problem with this model was that advertisers paid regardless of how many people watched their ads, or how many people actually acted differently after seeing or hearing them. In fact, a famous comment in advertising in the 1960s ran, "I know 50% of my advertising budget is wasted, but I don't know which 50%."

However, Google charges advertisers only when their ads are viewed. The moment a Google user accesses a page on which an ad appears, Google charges the company that placed the ad. Typically several views of an ad cost the advertiser less than a penny. And how does Google determine how much a click should cost? Google's Ad words, which is essentially an auction service for advertisers, calculates prices for ads in real time, depending on the popularity of the words or phrases an advertiser wants reserved and according to the laws of demand and supply. Through Google's Ad sense service, owners of other websites join Google's network and run Google-branded ads. Google's algorithms actively search the web for websites that the advertiser's target customers are likely to visit and then displays the company's ads in those specific, and relevant, websites. For example, if you run a popular cooking blog, you can allow manufacturers of kitchenware to advertise on your site. Google collects fees from the advertisers and shares some of the revenue with you.

Google's pricing model is an example of a broader trend in many industries, from advertising to consulting to health care. The pay-for-performance model is conceptually appealing because it ties compensation to the outcomes promised to a client. Pay for performance helps integrate pricing into the rest of our company's strategy, as the element of execution that allows us to capture some of the value we have created for our customers. ∎

Sources: Page, Larry and Eric Schmidt. Lecture at Stanford, May 1, 2002. http://www.academicearth.org/lectures/how-does-google-actually-make-money.

Jerum, Greg. "Net return marketing's groundbreaking 'pay for performance' Google Ad Words management model minimizes risk while maximizing clients' pay-per-click ROI," *PR Newswire*. UBM Plc, May 20, 2012. Web.

Bruell, Alexandra. "Pay-for-performance starts to gain steam," *Ad Age: Agency News*. Ad Age, January 30, 2012. Web. January 2, 2013.

INTRODUCTION: THE MULTIDIMENSIONAL NATURE OF PRICING

For many organizations, pricing is the easiest executional element to change—in many cases price changes can be made simply with a few strokes on a computer keyboard. This can lead to erratic and undisciplined pricing actions that confuse consumers and ultimately reduce perceived value. A primary reason we change price is because we know we can induce short-term change in customer behavior: a timely discount will increase sales and top-line revenues, at least in the short run. These increases occur often enough to seduce us into casting long-term strategic issues aside when it comes to pricing, making pricing the most dangerous box in the Big Picture framework. Inevitably, though, the strategic questions we have ignored will come back to haunt us. It is therefore crucial that when we examine pricing issues, we maintain our strategic mindset in the face of short-term temptations.

Pricing strategy and implementation require the use of both sides of the brain. The fact that a price is a number naturally leads us in the direction of quantitative analysis. Performing this type of analysis is necessary to understand the impact of pricing changes on profitability, to estimate their effect on quantity demanded, and to quantify the value of our products and services to customers. Pricing is also inherently tied to strategy, and sound pricing requires careful and disciplined customer and competitive analysis.

Sound pricing also requires an understanding of consumer psychology. Consumers evaluate the price of our products and services relative to the price of similar offerings, and they perceive both price and value subjectively and sometimes emotionally. They also evaluate price in the context of the overall budget available for a particular use, the price they paid for a similar item last time around, and what they know of prices for similar brands. For this reason, in order to manage pricing, we need to manage how customers perceive the price of our product and whether and how they compare it to other products. We need to identify for ourselves, rather than take as given, the answers to key strategic questions including: What business category are we in? Who are our primary competitors? What products are perceived as good substitutes for ours?

In summary, developing effective pricing requires quantitative skills to address issues of price setting and financial analysis, and qualitative skills to properly address issues of strategy and consumer behavior.

HOW COMPANIES SET PRICE: COSTS, COMPETITION, CUSTOMER, AND STRATEGY-BASED PRICING

There are four widely used approaches to setting prices (see Figure 11.1). We can think of them as evolving from cost-based pricing, the most basic form, to competition-based pricing, value-based pricing, and finally strategy-based pricing. We will explore the approaches in that order, focusing on their logic and effectiveness and also on their potential pitfalls.

The Evolutionary Nature of Pricing Approaches

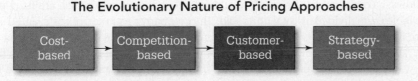

Figure 11.1 The four major approaches to price setting are cost-based, competition-based, customer-based, and strategy-based. We can think of them as evolutionary, from cost-based to strategy-based.

Figure 11.2 The basic cost-based pricing process works as follows:

1. Design a product.
2. Calculate the cost of producing the product.
3. Set price to recoup full cost (fixed plus variable cost).
4. Articulate the value of the product at the set price.
5. Find customer who will purchase the product.

COST-BASED PRICING

Cost-based pricing. The practice of setting prices by estimating the average cost of producing and selling the product plus a profit margin.

A widespread approach to pricing, particularly in business-to-business companies, is to design and manufacture a product, have the finance department calculate a minimum price based on the average cost of production plus a profit margin, and allow any transaction priced to clear that threshold. The logic for this **cost-based pricing** method is that companies are in business to return a profit to shareholders, and the best way to do that is to sell products at a price that exceeds the cost of production. The marketer in the cost-based pricing company is challenged to justify the price the company wishes to get for the product, which may or may not represent a fair value to consumers (see Figure 11.2).

There is a fundamental problem with setting prices based on production costs, however, and that is circularity: in order for companies to calculate costs, they must make an assumption about how many units they will sell, and this number is driven by the price. Calculating prices that are adequate for market conditions is impossible to do based just on production costs unless the company has customers under a long-term contract to purchase a pre-determined number of units at the estimated cost of production. In all other instances, setting price levels based on production costs is sure to lead the company to overprice its products when demand is depressed and under-price them as demand rises. A cost-based pricing strategy can thus lead to either a "death spiral" or loss of customers, or a "growth spiral" and loss of profits.

Cost-Based Pricing and the Death Spiral

Average costs. The sum of fixed plus variable costs divided by total units sold.

Examples of cost-driven death spirals abound; they all boil down to the company's overpricing its products and becoming uncompetitive. The basic problem unfolds as follows: a company sets its prices to equal total **average costs**, which are fixed plus variable costs divided by total units sold. The company's estimate of costs, and therefore its price, is based on current volume in a relatively stable market. As long as the market continues to be stable and there is no increased competition, things are fine. However, if market conditions suddenly shift, the death spiral is triggered (see Fig. 11.3). Market changes may occur if a lower-cost competitive option becomes available due to new market entry or technology change, or if there is a generalized economic

Traditional Cost-Based Pricing: The Death Spiral

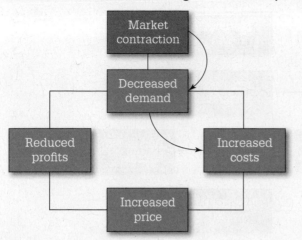

Figure 11.3 Cost-based pricing can cause a death spiral when the market contracts and fixed costs are spread over a smaller number of units, pushing average costs up and therefore driving prices up. The higher prices cause further reduction in profits as customers buy even fewer products due to the higher price.

downturn. If there is a sudden drop in quantity demanded, the company's fixed costs will be suddenly spread over fewer units, and therefore the average costs per unit will increase.

With higher average costs, the company's cost-based pricing approach forces an increased price, which makes its products less attractive to customers, so some of them leave. Higher prices might also invite more competition, which further lowers demand and increases costs. A well-known example of a death spiral is the experience of Wang Laboratories in the late 1980s. The company had successfully manufactured and sold word processors, but when computers became more popular and demand for word processors decreased, the company increased the prices of its word processors, accelerating its own demise.

Cost-Based Pricing and the Growth Spiral

In the case of the growth spiral, the company gets into trouble by pricing its products too low. This situation can develop if there is a sudden increase in demand, either because an external condition causes the market to grow, or because competition decreases. Higher demand means an increased volume is spread over the same fixed costs. This then brings economies of scale in manufacturing and lower marginal costs of production.

With lower marginal costs, a cost-based strategy means the company lowers price to take advantage of its low-cost leadership. Lower price results in lower profits on each product. It should also result in increased demand, but unless the increase in volume is asymmetrically large, the company may end up worse off in the long run (see Figure 11.4a and b). It may take advantage of the increased economies of scale to further lower price and slim its margins. At its limit, this process results in insignificant marginal profits on each sale, but a lot more sales and capacity shortages.

This situation actually occurred in Europe in the late 1990s as the rise of Internet-based sales increased freight volumes. Courier services lowered their pricing, causing capacity constraints and decreased service levels. Although the cost growth spiral

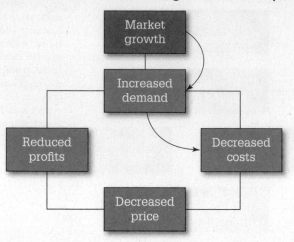

Traditional Cost-Based Pricing: The Growth Spiral

Market growth → Increased demand → Decreased costs → Decreased price → Reduced profits

Figure 11.4 Cost-based pricing can cause a growth spiral when the market expands and fixed costs are spread over a larger number of units, reducing average costs and therefore driving prices down. The lower prices cause customers to buy even more of the company's products. This can cause reduced profits either directly or indirectly when capacity constraints reduce service levels and drive customers away.

may not sound as serious as the cost death spiral, it can be, because capacity bottle-necks and poor service can lower profits in the short term but also damage the image of the brand in the long term.

How to Use Cost-Based Analysis for Pricing

We avoid the boom-and-bust cycles associated with cost-based pricing by basing our prices not on the cost of production, but rather on the value we create for customers, on our brand positioning. Rather than starting our pricing analysis with costs and ending with value, we should instead start with value and end with costs.

The right question to ask is: "Given the value we provide to our target audience, what is the right price for our products?" Once we know that, we can also ask: "What is the impact of pricing at different levels on profitability?" Cost-based analysis is critical as the marketing and sales teams discuss whether to discount to get more volume, or hold price high and work to increase the perceived value of the product. Conducting financial analyses is therefore fundamental to our understanding of what the minimum sales volume should be to break even, and how to maintain profitability in the face of changing market conditions. Two important cost analysis concepts every marketer should know are contribution margin and breakeven quantity. The Marketing Tool at the end of the chapter explains how to perform basic financial analysis for pricing using these two concepts.

The financial **contribution** of a product or service is the difference between the price paid and the variable costs associated with making that product. This is expressed as P–VC, where P is price and VC is the **variable cost** per unit. Often, contribution is also expressed as a percentage, called the **contribution margin**, by taking the price minus the variable cost and dividing it by the price (CM = (P-VC)/P). Companies have

Variable costs. Costs of producing and selling a unit of our product that vary with the volume we sell.

Contribution and contribution margin. The difference between the price and the variable cost of producing and selling a unit of our product or service. Contribution is generally expressed as a percent, by dividing the dollar contribution by the price, and called contribution margin.

two types of costs, variable and fixed. A cost is **variable** if it changes with the number of units that we sell, and **fixed** when it is the same regardless of how many units we sell.

For example, if we run a manufacturing company, the cost of office space, utilities, and employee salaries are generally fixed, meaning we will need to pay the same amount for these expenses regardless of how many units of the product we sell. However, the cost of the raw materials we use to make the product and the cost of packaging and shipping vary depending on how many units we sell. The reason the difference between price and variable cost is called "contribution" is that the price minus the variable cost is the amount of money that selling each unit contributes to profits and to paying the fixed costs.

The concept of **breakeven volume** is similarly simple but also very useful. The breakeven volume is the minimum volume we need to sell in order to break even, meaning that at that level of units sold, we have exactly enough sales to cover our fixed costs and all the variable costs of making and selling those units.

Consider two companies that have similar fixed costs but different contribution margins. The company with a high contribution margin has a greater incentive to sell more units of the product and more room to lower price than a company with a low contribution margin. Let's see why. Companies with high contribution margins are generally capital-intensive or labor-intensive companies. Their contribution margins are likely to be high because most of the cost of production or servicing is fixed, and therefore variable costs are low relative to fixed costs (*price − variable cost* is high). When this is the case, each additional unit of product these companies sell helps them utilize their fixed cost base (their buildings, their employees, their overhead) and therefore lower their average costs per unit. This explains why high-contribution companies will try to sell as many units as they can even if they have to lower prices. For example, orchestras often sell leftover tickets at half-price one hour before the show, hotels are willing to participate in Priceline.com to sell empty rooms just before the weekend, and manufacturers have a short-term financial incentive to discount product in order to keep the entire manufacturing plant running.

Fixed costs. Costs of producing and selling a unit of our product that do not vary regardless of how many units we sell.

Breakeven quantity. The number of units we need to sell in order to break even are reached when our revenues are exactly the same as the sum of our fixed and our variable costs.

Priceline.com is an example of a company that has emerged to allow high-contribution margin businesses, like hotels and airlines, to sell the last few units at a deep discount and try to cover fixed costs. Priceline's business model is based on lowering the negative impact to the hotel's brand image by making hotel rooms available at the last minute to customers who bid knowing the approximate address and hotel star rating but not the name of the hotel until the reservation is completed, often just 24 hours before scheduled check-in.

Kramer knives is an example of a high variable-cost business that is able to maintain premium pricing for its products.

Conversely, companies with relatively high variable costs as a proportion of the cost base will not be as willing to trade price in order to increase their volumes. The epitome of a high variable-cost business is a company like Kramer Knives. Kramer takes expensive raw materials like stainless steel, nickel, and rare woods and transforms them into one-of-a-kind made-to-order knives that can sell in the $5,000 to $10,000 price range. http://www.kramerknives.com.

The natural pricing incentives created by the cost structure are summarized in Figure 11.5. Companies with high fixed costs relative to their variable costs, and therefore high contribution margins, will tend to focus on achieving high volumes as a business goal and price close to their variable costs. Companies with high variable costs relative to their fixed costs, and therefore low contribution margins, would rather sell lower quantities of their products than deeply discount them.

We have discussed how differences in the allocation of fixed vs. variable costs impact pricing incentives. Now we focus on the overall cost level. Having a lower cost structure than our competitors can be a tremendous strategic strength; it provides flexibility and a natural protection against potential competitors. However, a low-cost core competence does not necessarily mean the company should position itself on price. For example, in the late 2000s, Copa Airlines, a Panamanian-based airline, kept low-fare competitors from Brazil and Argentina away from its market by promoting itself as highly operationally efficient (i.e., it had low costs). It was not positioned as a low-priced airline, but competitors realized that if they started a price war with Copa, it could drop its prices to levels they might not be able to match profitably. Knowledge of this low-cost structure deterred price-cutting by competitors.

Of course, in making pricing decisions, costs matter. Although the cost structure should not be the primary driver of a company's pricing levels, if we do not know what our costs are, we are flying blind when it comes to pricing. We started the discussion on cost-based pricing by demonstrating that pricing based on costs can generate negative feedback loops. On the other hand, we can use costs and financial analysis in pricing to help us rationally answer questions like: What will happen to our profits if we change price to get more volume, and how much volume can we afford to lose

Figure 11.5 Companies with high variable costs relative to fixed costs (and therefore low contribution margin) will be willing to hold prices high and give up some volume, whereas companies with high fixed costs relative to their variable costs (and therefore high contribution margin) will be willing to lower price in order to sell more volume.

Contribution Margin and Business Goal

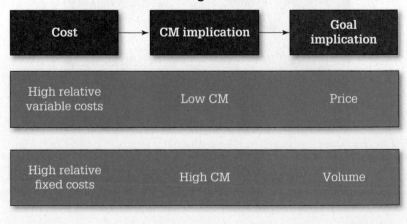

Cost	CM implication	Goal implication
High relative variable costs	Low CM	Price
High relative fixed costs	High CM	Volume

Copa is a low-operating-cost company that does not position itself as a low-fare airline. This company's low cost structure serves as competitive protection from market rivals and helps prevent price wars.

when we increase price before it affects our profits? The relatively simple concepts of contribution margin and breakeven can help us run some helpful back-of-the-envelope calculations. If we understand how costs affect profitability, we will be able to have reasoned discussions with others in the company who either want to price based on costs alone and ignore value, or ignore costs altogether.

COMPETITIVE-BASED PRICING

Pricing relative to the competition often results from adopting a market share goal: as competitors threaten our share, lowering price seems like the quickest and most direct way to regain our market position. However, in pricing reactively to competition, companies might regain some lost share but sacrifice other long-term strategic objectives. **Competitive-based pricing** assumes our competitors have better information about what products and services are worth than we do (see Figure 11.6).

Competitive-based pricing. The practice of setting prices by selecting a competitor's product price and pricing at the same level, or slightly below or above.

The drawback of pricing relative to the competition is that because pricing helps articulates the positioning of the product. When we merely copy the competitors' pricing approach we are also, in essence, copying their strategy and positioning.

Competitive-Based Pricing Process Steps

Figure 11.6 Generally, companies following a competitive pricing approach will set their price based on a competitor's price for a similar product and try to adjust costs and product. Competitive-based pricing often works as follows:

1. Examine the competition's product offering.
2. Evaluate the competitive price.
3. Assess whether our company could offer a similar product for a similar price.
4. Determine the costs of the product.
5. Price the product at some reasonable margin (slightly above or below) the competition.

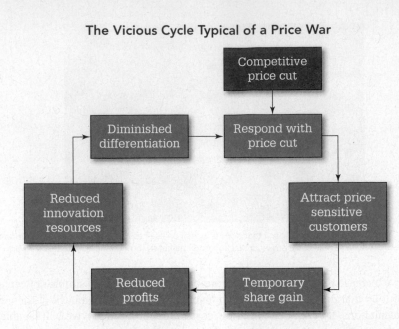

The Vicious Cycle Typical of a Price War

Figure 11.7 In markets where the competitors are constantly trying to match or beat competitor's prices, a competitor's price cut can result in a series of price cuts, which are cumulatively destructive for both companies and for the category as a whole.

Price Wars

A competitive-based pricing approach is particularly dangerous when the competition lowers price. In these situations, competitive-based pricing might result in a price war vicious cycle (see Fig. 11.7)

Scholars who study game theory distinguish three types of competitive games, positive-sum, zero-sum, and negative-sum. **Positive-sum games** are those in which the more intense the competition, the greater the rewards to be shared because both players improve their skills as a result of competing. Even the loser gains from competing, through improved performance or market expansion. Positive-sum games tend to happen in markets where competitive pricing drives category expansion, as long as the competitors show some restraint and avoid pricing so aggressively that they don't have enough resources to invest in innovation and growth. In these instances, all competitors can benefit if price goes down across the board and as a result the category grows. The initial growth phase of the market for massively multi-player online games like World of Warcraft is an example. This category saw huge gains in the late 1990s with the expansion of the Internet and of internet-based communities even as pricing for games was going down.

In **zero-sum games** competitors must share a fixed reward, so one's gain is the other's loss. This type of game is typical of mature markets with little innovation and markets with fixed competition due to high barriers to entry but little differentiation causing firms to compete fiercely. For example, Energizer and Duracell faced this type of dynamic in the 1980s, when both were making claims regarding battery life and competing on features and pricing. Consumers became confused about the benefits of each and ultimately indifferent between the two, buying what was most available or on sale. This situation occurred, in part, because the two companies were using their resources to compete against each other rather than bring meaningful innovation to

Positive-sum games. Those in which the more intense the competition, the greater the rewards to be shared because both players improve their skills as a result of competing.

Zero-sum games. Those in which competitors share a fixed reward, so one's gain is the other's loss.

consumers. There was also little threat of competitive entry because of the high invest-ment needed to set up a new battery-manufacturing company.

Competitive-based pricing degenerates into **negative-sum games**. In negative-sum games, the more intense the competition, the smaller the rewards available to be shared; even the winner loses from competing. Price wars start because companies price based on competitors' actions. Sadly, price wars have no winners. In the long run, not even consumers win: price wars stifle innovation because the competitors end up with insufficient resources to invent new products or services. Rather than blindly cutting prices when our competitors cut prices, we need to adopt a more thoughtful approach to addressing price competition.

Negative-sum games. Competitive games for which the more intense the competition the smaller the rewards available to be shared; even the winner loses from competing.

Thoughtful Reactions to Price Competition

Reacting thoughtfully to competitors when they undercut our prices requires con-ducting a careful analysis of the impact of a competitive price cut on our own custom-ers, and then taking the time to collect some competitive information before readying an appropriate response as illustrated in Figure 11.8.

Analyze the Impact of a Competitive Price Cut

When a competitor launches a pricing attack, the first thing we should do is to ana-lyze the true impact on our customers. News of the threat of a competitive attack is often exaggerated, particularly in business-to-business markets where competitive intelligence is scarce and often obtained through customers or the sales force. Cus-tomers are always trying to get the lowest price and salespeople are in constant fear of losing their customers. Also, in many companies, salespeople are compensated as a percentage of sales, so they are better off selling at low prices than completely losing a deal.

In assessing the information, we first must painstakingly ensure that the competi-tive price is for a truly comparable product with similar performance, service levels, and warranty coverage, or we must adjust for these factors. We must also make sure that we are comparing similar-sized transactions and similar contractual terms, to control for large-deal discounting. After we make all these adjustments, we need to do some analysis to figure out exactly how many accounts we are likely to lose to the cheaper competitor, and how many are likely to stay with us even if there are cheaper alternatives.

In preparing a thoughtful reaction to competitive price drops, we need to estimate both their seriousness and the strategic strength of the competitor. We estimate the

Steps to Preparing a Response to Price Competition

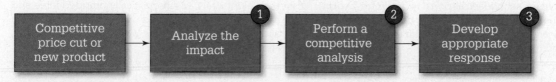

Figure 11.8 Preparing a thoughtful response to a competitive price cut requires doing some analysis and data gathering to estimate the volume at risk and to understand the nature of the competitor's core competence and strategic strengths.

true cost of the competitive attack by tallying the number of customers likely to defect on price (geographically and by type) and the volume they represent. As we conduct this analysis we will want to make sure we include both the top-line sales loss and the more qualitative strategic impact of the loss. We conduct the strategic assessment of the loss by asking:

(a) What is the loyalty type of the lost accounts?

- Were they exclusive or multi-brand customers?
- Were these heart or hand accounts or head accounts? Did their loyalty type align to our capabilities?
- Were these accounts difficult to serve? Always asking for discounts?

(b) What is the strategic value of these accounts?

- How much were they buying?
- Are they reference accounts, which generate positive word of mouth?
- Are they innovation accounts, which help develop new products?
- Are they high-growth accounts, with lots of potential for cross-selling and business development?

GLOBALMARKETING

SOUTHWEST AIRLINES: THE CREATION AND EXPORT OF THE LOW-FARE BUSINESS MODEL

Southwest Airlines started as a small regional carrier flying in and out of Dallas's Love Field Airport in 1979, but it grew quickly, becoming the seventh-largest U.S. passenger carrier by 1993 and a top-three domestic carrier by 2010. Although Southwest has had some trouble maintaining its performance in the United States since 2010, its early success spurred the creation of similar airlines around the world.

Thanks to deregulation in the European market, by 1993, low-cost Ryan Air was able to fly between the UK and Continental Europe, and it was quickly imitated in Europe by Easy Jet and others. By about 2005, there were over 60 low-cost airlines in Europe, flying more than 25 percent of the scheduled intra-European flights.

The European low-fare business model is based on the same basic principles developed by Southwest Airlines:

- Flying between secondary airports to minimize airport landing fees and other airport-related costs.
- Flying only one or two models of aircraft to minimize staff training and maintenance costs.

- Flying short routes.
- Minimizing onboard services, including food and drinks, and not offering seat assignments, to both lower costs and shorten turnaround time at airports.
- Flying full planes.

Despite handicaps like longer routes and slower deregulation, budget airlines in Asia already account for more than 20 percent of total seats flown there. Low prices are even more important in this market because so many people are only now entering the middle class and can afford to fly. The expansion of the low-fare model started in Southeast Asia, with airlines like Air Asia from Malaysia (whose tag line is "Now everyone can fly"), which has flown more than 100 million passengers so far. Spring Airlines is China's first low-fare carrier. Just as U.S. low-fare carriers forced a response from their older rivals, which drastically dropped fares and even created their own low-fare divisions (like United's TED), Australia's major carrier, Quantas, owns the low-budget carrier Jetstar. ■

Sources: ELFAA, "Liberalization of European Air Transport: The Benefits of Low Fares Airlines to Consumers, Airports, Regions and the Environment," 2004. http://www.elfaa.com/documents/ELFAABenefitsofLFAs2004.pdf.

Chu, Kathy. "Discount airlines change air travel in Asia," *USA TODAY*, November 27, 2011. http://travel.usatoday.com/flights/story/2011-11-27/Discount-airlines-change-air-travel-in-Asia/51426118/1.

The loss of strategic accounts is more devastating than a simple tally of revenues can reveal, and it might indicate that we are facing a compelling competitor. Does the competitor offer simply a cheaper but lower-quality product, or a high-quality product for a low price? When we perform this type of analysis, we cannot expect to be able to develop a very accurate prediction, but we should be able to bracket, come up with a high and a low estimate, for the potential sales loss.

Perform a Competitive Analysis

A second and integral step to readying a thoughtful competitive reaction is to ask why the attack has happened. Were our prices too high? Perhaps through lack of innovation or customer service, we opened the door for this competitor. We are not looking here for a reason to blame ourselves, but rather conducting an exercise in introspection and self-reflection. To the extent that our marketing promises are no longer met by the reality of our execution, asking why the attack happened should help us garner the internal momentum necessary to get the company back on track. In addition to estimating the true cost of the competitive attack, we should also assess the competitor's relative strength. A useful way to do this is to conduct a competitive core competence audit. (Please see the core competence audit Marketing Tool in Chap. 2.)

A competitive core competence assessment tells us how serious the competitive attack may be, but more importantly it informs our competitive response. A core competence audit of Southwest Airlines (see the Global box) would have given established carriers cause for concern very early in the low-cost airline's history (see Fig. 11.9). Southwest's innovative business model, and its benefits of low price and convenience, had great appeal to price-sensitive customers. Although older carriers needed to act, given Southwest's low-cost core competence, lowering prices and service offerings in shared routes would be exactly the wrong response. However, this is exactly what they did. Preparing a thoughtful response to price competition requires combining analysis of the potential sales loss with an analysis of the competitor's core competence.

Southwest Airlines Core Competence

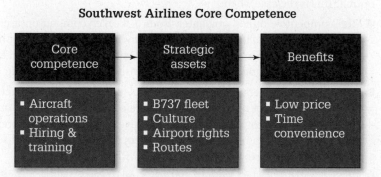

Figure 11.9 In the late 1990s and early 2000s, Southwest's core competence in aircraft operations and hiring and training was supported by related strategic assets. These included flying only one type of aircraft (B737s), which lowered maintenance costs, and flying only into secondary airports. The airline offered customers a fun, low-frills, and low-cost travel experience.

Figure 11.10 There is a range of potential responses to price competition, from doing nothing to responding with price. The appropriateness of each type of action depends on the relative amount of sales we are likely to lose and the relative strength of the competitor's core competence.

Source: Nagle, Thomas T., Holden, Reed K. "The Strategy and Tactics of Pricing. A guide to Profitable Decision Making." Third Edition, © 2002. Reprinted by permission of Pearson Education, Inc. Upper Saddle River, NJ.

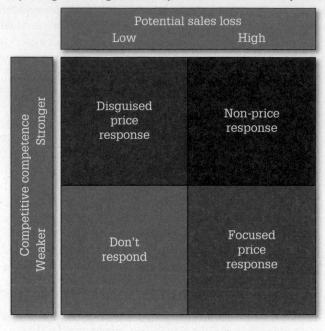

Preparing a Thoughtful Response to Price Competition

Respond to Price Competition

Responses to price competition can range from doing nothing to responding with price (see Figure 11.10). For most companies and in most situations, a price response should be an option of last resort. However, the frequency and severity of price wars suggests that many companies across industries respond to price attacks with price cuts.

Let's look at each type of response to price competition and when to use it:

1. ***Don't Respond.*** Not responding to price competition is sometimes the best option. This is the case when:

   ■ The competitive attack originates from a weaker competitor, a company that does not have a lower cost structure and is simply pricing incoherently. Although it is often a bad idea, companies entering an established category often compete on price even if their cost position does not justify it.

   ■ The competitor offers lower prices but provides an inferior product. In this case, we can expect to lose our most price-sensitive (and lowest customer lifetime value) customers. Assuming we have differentiated our brand on a non-price benefit, price-sensitive customers are probably a small segment, and it might be worth relinquishing them without retaliation.

   ■ The potential sales loss from the attack is relatively small because the competitive threat has been overstated. This might happen if we have received misleading competitive information. In the supermarket business, for example, during the late 1990s competitors like Web van came to market offering a new shopping option for groceries that proved less of a threat than expected. Most people still preferred to shop for groceries.

- We have such an excellent product and service reputation, and therefore such a high level of customer loyalty, that at least in the short term we are unassailable. This was the position Apple enjoyed when the first Android phones came to market. Despite proven claims of technical superiority for Android phones, Apple users were highly resistant to competing arguments.

Some strategists suggest that when the price competitor is relatively weak (meaning its cost structure is higher than the market leaders'), the market leader should be willing to engage in a price war until the new entrant backs down or is driven out of the market. However, although war analogies are used often in business, decades of devastating price wars and feature wars provide ample evidence that they are inappropriate for business strategy. It is now widely accepted that combining aspects of competition while considering the potential for cooperation, or at least mutual survival, is much preferable (Adam Brandenburger, 1996).

When our company possesses a strategic advantage over the competition, we are better off not responding. In any case, we should consider a medium or longer-term horizon and try to establish whether the competition might be able to learn and overcome its production or commercial weaknesses over time. Low-cost competitors in many markets start out with a weak product offering and are ignored by incumbents but later come back much stronger, posing a real threat to the market leader. For example, Mizuno entered the U.S. performance running shoe market in the late 1990s as a low-cost competitor and emerged years later as a high-end performance shoe brand. Applied Medical started as a low-cost and low-quality provider of surgical devices in Asia and later reemerged as a threat to very established companies such as Covidien and Johnson & Johnson in their core European and U.S. markets.

2. *Undertake a Non-Price Response.* If the competitive entrant has a low-cost core competence, or if consumers become more price-sensitive or start switching to a new technology, we cannot ignore the competitive threat. However, lowering price is not the best response. It will increase the importance of price while reducing the resources we have to invest in differentiation (see the price war vicious circle in Fig. 11.7). For example, as Walmart, the low-cost U.S. retailer, started to grow aggressively in the early 1990s, smaller local retailers lowered price. This was exactly the wrong response and drove many competitors out of business.

Non-price responses that can fend off low price competitors include:

- *Improve differentiation by investing in product and service improvements.* Many companies have successfully incorporated value-added services to differentiate their offerings without giving away price. In addition to product improvements, which might take a long time to be implemented, extended warranty and other service agreements improve the value proposition without changing the product price. As an example, in response to price pressures in the U.S. market, BMW and other luxury car makers have added a free maintenance plan and longer warranties, effectively lowering the cost of ownership without changing the price.

- *Strengthen relationships with market collaborators.* An effective way to protect against competition is to improve supply-chain processes, such as by securing exclusive supply agreements. Whole

BMW Maintenance Plan: The BMW maintenance plan makes BMW cars more competitive with other luxury vehicles by lowering the cost of ownership of the car without lowering the purchase price outright.

Guenter Schiffmann/Bloomberg/Getty Images

Foods, the U.S. leader in retail organic and natural food products, can effectively combat competition by buying up a producer's entire supply of a particular crop. AT&T signed an exclusive agreement with Apple to sell iPhones in the U.S. market, providing the phone carrier with a tremendous advantage over the competition.

Another way to fend off competition is to lock customers and/or distribution into long-term supply contracts. For example, in the medical device market in the United States, long-term supply contracts effectively limit the speed with which low-cost entrants can displace large established providers like Johnson & Johnson and Covidien. Companies have also appealed to regulatory authorities for competitive protection. For example, aluminum extruders in the United States successfully appealed to the government to obtain pricing protection alleging Chinese manufacturers were "dumping" in their market (selling below raw material costs). As a result, the Commerce Department imposed a 59 pecent duty on Chinese imports.[1] Enlisting third-party collaborators to help generally provides only temporary relief, however, and is not a substitute for the long-term sustainable differentiation that comes from product or service superiority and customer loyalty.

■ *Use communications strategically.* Tactfully communicate the risks of switching to a low-price and low-quality competitor. Ethicon Inc., a manufacturer of high-quality suture products, has tracked customers defecting to low-cost competition and learned that up to 60 of these customers percent return to Ethicon within a year, due to product reliability problems. The company uses that data to market itself to hospitals considering low-cost alternatives. Other companies have used the threat of lower quality as a powerful motivator to keep customers from switching to low-cost competitors. IBM's long-running tag line "Nobody Got Fired for Buying an IBM" motivated countless purchasing managers to continue buying IBM hardware at a premium.

■ *Cut costs.* If the presence of low-cost competition is a sign that our margins were too high, adapting to an environment of lower prices will require lower costs. This does not mean that we should compete on price; rather it means that cost containment is one of a group of measures the company needs to undertake for long-term survival. Earlier in the chapter we saw how Copa Airlines was able to communicate its low operating costs as a way to keep low-fare airlines away.

■ *Switch to solution selling.* Although it can be challenging and take some time, companies have successfully shifted their business model from product selling to services in response to price competition. For instance, IBM shed its laptop division to Lenovo, a Chinese company, in 2006. This sale was a milestone in the company's move away from hardware and into integrated solution selling and software. Implementing a successful products-to-service business model shift is challenging and requires deep strategic and executional changes, including retraining the sales force, reeducating the distribution channels, and rethinking the product development and product model.

IBM's "No One Ever Got Fired for Buying an IBM" tag line served to increase the perceived risk of switching away from IBM to a cheaper, and potentially lower quality, alternative. This helped temporarily lower the importance of price among IBM's customers.

[1]Zhang Qi. "US to impose duties on aluminum," *China Daily*. March 3, 2011. http://www.chinadaily.com.cn/business/2011-03/31/content_12257467.htm.

3. **Execute a "Disguised" Price Response.** When the sales loss from low-cost competition does not yet warrant an all-out business model shift but the competitor has an advantageous cost position, the incumbent company might respond with price but in a way that minimizes price sensitivity. These actions amount to a price discount, but they are undertaken to reassure hesitant customers and prevent a mass defection and the price war that might ensue. They include:

- **Change the price structure.** One classic tactic is to *change customers' choices,* reframing the way they consider competitive choices and prices. In the 1980s, when Taco Bell introduced the 99-cent taco, McDonald's responded by bundling burgers, fries, and drinks into "value meals." McDonald's used this price-bundling tactic to redirect customers' attention away from the tacos *versus* burgers comparison. Instead, retained customers felt they were getting a better deal on a lunch-to-lunch basis. While Taco Bell eventually followed suit and offered a similar meal bundle, McDonald's tactic provided a reason for retained customers to stay without directly triggering a product-to-product price war. Similarly, smart managers use quantity discounts or loyalty programs to insulate themselves from price wars. These tactics do not provide permanent price protection, nor do they retain price-sensitive customers willing to search for the lowest price. However, they do provide temporary relief and serve to keep loyal customers.

By introducing a bundled meal price for its Combo Meal, McDonald's was able to divert attention from Taco Bell's $1 items, temporarily decreasing pricing pressures and averting an all-out price war.

- Discount through the Channel. By collaborating with channel members, the incumbent company might be able to issue rebates on particular products that are most at risk without sounding discounting alarm bells. In 2007, just a few months after the release of the innovative iPhone 3G, Apple's Steve Jobs announced the company would slash the price of its first generation iPhone by $200. This announcement, made at a user conference, is considered one of the worst marketing mistakes the company ever made. The across-the-board price drop on a product launched only a few months before angered the many heart loyal customers who had stood in line to pay a very high premium for this innovative product. The company could have instead considered an action through its channel member, AT&T, such as issuing rebates on its cell phone service contract. Apple could have also made use of its stores to issue rebate checks or provide free product accessories to early adopters of its high-priced product.

Steve Jobs announced Apple would be cutting $200 off the price of the iphone 3G on September 7, 2007.

- Develop flanker brands. Sometimes we can "de-feature" our product and sell it under a different model name or even a different brand name. Generic drugs and private-label grocery products are sold under the brand name of the grocery store rather than of the manufacturer. Another example, in B2B, is Xiameter, a brand of Dow Corning. Dow Corning sells thousands of specialty silicones, and Xiameter sells more standard products and offers a lower level of service. Also, Xiameter is only available online.

4. **Execute a Focused Price Response.** A price response is justified when we estimate that, based on our lost sales, our revenue loss will be severe, and the competitor is weaker than we are. The advantage of a focused action is that it will

help us contain the losses from the price cut while averting an all-out price war. We will limit price reductions to accounts, geographies, or products where we are vulnerable. In this way, we cut down the opportunities for the war to spill into other markets. However, regardless of the footprint of our pricing action, we need to act swiftly. Swift strategic discounting can send a message to a weaker competitor that we are willing to defend our customer base from further attack.

The actions the incumbent company should consider include:

- ■ **_Proactively discount to customers at risk._** These might be large yet price-sensitive customers who are at risk of defection but who represent profitable customer lifetime value relationships. In providing discounts to these accounts, we must understand just how many there are and the overall impact of the discount. We also need to execute in a way that maintains the integrity of the pricing policy and processes of the company. A flawed execution of this tactic will result in each customer's demanding a different discount according to its negotiating power and the influence of the salesperson representing it. It is critical that we do not negotiate one discount at a time, but rather change the pricing policy to include specific customer types facing specific circumstances.

- ■ **_Discount vulnerable products and non-core markets._** Focus on the area where we have the least to lose and the competitor has the most to lose. For example, a market leader may discount in overlapping markets or in product categories where leadership is reversed. Tweeter, an East Coast electronics retailer, when faced with low-cost competition from retailers such as Best Buy, offered an automatic price protection guarantee. Tweeter's promise was that the company would scan newspaper ads itself and mail customers a rebate check for the difference between its price and the lowest competitive price in the local market. Because Tweeter was positioned as a premium electronics retailer, it shared only a small percentage of its competitors' product portfolio. This meant it could maintain its higher prices on high-end, high-margin brands and match prices on lower-end brands. We can generalize the Tweeter example to overlapping products that are not central to the companies' positioning. Discounting on these products serves both to create customer goodwill regarding the fairness of our pricing policies and to signal to competition our willingness to compete on price in specific niches (Gourville and Moon, 2004).

Blind reaction to low-cost competition or price cutting in the face of competitive product introductions can quickly degenerate into a price war where everyone—companies and customers—loses. However, we must continually gather competitive information and benchmark our prices against competitors' to avoid being caught by surprise, particularly if we are trying to earn share from a competitor. We will revisit this case later in the chapter. Ultimately, our pricing policies should be based not on our costs, not on the competitor's cost base, but rather on the value we provide.

CUSTOMER VALUE-BASED PRICING

Customer value-based pricing is a preferred alternative to cost-based and competitive-based pricing. The value-based marketer will try to set prices based on the perceived value of the product. In customer value-based pricing, finance and

Customer Value-Based Pricing Process Steps

Figure 11.11 The pricing process from a value-based approach flows as follows:

1. Define our target customers.
2. Identify the benefits we will provide to those customers.
3. Design a product to deliver the benefits identified in Step 2 above.
4. Set the price of the product.
5. Ensure the product is viable at the market price given our cost structure.

accounting still play a role in the pricing decision by providing inputs regarding the level of pricing that will clear variable costs and provide an adequate margin (see Figure 11.11). In this approach, we manufacture the product while taking customer preferences into account, and in an ideal scenario, we charge customers according to their willingness to pay.

The difficulty here is that charging each customer according to willingness to pay will generally lead us to under-price, since customers may not realize the value we provide without further intervention on our part. This is especially true for new products and in particular those that are rich in experience attributes; for these, customers really cannot understand the value until they have tried them and we have managed their consumption experience to ensure they understand all the ways in which these products are helping them. Also, the same product has different value to different customers; we could try to charge prices accordingly, but in many industries it is actually illegal to charge different customers different prices for the same product. Even when it might be legal, from a practical standpoint it may simply be too difficult to use this type of approach; it can create a lot of complexity and make customers feel they are being treated unfairly. In practice, we think not just about how to charge what the customer will pay, but also how to influence the customer to raise his or her willingness to pay based on our strategy. This is the difference between customer value-based pricing and strategic pricing.

The potential pitfalls of value-based pricing reside in the relationship between perceived value and positioning. If we have not positioned our product in a way that correctly articulates value to maximize customer's willingness to pay, then pricing based on perceived value will lead us to under-price the product. Value-based pricing is theoretically the right way to price, but we distinguish it from strategy-based pricing more precisely to emphasize that strategic pricing seeks not just to understand but to *direct* customer's perceived value based on our chosen strategy. With strategic pricing we go beyond the important fundamentals of value pricing to raise customer willingness to pay by uncovering new sources of value for our customers through better communication.

Value-based pricing is a natural extension of the segmentation, targeting, and positioning process. We identify a group of consumers most likely to be interested in our product and price it based on the value it provides. This process requires identifying key segmentation variables, and subsequently key product benefits, that are likely to be appealing to our target. By selecting and emphasizing the appropriate product benefits for our target audience and as much as possible monetizing those benefits—that is, calculating their value—we can increase perceived value within that specific group.

This can be challenging in practice. Consider the following example: our R&D department has developed a computer keyboard that allows people to type 10% faster. Current keyboards that are comparable on all other features are priced at $100. How should we price this product? A common answer is $110, based on the idea that a 10% increase in speed should somehow translate to a 10 percent increase in price. A deeper analysis, however, is necessary.

Speed is a *feature* of the product; in order to assess value we must consider the *benefit* it provides by looking at how the product is used. For example, if the keyboard is used in the home, perhaps the 10% increase in speed will allow the user who usually works two hours a day on the computer to reduce her computer time to one hour and 40 minutes, giving her an additional 20 minutes per day to spend with her family. When the benefit is expressed in this way, the incremental value of this feature to customers may be much higher than $10. To derive the value of the product in this manner we start by building a feature-benefit-value ladder, as we did in Chapter 5 for segmentation, and monetize each of the benefits of the product by looking at how it is used.

Perhaps our keyboard has a second opportunity in the large corporate account market. We might find that the typical user here is a research associate at a consulting firm generating $100,000 in income for his company. If our keyboard can increase this person's productivity by 10%, we could infer that he will create an additional $10,000 in income. This amount arguably represents the true value of the keyboard. Can we charge $10,000 for the item? Probably not, but by emphasizing the benefit of increased productivity, we can increase its perceived value, thus increasing **consumer surplus**. Consumer surplus is the difference between a customer's willingness to pay and the price paid. We can then elect to capture some of that increase through price; we might price the keyboard at $500 rather than $100. Or we might maintain the price, effectively "leaving money on the table," and use the consumer surplus we've created to gain additional market share and/or increased customer loyalty.

The value-pricing process is quite useful in business-to-business (B2B) as well as business-to-consumer (B2C) contexts. In the case of B2C, however, we might find, depending on the particular product attributes, that monetizing product benefits is more difficult. Companies that sell their products and services to other companies must show how they are able to increase the revenues or decrease the costs of their customers. However, it is difficult to put a value on consumers' well-being,

Consumer surplus. The difference between a customer's willingness to pay and the price paid.

NEW PRODUCTS/INNOVATION

VIRTUALLY FREE SMARTPHONES (WITH A TWO-YEAR CONTRACT)

The practice of pricing one part of a two-part product relatively cheaply and making up the profit in sales of the other part, usually a service or consumable good, is called 'Razor and Razorblade' pricing, because Gillette was the first to use this pricing model, in the 1970s. It now covers many products and services, including printers, Nespresso coffee machines,

Seong Joon Cho/ Bloomberg/Getty Images

and smartphones. In the United States, AT&T and other major wireless companies offer Apple iPhones and other blockbuster smartphone products virtually free with a two-year service contract. Of course, the phones are not free but rather are paid for over time, with each monthly service bill. ■

comfort, self-esteem, and so on. Products rich in credence attributes generally have psychological or emotional benefits, which are difficult to monetize. Of course, just because a benefit is difficult to monetize does not mean we should disregard it when attempting to raise willingness to pay. For example, the reason customers are willing to pay more for Tylenol is the perception of safety and peace of mind they associate with that brand. For years marketers at Johnson & Johnson have touted the safety processes and highly ethical stance to which the company adheres.

STRATEGY-BASED PRICING

Strategic or **strategy-based pricing** is born of our core competence and builds upon a value-based pricing foundation. The strategic pricing process begins by defining our strategy and value proposition that arises from our core competence, in the context of our chosen business category. The second step is to identify the true benefit of a particular product. Then we set a price, taking into account our customers' current willingness to pay and whether our goal is to capture additional consumer surplus or earn additional market share. We also align the delivery of our price, our pricing tactics, to our marketing objective of either customer acquisition or customer retention. Finally, we communicate value to consumers, to align perceived value and price.

Strategic pricing seeks not simply to understand a customer's assessment of product benefits, but also to shape that assessment based on our core competence and overall market intent. By approaching pricing from this perspective, we ensure that the price-setting process is driven by sound strategy, as opposed to opportunistic tactics.

In strategic pricing we control the valuation of the product by developing a core skill that allows us to solve some customer problem better than our competitors, and then convincing our customers that the price they are paying for that solution is appropriate. Philosophically, customer-based pricing and strategic pricing are closely aligned. The subtle but important distinction between the two is that in strategy-based pricing we set the strategy and value for our product as *informed* by our customers; in customer-based pricing our customers set our strategy purely based on their current willingness to pay, without considering the possibility that we can influence that willingness. We distinguish two types of strategic pricing strategies: value and benchmark.

> **Strategy-based pricing.** The practice of setting prices by creating value for our product and communicating it to our customers, thus adapting their willingness to pay.

iTUNES PRICING INNOVATION

© Aratoliy Babiy/ iStockphoto

Apple's contribution to pricing has been simplification. When the company launched iTunes in 2003, it introduced single-song pricing at a one-price-fits-all $.99 per song. Since then, iTunes has raised its prices, but the service has retained the benefits of simplified pricing. These include: (1) allowing listeners to easily try the work of new artists, (2) lowering the barriers for new artists to sell their music, and (3) increasing the perceived transparency in the music retailing business, (4) better aligning value (songs that are well liked) with price by de-bundling albums. Listeners are able to pick and choose what they want without having to purchase an entire album; this undoubtedly raises customer satisfaction, not just with iTunes, but more importantly for the industry and the artists whose music iTunes distributes. ■

Strategy-Based Pricing: Value

When we are attempting to stimulate demand in the category, our focus needs to be on creating value, and we will use pricing to highlight the value of our product. In this case, we are not just acting like market leaders; we are also acting like price leaders.

For example, when the market for small-business customer relationship management (CRM) software first developed in the mid-2000s, providers were targeting companies that had never used similar software and were keeping their client lists in Excel, generic databases, or paper-based Rolodexes. Thus, CRM companies had to communicate the value of their products benefit by benefit. For example, they had to show how having their software might increase companies' close rates on their sales or increase the productivity of their salespeople.

Benchmark Pricing

In general, we apply value pricing strategies when we are seeking to stimulate demand. When we are seeking to earn share, we still need to price based on the value we create for customers; however, now we must recognize that our target customers currently purchase from a competitor and therefore will be benchmarking our value and

CUSTOMERFOCUS

CONTINUITY PRICING: THE HYATT RANDOM REWARDS PROGRAM

In 2009, Hyatt Hotels unveiled its "random acts of generosity" program, which rewards randomly chosen guests by picking up the tab for services like a hotel-spa massage or hotel-bar drinks. Hyatt hopes these customers will repay the unexpected perks with loyal repeat business, and that word of the program will attract new clients from competitors. Gratitude can be a powerful marketing tool if executed well; if done poorly, however, this type of program can make other guests feel they were treated unfairly compared to friends who received the rewards. Guests who get rewards with some frequency might also come to expect them and feel disappointed when they don't.

Traditional reward programs fail to inspire gratitude because customers must earn the benefits through time and money spent on the company. Hyatt took a gamble by introducing something new, based not on merit but on the simple fact of being a Hyatt customer. The company hoped to reap the rewards of research indicating that people feel

© Blue Images/Corbis

guilty when they fail to reciprocate out of gratitude—and pleasure when they do. The element of surprise is a key to this program; the company empowered on-the-ground employees to decide when and upon whom to bestow the favors, instead of mandating their distribution through top-down corporate policy. Hyatt hoped the employees' spontaneous acts would convey a sense of genuine warmth and hospitality to its clients, who in turn would feel loyalty and a personal connection to the company.

Although Hyatt has not publicized the scorecard for the program, customers appear pleased. One patron commented that he was "delighted" after receiving a complimentary upgrade to a suite as part of one Hyatt's random "Guest of the Day" initiative. If these serendipitous occurrences do indeed lead to long-term customer gratitude and future earnings for the company, more companies may begin to experiment with substituting unexpected perks for more standard targeted rewards programs. ■

Sources: McClain, Al. "Hyatt offers random lesson in loyalty building," *Retail Wire*. N. p., March 29, 2011. Web accessed January 2, 2013.

Walker, Rob. "Hyatt's random acts of generosity," *The New York Times*. June 17, 2009. Web accessed January 2, 2013.

"Hyatt random acts," *Inside Flyer*. Frequent Flyer Network, July 2009. Web accessed January 2, 2013.

"Hyatt promises 'Random Acts of Generosity,'" *Hotel Chatter*, May 22, 2009. HotelChatter.com. Web accessed January 3, 2013.

our price against the competitor's offering. For this reason, when we are earning share from a competitor we will adopt a **benchmark** pricing strategy. This is not to say we *must* match or beat our competitors' prices; we will attempt this only if we have selected price sensitivity as our dynamic variable and low cost as our core competence. Then we will compete by executing on the main benefit in the category and differentiating, and by increasing the importance of price as our dynamic benefit. In all other cases, we will seek to keep the price differential between ourselves and our competitor at a level that optimizes our profitability, while emphasizing whatever dynamic benefit we have chosen.

For example, when Subway entered the fast-food market and earned share from McDonalds, it benchmarked the price of a meal at McDonalds and priced slightly higher, at a level Subway felt maximized its profitability. When we are earning share and pricing higher than our competitor, the price difference between the market leader and us articulates the value differential between them and us. Subway, which positioned itself on health, felt the price premium of its meal helped articulate the value of health (the dynamic benefit) over simply convenience (the main benefit).

PRICING TACTICS: TRIAL AND CONTINUITY PRICING

While we will always engage in strategic pricing, we must also consider our short-term, or tactical, pricing approach. Our first challenge is to clearly identify which pricing decisions are strategic, and which are short term, and to clearly distinguish between the two approaches. Our worst-case scenario is when a short-term pricing tactic such as a price promotion somehow becomes a permanent price reduction. Tactical pricing is often used to directly change behaviors, and our tactics should correspond to our marketing objective of customer acquisition or customer retention.

Trial Pricing

Trial pricing is intended to encourage non-users of our brand (whether competitors' customers or non-users of the category) to try our product with the expectation that, after doing so, the consumer will buy additional units at the regular price. Trial pricing tactics often take the form of deep discounts or samples, usually on a single-unit purchase of the product. One of the key challenges associated with this tactic lies on how to deliver the discount. Because we wish to offer the reduced price only to first-time buyers, we must somehow distinguish them from our current customers. If we cannot do so and simply offer a lower price to all consumers, we run the risk of giving a substantial amount of surplus away. If our product is new to the world, this is clearly less of a concern, but as soon as the first group of buyers accepts the discount and experiences the benefits, the concern will arise. Thus, delivering the reduced price solely to non-users is our first tactical challenge.

Of course, we *assume* a substantial price reduction will provide a sufficient incentive for potential customers to purchase a product they likely would not have purchased at the regular price. The real test of a successful trial pricing strategy, however, lies in the consumer's experience of the product. Based on this experience, the perceived value of —and, therefore, willingness to pay for—the product should increase. Thus, for trial pricing to be a sound tactic, we must ensure our customers have a positive enough experience that they will be willing to spend more on subsequent purchases. Our ability to retain trial users and convert them into long-term customers is thus crucially dependent on our emphasizing an experience attribute of our product. For this reason our emphasis in implementing a trial pricing tactic should be on the experience of the product, as opposed to the appeal of the lower price.

Continuity Pricing

A **continuity pricing** tactic is used to offer existing customers a lower price, generally across multiple purchases, in an effort to keep them in the franchise. If a customer buys eight rolls of toilet paper at a discount instead of four at the regular price, we have essentially locked in that customer, at least for the near term. Continuity pricing strategies tend to be most effective for products that are perishable, used on a regular basis, or difficult to store. For these types of products, a lower price will lead to increased purchase and consumption. If, on the other hand, a consumer loads up on our product due to a price promotion but does not increase his or her consumption, our promotion has failed.

In some cases we may use rebates so rewards *follow* the behavior we are trying to create. Only after the customer has bought the product and used it can he or she access the coupon that lowers the price of a subsequent purchase. In other cases marketers try to elicit consistent buying by giving away in-box or in-package coupons. Coupons can also be used for a specific time period to accomplish a specific goal, such as preventing regular customers from defecting to a new competitor. It may seem that the company is offering a perpetual discount to its current users, but coupons can also serve in price discrimination. For example, Johnson & Johnson could offer a lower price to the regular buyers of BAND-AIDS® through an in-box coupon and reserve a higher price for people who are buying the product in an emergency. However, while these types of tactics might be effective, using them excessively often simply increases price importance and price sensitivity among our customers, decreasing loyalty across the board.

Another danger of continuity pricing is that it can increase the time between purchases. If our customer has developed a habit of purchasing our product every two weeks, then a continuity promotion such as a deep discount on a purchase of a larger package size may break this habit. This can lead to unforeseen consequences. When the consumer finally runs out of our product and returns to the store to replenish, he or she may take more time to evaluate the competitive offerings than otherwise.

Ideally, as we structure our continuity pricing tactics we should try, whenever possible, to emphasize non-price rewards, ideally offered in a random way rather than in a predictable fashion. These types of tactics enable us to encourage customer loyalty while reducing the risk of increased price importance. Loyalty programs such as frequent flyer miles are a type of non-price reward, although they are not random. The Hyatt Random Rewards program described in the Customer Box is a great example of a random and non-price continuity pricing initiative.

Both continuity and trial tactics can be effective under the appropriate circumstances. We need to realistically consider their potential costs and benefits and apply them appropriately to each specific situation as discussed below.

GLOBALMARKETING

GLOBAL PRICING—U.S. PATIENTS BUY LOWER-PRICED DRUGS FROM CANADA

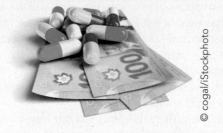

In the pharmaceutical drug business there are huge fixed costs related to research and development and regulatory approvals, but once those have been satisfied and the company has made a decision to go ahead, the costs of making and selling additional units are generally much lower. In the United States, where a lot of drug companies are headquartered and drugs are first introduced, prices are set high enough so that researching, creating, and selling the drug is economical for the pharmaceutical company. However, the Canadian market presents very different conditions, especially a government-run health care system that negotiates much lower prices than in the United States for the same drugs. It is in the interests of pharmaceutical companies to maintain these two different price levels, but the disparity also creates an incentive for U.S. consumers to import drugs from Canada back into the United States, reducing drug company profitability. The practice is technically illegal, although the Food and Drug Administration (FDA) website states that the FDA does not object to personal importation of drugs in small quantities and not for resale. ∎

Sources: "Is it legal for me to personally import drugs?" http://www.fda.gov/AboutFDA/Transparency/Basics/ucm194904.htm.
Pear, Robert." Plan to import drugs from Canada passes in Senate, but Bush declines to carry it out," *The New York Times*, July 18, 2002.
Roberts, Russell. "The high price of cheap drugs," *Hoover Digest 3*, July 30, 2004. http://www.hoover.org/publications/hoover-digest/article/8083.

PRICING AND THE BIG PICTURE

We have broken pricing into two basic stages: strategy and execution, shown in Figure 11.12. **Price strategy** addresses questions about value creation and our long-term approach to pricing. The key strategic question we ask is: "What should the general price level be for the products, given our brand name and positioning?" The answer is given by decisions made in the Business Objective, Marketing Objective, Source of Volume, and STP chapters. For example, if our business objective is tied to profitability, we will tend to increase prices because price is the most direct way to affect profits.

Price Strategy. The overall price level for our products, based on our overall strategy and on our positioning.

Our choice of a strategic quadrant also has price-setting implications, because it determines whether and how we (and our customers) will benchmark our product. For example, if we choose an acquisition/stimulate demand strategy, our target audience is a population of non-users who might be heterogeneous and might not have any type of reference for our product and therefore little awareness of prices in the category. Conversely, if we are implementing an acquisition/earn share strategy, targeting users of a key competitor, our target audience will be made up of competitive customers who are currently loyal to the competitor and benchmark our prices against the competitor's price for a similar product.

Segmentation is also critical to issues of pricing strategy. Within the strategic focus quadrant we have chosen, we can further segment customers by their value assessment of our product and by their relative degree of price sensitivity. Let's think about grouping customers by their value assessment. A company selling medical sutures should recognize that a suture delivers higher value in facial plastic surgery than the same suture used in a part of the body that is not generally exposed. If we are able to separate these two customer groups, targeting facial surgeons separately from body surgeons, we could in theory maximize consumer surplus by selling the product at different prices. In practice, customers will not accept paying a higher price for a product that we also sell for a lower price, so we must justify pricing differences through differences in value. For example, we could tweak the product and sell a slightly different version to the two customer groups. In B2B settings, we can calculate the value of the product to different customer groupings relatively easily by examining how customers use our product. Value-based segmentation has critical strategic and executional implications for pricing.

Price sensitivity differences in our target market also play an obvious role in segmentation. If a very large segment of the market is very price-sensitive, we may elect to use price sensitivity as a main or dynamic benefit, positioning the Fundamental Entity on price. We may do this either to earn share from a competitor or to stimulate demand of the category. This is the strategy that low-cost competitors like Walmart in retail, Southwest Airlines and Ryan Air in air travel, and many others have used so successfully.

If we use price to earn share, we will price lower than our key competitor while delivering similar or slightly lower performance on the main benefit. If we use price to stimulate demand, then price will be our main segmentation benefit. In this case we

Pricing and the Big Picture

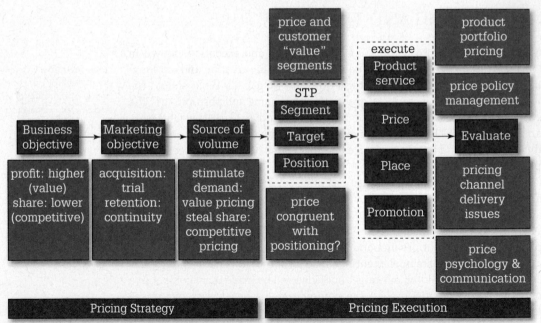

Figure 11.12 Pricing Strategy decisions help us determine the overall price level for our products, based on our Strategy decisions up to this point and on our positioning. Pricing Execution takes up the implementation of strategic decisions we made earlier in the Big Picture framework. Pricing Execution questions generally relate to the 4 P's, specifically: the customer experience of price (or Promotion/Price Communications), price structuring (Price), pricing relative to the product portfolio (Product), and our ability to maintain pricing discipline as our sales channel partners deliver our products in the marketplace (Place).

are implicitly working the assumption that lower prices will help expand the category (though this rarely happens in practice). Regardless of the relative importance of price in our business category, we should position our Fundamental Entity on price only if we have identified a core competence that enables us to establish ourselves as a low-cost producer relative to other companies in the category.

Pricing execution deals with the implementation of the general pricing level we have developed as a result of our strategic decisions. Under pricing execution, we consider topics that relate pricing to the other P's (product/service, promotion, price structuring, and place). Here are the sorts of questions we ask under pricing execution:

Pricing Execution. The implementation of the general pricing level we have developed as a result of our strategic decisions.

- **Product:** how should we price products in a portfolio relative to each other?
- **Promotion:** how should we communicate our prices to maximize the perceptions of value of our products?
- **Price:** how should we structure our prices to best align the perception of value to the cost of purchasing and owning the product?
- **Place:** how should we allocate discounts and price promotions within the distribution channel?

Another way to think about this is to consider that for our pricing tactics to be worthy of implementation, they must tie short-term outcomes of customer acquisition and customer retention to our long-term strategy. This integration of strategy and execution will happen only if we match pricing tactics (which encourage *behavior* change) to our company's strategies (which deal in the realm of *bodies* and *beliefs*) (see Figure 11.13.)

Pricing issues must be considered throughout the framework. In addition, as with other executional elements, we can consider pricing strategies and tactics from the perspective of the strategic quadrant illustrated in Figure 11.14.

For *acquisition/stimulate demand*, we are interested in leveraging price actions to set perceived value in the category. We will therefore use a value pricing approach, acting as category leaders to convince consumers of the value of our product and of

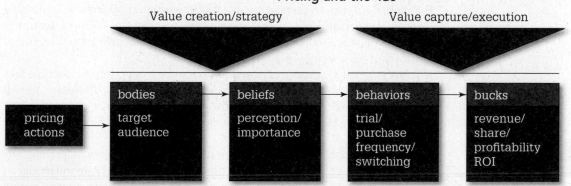

Figure 11.13 The strategic marketer will always evaluate tactics designed to result in a behavior change, such as deep discounts, promotions, and loyalty programs, by asking whether they fit with the overall strategy, designed to act on a specific group of customers and change their beliefs. In aligning beliefs and behaviors, we are also aligning marketing strategy with execution.

Pricing Strategies and Tactics and the Strategic Quadrants

Figure 11.14 When we execute a stimulate demand strategy, we emphasize the *value* of the product to our target customers, whereas when we execute an earn share strategy we emphasize the value difference between ourselves and a competitive benchmark . When we seek to acquire customers, we use trial pricing tactics if there are strong experiential attributes to our products. When seeking to increase loyalty among existing customers, we use continuity pricing tactics.

the category. From a tactical perspective we will use trial pricing to introduce non-users to our product or service benefits, particularly if a direct experience with our product will increase perceived value.

For *retention/stimulate demand* we are still interested in taking a value pricing strategy, this time maintaining perceived value among existing customers. Tactically, however, we will pursue continuity pricing, attempting to reinforce current users and reward loyalty with our price promotions.

If we are engaged in *acquisition/earn share*, our price strategy must reflect the fact that our target audience is familiar with our competitor's price. For this reason we will engage in benchmark pricing, setting a price that takes our competitor's price into account. Our pricing tactic will include trial promotions that invite consumers to try our product instead of the competitor's.

Finally, for *retention/earn share* our price strategy will be benchmark pricing, setting a price that takes our competitor's price into account. Tactically we will engage in continuity promotions appropriate for our current users, again encouraging loyalty and repeat purchase.

☐ SUMMARY

1. Identify the multi-dimensional aspects of pricing

Numerical analysis is necessary to understand the impact of pricing changes on profitability, to estimate their effect on quantity demanded, and to quantify the value of our products and services to customers. Pricing is also inherently tied to strategy, and sound pricing requires careful and disciplined customer and competitive analysis. We need to identify for ourselves, rather than take as given, the answers to key strategic questions, including: What business category are we in? Who are our primary competitors? What products are perceived as good substitutes for ours? Finally, pricing strategically also requires that we understand and manage the way we structure pricing and communicate it to customers.

2. Describe how companies commonly set prices

Companies generally set prices by estimating their costs and adding a margin in cost-based pricing; by pricing to match the competition with competitive pricing; by estimating customers' willingness to pay through customer-based pricing; or by using their positioning and strategic choice to estimate the value of their products.

3. Explain the logic of cost-based pricing

The logic of cost-based pricing is that companies are in business to return a profit to shareholders, and the best way to do that is to sell products at a price that exceeds the cost of production. The challenge in cost-based pricing company lies in justifying the price the company wishes to get for the product, which may or may not represent a fair value to consumers.

4. Describe competitive-based pricing

Competitive-based pricing is the practice of taking pricing cues from our competitors and pricing within the range they set. An important drawback of pricing relative to the competition is that because pricing articulates the positioning of the product, when we merely copy the competitors' pricing approach we are also copying their strategy and positioning. Also, when we react to competitors' lower pricing by cutting our price, we are likely to generate a price war.

5. Explain customer value-based pricing

Value-based pricing aims to price products based on customer preferences and what customers are willing to pay. The difficulty here is that charging each customer according to willingness to pay will generally lead us to under-price, since customers may not realize the value we provide without further intervention on our part.

6. Discuss how to align pricing to the firm strategy

Strategy-based pricing is born of our core competence and strategy and builds upon a value-based pricing foundation. We begin by defining our strategy and value proposition, arising from our core competence, in the context of our chosen business category. The second step is to identify the true benefit of a particular product. Then we set a price, taking into account our customers' current willingness to pay and whether our goal is to capture additional consumer surplus or earn additional market share. Finally, we communicate value to consumers, to align perceived value and price.

7. Integrate pricing with other elements of the Big Picture framework

While pricing is often considered a tactical tool, from the point of view of the Big Picture framework it is integral to the success of our overall strategy, and significantly influenced by each of the other chapters. Pricing Strategy decisions help us determine the overall price level for our products, based on our Strategy decisions up to this point and on our positioning. Pricing Execution takes up the implementation of strategic decisions we made earlier in the Big Picture framework. Pricing Execution questions generally relate to the 4 P's, specifically: the customers' experience of price (or Promotion/Price Communications), price structuring (Price), pricing relative to the product portfolio (Product), and our ability to maintain pricing discipline as our sales channel partners deliver our products in the marketplace (Place).

☐ KEY TERMS

Average costs. (p. 288) The sum of fixed plus variable costs divided by total units sold.

Breakeven quantity. (p. 291) The number of units we need to sell in order to break even are reached when our revenues are exactly the same as the sum of our fixed and our variable costs.

Competitive-based pricing. (p. 293) The practice of setting prices by selecting a competitor's product price and pricing at the same level, or slightly below or above.

Consumer surplus. (p. 304) The difference between a customers' willingness to pay and the price paid.

Contribution and contribution margin. (p. 290) The difference between the price and the variable cost of producing and selling a unit of our product or service. Contribution is generally expressed as a percent, by dividing the dollar contribution by the price, and called contribution margin.

Cost-based pricing. (p. 288) The practice of setting prices by estimating the average cost of producing and selling the product plus a profit margin.

Customer-based pricing. (p. 288) The practice of setting prices by estimating the willingness to pay of our customers.

Fixed costs. (p. 291) Costs of producing and selling a unit of our product that do not vary regardless of how many units we sell.

Negative-sum games. (p. 295) Competitive games for which the more intense the competition the smaller the rewards available to be shared; even the winner loses from competing.

Positive-sum games. (p. 294) Those in which the more intense the competition, the greater the rewards to be shared because both players improve their skills as a result of competing.

Price Strategy. (p. 309) The overall price level for our products, based on our overall strategy and on our positioning.

Pricing Execution. (p. 311) The implementation of the general pricing level we have developed as a result of our strategic decisions.

Strategy-based pricing. (p. 305) The practice of setting prices by creating value for our product and communicating it to our customers, thus adapting their willingness to pay.

Variable costs. (p. 290) Costs of producing and selling a unit of our product that vary with the volume we sell.

Zero-sum games. (p. 294) Those in which competitors share a fixed reward, so one's gain is the other's loss.

☐ QUESTIONS FOR DISCUSSION

1. Identify the four approaches to price setting and the pluses and minuses of each.
2. Differentiate between a pricing strategy and a pricing tactic.
3. Your school has just purchased a printer that students can use, but only to print homework assignments. Describe in general terms how you might be able to monetize the value of this perk to the parents paying tuition.
4. Your mother runs a popular store in your city that sells delicious home-made prepared foods.
   (a) Design a trial pricing program for the store.
   (b) Design a continuity pricing program for the store.

Discuss implementation issues you foresee in carrying out these two programs.

☐ APPENDIX: MARKETING ANALYSIS AND PLANNING

Marketing Tool #11.1: Breakeven Financial Analysis for Pricing

Discriminating between Variable and Fixed Costs

Before conducting breakeven analysis for pricing, we must verify that we have the right inputs. To estimate the effect of pricing on profits, we need to understand which costs are **fixed** and which are **variable.** Fixed costs are those that we incur regardless of how much product we produce. An example of a fixed cost might be our mortgage payments on our factory, or salaries paid to our administrative staff. In contrast, variable costs go up and down based on how much product we produce. For example, the cost of leather used in a car is a variable cost that will increase with each car we produce. We must cover our fixed costs in order to break even.

To price properly analysts must make reasonable assumptions about what is fixed and variable. For example, they may assume all equipment and labor costs are fixed or all raw materials costs are variable. Of course, over time the cost of labor may vary with how much we produce, but over the short run we must generally pay our workers regardless of whether production is high or low. On the other hand, we may choose to treat some labor costs as fixed and others as variable. For example, all administrative, marketing, and management labor costs might be fixed over the near term, while only sales reps' travel and entertainment expenses are truly variable. For pricing purposes, we need to carefully identify variable costs, the incremental costs associated with product sales. Variable costs generally include the cost of supplies, raw materials not purchased under long-term contracts, product processing costs, and shipping costs. Variable costs are directly tied to how many units we sell; and if we sell fewer units than we expected, we will not incur those costs. Many fixed costs are not incremental, but others may be incremental in some situations, as we see next.

When considering a price change, we can disregard non-incremental, that is, fixed costs because we will incur them regardless of the price. For example, if a company is in business already and sells a particular product, the cost of its business licensing, administration, website maintenance, permanent staff salaries, office space rental, and machinery are not related to how much volume changes as a result of a price change. All these fixed costs should be ignored when we conduct what-if analyses for a price change.

What can complicate matters is that a price change can radically change the amount of volume we sell, forcing us to make drastic changes to our resources and therefore changing our cost structure. For example, imagine that a company is contemplating a big price decrease, and if it lowers price, volume will likely increase tremendously. If the company is already operating at or near production capacity, dropping price might require buying additional machines or hiring more people, increasing fixed costs. When contemplating what price to charge, we should also estimate how the price will affect the number of units we sell and when we can count as semi-fixed the additional costs we would need to incur at the different volume tiers. If we are thinking about making huge price changes, we should include semi-fixed costs in the analysis.

One final case we need to consider is that of a company that is a start-up or is contemplating going into a new market but has not yet launched its products or purchased its equipment. For this company *all* costs (including fixed costs) associated with starting or expanding operations are incremental.

In summary, the costs that matter for pricing financial analysis are incremental costs, the costs that change as a result of the volume changes that result from the price level. These are:

- All costs we know vary with the number of units we sell (variable costs).
- Semi-fixed costs (costs we will incur if we have to increase capacity to meet increased demand).
- Fixed costs for start-ups, new market entries, or introducing new products.

Calculating Breakeven

We are now ready to look at the two cost concepts required for pricing analysis. The first one is breakeven.

1. **Breakeven Volume.** Breakeven volume identifies the minimum acceptable number of units of a product we should be selling for a given price in order to just cover all our costs. We derive this formula easily by setting Total Costs equal to Total Revenue. The quantity sold that makes total costs equal total revenue is the breakeven quantity.

$$\text{Total costs} = \text{Total revenue}$$

or, written another way:

$$\text{Fixed Costs} + (\text{Variable Cost per unit} \times \text{Quantity}_{breakeven}) = \text{Price} \times \text{Quantity}_{breakeven}$$

Now we solve for $Q_{breakeven}$ by dividing both sides of the equation by $\text{Quantity}_{breakeven}$

$$(\text{Fixed Costs}/\text{Quantity}_{breakeven}) + \text{Variable Cost} = \text{Price}$$

and

$$(\text{Fixed Costs}/\text{Quantity}_{\text{breakeven}}) = \text{Price} - \text{Variable Cost}$$

and

$$\text{Fixed Costs} = \text{Quantity}_{\text{breakeven}} \times (\text{Price} - \text{Variable Cost per unit})$$

or

$$\text{Quantity}_{\text{breakeven}} = \text{Fixed Costs}/(\text{Price} - \text{Variable Cost per unit})$$

We can calculate the number of units we need to sell to break even by dividing the Total Fixed Costs by the result of subtracting the variable costs per unit from the price. As was mentioned in the chapter, Price − Variable costs per unit is also called Contribution in dollars. So the Quantity$_{\text{breakeven}}$ is equal to Fixed costs divided by the Contribution.

Breakeven analysis is helpful not just when we are looking at price decisions, but also when we are debating whether to undertake a potential new investment such as a product upgrade, because it allows us to examine the project's worthiness in terms of the additional sales it may generate.

We included fixed costs in our analysis because we were looking at a go-no-go decision. Later we will consider a company looking at a price change with no impact on its fixed costs.

2. **Contribution Margin.** As we discussed above, it is worth producing and selling a product if the price we can get for it in the marketplace exceeds at least the variable cost of producing it. A company already in business, for which fixed costs are sunk, should set its minimum acceptable price as follows:

$$\text{Price} = \text{Variable Cost}$$

The difference between price and variable cost is called *contribution*. We can think of contribution as the dollar amount that "contributes" to covering fixed costs (once we have paid for the marginal cost of production), and leave some profit (Figure 11.15). The contribution is often expressed as a percentage of price, and is called contribution margin.

$$\text{CM\%} = (P - VC)/P$$

The company's relative cost structure, that is, the relative value of fixed vs. variable costs, determines the contribution margin. The contribution margin, in turn, plays a critical role in the sensitivity of breakeven volume to a price change. We will look at two companies with different cost structures to illustrate this important point.

Companies A and B offer a similar product and sell the same quantity, 1000 units, at the same price of $10 with $1,000 in fixed costs (Fig. 11.16). However, A and B have different variable cost

EXAMPLES

Imagine a company contemplating entering a new market where it will be able to sell its product for $10 per unit. The variable cost of production is $2 per unit, and the total fixed costs (plant operation, business licensing, establishing distribution) are $3 million. How much volume must this company be able to sell in order to break even in this new market?

Breakeven Volume = Fixed Costs/(Price − Variable Costs)

Breakeven Volume = $3,000,000/($10 − $2)

The breakeven volume, that is, the minimum volume the company needs to be able to sell to want to enter that market is 375,000 units. ∎

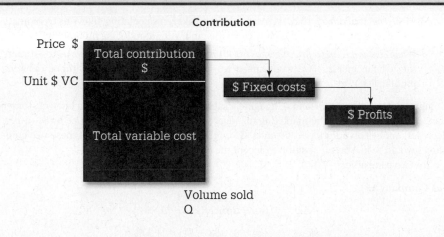

Contribution

Price $

Total contribution
$

Unit $ VC

$ Fixed costs

$ Profits

Total variable cost

Volume sold
Q

Figure 11.15
The contribution is the difference between the price and the variable costs per unit. Given the price we collect for a product, the contribution is the dollar amount left over to pay for a portion of the fixed costs and to add to the profits of the company. Contribution sometimes is expressed as a percentage. Contribution = Price − Variable Cost per unit and Contribution % = (Price − Variable Cost per unit)/Price.

structures, and therefore they have different breakeven quantities as well as different contribution margins. Company A's breakeven volume is 500 units; Company B's is 143 units. Whereas company A's breakeven volume is 50% of its current sales, Company B's is a much more comfortable 143 units, only 14.3% of its current sales. The simple breakeven calculation below will show how sensitive profitability is to volume.

We combine the concepts of breakeven and contribution margin to estimate the sensitivity of these companies' customers to changes in price. Assuming A's and B's fixed costs are truly fixed (rather than semi-fixed), we will use a different breakeven formula to perform sensitivity analyses and understand the relationship between price and quantity while maintaining profitability fixed. The equation we will use is:

$$\%\Delta_{breakeven} = -\Delta price/(CM + \Delta price)$$

Where Δ ("delta") means "change in."
To convert from Percent Units to Unit Sales Change we use the following:

$$\text{Unit Breakeven Sales Change} = \%\text{Breakeven Sales Change} \times \text{Initial Sales Volume}$$

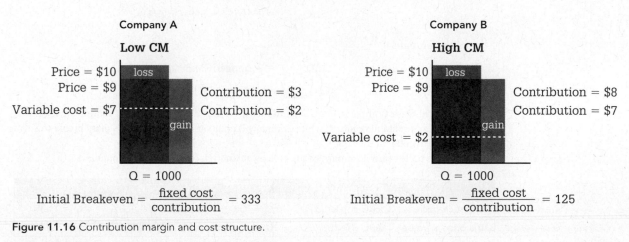

Company A

Low CM

Price = $10
Price = $9

loss

Contribution = $3

Variable cost = $7

Contribution = $2

gain

Q = 1000

$$\text{Initial Breakeven} = \frac{\text{fixed cost}}{\text{contribution}} = 333$$

Company B

High CM

Price = $10
Price = $9

loss

Contribution = $8

Contribution = $7

Variable cost = $2

gain

Q = 1000

$$\text{Initial Breakeven} = \frac{\text{fixed cost}}{\text{contribution}} = 125$$

Figure 11.16 Contribution margin and cost structure.

Contribution for Company A = ($10 − $7) = $3
Contribution margin for Company A = ($10 − $7)/$10 = 30%
Contribution margin for Company B = ($10 − $2) = $8
Contribution margin for Company B = ($10 − $2)/$10 = 80%

When contemplating a price increase. . . . The breakeven calculation allows us to estimate the volume decrease the company can withstand without reducing profitability.

When contemplating a price decrease. . . . The breakeven calculation allows us to estimate the volume increase we would need to justify a price decreasing without reducing profitability.

Going back to Companies A and B, imagine a sales person is trying to close a large customer transaction and presents the marketing manager with a proposal to lower price by $1 (a 10% decrease) and sell an additional 200 units. Given their cost structure, which of these two companies would be in a better position to accept the proposed price decrease?

The two companies:

For Company A:

$$\%\Delta Q_{breakeven} = -\Delta price/(CM + \Delta price)$$

$$\%\Delta Q_{breakeven} = +\$1/(\$3 - \$1) = +50\%$$

For Company A to break even after the price drop, it must increase its volume by 50%. Given the original breakeven unit level of 333, a 50% increase is 167 units. (333*50%).

For Company B:

$$\%\Delta Q_{breakeven} = -\Delta price/(CM + \Delta price)$$

$$\%\Delta Q_{breakeven} = +\$1/(\$8 - \$1) = +14.3\%$$

Company B can afford to drop price and keep its profit intact with just a 14.3% sales increase; this translates into 125*14.3% = 18 additional units sold.

Now, let's now assume that instead of a price decrease the two companies were contemplating a price increase. The same formula will help us see how many units of product sales the two companies will be able to forego before they start losing money.

For Company A:

$$\%\Delta Q_{breakeven} = -\Delta price/(CM + \Delta price)$$

$$\%\Delta Q_{breakeven} = -\$1/(\$3 + \$1) = -25\%$$

For Company B:

$$\%\Delta Q_{breakeven} = -\Delta price/(CM + \Delta price)$$

$$\%\Delta Q_{breakeven} = -\$1/(\$8 + \$1) = -11.1\%$$

In this case, Company A could afford to lose up to 25% of its breakeven volume (or 125 units) and keep profitability intact, while Company B could afford to lose 11.3% of its breakeven volume (16 units).

The table below summarizes the breakeven analysis for these two companies:

	Company A	Company B
10% price decrease	%BE = 10%/(30% − 10%) = 50%	%BE = −10%/(80% − 10%) = 14.3%
10% price increase	%BE = −10%/(30% + 10%) = −25%	%BE = −10%/(80% + 10%) = −11.1%

Clearly, Company B, the company with the higher contribution margin, is more likely to be willing to lower the price to get the incremental 200 units in volume, whereas Company A, the company with the lower contribution margin, is more likely to pass up the customer demanding a low price. Company A will keep prices up and sacrifice volume. This key insight from cost analysis for pricing can be generalized in Figure 11.6. Companies with high contribution margins, that is, with relatively high fixed to variable cost ratios, are likely to be willing to sacrifice some price to obtain additional volume.

Marketing Tool #11.2: The Economics of Pricing

This tool helps us conceptualize the foundational principles of value-based pricing by reviewing the economic model of surplus. Economists believe that value is transferred between consumers and producers whenever a transaction takes place. Consumers consider purchasing a product because they believe it will have value to them that is greater than the purchase price. Producers sell products because they have some ability to create value that exceeds the costs of producing and selling products. The difference between the consumer's willingness to pay for a product and the supplier's cost of production defines the amount of value created by a transaction; this value is termed *surplus*.

Total surplus is the total value of a product to the customer who buys it, minus the total cost (fixed cost per unit + variable cost per unit) of producing it. Economists assume that in each transaction total surplus is divided between consumers and producers by the price paid. Clearly, both parties would like to maximize their share of the total surplus (the benefit they receive from the transaction), but both parties must receive more benefit than they could gain through an alternative transaction or neither will be willing to transact. Accordingly, total surplus is split into three types: producer surplus, consumer surplus, and unrealized surplus. See Figure 11.17

Producer surplus is the value captured by the firm providing the product; it is the difference between the selling price and the (variable) cost of production after fixed costs have been covered. A company that increases its producer surplus is increasing its profits, at least in the short-term. We can manipulate two variables to change producer surplus: price and cost. Increases in price, decreases in cost, or both will increase producer surplus. Producer surplus is

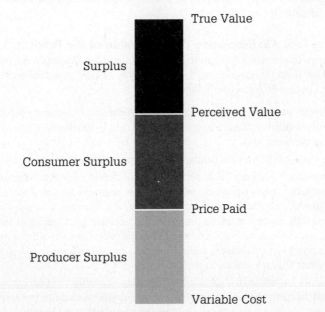

Figure 11.17 Economic Surplus and Pricing Strategy
Marketer's focus in pricing goes beyond tactically allocating surplus between producers and consumers and focuses instead on increasing perceived value through innovation and communication, thus diminishing unrealized surplus.

theoretically easy to quantify because it concerns simple dollars and cents; we assume we can calculate true economic costs and correctly distinguish variable and fixed costs. In practice, however, accounting rules and economic principles categorize these costs differently.

Consumer surplus relies on *perceptions of value* and consists of the difference between the consumer's perceived value of the product (assuming the purchase is a choice) and the price paid. Our challenge is to quantify the maximum amount the consumer would be willing to pay for the good. In many cases customers don't know themselves; they just know they would have been willing to pay more than they did. In addition, even for a specific consumer, the perceived value of a particular product is likely to change over time. Consider some situational factors. A consumer buying Advil to stock the medicine cabinet places a much lower value on the pain reliever than the same person suffering from an intense headache just before a job interview. If she looks in her pocket and finds she has only $4.32, her willingness to pay will also be affected.

Unrealized surplus, the third category of surplus, forces us to reexamine our habitual assumptions that we have positioned the brand in a way that maximizes perceived value and that consumers recognize that value fully. For example, a consumer may value her cell phone as a tool for increasing her efficiency but not fully realize its value for her personal safety if she should ever need to call for help in an emergency. However, marketers' job is to reveal value of which consumers were not aware. The customer whom we educate about the full value of her cell phone will then be willing to pay a higher price for it; the difference between this price and the actual price paid is unrealized surplus.

The existence of unrealized surplus is one of the key reasons the field of marketing exists. By helping consumers recognize how much value they personally will be able to capture by purchasing the product, the marketer increases their willingness to pay and then creates an opportunity to increase price (and therefore producer surplus). From the opposite perspective, unrealized surplus represents a failure of marketers to help consumers understand the true benefits of a product. This unrealized surplus creates an opportunity to increase perceived value in a strategic manner; it yields potential surplus for both the company and the consumer, rather than sacrificing one for the other.

Marketing Tool #3: Estimating the True Value of the Product

This tool helps us develop a maximum price recommendation based on the positioning of the brand and the strategic quadrant we have selected by helping us estimate the true value of a product to a customer. Follow these steps:

1. Select your strategic quadrant (Acquisition/Stimulate Demand; Retention/Stimulate Demand; Acquisition/Earn Share; Retention/Earn Share) based on the decisions made earlier in the framework.

2. Build a value-ladder for your Fundamental Entity. (See the Marketing Tool in Chapter 5.)

3. If your product or service could be targeted at different segments who are sure to attach different value to your product, select just one segment for this exercise. Alternatively, complete this exercise for each value segment. For example, a brand like Bubble Wrap targeting B2B customers would complete this exercise for its different industry segment targets (e.g., computer manufactures vs. industrial parts), as each of these types of customer segments will place a different amount of value on its products based on the value of the end-product they are seeking to protect.

4. Select all the benefits in the value ladder that generate value for your customer and develop a benefit list using the table below. In the first column write down the specific benefit you are monetizing. In the second column note its type; benefits can be functional, economic, or psychological. For example, for Michelin tires, a functional benefit is that the tires provide better handling performance; an economic benefit is that they save money because they use less gas; and a psychological benefit is safety.

5. Brainstorm how you might be able to monetize the value of each benefit on the list. Benefits bring value to customers either by helping them avoid costs or by increasing their revenues. It is critical that you consider both sources of value. Also, you will notice that some costs are easier to monetize than others. For example, if Michelin tires help drivers save gas we can easily translate that benefit to a dollar value for each tire. We would calculate how many miles a tire generally lasts and then we would apply a miles per gallon ratio to figure out how many gallons of gas a driver would use in the life of a Michelin tire. We would need to have data about the gas consumption of a non-Michelin tire. We would then estimate the gas consumption difference between the two tires along the life of the tire and translate it into today's dollars at the current gas price. Other benefits, such as safety, are not easily quantifiable. We will still consider them in our true value estimate. One way to do this is to look at the price premium that other products in the category with a similar benefit obtain. This is of course highly subjective, but finding an appropriate benchmark can increase our confidence in the pricing decision.

6. Write down the value of the product. If the product will be used over a long period of time, you will need to develop a cash-flow estimate, taking into account how long the product will last and how many times your target customer will use it.

Table 11.1 Estimating True Value

Benefit	Benefit Type	Value Formula	Estimated Value (in dollars)

Note that to estimate value you will have to make a series of assumptions. In practice a company would be able to validate these assumptions by interviewing several customers and noting the actual values by type of customer. Even when we feel that we are guessing, by guessing we are uncovering the key assumptions we make and which require further research and validation. This is tremendously helpful.

☐ **RESOURCES**

Brandenburger, Adam B. N. (1996). *Co-Opetition: A Revolution Mindset That Combines Competition and Cooperation.*

Gourville, J. and Y. Moon (2004). "Managing price expectations through product overlap." *Journal of Retailing 80*(1): 23–35.

King, S., J. Gans, R. Stonecash, and N. G. Mankiw, (2011). *Principles of economics.* Cengage Learning.

Nagle, Thomas T. and Reed K. Holden. *The Strategy and Tactics of Pricing: A Guide to Profitable Decision Making.* Englewood Cliffs, NJ: Prentice Hall, 5th edition, 2011

Rao, Akshay R., Mark E. Bergen, and Scott Davis. "How to fight a price war." *Harvard Business Review 78.2* (2000): 107–120.

Holden, Reed and Mark Burton. *Pricing with Confidence: 10 Ways to Stop Leaving Money on the Table.* John Wiley and Sons, Inc., New York City, 2008.

Raju, Jagmohan, Jagmohan Singh Raju, and Z. John Zhang. Smart Pricing: *How Google, Priceline, and Leading Businesses Use Pricing Innovation for Profitability.* Pearson Prentice Hall, New Jersey, 2010.

chapter twelve

"… and reducing the
indivisibles into cash, he
shared the whole among
his company, with such
equity and discretion, that
in the most minute article
he neither exceeded nor fell
short of distributive justice.
Having made this partition,
with which every individual
was perfectly well satisfied
and contented; Roque,
turning to Don Quixote,
'if we did not observe this
punctuality,' said he, 'there
would be no living among
such a crew.'"

Cervantes, Saavedra, M. de. (1803).

The adventures of the renowned Don Quixote de la Mancha. Glasgow: Printed by Chapman & Lang. Volume 4, page 238.

CHANNELS

After studying this chapter you should be able to:

1. *Describe the key challenges of managing channels*

2. *Identify the key purpose of a channel*

3. *Explain how channel members add value*

4. *Identify different channel flows and functions*

5. *Define the different elements of channel structure*

6. *Integrate channels with other elements of the Big Picture framework*

I n the late 1990s, Walmart became interested in Vlasic's gallon jar of pickles, nearly double the standard 80-oz. size, and began sales-testing at a price somewhere over $3 per jar. Consumer enthusiasm led Walmart to propose selling the pickles at just $2.97 per gallon. Vlasic agreed (Walmart accounts for 30 percent of its total retail market), so the larger size soon became available in Walmart stores nationwide. Through Walmart alone, Vlasic began moving an average of 80 gallon jars a week per store, totaling approximately 240,000 units each week.

Vlasic was soon scrambling to keep up with demand, however, pouring resources into a product that yielded

profits of only a few cents per jar. The result for the pickle company was millions of dollars in lost profits each year.

Vlasic wanted to raise the price of the gallon jar, but Walmart refused to renegotiate the contract, threatening to cut sales of all Vlasic products if the company persisted. The "Walmart squeeze" forced the company to restructure numerous aspects of its operations, a story echoed by many of Walmart suppliers that are forced to lower prices or lose out to domestic or foreign competitors. ∎

Fishman, Charles. The Walmart You Don't Know, December 3, 2003. http://www.fastcompany.com/magazine/77/walmart.html. Accessed May 13, 2013.

Freeman, Richard. Walmart 'eats' more U.S. manufacturers," *Executive Intelligence Review*, 11/25/03. http://rense.com/general45/manuf.htm. Accessed May 13, 2013.

Cary, W. P. "'The Walmart Effect' Probes the Good, the Bad and the Ugly," March 29, 2006. http://www.knowwpcarey.com/article.cfm?aid=792.

THE CHALLENGE OF MANAGING CHANNELS

The final executional element we consider in the framework is channel strategy. While the discussion in this chapter will focus on business-to-consumer (B2C) markets, the concepts we present here (and throughout the Big Picture framework) apply equally to business-to-business (B2B) markets. As Louis Stern, Emeritus professor of Marketing, has said, the ultimate goal in either scenario is to deliver a benefit to the end consumer, regardless of where we are in the supply chain or how distant the end consumer may appear. When channel members act as partners to deliver an end benefit, the channel is more robust and has the best chance of creating value for the end consumer in an effective and efficient manner. The more value the channel creates, the more likely its members will enjoy sustained growth and profitability.

Of all the executional steps in the Big Picture, channels present the biggest challenges. The main reason is that a channel is a *system* consisting of many interrelated organizations. Some we may control directly, others we may not control at all; some share our goals, and others have goals of their own. Further, these goals are not static, and market conditions are increasingly volatile as well, so our ability to forecast future conditions has become more limited. This limitation means that often we must rely on our executional abilities—our ability to change our channel strategy and implementation as conditions

CUSTOMERFOCUS

THE IMPACT OF DIGITAL DISTRIBUTION ON CUSTOMER SATISFACTION WITH MUSIC

In the 1980s, the success of recording artists depended largely upon their getting signed to a big record label. Labels financed the bands until they started making money, at which point the label kept most of the bands' profits because they had negotiated lucrative contracts by which they owned the artists' master recordings. This structure gave the labels a strong incentive to put all their support behind a few popular groups and push them to churn out regular hits, often at the expense of dozens of smaller but arguably more talented bands. Large record labels were necessary when the cost of manufacturing and distributing music was high. They had their own plants and controlled the worldwide shipping of their CDs. They also had representatives, who visited stores to ensure their artists were getting adequate shelf space and also dealt with defective and returned merchandise. Hence the channel was fairly efficient, but consumers were not gaining access to a wide variety of music.

When music became fully digital, this began to change. Artists and their potential audiences were able to connect with each other through a variety of other means, including iTunes, Napster, Pandora, Spotify, Satellite Radio, and a host of others. Artists were also able to reach listeners directly through sites such as YouTube. Two notable examples were Justin Bieber, who was discovered on YouTube, and Psy, whose music video "Gangnam Style" became the most watched video on YouTube in 2012.

As of 2013, an unsigned artist can now use a service such as Tune Core to distribute music through a variety of digital sources including iTunes and Spotify for as little as $10. This unprecedented access has had unprecedented impact: changes in music distribution brought an increase in sales of digital music. By the end of 2012, digital album sales had reached 118 million units, and digital track sales exceeded 1.3 billion. Perhaps more importantly, overall music purchases also reached an all-time high, presumably because the increased access and interaction of the digital channel enabled created an environment where artists could produce music that consumers valued.

The rise of digital has changed the essential structure of the music channel. High-paid studio executives used to act as the filter between bands and the public, going from club to club searching for promising new talent. Now music fans do this for free, posting their discoveries on blogs that reach wide audiences and provide excellent free marketing for bands. Because the music is recommended by peers instead of paid marketers, potential buyers receive what they perceive to be higher-quality information about the music that might interest them. In essence, the digital channel allows artists to use social media to access not just a large audience, but more importantly the right audience, those who are likely to value their music more. ■

Topping, Alexandra. Quiet Revolution Rages as Web-savvy Bands Learn How to Rule the Air Waves, May 18, 2009. http://www.guardian.co.uk/music/2009/may/18/web-music-revolution. Accessed May 12, 2003.

Stone, Brad. "Artists find backers as labels wane," *The New York Times*, July 1, 2009. http://www.nytimes.com/2009/07/22/technology/internet/22music.html?_r=0.

The Nielsen Company & Billboards' 2012 Music Industry Report, January 4, 2013. http://www.businesswire.com/news/home/20130104005149/en/Nielsen-Company-Billboard%E2%80%99s-2012-Music-Industry-Report. Accessed May 12, 2013.

change. But changing a channel is not simply a matter of having a quick strategy meeting and then sending out a memo. For all these reasons, sound channel strategy is developed on a foundation of advanced planning and skill at forecasting future market conditions, and it is realized with consistent, effective execution.

CHANNEL DEFINITION AND PURPOSE

Our first and most important goal in developing and implementing channel strategy is *channel alignment*. An aligned channel is one in which all the members understand that their ultimate goal is to create and capture value for and from the end consumer. No matter how far away in time and space a particular channel member

Value chain. The terms value chain and supply chain are used to refer to firms who collaborate to bring value to an end consumer. These terms are also used to refer to the activities entailed in the design, manufacturing, and logistics of products and services.

is from this end consumer, the member's long-term survival depends not on how well it satisfies its direct customers, but on how well *all* the channel members satisfy the *end consumer*.

Of course, the farther away a channel member is from this end consumer, the less feasible this goal may seem. The immediate pressures and demands of our nearest neighbors in the channel, a set of firms often referred to as the **value chain**, can loom larger than the remote needs of our end consumers. However, if channel members lose sight of the channel objective of delivering value to the end consumer, the consumer will sooner or later abandon that channel in favor of a more responsive one. Without the end consumer, there is no channel.

Thus, regardless of how distant the end consumer may seem, the first purpose of all channel members is clear: maximize profits for the channel as a whole by profitably meeting the needs of this end consumer. Once they have achieved profit maximization, the channel members can allocate profits among themselves. Most will consider themselves deserving of the lion's share. If, however, a *channel leader* can emerge who successfully maximizes value chain profit and can also negotiate an equitable allocation of these profits among the value chain members, this firm will ensure the long-term survival of the channel. To accomplish this task, marketers must meet several challenges.

First, in order to lead, the channel member must recognize and attempt to mitigate the negative impact of conflicting goals within the channel. One classic example of this impact occurred in 1990, when Mazda identified an opportunity for an "affordable roadster."[1] It introduced the Mazda Miata, a two-seat convertible intended for sale at a very attractive $13,800 base price point. The car was so popular that dealers were not able to keep up with demand, and some tacked on "delivery fees" as high as $5,000, effectively moving the car into another price class. From the dealer's short-term perspective, this action made sense: demand exceeded supply, so prices (and their profits) went up. In the long run, however, this action had negative consequences for Mazda within the channel.

On one hand, by pricing the car too low and having insufficient supply to meet demand, the firm failed to capture an appropriate share of the value it created. On the other hand, because of the dealers' inflated price, Mazda failed to deliver on expectations it had built up for a fun sports car that was reasonably priced, and customers were disappointed. Because channels are essentially systems, it is often difficult to observe and measure the medium and longer-term impact of our actions on the end consumer. Nonetheless, greater alignment of dealer and manufacturer goals would have generated greater consumer satisfaction with Mazda, and likely more sustainable profitability.

Second, in order to create value, all members of the channel must effectively and efficiently transmit information, particularly information about the end consumer. Companies that market and deliver the product directly to the end consumer are in a good position to observe and interpret consumer feedback; for example, Amazon and Target have gathered extensive data about customer buying behavior that they mine in order to develop product promotions. While Target benefits from this information in the short run, the entire retail channel might benefit to an even greater extent if the

---

[1]Long, Brian (2002). *Mazda Miata: The Full Story of the World's Favorite Sports Car.* Veloce Publishing, Dorchester, England.

store were to transmit this information to *upstream* channel members, such as manufacturers, who might use it to create new and improved products.

Walmart implemented an EDI (Electronic Data Interchange) system in the 1990s with suppliers such as P&G and Kraft. Through this system, the manufacturers gained timely access to information about sales of their products and were able to supply the stores in a more efficient and effective manner. In this case, information sharing in the channel benefited the end consumer in two ways: first the information sharing made the channel more efficient and therefore reduced costs; second this information reduced occurrences of out-of-stocks, thus giving consumers more consistent access to the product. Consumer information is always of value; however, we have an opportunity to maximize this value if we use the information in a holistic manner, considering the total value chain.

CUSTOMERFOCUS

INTEL EMERGES AS A WORLD LEADER IN SEMICONDUCTOR MANUFACTURING

Intel, a world leader in semiconductor manufacturing, was founded in California in 1968 and controlled 90 percent of the world's personal PC microprocessor market by 1997. Its success is due largely to its creation of brand value among end consumers for a small, unseen computer subcomponent of which most computer users are unaware. Through extensive market research and a series of global advertising campaigns to raise the visibility of Intel chips, however, the company transformed a commodity product into a necessity.

The "Intel inside" branding campaign was launched in 1991, and the company not only educated dealers and customers about the value of its microprocessor but also persuaded computer manufacturers to carry the Intel logo on the exterior of their products. The campaign created a question in the minds of consumers about the quality of products that didn't have "Intel inside," and the only answer was Intel. The company's premium branding strategy worked, and brand recognition in the European market soared from 24 percent in 1991 to nearly 80 percent a year later. In 2009 Intel unveiled the "Sponsors of Tomorrow" campaign in Asian, European, and U.S. markets, along with a re-designed "Intel Inside" seen on new computers and retail outlets around the world.

Intel's success is linked to the success of the entire channel on a number of fronts. First, Intel's cooperative advertising program, which provides advertising dollars to retailers

Jason Kinch/Intel Corporation

and manufacturers if they feature the Intel logo, generated enormous awareness and improved value perceptions among consumers. This in turn presumably increased consumers' willingness to pay in a product category where price pressures are quite strong. Further, Intel's access to global markets and resultant sales growth has enabled it to take advantage of huge economies of scale that accompany such growth. Finally, broad acceptance of the Intel chip has made it a standard in most computers, increasing the efficiency of computer manufacture and distribution thanks to consistent quality and supply. ■

"The semiconductor industry: Space invaders," *The Economist*, briefing, January 7, 2012.

Perry Douglass, "Intel outgrows Samsung in sluggish semiconductor market," *Tom's Hardware Blog*, December 2, 2011. http://www.tomshardware.com/news/intel-samsung-nvidia-amd-semiconductor, 14141.html. Accessed August 15, 2013.

Whitewell, Stuart. "Ingredient branding case study," *Intel*. November 2005. http://www.intangiblebusiness.com/Brand-Services/Marketinservices/News/Ingredient-branding-case-study-Intel~466. html. Accessed May 15, 2013.

Intel India unveils its new "Sponsors of Tomorrow" Global Campaign. Also announces new Processor Rating System and "Intel Inside" logo design. May 28, 2009. http://www.intel.com/cd/in/corporate-pressroom/apac/eng/archives/2009/422109.html. Accessed May 15, 2013.

EXAMPLES/CAPTIONS

THE AMICABLE DIVORCE OF FACEBOOK AND ZYNGA: CHANNEL MEMBER COLLABORATION AND CONFLICT

Zynga's mission statement is to "connect the world through games." The company's Farmville game grew to 10 million daily users within six weeks of launch, and by the beginning of 2013 it had over 250 million daily users. Zynga originally made its games accessible through Facebook, which greatly benefited from the arrangement because Zynga aficionados would join Facebook to access their Farmville accounts, and because advertisers wanting to target Zynga's customers placed ads of Facebook

David Ko/Bloomberg/Getty Images

to reach them. Zynga also benefited because it used its customers' Facebook accounts to target their Facebook Friends. As Zynga grew, however, its power in the channel grew as well, enabling it to demand a greater share of the resources it was helping to create than Facebook was willing to part with. Though the two companies ended their special relationship in November 2012, it remains an example of the thin line that exists between collaboration and competition with channel partners. ∎

Sources: Martin, Scott and Jon Swartz. "Facebook earnings due Thursday, after Zynga loss," *USA TODAY.* July 25, 2012. http://usatoday30.usatoday.com/money/companies/earnings/story/2012-07-25/zynga/56486436/1.

Pepitone, Julianne. "Facebook and Zynga tear up their contract," *CNN Money.* November 29, 2012. http://money.cnn.com/2012/11/29/technology/social/facebook-zynga/index.html.

Last, but not least, marketers must consider the human element. A price is a price; an ad is an ad; a package is a package. These elements of the marketing mix are observable, stable, and for the most part within our control. In contrast, *humans* inevitably execute a channel strategy, and as we all know, humans don't always do exactly what we want them to do. Even if we manage to fully align the objectives of all channel partners, humans differ in their emotional, physical, social, and intellectual capacity to execute tactics that will achieve these objectives. Humans make mistakes, they get tired, they get confused, they get frustrated, and they get angry.

For these reasons firms often simply reach for technology solutions such as ATMs or voice recognition systems to replace humans. However, humans also have the ability to adapt, to navigate complex and dynamic situations, to recognize emotional cues, and to customize their responses on an individual basis. Hence, while we might seek to eliminate humans from the supply chain by replacing them with technology, this approach will only take us so far. Humans play an important part in even the most technological or standardized supply chain. In the end, managing a channel effectively requires managing humans effectively. Because humans deliver the added value delivered by virtually every channel member, training, service operations, and quality control are crucial.

The above discussion establishes the significant executional and strategic challenges we face in developing channel strategy. To meet these challenges we use the Big Picture framework and apply a disciplined strategy that will increase the efficiency of our decision-making. We must develop an understanding of (1) the value-added benefit of each channel member, which we will then use to (2) structure the channel.

THE VALUE-ADDED BENEFIT OF A CHANNEL MEMBER

With the primary objectives and challenges of the channel understood, our task is to conceive and implement a channel strategy in which each channel member adds value to the supply chain and understands the nature of that added value. In general, the value a particular member or members of the value chain might add falls into three basic categories, often referred to as utilities. Let's look at product, time, and place utility.

Product Utility

Of course, all channels are concerned with delivering products or services of some kind. However, **product utility** refers to the specific benefit each channel member provides with relation to our products, such as *product assortment*, *product inventory*, or *product selection*.

Product Assortment

Home Depot provides an amazingly broad assortment of **SKUs**, or **stock-keeping units**. Each SKU represents a unique hardware or building product available in the store. For some customers this assortment is overwhelming; the in-store experience can be confusing and frustrating. In contrast, customers loyal to Home Depot value this wide range of choices; the challenge of dealing with the complex in-store environment is worth it, because they are able to find virtually any home-improvement or hardware product in one location. This is the product utility of product assortment.

Product Inventory

Costco Wholesale stores are generally the same size as The Home Depot stores and stock roughly the same number of products, but they carry a very limited number of individual SKUs. Instead they use their floor space to offer customers large quantities of items, so Costco is able to charge much lower prices. The specific product utility offered here is not assortment, but rather inventory; customers come to Costco to stock up on staple items such as cereal, copy paper, and liquid detergent that are discounted heavily.

Product Selection

In contrast to Costco, few customers go to a Tiffany store to stock up. The product benefit Tiffany provides is product selection, in this case an exclusive selection that customers can find only at a Tiffany store. While Home Depot loyals may tend to rely on their own expertise to make the right choice of products, those loyal to Tiffany prefer to rely on the expertise of the store buyers and merchandisers to create a limited but appealing product selection.

Firms can also provide product selection utility by capitalizing on the expertise of in-store sales and service providers, such as when the channel member helps the customer select the perfect product for him or her. At a Sure foot boot shop, for example, skiers receive individual attention from a boot-fitting specialist to choose and customize what the store calls "the world's most comfortable ski boot."

Product utility can thus take many forms, and different customers value different types of utility. When a particular channel member has decided to offer a product utility, it will first need to identify the specific benefits sought by its target customer and then develop the skills and assets necessary to deliver these benefits. The skills and

Product utility. The benefit provided by channel members that delivers product expertise, assortment, or selection.

SKU. Stock keeping unit. A unique code that identifies each individual product in a retail store; used to track inventory in the channel.

strategic assets necessary for providing an assortment benefit similar to Home Depot's are quite different from those needed to provide the selection benefit of Tiffany.

Time Utility

Any firm that helps reduce search time, increase speed of delivery, or ensure sufficient inventory at times of peak demand is essentially adding **time utility** to the value chain. Different types of time utility have varying importance to different consumer groups and channel members. For example, a consumer shopping at drugstore.com may value the website's instant search capability and easy payment process. Technology has radically raised consumers' expectations about time utility; even the few seconds saved by having a data field pre-populated with the customer's name and address are of value. On the other hand, a different customer may value delivery speed over checkout speed and so prefer a nearby brick-and-mortar drugstore such as Walgreens.

Time utility also means the product is available when needed. Street vendors who magically appear selling umbrellas during a rainstorm are providing time utility. Finally, those channel members who provide product support and parts are delivering a form of time utility as well. For example, if a customer loses a cable for a pair of Bose noise-cancelling headphones, the firm will often send a replacement cable in 24 hours. This type of after-sale support is particularly important for firms selling specialized equipment that customers depend on. For example, Animas Corporation provides insulin infusion equipment that patients depend on to regulate their insulin levels. The company maintains a seven-day, 24-hour customer care line to offer crucial support whenever it is needed. Much of the added value of this product is accounted for by this service.

Place Utility

The final value added by channel members is **place utility**. The shorter the distance the consumer must travel to inspect, pay for, or receive the product, the greater the place utility. Willingness to travel depends on the product; we are obviously more disposed to travel a distance to purchase an automobile than to buy a stick of gum. This is why place utility is particularly important for low-involvement, frequently purchased products such as coffee. In some cities in the world it is possible to stand in one place and see two different Starbucks stores within a short walking distance; when a customer feels like having a cup of coffee, Starbucks is there.

These three utilities represent broad categories of possible benefits a channel can provide. To understand clearly the potential value added by a channel member, however, we must dig deeper and characterize the specific nature of the benefit. Even as simple a concept as "assortment," a specification of product utility, can mean very different things to different people. For example, a retailer can offer brand assortment—a broad selection of different brands—or product assortment—a broad choice of products from a narrower set of brands. Our understanding of the various utilities provided by channel members will help us as we begin to evaluate the structure of the channel.

CHANNEL FLOWS AND FUNCTIONS

The best way to think about channels is to remember that they deal with *flows*, most notably flows of product, information, and money.

Product Flow

The most obvious thing that flows through a channel is product. The product must make its way from the manufacturer to the end consumer, and the raw materials that make up the product must get to the manufacturer as well. The path these products take will affect how efficiently and effectively the channel functions. When we add a channel member, such as a distributor, we are adding another step to the distribution process, and this may add cost in terms of time and money. On the other hand, a distributor may increase the efficiency of distribution by reducing the total number of transactions in the channel: instead of having to contact several different suppliers to buy several different products the purchaser can simply go to a single source for several products.

The flow of physical product doesn't necessarily coincide with legal possession. In many cases the product is physically possessed and legally owned by different channel members; an agent may purchase inventory and resell it without ever holding the physical inventory (a stockbroker), or an agent may "hold" the inventory and offer it for sale without ever taking title (a real estate broker). The magazines available in grocery stores are generally owned by a third party known as a "rack jobber." This firm is responsible for ensuring that magazine displays are well stocked and presentable, and when the products have been sold the grocer compensates the jobber for them. The competencies associated with holding and transferring physical product (e.g., ensuring that the displays look good) are quite distinct from those associated with holding and transferring ownership (e.g. having efficient legal and accounting processes in place); it is thus quite sensible to break up these two elements of product when appropriate.

Information Flow

While we tend to think of channels as dedicated to moving product, they enable many other assets to flow as well. One key commodity that flows backward and forward through a channel is *information*. Information, primarily about the product or service, flows forward through the channel to the end consumer. Channel members may add value to this information by amassing and presenting it (a pitch by a technical salesperson), transforming it (unit pricing provided in the grocery store), or interpreting or reinforcing it (advice from an art dealer or ad agency).

Perhaps more importantly, information flows from the customer back up the supply chain as well. Ideally, value also is added to information as it flows in this direction; for example, our in-house sales force returns from the field with crucial information about customer preferences. Unfortunately, quite often, important consumer information traveling back up the channel is blocked or distorted in some way. Our sales force or retailer may have a detailed understanding of certain aspects of consumer needs but lack the motivation, the ability, or the opportunity to share it with relevant upstream channel members.

When information is not flowing efficiently, channel members may emerge whose sole purpose is to ensure that it does. A research firm, such as AC Nielsen, will collect, aggregate, and analyze grocery sales data across all product categories and then sell this information to manufacturers. When all competitors are accessing the same data, however, it is less likely to be a source of differentiation for the firm and becomes simply a cost of doing business. This is why direct marketers and those using fewer intermediaries generally have an advantage. For example, Dell's decision to sell personal computers direct to customers not only enabled it to cut costs; it also gave the company access to information about specific consumer preferences. Thus Dell was able to reduce inventories by building to order and, in the process, compile and analyze incoming customer data for future use in product development and strategic planning.

Money Flow

Channels also facilitate a number of other key flows, such as the flow of money and financing. Once again, channel members dedicated to this function must add value in a specific fashion, such as by providing financing or handling payments for or between other channel members and/or the end customer. A specific channel member also may assume the task of negotiation, as do car dealers. In this case the salesperson interacting with the customer has immediate and crucial information about him or her that can help the dealer extract the highest price the customer is willing to pay. With the rise of digital marketing, a new crop of third-party payment processors have arisen, such as Paypal, a payment option that appears on many web retail pages, Square, a company that enables small retailers to accept payments using smartphones, and Google Wallet, a mobile app that provides consumers a single method of payment online and in stores.

EXAMPLES/CAPTIONS

THE GOVERNMENT TRIES TO SUBSIDIZE THE COST OF DRUGS: IS THE CHANNEL ABSORBING THE SURPLUS?

Channel conflict arises when channel members are not fully aligned in providing value to end-users. Consider the federal 340B Drug-Pricing Program, signed into law under the Veterans Health Care Act of 1992 and expanded in 2010 to cover one-third of the country's hospitals. The apparent objective of this program was to reduce the price of drugs for patients by requiring most drug companies to discount their products, usually by about 20 to 50 percent, to qualifying hospitals. In fact, however, the 340B program was meant to provide a benefit not directly for patients, but rather for "safety net" hospitals, those serving rural and or poor communities. These facilities were expected not to

© age fotostock/Alamy Limited

pass the discount on to patients but rather to keep the profits in order to generate more income and thus ensure their survival in, and service to, the community. In some cases, however, it is not only these safety-net hospitals that benefit. When a qualifying hospital is part of a larger group, all the hospitals in that group can benefit. The University Medical Center of Southern Nevada qualified, for example, and was able to realize an estimated $9 million per year, some of which went to clinics and hospitals in the same system, including those that would not directly qualify. In this case, and many others, the surpluses generated by the value chain are not necessarily reaching those for whom they are intended. ∎

Sources: Pollack, Andrew. "Dispute develops over drug program," *The New York Times*. February 12, 2013. http://www.nytimes.com/2013/02/13/business/dispute-develops-over-340b-discount-drug-program.html?pagewanted=all&_r=0.

Barlas, Stephen." Health Care Reform Bill expands access to Section 340B discounted drugs for hospitals." *Pharmacy and Therapeutics*. November 2010, 35(11): 632-634.

Keough, Christopher L. and Stephanie A. Webster: "340B program presents opportunities—and challenges, "*Healthcare Financial Management Association*. November 2009, pp. 1-4.

As we think about these various channel flows, to assess or design a channel we must recognize (1) the various functions channel members may perform, and (2) the value of each of these functions to the end customer. In this way we can envision the ideal channel for efficient delivery of value to the end consumer, and the part each channel member will play in this process.

CHANNEL STRUCTURE

Like most executional elements of the Big Picture, our decisions about channel structure should tie directly back to our business and marketing objectives, source of volume, and most importantly, our customer. We also want to establish a strategic link between these decisions and our overall marketing strategy. Let's next consider three strategic channel structure decisions we must make: channel length, channel breadth, and channel depth.

Channel Length

Channel length refers to the number of channel members engaged in delivering the product to the end customer. At one end of the spectrum is **direct distribution**, a structure with few or no intermediaries between the manufacturer and the end customer. Direct channel users like Dell and Amazon.com enjoy a number of benefits, most notably increased control over product, money, and information flows.

Direct distribution represents a short channel length; as we move to longer channels with more members, we are moving toward **indirect distribution** (Figure 12.1). A packaged goods manufacturer, for instance, processes its goods through a wholesaler, a distributor, and then a retail grocer before they reach the end customer. Intermediaries add value to the channel by performing the various functions mentioned above. In addition, they improve exchange effectiveness and efficiency by reducing the number of transactions; the reason is that instead of visiting 60 different wholesalers to buy 60 different products, a retailer can elect to go to a distributor to get all of these products, and 60 transactions become one.

The wholesaler that supplies the distributor experiences the same benefit: instead of shipping its product to 100 different customers, it can ship 100 products to the distributor and all those customers can simply visit that distributor. Consider an extreme case in which each manufacturer of packaged goods such as frozen food, paper towels, and laundry detergent elects to sell directly to the end consumer through company-owned stores. By removing the grocer, the manufacturers are able to save money and lower prices. However, in order to fill his or her pantry the consumer would have to visit 20 different stores instead of one. This is one basic reason for the use of indirect rather than direct channels.

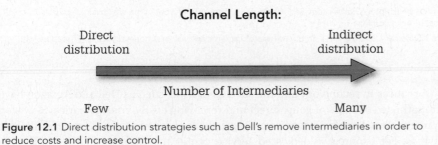

Channel Length:

Direct distribution

Indirect distribution

Number of Intermediaries

Few

Many

Figure 12.1 Direct distribution strategies such as Dell's remove intermediaries in order to reduce costs and increase control.

social**media**

Borders vs. Amazon: Using Social Media to Deliver Product Utility

In February 2011, the 40-year-old retail bookseller Borders Inc. filed for bankruptcy, citing unwise expansion as a core problem leading to an overabundance of long-term leases on unprofitable stores. But several other factors contributed to its collapse as well. Among them was the rise of popular online retailers, including the heavily diversified Amazon.com, and a failure on the part of the Borders management to understand the potential value to book buyers of social media.

Instead of channeling more resources into keeping up with increasing Internet demand, Borders outsourced its online business to Amazon from 2001 until 2008. This meant that visitors to the Borders website were automatically redirected to Amazon.com. Once at the Amazon site, consumers experienced the positive benefits of being among a community of online book buyers: they could sort books based on reviews by other readers, see what other readers with similar purchase patterns were buying, post "Listmania" lists of book recommendations on a particular topic, and create or browse a gift registry. For many Borders customers who already appreciated information and recommendations for books, these social media features created lots of value.

Ironically, at the same time that Amazon was using social media to deliver more value, Borders' management elected to discontinue many long-standing hiring, training, and incentive policies that were intended to maximize employees' product knowledge, expertise, and general passion for books. For example, all prospective employees had been asked to take a quiz testing their general knowledge of books and literature. This practice had ensured a positive in-store experience for customers looking for good book recommendations.

For consumers searching for just the right book to read among the millions available, the added value of product

© KingWu/iStockphoto

© nazdravie/iStockphoto

expertise and product selection provided by the channel member can be crucial. For many years, Borders delivered this value through its employees, and an increasing number of independent booksellers are now filling the void left by Borders by continuing the tradition of "hand-selling" books. In the meantime, Amazon's clear understanding of the value of social media in delivering product selection and product expertise demonstrates what the proper use of social media tools can drive.

"So you think you could have worked at Borders?" *CNN U.S.* September 12, 2001. http://www.cnn.com/2011/US/09/09/borders.quiz/index.html. Accessed May 15, 2013.

Frazier, Mya. "The three lessons of the Borders bankruptcy," *Forbes.com*. February 16, 2011. http://www.forbes.com/sites/myafrazier/2011/02/16/the-three-lessons-of-the-borders-bankruptcy/. Accessed May 12, 2013.

Lowrey, Annie. "Readers without Borders," *Slate.com*. July 20, 2011. http://www.slate.com/articles/business/moneybox/2011/07/readers_without_borders.html.

Advances in technology and the success of firms such as Dell and Amazon have strengthened the lure of going direct and removing costly intermediaries. However, in many cases benefits lost by removing a channel member can far exceed the cost savings. For example, a dedicated service center may seem expensive until it is

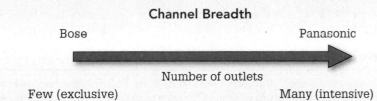

Channel Breadth

Bose   Panasonic

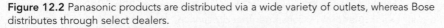

Number of outlets

Few (exclusive)   Many (intensive)

Figure 12.2 Panasonic products are distributed via a wide variety of outlets, whereas Bose distributes through select dealers.

eliminated, service levels decline, and long-term customers go elsewhere. No channel member should be eliminated until its added value has been realistically assessed. The channel should be long enough to ensure that key benefits and functions are performed, and short enough to ensure sufficient control of product, money, and information.

Channel Breadth

Channel breadth refers to the number of outlets that participate in distributing the end product to the consumer. As represented in Figure 12.2, it can range from *exclusive* distribution through a very limited number of outlets, to *selective* distribution through more outlets with a certain level of sales training and service, to *intensive* or *mass* distribution via as many outlets as possible, which minimizes travel and search costs for the end consumer.

Very often the breadth of the channel depends on the type of product attribute the firm is seeking to promote. Consider a case of exclusive distribution: Cartier watches, distributed only in limited, upscale locations by authorized retailers. These high-end watches are awash in credence attributes, and the channel itself helps establish these attributes for consumers. The exclusive Cartier retailer is thus an important part of the packaging and promotion for the product.

When the firm seeks to emphasize search attributes, particularly for a more complex product such as an automobile, a selective distribution strategy is more appropriate. Here we limit the number of outlets not only to establish an image, but also to ensure our ability to properly educate the sales force as they market our product. The added value of the Volvo dealer is product utility in the form of the salesperson who can identify the needs of the customer and match them to the right product and features.

Finally, a product may be distributed on a mass or intensive scale. Most items that are low in cost and complexity and high in experience attributes, such as packaged goods, fall into this category: Huggies diapers are available in grocery stores, drug stores, Walmart, Target, and other outlets. The key benefit added by the channel for mass distribution is time utility in the form of ease of access. Wide availability encourages consumers to try and experience these low-involvement products without expending substantial effort.

Channel Depth

Channel depth refers to the extent to which the channel is controlled, via forward and/or backward integration, by one or a few key channel members. In a highly

Channel breadth. The number of distribution outlets at which the product is available.

Channel depth. The degree to which a particular channel member controls a substantial portion of the channel via forward and/or backward integration.

NEW PRODUCTS/INNOVATION

AMAZON, ONLINE BOOK RETAILER OR MASS DISTRIBUTOR?

With a wave of new technological innovations, the web-based retail company Amazon.com is positioning itself as a mass distributor of goods, now that thousands of web-based merchants use it as a distribution platform for their own companies. Investments in new technology have made the site a central, easy-to-use hub of free services and information around which tens of thousands of external retailers have written applications and started businesses. ScoutPal, for instance, allows a user to instantly access a book's selling price on Amazon, and other programs help users instantly list products they would like to sell on Amazon.

Other fast and convenient tools like Amazon's one-click purchasing system attract merchants who want to sell directly to the 121 million consumers in its worldwide customer base. Amazon receives a commission of around 15% on such sales. By the end of 2012, 40% of the units sold on Amazon came from outside merchants, compared to 22% in 2003.

Advances in internal technologies have liberated Amazon from some of the ordinary demands of a retail company. Between 1999 and 2003, for instance, the company tripled the volume of goods it could handle and halved its cost of operations. These improvements allowed it to offer more consumer-friendly services, such as free shipping on orders over $25 and two-day product delivery for an annual fee of $79 through Amazon Prime, which other retailers struggle to compete with. It also meant an increase in the capacity of Amazon's Merchant.com business to run the e-commerce divisions of other retailers.

E-commerce currently represents 6.3% of all retail sales, but this figure is growing by 10 to 14% a year and may reach 30% in the next decade. Amazon's revenue jumped from $3.93 billion in 2002 to $9.91 billion in 2011; the company held a 10% market share in online retail sales for North America in 2010 and a 22% market share worldwide in 2012, followed by E-bay at 14%. By transitioning from an online retail outlet to a singular distribution service center, Amazon is quickly becoming indispensable to the daily operations of thousands of web users and their businesses, and as such a mass distributor in the online world. ∎

Shaughnessy, Haydn. "Why Amazon succeeds," *Forbes.com.* April 29, 2012. http://www.forbes.com/sites/haydnshaughnessy/2012/04/29/why-amazon-succeeds/. Accessed May 12, 2013.

Barr, Alistair. "Amazon revenue surges, stock jumps," *Reuters.* July 26, 2011. http://www.reuters.com/article/2011/07/26/us-amazon-idUSTRE76P6KB20110726. Accessed May 12, 2013.

Schrage, Michael. "Amazon's fire and the new integrated platform," *Harvard Business Review, HBR Blog Network.* September 29, 2011. http://blogs.hbr.org/schrage/2011/09/amazon-plays-with-fire.html.

integrated channel, the same company may own firms that perform many different channel functions: raw materials procurement, manufacturing, transportation, warehousing, and/or retail distribution. In a less-integrated channel, different, independent companies perform each of these functions. A deeper channel has more backward/forward integration, whereas a shallower channel is relatively less integrated.

Of course, the key advantage of integration is the increase in power and control it confers on the manufacturer. Gallo Winery (Figure 12.3) owns vineyards, cork and bottle manufacturers, trucks, and distributors, enabling it to control virtually all aspects of the wine production and distribution process. However, to the extent that performing each of these functions requires mastering different competencies, a single company might find it quite difficult to administer a substantial portion of the channel. For this reason, in the 1980s many firms began outsourcing channel functions, from customer service to R&D, by finding other, more specialized firms to perform them.

In many cases this strategy has been successful, but if the particular channel function has a high value-added benefit, outsourcing it can put the firm's customers at risk.

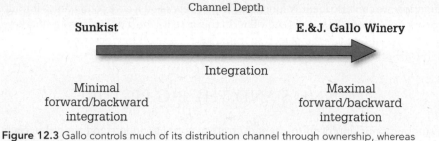

Channel Depth

Sunkist   **E.&J. Gallo Winery**

Integration

Minimal   Maximal
forward/backward   forward/backward
integration   integration

Figure 12.3 Gallo controls much of its distribution channel through ownership, whereas Sunkist does not.

For example, in the late 1990s Dell decided to outsource its customer-service phone lines. However, since the firm was using a direct-to-consumer strategy, its customer-service representatives were responsible for a crucial function that actually helped to differentiate the brand. Negative customer response was instant and powerful. By 2003, Dell had resumed providing its own customer service in order to address these issues.

Dell's experience should inform our decisions about outsourcing. Some managers have believed they could outsource any function that was not a core competence, and this remains true. However, if a function does or should contribute substantially to brand value and differentiation, it should not be outsourced. This decision is represented in Figure 12.4. When we are evaluating core competence and value added by

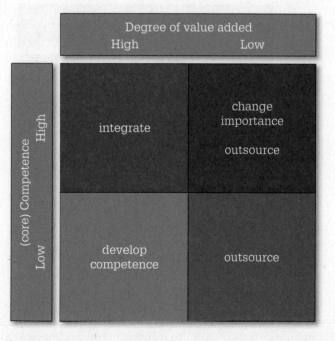

Figure 12.4 Channel depth decision matrix. Firms should seek to outsource functions for which they do not have a core competence and that do not provide a high added value, or differentiation.

a function, we can also identify functions that do represent a core competence for our firm but do *not* contribute to brand value. In this case we must either leverage marketing activities to change the perceived importance of this function or reduce our resource investment in it.

CHANNELS AND THE BIG PICTURE

In summary, our approach to channel strategy is to (1) understand the value each channel member adds (product, place, and/or time utility), and then (2) structure the channel to effectively and efficiently deliver that value. While channel strategy decisions are complex and tend to vary widely from industry to industry, our choice of marketing objective and source of volume can still help to focus and direct channel strategy, particularly with regard to the value our channel member adds. These relationships are illustrated in Figure 12.5, which recommends the type of utility to emphasize in each case.

Our choice of goal and time frame will also influence our channel strategy. A short-term time frame may lead us to rely on existing indirect channels to quickly build distribution. On the other hand, a profit goal suggests that we might want to remove channel members in order to lower our cost basis.

Figure 12.5 Channels and the Big Picture. The key benefits of channels change with each strategic quadrant. When we are stimulating demand, channel members play a critical role in helping us position the product appropriately. When we are earning share, channel members make the product available in the right places and in the appropriate level of intensity.

- In the case of acquisition/stimulate demand, our most important task is educating new customers about the benefits of our products, our brands, and the category. This task requires the delivery of product utility in the form of product selection, assortment, and the expertise to match consumers with products. It is in this quadrant that we ensure our consumers' first experience with our product is a positive one.

- In the case of retention/stimulate demand, we are still concerned with delivering product utility as the relationship between consumers and our brands deepens. In addition, though, we now want to offer time utility—having the right product, as well as the right parts and service, available when our consumers need it.

- For acquisition/earn share, we will continue to provide product utility, taking the competition into account. For example, our product assortment or selection should be comparable to our competition's, and we should use the channel to help our potential consumers understand why our benefits are superior.

- Finally, in the case of retention/earn share, our primary objective is to manage the channel in order to have our product, parts, and service conveniently available to our consumers when they need it. This ensures place and time utility.

Proper channel strategy and implementation are crucial for the success of our marketing efforts. Because channels are pervasive and difficult to change, we must employ the Big Picture framework in a disciplined fashion to ensure that our channel strategy is fully integrated with our overall marketing strategy.

☐ SUMMARY

1. Describe the key challenges of managing channels
Channels are *systems* consisting of many interrelated organizations. Some we may control directly, others we may not control at all; some share our goals, and others have goals of their own.

2. Identify the key purpose of a channel
The first purpose of all channel members is to maximize profits for the channel as a whole by profitably meeting the needs of the end consumer. Once they have achieved profit maximization, the channel members can allocate profits among themselves.

3. Explain how channel members add value
Channel members provide product utility, time utility, and place utility. Product utility refers to the specific benefit each channel member provides in relation to our products, such as product assortment, product inventory, or product selection. Time utility is the value channel members provide by helping reduce search time, increase speed of delivery, or ensure sufficient inventory at times of peak demand. Place utility is the value that channel members add by shortening the distance the consumer must travel to inspect, pay for, or receive the product.

4. Identify different channel flows and functions
Channels handle product, money, and information flows. The path raw materials and products take will affect how efficiently and effectively the channel functions. Channel members dedicated to facilitating the flow of money add value in a specific fashion, such

as by providing financing or handling payments for or between other channel members and/or the end customer. A specific channel member also may assume the task of negotiation, as do car dealers. Finally, in handling information flows, channel members may add value by amassing and presenting information, transforming it, or interpreting or reinforcing it.

5. **Define the different elements of channel structure**
Channel length refers to the number of channel members engaged in delivering the product to the end customer; from this perspective channels can be direct or indirect. Channel breadth refers to the number of outlets that participate in distributing the end product to the consumer. Breadth ranges from exclusive distribution to intensive or mass distribution. Channel depth refers to the degree of control the firm exerts over its channel members, generally through forward and/or backward integration. In a highly integrated channel, the company owns or controls many different channel functions; in a less integrated channel independent companies perform each of these functions.

6. **Integrate channels with other elements of the Big Picture framework**
Our choice of marketing objective and source of volume can still help to focus and direct channel strategy, particularly with regard to the value our channel member adds. In the case of acquisition/stimulate demand our channel should deliver product utility. In the case of retention/stimulate demand, the channel should deliver product utility and time utility. For acquisition/earn share, the channel should deliver product utility relative to the competitive brand. And finally for retention/earn share, the primary channel objective is delivering place and time utility.

☐ KEY TERMS

Channel breadth. (p.335) The number of distribution outlets at which the product is available.

Channel depth. (p.335) The degree to which a particular channel member controls a substantial portion of the channel via forward and/or backward integration.

Channel length. (p.333) The number of channel members in a particular value chain.

Direct distribution. (p.333) A structure with few or no intermediaries between the manufacturer and the end-customer.

Indirect distribution. (p.333) A longer channel structure with more members.

Place utility. (p.330) The benefit provided by channel members that provides convenient access to products.

Product utility. (p.329) The benefit provided by channel members that delivers product expertise, assortment, or selection.

SKU. Stock keeping unit. (p.329) A unique code that identifies each individual product in a retail store, used to track inventory in the channel.

Time utility. (p.330) The benefit provided by channel members that have the right product, parts, and services when consumers need them.

Value chain. (p.326) The terms value chain and supply chain are used to refer to firms who collaborate to bring value to an end consumer. These terms are also used to refer to the activities entailed in the design, manufacturing, and logistics of products and services.

☐ QUESTIONS FOR DISCUSSION

1. Channels facilitate flows not just of product, but also of information and money. If your firm is particularly concerned with collecting and disseminating information, how might this function affect your channel structure?

2. Most firms have outsourced functions in the channel that are *not* their core competence. However, sometimes this is not the best strategy. What other considerations are important when a firm decides whether to outsource?

3. The most profitable channels are those aligned with the marketer's purpose of creating value for the end consumer. Many well-managed channels also benefit from the direction of a *channel leader*, a strong channel member who protects the long-term sustainability of the value chain. Consider current examples of channel leaders such as Amazon and Intel, and discuss how they established this leadership.

Marketing Tool #12.1: Aim and Align the Channel

Managing channel partners is one of the most challenging elements of marketing execution. A key to effectively managing distribution channels is to understand the power dynamics. In mapping the current pathways to our customers, we seek to understand:

- Who are the channel players at each step?
- What role do they perform?
- What capabilities do they have?
- What are their motivations?

In turn, this information is critical in understanding:

(a) Whether the channel structure supports our chosen strategy, given our strategic focus and our positioning variable.

(b) What changes we might be able to make within the channel to enhance our overall marketing effort.

(c) Which channel member to target directly to help us shape our channel strategy. We will make this determination considering which channel member is most naturally aligned to our strategy and holds the most within the channel.

The following example maps the car distribution channel, listing all intermediaries between the manufacturer and the end user. We describe each channel member in terms of the added value it brings to the end user; the degree of power or control it has over the end user; the relative cost it adds to the overall channel, which also drives how it is compensated; the challenge it represents given the overall objectives of the manufacturer; and some potential alignment actions. In other words, how we can bring the channel member's actions in line with the manufacturer's overall strategic objectives.

In looking through the example in Table 12.1, you can assume the car manufacturer is executing a retention/stimulate demand strategy and has an objective of increasing profitability.

The manufacturer might decide to aim communications primarily at the dealers and Internet information sites and might try to enlist their help in aligning the rest of the channel members. You may use a similar format (Table 12. 2) to map the pathways to customers in a different industry, as a way to see the potential for channel conflict and to devise a way to resolve it.

1. **Channel Member.** List the channel members involved in getting the product from the manufacturer or supplier to the end user. Be sure to include any members engaged in the flows or product, money or information.

2. **Value-Added Benefit.** Describe the channel members' value-added benefit: what is the role of each channel member? Think about the members' overall role and their specific roles in relationship to end customers. In terms of end-customer benefits, channel value generally falls into one of the following categories:

(a) *Place or Spatial Convenience:* Providing convenient access to products and services.

(b) *Time:* Shortening order-delivery times, including facilitating financing and money flows.

(c) *Product:* Providing assortment or breadth of selection; facilitating small purchases, including delivering information.

Table 12.1 Aim and Align the Channel, Car Distribution Channel Example

Channel Member	Value Added	Degree of End-Customer Power	Relative Cost	Challenge	Alignment Actions
Manufacturer sales force	Product	Control product availability and dealer relationships	(1–5 or quantified) ~1 to 2% of new car pricing	Short-term focus	Back-end incentives to encourage support of profitable dealers
Dealers	Product, Time, Place	High customer control depending on service level and CRM systems	~5 to7% of new car pricing	Different incentives based on local relationships	Shift from top-line to profit incentives. Provide second-car purchase incentives
Used car dealers	Product (Selection), Time	Low control, acquisition-only business	>10% higher than private sale	One-time sale mindset	Sales reporting in exchange for limited promo $. Training support
Internet info sites	Product (Information)	High during the research process	low direct cost	Focus on enabling comparisons	Training and new product introduction "'peek preview". Co-promotional dollars.
Financing arm	Time (Financing)	Low product positioning impact	1% of new car pricing	Lack of price transparency	Collaborate on a model-by-model basis through co-financing offers to increase transparency

3. **Degree of End-Customer Power.** Describe how the channel member influences the end user's brand choice and purchase decisions. If possible, rate each channel member in terms of its relative power over the end user using a scale of 1 (low) to 5.

4. **Relative Cost.** Estimate the cost this channel member adds to the channel through a commission or markup to the product price. If you cannot easily obtain this information, rate each channel member in terms of the estimated cost using a scale of 1 (low) to 5.

Table 12.2 Mapping the Distribution Channel

Channel Member	Value Added	Degree of End-Customer Power (1–5)	Relative Cost (1–5 or quantified)	Challenge	Alignment Actions

5. **Challenge.** Given the information you have about the channel member, describe potential sources of conflict between the channel member's and the manufacturer's interests.

6. **Alignment Actions.** Brainstorm potential alignment actions to better integrate the channel member and to increase the overall value of the channel to the end user.

☐ RESOURCES

Coughlan, Ann, Erin Anderson, Louis Stern, and Adel El-Ansary: *Marketing channels*, 7th Edition. Prentice Hall, January 2006.

Hau, L. Lee. "The Triple-A supply chain," *Harvard Business Review*, October 2004, 1–11.

Rangan, V. Kasturi. *Transforming your go-to-market strategy: The three disciplines of channel management.* Harvard Business Press, 2006.

chapter thirteen

"A good thing it is," answered
Sancho, "to know those
herbs, for to my thinking it
will be needful some day
to put that knowledge into
practice."

The Project Gutenberg EBook of the History of
Don Quixote, Volume I, Complete by Miguel
de Cervantes, July 19, 2004 [EBook #5921],
Chapter 10.

INTEGRATED MARKET RESEARCH

After studying this chapter you should be able to:

1. *Explain the importance of discipline in market research*

2. *Assess the need to conduct market research*

3. *Effectively articulate a research question*

4. *List the major steps in designing a research project*

5. *Choose appropriate data collection methods and sources*

6. *Analyze and communicate the research results*

7. *Integrate research with other elements of the Big Picture framework*

Data-Driven Decision-Making: Gartner Research

Baran Özdemir/Getty Images

Gartner Research estimates that during any given minute in 2012, about 204 million emails were sent, 61,000 hours of music were heard on the online radio service Pandora, 3 million photos were uploaded to Flickr (and viewed 20 million times), 100,000 tweets were posted on Twitter, 6 million views occurred on Facebook pages, and 2 million Google searches were initiated.

It is no wonder the average company is increasing its data storage needs by almost 60 percent every year. However, most companies feel they underutilize their customer data. For example, the Marketing Leadership Council found that fewer than 30 percent of its financial institution members are effectively using customer data for such important activities as customer prospecting, product and service cross-selling, or customer segmentation. Today it is relatively cheap for marketers to acquire and store customer data, due to a continual decrease in technology costs. As a result of its ubiquity, using data for decision-making is becoming a competitive requirement rather than just a potential source of competitive differentiation.

In 2010 three researchers completed a research study of 179 corporations designed to understand the performance difference between firms that based their decision on data

analysis and those that simply used intuition. The study was primarily based on interviews and secondary research of company performance indicators. It compared firms on how much data they collected and whether they used that data to make strategic and executional decisions (what markets to enter, what products to develop, and the like). The researchers discovered a significant difference between companies using the science of "data and analysis" and those still managed through the art of "experience and intuition." Those that adopted data-driven decision-making achieved 5 percent to 6 percent higher productivity than could be explained by other factors, including how much they had invested in technology.

The purpose of research is to link the marketer to current and potential customers and the competitive environment through information. However, as the amount of data at our disposal increases enormously, thanks to websites, CRM systems, loyalty programs, and other streams, marketers face the challenge of distilling the relevant information from the vast amounts of data available. Yet strategy, not chance, should still drive our decisions about what data to collect and how to translate it into useful information. ■

Sources: Davenport, Thomas H., Jeanne G. Harris, and Robert Morison. "Analytics at work: Smarter decisions, better results," *Harvard Business Press*. February 8, 2010.

Lohr, Steve. "When there's no such thing as too much information," *The New York Times*. April 23, 2011. Accessed April 18, 2013.

Cooney, Michael. "Gartner: How big trends in security, mobile, big data and cloud computing will change IT. A quick roundup of IT trends, from Android adoption to cloud security," *Network World*. October 30, 2012. http://www.networkworld.com/news/2012/103012-gartner-critical-trends-263793.html.

ADOPTING A DISCIPLINED APPROACH TO MARKET RESEARCH

A disciplined approach to marketing research yields not only improved decision-making but also, more importantly, an enhanced ability to learn from our mistakes. While there are research projects we will always engage in as a matter of course, the best research is developed in response to specific, well-thought-out questions. At its core, research is the simple process of generating and attempting to test key hypotheses. As managers, we should constantly be engaged in the research process as we act, observe the results of our actions, and draw conclusions on which to base further action.

This chapter addresses some fundamental points about marketing research and decision-making and introduces the main marketing research techniques. The goal is to establish a baseline understanding of the marketing research discipline and its links to the key elements of the firm's strategy. We present the foundations as a series of logical steps, from assessing the need for research to ensuring the capture of organizational learning from the research process. The steps are:

1. Assess the need for research.
2. Articulate the research question.
3. Choose the research design.
4. Choose the methods and sources of data.
5. Analyze and communicate.
6. Evaluate the results.

ASSESSING THE NEED FOR RESEARCH

All marketing decisions are made under some uncertainty. No matter how much information we have, we can never predict outcomes with 100 percent confidence. Thus, it should be a given that the purpose of research is not to *eliminate* uncertainty, but instead to *reduce* it to a reasonable level. To reach this level, we need to estimate the return on investment of our research expenditure by asking a few simple questions:

> First, *how much uncertainty will I eliminate with this research project, and at what cost?* When we estimate cost we should consider both time and money resources, internal and external, that we will use in the research project.

> Second, *what is the value of this uncertainty reduction?* While we cannot perfectly assess this value, we should consider how we will benefit from the information. We are specifically concerned with potential incremental benefit vs. incremental cost.

> And finally, given the value of this uncertainty reduction, *is the return on this investment acceptable*, or would the firm be better served by allocating those resources elsewhere? The best market research, like the best marketing, is that which yields the highest return on our investment.

In general, the best return on our research investment will come from projects further to the left in the framework, where we are answering more strategic questions, because the decisions we make here constrain us substantially as we move toward execution on the right. Put another way, no amount of executional research can make up for a bad strategic decision—it is like trying to choose between

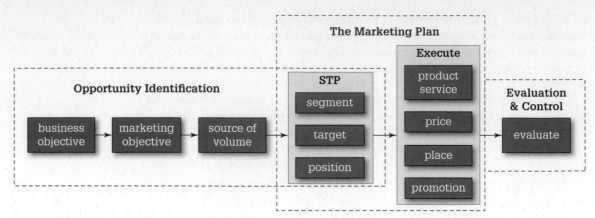

Figure 13.1 Market Research and the Big Picture.

Cross-sectional research. Research that collects data at one point in time across different samples of people or phenomena.

Longitudinal or time-series research. Research that collects data over a period of time, seeking to understand how the variable under study changes over time.

different grains of sand on a beach when we have chosen the wrong beach. All things being equal, a dollar spent to validate our choice of marketing objective will yield substantially higher returns than a dollar spent to substantiate our positioning strategy.

A final question we need to answer before embarking on any research project is whether it will be a one-time project or one that we will conduct repeatedly. For some types of research, such as collecting physical or demographic data like age, income, and geographic location of a target population, a large **cross-sectional** study—one that collects lots of data in a single time period—make sense. On the other hand, if we are interested in more dynamic data such as attitudes and purchase behavior, we are better served if we collect **longitudinal** information that captures trends in these attitudes or behaviors by taking similar measurements over time. For example, information about our customers' perceptions of our product or service is much more valuable if we can observe changes in these perceptions over time. We will thus maximize our learning from attitudinal market research when we ask the same questions frequently and observe the trends.

ARTICULATING THE QUESTION: MODELS

What will we do with our research information? If it is unlikely to generate any further action, then we should not undertake it. An effective research objective statement, on the other hand, *concisely* articulates the problem the research is meant to address, that is, the reason for conducting it. It then states the research question in a simple, straightforward manner. And finally, it formulates a hypothesis or model, the relationship among the variables that we hypothesize going into the research. The question we articulate will thus express a single-minded purpose for the research that the research methods available to us can address.

Problem: The management team of Phoenix Leasing Inc. is concerned that customer loyalty for their brand is decreasing. Over the last six months, the company's sales team has found itself in a number of highly competitive bidding situations in leasing program renewals for key customers. The management team fears that Phoenix's products and services are not perceived to be differentiated from their competitors'.

Question: What are the key benefits Phoenix's customers seek when choosing a provider? How do customers perceive Phoenix Leasing on these key benefits, and how does it compare to its main competitors?

The decline in customer loyalty is being driven by low approval rates and low perceptions of customer service relative to Phoenix's main competitors.

Figure 13.2 Example of a research statement for a fictitious leasing company, Phoenix Leasing.

The Research Statement

A classic research statement for experimental research contains the **independent** and **dependent variables**. In essence, we can think of independent variables as *cause* and dependent variables as *effect* in the cause-and-effect relationship. For example, when the outside temperature drops below 32 degrees for a period of time, we will likely observe the pond freezing. In this case the outside temperature is the independent variable and state of the pond (frozen or not) is the dependent variable. In the example presented in Figure 13.2, the independent variables are the key benefits Phoenix Leasing might offer its customers, including approval rates and customer service. The dependent variable is customer loyalty. Our hypothesis is that if we enhance our approval rates and customer service, we will see an increase in customer loyalty.

All good research is founded on good hypotheses about cause and effect. This can mean the difference between conducting cost-efficient and effective marketing research and wasting precious resources. If our going-in hypotheses are poorly framed, our research outcomes can lead to erroneous conclusions. Consider the case of the Nissan "Toys" advertising campaign, which aired in 1996 in the United States.[1] The TV commercial developed for this campaign was considered wildly successful; it generated significant awareness and a positive attitude toward the company. After about a month, however, dealers began to complain that the campaign was a failure: sales had not increased at all as a result of the ads. Despite the fact that, at the outset, the ad was popular among consumers and had won numerous awards, it was eventually deemed ineffective and pulled off the air.

Independent variable. A factor or variable that influences another factor (called dependent).

Dependent variable. A factor or variable that is influenced or is the outcome of other variables, called independent.

It is likely that the disappointing sales of the Nissan 300ZX were a result of poor alignment between communications and sales execution. Measuring marketing effectiveness requires having the right hypotheses in place about the relationships between marketing variables.

© Car Culture/Corbis

[1]http://vimeo.com/54537311#.

Obviously, there was a failure somewhere—the company did not achieve its sales targets. However, identifying the ad as the cause of the failure was a misdiagnosis based on a simplistic hypothesis that advertising increases sales, and that if sales do not increase, the advertising has failed and should be discontinued.

$$\text{Advertising} \rightarrow \text{Increased Sales}$$

This type of response can be quite costly. Marketing managers operate in an uncertain and dynamic environment; under such conditions we must naturally expect an inevitable number of failures. If we rely on simplistic models, we compound our failures because then we cannot learn from our mistakes and correct them going forward. By spending time to develop a more accurate model, we increase our chances not only of success, but also of identifying the true source of our failure in order to fix it going forward. It is this approach that will drive good research. In the case of Nissan, a better model might look something like this:

$$\text{Advertising} \rightarrow \text{Awareness \& Attitude Change} \rightarrow \text{Increased Dealer Visits} \rightarrow$$
$$\text{Increased Sales}$$

This model is a much better representation of the cause-and-effect linkages that connect advertising exposure and the actual purchase behavior we are seeking, and would be a much better foundation for any research we might wish to conduct in this case. The objective of the advertising campaign is to change attitudes toward the car, not to directly increase sales. Our further hypothesis is that attitude change will result in increased dealer visits, and this increase will in turn generate an increase in sales. Now we might draw a very different conclusion about the source of the failure.

The "Toys" campaign *did* in fact succeed in generating awareness and attitude change, and we should therefore consider it successful. Furthermore, the change in attitudes did increase dealer visits, supporting a potential research hypothesis that there is a relationship between attitude change and dealer visits. Unfortunately, these increased visits didn't lead to more sales, presumably because the product at the dealerships did not meet the expectations created by the advertising. Viewers of the ad campaign liked it because it was hip and cool, featuring a popular rock song, great visuals, and a very entertaining storyline. Unfortunately, when they went to the dealership they did not have a "hip" experience, and the product line, with the exception of the Z car, was composed of mini-vans and family coupes, decidedly un-cool. In essence, the same attitudes that drove people *into* the dealership drove them *right back out.*

The more sophisticated model allows us to better identify the specific failure so we can do further research, and, ultimately, fix our problems. In the Nissan case the executional failure occurred between the attitude change and the experience at the dealer. To fix this problem, we need to modify either the in-store experience (so it matches the expectations created by the advertising) or the expectations created by the advertising (so we can meet them at the dealership and in the product). This case demonstrates the importance of good models. Good models are key to good research and a good diagnosis of our problems.

Types of Models

The type of model we have decided to use drives the research process. These different models represent different approaches to research we use in order to (1) analyze the

CUSTOMERFOCUS

NESTLE'S SUCCESSFUL REPOSITIONING OF THE NESPRESSO BRAND THROUGH RESEARCH

In 1987 Nestlé purchased the intellectual property of a complete coffee system called Nespresso and hired Jean-Paul Gaillard to grow the brand around a single-serve coffee machine. Customers of Nespresso likened its brewed coffee to the best Italian espresso they'd ever had. Despite initial excitement about the venture, the first few years of the company's history were marked by slow growth. Gaillard summed up his early experience at Nestlé by saying: "For the first four years, I spent most of my time fighting the bureaucracy. . . . Nestlé didn't really believe in the product.[2]" Gaillard left Nespresso in 1996, when the brand's sales were only $250 million a year. Although it was growing, its parent company was disappointed.

In 2000 Nespresso conducted a large market research study and hired Future-Brand, a brand-consulting firm, to help reposition the firm and specifically target affluent coffee aficionados. By that

Interior of a Nespresso boutique, designed to create a luxurious experience as an integral part of the Nespresso brand image.

time, Starbucks had effectively redefined the coffee world for mainstream consumers, recreating the atmosphere of a European coffee shop and educating affluent consumers across the world about how to recognize and appreciate premium coffee. The stars were aligned for Nespresso's growth.

This market research information provided the impetus Nestlé needed to make a very large investment in propelling the brand forward. The company repositioned the brand as super-premium, targeted to the affluent world coffee aficionados identified by their market research study. In 2000 the company opened its first of what became more than 300 luxury coffee boutiques. Appropriately, the first was located on the elegant Champs-Elysées in Paris. By the end of 2012, Nespresso had reported 10 years of 30 percent compounded annual revenue growth. ■

Source: Levine, Joshua. "Pod of gold," *Time Magazine*, March 7, 2011. http://www.time.com/time/magazine/article/0,9171,2053573,00.html#ixzz2ll5e1D7v . Khamis, Susie. "Coffee," *M/C Journal 15(2)*, May 2012. http://journal.media-culture.org.au/index.php/mcjournal/article/viewArticle/476.

---

relationships between variables and (2) to predict outcomes from marketing actions based on those relationships. The Big Picture is an example of a *strategic model;* it is based on assumptions about the relationship between Marketing Objective and Source of Volume, and between the strategic elements on the left side of the framework and the tactical elements on the right side of the framework. When we are making specific choices within this model structure (e.g., how much money to spend to grow revenues from retained customers versus trying to acquire new customers) we can use market research to test the relationship between elements in this model (e.g., the relationship between spending on customer acquisition and average customer lifetime value).

A **behavioral model**, like our model of the consumer purchase process, attempts to predict consumer behavior based on the relationships among different types of key variables based on different assumptions. It assumes, for example, that attitudes drive behaviors. Although we may think this is obvious, the relationship between attitudes and behavior is not always strong. For example, people may report a very

Behavioral model. A model that attempts to predict consumer behavior by looking at relationships between variables, such as the relationship between attitudes and awareness and purchase behavior.

[2]Baxter, Andrew. "Nestlé Nespresso: Fast-rising brand," *The Financial Times*. April 27, 2009, 10:22 AM (www. ft.com). Last updated: April 27, 2009, 10:22.

positive attitude and intention toward charitable giving or health club attendance, but they do not always give to charity or go to the health club. Nonetheless, behavioral models can be the foundation of extremely valuable market research. This is particularly true for companies that have access to large amounts of behavioral data, such as Amazon, Spotify, and Netflix.

Another class of models of interest to market researchers is the **psychological model**, which describes how people process information and form attitudes. For instance, decision-making research looks at how consumers process information when comparing various products and how different approaches can lead to different attitudes. Do consumers evaluate products one at a time or do they collect product information to compare all products side-by-side? These different modes in processing style have different implications for marketing tactics ranging from pricing to distribution. For example, if market research reveals that customers are taking a side-by-side approach, the firm may produce materials that enable this type of comparison while presenting their product in a favorable light. On the other hand, if customers are using a sequential approach, retailers will encourage them to "shop us last."

Psychological model.
A model that describes how people process information and form attitudes.

RESEARCH DESIGN

Research design is our plan for addressing our research questions and hypotheses. A good research design gives us solid, actionable information. That said, selecting the design often requires us to make trade-offs between the quality of the data we are likely to collect and the cost of undertaking the research. Clearly we need to begin with a good understanding of the benefits and disadvantages of alternative designs. This chapter looks at general research designs, which we can categorize either by the *research methodologies* they use or by the *type of data* they collect. We look at each type next.

Research Methodologies

If we look at research designs in terms of their methodology, we find three broad types: **exploratory, descriptive**, and **experimental** *(or causal)*.

Exploratory Research

Exploratory research.
Research to determine whether we should pursue further research, and if so, in what particular area and manner.

Descriptive research.
Research that characterizes markets, industry competitors, target populations, customers, or a set of product features.

Experimental research.
Research that studies the impact of some *manipulation* on a particular outcome.

At any point during our strategic or executional analysis, we may need to gain additional insight into the environment in which we are operating. Exploratory research is just that: exploratory. We do this type of research to determine whether we should pursue further research, and if so, in what particular area and manner. For example, we may wish to explore market opportunities in a particular region or consider different possible ways to segment a market. Exploratory research can serve as a foundation on which to build hypotheses that we can subsequently test. Its purpose is thus not to test hypotheses, but rather to generate them so we can engage in further testing.

The types of exploratory research studies we use more often are *pilot studies*, surveys of a limited number of respondents via non-rigorous sampling techniques; *experience surveys*, input from experts who can provide guidance and insights into the research questions; *case study analysis*, reviews of similar situations to clarify the keys to the research question; and *secondary data analysis* or literature searches.

Descriptive Research

We use descriptive research to characterize markets, industry competitors, target populations, customers, or a set of product features. Descriptive research can be as simple as counting things—a retailer, for example, might count the number of cars passing through a particular intersection on an average day in order to decide whether to locate a store there. Marketers also often conduct descriptive research during segmentation, to understand the demographics in a particular market and decide whether it represents a substantial opportunity.

We may also utilize descriptive research to identify the attitudes and aspirations of a particular group of customers and, in doing so, test hypotheses about segmentation that we developed during exploratory research. We may, for example, have hypothesized that consumers who are strongly concerned with safety represent a viable target audience. We could conduct descriptive research to collect purchase information about other safety-related products such as insurance policies and home alarms to begin to quantify the size of our potential market.

Descriptive research is by no means limited to *STP* (segmentation, targeting, and positioning). We can use it to identify industry size, competitive share levels, color and fashion trends, frequency of new product launches, and so forth. The challenge is really choosing what to describe and at what level of detail. Instead of fielding omnibus studies to describe every aspect of a market or segment, we should use descriptive research (and all research) to answer specific, well-articulated questions, and to understand cause-and-effect relationships among variables, by observing how changes in one factor affect other factors in our model.

Experimental Research

Experimental research measures the impact of some *manipulation* on a particular outcome. For example, we might collect customer evaluations of a particular product (baseline data), then expose half of those respondents to a commercial (the manipulation) and collect evaluations of the product again (post-manipulation data) to identify the effect of the commercial, if any. Experimental research aims to uncover specific causal relationships as evidenced by two important qualities: first, the effect should follow the hypothesized cause, and second, when the independent variable (the cause) changes, there should be some *effect* on the dependent variable.

True experiments are also characterized by *random assignment to conditions;* that is, some consumers are chosen at random from the larger group exposed to the commercial or other stimulus. In many cases, for practical or ethical reasons it is not possible for us to perform a random assignment; then we are conducting a *quasi-experiment* and are somewhat more limited in the strength of the conclusions we can draw. Experiments and quasi-experiments help us understand the exact relationship between two variables. Therefore, marketers commonly use them to estimate the potential impact of, for instance, a price increase, a new product introduction, an ad campaign, or a shift in primary source of volume on outcomes like volume, top-line sales, or purchase frequency.

A common type of quasi-experiment is an in-market test in which we evaluate the impact of one specific action in certain markets. Companies like GfK BehaviorScan® conduct extensive in-market tests in carefully selected markets where many variables such as distribution, price, and product promotions can be monitored and controlled. Many academics and research firms also conduct true experiments under even more

Social Media Can Predict Elections: The 2012 Presidential Campaign

On November 3, 2012, Republicans expressed shock at the results of the presidential election: Barack Obama won 332 electoral votes to Mitt Romney's 206, and 51.4 percent of the popular vote. While traditional polling prior to the election tended to favor Obama, many polls were within the margin of error and some predicted a Romney victory.

Social media, however, told a different story. While both candidates had a presence on key social media sites such as Tumblr, Facebook, and Twitter, participation in the social media world was much richer and stronger for the Obama campaign. For example, Obama had more than 20,420,000 Twitter followers, while Romney had 1,225,000. Facebook likes exceeded 29,101,000 for Obama, while likes for Romney were less than 8,000,000. This trend was mirrored on YouTube, Pinter-est, Instagram, and even Spotify, where Obama's campaign playlist had 14,600 subscribers compared with 402 for Romney.

Obama's dominant relationship with voters in the digital world began with the 2008 election, when he recruited Chris Hughes of Facebook to help launch the online campaign. It was at this time that Obama's team learned that the interactive nature of social media makes it not simply a tool for communication, but also a tool for learning. In that campaign a key tool was My.BarackObama.com, a networking site that allowed Obama supporters to connect with one another. This page eventually spawned 400,000 blogs and raised $30 million. More importantly, the campaign was able to collect information about supporters and attitudes by monitoring blog posts and comments on a minute-by-minute basis.

Sources: Wortham, Jenna. The *Presidential Campaign on Social Media*. October 8, 2012. http://www.nytimes.com/interactive/2012/10/08/technology/campaign-social-media.html?_r=0. Accessed May 14, 2013. 2012 Presidential Election. Last updated November 29, 2012. Politico.com. http://www.politico.com/2012-election/map/#/President/2012/. Accessed May 15, 2013.
McGirt, Ellen. "How Chris Hughes helped launch Facebook and the Barack Obama campaign," *Fast Company*. April 1, 2009.

Qualitative research.
Research that collects data from a relatively small sample that is not randomly selected. Qualitative data is not generalizable to a larger population. However, it provides a nuanced or deep understanding of a particular phenomenon or sample.

Quantitative research.
Research that collects numerical data generally drawn from a sample which is representative of a larger population. Quantitative data is expressed numerically, and is amenable to mathematical manipulation enabling the researcher to draw conclusions that are generalizable to a larger population.

carefully controlled laboratory conditions; articles in academic publications such as *The Journal of Consumer Research* report their findings and serve as invaluable secondary research sources for managers.

Data-Driven Approaches

Another way we can describe market research is as **qualitative** or **quantitative**. While these two types of research often are considered distinct, they are better understood as two ends of a continuum.

Qualitative Research

At the qualitative end of the continuum are data commonly collected and reported in the form of words or other non-numerical means; this type of research takes a flexible, open-ended approach to discovery. For example, we may choose to do a day-in-the-life study of several customers, following them around and noting their behaviors and responses. We may or may not ask specific questions, and our questions may be open-ended queries from an interview guide or generated on the spot based on individuals' specific responses to stimuli.

We may also wish to understand what aspects of the service we provide are important to our customers, through a method such as **Critical Incident Technique (CIT)**. In a typical CIT interview, we ask a customer to review a recent service experience with our company and describe the most memorable aspects, either very good or very bad. CIT can uncover potential segmentation variables for further study, areas for service improvement, or salient aspects of a service experience that we can further develop based on our positioning variable (see Marketing Tool 13.1).

Qualitative research can generate exceedingly rich information and often leads to deep insights, particularly about customer attitudes. Because of the inherent flexibility of most qualitative research techniques, however, the skill level of the researcher is of paramount importance. For research in general and for qualitative research in particular, the researchers themselves will always somewhat influence both the outcomes and the conclusions. Even in pure observational research, in which data collection is conducted unobtrusively without interacting with the customer, the researcher can influence both what specific data is collected and how it is analyzed and reported.

Qualitative research generally relies on a small number of respondents, because its nature requires that we spend more time with each. This means that when we analyze the data, we must avoid creating averages or percentages and assuming they are generalizable to a larger population. Most often we use qualitative research in a more exploratory fashion instead, to generate insights and ideas for possible further research. Averages and other numerical conclusions require larger samples and are better suited to quantitative methods, which we look at next.

Quantitative Research

At the extreme quantitative end of the data-driven research continuum, we collect and report data in strictly numerical form. Quantitative data includes market share data, industry growth trends, or responses to specific survey questions. Quantitative data must be collected systematically and in sufficient quantities to allow us to apply standard statistical techniques. This illustrates one of the essential trade-offs between qualitative and quantitative research: we give up the richness, depth, and flexibility we can obtain with a small number of respondents for the breadth and statistical reliability we find with quantitative research on a larger group. In qualitative designs an interviewer is free to modify, add, or delete a question based on an earlier response; in contrast, in quantitative research *consistency* is key. An interviewer in a quantitative study must try to ask the same questions of all respondents *in the same manner and under the same conditions*.

Many managers feel more comfortable with quantitative than qualitative research; when information appears in numerical form it seems more objective. We can also perform statistical analyses on numbers to test our results for validity and reliability. **Validity** is a measure of how verifiable and true a piece of information is; for example, we may ask someone to report his age and validate this information with birth records. **Reliability** is simply consistent predictability over time regardless of validity; for example, if a watch is consistently five minutes fast it is always *wrong*, but we can still rely on it for a certain type of information. While it is true that with quantitative data we can leverage statistical tools to test for reliability and validity, this does not necessarily mean that quantitative data is more objective or valuable than qualitative research. In both cases the assumptions and attitudes of the researchers can interact with and influence the data; this influence is simply felt in different ways. In a quantitative survey project, for example, our choice and wording of questions reflect our personal assumptions and attitudes.

Critical Incident Technique (CIT). A qualitative research technique designed to uncover memorable experiences, either very good or very bad, as a way to discover the most salient attributes of a product or service.

Validity. The extent to which our data accurately captures the information we are seeking.

Reliability. The extent to which repeated measurements of a variable yield the same answer.

A telling example occurs when college-age students are asked to create a questionnaire that includes demographic data. A fair number devise categories for ages as follows:

— Less than 16 years old

— 16–20 years old

— 20–30 years old

— Greater than 30 years old

NEW PRODUCTS/INNOVATION

INNOVATION: NEUROMARKET RESEARCH

Neuromarketing is a science based on the fact that up to 95% of our thoughts, emotions, and learning occur before we are ever aware of them, according to Roger Dooley, author of *Neuromarketing* and *Brainfluence*.[3] Consumer decision-making, too, combines immediate unconscious emotional response with slower conscious response. We have all made an impulsive expensive purchase that we later rationalized as being good, for example. The fact that many of our strongest responses happen in our subconscious, and up to 200 times faster than our conscious verbal or conscious responses, also means that sometimes what we say and what we end up doing are quite different. This poses difficulties for attitudinal research. However, it also opens up possibilities for deeper research into subconscious responses that maps the brain and its electrical firings in response to different marketing messages. This is just what neuromarketing research does.

A now-famous use of neuromarketing research is a study performed by Professor Read Montague, who was interested in the puzzle of the Pepsi Challenge. According to blind tests shown in television advertising during the 1970s and 1980s, people prefer Pepsi's taste to Coke's. So why is it that Coke has maintained higher global market share than Pepsi? Montague used brain imaging to conduct his

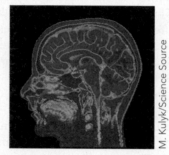

M. Kulyk/Science Source

own Pepsi Challenge in 2003. With an MRI machine, he tracked subjects' brain activity while they drank Coke and Pepsi and found that half said Pepsi tasted better in a blind taste as advertised, and neural activity was consistent with this response. However, when he let people see the brand of the drink they were sipping, 75 percent said Coke tasted better, and observations of brand activity also reflect this difference.

Since then, many companies have taken advantage of this new market research technique that involves the use of MRI and other monitors of brain activity. For example, Campbell's used neuroresearch as the basis for making a major change to its iconic soup labels for the first time in decades. Chrysler, Jack Daniels, and others are also using neuromarketing techniques to better capture people's emotional responses to their product designs and advertising visuals.

Some of the early general insights arising from neuromarketing research are that people react more strongly to visuals than to long text; that they connect better with advertising when it appeals to a specific need than when it is generic; and that concise, focused communications are always better than lengthy and complex ones. These insights are not new, but they should inspire advertisers to reduce clutter and develop more effective and transparent messaging. ∎

Sources: McClure, Samuel, Jian Li, Damon Tomlin, Kim Cypert, Latane Montague, and P. Read Montague. "Neural correlates of behavioral preference for culturally familiar drinks," *Neuron,44*(2): 379–387, October 14, 2004.

Megget, Katrina. "The neural frontier," *Pharma Times UK.* November 2012. http://www.neuroinsights.com/.

Mueller, MP. "The secret of neuromarketing: Go for the pain," *The New York Times.* August 7, 2012. http://boss.blogs.nytimes.com/2012/08/07/.

[3]Doyle, Roger. *Brainfluence: 100 ways to persuade and convince customers with neuromarketing.* Wiley, February 2012.

Of course, in the general population more than half the people are older than 30 years; however, to a college-age student the most relevant categories seem to be in the under-30 set! This example underlines the fact that numbers are not necessarily more objective than words.

The Data-Methodology Relationship

We've now seen why, when we engage in research, we must decide what type of data we are interested in and what research method we will employ. These two decisions are not independent; we must also consider the relationship between data and research methodology. Qualitative research is often exploratory, for instance, and descriptive research is often quantitative. Nonetheless, many combinations are possible, as Figure 13.3 illustrates.

While exploratory research is often qualitative, it is quite reasonable to conduct exploratory research using quantitative data as well, such as whenever we want to brainstorm options for further exploration. **Data mining** is an electronic means of combing through extremely large quantities of data (such as sales, demographic, or behavioral data) to uncover possible relationships or insights for this purpose. Exploratory research is generally undertaken to encourage openness and creativity, rather than to seek confirmation and certainty. It is generally followed by some type of descriptive or experimental research to help us select from among the alternatives we have developed and is thus a natural first step in a two-step process.

The exploratory step can occur at any point in the Big Picture framework. In the Business Objective chapter, for example, we might generate hypotheses about potential core competences, possibly by having open-ended discussions with managers, customers, and opinion leaders. At the executional end of the framework, in Marketing Communications, we might engage in research to identify different promotional options by doing an in-depth exploration of competitors' promotional tactics and customer responses to them.

On the other hand, while we usually think of quantitative research in connection with experiments, we can also apply an experimental approach to it. For example, suppose we have several different positioning concepts for a particular product. We might test these concepts by sharing different ones with different groups of consumers and then observing how they behave on a simulated shopping trip.

Whatever our research needs, we will want to consider a wide variety of research plans before committing valuable time and resources to the process. This careful consideration will increase our chances of efficiently generating knowledge and insights we can act upon.

	Qualitative	**Quantitative**
Exploratory	focus groups, depth interviews	data mining, initial market assessments
Descriptive	projective research	share data, usage and attitudes survey
Experimental/ Quasi-experimental	concept testing	in-market tests, simulated test market

Figure 13.3 Types of research designs.

DATA COLLECTION: METHODS AND SOURCES

Once we have stated and prioritized exactly *what* information we are looking for, we must decide *how* to collect it. Further, we must find out whether the information already exists, or we need to undertake new research to obtain it. Efficiency is the goal; that is, we want to reduce uncertainty as much as possible for each dollar we spend in research. In practice, this means selecting research techniques that have the greatest chance of providing us with accurate, actionable data given our research question.

In marketing, continual demands for more information coupled with ongoing technological advances have spawned countless market tools, techniques, and trends. A manager seeking to choose from among these should be aware of the "tools to theories" effect.[4] This occurs when, instead of developing a hypothesis and then searching for the appropriate tool with which to test it, we become enamored of a particular tool and let that tool drive our hypothesizing. When we are working with market research firms that specialize in a particular approach and toolset, we may be encouraged to choose the tool first. To avoid this urge, instead let our information needs drive our decisions regarding how we will collect information.

Collection Methods

There are two basic methods of data gathering, interactive and observational. **Interactive** methods use questionnaires or face-to-face communication with the subjects of the study to obtain facts, attitudes, or opinions. These methods can be qualitative (e.g., focus groups and in-depth interviews) or quantitative (surveys and questionnaires). **Observational** research records subjects' actions or responses without direct interaction. It includes a variety of techniques ranging from human observation (such as following customers in a retail store as they walk through the aisles) to electronic or computer-based means (recording click patterns on the Internet or scanner data at

GLOBALMARKETING

SIMPLIFYING CUSTOMER SATISFACTION RATINGS: CHINA AND TAIWAN

While many companies field customer satisfaction surveys to their customers, response rates are generally a problem. This problem is compounded for service companies serving a multilingual customer base. The Chinese government has come up with a solution to this problem for its customs and immigration "customers." It has installed electronic customer satisfaction meters in its immigration counters so that travelers can easily provide feedback to the authorities about their experience with the immigration staff. ■

Sample customer satisfaction ratings

© Olga Danylenko/ iStockphoto

Sources: The China Post News Staff. "Immigration Agency installs device allowing instant feedback," *The China Post.* August 3, 2010, 9:26 AM.

---

[4]Gigerenzer, G. (1991). From tools to theories: A heuristic of discovery in cognitive psychology, *Psychological Review, 98*: 254–267.

supermarkets). Netflix employs observational data about customers' viewing choices in combination with an algorithm to recommend additional movies and shows.

Data Sources

Our decision about data sourcing will have important implications from both a cost and a control perspective. We need to decide whether we are going to do **primary research**, in which we collect the data ourselves, or obtain **secondary research** that has already been conducted.

Primary research is customized; we develop it for our specific firm and our specific research question. This type of research is **proprietary**; that is, it may be used only by the sponsoring firm. Because it is developed specifically to meet our research needs, primary research is more likely to yield useful and actionable information. Furthermore, because this information is not publicly available, it is unlikely that our competitors will be able to benefit from it, at least not in the short term. Many Internet-based firms including Amazon, Pandora, and Facebook have recently sought to develop a core competence based on primary research, predicting their customers' buying behavior and attitudes toward particular books, movies, and songs.

Because primary research is customized, it is usually relatively expensive in terms of both time and money. In dynamic markets where short time to market and flexibility are critical, the opportunity cost of primary research can be high, particularly when measured in terms of time. Furthermore, while primary research is proprietary, our competitors may be able to deduce from the market actions we take what we have spent so much time and money to find out. For example, if we launch a campaign targeting a particular demographic group, our competitors may quickly realize that we have identified this group as a potentially lucrative opportunity. In this case we are simply serving as a market research firm for our competitors. On the other hand, sometimes we can successfully use primary research to establish a **first-mover advantage,** a market share advantage sometimes enjoyed by the first firm to introduce a product in a category. This occurs if we can protect the benefits of early market entry with patents or strong market position.

Secondary research is collected by a third party and then made available for sale or simply disseminated for public use. Many government agencies and regulatory bodies collect and distribute vast quantities of demographic information each year; universities around the world generate mountains of freely available data and information; and a number of trade organizations and research firms issue periodic studies on a variety of topics and industries. Thanks to the Internet, this information is now readily accessible and easy to search and analyze. Of course, it is equally available to our competition, which can make it more difficult to establish a sustainable competitive advantage with it. Nonetheless, a firm that can leverage secondary data efficiently and effectively can realize tremendous advantages.

Using secondary research demands relatively fewer time and money resources than generating primary research. Perhaps the most important implication of this is the speed with which it can be obtained: all we need to know is where to find it. Unfortunately, this resource benefit comes at a cost in terms of loss of customization and confidentiality. Secondary data is not proprietary. Nonetheless, the sheer quantity and variety available in most markets makes secondary research a valid consideration for many needs.

Primary research. Carrying out data gathering first-hand, that is, by sourcing it from the population we are seeking to investigate. Primary research can be conducted through a third party.

Secondary research. A gathering of second-hand data, that is, data collected by a third party for their own purposes.

GLOBALMARKETING

MARKET RESEARCH AND PRIVACY RESTRICTIONS

Privacy laws in Europe are a lot more restrictive than in the United States, making data collection about shoppers' habits more challenging, particularly online. For example, European data protection laws prohibit companies from tracking users via web bugs and cookies unless they have consent from the user. Tracking users with cookies can allow web pages to tailor ads, which is commonplace in the United States but not allowed in Europe. As of March 2012, Google changed its internal privacy policy to be able to pool data across all its products (YouTube, Google+, Google Apps, and Android Apps) as a way to obtain a more holistic view of Internet user patterns. This might have gone unnoticed in the United States, but European regulators immediately contacted the company, and by the end of

Baris Simsek/Getty Images

2012 they had issued a notice to Google telling it to change its privacy practices or risk being sued by the European Commission. ∎

Sources: Cellan-Jones, Rory. "Google told to fix privacy policy by EU data regulators," *BBC News/Technology.* October 16, 2012. http://www.bbc.co.uk/news/technology-19959306. Accessed February 3, 2013.

Gray, Peter. "Protecting privacy and security of personal information in the global electronic marketplace," http://www.ftc.gov/bcp/icpw/comments/ico2.htm. Accessed February 13, 2013.

ANALYZE AND COMMUNICATE RESULTS

The final step in the research project is the analysis and interpretation of results. Of course, good researchers avoid wasting research resources by doing a great deal of preparation before collecting the data to ensure the results are valid and generalizable. They choose appropriate measurement scales, use phrase survey questions, construct valid samples, and conduct trial runs to help ensure the success of the study.

The market researcher should therefore have a detailed plan prior to collecting the data that considers what form the finished results will take and how they will be used. Our vision of the research report combined with the type of data we have collected will determine the specific analysis we conduct. This analysis may be as simple as a synopsis of important quotes and themes from depth interviews, or as complex as an extensive statistical analysis. Regardless of the specific type of analysis, it is always advisable to consider in advance how this report might look.

In preparing to communicate our results, we first need to think about our audience. Their degree of familiarity with the issue at hand, their technical competence, and the setting for the delivery of the research results are all factors that will determine how we approach the report. An effective research report restates the research objective and then concisely and clearly summarizes the research design, research methodology, sources of data, and analysis methodology. Then it goes on to present the answers to the research question. Ideally it is a succinct document. Analyses that do not relate to the hypothesis or yield irrelevant results should not be presented, and low-level detail should be confined to the appendices.

INTEGRATION: MARKET RESEARCH AND THE BIG PICTURE

Continuous success in the marketplace requires that we abide by two tenets:

$$\text{Fail} \rightarrow \text{Correct}$$
$$\text{Succeed} \rightarrow \text{Replicate}$$

In other words, when the results of our marketing efforts are not as hoped, we need to be able to identify quickly and specifically the point of failure in order to correct it for future efforts. When we succeed, we should seek to understand how to replicate that success. To do so, we must ensure that we succeeded for the right reasons, that is, that tactical events unfolded according to our strategy. If we grow overconfident in the face of success and don't seek to understand *why* we have done well, we will not be able to sustain our success.

In the service of continuous learning, we will generate questions and collect information to answer these questions as we work through the framework. These questions will range from strategic to executional as we move from left to right in the framework as presented in Figure 13.4. The most important questions we will answer are the strategic questions related to business objective, marketing objective and source of volume. By gaining a clearer understanding of our core competence, goals, customers, and competition we will ensure that our work in execution will produce results not just in the short run, but over time.

Research in STP is crucial to ensure that our execution reflects our strategy. All too often firms get lost at this stage of the process, engaging in extensive communications research projects that can sometimes confuse and complicate issues instead of keeping them clear and defined. Research here should be focused on (1) selecting the correct main and dynamic benefits, and (2) assessing our success and changing perception and importance of these benefits.

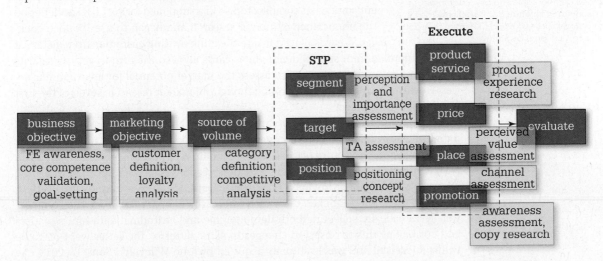

Figure 13.4 Market Research and The Big Picture

As we move into execution we may engage in more detailed research that is specific to the tactics we are implementing. Much of the task of measuring execution is an issue of metrics, as opposed to market research as presented here. In Chapter 14 we present this important topic in detail.

It is also important to note that the nature of our market research will be driven by our choice of strategic quadrant. Our strategic quadrant determines who we will be talking to, and what we are interested in learning from them.

For acquisition/stimulate demand, we are interested in learning from people who are outside the category. These consumers may or may not have knowledge or awareness of the category benefits. Our job here is to understand what they do and do not know, and what is preventing them from entering the category.

If we are pursuing an acquisition earn share strategy, we are interested in gaining insights from users of a competitive brand or segment. In particular, we wish to identify those users who might be willing to switch, and then understand how we can persuade them to switch.

For retention stimulate demand we will be speaking with current users of our brand, seeking to understand what they value about our brand, and what could make them value us more.

The Dummies book series used feedback cards to assess consumer reactions to its titles and combined demographic and psychographic information to plan future book releases. The series became wildly successful and had more than 250 million copies in print by Spring 2013.

Finally, for retention earn share we will conduct our research amongst multi-brand users. For these consumers we need to determine why they are using two or more brands, and whether and how we might persuade them to become loyal to our brand.

Market research is a process, not a project. In this chapter we have considered how to develop and test hypothesis about how our markets and consumers respond to our marketing activities. In the next chapter we will consider how to measure our impact on a continuous basis using metrics.

After the successful launch of its first few computer-related books for nontechnical people, IDG Books Worldwide, creator of the Dummies™ series, sought to expand by publishing more titles with the same friendly tone and Dummies trademark. All of these books present somewhat complex topics in a simplified format. IDG understood the importance of market research and began to use "bounce back" cards, cards placed inside the book inviting customers to register for further information or special deals. These cards allowed the firm to get to know its customer base a little better and to assess the market potential for its expanding series. However, despite some apparently thoughtful market research, seven of the first nine publications failed.

It turned out that IDG had not carefully thought through its research design and data integration questions. The company's president later recounted that his firm had failed to create an inventory of those customer names or perform any data analysis on psychographic information (including readers' responses to the important question, "How do you feel about buying a book that describes you as a 'dummy'?"). By 1991, however, when IDG launched the widely successful *DOS for Dummies,* the company was systematically collecting both demographic and attitudinal data on its readers and correlating this to observed changes in sales patterns. The series went on to be wildly successful and was eventually acquired by John Wiley and Sons. By 2013, the

Dummies ™ series had more than 1,800 titles, with total books in print of over 250,000,000.[5]

By using research to learn from failures, we can extract value from an otherwise negative situation and learn what we need to do in order to replicate successes. We'll return to this point in greater detail in the discussion of metrics in Chapter 14.

Market research is an enormous, dynamic area of study that we can only touch on in this book. Even the most seasoned marketer can easily get lost in the research, wasting valuable resources finding out something the organization already knows or doesn't really need to know. It is thus crucial to have a clear question in mind *before* undertaking any research, a clear plan of action based on potential research outcomes, and a confidence that the potential value of the research in terms of uncertainty reduction will justify the cost. The questions listed in Figure 13.5 should serve as a checklist as you develop your research plan.

MARKET RESEARCH PROCESS AND KEY QUESTIONS

1. Assess the Need for Research
   (a) What is the general problem or decision the research will address?
   (b) How much is the outcome of the research worth?
   (c) What is the total cost of the research?
   (d) Are there specific action plans for each outcome?
   (e) Is the research worth doing, given the above?

2. Articulate the Research Question
   (a) What are the specific questions the research can answer?
   (b) What are the hypotheses or models we would like to test?

3. Determine the Research Design
   (a) What type of methodology (exploratory, descriptive, experimental) is best suited for the type of research question we are asking?
   (b) What type of data would we like to collect?

4. Determine the Methods and Sources of Data
   (a) Has anyone already answered all or part of the research question?
   (b) Who is my research target?
   (c) How will we reach them (communication, observation) and through what means?
   (d) Do we need a statistically-significant sample?
   (e) Have we made sure the research instrument is *limited to the research scope*?
   (f) How will we collect, tabulate, code, and store the data?

5. Analyze and Communicate
   (a) How will we analyze the data?
   (b) Is the presentation as *concise* as possible?
   (c) Is the presentation of the research results appropriate for our audience?

6. Evaluate
   (a) Has the research provided specific answers to the questions at hand?
   (b) What have we learned?
   (c) What are our next steps?

Figure 13.5 Sample questions of the market research process.

---

[5]http://www.dummies.com/Section/Ten-or-So-Eye-Popping-Statistics.id-420239.html. Accessed May 15, 2013.

1. Understand the importance of discipline in market research

A disciplined approach to marketing research yields not only improved decision-making, but also, more importantly, an enhanced ability to learn from our mistakes. Without a disciplined approach, we run the risk of making bad decisions or at least wasting precious time and money resources. With a disciplined approach, we step through the processes to develop a sound research project.

2. Assess the need to conduct market research

The first step in the research process is assessing the need for research. This includes a cost-benefit analysis, when we consider the potential value of the research in terms of uncertainty reduction. If the potential value of this research exceeds the cost of doing it, we must consider whether the expected return on investment justifies going ahead.

3. Effectively articulate a research question

An effective research objective statement *concisely* articulates the problem the research is meant to address, that is, the reason for conducting it. It then states the research question in a simple, straightforward manner. And finally, it formulates a hypothesis or model.

4. List the major process steps in designing a research project

Exploratory methods are helpful when we need to further define the phenomenon we are studying, or we need to understand the population in which we are interested, in more detail prior to doing more in-depth research. Descriptive methods are useful if we just need to draw broad information about the attitudes, demographics, or other characteristics of the category, market, or population we are trying to study. Finally, experimental research is designed to understand quite specifically the relationship between two variables that we are able to manipulate. We combine these three methods of conducting research with two types of data, qualitative and quantitative, as a way to visualize different options available to us. We choose the combination of methods and data that best fits our overall research purpose, given our question.

5. Choose appropriate data collection methods and sources

Once we have designed our research, we begin to collect data. The key here is to efficiently and effectively collect high-value data. We may choose, for example, interactive methods such as questionnaires or interviews, observational research, where we do not touch our research subjects directly. In addition, we will determine whether to use primary research, where we collect the data ourselves, or secondary research that has already been collected by another party.

6. Analyze and communicate research results

After we have collected data, we need to analyze and communicate our results. If we have carefully structured our design, this part of the process will be quite natural. The end result of our analysis is usually a written report that summarizes our objectives, methods, and results.

The final piece of the puzzle is to actually act on the information. If we do not act, there was no reason to do the research in the first place. Firms that do the most effective research consider this work not as a one-time process, but rather as an ongoing process of collecting information, acting on it, then collecting more. This approach will lead to continuous improvement within the firm.

7. Integrate research with other elements of the Big Picture framework

When the results of our marketing efforts are not as hoped, we need to be able to identify quickly and specifically the point of failure in order to correct it for future efforts. When we succeed, we should seek to understand how to replicate that success. To do so, we must ensure that we succeeded for the right reasons, that is, that tactical events unfolded according to our strategy.

☐ KEY TERMS

Behavioral model. (p. 351) A model that attempts to predict consumer behavior by looking at relationships between variables, such as the relationship between attitudes and awareness and purchase behavior.

Critical Incident Technique (CIT). (p. 355) A qualitative research technique designed to uncover memorable experiences, either very good or very bad, as a way to discover the most salient attributes of a product or service.

Cross-sectional research. (p. 348) Research that collects data at one point in time across different samples of people or phenomena.

Dependent variable. (p. 349) A factor or variable that is influenced or is the outcome of other variables, called independent.

Descriptive research. (p. 352) Research that characterizes markets, industry competitors, target populations, customers, or a set of product features.

Experimental research. (p. 352) Research that studies the impact of some *manipulation* on a particular outcome.

Exploratory research. (p. 352) Research to determine whether we should pursue further research, and if so, in what particular area and manner.

Independent variable. (p. 349) A factor or variable that influences another factor (called dependent).

Longitudinal or time-series research. (p. 348) Research that collects data over a period of time, seeking to understand how the variable under study changes over time.

Primary research. (p. 359) Carrying out data gathering firsthand, that is, by sourcing it from the population we are seeking to investigate. Primary research can be conducted through a third party.

Psychological model. (p. 352) A model that describes how people process information and form attitudes.

Qualitative research. (p. 354) Research that collects data from a relatively small sample that is not randomly selected. Qualitative data is not generalizable to a larger population. However, it provides a nuanced or deep understanding of a particular phenomenon or sample.

Quantitative research. (p. 354) Research that collects numerical data generally drawn from a sample which is representative of a larger population. Quantitative data is expressed numerically, and is amenable to mathematical manipulation enabling the researcher to draw conclusions that are generalizable to a larger population.

Reliability. (p. 355) The extent to which repeated measurements of a variable yield the same answer.

Secondary research. (p. 359) A gathering of second-hand data, that is, data collected by a third party for their own purposes.

Validity. (p. 355) The extent to which our data accurately captures the information we are seeking.

☐ QUESTIONS FOR DISCUSSION

1. You are trying to increase customer satisfaction with your Italian restaurant. Using CIT, develop a plan for identifying where you need to improve your services or products.

2. Develop three research plans using the three approaches below. Try to determine whether you should introduce a new product in Atlanta, Georgia.
   (a) Qualitative research
   (b) Quantitative research
   (c) Experimental research

3. Take a look at the research questions below. How would you use market research to answer them?
   (a) How many pairs of skis were sold in the United States last year?

   (b) What are the most effective ways for executive MBA students in Western Europe to find a job in the United States?
   (c) What are the most preferred bottled water brands in your urban area?

4. Review the list of market research questions in Figure 13.3. For each, list at least one impediment to correctly answering it, given the practical difficulties organizations face.

☐ APPENDIX: MARKETING ANALYSIS AND PLANNING

Marketing Tool #13.1: Using Critical Incident Technique to Understand Customers' Experience Cycle

Background: The critical incident technique (CIT) was originally developed by psychologists in the 1950s and has been adapted to different types of research settings in the social sciences, including marketing. In the seminal paper on the topic, Flanagan (1954) describes a critical incident as one that makes a "significant contribution, either positively or negatively, to the general aim of the activity" and it "should be capable of being critiqued or analyzed" (p. 338).

We can use the critical incident technique to surface themes or specific needs of customers that are particularly important and are accessed by them when we ask them about what they like and dislike about interacting with the business category or with our company. For example, a bank interview customers of its consumer branch, asking them to describe all aspects of their experience with the bank, such as opening accounts, making deposits, cashing checks, and applying for loans. In conducting these interviews, the researcher is looking for specific themes that emerge when customers report similar positive (or negative) experiences. For example, we may notice that a number of customers report feeling nervous when they withdraw money from the ATM at night. In exploring the context of this feeling, we may find that this is a result of poor lighting around the ATM as well as the fact that the machine is difficult to operate at night, extending the amount of time customers have to stand in front of it. The results of this research can give us critical insights that will enable us to improve our products and services.

Description: Critical Incident Technique (CIT) interviews can be particularly helpful for exploring the customer experience cycle. Although we can gather critical incident data using direct observation or surveys, semi-structured interviews allow us to collect fuller and more nuanced responses than the other two methods. The steps in the process are:

1. **Gather all available secondary research.** If we are doing research with our own customers, we should review any surveys already conducted. If possible, we should observe customers and start to understand the broad stages in their particular purchase experience; as we note in Chapter 14, these are usually need recognition, search for alternatives, purchase, use, and evaluation. We should also start noting the benefits customers expect from the product or service.

2. **Prepare the interview questionnaire.** Divide the interview questions into groups that correspond to the phases of the customer experience—from the perspective of the customer. For example, in the case of an airline, we will ask fliers about their experience before, during, and after the reservation process; at the airport and pre-flight; during flight; and upon arrival. We want customers to focus on *recent and specific* experiences they have had with the product or service, not their general views, and to provide factual reports, rather than interpretations, of what happened. CIT seeks to evaluate activities *in context;* that is, we are interested in what is going on around the consumer when they report their experience. The questions typically follow a pattern. For each phase in the customer experience, we will prompt the respondent for both positive and negative incidents as follows:

    Think of a time you had a positive/negative experience with this brand.

    ■ Describe the circumstances and nature of this incident.
    ■ Explain why you consider this incident to be significant.
    ■ What did the company's representatives do that was effective/ineffective?
    ■ Why was it effective/ineffective?
    ■ Describe the outcome(s) or result of the incident.

3. **Conduct the interviews.** Once we have prepared the interview questions, we should pretest them with a few customers and ensure the questions are relevant and customers can answer them easily, tweaking as necessary in between pre-test interviews. There are no firm rules about appropriate sample size for CIT interviews. The determining factors are the complexity of the activity we are trying to study and the variety and quality of the critical incidents, rather than the number of participants. We should collect incidents

until redundancy occurs, that is, until no new critical behaviors appear. Often after 20 to 25 interviews per customer segment, clear themes begin emerging and we no longer learn new information from additional interviews.

4. **Analyze the data.** We then evaluate the transcripts in order to identify themes and insights to help organize, reduce, and analyze the qualitative data. We will organize this analysis based on the customer experience. In the case of the airline example, we can code our CIT data by phase of the customer experience (e.g., reservations, purchase, pre-check in, gate processes, boarding, in-flight...). Because the purpose of these interviews is to explore customers' salient experiences when using a product or service, we will seek to discover attributes that are important to customers and how they refer to the different benefits they seek.

    CIT is best suited for exploratory research that seeks to build an information base for further research. The output might be a set of attributes that customers seek within our product or service category, highlighting areas where there are unmet needs. For example, one airline that conducted CIT research discovered important unmet needs related to time convenience in its airport processes, communications, in-flight productivity, and baggage handling. While the airline had procedures in place for handling all these functions, it had not realized how critical some of them were to passengers' overall perception of their brand. The CIT process can be tremendously helpful in understanding the links between operational processes and customer perceptions.

☐ RESOURCES

Bearden, William O. and Richard G. Netemeyer. *Handbook of marketing scales: multi-item measures for marketing and consumer behavior research*. Third Edition. Sage Publications, Incorporated, Thousand Oaks, CA, December 10, 2010.

Churchill, Gilbert A. and Dawn Iacobucci. *Marketing research: methodological foundations*. South-Western Publishers, Cincinnati, OH, September 9, 2009.

Flanagan, J. C. (1954). The critical incident technique, *The Psychological Bulletin*, 51(4), 327-358.

Field, Andy. *Discovering statistics using SPSS*. Sage Publications Limited, London, England, January 21, 2009.

Johnson, Michael and Andres Gustafsson. *Improving customer satisfaction, loyalty and profit: an integrated measurement and management system*. John Wiley & Sons, Hoboken, NJ, August 2000.

Hayes, Bob E. "Measuring customer satisfaction and loyalty: Survey design, use, and statistical analysis methods." *ASQ Quality Press*, July 2008.

Kardes, Frank, Maria Cronley, and Thomas Cline: *consumer behavior*. South-Western Cengage Learning, Mason, OH, 2010.

chapter fourteen

"Every proverb is strictly
true; indeed all of them
are apothegms dictated
by Experience herself, the
mother of all science."

Cervantes, Saavedra, M. de. (1793).

*The history and adventures of the renowned Don
Quixote. 6th ed. corr. London: Printed for A. Law,
W. Miller, and R. Cater. Volume 1, page 139.*

MARKETING METRICS

After studying this chapter you should be able to:

1. *Describe the reasons companies set metrics*

2. *Develop metrics that reflect the Big Picture strategy*

3. *List the key steps in setting operational marketing metrics*

4. *Use evaluation metrics to evaluate the connection between our strategy and our execution*

5. *Relate key strategy and evaluation metrics to other elements of the Big Picture framework*

FedEx and Time-Critical *Metrics*

© wdstock/iStockphoto

FedEx, the largest global small-package shipping company, ships over 3.5 million packages on an average day. Ensuring that each one is correctly booked and delivered is the job of more than 300,000 employees, who use computer systems, miles of conveyor belts, and a fleet of planes and trucks to handle shipments. These tools alone cannot ensure FedEx is delivering packages accurately and on time, however. The company also relies on real-time data about its operations and a system that organizes that data into information to enable decision-making at all levels. Understanding how customers experience FedEx's service at each step of the process and establishing operational metrics that capture the subtleties of these perceptions are key to FedEx's success.

For instance, even though the company consistently achieved higher than 90 percent on-time delivery rates, FedEx management initiated a thorough review of the customer experience at its drop-off locations in the year 2000, due to negative customer feedback. A large observational research study identified two types of customer patterns at its stores. About 10 percent of customer visits were very brief; a customer walked into the store with a prefilled shipping bill, dropped packages off, and left. However, a very large percent of customers stayed in the store until they felt their packages had been fully processed and were on their way.

In observing and speaking to customers, FedEx identified a source of dissatisfaction. At peak times, when the office was crowded with many customers requiring the help of a team member, FedEx employees would process shipments, place them in a pile (which they called "the leaning tower of packages") on the customer-facing counter, and ship them later. It surprised FedEx to learn that seeing the large pile of packages made some customers

worry about whether their shipment would make it to its destination on time. So even though FedEx's on-time operational metrics looked fine, customers' perception of timeliness was actually decreasing.

Upon making this discovery, FedEx changed its package processing procedures by placing a wall with five presort windows behind the service counter. Now, when a FedEx employee takes a package from a customer, he or she says thanks and slides the package through one of the windows. This sends a highly visible signal that the package is being handled immediately.

Today, FedEx organizes its operational metrics around an index known as the Service Quality Indicator, with 12 weighted components that affect overall customer satisfaction. The company runs frequent customer satisfaction surveys to continually update the metric weights, and senior management reviews the Service Quality Indicators daily, reallocating resources as needed to hit target levels. FedEx is well aware that effective metrics must be informed by customers' perceptions of performance. ■

Sources: Manning, Harley and Kerry, Bodine. "How FedEx revamped its brand by fixing its leaning tower of packages," *Fast Company.* August 21, 2012.

Bauer J. Pecheux K., Smith M., Fletcher Z."The use of operations objectives and performance measures in private and public organizations."*White Paper*, February 15, 2010. Prepared for the Federal Highway Administration, Federal Transit Administration. http://ops.fhwa.dot.gov/publications/fhwahop10029/fhwahop10029.pdf.

Howell, M. T. "Actionable performance measurement: A key to success, "*American Society* for *Quality*, 2006.

THE PURPOSE OF MARKETING METRICS

A key to becoming a great marketer is to always pay attention to what is working and what is not. This continuous learning process depends on upon information that allows us to uncover relationships between our actions and their outcomes; that is the role of metrics. A **metric** is a system that quantifies a trend, a dynamic, or a characteristic. In marketing we use metrics to quantify the assumptions we use to develop strategies, to operationalize those strategies, and to measure their results. It is thus difficult to be effective marketers today if we feel squeamish about math, and in particular statistics. Understanding market research fundamentals, statistics, and basic marketing metrics is essential for all of us practicing marketing.

We can categorize metrics based on the kind of data they help us quantify and track, whether the data is about our company, our customers, our competitors, or our distribution partners. In any case, our metric systems should be closely aligned to our strategy. For this reason, within the Big Picture framework we refer to **Strategy-Integrated Metrics (SIMs)**, which reflect the strategy of the company and link multiple aspects of its performance by identifying causal relationships between them. We divide SIMs into measurements that help us develop and execute our strategy, and metrics that measure the impact of that strategy. We look at both types in this chapter, beginning with strategy-integrated metrics.

DEVELOPING STRATEGY-INTEGRATED METRICS

In 1992, two professors from Harvard Business School argued in a seminal article that in order to manage a company, executives needed not merely a financial perspective but rather a balanced and more complete view of the firm.[1] They proposed that business metrics should include a financial perspective, a customer perspective, an innovation and learning perspective, and an internal business perspective. This **balanced scorecard (BSC)** approach aligns the customer perspective with marketing and sales, the financial perspective with finance, the internal perspective with operations, and the innovation and learning perspective with human resources.

Since the release of the balanced scorecard approach to business metrics, thousands of companies all over the world have adopted some version of it, but often without realizing that it cannot work well when metrics are developed without a means of prioritizing them or integrating them across departments in the organization. For example, the marketing team might set metrics aimed at increasing product margins by raising prices, while the operations department sets cost-reduction metrics. In working to meet their separate goals, the two departments might actually be working against each other.

The SIMs metrics system builds on the BSC concept by accepting the strategic philosophy behind it and acknowledging that all good metrics exhibit several key criteria. Therefore, good metrics:

1. Are aligned to the strategy.
2. Establish linkages between higher- and lower-level measures.

Metric. A system that quantifies a trend, dynamic, or characteristic. In marketing we use metrics to quantify the assumptions that we use to develop strategies; to operationalize those strategies; and to measure the results of those strategies.

Strategy-Integrated Metrics (SIMs). Metrics that reflect the strategy of the company and link multiple aspects of organizational performance by following logical causal relationships.

Balanced scorecard. A business metrics system developed by Kaplan and Norton in the early 1990s which divides the firm into a financial perspective, a customer perspective, innovation and learning perspective, and an internal process perspective.

---

[1] Kaplan, Robert S. and David P. Norton. "The balanced scorecard–Measures that drive performance." *Harvard Business Review 70*(1): 71–79 (1992).

3. Integrate operations and marketing.

4. Identify causal relationships.

5. Enhance the core competence.

SIMs Are Aligned to the Strategy

Many companies measure themselves using standards established by equity research analysts or market leaders in their industries. However, equity analysts frequently change the way they look at industries, and when they do, companies that use their metrics can be exposed to the considerable expense of changing their reporting systems and employee incentives. More importantly, blindly adopting industry standard metrics can limit our creative and market-shaping opportunities by focusing us too much on the competition instead of on innovating and expanding the category. For these reasons SIMs emphasize and reflect the strategy of the firm, not just industry convention.

In the 1980s and early 1990s, airlines that had existed prior to the 1978 deregulation of the industry were accustomed to gauging their performance by comparing their yields (or capacity utilization) against those of other airlines. This narrow focus on revenue management left them open to the entry of low-cost competitors like Southwest Airlines, which measured the execution of their cost-focused strategy using aircraft and employee productivity metrics. These new entrants checked their prices and yields against those of alternative forms of transportation, such as buses. Southwest's differentiated approach to its strategy, captured by its metrics, enabled it to become and remain competitive in a much broader transportation category. Viewed through Southwest's metrics, which are now an industry standard, the performance of the older, legacy carriers was less than satisfactory.

In establishing business metrics, then, the firm should focus on its strategy rather than on the strategy of its immediate competitors or on metrics that have become an industry standard. After all, metrics standardization benefits analysts more than it does individual companies; this standardization allows analysts to quickly compare companies within an industry. However, it is unreasonable to expect that an industry will be differentiated if the metrics driving the actions of all competitors are not.

SIMs Are Linked to Higher- and Lower-Level Metrics

Metrics should be organized and hierarchical; that is, they should follow a focused, top-down approach. At the top of our metrics tree is the overall business objective of our company, the business goal, followed by lower, complementary goals necessary to make the overall objective a reality. Unfortunately, many businesses implementing performance measurement dashboards set many parallel, equally important, objectives. This can be both confusing and wasteful because it splits resources among many (too many) initiatives with potentially conflicting priorities.

Consider the case of a major equipment leasing company, now out of business, whose major functional departments each held separate metric-setting sessions. The sales teams adopted double-digit revenue growth targets; the customer service department set cost-reduction metrics; and finally, the asset management department, a profit center, adopted profitability metrics. Under the incentive system that these broad metrics created, the asset management department changed its policies so that customers who returned leased equipment with light damage or missing the user manual were charged stiff fees. Meanwhile, the customer service department had out-sourced its call center to reduce call times and thus lower costs. As soon as the new equipment-return policy went into effect, the 1-800 number was overwhelmed by angry customers whose only recourse was a third party attempting to handle the calls without a detailed understanding of the equipment, the delicate customer issues the new policy created, or a flexible approach to resolving complaints.

Needless to say, the sales team missed its revenue target as unhappy customers refused to work with the company again and spread the word about its punitive return policies. The company could have saved precious resources and increased its chances of meeting its sales targets if it had first prioritized goals, selecting either profitability or sales growth, and aligned actions and metrics with those goals. Effective metrics focus and simplify decision-making and lead us quickly toward sustainable growth.

SIMs Integrate Operations and Marketing

The metrics system should integrate internal and external perspectives of firm. SIMs link the company's success criteria—its overall business goal and overall brand positioning—to desired customer and employee behaviors, and to the operational processes necessary to achieve them. For example, a metric measuring "growth" does not provide managers and employees with any information about exactly how to achieve that growth. One manager may elect to achieve growth by lowering price to increase unit sales; the other might choose to increase advertising spending. In contrast, if a firm has identified a relationship between customer retention rate and sustainable revenue growth, it may choose to measure and provide incentives for a SIM of customer retention. Managers would then likely engage in strategies and tactics that improve customer service, satisfaction, and perceived value of the firms' products. These efforts would have substantially more focus as they are driven by a SIM that suggests interrelated tactics and strategies.

The best way to ensure that operations and marketing are integrated is to communicate the brand positioning not just within the marketing department, but across the different functional areas of the firm. Even the most intangible positioning can be influenced by actions (and therefore metrics) in, for example, the operations or finance department. For example, Walt Disney World has long positioned the amusement park as a place where "dreams come true." From an operational perspective, this means that all park employees must have the necessary mindset and training to make this happen. This is operationalized in a number of training programs including the "Traditions" orientation process, which is required of all new Disney employees and is an immersive exposure to the Disney philosophy of customer care. Operational metrics such as number of hours of training are therefore clearly linked to the brand metric based on the brand positioning.

The metrics-setting process should reflect this connection between actions in different functional areas. The best way to achieve this is to set metrics in a sequential and iterative process. First, the management team will select overall business goals and the overall company positioning; they will then define required employee and customer behaviors, internal processes, and metrics. This process should continue until a realistic and congruent combination of goals, behaviors, and processes has been found. We discuss the process for establishing SIMs in more detail later in the chapter.

SIMs Reflect Causal Relationships

SIMs address root causes of different outcomes rather than merely identifying symptoms. For example, a SIM that measures advertising spending and brand awareness helps us to determine not just that awareness is low, but also whether the cause of this problem is insufficient spending on advertising. By building metrics based on causal models that reflect relationships between our marketing activities and their impact, managers can learn from their mistakes and replicate their successes.

SIMs require us to continually test the key hypotheses upon which we are building our strategy, rather than simply assuming they are correct. For example, a manager may believe 100% customer satisfaction is required to increase customer retention and in turn achieve revenue goals. Yet achieving 100% customer satisfaction may be difficult and extremely expensive, and 90% satisfaction may have a nearly equal impact on retention. In order to set a specific objective, the manager, should test the relationship between customer satisfaction and retention. Otherwise, he or she will risk wasting precious resources by establishing metrics that may or may not contribute to strategic goals. While it may seem overwhelming to test several hypotheses on a regular basis, wasting resources on implementing the wrong metrics is infinitely more expensive.

SIMs Enhance the Core Competence

SIMs should reflect and foster the core competence of the firm. The positioning of the company is directly tied to the benefits it offers its customers, and those benefits in turn are directly linked to the company's core competence. Therefore, the company's business metrics should measure and continually enhance the core competence of the firm. Consider the case of a large supermarket chain that repositioned itself on the main variable of freshness based on its core competence in sourcing, processing, and handling produce and fresh products. The company selected a financial goal consistent with that positioning by carefully mapping salient customer experiences at the supermarket. For example, the firm observed that customers identified the look of meat, the appearance of produce, and the overall lighting in the stores as basic signals that the store had fresh products. Managers then outlined how to manage these elements, and then set operational metrics to ensure they would meet the expectations of freshness promised in the company's advertising and other marketing communication.

The new company strategy hypothesized that improved perceptions of freshness would motivate customers to buy higher-value products such as fish and meat; management therefore estimated the potential positive financial impact these improved perceptions might have. Further, they identified the operational metric that would help to support this freshness perception. For example, at the operational level, the firm began to monitor temperatures in store refrigerators on a more frequent basis to ensure that fresh meats stayed that way. Other metrics required the company to have best-in-class agro-sourcing, cold distribution chain, and in-store display and merchandising. Successfully meeting the company's operational metrics simultaneously enhanced the company's core competence, its competitive position, and, most importantly, the bottom line.

SETTING SIMS TO OPERATIONALIZE THE STRATEGY

The process of establishing SIMs goes hand-in-hand with the process of executing the company's strategy. In establishing SIMs, we need to think back to each chapter of the Big Picture and follow an iterative process by which we formulate hypotheses, gather data that proves or disproves our hypotheses, and prioritize projects across the organization based on the result. Thus, although we address metrics as the capstone chapter of the Big Picture, many of the ideas and activities included in this discussion have already been presented in other chapters of the framework. Metrics setting is a process consisting of the steps outlined in the sections below.

Step 1: Establish and Measure the Core Competence

The company's ability to establish SIMs is tied to its understanding of its core competence. This understanding should be reality-based rather than merely intuitive. So, for example, an executive team that claims the company has a core competence in process operations must be able to demonstrate quantitatively that its process operations capabilities are best-in-class. This means that when a firm assesses its skill level, it should compare the competence not to competition within the industry, but rather to the best performer across industries. If, for example, The Four Seasons hotel chain identifies its core competence as skill at customer service, it might develop metrics that allow it to compare its performance to that of other firms known for customer service, such as Singapore Airlines, Zappos, and Disney World.

This approach to measuring core competence is known as **cross-industry benchmarking**, and it involves setting our performance standards not based on our direct competitors, but rather based on those firms who perform best on those activities. Our tendency is generally to look within the industry and compare ourselves to our competitors. However, for core competence purposes, we are better off benchmarking against best-in-class companies across industries, because this holds our firm to the high standards necessary for development of a true core competence. In addition to being more useful, this data will also be easier to collect because companies are more open to sharing with non-competitors. For example, a company looking for benchmarking data on process operations should probably look among the market leaders of process-intensive industries, including fast food and logistics.

Once the company has a credible definition of its core competence, it must then seek to understand whether it is currently translating the core competence into differentiating customer benefits and superior economic returns. If the company has a

Benchmarking. The practice of pricing relative to a competitor's price, justifying the price difference between the two brands by the difference in their relative value of their offerings.

core competence but is unable to translate it into a tangible customer benefit, then it is not coherently linking its strategy to execution. If the firm is effectively translating its competence into benefits but is failing to generate superior economic returns, then it has chosen a strategy that is not sustainable.

Step 2: Detail the Positioning from a Customer Perspective

The positioning of our firm must always be expressed in terms of clear customer benefits. People often confuse brand tag lines with true strategic positioning statements. As we already covered in Chapter 7, a positioning statement is a clear and focused statement designed to reveal the primary benefit of the brand to the customer in a compelling way. An integral part of positioning is a clear statement of our target customer's current and desired behavior, and the beliefs that drive those behaviors. These statements are critical to operationalizing the positioning and setting metrics.

The starting point for setting metrics is to develop deep understanding of the customer experience, with our brand and in the category more generally. To do this, we can use qualitative research technique to gather data for a customer experience diagram. In this diagram, presented in Figure 14.1, we detail each step in the purchase and use process.

Detailing Salient Aspects of the Current and Desired Customer Experience for a Hypothetical Airline

	Current customer experience	Desired customer experience
Reservations & purchase	• I check several sites until I find the absolutely lowest prices • I try not to call the airline; their call center is terrible	• I check *Fast* airlines first, and then confirm their fares are competitive • My calls are answered quickly • My issues are resolved when I call
Arrival & check-in	• I never know how long I'll have to wait so I try to get to the airport as early as possible	• I don't have to wait in line for more than 10 minutes
Pre-flight experience	• You have to be an expert to navigate the airport • I rarely get a plug by the gate • Delays are frequent and unexpected	• I know where I am going • I can be productive while I wait • There are no unexpected delays at the gate
Flight experience	• The aircraft changes all the time, often the computer plug and entertainment system situation is terrible	• I am productive on board • My flight arrives on time
Connections	• If I connect through a new airport I am not sure my airline will be easy to find • Connecting can be extremely stressful due to short times	• I know where to go to make my connections • I have reasonable connecting times • I can be productive while I wait
Baggage	• I breathe a sigh of relief when my bag finally rolls out of the baggage claim belt	• My bag is there when I arrive • I have heard that their baggage customer service is top notch

Figure 14.1 A foundational step to setting operational marketing metrics is detailing the current customer experience by phase, and then describing the customer experience we hope to create given our brand positioning.

The example in Figure 14.1 depicts an airline that is positioning itself on *time convenience*, that is, showing passengers the airline values their time. We use the customer experience process to illustrate the steps customers move through as they search for, compare, buy, and use our products. Next to the current experience we develop the *desired* experience, the steps our customers will experience once our marketing strategy has been implemented. Writing both columns in the first person helps us adopt a customer perspective instead of our *opinion* of a customer's perspective. By putting ourselves in the mindset of the consumer, we are likely to notice certain aspects of our product or service more than others, and we will be most efficient when perfecting those aspects that are most salient and therefore have the greatest impact on overall brand perception.

A number of qualitative techniques, discussed in Chapter 13, can help us elicit this information from customers. These include observational methods such as Critical Incident Technique (CIT), in-depth interviews, and focus groups. Once the marketer has identified the highest-impact customer experiences, the company will need to look internally for ways to deliver and enhance those experiences. In our airline example, the company can generally improve time convenience perception by: (a) minimizing wait times, (b) ensuring passengers always have updated information regarding flight and airport processes, (c) setting expectations when waiting or when disruptions are unavoidable, (d) maximizing the value of passengers' time at gate areas and lounges, during flights, and at baggage check-in, and (e) scheduling frequent flights. Note that these elements are specifically related to our positioning of time convenience, and would change if we were to change our positioning to, for example, superior service or low price.

Now that we have a sense for what we want our customers to experience, and therefore to believe, we are ready to identify the internal actions our organization must take to operationalize our positioning by mobilizing our functional resources. Note that the distance between the current and desired customer experiences parallels the distance between the current and desired beliefs in the five-box positioning tool from Chapter 7. From this we know the resource requirements we must marshal for to create these desired experiences for our customers. In the airline example, by reading through the list in Figure 14.1, we can quickly get a sense for the breadth of resources required—from customer service, to check-in agents, to airplane furnishings, to baggage operations. It is obvious that the internal activities required to execute on our marketing strategy go well beyond marketing and include all functional departments.

Step 3: Operationalize the Positioning

Once we have translated our positioning into specific customer experiences, we are ready to detail the internal actions and measurement systems we will put in place to ensure we are executing as planned. Figure 14.2 shows how our airline trying to position itself on time convenience might go about resourcing appropriately. The left column lists the inputs or internal activities we must execute; the right column shows the outputs and operational tasks, as well as the customer metrics we will track. Ultimately, we are attempting to change customer perceptions to cause a change in customer behavior, so customer perceptions should always take primacy over objective operational numbers.

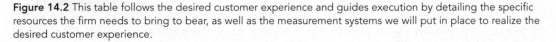

	Internal activities/inputs	Metrics/outputs
Reservations & purchase	• Staff adequate at peak times • Encourage call backs • Reward issue resolution and not call quantity	• Speed of answer • Perceptions on issue resolution
Arrival & check-in	• Adequate staffing at peak times • Install e-check in kiosks	• Waiting time • Total time to check-in • % e-check in
Pre-flight experience	• Install better signage • Ensure electrical outlets and wifi are widely available • Provide access to clubs	• Airport signage and outlets • Total process time
Flight experience	• Offer flexible meal times • Ensure electrical outlets and wifi are available on flights • Provide continuous entertainment	• % on time • % of planes with outlets/wifi • % uptime for entertainment systems
Connections	• Install better signage • Ensure electrical outlets and wifi are widely available • Provide access to clubs	• Airport signage • Capture connection time outliers
Baggage	• Honor priority baggage • Staff baggage operations adequately	• Time to last bags • % lost bags/claims

Figure 14.2 This table follows the desired customer experience and guides execution by detailing the specific resources the firm needs to bring to bear, as well as the measurement systems we will put in place to realize the desired customer experience.

Once we have established operational metrics around the most salient customer experiences, we will need to establish stringent standards for delivering on those metrics. As we saw in the zone of tolerance discussion in Chapter 9, we need to set and consistently meet customer expectations all the time to avoid falling into vicious profitability cycles.

Step 4: Set Operational Targets

As we establish delivery standards for our metrics, we must make decisions that balance the benefit against the cost of delivering. Detailed questions like "How long should our customers wait in line?" or "How often should we make flight status announcements in the waiting area?" will arise at this point. When we are setting targets for metrics that directly affect customer perception of our brand positioning, we will be more aggressive than our competitors. When setting targets for all other operational metrics, we will simply match our competitors' performance standards or perform slightly below if the metrics cover an area unrelated to our core competence.

For example, an airline delivering excellent time convenience might deliver slightly lower customized service than a competitive airline positioned on service. When we are setting metrics targets we can use simple statistical techniques like correlation and more advanced techniques like principal-components regression and factor analysis to estimate with precision the relationship between specific operational metrics and overall customer perceptions of our brand. We can then relate customer perceptions of our brand to overall customer satisfaction and loyalty.[2]

An important component of any SIM system is customer perception and importance data. These attitudinal metrics are leading indicators of brand performance. In the context of metrics, customer perceptions help us figure out whether the company is effectively translating the core competence into tangible customer benefits. When linked to customer behavioral data, these perceptions also help us develop an understanding of the relationship between attitudes, behaviors, and financials.

EVALUATION SIMS: STRATEGY AND EXECUTION

Metrics play a two-part role in linking strategy and the business objective of the firm: they provide the information we need to establish realistic performance goals (strategy), and they allow us to evaluate our results against those goals (execution). To forecast performance it is not sufficient to assume that our business will grow with general economic trends, or that we will do marginally better than last year. We

GLOBALMARKETING
THE HAPPINESS INDEX

As we begin to understand the importance of using SIMs to connect strategy and execution, we start to see how our choice of higher-level strategies and goals will drive tactics. For example, most businesses and governments identify financial goals, such as revenues or profits for businesses, or gross domestic product for governments. These goals naturally drive behaviors that focus on money. However, there has been an increasing interest in business and government in identifying other, non-financial metrics, that may actually drive behaviors in a different way. For example, in 2008 the country of Bhutan adopted the goal of measuring Gross National Happiness (GNH) rather than Gross Domestic Product, specifically stating in its Constitution, "The State shall strive to promote those conditions that will enable the pursuit of Gross National Happiness."

To achieve this goal, Bhutan has created a number of lower-level metrics, seeking to identify those that contribute most to the overarching goal of happiness within the country. Some of these metrics are financial, while others measure domains such as community vitality, education, physical health, and psychological well-being.

These results are published each year so that other countries can learn about Bhutan's approach to metrics. The availability of this information has fueled a growing movement to reconsider how countries around the world measure growth. In April 2012 the United Nations sponsored a conference on happiness, inviting leaders from around the world to explore what metrics drive happiness. A number of researchers agreed that while economic well-being has been identified as one driver of happiness, it is not the only important metric. Furthermore, while financial and health metrics appear to drive happiness, researchers found that the reverse can also occur: happiness can drive the productivity, health, and ultimately financial performance of a country.

This global trend toward choosing metrics outside the financial realm, and also seeking to understand more deeply the relationships between these metrics, is the ultimate expression of a great use of SIMs. ■

Sources: Williamson, Mark "The serious business of creating a happier world." *The Guardian*, April 11, 2012. http://www.guardian.co.uk/sustainable-business/united-nations-happiness-conference-bhutan. Accessed May 15, 2013.

Helliwell, John, Richard Layard, and Jeffrey Sachs (Eds.) The World Happiness Report. The Earth Institute, Columbia University, New York, New York, 2012.

Ura, Karma, Sabina Alkire, Tshoki Zangmo, and Karma Wangdi. *A Short Guide to Gross National Happiness Index.* Centre for Bhutan Studies, Thimpu, Bhutan, 2012.

---

[2]Johnson, Michael and Andres Gustafsson. *Improving Customer Satisfaction, Loyalty and Profit: An Integrated Measurement and Management System.* John Wiley & Sons, Hoboken, NJ, 2006.

must understand the source of our past successes, the value of our existing and potential customer relationships, and the attitudes and purchase patterns of our target customers.

To assemble forecasts and tie them to our business objective, we must therefore start by defining a customer, as explained in Chapter 3. We must then estimate how many customers our company has, how many of them were acquired during the last planning period, and how many are left in the acquisition pool. We should then estimate our acquisition and retention rates, and our per-customer purchase quantities and price levels. We must constantly relate overall business goals to our SIMs. We do this by asking questions such as: "What do our financial results from the last performance period say about the behaviors of our customers? About our success in attracting new customers? About our ability to execute our strategic plan?"

social**media**

Measuring the ROI of Social Media Marketing

How can we estimate the return on investment from social media initiatives? Return on investment (ROI) works well for measuring the value of hard assets with certain outcomes, like machinery in a manufacturing plant. However, while we can measure the amount of our investment in blogs, YouTube, or a consistent Twitter or Facebook presence, measuring outcomes is more complex.

We can measure these outcomes, however, just as we would for other marketing investments, by going back to our Bodies, Beliefs, Behaviors, and Bucks tool and brainstorming how to measure at each stage. We can measure beliefs like brand awareness and even brand perception by counting the number of Facebook "likes." We can measure behaviors by counting the number of unique visitors to our website, by looking at metrics of brand engagement, and by creating metrics for online word of mouth. For example, through an Amazon storefront we can measure brand awareness using metrics like the number of reviews posted, the number of times people have placed our product in their wish list, or our place in Amazon's product ranking for our category.

In our blogs, we can track our place in web searches as a proxy for awareness. We can count the number of members who read our content weekly, or the number of comments, as proxies for brand engagement behavior. We can also measure word of mouth behavior by tracking the number of references to our blog or the number of tweets about our content people have posted. Vocalpoint.com, P&G's social networking site created in 2006, has more than 1 million members, enabling the company to gather information from its core loyal customers. The company uses Vocalpoint to engage moms by providing relevant content on topics from health to parenting, asks retained users to provide feedback on products, and even efficiently conducts positioning market research.

A nice example of how P&G used SIMs to assess the value of its Vocalpoint investment is illustrated through a specific example for Dawn Direct Foam. In traditional ads for Dawn Direct Foam, a dishwashing soap, P&G stressed its grease-cutting power. However, P&G used Vocalpoint moms to test a different message: that "the soap is so much fun to use, kids will want to help with the dishes." P&G mailed the moms packets showing the detergent and a smiling girl with these words in big letters: "Mom, can I help?" To reinforce the point, the packet included a little sponge in the shape of a child's foot, plus a dozen $1.50 coupons. By checking the coupon redemption rate and overall sales for Dawn Direct, P&G was able to connect its Vocalpoint investment to bucks.

Sources: Berner, Robert. "I sold it through the grapevine," *Business Week Magazine*, May 28, 2006. http://www.businessweek.com/stories/2006-05-28/i-sold-it-through-the-grapevine .

Hoffman, Donna L. and Marek Fodor. "Can you measure the ROI of your social media marketing?." *MIT Sloan Management Review 52*(1): 41–49 (2010).

Fisher, Tia. "ROI in social media: A look at the arguments," *Journal of Database Marketing & Customer Strategy Management 16:* 189–195(2009).

Table 14.1 Evaluation SIMs by Strategic Quadrant

Strategic Quadrant	Bodies	Beliefs	Behaviors	Bucks
Acquisition/ Stimulate Demand	• number of non-users who meet target profile • key demographic characteristics of target bodies	• brand awareness • perception/ importance of key benefits delivered by category	• number of inquiries • number of trials (first time purchases) • overall category purchases • acquisition rate • key behavioral characteristics of target customers	• $ or unit sales • category growth • % category penetration
Retention/ Stimulate Demand	• number of retained customers	• perception/importance of main benefit	• number of purchases (per customer/overall) • number of upgrade products sold • % of customer base upgraded • retention rate	• $ CLV • $ profit • $ revenue
Acquisition/ Earn Share	• number of competitive customers who meet target profile	• brand awareness • perception/ importance of dynamic benefit	• number of trials by competitive customers • number of customers acquired • competitive acquisition rate	• unit market share • revenue share
Retention/ Earn Share	• number of multi-brand customers	• perception of our brand on dynamic benefit	• number of incremental product purchases by multi-brand customers • % loyalty	• % unit share of wallet • % share of revenue

Based on this evaluation, we can make any requisite changes to our strategy and forecast how our execution is likely to affect customer attitudes, behaviors and our performance. Our strategy evaluation metrics must elucidate the relationships described in the 4 B's; we are interested in the connections between our target bodies *(the size of our target segments),* their beliefs *(perception and importance of our main or dynamic variable)*, their behaviors *(retention and acquisition)*, and bucks (business objective).

SIMs to Evaluate the Strategy

An effective SIMs system will help us evaluate our strategy covering all intervening marketing variables: bodies, beliefs, behaviors, and bucks. Displaying metrics for all 4Bs in a table reminds us that strategy is, in essence, the process by which we develop hypotheses about members of our target market, and specifically about how changes in salient beliefs about our category and brand drive their behaviors. We will have different metrics depending on the strategic quadrant we have chosen. Table 14.1 shows a few sample metrics intended to provide a feel for the types of measures we can use, and also for how those measures vary slightly depending on our strategic quadrant.

Most of the metrics in Table 14.1 have appeared elsewhere in the text. As we've seen earlier, when pursuing a stimulate demand strategy we will use absolute performance metrics, such as the overall number of customers or potential customers (for acquisition), the perceptions of our brand on our main benefits, the number of customers who have been acquired or retained, and overall profits or revenues. Conversely, when pursuing an earn share strategy, we will use relative performance measures, including importance of a dynamic variable, perception of our brand on the dynamic variable, and market share or share of customers' wallets. Note that the **wallet share** is calculated as the average spend on our brand divided by the total customer spend on the category.

SIMs to Evaluate the Execution

Just as overall strategy metrics incorporate all 4Bs, executional evaluation metrics incorporate all 4 P's. As we did with operational metrics, in setting evaluation metrics we develop hypotheses and then test them by looking at both the inputs of our marketing efforts and their expected outputs.

Product Metrics

Product input metrics help us track whether we are effectively delivering products that are relevant to our stated strategy. In Chapter 9 (see Marketing Tool 9.2), we discussed the need to analyze our product portfolio by seeing how well it is aligned to the positioning, and by also classifying each product depending on whether it was most useful to acquiring or to retaining customers. For example, the iPod is generally considered a product that helps to attract new customers to the Apple franchise because it is relatively inexpensive and easy to start using. In contrast, the MacBook Air is considered more of a retention product, one that customers who already value Apple's benefits would consider even though it is quite expensive. Product metrics help us to track our efforts to develop and update retention and acquisition products and features in accordance with our overall strategy.

The output side of Table 14.2 shows metrics that will help us track the effectiveness of our product effort with customers. As an example, for acquisition we measure the number of inquiries and the **trial** rate of our products. (Trial counts first-time users as a percent of the target population.) For a stimulate/demand strategy, we count trial customers who are new to the category, while for earn share we count trial customers who come from our competitive target.

Pricing Metrics

In many ways, pricing metrics are both the easiest and most difficult metrics to develop. They are easy because a price is already a number, so measurement is fairly simple. They can be more difficult because we run the risk of creating metrics that drive short-term as opposed to long-term growth. For example, airlines commonly measure the relationship between price and percent capacity utilization of planes. These metrics drive managers to raise or lower prices of particular tickets at certain times to ensure that as many seats as possible are full. Unfortunately, solely focusing on these metrics, airlines ignore the relationship between price and value, and eventually satisfaction may drop.

Ideally, our pricing efforts aim to capture some of the value we have created throughout the entire marketing and commercial efforts of our firm. The pricing metrics should measure our short-term pricing efforts related to the *trial* and

Wallet share. Customers' spend on our brand as a percent of their spend on the category as a whole.

Trial. First-time users as a percent of the target population.

Table 14.2 Product Evaluation Metrics

Strategic Quadrant	Input	Output
Acquisition/Stimulate Demand	• number of acquisition products in pipeline/ total • number of acquisition products available/total • number of search features in key products • percent of products enhanced/ number products in portfolio	• number of inquiries from non-users • trial rate percent • percent of new product revenue • target customer perceptions of search features
Retention/Stimulate Demand	• number of products iterated/total products in portfolio • number of premium products/ total products in portfolio • number of retention products in portfolio/total • number of experience/credence features by stakeholder	• percent of repeat purchases • number of products per customer • percent heavy users/total customer base • percent premium product users/total customer base • percent premium product revenue • customer perceptions of experience features
Acquisition/Earn Share	• percent or number of products with advantage over competitive equivalent • gaps in product portfolio over competitor	• number of inquiries from competitive customers • percent of competitive trial rate • percent of competitive product cannibalization • percent of unit share in product category
Retention/Earn Share	• number of complementary features across product portfolio	• cross-selling rate • number of products per customer • perception of experience features

continuity pricing tactics discussed in Chapter 11; for example, if we have decided to use trial pricing, we may want to measure how many of our recently acquired customers came to our franchise because of a promotional price, whether they continued to purchase, and whether their attitudes toward our brand improved. Because trial pricing does not apply to all products but only to those with experience attributes, we might also look at the number of trial tactics available as a percentage of the number of products for which trial pricing is appropriate (see Table 14.3).

In the output column of Table 14.3 we measure the effectiveness of our trial pricing programs by measuring the percent of customers we acquired through a trial pricing program, the cost of trial pricing programs relative to sales, and the retention rates of customers acquired through trial pricing programs. This last metric will help us track whether our price discounts are helping us acquire the right customers, that is, customers who stay with the firm after we switch from the trial to the regular price.

In addition to measuring trial and continuity tactics, we measure overall price levels as well as customers' perceptions of our value. Note that we obtain value metrics (overall value perception) through a generally phrased survey question such as, "How would you rate the value you receive considering the cost of our products?", where the rating is generally given on a scale of 1 to 5 or 1 to 7.

As we do with all perceptual metrics, we must measure value perceptions often in order to collect valuable information. The metrics in the earn share quadrants are similar to those for stimulate demand except that we measure them against a

Table 14.3 Pricing Evaluation Metrics

Strategic Quadrant	Input	Output
Acquisition/Stimulate Demand	• trial pricing tactics/number products with experience features • price premium vs. market average	• number of new customers in trial pricing programs/ total new customers • trial pricing program cost/ sales from new customers • trial pricing participant retention rates • overall value perception of our brand (percent good value)
Retention/Stimulate Demand	• number of continuity pricing tactics available • price premium vs. market average	• percent of sales booked under continuity pricing programs • overall value perception of our brand (percent good value)
Acquisition/Earn Share	• number of competitive trial pricing tactics available • price premium vs. competition	• number of new customers from completion in trial pricing programs/ total new customers from competition • trial pricing program cost/ sales from new customers from competition • trial pricing participant retention rates • overall value perception of our brand (percent good value) vs. competition
Retention/Earn Share	• number of cross-selling trial pricing tactics available • price premium vs. competition	• percent of multi-brand customers successfully cross-sold • value perception of our brand vs. competition

competitive benchmark. For retention earn share we also look at the number of "cross-sell" pricing programs. These programs might offer discounts specially targeted to multi-brand customers, to encourage them to purchase several types of products from us.

Channel (Place) Metrics

Our channel (also called place) efforts are aimed at distributing our products and services to our target customers with a degree of availability that matches their **willingness to wait or search** in order to buy from us. Here we are interested in operational metrics that can help us drive the flow of product, money, and information in the channel.

For example, packaged goods manufacturers such as Kraft use Nielsen data to track whether their products are in stock in grocery stores. From an operational perspective, they would track inventory levels at the factory, warehouse, and distribution centers in order to begin to understand how these levels affect the level of stock in the stores.

The channel metrics in Table 14.4 helps us track the degree of focus of our sales channel on each of our target populations. For example, metrics like number of salespeople/number of customers tell us the relative coverage we have allocated to a particular group of customers. In addition we may consider metrics dedicated to measuring the relative efficiency of our sales force; for example, $sales expenses/$sales will give us a sense of how much money we are spending to successfully sell our products and services.

Finally, perhaps the most important metrics in the table are dedicated to understanding customers' willingness to search or wait if our product is not available. This is a very important metric. Because it is based on a customer survey question, we need to measure

Willingness to wait or search. The percent of customers willing to delay purchases or change stores (or distribution outlets), rather than purchase a different brand.

Table 14.4 Channel Evaluation Metrics

Strategic Quadrant	Input	Output
Acquisition/Stimulate Demand	• sales training programs/new product launches • number of sales personnel/number of potential clients • account data available/number of contacts in prospect database • number of sales visits logged/number of contacts in prospect database • number of stakeholder relationships/number companies in prospect database	• sales (dollar)/number sales visits • number of sales personnel/number new customers • dollar sales expenses/dollar sales • number of outlets carrying our brand/total number of outlets
Retention/Stimulate Demand	• number of sales visits logged/number of contacts in existing customer database • number of sales personnel/number of existing customers	• number of outlets carrying our brand/total number of outlets • percent on time deliveries • percent customers willing to search
Acquisition/Earn Share	• sales training programs/new product launches • number of sales personnel/number target competitive customers • number of sales visits/number of competitive prospects in database • number sales visits logged/ number of competitive customers	• number of outlets carrying our brand/total number of outlets carrying competitor's brand • percent of outlets out of stock
Retention/Earn Share	• number of sales personnel/number target multi-brand customers • number of sales visits/number of multi-brand customers	• number of outlets carrying our brand/total number of outlets carrying competitor's brand.

it frequently. The survey question might read something like: "*Please rate your agreement with the following statement using a scale of 1 to 7, where 1 means that you completely disagree and 7 means that you completely agree. 'If brand x's product were not available, I would rather wait until it became available than buy another brand.'*"

Note that the earn share metrics measuring intensity of distribution (such as number of outlets carrying our brand/ total number of outlets) are stated in terms relative to the competitive brand. As with other elements of execution, when we earn share, we seek to benchmark our execution and exceed our benchmark company's performance only as it pertains to our dynamic variable.

Promotion Metrics

Our promotional, or communications, efforts are aimed at achieving effective and concise articulation of our positioning. Our input metrics measure the intensity of our promotional efforts: how much we are spending, how many people we have reached, how many times we have reached them. For example, Volkswagen (VW) purchased a 60-second spot during the 2013 Super Bowl broadcast, at a cost of $4 million. In addition, the company posted three different versions of the ad online, with three different endings, asking fans to vote on which version they wanted to see in the broadcast. The cost metric is clear; in addition, VW knows that 108.4 million people watched the Super Bowl, and YouTube visits exceeded 2 million.[3] These figures represent input

---

[3]http://www.usatoday.com/story/money/business/2013/01/27/super-bowl-commercials-pressure-volkswagen-of-america/1836881/. Accessed May 10, 2013.

NEW PRODUCTS/INNOVATION

YOUGOV BRAND INDEX MEASURES BRAND PERCEPTIONS

Through much of 2011 and 2012, Apple and Samsung were locked in a series of patent lawsuits regarding technology and competition in the smartphone category. Interestingly, the two companies have been going head-to-head by targeting consumers with similar demographics, yet they have very different strategies. In 2012, Apple released just one model, the iPhone 5. In contrast, Samsung has "bombarded the market with 37 variants tweaked for regional and consumer tastes, from high-end smart-phones to cheaper low-end models" (Reuters). Who is winning the smartphone war?

Until recently, analysts would just compare unit sales and revenue numbers across the two companies to answer this question. Today, however, equity and brand analysts are also looking at metrics that capture customer brand perceptions and thus provide a leading indicator of company performance. One such index is YouGov, originally based in the UK but now a global presence, which publishes a daily Brand Index that tracks perceptions of brands. Brand Index captures traditional metrics like perceptions of quality, value, customer satisfaction, reputation, general impression, and recommendation. It also captures more innovative metrics like "buzz"—whether people have heard anything positive or negative about the brand in the media or through word of mouth.

Consumer perception data from Brand Index showed, for example, that in the last quarter of 2012 Samsung made some advances in consumer perception, and the two brands were essentially neck and neck. While Brand Index data shows perception of the iPhone is outpacing perception of the Galaxy, those scores have recently been trending closer. In mid-September 2012, iPhone outscored Galaxy on recommend scores by 16 points— 26 vs. 9. But as of January 15, 2013, Galaxy had shrunk the difference to 11 points — 25 for iPhone vs. 14 for Galaxy (Fig. 14.3). Today, customer perception metrics are gaining ground not just in marketing, but also among financial analysts and others trying to predict the future of brands. ■

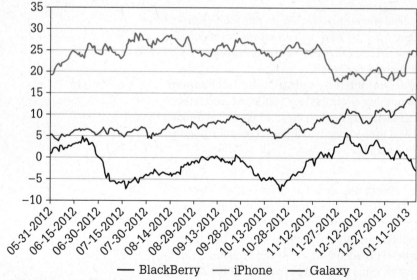

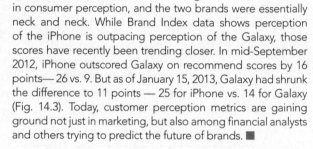

Figure 14.3 Customer perception of the iPhone is higher than that of the Samsung Galaxy, although by the end of 2012 those scores started to trend closer to each other.

Sources: Ansolabehere, Stephen and Brian F, Schaffner., Does Survey Mode Still Matter? Findings from a 2010 Multi-Mode Comparison (June 13, 2011). Available at SSRN: http://ssrn.com/abstract=1868229 or http://dx.doi.org/10.2139/ssrn.1868229.

"Samsung sees fourth-quarter profit at $8.3 billion on note sales, components,"

Reuters. Monday, January 7, 2013 | 7:14 PM ET. http://www.cnbc.com/id/100360820/Samsung_Sees_FourthQuarter_Profit_at_83_Billion_on_Note_Sales_Components .

Marzilli Ted. "Perception scores show Samsung, Apple at parity," *Forbes Magazine.* CMO Network, January 17, 2013. Ted Marzilli. Accessed May 15, 2013.

Table 14.5 Promotion (communication) Metrics

Strategic Quadrant	Input	Output
Acquisition/Stimulate Demand	• number of acquisition promotional materials/number total promotional materials • dollar acquisition spend/$ total promotional budget	• percent of brand recognition • percent of open-ended information recall • brand perception on main variable • number new customers converted/number new customers targeted • percent of purchase intention
Retention/Stimulate Demand	• number of image or behavior promotional materials/number total promotional materials • dollar retention promotion spend/dollar total promotion spend	• percent of brand preference • percent of heart loyal customers • percent of upgrade purchase intention • percent of top-of-mind awareness
Acquisition/Earn Share	• number of competitive promotional materials/number total promotional materials • dollar acquisition earn share spend/dollar promotional budget	• percent of competitive customers willing to try our product • percent of target competitive population unaided brand recall • percent of target competitive population unaided information recall
Retention/Earn Share	• dollar retention earn share spend/ dollar total promotional budget • number of switching promotional materials/number of total promotional materials • number of cross-sell promotional materials/number of promotional materials	• percent of top-of-mind awareness • perception of dynamic variable • percent of population who prefer our brand

metrics. To measure the impact of its efforts, VW would gauge the quantity and quality of online chatter about the ad, ad awareness, and, ultimately brand perceptions. Table 14.5 outlines potential input and output metrics by strategic quadrant.

EVALUATION: METRICS AND THE BIG PICTURE

Strategic business metrics help the company translate strategy into execution and stay focused on a single goal with prioritized tactical objectives. SIMs also enhance organizational cooperation: because all functions are working on a common goal and resources are naturally allocated to their most productive use.

We organized our discussion of metrics according to elements in the Big Picture framework. At a high level, we maintain alignment between strategy and execution by prioritizing initiatives that help us articulate the benefits of our brand to our target customers; this is precisely what operational metrics help us do. Our overall business goal, which is presented in Chapter 2, has two components: a numerical target and a metric type, both derived from the strategy of the company. If we seek to stimulate demand, we will emphasize category expansion or market development initiatives and our metrics will be absolute (number of customers, overall category growth, and so on). When we are trying to earn share, we will seek to grow at our competitor's expense and measure success by selecting a relative metric (such as market share, revenue share, or share of customers' category spend). Our choices in segmentation, targeting, and positioning will also affect our choice of operational metrics, that is, whose behavior we measure, what we measure, and how we measure it.

Our input metrics help us understand whether, as a team, our organization is allocating resources as dictated by our stated strategy. We also set *output* metrics to test whether our efforts are having the financial and customer perception impact we planned. And although we organized the discussion of strategic and executional evaluation metrics by each of the 4 P's, the metrics system needs to stand as a coherent whole, in which the business objective and the overall perception of the brand stand at the very top of the system and lower-level metrics cascade down.

Our primary objective is to organize our metrics by customer rather than function. In doing so, we integrate strategy and execution, avoiding organizational silos that lead to inefficiencies. By using metrics to analyze firm strategy and execution holistically, we can uncover root causes to problems that we might otherwise address at a superficial level or miss altogether. Business metrics are a the tool to diagnose root causes and to improve firm performance in a sustainable manner.

☐ SUMMARY

1. Describe the reasons companies set metrics

The purpose of marketing metrics is to operationalize the firm's strategies and to track the impact of those strategies on target customers and our financial objectives. A metrics system allows us to quantify this impact and, in doing so, understand key relationships between strategic variables and executional variables.

2. Describe the criteria of metrics that reflect the firm strategy

SIMs or Strategy-Integrated Metrics, reflect the firm strategy and meet five key criteria: (1) Metrics are aligned to the strategy of the organization. This happens in two ways: operationally and from an evaluation perspective. (2) Metrics help us focus and prioritize initiatives; we set top-level metrics to address the overall business goal and the overall brand perception of the firm, and then integrate focus on achieving overall goals by integrating all functional areas. (3) Metrics integrate an internal and external perspective of the firm. (4) Metrics are arranged in a system linked through hypothesized causal relationships. We develop *input* and *output* metrics as we engage in a continuous process of hypothesis-development and hypothesis testing. (5) Our metrics system is aligned to the core competence and helps us continually enhance and evolve our firm's core skills—those that are unique, rare, and difficult for our competitors to imitate and that help us deliver relevant customer benefits.

3. List the key steps in setting operational marketing metrics

Once we have set operational metrics, we can set evaluation metrics by linking our overall goals and strategic objectives to each part of the Big Picture framework. As we do this, we must address both inputs and outputs of the marketing process. Although this chapter organizes evaluation metrics by functional discipline (product, pricing, distribution, communications), the metrics system draws from all required departments of the firm in the assembly of a holistic measurement dashboard.

4. Use evaluation metrics to evaluate the connection between our strategy and our execution

The overall goal of metrics is to help us diagnose failures and identify the reasons for our success in an effort to enable continuous learning in the organization. An effective SIMs system will help us evaluate our strategy covering all intervening marketing variables: bodies, beliefs, behaviors, and bucks. Specifically, we use metrics to test key hypotheses about members of our target market, and about how changes in salient beliefs about our category and brand drive their behaviors.

5. **Relate key strategy and evaluation metrics to other elements of the Big Picture framework**
In order to ensure that we meet our objective of developing strategy-integrated metrics, we can organize their development based on the Big Picture framework. Working from strategy to execution, we should develop metrics relative to each box in the framework, ensuring that the metrics are related to one another.

☐ KEY TERMS

Balanced scorecard. (p. 371) A business metrics system developed by Kaplan and Norton in the early 1990s which divides the firm into a financial perspective, a customer perspective, innovation and learning perspective, and an internal process perspective.

Benchmarking. (p. 375) The practice of pricing relative to a competitor's price, justifying the price difference between the two brands by the difference in their relative value of their offerings.

Metric. (p. 371) A system that quantifies a trend, dynamic, or characteristic. In marketing we use metrics to quantify the assumptions that we use to develop strategies; to operationalize those strategies; and to measure the results of those strategies.

Strategy-Integrated Metrics (SIMs). (p. 371) Metrics that reflect the strategy of the company and link multiple aspects of organizational performance by following logical causal relationships.

Trial. (p. 382) First-time users as a percent of the target population.

Wallet share. (p. 382) Customers' spend on our brand as a percent of their spend on the category as a whole.

Willingness to wait or search. (p. 384) The percent of customers willing to delay purchases or change stores (or distribution outlets), rather than purchase a different brand.

☐ REVIEW AND DISCUSSION QUESTIONS

1. Identify four ways we categorize marketing metrics.
2. Imagine that Singapore Airlines, an Asian carrier, acquired the airline described in the chapter example (Figs. 14.1 and 14.2). You are in charge of reshaping the acquired airline as a luxury carrier positioned on customer service rather than time convenience. Redraw Figures 14.1 and 14.2 given the new positioning.
3. Discuss the difference between input and output metrics for product, place, price, and promotion.

☐ APPENDIX: MARKETING ANALYSIS PLANNING

Marketing Tool #14.1: Assembling Operational Metrics
To assemble operational metrics to implement our strategy, complete the following steps, using the appropriate columns in Table 14.6:

1. Define salient aspects of the current customer experience by process step. In particular, isolate specific customer pain points. This list of current experience attributes should be completed after conducting primary and secondary research as necessary, to ensure it is realistic. See Figure 14.1 for an example.
2. Given the customer proposition (see Chapter 7) for the brand or company we represent, describe a desired customer experience. (See Figure 14.1 for an example.)
3. Write down a series of activities (internal actions) the company will need to undertake to transport customers from the current to the desired experience. (See Fig. 14.2 in the chapter for an example.)

Table 14.6 SIMs: Setting Operational Marketing Metrics

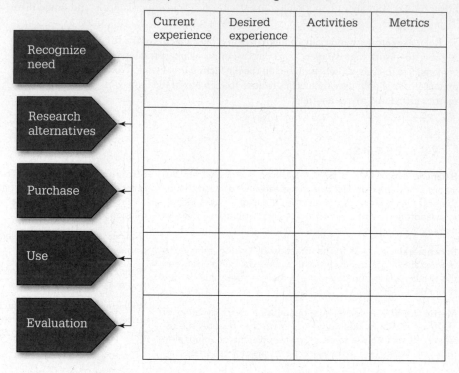

	Current experience	Desired experience	Activities	Metrics
Recognize need				
Research alternatives				
Purchase				
Use				
Evaluation				

4. Define output metrics, that is, operational and customer perception measures that will help us track whether we are executing to facilitate the customer experience. (See Figure 14.2 in the chapter for an example.)

Marketing Tool #14.2: Defining Overall Evaluation Metrics for the Fundamental Entity

The Bodies-Beliefs-Behaviors-Bucks structure is a helpful guide to setting overall strategy metrics. Use Table 14.7 to complete the following metrics table for a specific company, after you have determined its strategic priorities.

1. **Bodies.** Define relevant metrics for the number of target customers for the company within a particular planning period.
2. **Beliefs.** Summarize the key change in beliefs the company requires in order for its strategic goals to be realized.
3. **Behaviors.** Use behavioral metrics to track the specific behaviors you expect from the company's target audience given the strategy (conversion to the brand, upgrade, or increased usage).
4. **Bucks.** Use financial metrics to track progress toward the financial goals that logically follow from the strategic metrics already used for bodies, beliefs, and behaviors.

See Table 14.1 in the chapter for an example of Overall Strategy Evaluation Metrics.

Table 14.7 Overall Evaluation Metrics for the Fundamental Entity

Strategic Quadrant / Goals	Metrics			
	Bodies	Beliefs	Behaviors	Bucks

Marketing Tool 14.3: Defining Executional Evaluation Metrics

We use evaluation metrics to measure the impact of our strategy. A comprehensive metrics dashboard will cover all aspects of strategy development and executional planning. For each Big Picture executional module, you will want to select input and output metrics that enable a company to measure its intended strategy. Using Table 14.8, complete the process steps below (see Tables 14.2 through 14.5 in the chapter for examples):

1. Define input metrics, that is, our own measures of the resources that we are dedicating to executing on the strategy.

2. Define output metrics, that is, the customer beliefs or behaviors we expect given our strategy.

Table 14.8 Executional Metrics

Chapter	Key Input Metrics	Key Output Metrics
Product		
Pricing		
Communications		
Channels		

☐ RESOURCES

Srivastava, Rajendra, David J. Reibstein, and William S. Woodside." Metrics for linking marketing to financial performance," Institute, Issue 5, Part 200 of Report, Marketing Science, 2005, 26 pp.

Farris, Paul W., et al. *Marketing Metrics: 50+ Metrics Every Executive Should Master*. Pearson Prentice Hall, 2006.

Gupta, Sunil and Valarie Zeithaml." Customer metrics and their impact on financial performance," *Marketing Science 25.6* (2006): 718–739.

Srinivasan, Shuba and Dominique Hanssens. "Marketing and firm value: Metrics, methods, findings, and future directions," *Boston U. School of Management Research Paper No. 2009-6* (2008).

Johnson, Michael and Andres Gustafsson. *Improving Customer Satisfaction, Loyalty and Profit: An Integrated Measurement and Management System*. John Wiley & Sons, 2006.

GLOSSARY

Aspirational variables. Variables that reflect beliefs and attitudes about the future: the wishes, hopes, and dreams of our target audience.

Attitudinal variables. Variables that describe the thoughts, feelings, and beliefs of consumers. Marketers have implicitly used attitudinal segmentation strategies for years by appealing to consumers' need for safety or self-esteem or desire to be "hip" or "cool."

Augmented product. Product innovation that represents the dynamic benefit.

Average costs. The sum of fixed plus variable costs divided by total units sold.

Average customer life. The average number of years a customer can be expected to stay with the company given the current retention rate.

Balanced scorecard. A business metrics system developed by Kaplan and Norton in the early 1990s which divides the firm into a financial perspective, a customer perspective, innovation and learning perspective, and an internal process perspective.

Basic awareness (also called aided recognition). Consumer's ability, when presented with the brand name or logo, to acknowledge that he or she has seen it before.

Behavioral model. A model that attempts to predict consumer behavior by looking at relationships between variables, such as the relationship between attitudes and awareness and purchase behavior.

Behavioral objective. Communication with a goal to cause an action or specific behavior in our target audience.

Behavioral segmentation variables. Variables that describe the specific actions of consumers or potential consumers.

Benchmark pricing. The practice of pricing relative to a competitor's price justifying the price difference between the two brands by the difference in the relative value of their offerings.

Benefit-based category definition. The business category (or market) is the field within which companies deploy their products and services and customers satisfy needs through the purchase of products and services. Traditionally, companies defined business categories by adding up their sales of particular types of products; today we do it by adding up the revenues of products that fill a particular customer need.

Benefit plot. A graphic showing importance and perception ratings. Sometimes these plots are also called perceptual plots.

Brand. A name, term, sign, symbol, or design, or a combination of them which is intended to identify the goods or services of one seller or a group of sellers, and to differentiate them from those of competitors. In practice, the brand is synonymous with the overall benefit the company promises to deliver to its customers.

Brand comparisons. One way in which consumers make purchase decisions is by evaluating the benefits of the products and services of a particular brand against the cost of purchasing those products and services.

Brand preference. Customers' stated ranking of our brands relative to substitute brands in the category.

Breakeven quantity. The number of units we need to sell in order to break even are reached when our revenues are exactly the same as the sum of our fixed and our variable costs.

BUMP. Mnemonic for assessing marketing communications execution. This acronym stands for *Believable, Unique, Memorable, and Pertinent*.

Category penetration. Purchasers of a category as a percent of the relevant population in a given market and over a specific period of time.

Categorical variables. A categorical variable like gender, occupation, or marital status that is used to represent discreet types, or categories, or numerical categories on a scale.

Channel breadth. The number of distribution outlets at which the product is available.

Channel depth. The degree to which a particular channel member controls a substantial portion of the channel via forward and/or backward integration.

Channel leader. A company that holds the greatest power in the distribution channel; as a result, it is able to set standards for how the channel will be managed and bring channel members together around key activities and behaviors.

Channel length. The number of channel members in a particular value chain.

Communications objective. The type of change in beliefs or, in some cases, behavior we wish to accomplish through communications.

Comparative advertising. Refers to the practice of advertising products or services relative to other products sold by competitors rather than in absolute terms.

Competitive-based pricing. The practice of setting prices by selecting a competitor's product price and pricing at the same level, or slightly below or above.

Competitive plot. A plot of just a couple of benefits that define our specific market space and help us locate brands in that space.

Consideration set. A list of companies or brands that are simultaneously considered by consumers seeking to make a purchase based on a need they have identified or a benefit they are seeking to obtain. As consumers engage in research of a category, they may discover options that were not in their initial consideration set.

Consumer surplus. The difference between a customer's willingness to pay and the price paid.

Continuous variables. Variables that can take any value within the scale used to measure them (not simply the whole numbers on the scales, but including fractions).

Contribution and contribution margin. The difference between the price and the variable cost of producing and selling a unit of our product or service. Contribution is generally expressed as a percent, by dividing the dollar contribution by the price, and called contribution margin.

Core business. The core business of the firm is the central focus of a company's activity.

Core competence. A skill of the firm that is pervasive throughout the organization and can lead to a sustainable, competitive advantage.

Core competence. Key organizational skills that drive sustainable growth. The core competence is the source of differentiation for the firm.

Corporate self-esteem. The organizational confidence that arises from a shared understanding of the company's purpose and core competence.

Cost-based pricing. The practice of setting prices by estimating the average cost of producing and selling the product plus a profit margin.

Cost of entry. The cost of entry into a category is the minimum acceptable product or service standard that a company must be able to deliver in order to be considered by consumers in that category as being part of their consideration set in that category.

Cost per Thousand (CPM). The cost to reach one thousand customers with a marketing message.

Creatives. Writers and designers responsible for bringing a copy strategy to life, transforming it from a simple set of words in five boxes of the positioning statement.

Credence attributes. Attributes that we cannot assess even after consumption (airline safety, beauty claims).

Critical Incident Technique (CIT). A qualitative research technique designed to uncover memorable experiences, either very good or very bad, as a way to discover the most salient attributes of a product or service.

Cross-sectional research. Research that collects data at one point in time across different samples or people of phenomena.

Customer acquisition. A series of activities designed to bring new customers to our brand or franchise, including awareness creation, information delivery, and activities designed to encourage trial.

Customer acquisition cost (per customer). The one-time cost of all marketing and sales activities plus all physical infrastructure and systems required to motivate a customer to purchase.

Customer attrition or customer churn. The rate at which customers are leaving the company.

Customer-based pricing. The practice of setting prices by estimating the willingness to pay of our customers.

Customer experience process map. A tool that reviews the customer experience with a particular brand or an entire product category and the factors which influence that experience.

Customer Lifetime Value (CLV). The total net present value of current and future profits that a particular customer will generate over the lifetime of his or her relationship with a firm. CLV = $m(r/1 + r - d)$, where m is the $ margin per customer, r is the retention rate, and d is the weighted-average cost of capital of the company or discount rate.

Customer loyalty. Customer loyalty is generally defined as the combination of repeat purchases and commitment to a brand on the part of a customer; both attitudinal and behavioral components are necessary for loyalty to exist.

Customer Relationship Management (CRM). A set of processes to manage the connection between the company and the customer.

Customer retention. Activities designed to help keep customers longer.

Customer satisfaction. The gap between the customer's expectation of company performance and the perceived experience of performance.

Demographic variables. Those variables that we can physically observe and measure such as age, gender, educational status, household size, income, marital status, and geographic information like country of origin, population income, and population density.

Dependent variable. A factor or variable that is influenced or is the outcome of other variables, called independent.

Derived importance. Also called "revealed" importance as the researcher uses statistics methods to estimate importance indirectly, based on answers to other questions rather than by asking directly.

Descriptive research. Research that characterizes markets, industry competitors, target populations, customers, or a set of product features.

Direct distribution. A structure with few or no intermediaries between the manufacturer and the end-customer.

Discount rate. If F is a payment that will be made t years in the future, then the discounted value of this payment (P), also called the present value, is $P = F/(1 + d\%)^t$.

Distinct branding. A branding approach whereby the company creates different brands for its different products and services.

Dynamic benefit. The differentiator we will emphasize as our point-of-difference, and which will be the foundation of our earn share strategy. These benefits are called *dynamic* because they have the potential of becoming "main" benefits of a new category.

The benefit used by a competitor to take share from the category leader.

4 Bs: Bodies, beliefs, behaviors, bucks. The foundation of any sound strategic marketing investment is thoughtful analysis of the target audience we are trying to reach (bodies), the beliefs we are trying to change (beliefs), the behavioral change we hope will result from the belief change (behaviors), and the financial impact of that behavioral change (bucks).

Earn share strategy. A competitive strategy characterized by comparisons to a company or group of companies (market segment).

Emotional involvement. The degree to which consumers evaluate products based on their emotional needs.

Emotional risk of loss. A loss incurred when a product fails to perform and causes emotional distress to a customer because that customer felt emotionally involved with the product.

Ethical practice. Our ongoing effort to act in accordance with the guiding moral principles we have identified that reflect our assessment of right and wrong and to consider the impact of our actions.

Ethics. The moral judgments, standards, and rules of conduct by which we live.

Expected product. The basic product attributes and benefits that customers expect when purchasing a product. Generally all products in the category deliver an expected product.

Expected value analysis. A technique that can help us estimate the potential impact of our actions in a systematic manner by considering the probability of an event and the value of the outcome.

Experience attributes. Attributes we can assess only after the product has been consumed (taste, performance, durability).

Experimental research. Research that studies the impact of some *manipulation* on a particular outcome.

Exploratory research. Research to determine whether we should pursue further research, and if so, in what particular area and manner.

Features war. When both parties engaged in competition retaliate in succession, their competition is called a *features war* if they primarily compete by trying to improve on each other's product features, or a *price war* if they primarily compete on price.

Five-Box Positioning Tool. A connected set of boxes that outline our positioning statement. These include the five descriptions listed below:

Current belief. Focused description of the single-most significant belief held by the target audience that most directly impacts the current customer behavior we are attempting to change with our marketing effort.

Current do. Single-minded description of the primary behavior of the target audience that we are trying to change with our marketing effort.

Customer proposition. A singled-minded statement that contains the essence of the value proposition to our target audience. The customer proposition is designed to achieve a belief change from the current to the desired belief such that the target audience will change their behavior, moving from the current to the desired do.

Desired belief. Focused description of the future belief that, if held by the target audience, will result in the specific behavioral change we are attempting to create with our marketing effort.

Desired do. Singled-minded description of the future behavior that will be exhibited by our target audience once the desired belief is achieved.

Fixed costs. Costs of producing and selling a unit of our product that do not vary regardless of how many units we sell.

Forward buying. The practice of purchasing retail inventory in quantities exceeding current demand, usually motivated by suppliers' offers of temporary discounts.

Functional involvement. The degree to which consumers are engaged in evaluating and considering practical aspects of the product's performance. For example, when consumers consider the gas mileage, safety ratings, or type of sound system in an automobile, they are assessing functional attributes.

Functional risk of loss. A loss incurred when a product fails to perform as promised from a utilitarian perspective.

Fundamental entity. Our choice of fundamental entity determines the perspective from which we will conduct our strategic analysis, whether it be brand by brand or from a more global, corporate point of view.

The brand level from which we conduct the strategic analysis. The Fundamental Entity might be the Corporate Brand, a Brand Line, or a Product Brand, depending on the company's brand structure.

Goal. Company goals function as success criteria and also help prioritize our actions and our allocation of resources.

Hand loyalty. Customer loyalty characterized by habitual re-purchase and low interest in product information, that is, low commitment to the brand.

Head loyalty. Customer loyalty based on specific benefits of a brand, such as product performance.

Heart loyalty. Customer loyalty based on personal identification with the brand.

Heterogeneity of services. Variability in service quality that arises because services are provided by humans.

Household penetration. The percentage of a particular group who use a particular product, product type, or service. For example, the household penetration of smartphones in the United States in June, 2013 was 56%.

Hybrid banding. A branding approach that combines two brands—the corporate brand plus separate brands—to designate differences in product or service lines.

Image objective. Communication created to capture share of heart, evoking an emotional response in consumers. The focus of an image objective is the *person* in the target audience, as opposed to the *brand*.

Independent variable. A factor or variable that influences another factor (called dependent).

Indirect distribution. A longer channel structure with more members.

Information objective. Communications intended to provide specific information about the brand; the information must be focused on the positioning.

Inseparability of production and consumption. The simultaneous production and consumption that characterizes most services.

Intangibility of services. A characteristic of services that means they cannot be touched or felt.

Life-stage marketing. Life-stage marketing more generally refers to the practice of adapting marketing messages and offerings to customers' specific life phases.

Longitudinal or time-series research. Research that collects data over a period of time, seeking to understand how the variable under study changes over time.

Main and dynamic benefit plot. A benefit plot that illustrates the basis of competition in a particular market space by showing target customers' perceptions of the different brands' performance of the main and dynamic variable.

Main benefit. The primary customer benefit emphasized by the market leader of a category. The main benefit becomes a "cost of entry" into the category because companies wishing to enter that market have to deliver the main benefit to an acceptable level in order to be considered part of the category.

The primary benefit provided by the category and that differentiates the category leader.

Metric. A system that quantifies a trend, dynamic, or characteristic. In marketing we use metrics to quantify the assumptions that we use to develop strategies; to operationalize those strategies; and to measure the results of those strategies.

Millennials. The generation born between 1980 and 2000 (approximately). Millennials are sometimes referred to in the media as "Generation Y."

Negative-sum games. Competitive games for which the more intense the competition the smaller the rewards available to be shared; even the winner loses from competing.

Panel data. Information regarding customers' behavior and attitudes toward products and services that is collected from a group of consumers (a panel) over time. This enables the researcher to track trends among a group of consumers.

Path to purchase. The stages that a customer goes through in identifying a need and eventually purchasing, using, and evaluating a product purchase.

Pay per Click (PPC). A method of paying for Internet advertising in which the advertiser does not pay for the placement of the ad, but rather pays each time a consumer clicks on the ad to view more information or place an order.

Perception and importance plot. A benefit plot that illustrates the relative importance of the key benefits in the market space and how customers perceive each of the brands' performance on those key benefits.

Place utility. The benefit provided by channel members that provide convenient access to products.

Porter's 5 Forces. A framework advanced by Michael Porter that provides a systematic means of quickly assessing the competitive space by highlighting the primary external factors that drive company performance. The five forces are: supplier power, buyer power, threat of competitive entry, threat of substitute products, and threat from existing competitors.

Positionality. The most important criteria for adding products to our portfolio. A positional product does more than simply create revenues through sales; it also builds brand equity and enhances our relationship with our customers.

Positioning statement. This statement will marry our entity's core competence, strategic intent, and understanding of the target consumer.

Positive-sum games. Those in which the more intense the competition, the greater the rewards to be shared because both players improve their skills as a result of competing.

Potential products. Products with new attributes (and therefore a new dynamic variable) that marketers evaluate in considering innovations.

Price elasticity of demand. A measure of the degree to which the quantity demanded of a good or a service changes with its price.

Price Strategy. The overall price level for our products, based on our overall strategy and on our positioning.

Pricing Execution. The implementation of the general pricing level we have developed as a result of our strategic decisions.

Primary research. Carrying out data gathering first-hand, that is, by sourcing it from the population we are seeking to investigate. Primary research can be conducted through a third party.

Product assortment. The different products within a set that a particular company offers.

Product attributes. Characteristics of products that drive the way customers learn about them and that we categorize as Search, Experience, and Credence.

A product attribute is a relatively concrete physical or functional characteristic of a product or service.

Product benefit. What a customer stands to gain from using a product. Product benefits arise from product features and they represent the external, customer-based perspective on a product or service.

Product feature. Physical or functional attribute of a product or service. Product features reflect the company's internal perspective of a product or service.

Product life cycle. This concept describes the growth, maturity, and eventual decline of a product as if it were a living being.

Product or brand benefit. An abstract, psychological, or emotional benefit sought by a customer in consuming a product or service or choosing a brand.

Product proliferation. A situation in which firms find themselves attempting to manage an unwieldy number of products, including many that may not deserve the time and resources they receive.

Product utility. The benefit provided by channel members that deliver product expertise, assortment, or selection.

Productization of services. Transforming services offerings so they resemble tangible products. This is accomplished, for example, by creating a name/logo/identity for the service and marketing it as similarly to a traditional tangible product as possible.

Psychographic variables. Variables that combine demographics, personality, values, attitudes, interests, and lifestyles of consumers for segmentation purposes.

Psychological model. A model that describes how people process information and form attitudes.

Qualitative research. Research that collects data from a relatively small sample that is not randomly selected. Qualitative data is not generalizable to a larger population. However, it provides a nuanced or deep understanding of a particular phenomenon or sample.

Quantitative research. Research that collects numerical data generally drawn from a sample which is representative of a larger population. Quantitative data is expressed numerically, and are amenable to mathematical manipulation enabling the researcher to draw conclusions that are generalizable to a larger population.

Recency, Frequency, and Monetary value (RFM). Analysis which ranks customers by examining how *recently* they have purchased (recency), how *often* they purchase (frequency), and *how much* they spend (monetary) with the company.

Reliability. The extent to which repeated measurements of a variable yield the same answer.

Repeat usage. Volume (or sales) by retained customers as a percent of total volume or sales.

Retention elasticity. The change in customer lifetime value with a 1% improvement in the retention rate.

Revenue market share. The revenue of our brand divided by the total revenue corresponding to all brands in a category within a specific time frame.

Risk of loss. The potential negative outcome the consumer incurs when making a product choice. Consumer involvement level is driven by this risk of loss, which has emotional and functional components.

Search attributes. Attributes we can evaluate prior to consumption (price, physical product characteristics).

Secondary research. A gathering of second-hand data, that is, data collected by a third party for their own purposes.

Segmentation. The process of identifying a group of customers who share at least one characteristic that will make them more responsive to our marketing message.

SKU. Stock keeping unit. A unique code that identifies each individual product in a retail store, used to track inventory in the channel.

Source of volume. A process by which we attribute customer purchases to groups of consumers in each of the strategic quadrants: retention/stimulate demand, retention/earn share, acquisition/stimulate demand, acquisition/earn share.

Stated importance. Perceptual estimate obtained from a survey in which customers are asked directly to rate the importance of a benefit or product attribute.

Statistical reliability. The ability of a statistical measurement to produce the same results when the same phenomena are measured under different conditions.

Statistical validity. Evidence that a statistical study measures what it was set out to measure.

Stereotyping. The practice of considering any individual in a segment or population as a representative of the population as a whole by emphasizing physical or demographic variables to draw unrealistic and potentially offensive conclusions regarding attitudes and behaviors.

Stimulate demand strategy. The market leader's strategy based on growing the category. This is done either by attracting non-users to the category (acquisition) or by motivating current customers of the brand to purchase more or to pay more (retention).

Strategic asset. A strategic asset is a resource of the company that is supported by a core competence and is critical to differentiating the brand.

Strategic customer insights. Information about customers or potential customers that holds special value to our firm given our capabilities and marketing strategy.

Strategic focus. The key intersection of customer and competitive attention that represents our best strategic opportunity.

Strategic focus choice. Based on the sources of volume and an opportunity assessment, the company chooses a strategic quadrant as the primary focus of its strategic execution.

Strategic quadrants. The strategic quadrants are a 2x2 that results from a combination of the marketing objective decisions (customer focus) and the source of volume choice (competitive focus). There are four strategic quadrants: acquisition/stimulate demand, retention/stimulate demand, acquisition/earn share, retention/earn share.

Strategy-based pricing. The practice of setting prices by creating value for our product and communicating it to our customers, thus adapting their willingness to pay.

Strategy-integrated metrics (SIMs). Metrics that reflect the strategy of the company and link multiple aspects of organizational performance by following logical causal relationships.

Survival rate. The expected probability that a customer will still be with the firm in a particular time period.

Switching costs. The costs customers will incur if they switch companies, including financial costs, but also the cost of time to apply for a new service or learn to use a new device.

Tag line. A short statement that is meant to capture the essence of the brand positioning; accompanies the brand logo and is an integral part of the brand identity of the firm.

Target audience description. A rich description of a member of the market segment we are pursuing, leveraging demographic, behavioral, and attitudinal characteristics.

Targeting. The process by which we locate and describe specific groups of customers who we hypothesize are most likely to be interested in obtaining the benefits we offer through products and services.

The Big Picture framework. An integrated framework designed to help you analyze and address the myriad marketing problems you will face during your career.

Time utility. The benefit provided by channel members that have the right product, parts, and services when consumers need them.

Top of mind (or **unaided**) **awareness.** Customers' ability to identify the brand or product with the business category.

Trial. First-time users as a percent of the target population.

Umbrella branding. A branding approach whereby the company uses just one brand for all of its products and services.

Unit market share. The number of units sold by our brand divided by the total number of units sold in a category within a specific time frame.

Validity. The extent to which our data accurately captures the information we are seeking.

VALs. Acronym for Values, Attitudes, and Lifestyles. VALs is a system for grouping consumers according to certain attitudes and demographics (together known as psychographics) in order to predict their response to marketing and advertising initiatives.

Variable costs. Costs of producing and selling a unit of our product that vary with the volume we sell.

Viral marketing. A communications tactic intended to increase awareness using social media as opposed to traditional paid advertising. This awareness spreads like a virus as users come in contact with one another and "infect" their friends and associates with information about a product.

Wallet share. Customers' spend on our brand as a percent of their spend on the category as a whole.

Willingness to search. The percent of customers willing to delay purchases or change stores (or distribution outlets), rather than purchase a different brand.

Zero-based communications budgeting. The practice of building communications budgets by starting from zero and considering the size of the target audience, the positioning message, and the communication objective and then selecting the most appropriate media channel and number of exposures to arrive at a total budget.

Zero-sum games. Those in which competitors share a fixed reward, so one's gain is the other's loss.

Zone of tolerance. The range of acceptable or expected outcomes in a service experience.

INDEX